THE GLORIOUS MOUNTAINS OF VANCOUVER'S NORTH SHORE

A PEAKBAGGER'S GUIDE

THE GLORIOUS MOUNTAINS OF VANCOUVER'S NORTH SHORE

A PEAKBAGGER'S GUIDE

David Crerar
Harry Crerar
Bill Maurer

RMB

RMB | Rocky Mountain Books Ltd.
rmbooks.com @rmbooks facebook.com/rmbooks

Cataloguing data available from Library and Archives Canada
ISBN 9781771602419 (paperback)
ISBN 9781771602754 (electronic)

All photographs are by the authors unless otherwise noted.

Cover design: Chyla Cardinal
Layout design: Lin Oosterhoff

Printed and bound in Canada by Friesens

Distributed in Canada by Heritage Group Distribution and in the U.S. by Publishers Group West

For information on purchasing bulk quantities of this book, or to obtain media excerpts or invite the author to speak at an event, please visit rmbooks.com and select the "Contact Us" tab.

We acknowledge the financial support of the Government of Canada through the Canada Book Fund and the Canada Council for the Arts, and of the province of British Columbia through the British Columbia Arts Council and the Book Publishing Tax Credit.

DISCLAIMER

The actions described in this book may be considered inherently dangerous activities. Individuals undertake these activities at their own risk. The information put forth in this guide has been collected from a variety of sources and is not guaranteed to be completely accurate or reliable. Many conditions and some information may change owing to weather and numerous other factors beyond the control of the authors and publishers. Individuals or groups must determine the risks, use their own judgment, and take full responsibility for their actions. Do not depend on any information found in this book for your own personal safety. Your safety depends on your own good judgment based on your skills, education, and experience.

It is up to the users of this guidebook to acquire the necessary skills for safe experiences and to exercise caution in potentially hazardous areas. The authors and publishers of this guide accept no responsibility for your actions or the results that occur from another's actions, choices, or judgments. If you have any doubt as to your safety or your ability to attempt anything described in this guidebook, do not attempt it.

David dedicates this book to Harry, Philippa, Isla,
and Angus: the youngest baggers.

Harry dedicates this book to his parents
and grandparents.

Bill dedicates this book to his parents,
Fred and Fritzi, for making Vancouver their
home and his birthplace in this beautiful natural
environment, and to his children, Andrew and Annie,
for continuing the family tradition of adventure and
exploration in the great outdoors.

NORTH SHORE RESCUE AND
LIONS BAY SEARCH AND RESCUE

North Shore Rescue (NSR) was founded in 1965. Since then, it has grown to be one of North America's most active and prominent mountain search and rescue teams.

Lions Bay Search and Rescue (LBSAR) was founded in 1983, after the debris torrent that killed Tom and David Wade in February of that year.

These teams of volunteers have saved countless lives in the mountains surveyed in this book. Even those who go into the mountains properly prepared know that this dedicated army stands on guard to help if the hiker unexpectedly breaks a leg or worse. We are all in their debt.

A portion of the proceeds from this book will be given to NSR and LBSAR, registered non-profit societies dedicated to saving the lives of people in distress on local mountains. We encourage you to donate to them as well:

NORTH SHORE RESCUE TEAM SOCIETY
147 East 14th Street
North Vancouver, BC V7L 2N4
canadahelps.org/en/charities/north-shore-search-and-rescue-vancouver-sr-team

LIONS BAY SEARCH AND RESCUE SOCIETY
PO Box 629
Lions Bay, BC V0N 2E0
canadahelps.org/dn/9468

If you are ever rescued by one of these organizations, donate generously and regularly. How much is your life worth? How many hundreds of hours were spent rescuing you? Repay your debt, in full, now, or over the remainder of your but-for-your-rescue lifespan.

This book is not associated with or published by these organizations.

CONTENTS

DIVISION OF LABOUR

David and Harry Crerar were primarily responsible for the route descriptions and for the historical and natural history research. Bill Maurer was primarily responsible for the maps and measurements, as well as the bagger tips.

ACKNOWLEDGEMENTS

Loud thanks go to Ean Jackson, who makes the world a finer place with his energy, enthusiasm, and generosity, through his trail-running group, Club Fat Ass, and all of his other endeavours. Ean was instrumental in our full immersion into the religion of trail running and the worship of nature, and we, along with the thousands of others he has helped, will always love and revere him.

Special thanks to Dr. Glenn Woodsworth, who graciously shared his wisdom of the mountains with us, and who provided invaluable comments on an early draft of this book. We were heartened to see that Glenn received similar thanks in Dick Culbert's classic 1965 *A Climber's Guide to the Coastal Ranges of British Columbia*, and here he is, helping us, 50 years later.

We also here acknowledge that the legendary Dick Culbert (1940 Winnipeg – 2017 Gibsons) died just before publication of this book. All devotees of British Columbia mountains are in his debt.

A warm thanks to our friends and fellow adventurers Julia Lawn, Mick Bailey, Ran Katzman, Christine Moric, Bill Dagg, Dr. Neil Ambrose, Glenn Pacé, Simon Chesterton, Doris Leong, Avery Gottfried, Michael Kay, and Rick Arikado, who helpfully read early drafts of this book and provided useful thoughts. And to our adventurers-in-crime Ken Legg, Tundra, Tom Hamilton, Simon Cowell, Roy Millen, Magnus Verbrugge, Rían Ó Maoil Chonaire, Anders Ourom, Mike Wardas, Ferg Hawke, Bill Hawke, Rob Letson, Sean Muggah, and Gavin Marshall. And our profound thanks to the professional, enthusiastic and dedicated team at RMB | Rocky Mountain Books: Don Gorman, Joe Wilderson, Chyla Cardinal, and Jillian van der Geest.

Our hearty thanks as well to Daien Ide and Janet Turner (North Vancouver Museum and Archives); Evelyn Chui; Robin Tivy; Allan McMordie; Allison Hunt; Curtis Jones; Craig Moore; Tim Logie; Tony and Maureen Crerar; Philippa Crerar; Craig Williams; Angus Gunn QC; Katie Heung, Pippa Sugimoto; Ken Tyler; Doug Keir; Paddy Sherman; Deidre Cullon; Linda Dorricott; Fiona Hamersley Chambers; Dr. Michael Pidwirny (Associate Professor, Department of Earth, Environmental and Geographic Sciences, UBC), Dr. Elizabeth Moore; Diana Cooper (Archaeology Branch, British Columbia Ministry of Forests, Lands and Natural Resource Operations); Jon Whelan; Lindsay A. Stokalko and Elizabeth Kundert-Cameron (Whyte Museum of the Canadian Rockies); Michael Kennedy, Liz Scremin, Jay MacArthur and Paul Geddes (ACC); Martin Kafer and Dr. Michael Feller (BCMC); Tony Cox (Lions Bay Historical Society); John Taylor; Jim Slight (Deep Cove Heritage Society); Andrew Durnin (District of North Vancouver); Kris Holm (BGC Engineering); Reto Tschan (West Vancouver Archives); Carla Jack (Provincial Toponymist, BC Geographical Names Office) and Susan J. Green (Registrar, BC Register of Historic Places, Heritage Branch, Ministry of Forests, Lands and Natural Resource Operations); Melissa Adams (Union of British Columbia Indian Chiefs Resource Centre); Ann Stevenson (Museum of Anthropology Library); Dr. Jesse Morin; Lyle Litzenberger; Maria Bremner; Alan Martin; Murray Comley; Aleksandra Brzozowski (Islands Trust); Trudi Luethy; Chris Cryderman; Hugh Kellas; Lid Hawkins; Donald Grant and Iola Knight (Hollyburn Heritage Society); Katharine Steig (Friends of Cypress Provincial Park); the staff at the City of Vancouver Archives and Vancouver Public Library Special Collections; Candice Bjur (UBC Archives); Chelsea Shriver (Rare Books and Special Collections Librarian, UBC); Jesse Morwood (Ministry of Transportation and Infrastructure); Drs. Ryan Janicki, David Briggs, Elna Johnson, and Bob Sharma; the late Major James Skitt Matthews (the City of Vancouver's first archivist), and Bob Dylan.

Artaban: views of Harvey and Lions across Howe Sound

INTRODUCTION

I have watched the population grow from twenty thousand to nearly half a million, and the tax burden become heavier every year as the population increased. That odious word "parking" had not yet been coined, and traffic was regulated by the good sense of those who used the roads. An hour's walk would take us out into the woods, where nature could be enjoyed by the poorest without cost. Progress we have attained in great measure. Yes, but it seems we have paid a heavy price. Freedom and contentment have had to go down under the Juggernaut of progress. Through all the changes that Vancouver has passed, from a small town to a seething metropolis, The Lions have looked down unperturbed by the hectic scramblings of restless, ambitious men. Their unchanging serenity is a tonic to the souls of those who, in their perplexity, wonder what it is all about and how it all will end. We can be thankful that God made something that man, in all his conceit, cannot destroy. When we look up to The Lions, in their calm, enduring majesty, we feel comforted and assured that, so long as they stand guard over our destiny, no great harm can befall.

— John F. Latta, *The Ascent of The Lions*, 1903

Is it not wonderful that mountaineering has taken its place among the elect of the world's pastimes? The game is played in the most sublime of playgrounds, where in the clearest, purest air lofty ridges and snowy peaks rise from dark forests in beauty ever changing in charm and colour, from hour to hour and season to season. There, in the safest solitude of the everlasting hills, nothing is ordinary or trivial, and the petty anxieties which loom so large in the world of cities, give way to a delightful sense of absolute freedom and the joy of living.

— Basil Stewart Darling, "The Passion for Mountain Climbing," 1910

… though not my first introduction to the mountains, [this trip] was the means of ushering me into a circle of mountaineers among whom I was destined to win friends, few, but true friendships, that have stood the tests of all vicissitudes of trail and camp and climb, severer tests than those to which more conventional friendships are subjected. Are not such friend-ships sufficient reasons alone for feeling not far removed from Mountain-Worship?

— Don Munday, "The Cathedral Group," 1913,
after climbing White Mountain (now Mount Burwell) for the first time

… imagine you are driving north, across the Lions Gate Bridge, and the sky is steely gray and the sugar-dusted mountains loom blackly in the distance. Imagine what lies behind those mountains – realize that there are only *more* mountains – mountains until the North Pole, mountains until the end of the world, mountains taller than a thousand me's, mountains taller than a thousand you's.
Here is where civilization ends; here is where time ends and where eternity begins.

— Douglas Coupland, *Polaroids from the Dead*, 1996

Vancouverites are the most privileged people on the planet to live in this paradise. Mountains define our city, and we exult in their natural beauty. But Vancouverites of all stripes take the North Shore mountains for granted. Most Vancouverites, glancing up from their lattés, barely register the background wallpaper of the North Shore peaks. If pressed, most could only name Seymour and Grouse, and misname Cypress, as the three known mountains of the North Shore, owing solely to their status as ski hills. Beyond that, our peaks are a nameless and amorphous blue-green backdrop.

Until a decade ago, the authors felt some degree of shame over their ignorance. Despite avidly hiking, running, and, indeed, living on their slopes, we remained largely unaware of these mountains in their fullest beauty and adventure. On the commute home, the supports of Lions Gate Bridge framed a lovely pyramidal peak: what was it called? I made enquiries among online hiking enthusiasts. Most were stumped on this most impressive of the front-row peaks: West Crown (sometimes called "Sleeping Beauty"). From my office, I gazed up the Capilano Lake reservoir to a distant rounded bump: what was it? Some sleuthing revealed it to be Capilano Mountain. Rare write-ups of its ascent gave it mixed reviews. These proved to be horribly unfair: actual exploration revealed it to be an adventure playground of lakes, tarns, and lovely granite slabs, all electrified by the tingling sense of an adventure very close yet very far.

Historically, European settlement in the area now known as Vancouver and the rise of mountaineering internationally occurred around the same time. Arrivals to Vancouver soon began exploring and climbing the peaks of the North Shore, with most of the first ascents (recorded ascents, at least) occurring on the front-range mountains in the 1890s and 1900s. Until the Second World War, members of the British Columbia Mountaineering Club ("BCMC": see **Appendix 3**) and other hikers and climbers enthusiastically explored our local peaks. With the rise of the automobile and expanded roadways, however, interest in local peaks waned as serious climbers looked elsewhere for new adventures, and as more casual hikers stuck to the same well-trodden trails in local provincial and regional parks. Over the past 30 years, the rise in the twin enthusiasms for green and healthy lifestyles, coupled with a greater public zeal for exploration and adventure, has rekindled interest in some of the lesser-known local peaks.

There are so many peaks, so many stunning sights, mere kilometres away, right in our own backyard. There is infinite adventure only a short drive, bus ride, bike ride, or jog away. Adventures like these create a rare and special camaraderie known only by hardy kindred spirits who, exhausted, glow from mountain conquest and the beauty of nature. The goal of this book is to open these doors and to allow you to sense the same wonderment that we did when we discovered that such scenery and adventure lies in our backyards. From the salamanders and emerald moss of the peaks of Gambier in the west to the hanging lake of Fannin in the east. From the ridge adventure of Howe Sound Crest Trail in the south to the remote grandeur of Capilano in the north. From the dolphin-leaping waters of Howe Sound in the west to the seal-snorting ripples of Indian Arm in the east. Over this land, streams burble and waterfalls roar; ancient, moss-covered trees still tower; ephemeral wildflowers bloom in abundance; myriad mushrooms stir at rain; salmon spawn; and deer, bear, cougars, and even mountain goats roam. We present to you the glorious peaks of Vancouver's North Shore.

WHY THESE PEAKS?

Any peak list is an inherently debatable and arbitrary process. We have started with the geographic boundaries of Howe Sound in the west (including the mountains on the Howe Sound Islands) and Indian Arm to the east. The northern boundaries are marked by Capilano and Dickens, but we have omitted some very remote northern peaks between them (such as Eldee and Bivouac).

In terms of difficulty, you will not find any peaks that require technical mountain climbing skills or ropes. In theory they are all non-technical or less technical (Class 3 or easier); you will not find the Camel, East Lion, Spindle, or Harvey's Pup in this book. That said, all mountain climbing has inherent danger. Several of these peaks are challenging and risky and should only be attempted by experienced mountaineers; in particular, West Lion, Hanover, Crown N1, and Coburg have considerable exposure where a fall would almost certainly result in death.

We have not included every hill on the North Shore. Mainland peaks must have a minimum elevation (height) of 1000 m, while Howe Sound island peaks, which start closer to the water, have a minimum elevation of 400 m. For mountains, elevation is the less interesting vertical measurement. In terms of climbing effort and isolated beauty, prominence is the key measurement: the distance one must first descend before starting up the next peak. The mountains in our book had to have a prominence of at least 45 m. Between these two measurements, many well-known "mountains," including beloved hikes such as Dog Mountain and Dinkey Peak, did not make the cut because they were, well, too dinky.

Finally, the peak must have either an official or a more-or-less established name. About half of the peaks surveyed herein have official Canadian Geographic Survey names. The remainder have names that have popular or historic use, either through use over time, or the more recent designation or proposal of a name for a peak. The latter course is sometimes controversial: for some, a mountain must acquire a name organically. We are more inclined towards the bestowing of some name, even an artificial and interim one, for a peak, to render concrete and consistent our conspired adventures, with points of reference. That said, in referring to an unofficially named peak by any particular name, we are not lobbying for that name to become official; we use these names as reference points only, and fully concede that those temporary names may well in the future be appropriately replaced with others. The most prolific recent bestower of names on our local peaks is Robin Tivy, whose bivouac.com provides an encyclopedia of local and international mountains and is itself a wonder of the modern world. We tip our hats to Robin for his great work.

Captain James Bowen
(1751-1835)

Our North Shore peaks derive their names from several primary sources, and most tell a story. In and around Howe Sound, most peaks, and indeed most landmarks, commemorate the Glorious First of June 1794 battle at Ushant, off Brittany, where the British Channel Fleet under Admiral Lord Richard Howe (1726–1799) defeated a French revolutionary fleet attempting to deliver grain to the Americas (see **Appendix 13** for Glorious First of June names). Captain Vancouver started off this naming tradition even before the battle, in 1792, with two names of persons who later gained greater fame at the battle. Vancouver named the sound after Lord Howe, the British commander, and Mt. Gardner, the tallest peak on Bowen, after Admiral Alan Gardner, a maritime mentor to Vancouver and commander of HMS *Queen* at the Glorious First of June (see **Appendix 17** for Captain Vancouver's Howe Sound journal entries).

Captain Richards's 1860 chart showing Gardner, Black, and Crown.

This Glorious First tradition continued 50 years later with the further exploration and surveying of the Lower Mainland's waters by Captain George Henry Richards in HMS *Plumper*, a man-of-war, in July and August 1859. Richards was an effective captain and administrator (eventually became an admiral and received a knighthood), and carried out the first survey of Howe Sound and its islands since Captain Vancouver in 1792. Richards was also a very prolific namer of places: he had a keen sense of history and appreciated his own historic role; he even named one of his own sons "Vancouver" Richards. His ship is commemorated by Plumper Cove at Keats Island in Howe Sound. It is a mark of great national, provincial, and municipal shame that almost nothing has been named after Captain Richards himself. (Richards Street in downtown Vancouver was named not after him but after Lieutenant-Governor Albert Norton Richards. Another Richards Street in Vancouver was briefly named after Captain Richards but was renamed Balaclava Street in 1907.) The only coastal feature today in British Columbia named after the captain himself is the uninteresting Richards Channel off the northeast coast of Vancouver Island. It would be apt to correct this neglect now, so soon after the 150th anniversary of the *Plumper* survey.

Most of the place names in and around Howe Sound are tied to the Glorious First. For example, Richards named Bowen Island after Admiral Bowen, present at the Glorious First. Brunswick and Harvey also have their names derived from a ship and a hero, respectively, of the Glorious First. Captain John Harvey of the *Brunswick* sank the French ship *Vengeur du Peuple* before succumbing to his wounds weeks later (and, notably, what is more popularly and somewhat prosaically known as Hat Mountain due to its shape has also been called Mt. Vengeur). Captain Harvey is the subject of a memorial in Westminster Abbey, but enjoys an even finer tribute: a pointy peak that is often mistaken for one of The Lions and that w provides an invigorating climb from both west and east approaches.[1] Captain Harvey's ship at the Glorious First was HMS *Brunswick*, and to the north of Mt. Harvey is found Brunswick Mountain, the highest on the North Shore.

Subsequent naming patterns went all to hell, however. "Brunswick" was mistakenly attributed to the royal family surname of the present monarch of the United Kingdom and Canada rather than to the ship. Thus, thereafter, other official and unofficial peaks in the area of Brunswick were named after various iterations of the House of Hanover and our present Canadian/British/German royal family, including Hanover, Windsor, and Gotha and Coburg looming over Deeks Lake (for royal family names, see **Appendix 14**).

Even Captain Richards himself didn't stick with the program, and the Battle of Trafalgar creeps into the naming of local peaks. He thus named the entire mountain range "Britannia," after HMS *Britannia*, a 100-gun ship that was present at Trafalgar and also St. Vincent but not the Glorious First.

Other themes creep in, with prophets and biblical figures in the Howe Sound Crest Trail peaks of St. Marks and possibly James. In the Fannin Range, Mt. Bishop (named not after the episcopal office in the Church of England and the Catholic Church, but rather after Joseph Bishop, the first president of the British Columbia Mountaineering Club, who died falling into a crevasse on Mt. Baker) led to the later false-etymological naming of Rector, Curate, Vicar, Deacon (Jarrett), and Presbyter (Clementine) after other clerical posts. Still other peak names commemorate the poor animals blasted by early hunters: Goat and Grouse.

Our research unearthed names bestowed on local peaks by the BCMC during early climbs and club trips: Jarrett (Deacon), Clementine (Presbyter), Echo (Perrault), and Rice (South Lynn). We have favoured those older names over more recent, more arbitrary, names, even though, arguably, those names failed the test of time. We prefer names that have a historical tie or anecdote, or were bestowed by early climbers, rather than a later name chosen to fit an imposed theme, like a suburban street plan.

We must acknowledge that many or all of these mountains have or have had names bestowed on them by the First Nations peoples who have lived in this area since time immemorial: the *Sḵwx̱wú7mesh*/Squamish in the west and north, and the Tsleil-Waututh (formerly called "Burrard") in the east. As set out in **Appendix 16**, the authors have extensively researched all popular, archival, and academic sources for Indigenous names of these peaks, including consultation with members of those First Nations. Unfortunately, apart from the traditional name for he Lions – Chee-Chee-Yoh-Hee ("The Twins") – there are few publicly available traditional names for these peaks under present scholarship. Nonetheless we have included as many traditional Squamish and Tsleil-Waututh names for rivers, creeks, islands, villages, and other places, as well as all Indigenous uses and legends concerning these mountains as could be located. It is hoped that the future will bring more study and writing on this important topic.

As a final note on names, generally where a mountain is named after a person, it is "Mt. X": Mt. Everest, Mt. Seymour, Mt. Strachan. Where a mountain is named after a thing, it is "X Mountain": Crown Mountain, Goat Mountain, Brunswick Mountain. Thus a mountain could be Mt. Bishop if it is named after Mr. Bishop (as the North Shore peak is) or Bishop Mountain if it is so named because it looks like a bishop's hat, or mitre; Crown Mountain if named because it resembles a crown (which it is, even if it does not), or Mt. Crown if named after Mr. or Mrs. Crown. And where a mountain is solitary and skinny or is a sub-component of a larger mountain, it is often referred to as a peak: Leading Peak, Pump Peak.

Finally, we acknowledge that some of these peaks are in the watershed, and that this might be a source of controversy. They are included not in order to encourage people to enter the watershed (and we discourage you from doing so), but rather in recognition that people will climb those peaks anyway, and will climb those peaks at greater danger to themselves and to others and to the environment absent guidance. That said, we have only included those peaks at the periphery of the watershed (Cathedral, West Crown, and Enchantment), and not those deep within (such as Daniel, Appian, Cardinal, and Magic: see **Appendix 20**). Vancouver is rare among municipalities in, first, having such a vast watershed reserve, and, second, excluding people from the natural beauty of such a reserve. Further, gaining access to these areas is a rigorous enough exercise to filter out the kind of human detritus that would contemplate despoiling the watershed: in all likelihood, only those who revere and respect nature will take the exhausting measures to venture to these areas.

PEAKBAGGING

Peakbagging is the enthusiastic and methodical climbing of mountains, usually in a specific area, following the Scottish traditions described below. Those who climb all delineated peaks are traditionally referred to as "compleatists" (after Izaak Walton's *The Compleat Angler*, a 1653 celebration of fishing, and not due to any simple misspelling). We confess we are enthusiastic peakbaggers who visited many of these peaks for the sole reason that "they are there." Some alpinists sneer at the concept of peakbagging: that is, encouraging the climbing of unworthy peaks at the expense of more interesting ones, and the frenetic drive towards the destination rather than the appreciative journey to get there. These sins too are acknowledged. But if these sins are recognized, they can be avoided: speed and diligent visitation give more time for contemplation of their beauty.

The idea of peakbagging was popularized by the Scottish mountaineer Sir Hugh Munro, 4th Baronet of Lindertis (1856–1919). Based on his writings (his Munros Tables were first published in the *Scottish Mountaineering Club Journal* in 1891) and adventures, alpinists generally recognize 282 Munros in Scotland, defined as those peaks 3,000 feet (914.4 m) or higher and generally regarded as separate mountains rather than subpeaks of larger mountains. Those with a topographic prominence of more than 150 m (492 ft.) are sometimes called "Real Munros." We acknowledge that not all of the peaks surveyed in this book would be considered Munros, either because they are too low (e.g., Gardner), insufficiently prominent (e.g., Pump Peak), or insufficiently distinct (e.g., North Needle).

For many alpinists, climbing all of the Munros is the quest and adventure of a lifetime: as of December 2017, more than 6,285 climbers had attained a compleat Munro Round. Others have sought to set speed records for ascending all Munros. The present record-holder is Stephen Pyke, who bagged all (then) 283 Munros in 39 days in 2010, at times climbing 12 peaks in a single day. Making this feat even more staggering is that he did so entirely self-propelled, travelling on foot, kayak, and bicycle. His final peak was Ben Hope, near Sutherland. Pyke staggered up to the summit cairn. There he found a surprise left by the previous record-holder, Charlie Campbell, who had hiked up the day before: a note of congratulations and a bottle of whisky.

Ean Jackson encountered a similar moment when he, accompanied by author sherpa Crerar (Senior), bushwhacked up the back side of North Needle, to make Jackson a compleatist climber of all of these peaks. Bloodied and bewildered, they pulled themselves onto the ridge, only to discover their friend Ken Legg with his noble mountain hound Tundra, who had secretly hiked the 9-km Lynn–Needles ridge route to meet them. Champagne was pulled out of a backpack, and cheers sounded all around. These tales epitomize the good spirits of the mountain: kindred souls who know there are few pleasures in life greater than pushing one's body and soul to the limits, to be rewarded by scenes of geologic and natural beauty, shared with good friends.

OUR WISHES FOR THIS BOOK AND FOR THE PEAKS

Our first wish is for you, the reader, to incrementally set your sights to the infinite adventures and beauties in our North Shore peaks. All of us were casual and unambitious hikers, driven largely by frenetic trail-running into looking beyond the basic North Shore trails to discover more obscure peaks. We stumbled through these adventures, often with minimum information in our heads and maximum blood on our legs. It would have been useful to have some advance intelligence on these routes, and a sense of the relative difficulty of each peak, rather than exposing ourselves to some anxiety and injury in scouting out these adventures. We hope this book will facilitate your gradual growth towards more ambitious adventures.

We will contribute a portion of the proceeds from this book to North Shore Rescue and Lions Bay Search and Rescue, literal guardian angels watching over all those who venture into the North Shore peaks. We strongly encourage you to contribute generously and often to these worthy volunteer organizations, whether or not you have ever needed their assistance in a dark, lonely time.

We hope also that this book will lead to the establishment of more solid trails for some of the more obscure peaks. Already the Bagger Challenge (see **Appendix 4**) has contributed to wider knowledge of many of these peaks and routes, and the boots and flagging tape themselves have forged new trails (Magnesia, Enchantment, and Apodaca) and revitalized overgrown ones (Indian Arm Trail, the Episcopal Bumps, Jarrett and Clementine, Dickens). While it would be arguably unfortunate to have too polished a trail system, it would be safer and more welcoming if the existing trails formed a better-marked and more cohesive and clear network of trails, with trail posts stretching from Dickens to Deeks. If you have ever visited Boulder, Colorado, you will have admired its hundred-mile-plus trail network that runs throughout and beyond the Flatiron Range overlooking the city. A similar network of trails here could provide greater safety without compromising adventure.

We hope this book will help contribute to a greater appreciation of our local history as well. This history is largely ignored and unknown in suburban North Shore, which assumes itself to be a commuter town with some prior logging activity thrown into the mix. We hope that the mentions of hardy BCMC pioneers, scampering up these peaks in hobnail boots and bloomers, will gird your loins and stifle any whingeing or pangs of discomfort you may have. Similarly, we hope to cast light on the unknown zinc mines in the far North Shore backcountry, and, more anciently, the history of Indigenous peoples in these mountains (see **Appendix 16**), and the old-growth trees that still survive here (see **Appendix 1: Best peaks for old-growth and giant trees** and **Appendix 10**).

Finally, we hope this book will help contribute to an appreciation of the North Shore peaks as a zone of unique natural beauty, so close to a city and yet so wild. The Howe Sound Islands should become a national park or be otherwise protected, to be preserved for generations to come, their peaks, mosses, lakes, deer, and dolphins part of a natural reserve so close to Vancouver as to be Stanley Park writ large. All of the mainland peaks, with their trees, plants, and animals, should similarly be preserved for all generations, resisting the ever-increasing pressure of expanding neighbourhoods and ever-larger mansions with even greater views ever higher up mountain slopes. As for bears and larger mammals, which city-dwellers assume live in abundance on the North Shore peaks, by this book we hope to wave a warning flag that there are fewer animals back there than you think. In our tens of thousands of hours clocked in these mountains, at all times of day and night, we have seen far fewer critters than you would expect (see **Appendix 10**). We should not be so glib with thoughts that there exists infinite wildlife "back there" such that if a bear or two is shot for rummaging in rubbish bins left out overnight by suburban idiots, it is no big deal. Mountain goats, wolves, elk, and grizzly bears used to inhabit the local mountains and valleys: all but the first of those species are now gone, and even the goats are rare. We've driven several dominant animals to extinction in our local peaks, and it can happen again.

Why not go beyond preservation, however, and try to reverse our past transgressions? A May 1923 issue of the BCMC's *BC Mountaineer* reported, of Mt. Bishop, that while bears and goats were usually seen on past trips, "both species seem to have been driven away by hunters." The October 1944 *BC Mountaineer* quoted a newspaper report from 1914: "Fred Maddison and Charles Mullen shot four mountain goats on Crown Mountain yesterday." The *Daily World* newspaper remarked that "Vancouver is the only city on the American continent where bear, deer and goats can be shot within sight of city hall," and lamented: "No wonder that mountain goats and other wildlife have fled from the coastal area from this unnecessary slaughter." Two years later the *BC Mountaineer* noted the marmots playing in Goat Mountain cirque. Today no marmots are to be seen. Elk roamed the alpine plateaus until they were hunted to extinction in the early 20th century. Let us rewild our North Shore peaks with mountain goats, which abounded on Grouse and Goat mountains, on mounts Seymour and Bishop, and everywhere in between. Let us bring back marmot colonies to the scree slopes of our North Shore peaks. Bring back the noble elks. Not only could and would we reverse the excesses of Edwardian hunters, but it would add further beauty to the pleasures of future adventurers and would also be superb for attracting tourist dollars.

The more people gain a zeal for exploring the North Shore peaks, the better these goals can be accomplished. Let joy and virtue unite and flourish in these mountains.

HOW TO USE THE BOOK

The text surveys and profiles the 67 peaks of Vancouver's North Shore. We have generally followed the same format for each: an introduction to the area and its arterial trails and history, followed by a peak-by-peak survey. Each description starts with a summary of 28 key facts about the peak at a glance. Next is an introduction to the peak, followed by a (non-comprehensive) turn-by-turn description of the route up. Where there are other trails up that are worthwhile or occasionally used, we will include those, although generally in briefer form. The more difficult the peak, the more the book relies on the reader to have appropriate route-finding skills and experience. Do not expect handholding for every peak.

The peaks are surveyed from west to east. We start with the Howe Sound Islands, and then go from north to south on Howe Sound Crest Trail, to the Grouse–Crown and Lynn–Cathedral peaks, and conclude with the Fannin Range above the Indian River and Indian Arm.

At the back of the book, we've put together a collection of appendices for deeper knowledge and appreciation of the local mountains:

- **Appendix 1** provides a bevy of lists – highest, most prominent, most beautiful peaks; best running routes, wildlife-sighting areas, blueberry patches, and swimming holes – to help you plan your next adventure.
- **Appendix 2** is a glossary of hiking and climbing terminology.
- **Appendix 3** gives a short history of the British Columbia Mountaineering Club and the Alpine Club of Canada.
- **Appendix 4** tells of the Bagger Challenge, an annual peakbagging event that drew the authors into exploring these glorious peaks.
- **Appendix 5** recounts the Tour de Howe Sound, the annual 'bagging challenge of the Howe Sound summits.
- **Appendix 6** reveals the secrets of whisky bagging in the North Shore mountains.
- **Appendix 7** similarly discloses the fun of geocaching in these high places.
- **Appendix 8** recounts the history of cairn building and summit logging.
- **Appendix 9** explains those "rocket radio towers" such as found atop Gardner, Hat, and Cathedral.
- **Appendix 10** provides a high-level overview of the most common animals, plants, and fungi you'll encounter on our local peaks.
- **Appendix 11** summarizes the geology of the area.
- **Appendix 12** describes the mighty watersheds of the North Shore and the creeks that drain them.
- **Appendix 13** transitions into naming history, surveying the captains and ships present at The Glorious First of June battle in 1794, one of the primary sources for names of local peaks.
- **Appendix 14** is an overview of the family tree of the Wettin–Hanover–Saxe-Coburg–Gotha–Windsor royal family of Britain and Canada, the other main source of Britannia Range peak names.
- **Appendix 15** details everything you ever wanted to know about the naming of peaks.
- **Appendix 16** outlines the relationship to these mountains of the two First Nations who have lived there for thousands of years: the Squamish in the west and north and the Tsleil-Waututh in the east.
- **Appendix 17** reprints the journal entries for Captain Vancouver's visit to Burrard Inlet and Howe Sound, and his impressions of the mountains.
- **Appendix 18** provides an 1864 description of Burrard Inlet and Howe Sound based on Captain Richards's survey.
- **Appendix 19** digs out some archival newspaper clippings about first ascents and peak names, specifically Seymour and Bishop.
- **Appendix 20** lists named peaks not profiled in this book, either because they are too technical or lack height or prominence or are deep within the off-limits watershed.
- **Appendix 21** gives you the best Robbie Burns peakbagging songs and poems, in the grand tradition of whisky, cairns, and Munros.
- **Appendix 22** contains a comprehensive bibliography of print, internet, and other resources for those hungry for more information.

- **Appendix 23** lists still-unsolved mysteries as to first ascents, name origins, Indigenous place names and more.
- **Appendix 24** is a gallery of panorama photographs with peak names.

In **Appendix 1** you will find the most important resource: we've sorted the peaks into beginner, intermediate, and advanced levels, and arranged them in rough order from easiest to hardest. In some ways, this book is presented as an incremental mountain education: the local peaks can serve as a gradated introduction to hiking, climbing, and scrambling, with progressively more difficult terrain and routes. Unless you are comfortable completing a peak of medium difficulty, you probably should not attempt a harder one, at least not without a companion whose competence and confidence can guide you through. For example, unless and until you are comfortable climbing Hollyburn, you should not even think of climbing Coburg.

And remember: the difficulty ratings are on a relative scale. A 1/5 score does not mean the route is an easy stroll. Seymour, for example – rated 1/5 – is beyond the fitness level and wilderness competence of most Canadians and is a frequent spot for North Shore Rescue call-outs.

Difficulty is based on perfect conditions: blue skies, perfect visibility, no lingering snow, no rain, no clouds. If the weather is doubtful, do not test your limitations! Even a "beginner" hike can be deadly in the wrong conditions.

HOW TO USE THE PEAK SUMMARIES

We've used a "dashboard" approach to give you a concise and consistent overview of each peak before delving into the details. To get the most from this guidebook, we recommend you become familiar with the dashboard. Where there is a scale, we've assigned 0 as the worst, or lowest, score and 5 as the best, or highest.

Kathleen Burke (later Crerar) and friends in front of Grouse Mountain Chalet March 30, 1923

The following box shows the general format of the dashboard data. The title gives the name and elevation for each peak. Where the peak is one of the highest, we have also included its elevation ranking.

CAPILANO MOUNTAIN
(CAP) (1692 M #5)

The first line of each information header, formatted like this, contains a pithy description of why you may (or may not) wish to climb that particular peak.

CAUTION:
Highlights dangers, such as cliffs, technical climbing, lack of trail, and remoteness.

PROMINENCE:
If you are going between peaks, this is the distance you will need to descend before you start up the next one.

LATITUDE/LONGITUDE:
Location.

BANG FOR BUCK:
(0–5) Quality of peak in relation to the effort involved. 0: punishing and unrewarding; 5: the views, features, and route are glorious enough to justify the effort.

PEAK VIEW:
(0–5) How's the view at the summit? 0: no view at all; 5: stunning views.

TRUE SUMMIT LOCATION:
Clarifies the precise location of the actual top, for purist or novice peakbaggers.

HEADWATERS:
Rivers and creeks that start their course to the sea from this peak.

BEST VIEWS FROM:
Best places to view the peak from afar.

TRIP INFORMATION

Round-trip distance: Total distance (in kilometres) from the start to the finish. When a peak can only be reached from another peak, this is the longest distance from the start.

Elevation gain: Total distance up from start to finish on the main route.

Time: We have provided a range that includes hikers from fast to slow. If you are especially speedy or particularly leisurely, adjust accordingly. The number in brackets is the actual time of one of the authors, an energetic trail-runner: you can measure your own average speed in "Maurer units."

Difficulty: (0–5) How much physical effort, technical expertise and navigational skills will be needed? 0: A walk in the park; 5: Experts only.

Snow free: Approximate date each year when the trail is mostly snow-free.

Must-sees: Blueberry patches; swimming holes; cultural modification; big trees, etc.

Scenery: (0–5) 0: nothing but trees and rocks; 5: impressive (old-growth, waterfalls, sweeping vistas).

Kids: (0–5) 0: get a sitter; 5: fun sights and a less technical, difficult, and dangerous route. Needless to say, this assumes kids are accompanied by a responsible, experienced adult; we are not endorsing any of these routes as solo kid trips.

Dogs: (0–5) How suitable is the route for dogs? 0: not suitable; 5: smooth footing and not too steep.

Runnability: (0–5) How runnable is the route (due to steepness, technicality, rolling rocks, or other hindrances)? 0: don't even think about it; 5: awesome.

Terrain: (0–5) 0: rough, bushwhacking, boulder fields, and devil's club; 5: lovely trail.

Public transit: Bus number: most routes are from Phibbs Exchange (near Ironworkers Memorial Bridge), Lonsdale Quay (central), Park Royal (west), or Horseshoe Bay (far west).

Cell coverage: How reliable and strong is cellular reception? Don't depend on this description! Signal strength depends on many factors, including the provider, the device, tree cover, even the weather. Cliff bands, gullies, and valleys block reception. Try to phone from a high point with minimal tree cover.

Sun: How's the sun on a sunny day on this route? Do you need sunscreen for the whole way, or can you judiciously zip to the exposed peak and back under tree cover before you start to sizzle?

Water: This entry will be in italics where there is no or little water along the route or the available water is not potable. Note: Giardia and related bacteria do occur in the North Shore mountains. While the water may look clean, we strongly recommend you purify or filter it before drinking.

Route links: Can you combine this adventure with a pleasing odyssey to other peaks?

HISTORY

Name origin: How the peak got its name, where that is known.

Name status: Whether official or unofficial (and if unofficial, recent or widespread, i.e., popularly used for a generation or more), and date of adoption.

Other names: Have any other unofficial names been given to this mountain?

First ascent: The first *recorded* climb to the peak. BCMC (British Columbia Mountaineering Club) members own this title for most peaks. Of course, the likely first ascenders of many of these summits were anonymous First Nations hunters, gatherers, or shamans, or early surveyors, explorers, hunters, or prospectors.

Other write-ups: Repeatedly useful references, abbreviated as:

- **Gunn** = Matt Gunn, *Scrambles in Southwest British Columbia* (Cairn Publishing, 2004)
- **Hanna** = Dawn Hanna, *Best Hikes and Walks of Southwestern British Columbia* (Lone Pine, 2006).
- **Hui** = Stephen Hui, *105 Hikes in Southwestern British Columbia* (Greystone Books, 2018)

Note that other editions of these books may omit peaks or add new ones.

Mountain essay: A long or short overview of the highlights of the mountain, including history.

Routes: We do not attempt to list every possible route up each mountain. Although we provide more detailed directions than most other hiking books, you should not assume that every turn and potentially confusing portion of the route has been mentioned. You will need to pay close attention to your own map and GPS, as well as the trail conditions. Snow, wind, treefall, signfall, logging, and human interference are common on these trails, and trail conditions and directions change every day.

Bagger tips: In the introductions to peak areas and ranges, co-author Bill Maurer has provided tips and routes aimed at the frenetic and energetic peak-bagger for optimizing speed and efficiency in a limited day. These observations are certainly not aimed at the casual hiker, and should only be followed by those with experience, stamina, and focus. The times provided in brackets (in bagger sections, as well as the time entries for individual peaks) are Bill's own times, to provide a consistent benchmark.

HOW TO USE THE MAPS

Just because a map (in this book or elsewhere) has a line on it, do not assume there is a trail or that the trail is in perfect condition. Some lines indicate a rough route with no flagged trail. Even on marked trails, conditions change all the time: treefall, spring growth, logging, floods, vandalism, and mud can all change trails beyond recognition. Some of the directions provided in the route descriptions and these maps are just that: routes rather than trails. You must be self-sufficient and experienced with compass and GPS, maps, and routefinding skills before you even consider attempting these routes.

DIFFICULTY, TIME ESTIMATES, AND PHYSICAL FITNESS

The baseline for this book is higher and harder than your typical hiking book, and higher and harder, for example, than the classic local guidebooks Bryceland and Macaree, *103 Hikes*, or Hannah, *Best Hikes*, or the newly released *105 Hikes*, by Stephen Hui. It is not intended as a general hiking guide with the assumption that every hike will be appropriate and enjoyable for every person. Many of these adventures are only suitable for a very few who have the experience, physical fitness, stamina, and preparation sufficient to survive the long, arduous, hazardous bushwhacks such routes entail. Again, if in doubt be cautious and conservative, and use the list of peak difficulty in **Appendix 1** as a means to determine where your limits are.

Time estimates are always difficult. Some readers are frustrated by trip times that wind up being wildly conservative; other, slower hikers may find themselves in peril through an estimate that is more ambitious than their ability. The suggested hike durations and commentary in this book are aimed at a fit hiker with some mountain and routefinding experience. You should calibrate your expectations up or down, as appropriate. We also strongly recommend that you use the list of peak difficulty in **Appendix 1** as only a relative measure: do not try a harder peak until you are comfortable with the peaks listed as easier.

An oft-cited rule of thumb for the average hiker's pace is 4 to 6 km/h on flat ground, with an extra half-hour for every 300 m of elevation gain. For most of the routes in this book, throw those estimates out the window, due to intermittent trails and steep climbs. Then again, a fit long-distance runner or experienced power hiker will find that benchmark to be woefully slow. The first rule of hiking, as of life, is "know thyself."

Unless specified, time estimates are based on the route referred to in the distance measurement in the peak table. Of course, distances and speeds will vary greatly between routes. We have provided a range covering a fast hiker to a slow hiker. If you are especially speedy or leisurely, adjust accordingly. The number in brackets is the actual time of one of the authors: you can measure you own average speed in Maurer-units (as in "I'm but half the speed of Bill") and plan your trips accordingly.

SAFETY

Vancouver's comfortable urbanity is jarringly proximate to remote danger. Each year, the number of rescue calls NSR receives has increased, and most of those could have been avoided had the distressed callers prepared or packed adequately. These people thought they were venturing only a few kilometres into the mountains and found themselves facing inclement weather, cliffs, wild animals, and death. Often these perils could have been easily avoided.

As a first step, again, know thyself. While your reach should extend your grasp, you should also always know your own limits, knowledge, ability, and experience. Only explore these peaks in perfect conditions; they will still be there on a nicer day. Assume that the worst will happen, not the best. You must be able to answer affirmatively to all three of these questions:

1. Can I find my way back?
2. Can I find my way back in the dark?
3. Can I survive one or two nights in the bush if I fail in 1 or 2 above?

THE TEN ESSENTIALS
ALWAYS (we repeat: *Always*) carry the Ten Essentials:

1. **light:** Headlamps are ultralight and cheap. LED lights last forever. Two lights are better than one (try changing batteries in the dark). Make sure that you bring an extra round of batteries. Our favourite entry-level headlamp is the Petzl Tikka XP, at less than $50.
2. **signalling device:** whistle (we recommend the Fox 40 whistle with a lanyard).
3. **firestarter:** matches (waterproof or in plastic bag) or lighter.
4. **extra clothes:** hat or toque, gloves or mittens, fleece jacket, Gore-Tex jacket, polypro underwear, good quality hiking socks, and Gore-Tex overpants. At a minimum, bring an ultra-lightweight puffy jacket. Models produced by companies such as Montbell weigh less and are smaller than a hotdog bun. Rain shells are now so small and light there is no excuse not to carry one, even when skies appear perfect. The Montbell Tachyon lightweight jacket, for example, is smaller than and half the weight of your wallet.
5. **pocketknife:** A multi-tool is better, but any good pocket knife with a quality blade will suffice. A small pruning saw to cut branches for a shelter or fire is also useful.
6. **shelter:** Large orange plastic bag and thermal tarp. An ultra-lightweight bivouac sack would also work. Survive Outdoors Longer (surviveoutdoorslonger.com) produces

emergency sacks that weigh only 100–200 g: not comfortable, but could mean the difference between life and death. Even a garbage bag is better than nothing.

7. **water** (electrolyte powder recommended) and **food** (high-energy food bars or gels).

8. **first-aid kit:** Should include ibuprofen or other pain-killers, splint, dressings, bandages, scissors, blister dressings, Benadryl or bee-sting medication.

9. **navigation:** Good quality compass, with topographical maps, and the ability to use both! We also recommend a GPS unit. The Garmin 64st or Montana GPS have superior reception. Load them with local base maps (e.g., from Backroad Mapbooks, backroad-mapbooks.com).

10. **communications:** Up-to-date smartphone, with a charged auxiliary battery. Store it in a plastic bag. Keep it turned off, and save it until you need it; don't drain it taking selfies or leaving location tracking turned on. Coverage in these mountains is notoriously spotty; assume you will not have coverage, and call when you can. Depending on the terrain and difficulty of your excursion, it may also be worth considering a satellite communications device such as the SPOT or the Delorme InReach (see below).

We are blessed with technology. All of the above Ten Essentials can fit in a small knapsack or trail-running pack. There is no excuse for not bringing all of these items. You will not notice they are there, and they may well save your life.

Of course, many people have a longer essentials list (a local Korean hiking group is rumoured to have a "400 Essentials" list). Other prudent and useful things to bring would be:

- **water purification:** Pills such as those produced by Aquatabs, or chlorine dioxide drops such as those produced by Aquamira, provide a simple and lightweight means of water purification, albeit with a delay of 15–30 minutes. MSR and Platypus produce several good purification systems. Lifestraw and Sawyer produce practical filtration systems ideal for quick swigs of water direct from the source.

- **SPOT or similar device:** Although expensive ($150–$200), consider its worth if it saves your life. This small device weighs almost nothing. It will send GPS signals confirming safety to a designated list of emails of loved ones, and allowing an emergency signal to be sent. Best if you do not use the step-by-step tracking feature; save that for an emergency.

- **sunscreen**
- **sunglasses**
- **hat**
- **snacks:** energy bars, gels, chews, trail mix
- **energy drinks or powder**
- **repair kit:** duct tape/Gorilla tape
- **toilet paper** or Wet Ones
- **hand sanitizer**
- **insect repellent**
- **binoculars**
- **trekking poles:** Invaluable if you have wobbly or sore knees. Just don't lean too hard on them on steep descents, lest you kebab yourself.
- **bags** for collecting trash
- **route description** or guidebook
- **field guides**
- **outdoor journal** with pen/pencil

- **quick-dry towel**
- **camera**
- **Go-Pro camera** (but leave the selfie stick at home)
- **two-way radios**
- **gaiters**
- **sandals** for fording
- **crampons or micro-spikes** for early-season climbs with snow underfoot. The locally made Hillsounds are our favourites (hillsound.com).
- **space blanket:** Available at marathons or outdoor stores, these weigh nothing and could provide additional emergency warmth and shelter.
- **beer/whisky** for triumphant peak celebration.

SAFETY TIPS

These tips will help you stay alive in these dangerous areas.
- **Bring the Ten Essentials** listed above.
- **Tell family or friends** your destination and route in detail, as well as your expected return time. Print out and leave a map and a route description with them. If you're late, rescuers will know where to look for you. If you have no local loved one, at least send an email or leave a Facebook post, or a note in your car window (although this sometimes attracts thieves). Where there is a trailhead logbook, sign in (and sign out!).
- **Check the weather report.** North Shore weather is unpredictable and can be deadly. Prepare yourself as best you can. Assume the worst and savour the best. Bring or wear worst-case clothing even if the skies are clear. Be willing to turn back if the weather becomes threatening. These are your local mountains: they will be there tomorrow and you can always hike them later.
- **Don't hike alone.** Even if you know the trail like the back of your hand and are experienced in the outdoors, what will you do if you break your leg in a gully out of cell range? Go with a friend. Or better yet, join a BCMC or ACC outing or trip organized by a trusted online hiking group.
- **If you get lost, stop and backtrack.** A trait most of us are guilty of is to persevere along a route even if all evidence indicates you are off trail. And then you try to backtrack on a hypotenuse to save time. These tactics fail 99 per cent of the time. You will rarely regret backtracking.
- **Know when to quit.** Frenetic and determined peakbaggers will sometimes keep going under adverse conditions. Purge this tendency. There is less shame in turning around than continuing, getting lost or injured and possibly dying. None of these peaks are worth dying for, and they will still be there next weekend. Remember: if you die, your adventures will likely be at an end.

WHAT TO DO WHEN THINGS GO WRONG
- **Do not panic.**
- **Stay positive.** Even if lost in these peaks, you are likely less than 20 km away from the city.
- **Refer to maps** and GPS.
- **If in doubt, stay put** rather than blindly travelling around and risking getting more lost or falling off a cliff. Resist the temptation to go downhill, which often leads to dangerous drainages and cliffs.

- **Conserve** your cellphone **battery**: turn off all unnecessary applications.
- **Blow a whistle**: three short blasts each minute to signal emergency.
- **Stay visible.**
- **Seek shelter.** If cold, safely light a fire if possible.
- If things appear to be going downhill, **call friends and family**, and, if appropriate, **911 or NSR** sooner rather than later.

SPECIFIC RISKS

Several of these mountains are scramble ascents or otherwise exposed, remote, or undeveloped and should only be attempted by properly equipped, experienced climbers. The most dangerous are West Lion, Cathedral, Echo, Hanover, Forks, Coburg, and Crown N1. Certain peaks have acute rockfall danger, Hanover being the most serious. Wearing a helmet is strongly advised. Do not try these routes in anything but perfect weather.

NIGHTFALL

Shockingly obvious, but many hikers forget that sundown in Vancouver ranges from 4 p.m. to 9 p.m. Always check sunset times online and be wary of daylight saving changes. While usable light may linger for an hour after sunset, this usually offers little solace in the dark forests of the North Shore.

WEATHER

The natural conditions of most North Shore mountains are less of a risk factor than weather and conditions at the time of climbing. The routes and ratings in this book are designed for fair weather, with clear, safe ground and rock underfoot. While some routes may work just as well in the winter, conditions are considerably different in cold and snow. Familiar and relatively easy routes in the summer are life-threatening in the winter. Goat, for example, is a pleasant summer climb that children can do with proper supervision. In the winter, though, a slip on its steep approach will propel you unprotected down a cliff into Kennedy Lake; several deaths have occurred here. Crown, similarly, is a pleasant and accessible hike in perfect summer conditions but an icy slide to death or grievous injury in winter or early spring, with ice or snow (or rain for that matter) on the steep, rocky approach. (That said, for additional relatively safe winter routes, see **Appendix 1: Best snowshoe trips**, but check avalanche.ca first!)

Hiking is particularly hazardous where snow lingers (as it does in most years) into May and June. By then, the snow has become a dense and slippery vertical ice rink. If you slip, stopping is nearly impossible. Many people have been seriously injured and even killed by losing their footing and sliding into a tree or over a cliff. If you do hike on snow, bring crampons and an ice axe and know well how to use them.

Even in warmer seasons, our local granite, rocks, and roots, covered in microalgae, become perilously slippery when wet. Use great caution when rocks are wet – slipping is the cause of most accidents on North Shore mountains. Fog and cloud can descend fast and hard here, reducing visibility to literally a metre; the writers have had to navigate by return GPS track in the dark too many times.

With our tall trees, wind creates its own danger. The abundance of treefall is proof that trees and large branches often snap and fall, and you do not want to be under them when they do. Even in Stanley Park, people have been killed by falling trees and branches. The risk does not end when the wind abates: damaged trees and branches can lean against each other, or hang by a sliver, waiting to fall on the unsuspecting. Be cautious of dead or leaning trees; assume that no tree is as solid as it seems.

In two minutes the weather went from blue sky to insane lightning storm: beware!

Lightning should never be underestimated, especially on a mountain. A direct strike will likely kill you or cause grievous injury. You can also be severely burned, knocked unconscious, rendered brain-damaged, or otherwise grievously injured by lightning striking the ground or a nearby rock, or simply electrifying the air around you. You are a sitting duck for death from above when on a ridge, in an open meadow, or on a peak. The authors have all personally experienced the sky turn from blue to thunderous black in a five-minute span; one author has been knocked unconscious by a nearby lightning strike while on a peak. If you see lightning or hear thunder, or see approaching hammer-like or tendrilled or black thunderclouds, get down from the peak or ridge immediately. If trapped on a high point, get below the highest boulder or tree. Instead of lying on the ground, squat or otherwise minimize contact with the ground or rock, as a near-strike can travel along the ground and still cause acute injury. Putting your feet on your backpack rather than directly on the ground may diffuse the shock. Avoid creeks, lakes, lichen, and wet surfaces. Give yourself some distance from your companions: if one of you is knocked out, the others can try first aid.

As keen as we are to get out and play, consider giving local mountain adventures a miss in less than perfect conditions. This is one of the joys of a locally focused hiking book: no date-stamped climbing permit or return air ticket restricts your opportunities. These mountains will be there for your entire lifetime, but if you ignore our advice and venture into the mountains in suboptimal conditions, that lifetime may be a short one. Be a fair-weather adventurer!

HYPOTHERMIA

In Vancouver's unpredictable, wild, wet, and cold weather, hypothermia awareness is critical. It is a common and potentially fatal condition. Weather is nastier in the mountains, and the temperatures are usually 5 to 10° colder. The day can be perfect in Vancouver and freezing on the peaks.

Contrary to expectation, most cases of hypothermia do not occur in freezing temperatures, but rather in surprisingly mild weather: 0 to 10°, exacerbated by inadequate clothing, fatigue, or persistent cold dampness.

The best advice is to avoid it altogether, by going into the mountains expecting the worst and bringing sufficient clothing. In today's age of ultralight shells and insulated jackets, there is no excuse for not bringing sufficient emergency clothing.

Hypothermia creeps in slowly, and often victims of hypothermia or their companions may not be aware that it is setting in. Watch for uncontrollable shivering, fast or shallow breathing, slurring of words, loss of coordination, fatigue, and nausea. As the condition worsens, skin turns pale, and lips and extremities turn blue. Perversely, a hypothermia victim may feel warm or hot; victims are often found with their clothes desperately torn off.

If you feel or see the signs of hypothermia, if at all possible: take shelter; replace wet clothing with dry; get warm; rehydrate, preferably with hot tea, soup, or water. Ideally, the rewarming will be gradual rather than rapid.

INSECTS

Mosquitoes are a nuisance in the North Shore mountains, particularly in spring and early summer. By late summer and early fall, when most seasonal tarns have evaporated, the mosquitoes vanish too. Bug spray and perhaps eating citrus fruit is the solution.

Bees and wasps usually nest in dry rotten trees but can be found anywhere in the North Shore mountains. Be sure to carry the appropriate level of medication if you have or suspect that you have allergies. An EpiPen is a potential lifesaver for those with serious allergies. A first-aid kit with Benadryl is useful for others.

Recently, there has been increased presence and awareness of deer ticks in the North Shore mountains, and the carrying of Lyme disease by these creatures. They are especially prevalent in spring. There is little to do to safeguard against them, except for wearing long clothing and avoiding brushing against trees: likely impossible in these parts. Have a buddy scope out your scalp and body for ticks after hiking. If a tick embeds itself, extract it as soon as possible: pull it out slowly with fine-tipped pliers; do not twist or yank, as you may leave its head in your skin. Though Lyme disease is very rare, it is compounded by the fact that it can manifest itself quickly or gradually, and that it has its symptoms which resemble other ailments and can come and go. Its usual first sign resembles the flu: sore throat, headaches, congestion, stiffness. While some victims contract a rash, particularly a circular, spreading "bulls-eye" rash, the majority do not. If untreated, the disease can shut down all systems of the body, causing neurological illnesses and paralysis. One can buy specially designed tick extractors; consider carrying one.

For safety considerations with other animals, see **Appendix 10.**

One should be careful when using ropes that are found on hikes. Always assume that the rope is old, frayed, goat-nibbled, UV-light-degraded, and poorly tied. Always have another grip or point of contact to save you if the rope fails. Never put your entire weight on the rope. Consider bringing your own fresh, safe rope to use.

CLOTHING AND EQUIPMENT

In addition to the thoughts above and among the Ten Essentials, here are a few more ideas.

UPPER-BODY CLOTHING

Dress in layers of lightweight synthetic (or Smartwool merino) materials that wick sweat and moisture away from the body. A lightweight, long-sleeve technical shirt, even in hot weather, will offer better protection from prickles, ultraviolet light, and unexpected drops in temperature. Avoid cotton. Carry or wear an ultralight shell jacket and puffy jacket; you can buy such products that compress to the size of a banana and weigh next to nothing. We also like hiking in light cotton-poly gloves, in all seasons: they offer sun protection as well as protection from branches and rocks as you descend and, at times, fall. A hat will protect you from ultraviolet light, and keep the heat in. We are fond of the wide brims of Tilley and similar hats.

LOWER-BODY CLOTHING

Again, lightweight synthetic materials are best. Sweatpants, jeans, and the like are terrible for hiking. We prefer knee-length hiking shorts. Lightweight synthetic underwear, as produced by such companies as Under Armour, are preferable to chafe-inducing cotton briefs. We love merino wool socks, and several manufacturers make this type of socks for hikers and runners that combine comfort and durability. In muddy conditions, gaiters may be useful. When bushwhacking, we sometimes use long-distance-running compression socks, which offer some protection against nasty shrubbery.

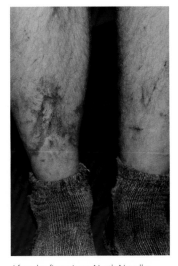

After the first trip to North Needle.

FOOTWEAR

Throw away those primitive torture devices – leather boots – and invest in some sturdy trail runners. The runners should provide good ankle support, with heavy-duty insoles and toe protection to guard against rocks. More important, they should have sufficient grip to travel over the moss-encrusted slickness of West Coast rock and skid-road bridges.

HYDRATION AND PACKS

Backpack technology has progressed in staggering bounds in the past 20 years: packs are now considerably lighter, tougher, and more comfortable. Find one that is perfect. We like packs with sternum and hip belts, to distribute weight and avoid chafe-inducing wobbling. We also like packs with decent pouches on the belt, to allow ready access to a camera, phone, map, and snack.

A good pack should have a good hydration system: you will stay hydrated if water is readily accessible. Nathan has perfected the art of running hydration packs. The best one for baggers is the HPL20; for shorter trips (less than three hours) the lighter, 1.5 litre HPL8 is perfect.

CAMPING

All of the peaks in this book can be and have been climbed as day hikes: however, an overnight adventure allows a more focused and leisured trek. As always, we recommend ultralight fast-pack equipment. Tents made by Montbell, Big Agnes, and MSR will make you happy.

FOOD

For short, intense trips, we generally bring an energy gel or other ultra-running carbohydrate supplement that is lightweight. For a more traditional experience, tote a PB&J sandwich or a submarine or maybe a smoked-salmon wrap. For longer trips that tax the muscles, consider a protein replenishment in the form of beef jerky or cured sausage. Bring lots of inter-meal snacks too: homemade trail mix, M&Ms, and fruit leather. For overnight trips, you can save weight by eschewing heated food. And single-malt whisky and craft beer taste finest on a peak.

ETIQUETTE AND ETHICS

While the North Shore's vast wilderness appears impenetrable at times, it is more vulnerable than it looks. Hikers are encouraged to respect the land and follow the Leave No Trace principles (leavenotrace.ca) to keep this national treasure alive for future generations. Beyond this, respect other hikers. Nobody came to the mountains to experience the joys of angry dogs, loud music, screaming morons, or garbage.

Some guidelines:

- **Don't litter:** There is nothing worse than seeing garbage on a trail. If possible, pick up litter left by previous idiots, and pack it out.
- **Leave space:** Many of these trails have many different kinds of users: hikers, trail-runners, bikers, horseback riders. Be courteous to all. Leave space on the trail for others to use; avoid walking two or three abreast on narrow trails.
- **Yield:** Downhill hikers yield to uphill hikers. Hikers yield to horses. Mountain bikes yield to everything. Stay alert for and let users who are faster than you pass.
- **Horses:** When meeting a horse, get off the trail on the downhill side (horses often bolt uphill when spooked). Quietly greet the rider and confirm that you are standing in a safe place. Stand quietly while the horse passes.
- **Obey the rules of the road:** Stay to the right on wider paths. Pass on the left.
- **Don't block:** Take breaks on the side of the trail, not on the trail or on a bridge.
- **Group hikers:** Yield to single or pairs of hikers. Avoid hiking in large groups. If you do, take special care not to block trails, be loud, or be annoying. Consider breaking up your group, possibly into different speeds, with all meeting at a given spot.
- **Hike quietly:** Blaring loud music or playing it through tinny phone speakers is obnoxious. If you must listen to music, wear headphones (but why would you want to commit a travesty of nature and etiquette by muting yourself off from birdsong, as well as the sounds of

approaching mountain bikers, hikers, cougars and bears?). Keep telephone calls to a minimum, and away from other groups. It may be a defence to a murder charge that the victim was engaged in a Facetime or Skype call on a peak in their final moments.

- **Avoid unsolicited advice or comments:** While some hikers think they are being helpful or friendly, unsolicited advice or comments ("It's too cold for shorts!" "Wait until you see how steep the next hill is!" "Only four hours to go!" "Don't look so glum!") are bloody annoying. If people want input from you, they'll ask.
- **Bear bells:** Leave them at home. Studies have shown that they may in fact attract young and curious bears. They also drive away other animals, including humans. (**Appendix 10** advises on what to do if you encounter a bear.)
- **Don't hog a viewpoint or a peak:** Give others their chance for a clean photograph or moment of glory.
- **You're responsible:** If you're leading a group of inexperienced hikers (we're looking at you, ESL teachers), brief them thoroughly beforehand on trail etiquette and safety.
- **Dogs:** Control your dog. If in doubt, leave the dog at home. Approaching hikers don't know if your dog is friendly or safe. Clean up after your dog, or have it poop well off the trail. There is a fecal hot-tub in hell reserved for dog owners who leave plastic baggies of dog waste at trailheads or along trails.
- **Human waste:** Do not defecate within 100 m of creeks or lakes or the trail itself. Try to find already disturbed land (upturned tree or bare earth) and dig a shallow pit in which to poop. Cover and bury it. Leave no trace.
- **Stay on trails**: Where a trail exists, use it. Trail-cutting causes erosion and kills life underfoot. It also confuses future hikers. Even on bare rock, avoid stepping on vulnerable lichen and algae. Stick to the bare rock.
- **Walk through a mud puddle, not around it**: Don't make it larger and erode the trail.
- **Never throw rocks or other objects below you:** Also take care not to accidentally dislodge rocks. In a place like Hanover, you will likely kill the person below you.
- **Fires:** In most areas of regional and provincial parks, which cover most of these peaks, fires are illegal. There should be no need to light a fire for most of these hikes, unless you face an emergency bivouac. If you do, build the fire on rock, and not flammable material on trails. Extinguish it thoroughly, bury it, and leave no trace.
- **Do not pick or take plants, flowers, rocks,** historical artifacts, or other things you find on the trail, regardless of whether the place is a park or not. You'd be taking that pleasure away from the next visitor. Berries and mushrooms can be responsibly taken if they are abundant and you leave some for others.
- **Eliminate invasive species:** The exception to the above is your treatment of invasive species like ivy, holly, dead nettles, and scotch broom. Pull those up root and branch! For photographs of invasive species, browse the database at nativeplants.evergreen.ca.
- **Do not move or destroy signs, blazes, flagging tape, or cairns:** these mark the trail and may be crucial for the safety of hikers, particularly in poor weather. Unless you are marking the trail or the trail is not obvious, try to avoid building new, potentially misleading cairns.
- **Maintain trails:** Be a trail saint. Clip bushes and branches growing over the trail. Move deadfall. Cover false paths.
- **Do not approach or antagonize wildlife:** While feeding wildlife may seem kind and cute, it interferes with the animals' natural hunting and gathering and unnaturally habituates them to humans. Plus, your human food could sicken them.

- **Rescue:** If you are ever rescued by NSR or LBSAR, donate generously and regularly. How much is your life worth? How many hundreds of staff hours were spent rescuing you? The average rescue costs thousands of dollars. Strive to repay your entire debt, now, or over the remainder of your but-for-your-rescue lifespan.
- **Smile and be friendly:** Greet people you meet. This tells them you are there, and makes them feel at ease. A simple "Howdy" or "Nice day" is fine.
- **Leave each place you visit in a better condition than you found it:** Take only pictures, leave only footprints (and only on the trail).

Hat Tarn with Mt. Hanover in the background.

MEANS OF PEAKBAGGING

TRAIL RUNNING

We list trail running first because it is the fastest and most fun way to explore the North Shore peaks. We do not encourage running every step of the way up a peak: even the best trail runners power-hike. But trail running shoes offer greater comfort and grip than traditional hiking boots. And many of the starts of North Shore peak routes, with arduous and somewhat dull climbs up gravel or logging roads, scream for a speedy approach or escape. Exhibit A: Howe Sound Crest Trail, of which 35 per cent is dull and 65 per cent is spectacular. The faster you cover these mediocre stretches, the more time you can spend exulting in the beautiful and remote places. See **Appendix 1** for most-runnable bagging adventures and best slalom run descents.

HIKING

Hiking is the most popular means of climbing the North Shore peaks. Even if you go at a hiking pace, we endorse using trail-running shoes and other ultralight equipment. Leather boots are almost never necessary, and will constrict the inevitable swelling of your feet after a long day.

CYCLING

None of the peaks (with the possible exception of Grouse) allow for a feasible all-cycle approach. Even with Grouse, the near-endless gravelly pedal up Mountain Highway would be life-denying, and bikes are probably not permitted up the peak itself. That being said, many of the peaks lend themselves well to a substantial cycle approach. For those peaks accessed from Seymour Valley Trailway (the LSCR road) (The Needles; Paton/Coliseum/Burwell/Cathedral; Bishop/Jarrett/Clementine, etc.) a bike will shave hours and fatigue off your approach time. And for all of the peaks, it is glorious as well as green to achieve a self-propelled ascent: pedalling or kayaking from your home to the trailhead, hoofing it up the peak, and returning home sans fossil fuel. See **Appendix 1** for the best bike and bag adventures.

KAYAKING/CANOEING

The Howe Sound peaks all lend themselves to the adventure of an aquatic approach. Do not be fooled by their proximity to Vancouver: weather and wave conditions on Howe Sound can change suddenly, and the waters are cold and potentially deadly. As for the other peaks, Dickens is the only one that would make sense as a water approach.

ROUTEFINDING

Many of the peaks included here do not have established trails; their directions are for routes only, rather than trails. But if you follow our recommended sequence of peaks, you will find your routefinding skills increasing with each adventure. The following are tips that may accelerate your comfort with bushwhacking and finding a trail.

- There is no shame and much wisdom in retracing your steps. If you feel like you have lost the path, go back to the last blaze, flagging, or other point of certainty. Many adventures turn ugly through ruthless perseverance and (more typically male) adamance at always going forward, thus compounding the initial error.
- If you lose track of a path, look for a fallen tree. Most times when you lose a trail, it is due to a fallen tree obscuring it. Often a storm will fell a whole copse of trees, making the exercise challenging. Use fallen trees as an asset rather than a liability: in most circumstances, you will find the trail right under them!
- Sometimes animal tracks are your enemy and sometimes they are your friend. Deer and bears have roughly the same flexibility and dexterity as we humans do, and they have the same aversion to cliffs and steep slopes. On the other hand, they don't seem to be as destination-obsessed as humans, and an encouraging path may ultimately lead you nowhere.

HIKING WITH CHILDREN

Our North Shore peaks are a playground, a classroom, and during berry season a candy store. It is not a hard sell: there is rough and ropey bark to be pawed, storybook mushrooms to be poked, and late-season snowball fights. Infinite piles of rocks lead to infinite inukshuks. Frogs and salamanders live in the lakes. Grey jays land on trail-mix-laden hands and on heads. Trolls live under trail bridges and older siblings jump out from behind fat trees yelling "Gruffalo!" Old man's beard plants make fine false moustaches. Erratics and granitic slabs invite modest rock climbing. Puddles need draining. Trail running comes naturally. And all children appreciate the epic glory of reaching a peak and spotting their tiny home so far away and below.

It is not difficult to keep hiking fun and adventurous. Always refer to a mountainous outing as an "adventure" rather than a "hike." It is a treat rather than a forced activity on a sunny day. Every step should be a discovery or a game. Be cautious but ambitious with hikes with your kids: they are capable of much more than you expect.

Many parents fret about safety. None of the "easy" hikes set out in **Appendix 1** have any inherent exposure. As for the peaks, and any dicey areas en route, most children have a keener sense of self-preservation than their parents, and the potentially dangerous parts of routes become a teachable moment. Hold their hands and explain the risks that come with reckless or undisciplined behaviour, whether on a mountain or on a road. (That said, know your own child. Some children lack self-control, good judgment, and a sense of self-preservation, due to temperament or upbringing or psychological or physical conditions, and should not be brought up a mountain; wait until they are ready.) Ultimately your children face a much greater risk of death or injury from being hit by a minivan frantically driven by a parent to drop their own child off at school.

The objective is to bend your children, not break them. Take lots of pauses, but control the timing yourself, rewarding toughness and never indulging whining. Bring lots of water and snacks, especially chocolate. Sports Beans (with electrolytes) and other packaged snacks work very well, both as an incentive and an invigorator. Make sure children are dressed appropriately, in layers, for any weather, and invest in good-quality shoes. Ultimately your success at being a superb hiking parent will be determined by your own imagination and stamina. Carry as much of the collective provisions as you can, and be capable of popping your child on your shoulders if the need arises. And never whine or falter yourself. You likely have only yourself to blame if your child is wimpy, flabby, or unadventurous.

For ideas on the best hikes to take your children on, see **Appendix 1** for the best mountain adventures with kids and the best granite slabby playgrounds, as well as the best mountain blueberry/huckleberry abundance and post-bag swimming holes.

North Strachan: the true summit, with Lions and Brunswick in background.

HIKING WITH DOGS

Dogs are stolid and enthusiastic peakbagging companions. As with children, your reach should extend your grasp: dogs are capable of far more than you would expect. Katey, a famous North Shore adventure dog, is neither husky nor elkhound, but a short-legged beagle. Famous and hardy North Shore mountain pooches Tundra, Bella, and Stetson have climbed most of the peaks in this book. Be sure to bring sufficient food and water, especially in late season: dogs do not sweat, and they need more water than we humans do.

Most of the peaks are in provincial or regional parks, so in theory dogs must be on leashes. In practice, though, this is neither feasible nor desirable, and generally a blind eye is turned by the authorities and by fellow hikers provided that the dog is well behaved. Maintain this decent equilibrium by being responsible dog owners: ensure that your dog is well disciplined and non-threatening, and clean up after your pet. If either the owner or the dog is incapable of these basic necessities, they should both stay home.

Burt's Peak, Gambier Island, from the meadow beside lovely Lost Lake.

HOWE SOUND ISLANDS

(9 PEAKS)

Howe Sound is the large, triangular body of ocean northwest of Vancouver between the communities of Horseshoe Bay, Gibsons, and Squamish. It includes Bowen, Gambier, and Anvil Islands, offering fun mountains and challenging routes for peakbaggers.

When Captain Vancouver exited Burrard Inlet (which in the original, 1798 edition of his book was called Burrard's "Canal") and visited Howe Sound on June 15 and 16, 1792, it is unsurprising that the mountains were a predominant vision. These peaks, however, probably contributed to his ill-ease and disappointment at the imposing inhospitality of Howe Sound:

> Quitting Point Atkinson, and proceeding up the sound, we passed on the western shore some small detached rocks, with some sunken ones amongst them, that extend about two miles, but are not so far from the shore as to impede the navigation of the sound; up which we made a rapid progress, by the assistance of a fresh southerly gale, attended with dark gloomy weather, that greatly added to the dreary prospect of the surrounding country. The low fertile shores we had been accustomed to see, though lately with some interruption, here no longer existed; their place was now occupied by the base of the stupendous snowy barrier, thinly wooded, and rising from the sea abruptly to the clouds; from whose frigid summit, the dissolving snow in foaming torrents rushed down the sides and chasms of its rugged surface, exhibiting altogether a sublime, though gloomy spectacle, which animated nature seemed to have deserted. Not a bird, nor living creature was to be seen, and the roaring of the falling cataracts in every direction precluded their being heard, had any been in our neighbourhood.[2]

While Captain Richards named most of the landmarks around Howe Sound, including its peaks, he too was ambivalent about the area:

> HOWE SOUND, immediately adjoining Burrard inlet ... on the north is an extensive though probably useless sheet of water, the general depth being very great, while there are but few anchorages. It is almost entirely hemmed in by rugged and precipitous mountains rising abruptly from the water's edge to elevations of from 4,000 to 6,000 feet; there is no available land for the settler, and although a river of considerable size, the Squawmisht, navigable for boats, falls into its head, it leads by no useful or even practicable route into the interior of the country.[3]

The peaks on the Howe Sound islands may not be as high as some of the others in this guidebook, but before you write them off, consider that most routes start at sea level. Given their lower altitude and the warming effect of the ocean, these peaks get far less snow than most on the mainland, so they are available to climb year-round.

BOWEN ISLAND
(3 PEAKS)

Bowen is the most populous of the Howe Sound islands (approximately 3,500 permanent residents) and is the nearest to Vancouver. The island is roughly 12 km long by 6 km wide and 50 km² in area.

The Squamish name for the island is Kwilakm, meaning "clam bay," after its bounty of clams. Another name was Xwlíl'xhwm, meaning "fast drumming ground." It has been theorized that the name does not refer to actual drumming but to the sound made by the ocean as it passes through the narrow pass between Bowen's northern point and Finisterre Island.

Originally named (together with neighbouring Keats Island) as Islas de Apodaca by Spanish explorer José Narváez aboard the *Santa Saturnina* in 1791, it was renamed in 1859 by Captain Richards after Rear Admiral James Bowen (1751–1835), who was master of HMS *Queen Charlotte*, Admiral Lord Howe's flagship at the Glorious First of June. Bowen served at Lord Howe's personal request, and Howe was a fond mentor of Bowen. Even during battle, Bowen would address Lord Howe by his formal title, prompting this response: "Mr. Bowen, you call me, my Lord!, and My Lord! you yourself deserve to be a Prince."[4]

Homesteaders arrived on Bowen in 1871, building houses and a brickworks. Surprisingly for its present character as a sleepy bucolic paradise, Bowen has had an active industrial history, including logging, mining, and milling, and an explosives factory. There is presently no heavy industry on the island.

Bowen has long been an outdoors playground for Vancouverites, with the Terminal Steamship Company and then the Union Steamship Company offering summer cruises from Coal Harbour throughout the first half of the 20th century.

Bowen is serviced by regular BC Ferries from Horseshoe Bay. There are frequent sailings and it is inexpensive to walk on or take your bike. Water taxis are also an option off hours.

There are three peaks on Bowen. If you aspire to climb them all in one day, prepare for a long day, as they are quite far apart. While it is possible to do a sweep on foot, you may wish to bring your bike and take out-and-back routes to save time and energy.

The village of Snug Cove near the ferry terminal is quaint and worth exploring before or after your bagging expedition. There are several decent restaurants and pubs where hungry peakbaggers may reward themselves for a fine day of accomplishments in the mountains, and many popular bed and breakfasts should you decide to stay the night.

The rocks underlying all of the Bowen Island peaks are among the oldest on the North Shore, predating the Jurassic period. They consist largely of the sedimentary rocks greenstone, chert, and greywacke, and are referred to by geologists as the "Bowen Island Group." Kilometre-wide bands of younger plutonic rock run west–east towards the north and south ends of the island, with the northernmost and southernmost ends returning to the predominant Bowen Island Group rock.

GETTING THERE

By car: from Lions Gate Bridge, take Highway 1 to Horseshoe Bay.

By transit: take the #250 or the #257 bus.

From Horseshoe Bay, take the Bowen Island ferry to Snug Cove on Bowen Island. Ferries leave roughly every hour during the day and take approximately 20 minutes. Be sure to check the current schedule at bcferries.com/schedules/mainland/biva-current.php.

Water taxis are also an option off hours. Services to Bowen Island include:

- cormorantwatertaxi.com
- bowentaxi.com/pages/schedule-fares
- oldschoolmarine.com/services/water-taxi

BOWEN BAGGER TIPS

The three peaks of Bowen can be bagged in an energetic day from Horseshoe Bay on foot or as a bike-and-hike. Reduce greenhouse gases and leave your car on the mainland.

Total distance:
18.3 km (hiking) plus 24.2 km
(paved road approaches) = 42.5 km

Estimated total time:
8 hours (from Snug Cove with bike)

Elevation gain:
2093 m

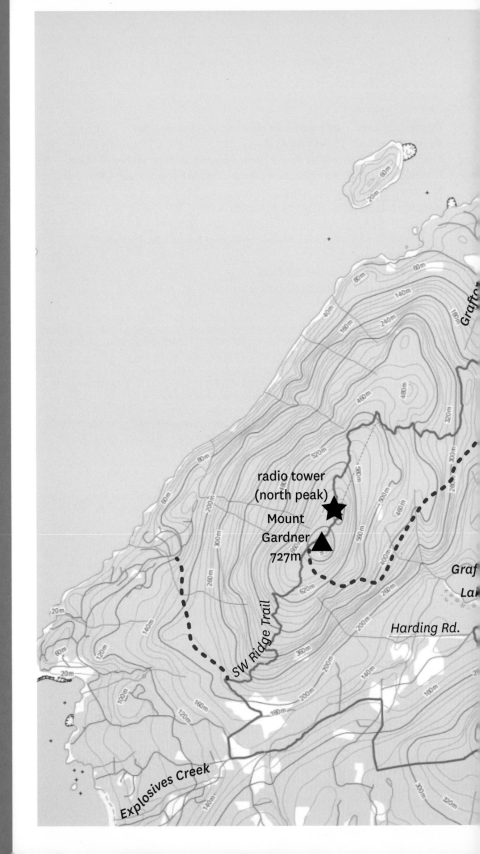

radio tower
(north peak)

Mount
Gardner
727m

SW Ridge Trail

Harding Rd.

Graf
La

Graf

Explosives Creek

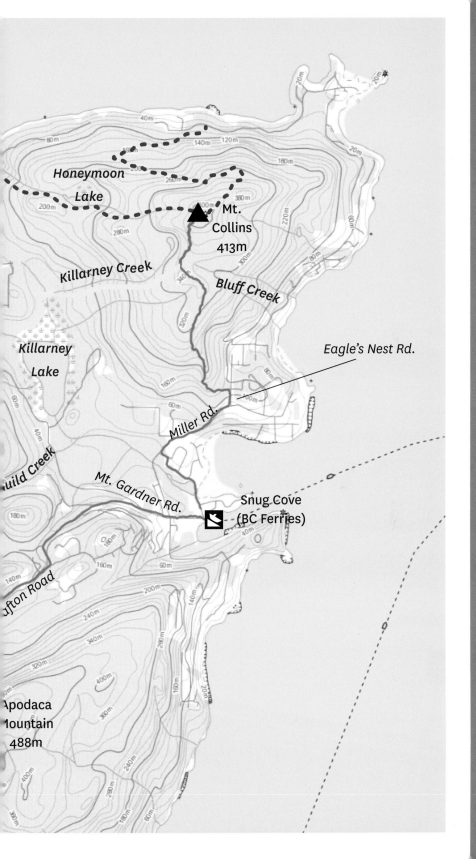

Honeymoon
Lake

Mt.
Collins
413m

Killarney Creek

Bluff Creek

Killarney
Lake

Eagle's Nest Rd.

Miller Rd.

uild Creek

Mt. Gardner Rd.

Snug Cove
(BC Ferries)

fton Road

Apodaca
Mountain
488m

MT. GARDNER

(GAR) (727 M)

A popular route with rewarding views, although the true peak, stuck in the woods about 1 km to the south of the microwave station, has none.

CAUTION:
Some steeper bits near the north peak. Potentially unreliable ropes.

PROMINENCE:
727 m.

LATITUDE/LONGITUDE: N49.37667 W123.39083, north summit; N49.37915 W123.38837, south (true) peak.

BANG FOR BUCK:
4/5

PEAK VIEW:
0/5. But splendid views on north peak near microwave station.

TRUE SUMMIT LOCATION:
The true peak is south of the popular viewpoint at the microwave station.

HEADWATERS:
Small streams.

BEST VIEWS FROM:
Howe Sound, HSCT peaks.

TRIP INFORMATION

Round-trip distance: 7.0 km from trailhead plus 5.8 km from Snug Cove to trailhead (up Route 1, down Route 2).

Elevation gain: 700 m.

Difficulty: 2/5. Main challenge is the rabbit warren of trails.

Time: 3–6 hours all routes.

Snow free: Year-round with rare exceptions.

Must-sees: Salmon ladder in Crippen Park; lily pads on Killarney Lake; the hamlet of Snug Cove.

Scenery: 3/5.

Kids: 4/5. Take care with the cliffs off the helicopter pad on the north peak.

Dogs: 1/5. Dogs must be on leash in Crippen Park. Short stretches require a rope.

Runnability: 4/5.

Terrain: 4/5. Second-growth forest.

Public transit: #250 or #257 bus to Horseshoe Bay. Ferry to Bowen Island.

Cell coverage: Good on peak; variable below.

Sun: Mostly in shade. Fully exposed on north peak.

Water: None.

Route links: Apodaca, Collins.

HISTORY

Name origin: Named by Captain Vancouver after his friend and mentor Admiral Lord Alan Gardner, Baron Gardner of Uttoxeter (1742–1809), who fought at the Glorious First of June and was instrumental in recommending Vancouver to command the exploration of the Pacific Northwest. Name used in Captain Richards's 1860 chart.

Name status: Official. Adopted December 7, 1937.
First ascent: First climbed by settlers before 1912. Likely climbed by First Nations before that.
Other write-ups: Hanna, Hui.

Gardner is the highest peak on Bowen Island. Getting to the trailhead is a good part of what makes this peak the most popular Howe Sound summit: it includes a short ferry ride, a visit to a quaint seaside village, and a circumnavigation of a pleasant lake. Bring your bike. Stay for dinner or even stay the night in one of the several B&Bs, and make it a mini-vacation.

Most hikers will head for the shorter north peak, with its radio towers and a helicopter landing pad that makes a good platform for sunbathing, resting, picnicking, and exulting in the views of Howe Sound and the Howe Sound Crest peaks. For most visitors, this is the destination. The true summit, however, is a forested viewless bump to the south, on the other side of a small hollow. Only purist baggers will bother.

On either peak, contemplate the folly of a 1969 proposal by a company named Maui Holdings to build an upscale resort, with a golf course, a thousand condominiums overlooking Killarney Lake, and skiing on Gardner, even though Gardner only receives a light dusting of snow each winter. Also appreciate the resilience of nature, rebounding with new forest from what was described in 1971 as the "slash-burned scars" of Gardner. Gardner's southwest slopes were also the subject of the exploratory Bonanza Mine in the early 20th century. One mine shaft is seen in the Bluewater area, near Mutiny Lane. Another is about 15 minutes off the Mt. Gardner trail, where a slag heap and an ore car can also be seen.

Although Gardner is popular and close to civilization, it is a rabbit warren of trails of various consistency. There are several ways to the peak. The fact that there are two peaks and so many trails requires you to pay even more attention to routefinding than otherwise. Bring a GPS and second-guess every turn you make. Happily, signposts have recently been placed at key intersections to offer some guidance. We also recommend bowentrails.ca, a useful website providing maps and information on this peak, whose routes as of this writing were being reorganized and better signposted.

Given the low elevation and plethora of trails, Gardner lends itself well to loop ascents and descents, with the warning above that you may get lost if you get too fancy. We usually ascend via Route 1 (gentle forest) and descend via Route 2 (steep trail and then dull gravel switchbacks), following the directions in reverse. The route down from the north viewpoint peak is easy to find: north of the radio tower, beside a large rock, and usually marked by a well-flagged tree. But the alternative routes below, and other sources such as bowentrails.ca, will give you nearly infinite variations.

To Bowen Island residents, the popular Gardner Hardener trail is a fair substitute for the Grouse Grind. It starts at Hiker's Trail / Bowen Pit Road (where there is a sign and scores for fastest climbing times), and follows existing trails to the peak (primarily Route 2, below).

The summit of Gardner consists of banded amphibolite and metasedimentary rock, the same as on Hollyburn. This younger mineralization originated as ocean or river sediments, and then was pressurized into metamorphic rock. The underlying stratum is Bowen Island Group pre-Jurassic metamorphic.

FROM SNUG COVE VIA KILLARNEY LAKE AND SOUTH GARDNER
TRAIL/MID-ISLAND TRAIL

This trail takes you on some lovely single-track around the mountain, then steeply uphill to the south peak (true summit).

- From the ferry, take your first right at the library. Continue along for about 25 m and then go left on trail into Crippen Regional Park. Pass a memorial garden and a fish ladder.
- Follow this wide, popular trail about 2.5 km to Killarney Lake.
- Go left and keep the lake to your right. After 700 m, watch for a steep trail on your left (if you reach a bridge across marshy swamp, you have gone too far). Cross Mt. Gardner Road, then go rightward along the shoulder about 200 m to Hikers Trail (Bowen Pit) Road. Follow this road uphill to the metal gate marking the trailhead.
- Continue uphill on dirt road until you reach a sign marking Skid Trail on your left (south). Follow this single-track through a forested area. After about 2 km the trail forks.

On Bowen Island, a fork in the trail. Either way takes you to the top of Mt. Gardner.

- Go straight, on the marked South Gardner Trail.
- The trail will gradually slope upwards. It also forks in places and the dominant trail appears to go downwards. *Don't go this way.* If you find yourself doing this, you have gone the wrong way; backtrack and go up.
- After a few steep sections the trail will continue to climb south. You will come to an intersection. A steep trail, marked "Mt. Gardner Summits," heads upward to the right, north. This is the most direct route to the summits. Ascend via a series of tight switchbacks to the south peak, the true summit. Go over two short bumps. The true peak is an uninspired, scrubby rock dome marked by a small cairn. There is no view.

- Alternatively, at the sign, you can continue straight on the South Gardner trail. This route will loop you around to approach the summits from the southwest. This is slightly longer, but nicer and less steep. There are some viewpoints. The trail pops out into the small dip between the peaks. You will see in the col nice new signs directing you to the two summits.
- Whichever way you approach, it is easy to climb both peaks: the south and north summits are close together, separated by a small dip, with a signposted trail connecting them.

ROUTE 2:

FROM SNUG COVE VIA GRAVEL ACCESS ROAD

This is the easiest and fastest, if dullest, route to the microwave facility at the north peak.

- At the end of Hikers Trail (Bowen Pit) Road veer right (north) up the gravel road. The road does about 12 switchbacks, steadily climbing. When you come to a switchback heading due north for a long distance, do not take it, but cut into the forest, onto Mt. Gardner Trail.
- The trail alternates between gentle climbs through glades of second-growth trees to very steep patches with ropes. You are never exposed, but this climb can be slippery when wet.
- At the end of the steepest stretch, you will pop out to the north peak microwave tower, beside a large rock. The tree at the mouth of the trail is usually covered in flagging tape.
- The south and north peaks are close together, separated by a small dip, with a well-marked trail connecting them.

ROUTE 3:

FROM WEST – MUTINY LANE

- Take Grafton Road to Adams Road to Bowen Bay Road across the island. Turn north onto Windjammer Road. Drive to end of Mutiny Lane. You will see a hiking kiosk.
- Travel southeast and up along Bluewater Trail, at first steep, then gradual.
- Come to a junction. To the right heads down to Laura Road. Turn left instead, up the steep Southwest Ridge Trail.
- After several switchbacks to climb the steep slope, hit a flattish section on Skid Trail.
- Go left and up. Within a few minutes, you will come to the saddle between the north and south peaks.

ROUTE 4:

FROM SOUTH – LAURA ROAD

- Take Grafton Road to Adams Road to Bowen Bay Road. Turn right on Westside Road, then left on Laura Road.
- There is a trailhead kiosk.
- Go north on Bowen Bay Trail.
- At a three-way intersection, turn right, up the steep Southwest Ridge Trail.
- After several switchbacks to ameliorate the steep slope, hit a flattish section on Skid Trail.
- Go left and up. Within a few minutes you will come to the saddle between the north and south peaks.

APODACA MOUNTAIN

(APO) (488 M)

A gentle bushwhack to an obscure bump in a nature preserve.

CAUTION:
No trail or trail markings.

PROMINENCE:
325 m.

LATITUDE/LONGITUDE:
N49.36194 W123.36500.

BANG FOR BUCK:
1/5. "Because it's there."

PEAK VIEW:
0/5. No views.

TRUE SUMMIT LOCATION: Marked
with a small rock cairn.

HEADWATERS:
Small streams.

BEST VIEWS FROM:
Eastern Howe Sound,
HSCT peaks.

TRIP INFORMATION

Round-trip distance: 4 km from ferry to turnoff for Grafton Road (one way); 6.3 km return to peak.
Elevation gain: 350 m.
Difficulty: 3/5.
Time: 1–3 hours.
Snow free: Year-round with rare exceptions.
Must-sees: Lots of deer skeletons; also live deer; alpacas down below.
Scenery: 2/5.
Kids: 2/5. An introduction to the joys of bushwhacking.
Dogs: 0/5. Not allowed in ecological reserve.
Runnability: 2/5.
Terrain: 2/5. Rolling hills. Bushwhacking.
Public transit: #250 or #257 bus to Horseshoe Bay. Ferry to Bowen Island.
Cell coverage: Generally good on peak; variable below.
Sun: Mostly in shade.
Water: No water other than murky ponds.
Route links: Gardner, Collins.

HISTORY

Name origin: The Spanish name for Bowen Island (together with neighbouring Keats Island) is Las Islas de Apodaca, named by Spanish explorer José Narváez in 1791 after Sebastian Ruiz de Apodaca (1747–1818), a Spanish admiral who was later appointed lieutenant general, the highest Spanish rank. Proposed as a name by author David Crerar in 2011 after Apodaca Provincial Park, on the southeast slope. The park was established in 1954 on land donated by Vancouver archivist Major James Skitt Matthews in memory of his son, who had died at age 22 in an accident. Major Matthews himself had proposed naming the peak "Apodaca," in a letter of September 27, 1953.

Name status: Unofficial. Apodaca Park named on November 22, 1954.

First ascent: Likely climbed by First Nations and settlers. David Crerar, Ean Jackson, and Ryan Conroy made first known report of climb, in 2009.

Apodaca is the unofficial name of the second-highest point of land on Bowen Island. The summit, a bump in the forest, is only distinguished from its neighbouring bumps by a small rock cairn. The peak is located in the Bowen Island Ecological Preserve, so tread lightly. At the time of this writing there were no access trails, so be sure to bring a compass, some extra GPS batteries, and a decent topo map. Also get ready for a good bushwhack.

Apart from bagging another peak, there is little obvious draw to Apodaca. That said, the bushwhack is not arduous or unpleasant if one follows the obvious contour-line route and the small lakes. Their radiant green and the sense of solitude so close to civilization make Apodaca a worthy adventure.

For some odd reason, Apodaca seems to be the region where Bowen deer go to die. You will almost certainly find a deer skeleton on your hike.

The "first bagger" co-exploratory jaunt to Apodaca was marked by three dead GPS units, a torrential downpour, discovery of massive tree blowdown from storms, near tumbling over cliffs, lacerated shins, and inadvertent 100 per cent retracing of paths. But that is a tale for another day. The route below is more pleasant and calm.

ROUTE 1:

DIRT ROAD FROM GRAFTON ROAD

Note: You may be approaching or crossing private property. Please be respectful of people's peace and quiet.

- The most direct way to access Apodaca from the ferry is to go about 4 km up Grafton Road. Take the unnamed gravel road that heads southeast from this junction just beyond a house. Bypass the driveway on the left that leads to the house. N49.36613 W123.3765.
- The unnamed road heads slowly uphill past some dumpsters and random garbage and construction debris.
- Pass three switchbacks until you get to a large open area at the fourth one. Elevation is 280 m at this point. If you are on a bike, this is where you would leave it. N49.36135 W123.37471.
- Hike a little farther along the road and then head uphill into the bush.
- As the crow flies, your destination is not much more than a kilometre away, but anticipate between 2 and 3 hours of gentle bushwhacking past a few steep bits and cliffs, a few swamps and some blowdown.
- The peak is marked by a lovely carpet of multihued moss, a considerable tree-root ball, and a pointy, rocky cairn. Through the trees one may see Mt. Gardner but only in perfect weather. At the time of writing there was also a broken white ski pole at the summit cairn.
- To return, either retrace your steps or take the more direct approach heading downhill in a westerly direction. This is much steeper than the ascent, but there are many easy routes through the somewhat bluffy terrain. You'll require a GPS but will end up right at the fourth switchback if you have threaded these correctly.

The map gives a good indication of a descent which forms a nice loop with the route taken uphill.

- Continue steeply downhill on a trail to your left that will return you to Snug Cove.

ROUTE 2:

HARDING ROAD

- Take Grafton Road approximately 5 km to Harding Road. The intersection is just beyond Grafton Lake.
- At the intersection, cross Grafton Road, heading south. Go uphill into the forest. Follow contour lines and avoid deadfall to the summit.

The bland, viewless Apodaca summit, with broken ski pole.

MT. COLLINS

(BCO) (413 M)

A lovely single-track trail leading to an unremarkable mossy bump with no view.

CAUTION:
No trail markings.

PROMINENCE:
358 m.

LATITUDE/LONGITUDE:
N49.40640 W123.33360.

BANG FOR BUCK:
3/5

PEAK VIEW:
0/5. No view.

TRUE SUMMIT LOCATION:
Small rock cairn.

HEADWATERS:
Bluff Creek, Honeymoon Creek, an unnamed creek flowing from Mud Lake into Killarney Lake.

BEST VIEWS FROM:
Gambier Island peaks, east-central Howe Sound, HSCT peaks.

TRIP INFORMATION

Round-trip distance: 5 km from trailhead plus 4.6 km from Snug Cove.
Elevation gain/loss: 350 m.
Difficulty: 2/5.
Time: 0.75–2.5 hours.
Snow free: Year-round with rare exceptions.
Must-sees: Partial views of Howe Sound peaks about halfway.
Scenery: 2/5. No peak view. Second-growth forest.
Kids: 4/5.
Dogs: 5/5.
Runnability: 5/5. Paved road sections. Fun roller-coaster running back, downhill.
Terrain: Varied. Some wide gravel trails. A bit of road.
Public transit: #250 or #257 bus to Horseshoe Bay. Ferry to Bowen Island.
Cell coverage: Generally yes.
Sun: Mostly in shade, except for road.
Water: None.
Route links: Gardner, Apodaca.

HISTORY

Name origin: After James Collins (1882 Glasgow – 1974) and his wife, Laura Irene Smith (1883 Manitoba – 1961), Bowen Island pioneers who had a dairy and vegetable farm stretching from Killarney Lake to Deep Bay. The Collinses were deeply religious and started the first church on the island. They donated a parcel of land and helped finance the building of the present United Church and Collins Hall, off Miller and Reed roads. Laura was the daughter of first-generation Bowen Island pioneers and served as the schoolteacher.
Name status: Official. Adopted September 15, 1982, on 92G/6, as submitted by

Margaret Fougberg (née Collins) and endorsed by Bowen Island Historians.

First ascent: Unknown. Likely climbed by First Nations, prospectors, and hunters.

The trail to Mt. Collins is a relatively undiscovered gem for runners, hikers, and peak-baggers. It is smooth and spongy underfoot, with just the right slope. En route you will see mature trees dappled with sunlight, many arbutus clinging to sunny bluffs, and small clearings carpeted in moss. The noises of civilization are masked by birdsong. The trails, particularly on descent, are a trail runner's delight: spongy switchbacks and a gentle grade give the sense of a child-friendly roller coaster.

Unfortunately, after such a lovely lead-up, the summit of the third-highest mountain on Bowen Island is a bit of a disappointment. The trail ends in a small grove of firs. A small cairn serves notice that one has arrived at the destination. While beautiful in its own way, there is no view of anything other than forest from the peak of Collins.

ROUTE 1:

FROM SOUTH AT EAGLE'S NEST ROAD

- From the ferry, take your first right at the library. Continue for about 25 m and then go left on trail into Crippen Regional Park.
- Follow wide trail about 600 m slightly uphill past Bowen Memorial Gardens. Go right on paved Miller Road for about 1.5 km. At the crest of the hill, go left onto Scarborough Road and keep climbing.
- In about a block (across from Eagle's Nest Road), go left into a short driveway. The trailhead is at the end of the driveway.
- A narrow, rocky trail goes steeply uphill past a white gate then a large, green water tower. Stay left of the water tower on a narrow trail that leads steeply uphill around a cliff. *Do not turn right here, despite what may appear to be a route up the rocks.*
- The trail flattens out along a ridge for about 1 km. After about 600 m, at 140 m elevation, the trail turns to the right, up and north. There are a couple of rocky outcroppings where you can get partial views of Mt. Harvey and of The Lions. Go up and down a few rolling hills. At 330 m elevation, the trail heads left (west), climbing up one knoll and then up again and to the modest cairn on the modest and viewless summit of Collins.
- A short bushwhack to the west of the peak leads to the tiny, well-named Mud Lake.
- Return the way you came. Turn on the jets for a very pleasing trail run.

ROUTE 2:

FROM WEST VIA HONEYMOON LAKE

<u>Note:</u> This route is not encouraged, as Honeymoon Lake is the Bowen Island reservoir. Further, this is a nasty bushwhack: bring a GPS and Band-Aids.

- From the ferry in Snug Cove, take Mt. Gardner Road for 4 km (just past the lake) to Woods Road. Follow Woods Road for 2 km to find a trail to your right.
- This unmarked but reasonably well-trodden trail will take you to the Bowen Island reservoir, Honeymoon Lake.

- At Honeymoon Lake the trail vanishes. Continue upward, following the contour lines. You will have to endure an arduous bushwhack past a series of bluffs and up some duffy slopes. None of it is particularly hard or dangerous, but it is a fairly life-denying exercise.
- After a few false summits, veer just south (right) of the sunlight streaming in from the north, to the cairned summit.

Route 3:
FROM NORTH VIA SMUGGLER'S COVE ROAD

<u>Note:</u> The north side of Collins is bounded by private land; get permission before you attempt this route.

- From the ferry in Snug Cove, take Miller Road about 2 km to Scarborough and then onto Eagle Cliff Road.
- At the end of the island, go left onto Finisterre Road, then left again on Smuggler's Cove Road.
- Just before the end of the road, and just before Porters Road, there is a gated gravel road heading up the slope in a series of switchbacks. The gate may be unlocked. This gravel road is mostly driveable. It leads almost to the peak of Collins, stopping about 80 m from the end of the road due to tree blowdown and alders.
- Walk to the end of the road. Bushwhack through a thin curtain of trees to see a few bumps. Venture straight south and up and down and up to the cairned summit.

Gambier: mossy paradise: west slopes of Liddell

GAMBIER ISLAND
(5 PEAKS)

Give Gambier a visit. It is a stunningly beautiful place and well worth a bagging adventure. Marvel at the manifold hues of green on the moss magnificently carpeting the whole island: Ireland cannot compete with Gambier. Say hello to the salamanders in Gambier Lake. Watch the sunlight diamonds sparkle off the ocean. Visit lonely, lovely lakes. Discover history, with ancient corduroy roads and logging cables and camps partially swallowed by the resurging moss, trees, and ferns. In the early spring, watch the meadows turn purple with foxglove. Gambier is the most beautiful of the Howe Sound Islands and holds many secrets.

Gambier is also the largest of the Howe Sound Islands. It is roughly 70 km² in size, rugged, and sparsely inhabited, with only about 125 full-time residents. The population grows to 600 in the summer. The shape of the island resembles a jellyfish or Pac-Man ghost, with four peninsulas dangling off its south end.

The Squamish called the island Cha7elknech (sometimes written Tcalkunts). Its spiritual name was St'apes. According to Squamish legend, Gambier Island was formed after Mink and his sister Skunk held a feast. Mink treacherously killed Wolf. Other animals opened boxes thought to be gifts for the guests, when in fact they held skunk spray. Whale could not fit in the longhouse and blocked the front entrance. Mink and Skunk fled out the back door. The longhouse came crashing down, trapping the spirits of the animals inside; the house was transformed into Gambier Island. The 1975 British Columbia Archaeological Survey identified 19 First Nations camps or village sites on the island.

The island was named by Captain Richards in 1859 for James Gambier (1756 Bahamas – 1833 Buckinghamshire), Lord Gambier, Admiral of the Fleet, who had a distinguished career in the Royal Navy. Having entered the navy at age 11, Gambier rose to become Lord of the Admiralty from 1795 to 1807. He was also a governor of Newfoundland and served as a negotiator of the Treaty of Ghent ending the War of 1812 between Britain and the United States. He commanded HMS *Defence* at the Glorious First of June. Despite this moment of glory, he was a notoriously dour officer nicknamed "Dismal Jimmy"; he was fervently religious, and some doubted that his "praying ships" could be fighting ships. Although later honourably acquitted, he was court-martialled in 1809 for allegedly failing to destroy the French fleet in the Battle of Basque Roads during the Napoleonic Wars.

Captain Richards described Liddell and Killam without, of course, naming them:

> GAMBIER ISLAND, lying in the centre of the sound, immediately northward of Bowen island, is almost square shaped, and 6 miles in extent either way. On its western side rise two very remarkable cone-shaped mountains over 3,000 feet in elevation; the southern face of the island is indented by three very deep bays or inlets, in the easternmost of which only is convenient anchorage found. Close off the south-west point of the island are the Twins, two small islets; they are the only part of its coast which may not be approached very close.[5]

In 1875 A.C. Fraser applied for the first homestead on Gambier. The island never attracted the settlers or tourists that flocked to Bowen, but it was exploited for its natural bounty. Gambier was heavily logged throughout the 20th century; from 1918 to 1925 seven timber companies operated there. The elongated, sheltered bays in the south (particularly West, Centre, and Long bays) also served as storage and sorting facilities for log booms which would be released to the mills in Vancouver, North Vancouver, and beyond, as needed.

Despite the increased appreciation of Gambier's unique beauty for recreation and cabins, the logging continues. During the writing of this book, both the Gambier Lake and the Mt. Killam trails have been greatly diminished by substantial clear-cuts. A 2014 proposal to log extensively around and near Gambier Lake was mercifully withdrawn after public outcry. It is hoped that government and private interests will act to protect rather than despoil this emerald island.

There are five peaks on Gambier. They are far apart and most require bushwhacking. There is no road connection between the west and east sides of the island and no plausibly bikeable routes at present. A trail connects the Lost Lake area in the east to Gambier Lake in the west, but it is a woolly old corduroy road that would not be a pleasant bike ride (and should not be biked, as it would destroy these remnants and the fragile existing trail). It is possible to do a sweep of all peaks on foot, either as a multi-day trip with a overnight camp at Gambier Lake, or as a one-day insane endurance feat.

A bike is wise for taking out-and-back routes to save time and energy, especially on your approaches to Killam and Liddell/Gambier. That said, it is more efficient to stash your wheel halfway to Gambier Lake when you hit the long uphill stretch.

The main wharf, settlement, and BC Ferries dock is at New Brighton, in the southwest. There are no stores and only one seasonal bed and breakfast; a general store appears to be generally closed. There are also wharves with small clusters of cabins at Brigade Bay (east) and Douglas Bay (northeast). Camps Artaban (Anglican) and Fircom (United) are on the south side of the island, while Camp Latona is in the north. Halkett Bay Provincial Park is located in the southeast corner.

Gambier has an impressive network of trails, of various degrees of maintenance and blowdown. Several years ago the Gambier Island Conservancy put out an impressive map and trail guide. Though the map is now discontinued, and the conservancy is discouraging its use, it is still an enormously helpful map. A new one will likely be released soon.

Geologically, most of north Gambier Island consists of mafic volcanic strata and associated sediments of the Upper Jurassic and Lower Cretaceous Gambier Group (approximately 100 million years old). Most of the south part of the island consists of granitic rocks of the Jurassic to Cretaceous Coast Plutonic Complex (approximately 160 million years old). These are referred to as the Bowen Island Group, and predominate on that island. The boundary between these two geological zones lies just south of the summit of Mt. Artaban. Liddell, Killam, and Burt's all consist of Gambier Group rocks. These rocks also make up Lions Bay and, above, Brunswick Mountain, on the mainland: geological islands surrounded by plutonic granodiorite, quartz diorite, and other plutonic rocks.

GETTING THERE

By car: from Lions Gate Bridge, take Highway 1/99 to Horseshoe Bay.

By transit: take the #250 or #257 bus to Horseshoe Bay.

BC Ferries: if you time it correctly, you can get to New Brighton on Gambier Island from Horseshoe Bay in about 90 minutes. First take the ferry to Langdale on the Sunshine Coast (40 minutes). The Gambier ferry, *Stormaway* (a small, 16-seat vessel), is located in the terminal complex, at a little pier just below and to the north of the main BC Ferries moorage. The *Stormaway* fare is $7.50 and there is no charge for the return trip from Langdale. The Gambier ferry travels first to Keats and then to Gambier (40 minutes). Be sure to check the current schedule at bcferries.com/schedules/mainland/vasc-current.php.

Water taxis are also an option and perhaps a necessity if you are late returning from adventures:

- cormorantwatertaxi.com: Brian, 604-250-2630
- www.bowentaxi.com: 604-484-8497
- Gambier Island Water Taxi, 604-740-1133
- Sunshine Coast Water Taxi, 604-989-9990

GAMBIER BAGGER TIPS

Gambier Island can be traversed by taking the Cormorant water taxi to Camp Fircom and then returning via the public *Stormaway* and Langdale ferries or vice versa. Unfortunately neither BC Ferries nor the regular Cormorant water taxis leave enough time to do the entire traverse and get to New Brighton in time for the last *Stormaway*, at 18:50. For the hardened bagger who would like to do the island in one trip, the best approach is to traverse Artaban, Burt's Peak, Gambier, and Liddell on the first day. The forest in the valley below Liddell is soft and pleasant for camping. Throw in a light sleeping bag and bivy sack and finish off Killam the following morning. Be careful to check the *Stormaway* sailing times before leaving, as there are many large gaps in their Sunday morning schedule.

Total distance:
19.5 km (day 1: Fircom to Liddell–Killam valley) plus 8 km (day 2: Liddell–Killam valley to New Brighton) = 27.5 km

Estimated times:
12 (day 1) plus 3:15 (day 2) = 15:45

Elevation gain:
2145 m (day 1) plus 513 m (day 2) = 2658 m

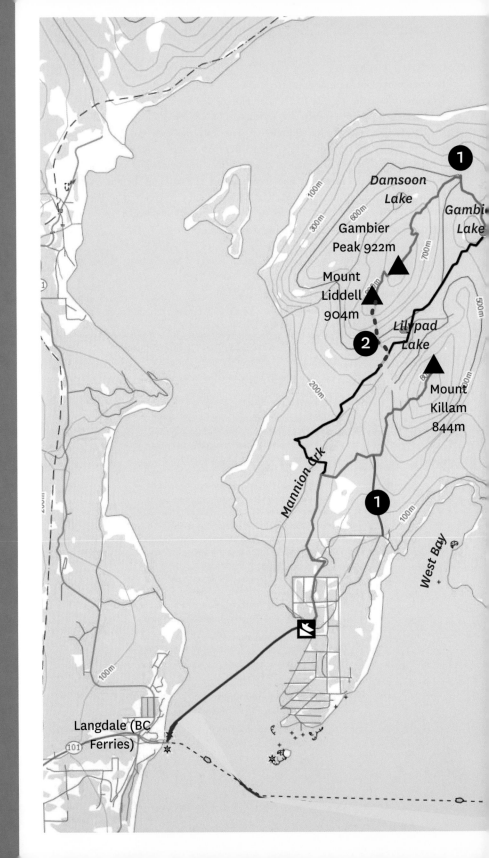

Damsoon
Lake

Gambier
Lake

Gambier
Peak 922m

Mount
Liddell
904m

Lilypad
Lake

Mount
Killam
844m

Mannion Crk

West Bay

Langdale (BC
Ferries)

101

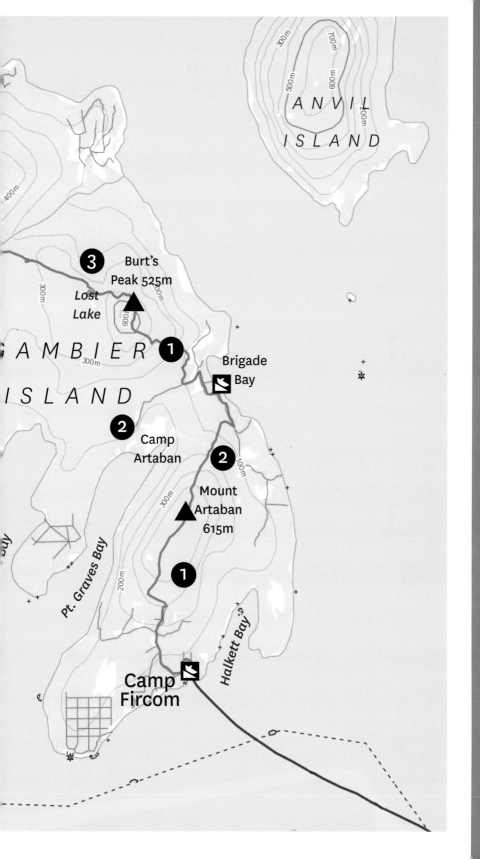

ANVIL

ISLAND

3 Burt's
Peak 525m

*Lost
Lake*

GAMBIER

ISLAND

1

Brigade
Bay

2

Camp
Artaban

2

Mount
Artaban
615m

1

Pt. Graves Bay

Halkett Bay

Camp
Fircom

MT. KILLAM
(KIL) (844 M)

A steep, scenic route with a stunning viewpoint near the peak.

CAUTION:
Steep. Slippery when dry.

PROMINENCE:
334 m.

LATITUDE/LONGITUDE:
N49.48924 W123.40933.

BANG FOR BUCK:
2/5

PEAK VIEW:
1/5
Nice view of Horseshoe Bay and southeastern Howe Sound just off the trail about 200 m below peak.

TRUE SUMMIT LOCATION:
Approximately 500 m beyond lookout. A cairn marks the spot.

HEADWATERS:
McDonald, Mannion, and Whispering creeks.

BEST VIEW FROM:
Langdale Ferry, HSCT.

Trip information **Round-trip distance:** 12.4 km from New Brighton.
Elevation gain: 844 m.
Difficulty: 2.5/5.
Time: 2.5–5 hours.
Snow free: Year-round with rare exceptions.
Must-sees: Old-growth trees; lookout near peak; moss-covered trails and clearings.
Scenery: 3/5.
Kids: 3/5. A good bike-and-hike adventure.
Dogs: 4/5.
Runnability: 4/5.
Terrain: Second-growth forest.
Public transit: None on the island.
Cell coverage: Only near peak; sporadic.
Sun: Tree cover for most of the route.
Water: Some small streams near the base; *no water above.*
Route links: Liddell, Gambier; longer: Burt's, Artaban.

HISTORY

Name origin: Named to commemorate Lt. David Allison Killam, RCNVR, DSC, from Vancouver, who was serving aboard MTB 460 when he was killed in action off the coast of France July 2, 1944, at age 26. With no known grave but the sea, his name is inscribed on the Halifax Memorial, panel 10. He received the Distinguished Service Cross. Killam was born November 8, 1917, at Vancouver and spent boyhood holidays on Gambier Island. He was survived by his wife, Elizabeth K. Killam, his son David, and his parents, Lawrence (president of British Columbia Pulp and Paper) and Edith Humphrey Killam, all of Vancouver.

Name status: Official. Adopted March 3, 1949, on C.3586.
Other names: Paul Mountain (Mt. Liddell was called "Peter Mountain").
First ascent: Unknown; likely climbed by Indigenous people.

L: Liddell; R: Killam.

Liddell (left, west) and Killam (right, east) are the two highest peaks on Gambier Island. From the ferry to Langdale, they present an impressive pair, rising anvil-like above New Brighton, and separated by Mannion Creek. They have sad histories, being named after two boys who spent summers on Gambier Island and who were killed in the Second World War. Originally, it was proposed that the peaks be named Mounts David (Killam) and John (Liddell), but the Geographic Board of Canada preferred using the surnames.

Despite being relatively low island peaks, they are both challenging climbs for which the treed-in peak views are somewhat underwhelming. The foliage and flattish tops of the Liddell and Killam mean there is no visible target to aim for; a GPS is strongly advised.

In pleasant contrast to Liddell, there is no bushwhacking on Killam, with minimal deadfall and undergrowth. Although the forest is mostly third-growth trees, there is not the usual West Coast blueberry shin-thrashing. Massive stumps, with ghostly eyes cut by loggers' springboard slots, abound. Occasionally you will see a giant old-growth tree. Pause to contemplate what an Eden, what a demi-paradise, Gambier Island would have been in its natural state, and enjoy what remains.

Route 1:
NEWER, SHORTER, SOUTH APPROACH
- From the pier at New Brighton, at the old general store, go straight on the main dirt road (West Bay Road).
- Head north up West Bay Road for about 2 km. Take the trail at the intersection of West Bay Road and Mountain Road. There is a signpost, somewhat hidden, at the end of a driveway.
- The start of the trail is charming, with a ceramic art panel, boardwalks, stairways, horsetails, and devil's club. A spongy trail leads up to another marker post, where the route network gets a little messier.
- Go east, following markers with a maple leaf on them. *Do not* follow the Wombat or

(counterintuitively) the Mountain trail (marked with wombat and mountain icons, respectively).

- The Maple trail soon cuts north, continuing for another 2 km or so, with Whispering Creek generally close to your right. It then dips down into Whispering Creek (at a pleasant lunch spot), crosses it, and rises to an old logging road. Proceed about 1 km north on the road.
- Come to the Mt. Killam trail turnoff up to your right. There is a hiking sign and flagging but they are easy to miss.
- Hike steeply upward, following grey trail markers and liberal flagging tape. If you don't see markings, you're likely off trail. Blowdown occasionally makes the trail confusing.
- You will pass over two pleasantly open fields of moss and granite. The trail gets increasingly steep and, in dry weather, slippery with needles.
- You will come to a stump that resembles a kappa monster of Japanese myth. It often sports sunglasses.
- Just after a steep notch, below a permanently wet wall, at around 700 m, you'll find a spectacular lookout about 20 m off and below the trail, with splendid views of the south peninsulas of Gambier, as well as Artaban, Bowen, and the southern Howe Sound Crest peaks.
- For the summit, continue left, north, upward on the trail, past a false summit. You will hit the peak, towards the north end of the mountain. The peak is identified by a small cairn next to a mossy rock: it's the perfect place for a snooze. Although there is no view, you can see how steeply the valley cuts between Killam and Liddell.
- Return to New Brighton via the same route.

Route 2:
TRADITIONAL WEST APPROACH

Caution: There is active logging in the area. New roads may be built and trail signs may be removed. We recommend Route 1 above.

- From the pier at New Brighton, take the dirt road (Andy's Bay Road) slightly left and uphill past the old general store and community centre.
- Follow the signs to the lake. You will pass by several houses. The road eventually narrows and the logging begins.
- Pass a recent cutblock and go down a hill. There is then a fork, marked as the Killam hike to the right and Gambier Lake to the left. Both signs are new, and high in the trees. Take the Killam road.
- You will come to a quarry. Note the giant tree near the entrance. A trail to your left is signposted "Gambier Lake (temporary route)." Take this option.
- This trail hugs the left side of the quarry and a clear-cut above it. Mannion Creek burbles below you to your left.
- Just past the clear-cut, you will see another sign for "Gambier Lake (temporary route)." Don't take it. Instead, follow the markings heading south (and down) along an old logging road that is perfect for running.
- Immediately after the first creek, look for the Mt. Killam sign. It is heavily flagged, and has a hiker sign. If you hit a second creek you've gone too far.
- Follow the above directions up to the peak.

View from the south end of Liddell.

MT. LIDDELL

(LID) (904 M)

The second-highest peak on Gambier Island; but the high point is no more than a treed chunk of rock with a partial view of the Port Mellon pulp mill.

CAUTION:
Largely unmarked and remote. Much deadfall. Some steep and cliffy sections.

PROMINENCE:
54 m.

LATITUDE/LONGITUDE:
N49.49944 W123.42333.

BANG FOR BUCK:
2/5

PEAK VIEW:
1/5. Pulp mill. Mt. Elphinstone on the Sunshine Coast.

TRUE SUMMIT LOCATION:
Rocky outcrop. Don't mistake for Gambier Peak, which is higher and to the north.

HEADWATERS:
Small streams flowing into Lilypad Lake or Gambier Lake.

BEST VIEWS FROM:
Northern Howe Sound, Leading Peak, HSCT.

TRIP INFORMATION

Round-trip distance: 26.8 km.
Elevation gain/loss: 1087 m.
Difficulty: 4/5.
Time: 4–9 hours.
Snow free: Year-round with rare exceptions.
Must-sees: Gambier Lake; moss.
Scenery: 2/5.
Kids: 1/5. Too far and bushwhacky.
Dogs: 3/5.
Runnability: 2/5. Only the approach.
Terrain: Second-growth trees; steep and cliffy sections.
Public transit: None on the island.
Cell coverage: Some on peak; inconsistent.
Sun: 20 per cent. Mostly tree-shaded.
Water: Bring your own. In emergency, small swampy lake and Gambier Lake at the foot of mountain.
Route links: Gambier, Killam, Burt's, Artaban.

HISTORY

Name origin: Named to commemorate RCAF Flying Officer John Raymond Liddell (1924–1945), J43745, from Vancouver, who, at age 20, was serving with 58 Squadron when his plane went down off the coast of Norway on April 26, 1945. With no known grave, his name is inscribed on the Runnymede Memorial, Surrey, UK, panel 279. He was born in Wallasey, Merseyside, England, and grew up in Vancouver, spending many childhood summers on Gambier Island; survived by his parents, Robert Roberts Liddell and Ottilie Anna Liddell (née Ranta) of Vancouver.

Name status: Official. Adopted March 3, 1949.

Other names: South Liddell Peak; Peter Mountain (in first edition of *103 Hikes* (1973); Killam was called "Paul Mountain").

First ascent: Unknown; likely climbed by First Nations.

We profile the two highest points on Gambier Island. They are nearly the exact same height, although the true Mt. Liddell, the one covered here, is slightly lower. It is located about a kilometre south along the ridge, down a short shoulder and up again via a largely overgrown trail. Access to both peaks is via the Mt. Liddell trail from Gambier Lake, partially marked with blue-and-white squares and flagging. You can also attain Liddell via a more direct but bushy straight shot up from Lilypad Lake. The old route, written up in early editions of *103 Hikes* and marked on the Gambier Island Conservancy map, approaches from the southwest and west via Muskeg Lake. It is heavily overgrown and requires crossing a dangerously dilapidated logging bridge, and thus is not recommended.

Liddell is a challenging peak. First, it is remote; getting to the base of the mountain in itself is not difficult, but it is time-consuming. Second, there's a steep, rough track from the Gambier Lake trail to the peak. Anticipate fairly open second-growth forest for the first half and then smaller, denser vegetation for the summit push. When you do finally get to the top, you'll find a flattish, tree-covered ridge with a few outcroppings. Were it not for the small cairn on a chunk of rock in a partial clearing, you'd be hard-pressed to know you are on the summit.

The good news is that it's a short skip along the ridge to Gambier/North Liddell peak, for manic peakbaggers.

Gambier trail to peak from Gambier Lake.

Route 1:

FROM NORTH – NEW BRIGHTON AND GAMBIER PEAK

Follow the Gambier Peak route, below.

- From Gambier Peak, continue south along the ridge. There will be occasional black-and-white markers, often on fallen trees, but for the most part you will have to make your own trail, following logical contour lines.
- You will descend a series of scrubby platforms. While there are portions of nasty bushwhack and cliff bluffs, at no time should you feel in danger of falling or laceration. Wiggle back and forth, finding a comfortable route. You will see beautiful moss covering former tarns.
- Eventually reach the bottom of the col between Gambier and Liddell. Then climb up, south, to Liddell Peak. If the route you have taken is excessively unpleasant, cut back or sideways and try again.

Route 2:

FROM SOUTH – NEW BRIGHTON AND BUSHWHACK UP FROM LILYPAD LAKE

<u>Caution:</u> There is active logging in this area. New roads may be built; trail signs may be removed. This describes a bushwhack route, with no trail at the end.

- From the pier at New Brighton, take the dirt road (Andy's Bay Road) slightly left and uphill past the old general store.
- Follow the signs to "Lakes" (i.e., Gambier and Lilypad). You will pass several houses. The road eventually narrows and the logging begins.
- Go down a hill. There meet a fork, with the Killam hike marked to the right, and Gambier Lake (the Liddell route) marked to the left. Both signs are new, and high in the trees.
- Take the road to Gambier Lake (left). The trail goes over a creek, and then veers north again. Continue about 2 km northeast and uphill past recent cutblocks.
- After a while the road becomes brighter due to the clear-cuts. To the right you will see a sign directing you to Gambier Lake, on a trail departing the logging road. There are several green and green-and-orange markers. Take this trail (note that there was, confusingly, a sign pointing westwards along the road to Liddell. This trail remains overgrown and unpleasant, and is not described here).
- The trail is obvious, cutting a track through the mossy floor, with berms to your left and right. Gradually ascend.
- After 1.5 km, look for a small lake (Lilypad) on your left.
- Just short of the lake, to the south, step off the main trail to the left and bushwhack upwards. There is no trail. There is much blowdown, and at times you will hit cliff bands. Veer left and right: at no point should you be exposed or in danger.
- Continue uphill for approximately an hour. You will probably cross the remnants of an old logging road running northeast on the slope. Eventually, you will come to the west slope of the ridge that bears Liddell and Gambier peaks.
- When the terrain flattens, turn right (northeast) and follow the obvious contour lines uphill. There will be a series of slightly steep portions and benches. Again, none of it should be precarious.

- The ground is covered with a thick blanket of glowing green moss and deer droppings.
- Towards the top, look for an opening in the tree canopy with several rocky outcroppings.
- The peak is marked with a small rock cairn.
- If you plan to continue to Gambier Peak and down to Gambier Lake, head north along the ridge. Sporadic white and black blazes and older orange flagging tape marks the route.

Gambier Lake, with Liddell behind.

GAMBIER (NORTH LIDDELL) PEAK

(GAM) (922 M)

The highest peak on Gambier Island. An interesting trek albeit with an unrewarding view.

CAUTION:
Remote. Limited trail markings above Gambier Lake. Especially challenging on final ridge.

PROMINENCE:
922 m.

LATITUDE/LONGITUDE:
N49.50389 W123.41750.

BANG FOR BUCK:
2/5

PEAK VIEW:
1/5

TRUE SUMMIT LOCATION:
Rocky outcrop.
Not to be mistaken for Liddell, which is lower and to the south.

HEADWATERS:
Small streams flowing into Gambier Lake.

BEST VIEWS FROM:
Howe Sound Crest Trail peaks, Langdale Ferry.

TRIP INFORMATION

Round-trip distance: 24.8 km from New Brighton.
Elevation gain: 1032 m.
Difficulty: 4/5.
Time: 4–9 hours.
Snow free: Year-round with rare exceptions.
Must-sees: Gambier Lake; side trip to Damsoon Lake; salamanders in both lakes; moss.
Scenery: 3/5. Only thanks to Gambier Lake.
Kids: 1/5. Far and involves bushwhacking.
Dogs: 4/5.
Runnability: 3/5. Most of approach, little of the final stretch.
Terrain: 2/5. Second-growth forest, reclaimed logging road.
Public transit: None on the island.
Cell coverage: Generally present.
Sun: Mostly under tree cover. Only exposed on peak and at lake.
Water: Gambier Lake. Small creek en route usually last chance for water and usually flowing.
Route links: Liddell, Killam, Artaban, Burt's.

HISTORY

Name origin: after Gambier Island.
Name status: Unofficial.
Other names: North Liddell Peak.
First ascent: Unknown; likely first climbed by Indigenous people. Tom Fyles climbed it in 1920.

Mt. Liddell, the highest officially named peak on Gambier, is not in fact the highest point on the island. That distinction belongs to the peak about 1 km to the north of Liddell, which bivouac.com calls "Mount Gambier." We call it "Gambier Peak," a name that was used in the early 1920s by BCMC members such as Tom Fyles.

The route from Gambier Lake to the peak could be pleasant. At the time of this writing, however, it is a rough trail to a remote location and should be approached with caution. While cleared in 2014, blowdown from subsequent storms litters the area and obscures the trail. A large section of the trail traverses a spooky forest of sticks: alders that reached a height of about 2 m and then died, leaving pointy booby traps for all who pass by. The years have taken their toll on the wooden signs and markers that can be seen occasionally on the ground or moss-covered and still attached to a fallen tree.

The first part of the trail, from Gambier Lake toward Damsoon Lake, is in theory traced with white markers, while the trail to Gambier and Liddell supposedly has black-and-white markings. However, most of these have vanished with time and blow-down, and you will have to fight through interlocking walls of juvenile pine trees. Eventually you punch out to the ridge leading to the peak. After clambering over considerable deadfall, you hit the peak (keep heading south for the true summit). To add insult to injury, the main views are Port Mellon and the clear-cuts above it.

Running clubmoss on Liddell/Gambier Trail.

As cautioned before with respect to Liddell, old editions of *103 Hikes* and the now discontinued Gambier Island Conservancy map provide a route that traverses Mt. Liddell on its west slope, and then ascends Mt. Liddell in the same manner as the route took. This hike is apparently unmaintained, densely overgrown, and nastily steep. It also involves crossing a rotting bridge over a deep chasm.

Despite these cautions, there is much of beauty – and weird beauty in particular – on this hike: salamanders at the lake abound, for example, as does running clubmoss, with its vertical tendrils, in early autumn.

ROUTE 1:

FROM SOUTH – NEW BRIGHTON VIA GAMBIER LAKE

Caution: There is active logging in the area. New roads may be built. Trail signs may be removed.

- From the pier at New Brighton, take the dirt road (Andy's Bay Road) slightly left and uphill past the old general store.
- Follow the signs to "Lakes" (i.e., Gambier and Lilypad). You will pass several houses. The road eventually narrows and the logging begins.
- Go down a hill. There meet a fork, with the Killam hike marked to the right, and Gambier Lake (the Liddell route) marked to the left. Both signs are new, and high in the trees.
- Take the road to Gambier Lake (left). The trail goes over a creek, and then veers north again. Continue about 2 km northeast and uphill past recent cutblocks.

Gambier: the fork. Go right to Gambier Lake and Gambier Peak.

- After a while the road becomes brighter due to the clear-cuts. To the right you will see a sign directing you to Gambier Lake, on a trail departing the logging road. There are several green and green-and-orange markers. Take this trail. (Note that there may be, confusingly, a sign pointing westward along the road to Liddell. This trail remains overgrown and unpleasant and is not described here.)
- The trail is obvious, cutting a track through the mossy floor, with berms to your left and right. Gradually ascend.
- After 1.5 km, look for a small lake (Lilypad) on your left. <u>Note:</u> If you prefer to reach Gambier via Liddell, pause here and refer to the route description for Liddell, above.
- Continue slightly uphill and then downhill on the overgrown access road about 2 km to the large and beautiful Gambier Lake.
- As you contour the south and east lakeside, look for salamanders in the deeper puddles and on the lakeshore.
- At the far end of the lake go left and along the east side of the lake for about 200 m. Cross some treacherous slippery logs.
- Head towards and past the toilets (marked with a sign; ideally, no one will be using these al fresco commodes as you pass by). The toilet trail leads to another track heading north along the east side of the lake and to another slippery log crossing.
- At a campsite and fire pit, head north, along an old skid road. Entering the forest, you will see an old sign to Damsoon Lake. The trail follows another old road.
- The road gets a little unpleasant with alders and other scrubby small trees.
- Now the trail (to Damsoon Lake) gets considerably wilder and woollier. It remains, however, marked with white markers and tape flagging. If you go for more than a minute without seeing a trail marker, backtrack and regroup: this is not a trail for improvisation.
- The trail follows a creekbed and then contours along a cliff band (including a rope) before cutting sharply northwest up a creek gully. There is much deadfall but the way is generally well marked.
- Eventually pop out of the gully, but there is still a steep climb west.

- The trail comes to an old logging road that is choked with small trees. A few paths and a log bridge of sorts cut through this scrub. Look for the continuation of the trail on the other side, up. It should be well flagged.
- The trail travels southwest around a knoll before diving farther southwest into a heavily overgrown, swampy corduroy road. This is where the marking gets thin and the treefall gets thick.
- Eventually you go up a little and punch out onto a rocky, former logging road that is choked with alders. Liddell Ridge is straight in front of and above you.
- Turn left and go about 200 m up the road until it crests and starts to descend. Take a deep breath and punch through a curtain of dense, scrubby pines to your right, uphill.

<u>Note:</u> This portion of the route is considerably different from that depicted on the old Gambier Island Conservancy map.

- The forest mercifully thins out after 200 m. Traverse southwest, gradually climbing.
- The peak is guarded by a cliff band above you. You will come to a pretty grove of bright green. Continue traversing up. Soon you will come to an obvious gully and gap up through the cliff band. Climb up. You will have to use your hands. Trees will assist. The gully may be slippery if wet or very dry.
- Pop out onto the peak ridge. Continue southwest to the peak along the relatively clear ridge, referencing the occasional black-and-white trail markers.
- The tree-covered "peak" is no more than another rocky outcropping. Look for a small rock cairn.
- To return, either retrace your steps to Gambier Lake or continue down and up along the ridge 1 km to Mt. Liddell (*see above for description of Gambier to Liddell*).

ROUTE 2:

FROM SOUTH – NEW BRIGHTON VIA LILYPAD LAKE

See above route to Liddell and then beyond to Gambier Peak.

Opposite page: steep muddy section at start of the gully northwest of Gambier Lake.

MT. ARTABAN

(ART) (615 M)

The best, most accessible, and well-trodden peak on glorious Gambier Island.

CAUTION:
Very little water.

PROMINENCE:
592 m.

LATITUDE/LONGITUDE:
N49.46722 W123.34028.

BANG FOR BUCK:
3/5

PEAK VIEW:
5/5. Panoramic view of the

Howe Sound Crest peaks from
Deeks to Black.

TRUE SUMMIT LOCATION:
Single peak.

HEADWATERS:
Small streams.

BEST VIEWS FROM:
Highway 99 southbound, other
HSCT peaks, Leading Peak, Porteau
Cove.

TRIP INFORMATION

Round-trip distance: 10 km return from Halkett Bay; 5 km return from Brigade Bay; 8 km return from Camp Fircom.

Elevation gain: 615 m.

Difficulty: 2/5. A good trail for beginners to intermediates.

Time: 2–4 hours.

Snow free: Year-round with rare exceptions.

Must-sees: Croaking tree frogs just below peak.

Scenery: 3/5. Coast. Cabins. Old growth.

Kids: 4/5. Ferry ride adds to adventure. Safe, well-marked trail.

Dogs: 4/5.

Runnability: 4/5. Gravel road and some single-track.

Terrain: Varied. A bit of gravel road. Lots of single-track. Well marked.

Public transit: None on the island.

Cell coverage: Some on peak; inconsistent.

Sun: 70 per cent covered.

Water: Little drinkable water; creeks dry in late summer.

Route links: nice combination with Burt's Peak. It would be a very full day to combine with the other Gambier Peaks (Killam, Gambier, Liddell), which are on the west side.

HISTORY

Name origin: Named in 1929 by Reverend Arthur T.F. Holmes, Vicar of Lulu Island, after the Church of England's Camp Artaban, located across the bay at the head of Port Graves. The camp itself is named for the main character in an 1895 novella by Henry van Dyke called *The Story of the Other Wise Man*. The tale recounts Artaban's arduous journey to meet the other three magi at Bethlehem, and how he never arrived there, because he could not ignore the hardships of the people he met along the way.

Name status: Official; adopted December 10, 1929, on 92G/6 (file B.3.26).

First ascent: Unknown; likely climbed by Indigenous people.

Other write-up: Hanna.

The trail to Mt. Artaban, the fourth-highest peak on Gambier Island, is accessible, marked, and well travelled, making it perfect for the intermediate bagger. A day on Mt. Artaban includes a short nautical adventure, as well, making it an excellent choice as a day trip with friends from out-of-town. Getting to the trailhead involves some additional logistics, as the only way to get there is by boat. The experience of taking a small water taxi or even kayaking makes the trip extra special.

There are two decent trails to the summit: one from the Halkett Bay Marine Park government dock in the south, and the other from Brigade Bay in the north. Both locations are served by semi-regular water taxi from Horseshoe Bay, and you may wish to do a loop route, going up and over Artaban, and then back to Fircom, thereby saving around 5 km and much climbing.

There are a small number of rustic campsites available in Halkett Bay Marine Park. The forest in the area abounds with ferns and moss – on both ground and trees – and smells rich and humid. In 2015 HMCS *Annapolis* was sunk in Halkett Bay to form an artificial reef, making this a popular destination for divers.

On a clear day, the views stretch from Harvey and The Lions to Mt. Collins and Mt. Gardner on Bowen Island. There are two interesting viewpoints farther down the mountain within the reserve, just off the main trail, one giving a view to the west and the other a view to the north and east, which may tempt you to make a short excursion off the main trail to the viewpoints.

Much of Artaban was burned by a human-caused fire that started on July 9, 1922. The mountain has been a regular destination for boys and girls attending Camp Artaban, administered by the Church of England since 1923, on Port Graves Bay, to the west. The campers erected a cross on the summit: now long gone. In 1957 a fire lookout tower was built on the summit. The tower was probably one of the first Forest Service fire towers to be constructed off-site and lifted to the site by helicopter. It fell into disrepair in the 1970s and collapsed. The wreckage of the tower was removed around 2011.

In June 2008 the Islands Trust Fund established the 107-hectare Mount Artaban Nature Reserve, which includes the summit of Artaban. The region was largely logged in the 1930s and '40s with further, less intensive logging in the 1960s; the forest today consists mostly of second-growth Douglas fir, western hemlock, western red cedar, red alder, and bigleaf maple. In the higher elevations are some unlogged forest, primarily of smaller shore pine and Douglas fir trees: none are terribly old or majestic.

Visible from the peak, on a bench to the east, below, is a pleasing tarn that retains water even in the hottest summer. This pond is fed consistently by water seeping into the peak rock above it, percolating down and then seeping out into the pond.

ROUTE 1:

FROM SOUTH – HALKETT BAY MARINE PARK

- From the dock, head inland through the campsite and left onto a well-travelled trail. Take this trail 2 km to a subdivision of newer cabins (Fircom Plateau).
- Take Jay Road uphill to where it ends at the trailhead in about 3 km. (There are several large, blue metal signs referencing the trail along the way.)
- The trail is well marked with orange metal tags. Note the old-growth Douglas fir and western red cedar as you climb.
- The trail is generally straight, except for a sharp turn to the left (west) after about 1 km. After 500 m, it then turns sharply again, this time to the right, and climbs up the ridge.
- The trail heads up the obvious ridge, along a series of wide benches. The steepest section is just before the peak, although it is not tricky or particularly steep. There is a sign marking the Mount Artaban Nature Reserve.
- The summit is obvious: a flat rocky bench with a few scrubby trees.

ROUTE 2:

FROM NORTH – BRIGADE BAY

- Brigade Bay is a popular spot for islanders to moor their boats and park their rough old vehicles they use only on the island.
- From the dock, take the gravel road left and uphill.
- Turn left onto the main road and head south for about 1 km. Look for a prominent trail marker opposite the water, in the trees just past a small creek.
- The trail is steeper and less established than the southern approach and occasionally obscured by deadfall and conflicting paths. At times, you may feel drawn to the gully running occasionally beside the trail; resist. That said, the trail is generally easy to follow and marked for the most part with orange flagging tape. When dry the needles underfoot can be slippery.
- Continue in an essentially straight line due south up the obvious ridge to the peak. It hits a few wider benches and eventually pops out of the trees onto the rocky peak.

Opposite page: Burt's Peak.

BURT'S PEAK

(GBU) (525 M)

A mossy green wonderland pleasantly tied into a trip to Lost Lake.

CAUTION:
No established trail.

PROMINENCE:
485 m.

LATITUDE/LONGITUDE:
N49.49834 W123.35336.

BANG FOR BUCK:
3/5

PEAK VIEW:
2/5. Deeks, Brunswick, and Hat across Howe Sound; Artaban and Killam on Gambier Island.

TRUE SUMMIT LOCATION:
Obvious central peak, with bumps to the north and south.

HEADWATERS:
Small streams flowing into Lost Lake.

BEST VIEWS FROM:
Highway 99 returning from Whistler; Unnecessary Mountain; Mt. Strachan.

TRIP INFORMATION

Round-trip distance: 6.4 km from Brigade Bay return.

Elevation gain: 525 m.

Difficulty: 3/5. No established trail.

Time: 2–4 hours from Brigade Bay.

Snow free: Year-round with rare exceptions.

Must-sees: Lost Lake; Burt's Bluff; old moss-covered corduroy logging roads.

Scenery: 2/5.

Kids: 3/5. Some bushwhacking and muddy spots but not particularly long or dangerous.

Dogs: 4/5

Runnability: 3/5

Terrain: Established trails to Lost Lake and Burt's Bluff. Then rough route with intermittent flagging.

Public transit: None on the island.

Cell coverage: Usually.

Sun: From Brigade Bay, 30 per cent exposed (on roads); rest entirely tree-shaded.

Water: Scarce; a few small streams.

Route links: Artaban, Gambier, Liddell, Killam.

HISTORY

Name origin: The popular scenic climb of Burt's Bluff is below to the south. Burt was apparently a Camp Artaban counsellor.

Name status: Unofficial.

First ascent: Unknown, but likely climbed by First Nations and then loggers in the early 1900s. Summit cairn erected by David Crerar, Ken Legg, and Michael Wardas in 2011.

Gambier Island's fifth bump, Burt's Peak, is located in the northeast quadrant of the island, above Brigade Bay and north of Mt. Artaban. It is a decent 525 m tall, with a prominence of 485 m from Mt. Artaban; one must almost hit water before climbing again up Burt's. The Islands Trust's Brigade Bay Bluffs Nature Reserve is located on its southeast flanks.

Although a lightly flagged trail exists, the peak is little visited or known. But it is a worthy and enjoyable climb, covered in the beautiful and abundant moss that Gambier is famous for. From the sunny and tranquil peak, there are pleasing views of the Howe Sound Crest Trail mountains.

If the weather is fine, we strongly encourage you to combine this trip with a visit to Lost Lake, to the west of the peak. It is a rarely visited, beautiful, meadowlike lake with the modest but worthwhile Burt's bump offering a pleasing background.

The rock in the area is composed of Gambier Group rocks of the Mesozoic era, made up of andesitic to dacitic tuff, breccia agglomerate, andesite, argillite, conglomerate, lesser marble, greenstone, and phyllite. Intrusive rock of the Coast Plutonic Complex, such as quartz diorite and diorite, also occur in the vicinity.

GETTING THERE
Water taxi from Horseshoe Bay to (best) Brigade Bay or (reasonably close) Camp Artaban or (longer) Halkett Bay or Camp Fircom.

ROUTE 1:

FROM SOUTH – BRIGADE BAY OR MT. ARTABAN OR CAMP ARTABAN
- From the south or east, travel a gravel road through a rough meadow to the well-established Burt's Bluff trail (faded green trail markers), which climbs uphill to the north from the connector trail between Mt. Artaban and Camp Artaban.
- After a steady but not steep climb, the trail follows an old logging road running between two bumps the scenic vista of Burt's Bluff (left) and Burt's Peak (right).
- Go another 200 m or so along the logging road, past some cliffy bits, until you see a natural route jagging sideways up the rock.
- Travel upwards on a steep but manageable slope (very minor bushwhacking: there is minimal undergrowth).
- Pass over three flattish washes that look like old logging roads. This will lead to another pair of uplands. Go left (although the right also has some flagging).
- This leads to an obvious peak.

ROUTE 2:

FROM SOUTH – CAMP ARTABAN

- Take the well-worn trail heading northeast to Brigade Bay (pink markings). At the three-quarters mark, turn left (uphill, north) to take the Burt's Bluff trail. Follow directions above to top of Burt's Peak.

ROUTE 3:

FROM NORTH – DOUGLAS BAY OR GAMBIER LAKE

- From Douglas Bay (blue markers) or Gambier Lake / Latona Beach, take the respective trails to Lost Lake. Both trails follow ancient cedar corduroy roads used for logging in the early 1900s. Massive stumps notched with axe scars evidence the now-lost forests of Gambier Island. Every hue of green soothes your eyes.
- Just to the north of Lost Lake, the two trails intersect. Make the short descent to the creek flowing north from the lake and cross. A (now) reasonably well-flagged route starts climbing steadily southeast up the Burt's Peak slope at a more or less steady 45° angle, following a draw and climbing over the occasional knoll. At times one must scramble over fallen trees and branches, but it is generally low-intensity and easy bushwhacking.
- After about 1 km you will catch a glimpse of the rocky cliffs off the west side of the peak. Continue the general southeast climb.
- After a while you will come to a flat area at the base of the summit. There is a small, shallow pond here and some old logging chains, buckets, and the like. Another bump rises to the south.
- A steep but manageable path climbs up; you should not have to use your hands. This stretch is at times slippery.
- The mossy peak is marked by a small cairn. There are views through the trees of the Howe Sound Crest Trail peaks.

Gambier: Brigade Bay
water diamonds

ANVIL ISLAND

(1 PEAK)

Anvil Island is the third-largest island in Howe Sound. On the drive between Vancouver and Whistler, it is the island opposite Porteau Cove. If you look at it upside down, it does look like the type of anvil Captain Vancouver would have had on board the *Discovery* when he named the island. As he wrote in his journal for June 14, 1792: "The sun shining at this time for a few minutes afforded an opportunity of ascertaining the latitude of the east point of an island which, from the shape of the mountain that composes it, obtained the name of Anvil Island."

Anvil Island and Leading Peak, with McNabb Lions on Sunshine Coast behind.

The Squamish called the island Lhaxwm or Tlaqom, and it has long been an important place for spiritual training. According to Squamish legend, the island was a transformed serpent, or a serpent lived at the summit of Leading Peak. Traditionally, Anvil Island was the home of the Smàýlilh (Wild People) who could change their shape, appearing as humans, dogs, or trees. They are sometimes identified with sasquatch. The Wild People kept pet wolves. They generally lived high in the mountains, away from Squamish villages. Kwelhaynexw ta elhkay, a giant mythical spirit, specifically lived on Anvil.

Captain Richards described the peak and island:

> In coming from the northward, Passage island, at the entrance of Howe sound, kept on or just open of a remarkable peak on Anvil Island within the sound, bearing N. by W. ¾ W., will clear the edge of the Sturgeon bank until the bearings just given are brought on for entering.

> … Anvil Island is oval-shaped, and 3 miles long, and its summit, Leading peak, 2,746 feet high and very remarkable, resembles the horn of an anvil pointed upwards. From almost all parts of the strait of Georgia this peak appears as a most prominent object; … it is … an excellent leading mark to clear the shoals off the Fraser River by being kept just open westward of Passage island, on a N. by W. ¾ W. bearing.[6]

The Columbia Clay Company operated at the southern tip of Anvil Island (at Irby Point) from 1897 to 1912 and apparently grew to be the largest in the province by 1905. A second works, run by the Anvil Island Brick Company, operated from 1910 to 1917. After that, at least in 1922, Ceramics Industries Limited made bricks on Granville Island from Anvil Island clay.

Most of the island rises steeply and fortress-like from the waters of Howe Sound. Given its relative inaccessibility, only a handful of people live on the island year-round.

Of the three islands in this book, Anvil is the most accessible by kayak. The distance from Porteau Cove Provincial Park seems manageable, at 5.7 km, but the trip is only recommended for experienced kayakers: the winds can whip up suddenly, with deadly results. In 2007 two experienced and hardy North Vancouver adventurers, Denis Fontaine and Richard Juryn (after whom Juryn Trail near Capilano University is named), died of hypothermia after their kayaks were overturned by a sudden storm arising on a day of otherwise perfect weather.

Anvil lies just north of Pam Rocks, home to a good-sized seal colony. You may also see porpoises and dolphins jumping in the waters below. As the water quality of Howe Sound has improved, orcas have returned, although sightings are still rare.

There are no campsites on the island, but boaters will find a lovely moorage at the bay located north of the southeastern peninsula, as well as unofficial campsites upslope (but be careful to keep the water supply pristine). There are no parks or public access points to the island, but the Gambier Island Local Trust Committee's 2013 official community plan contemplated future parkland in this area.

There is only one (obvious) peak on Anvil. Only two real trails lead to it. Both trails begin on the private property of Daybreak Point Bible Camp, so expect to be approached and asked to sign a waiver and pay a small fee ($25 at last check). There is also a steep bushwhack approach from the east for the frugal or atheistic.

Geologically, Anvil Island is identical to the predominant rock of Gambier Island: largely of volcanic origin (andesite, dacite, and rhyolite flows), with metasiltstone and associated sediments at the base. These strata date from the Upper Jurassic and Lower Cretaceous periods and are among the oldest on the North Shore: approximately 140 million years.

ANVIL BAGGER TIPS
The most direct way to bag Leading Peak is to paddle from Porteau Cove and then hike up via the East Creek route. Be careful of tides and wind before attempting this crossing as the weather conditions in Howe Sound can change dramatically while doing the hike.

Round-trip distance:
11.4 km (paddle from Porteau) plus 5.8 km (Route 3, East Creek route) = 17.2 km

Time:
3 paddling plus 3 hiking = 6 hours round trip

Elevation gain:
765 m

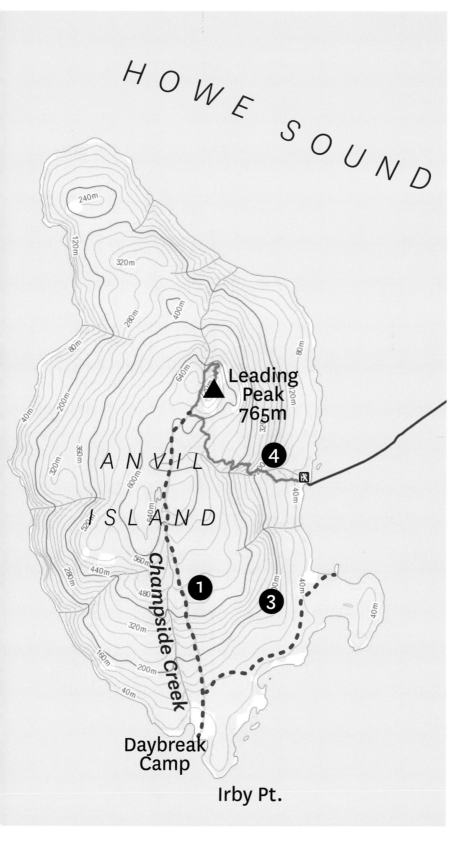

H O W E   S O U N D

Leading
Peak
765m

4

1

3

A N V I L

I S L A N D

Champside Creek

240m
120m
320m
400m
280m
80m
640m
80m
20m
320m
40m
200m
40m
350m
300m
600m
520m
560m
440m
280m
480m
320m
200m
180m
40m
40m
40m

Daybreak
Camp

Irby Pt.

Leading Peak as seen from Deeks Peak.

LEADING PEAK
(LEA) (765 M)

Outstanding views on an impressive peak that looks more difficult than it is.

CAUTION:
Final ascent can be slippery and potentially dangerous.

PROMINENCE:
765 m

LATITUDE/LONGITUDE:
N49.53889 W123.30417

BANG FOR BUCK:
4/5

PEAK VIEW:
5/5. Spectacular 360° views from peak.

TRUE SUMMIT LOCATION:
Single obvious peak marked by helicopter pad.

HEADWATERS:
Champside Creek, East Creek, various unnamed creeks, some small streams.

BEST VIEWS FROM:
Highway 99, returning from Whistler; HSCT.

TRIP INFORMATION

Round-trip distance: 5.8 km via East Creek; 7.5 km from Daybreak Point (southwest).

Elevation gain: 765 m.

Difficulty: 3/5. Seldom travelled. Good trail marking. Some excellent single-track.

Time: 3–6 hours from Daybreak Point.

Snow free: Year-round with rare exceptions.

Must-sees: White Spot viewpoint halfway up; beautiful fairy lake on saddle.

Scenery: 4/5. Second-growth forests; creeks; lake.

Kids: 3/5. Fairly steep in sections.

Dogs: 4/5. May require a permit.

Runnability: 3/5. Dirt road to trailhead. Some small stretches of single-track in centre of island.

Terrain: Well-marked single-track through second-growth; some steep portions. Rocky final ascent.

Public transit: None on the island.

Cell coverage: Generally available, especially towards peak.

Sun: Only the summit is exposed.

Water: Lake water murky; creek mostly dry in summer.

Route links: None.

HISTORY

Name origin: The dramatic point of the peak served as a guide for ships to get their bearings. "Leading" (pronounced as in "leader," not as in "lead-footed") is incorporated in many British Columbia coastal place names. Captain Vancouver noted that following a straight line from Passage Island (at the mouth of Howe Sound) to

Leading Peak leads the ship along a safe route, staying west of the mudflats at the mouth of the Fraser River. As stated by Captain Richards:

> In coming from the northward, Passage Island, at the entrance of Howe Sound, kept on or just open of a remarkable peak on Anvil Island within the sound, bearing N. by W. ¾ W., will clear the edge of the Sturgeon Bank until the bearings just given are brought on for entering.[7]

Name status: Official. Adopted in the 18th Report of the Geographic Board of Canada, March 31, 1924, as labelled on British Admiralty Chart 570, 1865 et seq.
Other names: Eagle Peak. Anvil Peak.
First ascent: Climbed by BCMC in 1931; almost certainly climbed much earlier than that by prospectors and by the Squamish.

Leading (or Eagle) Peak is the greatest of the Howe Sound summits. Thanks to its pointy prominence, it's the one that commands the attention of tourists and locals driving up the Sea-to-Sky Highway. We will work with the theory that its pointiness makes the island look like an anvil, provided the anvil is pointed nose-down for some inexplicable reason. Despite its steep appearance, it is not terribly difficult or dangerous to summit, and on a clear day the view is one of the best of the peaks surveyed in this book. You will stand on the helicopter pad on top and survey the entirety of the Howe Sound Crest Trail peaks, the Tantalus Range, and Howe Sound around you. You will marvel at sailboats and perhaps dolphins and whales playing in the ocean below. The primary challenge in your climb is the logistics of getting to the island and gaining access to the trailhead.

The easiest and logical route up Leading Peak is via Daybreak Point Bible Camp, which maintains the trail and owns the property where the trailhead is located. The majority of the trail, and the peak itself, however, is on Crown land. That said, the steep climbs skirting the island, and the steep topography generally, make alternative routes hardly worth the candle. Those routes may be necessary, though, if you wish to bag Leading in the summer, as it is the usual policy of the camp not to permit visitors then, in order to safeguard the young people attending camp during those months.

GETTING THERE
Take a water taxi to Daybreak Point Bible Camp, located at the southern point of Anvil Island.

If travelling by private boat or kayak, consider the small bay formed by the round peninsula 2 km northeast of the bible camp, and follow the good dirt road that parallels the shoreline to the trailhead. Please respect private property.

Route 1:
FROM SOUTH – DAYBREAK POINT BIBLE CAMP
<u>Note:</u> The Leading Peak trailhead is on private property at the Daybreak Point Bible Camp. The camp owns the first kilometre or so of trail, up to approximately 160 m. You may be asked to sign a waiver and pay a usage fee.
• The trail is marked with aluminum can lids as well as cryptic number signs (the

final one being "15," at base of the final ascent up the peak).

- From the dock at the camp, go uphill on well-marked trail beside a waterfall. The going is very steep at the start. There is a rope up a slippery patch that becomes a waterfall in foul weather.
- After a quad-busting 30–60 minute ascent, you come to a series of plateaus and outcrops. Look for a sign for the White Spot lookout. The short detour to the lookout is well worth it. A large cross, hooked up to an electric panel, provides no shade.

Fairyland Lake, en route to Leading Peak.

- Continue climbing up well-marked single-track to a beautiful pocket lake at the saddle. You half-expect to see fairy cottages around the lake amongst the glowing green moss and the bonsai-like trees.
- After the lake, descend and then briefly climb for an epic view of the cone-shaped peak to the north.
- Descend again through a narrow valley and over a small creek.
- On the next ascent, you will see that final numbered sign (15) before approaching a narrow and neat valley between two towering rock walls, the right (east) one being Leading Peak. Moss drips overhead.
- Continue north through this gap, proceeding from the east side to the west side and back to the east.
- At the end of the gap valley, begin to climb up the wall on an obvious tree handhold.
- While the climb may seem daunting from afar and up close, the way up, amazingly, is a calm one with no real exposure or anxiety. It is a masterpiece of trailbuilding.
- The trail winds around to the north side of the peak. Hands are only occasionally needed. The route is obvious, and occasionally marked with red dots.
- There are some relatively steep, rocky sections that could be slippery if wet. If dry, they provide an easy climb. You should never feel exposed.

At the helipad atop Leading Peak.

- Corkscrew up Leading Peak to the solar power station, microwave tower, and helipad at summit. Bask in the spectacular 360° views. The helipad makes the world's finest picnic table provided no helicopter is landing.
- Retrace your steps back down the same way or try the Night Hawk Trail variant about halfway down.

ROUTE 2:

NIGHT HAWK TRAIL

A new Night Hawk Loop was blazed around 2012. It is longer and more circuitous, but softer on the legs given its spongy surface, as it tracks the contours of the hill. It makes for a spectacular descent. It is a side route off the main Route 1 up Leading Peak described above, and the top and bottom rely on the main trail. Night Hawk Trail still requires one to cross through the bible camp property, however, with the same caveats as above.

- The trailhead is to the west of the main trail, next to the waterfall.
- Snake uphill on a series of wide switchbacks. After about 2 km, look for a sign marking "Night Hawk Peak." There is a good partial view here of the Howe Sound Crest mountains.
- The Night Hawk joins the main trail just below the saddle lake and is marked with a sign. Go left and uphill to the summit.

ROUTE 3:

FROM EAST (SOUTHERN ISLAND) – EAST BAY

<u>Note:</u> This route is not recommended, as it may involve unauthorized trespass over private, albeit generally unused, land.

- Moor or ground your boat at the crescent beach to the north of the fat peninsula sticking out of the southern east side of the island.
- Climb up the bluffs to the scraggly forest. Watch out for stinging nettles.
- Old roads will be discernible in the forest, hooking west and south. They will soon turn into a proper gravel road. Pass some properties and buildings.
- After about 1 km you will come to the main trail just after a bridge over Champside Creek.
- Continue up the way described in Route 1.

ROUTE 4:
FROM EAST (MID-ISLAND) – EAST CREEK
<u>Caution:</u> This is a very rough route: a steep, nasty bushwhack with some exposure.
- The route starts from the west side of the beach/bay into which East Creek flows. There are a few rough camping spots here.
- Follow flagging through the woods to the west, crossing a new service road a short way up.
- The route continues west up the steep, wooded slope, winding its way through numerous cliff bands. You may need to use your hands, but you should never feel in danger. If you do, backtrack or go sideways.
- At about 450 m, the gradient eases off and heads northeast ward to join with the main trail in the Anvil saddle.
- Follow the trail from the Anvil saddle to Leading Peak described in Route 1 above.

Paddle to East Creek from Porteau Cove

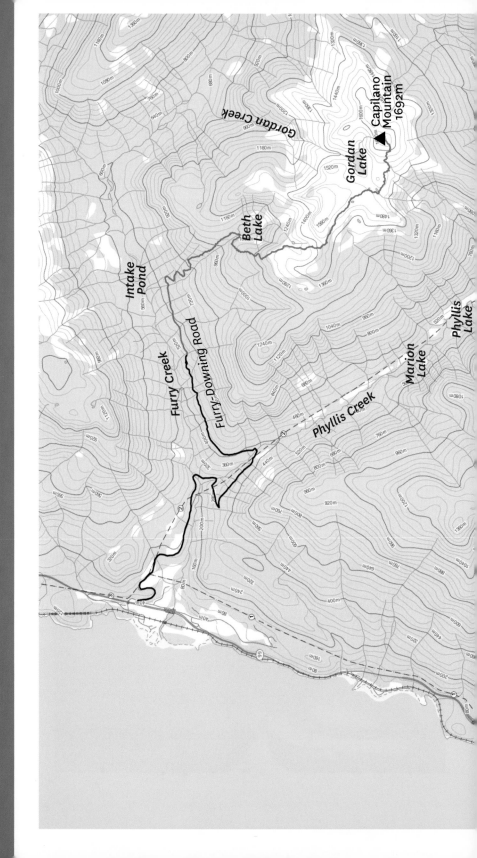

BRITANNIA RANGE

(23 PEAKS)

Picture yourself on the deck of the BC Ferry that runs between Horseshoe Bay and the Sunshine Coast. There's not a cloud in the sky. A salt-tinged wind tousles your hair. You close your eyes, breathe deeply, and turn toward the Lower Mainland. You open your eyes and are rewarded with one of the most magnificent urban vistas on the planet.

The wall of verdant mountains that thrusts almost vertically upward from the ocean on the east side of Howe Sound between West Vancouver and Britannia Beach is called the Britannia Range. The glorious and arduous Howe Sound Crest Trail (HSCT) stretches 30 km from the north end of the eastern horizon to the south.

The range provides a history lesson, dating back to when Britannia ruled the waves. Captain Richards of the Royal Navy named the range after the 100-gun HMS *Britannia*, which saw action at the Battle of St. Vincent in 1797 and the Battle of Trafalgar in 1805.

The British theme carries through to the individual mountains as well. Most of the peaks in the Britannia Range recognize current and former houses or dynasties of the British royal families. Windsor Peak, for example, is named after the House of Windsor, Queen Elizabeth II's family. Before the nastiness of the First World War, and a rebranding exercise, the Windsors were the Saxe-Coburg and Gothas, a German house, which included the House of Wettin (see **Appendix 14** for more details).

Access to the northern Britannia Range peaks overlooking Howe Sound changed significantly in 1956 with train access to Squamish, and again in 1958 when road access opened. No longer did hikers need to take a boat to St. Mark's Beach, Brunswick Beach, or Lions Bay to gain access to these peaks.

Beth Lake, Capilano Mountain.

CAPILANO MOUNTAIN

(CAP) (1692 M #5)

A grand adventure of varied terrain, leading to a granite playground and a pleasing lake.

CAUTION:
Remote. Long. Trail sometimes faint. Routefinding skills recommended.

PROMINENCE:
603 m.

LATITUDE/LONGITUDE:
N49.55640 W123.13580.

BANG FOR BUCK:
3/5. Superb but far.

PEAK VIEW:
4/5. Interesting view straight down Capilano Valley to downtown Vancouver, and back sides of North Shore peaks.

TRUE SUMMIT LOCATION:
Obvious, above Gordan Lake.

HEADWATERS:
Capilano River, Phyllis Creek, Furry Creek, Downing Creek.

BEST VIEWS FROM:
Windsor; downtown Vancouver, staring northwest up Capilano Valley.

TRIP INFORMATION

Round-trip distance: 14.2 km (trailhead) plus 12.4 km (road from Furry Creek) = 26.6 km.

Elevation gain: 1662 m.

Difficulty: 4/5. Far, but no exposure; some routefinding challenges.

Time: 6–12 hours.

Snow free: Late July–October.

Must-sees: Lovely Beth Lake; granite slabs; old growth; view of Vancouver.

Scenery: 4/5.

Kids: 2/5. Far, but possible for sturdy kids.

Dogs: 4/5.

Runnability: 4/5. Many runnable stretches.

Terrain: Second-growth forest; granite slabs.

Public transit: #C12 bus only goes as far as Brunswick Beach Road, just north of Lions Bay.

Cell coverage: Scarce and unreliable.

Sun: Minimal in first half (forested); second half mostly exposed.

Water: Ample along route.

Route links: Not convenient to other peaks. In theory, one could link to Windsor–Deeks col (see below at p. 111).

Name origin: After Squamish Chief Kiapalano (ca.1792 – ca.1875, buried in Mission Reserve Cemetery, North Vancouver). He was the father of Chief Joe Capilano (also known as Joe Matthias, or Sa7plek) (1850–1910), a leader of the Squamish nation. *Legends of Vancouver*, a collection of Coast Salish stories by Pauline Johnson, was based on Capilano's tales. Name was used for the river in 1867 (*Yale Examiner* article), 1880 (George Keefer map), and 1887 (when reserve was set aside). Name used for the mountain in 1912 North Vancouver map.

Name status: Official. Adopted May 6, 1924, in Ottawa file OBF 0836, as labelled on BC map 2D. Note that the official name is Capilano Mountain, not "Mt. Capilano" as should be the case, as it is named after a person.

First ascent: According to Don Munday, Edward LePage made the first climb, in 1913 or 1914. A Department of Mines survey party led by Kenneth Chipman (later chief topographer in the department) also climbed it in 1920.

Capilano Mountain marks the northern boundary of this book's domain, and is the northernmost peak visible from downtown Vancouver, framed between Crown Mountain and Magic Mountain, straight up the Capilano Valley. On the map it is about 13 km southeast of the golf resort at Furry Creek.

Capilano is a sinfully neglected adventure, with varied terrain including two magnificent cirque lakes and a blinding playground of white granite. On hot summer dats, there are splendid swimming opportunities in both Beth Lake and Gordan Lake, as well as in the several tarns up higher. The trail is also a mycologist's delight, teeming with gigantic boletes, amanitas, bears' heads, and other weird stuff. As well, the slopes harbour some of the finest preserves of the various species of mountain blueberries: big like Needles blueberries, and delicious like Crown blueberries. For those so inclined, there are good stretches of trail-running, especially when approaching Beth Lake, and the glorious granite rock field at the base of the mountain. The views from the summit on a clear day are stunning and yet odd: Vancouver is visible, far to the south. You will likely not see a soul, although you will feel you have covered a vast territory in the trip. One has that tingly "into the wild" sense throughout the adventure.

A May 1938 ACC Vancouver trip described it as a seldom visited peak; they boated to Furry and started their ascent. In the 1970s a trail linked Capilano to the Deeks–Windsor saddle meadow (see p. 109): heading due west from Gordan Lake (rather than down to Beth Lake as described below), to join the Marion Lake trail just northwest of the lake. It then continued southeast toward Marion Lake along Phyllis Creek before turning southwest, short of Marion, to head up the ridge to the meadows. Its present state is unknown but the trail has likely vanished. That said, it would be a worthy project to reblaze and link Capilano to the Howe Sound Crest peaks.

The first reference to the name "Capilano" is an 1859 letter from Captain Richards to Governor James Douglas, referring to "Ki-ap-a-la-no, chief of the Squamish tribe." The Squamish pronunciation is more akin to "Chlee-ap-a-la-noch," with the "ch" resembling the sound at the end of the Scottish word "loch." The name of Capilano River (formerly called a creek) predated the name of the mountain. The Capilano River itself was earlier referred to as "Homulcheson Creek" by local First Nations:

the village at the mouth of the Capilano River, now partly occupied by Park Royal Shopping Centre and Ambleside, was called "Homulcheson."

The rocks of the Capilano area are plutonic, consisting largely of quartz diorite with hornblende.

For peakbaggers, Capilano is a lone wolf, so there is not much optimization possible. For a short day the quickest approach is to bring a mountain bike to the start of the gravel road in Furry Creek. You can cycle 6.2 km up the road. Park the bike just before the large creek washout where the bush starts closing in on the road. There's not much to be gained with the bike beyond here.

GETTING THERE

From Lions Gate Bridge, take Highway 1/99 north toward Whistler. Exit the highway at Furry Creek. If you are taking transit, best to bring your bike, as the bus stops just north of Lions Bay.

Note: The approach is tricky. Follow the paved road that parallels the highway past the intersection with the entrance to the Furry Creek Golf and Country Club. About 600 m past the highway exit you will see a gravel road heading up to your right. Most drivers will want to park here. An all-wheel-drive or a 4-wheel-drive is recommended to proceed farther, but there is a gate a short ways up that is usually locked.

- Set your odometer at the gate. Go 1.5 km to a quarry. Keep right.
- At 2.5 km you will pass by a gate leading steeply downhill. Don't go here even if the gate is open.
- Cross two bridges (Furry Creek at 2.8 km and Phyllis Creek at 3.1 km).
- At the fork in the road at 3.7 km, stay left. Follow the power lines. At 4.3 km, take the smaller road left. We noted the number "283" on the hydro tower near this fork.
- Note: This is a narrow dirt road that goes from being driveable to almost impenetrable single-track through alders as you reach the trail to Beth Lake. If you are driving, go as far as you dare. We went 600 m to a small parking area and recommend you park here too. Cross a third bridge (Phyllis Creek again).
- Stay right at next fork. You will come to a deliberate ditch. All drives end here. Park.

ROUTE

- The start of the trail adventure is a bit of an act of faith. Follow an obvious but overgrown (and unmarked) former road through scrubby brush and over about five minor and three major creeks (none of which are difficult to cross) to the trailhead, marked "Beth Lake Trail."
- Pass a rocky, washed-out mudslide and a small creek.
- The second major creek, Beth Creek, appears forbidding but is readily crossed along judiciously selected rocks. Pick up a sturdy alder to help with balance.
- You will know you have arrived at the last creek, Beth Creek, because on the near side, you will note some big old logs that remain from a bridge.
- About 100 m past the creek, look for surveyor tape and metal reflectors in the trees on your right.
- **Access to Beth Lake:** The trail is steep but well groomed and marked, in contrast to the immediate approach. You will be reminded of Deeks Lake Trail as you ascend through damp second-growth forest.

- This nice trail with runnable sections takes you up to the lake. Watch for metal tags on the trees. Anticipate minor detours around blowdown.
- Eventually you punch out of the forest to behold the pleasing Beth Lake (1085 m), again reminiscent of a smaller Deeks Lake. It is surrounded by scree slopes and thick forest and very peaceful. Rocky ramparts tower above. A thin waterfall pours down rocks to the lake. Enjoy the view of this breathtaking amphitheater.
- **Beth Lake to tree line:** Follow the edge of the lake to the right (counterclockwise) over a series of logs bridging the outflow creek. Look for metal tags on the trees on the far side. Head slightly back downhill to the foot of the cliff.
- Head sharply uphill on west side of lake. Note some orange tape and metal markers on the trees. You will reach a boulder field below the ridge in about 30 minutes. Trail marking in this section is very hard to follow, as there are few places to hang tape. Generally stay left of the rocks up to the ridge.
- **Rock field:** The flagging is inconsistent along here, but trail finding is reasonably simple. After about 30 minutes, the trail leads to an open rock-field arena, with bluffs rising up to your left and ahead. The fat blueberries and boletes start in earnest, for your foraging pleasure on the return.
- Proceed straight through alongside a moss creeklet to an impressive boulder field.
- Scamper up this slope to the southeast. This leads to a ridge with a clear view of the destination peak.
- **Ridge to Gordan Lake tarns:** Another kilometre takes you to an enchanted heather meadow of suspended pocket ponds overlooking a vast white granite playground surrounding the base of Capilano.
- Gordan Lake, a cirque lake to the north of Capilano, invites exploration, but this is not the route up the peak. Instead, proceed south over the granite slabs and past a series of tarns. There may be (likely inconsistent) cairns for the rest of the route.
- The safe and sure route has you traversing the base of the ridge, to the base of a granite dome to the south that connects to the ridge leading up to the peak. Alternatively, you can scramble up the side of the ridge.
- On the ridge, follow the even-sloped path through heather to the summit of Capilano. A bit of scrambling and routeclimbing is necessary along the final ascent, but you should not feel at peril, or you have veered off course.
- Look for small rock cairns to the summit.
- On the peak you will be rewarded with views south to the Howe Sound Crest Trail peaks, with the city of Vancouver itself framed between the summits of Crown and Magic. To the southeast are the forbidden mountains of the Capilano watershed: Appian (west) and Daniels (east). To the east you will see Crown Mountain and in the distance, Golden Ears. Sky Pilot and the Garibaldi Peaks to the north and the Tantalus Range to the northeast complete the spectacular view.

HOWE SOUND CREST TRAIL
(19 PEAKS)

The Howe Sound Crest Trail (HSCT) is a glorious 30-km route that stretches high above Howe Sound along the spine of the Britannia Range, from Cypress Bowl to Porteau Cove. With 19 peaks accessible, this trail is a peakbagger's delight.

Before the arrival of Europeans, Native people hunted on these slopes, primarily for the treasured fur of mountain goats. Mountain goats are still seen, but rarely now: Harvey and Enchantment are the best viewing spots. There are abundant bears and deer.

The north part of the trail was originally a pack road for servicing the dam and flume at the mouth of Deeks Lake, itself used to provide water and electricity (through a pelton wheel) to the gravel works down below at Porteau Cove. In 1928 the BCMC's *BC Mountaineer* described a "possible new route" from Deeks Lake to Brunswick. By at least as early as 1937, 1940, 1946, and 1947 it was referred to as "mostly a good trail," used to gain access to Brunswick and Hanover mountains as an alternative to the traditional route up from Brunswick Beach and Lions Bay. In the 1960s the Porteau–Deeks route was largely ground over by a gravel service road used to log the mid-Deeks Valley. The present trail follows traces of both of these routes.

The south part of the trail started as an informal route to The Lions. In 1971 it was called Skyline Ridge Trail. In the 1960s UBC students improved the trail from Cypress Bowl to Strachan Meadows, and in 1977 the Varsity Outdoor Club further improved the route, particularly from Cypress Bowl to The Lions (although a 1977 BCMC report simultaneously complained of the roughness of the trail and the litter the improved access had attracted).

The central segment between Deeks Lake and The Lions was the last part of the trail to be groomed. The Deeks Lake to Harvey stretch was improved in 1983 on a federal grant. The tranche from Harvey to The Lions was not finished until the late 1980s. This section was first routed to dip deep into the watershed to the east of David and James peaks, although the more popular route these days (and the one favoured by these authors, of course) is to go over both peaks.

Due to its increasing popularity, and increased appreciation of its beauty, the HSCT was officially added to Cypress Provincial Park in 1982.

The high point of the trail proper is the 1542-m summit of Unnecessary Mountain. The terminus elevations are 100 m (north, at Porteau Road parking lot) and 920 m (south, at Cypress Bowl downhill ski parking lot). Hiking from south to north is thus generally easier, with net elevation loss, although ending closer to Vancouver will make a north–south hike more desirable for most. The different views make the route well worth hiking in both directions.

The trail is usually free of most snow from mid-July to late October. More so than any other area of the North Shore front peaks, this is a summer-only trip for all but the most experienced alpinists; much of the route follows a narrow ridge, and the risk of avalanche or collapsing cornices is significant.

Despite its modest length on paper, this is a very challenging trail with almost continuous climbing up and down. The *Don't Waste Your Time…* authors described it as "a feral, shaggy, hump-backed beast, beautiful from a distance, but a demon to ride." Many seasoned hikers return surprised and broken by its challenges. Most hikers will make an overnight trip of it. Fit trail-runners can run it in a long and tiring (but, if sunny, utterly exhilarating) day. It would be extremely difficult if not impossible to bag all 19 peaks in a single-day sweep. Those intent on summiting all of them should therefore plan for a multi-day effort or several day trips. Happily, this approach is facilitated by several trails leading back down to Lions Bay, allowing for a variety of interesting loop routes. Those are set out below.

The HSCT poses significant issues and logistical concerns that should be considered before getting to the individual peak descriptions.

WATER

There are several lakes, tarns, and creeks along the route – far more water at the north end than the south. Most, however, are dried out or unsavoury by August, the prime time to do this trail. Further, the exposed ridge hiking will leave you scorched on a hot summer day. There are long stretches where there is no water at all, most importantly the parched stretch between Magnesia Meadows and St. Marks. Take special care if you are travelling from north to south. It is wise to fully load up on water at Brunswick Lake, your last safe bet for water before Cypress Bowl some 20 km away. The Magnesia Meadows tarn is usually swampy by August. After that your only chances for water will be a semi-permanent snowpatch between James and Thomas or the small cirque lake between Thomas and West Lion. If you miss these, you will be delirious by Cypress Bowl on a hot day. Be sure to bring plenty of water with you as well as a filter or tablets in case you run out.

SAFETY

The peaks along the HSCT are remote. Clouds, fog, rain, lightning, and even unseasonal snow can arrive swiftly and without warning, turning pleasant ridgewalks into precarious slides. Be sure to take all precautions and bring the Ten Essentials as noted in the introduction. If you or a companion should come to grief in the alpine, there are two emergency shelters. Both have distinctive red metal roofs, and both are situated on the actual HSCT. The Brunswick one is above Brunswick Lake as you enter the alpine at the Porteau Road (north) end. The Magnesia Meadows shelter is obvious, located in the centre of the meadows in the shadow of Harvey.

GETTING THERE

The entire trail runs from the parking lot on the upslope (east) side of the Sea to Sky Highway just south of Porteau Cove Provincial Park, to the Cypress Bowl Provincial Park downhill ski area in the south. That said, the trail, and the peaks off the trail, are accessible from six main trailheads and several more tentative ones. The main access points, from north to south:

11. Porteau Road
12. Lions Bay (Sunset Road) to Brunswick Mountain
13. Lions Bay (Sunset Road) to Mt. Harvey
14. Lions Bay (Sunset Road) to Lions (Binkert Trail)
15. Lions Bay (Oceanview Road) to Unnecessary Mountain
16. Cypress Bowl

These variable access points allow for creative full-day loops focused on attaining summits rather than hiking the entire Howe Sound Crest Trail.

APPROACHING THE PEAKS

Depending on your destination and ability and the number of peaks you plan to bag, you may choose from different start and finish points. In the interests of saving paper, we have separated route descriptions into two parts for this area. The first part will get you to a familiar reference point on the HSCT, while the second part will get you from the reference point to the peak.

Deeks Lake and Brunswick Mountain.

A NORTH TO SOUTH OVERVIEW OF ENTIRE HOWE SOUND CREST TRAIL

I. PORTEAU ROAD TO DEEKS LAKE (DEEKS, WINDSOR, GOTHA, COBURG) (7 KM)

- Take the unnumbered exit east off Highway 99 at Porteau Road. There is a small parking lot for users of the HSCT with space for about 12 vehicles.
- Note: If the gate is open, and your vehicle is very sturdy and 4WD, it is possible to drive the first 4 km. Ordinary cars can only venture about 800 m up the road. There is no real place to park. It makes more sense to park in the main lot.
- From the parking lot, go right and uphill on a gravel road past a yellow gate.
- After 1.5 km you will see a left-hand turnoff for the Deeks Peak hike via Kallahne Lake Trail. (See the route description for Deeks Peak if you go this way.)
- Soon after, on the left, is a decent waterfall cascading down on granite face.
- The trail continues upwards on dull switchbacks, eventually, at 3.7 km, reaching a small lake and an HSCT signpost where the trail departs upwards from the road-trail.
- For the remaining 3 km up to the lake, the route alternates between reclaimed logging road and thigh-splitting, rooty trail.
- After about 1 km you will see a lookout over the valley on your right.
- You will see, to your right, an old trail down to Deeks Creek. Don't take it.
- Cross two boulder washes.
- After another 1 km you will see the base of the impressive Phi Alpha Falls (named after the UBC chapter of Delta Kappa Epsilon fraternity) on Deeks Creek, which cascades down 500 m or so.

Brunswick Falls, Howe Sound Crest Trail.

- You will pass by a massive spruce while hearing the distant roar of the falls. Soon you will come to the best view of the falls, on a short side trail. Take care: the path is slippery and a fall would have dire consequences.
- Well-travelled single-track trail continues steeply uphill with waterfall to the right.
- You will see the light filtering through the trees, indicating the lake above. Keep motoring upwards until the trail mercifully starts tilting downwards towards the lake.
- Come to a marked intersection with a campsite. More campsites are found in either direction around the lake.
- The left, north, clockwise direction around the lake leads to Windsor, Deeks, and Gotha–Coburg, as well as several prime campsites.
- The right, south, counterclockwise direction, continuing along Howe Sound Crest Trail, leads to Hanover, Hat, and Brunswick.

II. DEEKS LAKE TO BRUNSWICK MOUNTAIN TRAIL INTERSECTION (HANOVER, FAT ASS, HAT, WETTIN) (6 KM)

- The segment from Deeks Lake to Brunswick Mountain is one of the HSCT's most pleasing stretches.
- From the point where the trail meets Deeks Lake, head right, south (counterclockwise), passing by a campsite.
- Come to the Deeks Creek outflow, crossable over accumulated logs that are stable but slippery in wet weather.
- On the far side of the creek, meet the obvious trail and climb, steeply for a bit, up a muddy gully. The trail torques to the east.
- This next stretch is a celebration of mushrooms in the autumn. Boletes (porcini), bear's head, russulas, chicken of the woods, chanterelles, and massive bracket fungi abound.
- Roughly opposite from the point where the trail first meets the lake, you will leave the lake.
- Follow along upper Deeks Creek.
- After about 500 m, cross to the north side of the creek. The crossing is generally easy but can be dicey in wet weather or high water.
- The trail climbs steeply up over a rockfall, eventually reaching the pleasing green (in autumn) or turquoise (in summer) waters of Hanover (Middle) Lake with its waterfall at the south end.
- The naming of Hanover and Brunswick lakes is somewhat confusing in that Hanover towers over Brunswick Lake. That said, Brunswick is to the south of Hanover, in both lakes and peaks.
- More steep climbing, now assisted by a rope, and then a short, flat, lazy creek. Then up to Brunswick Lake (at around 10 km), a very beautiful double lake, the larger part a glacial cerulean, the smaller a muddy brown. There are granitic benches and islands. The place has the feeling of a fairyland. There are several campsites.
- Cross the log-and-rock bridge that separates the two parts of Brunswick Lake.
- There are several campsites here, with a handsome red-roofed shelter five minutes' climb above the lakes. A whisky cache is nearby.

Hanover (Middle) Lake, Howe Sound Crest Trail, with Brunswick behind.

Brunswick Lake is both glacial blue and muddy brown. Coburg and Gotha tower behind.

Brunswick Lake with Hanover behind.

- Climb up a dirt trail, which turns muddy in rain. Here there is a profusion of mushrooms – boletes and amanitas – in the autumn. At the top there are magnificent views of Hanover, Gotha and Coburg, and the three lakes.
- The minor but obvious side trail to Hanover leaves the HSCT about halfway between the Brunswick Lake hut and the Mt. Brunswick ascent trail. There is a loud creek here.
- The main trail climbs steeply up to Hat Pass and meadows.
- At Hat Pass you will see one of the most beautiful sights on Howe Sound Crest Trail: Hat Tarn, with a spectacular view of Hanover in the distance. Be sure to pause and look around.
- The small trail to Hat, Fat Ass, and Wettin, ascending sharply through the heather, is marked by orange flagging to the west. Depending on the amount of tape and boot-tread, it can be missed. For some reason this trail is better trod the farther you hike along it.
- The route descends to a meadow plateau with several small tarns.
- The meadow trail soon gives way to rock underfoot. In summer this stretch is hot and exposed.
- The trail then re-enters the forest and climbs up.

III. BRUNSWICK MOUNTAIN TRAIL INTERSECTION TO MT. HARVEY TRAIL INTERSECTION (HARVEY, MAGNESIA, BRUNSWICK) (3 KM)

- The intersection with the Brunswick Mountain trail is obvious, with several metallic markers in the trees, some flagging tape, and obvious trails up and down.
- After a long eastward traverse, the trail will suddenly turn south and down. At times the slope is steep, cut across by the trail. At all times, save for the occasional treefall, the trail is obvious.
- Continue south. You will reach Magnesia Meadows, with its lake and red A-frame shelter. There are fine views of Harvey from the meadows.
- To the east of the shelter is the route to Magnesia Peak.
- Continue south through the meadows. As unpleasant as the lake may seem, it may be your last opportunity for water for a long time. Get out the water purifier.
- Climb south to a ridge. At the top of the ridge, you will pass the Harvey side trail and then descend again onto the Harvey clear-cut slope.
- This section of the trail will take you through dense blueberry bushes on the gravelly, dusty slope facing south from Mt. Harvey. This is the densest concentration of mountain blueberry and black huckleberry bushes in these mountains, and perfectly situated with southern exposure and no tree cover. As a result, you will find some of the plumpest, sweetest berries you have ever tasted. You will probably also find a bear or two, especially in September, when the bears go into a state of manic eating, or hyperphagia, to store up nutrients for hibernation.
- The trail switchbacks down a logged slope. The thick berry bushes may obscure the route, making it is sometimes difficult to follow the trail down the Harvey slope to David Peak.
- At the base of that slope, now to the southeast of Harvey, you reach a small grassy meadow at the far southeast side of the Harvey clear-cut.

IV. MT. HARVEY TRAIL INTERSECTION TO WEST LION (DAVID, JAMES, THOMAS, WEST LION) (4 KM)

- The HSCT used to drop down below the mountain, traversing James and David to the east and nearly reaching a small lake (Hanging Lake) below. That trail is still used, but the new HSCT route, which goes over David and James and south to The Lions, is easier, despite the climbing, and gives better views.
- From the grassy area, it is sometimes difficult to find the start of the climb over David and James due to rapidly growing underbrush. If you head in the obvious direction, south and upwards, and through the shrubs, you will see the path. At all times, you should feel as if you are on a trail. If you don't, go back to the grassy patch and start again.
- The trail climbs steeply and steadily, over and under large roots of trees.
- Eventually you pop out of the underbrush to see an obvious trail up the rocks to David Peak, which has a cairn and a summit logbook. The rock towards the peak is somewhat crumbly; be cautious.
- Descend David Peak to the south, along a rocky route, again with some crumbling. Take care not to skid.
- At the south base of David is a pleasing meadow between David and James. The trail cuts and winds across the turf.
- The trail leading to James Peak is sometimes hard to follow but is a logical zigzag up a series of rocky balconies to the peak.
- Continue south and down from the peak of James. For those who are apprehensive about heights, there is a short section that will get your heart pumping. There is a cable to help you (although it is unnecessary except in wet or icy conditions).

From the base of David heading south to James Peak.

- At the south base of James there is a viewpoint over Enchantment Lake, with an odd ancient mailbox stuck to a tree.
- Ascend a scree slope that continues up and west, bypassing an unnamed peak bump between James and Thomas.
- Follow the HSCT towards West Lion. Climb up a steep rock face, where hands may be needed. The HSCT climbs Thomas Peak (the nubbin of a peak between West and East Lion), before passing a small tarn and descending to the left to the base of West Lion.
- Cut west toward the obvious pass between the two Lions. The trail follows the top of the scree slope and the base of West Lion. At one or two spots you will wish to slow down and use your hands. The crux is a narrow ledge in the rock face, with a slope down below. It looks scarier than it is. Just take it calm and slow, and only do it in non-wet and non-icy conditions.
- Then follow red paint dots to ascend a steep but manageable black rocky slope to the porch below West Lion.
- The trail is well marked throughout.

V. WEST LION TO CYPRESS BOWL (NORTH UNNECESSARY, UNNECESSARY, ST. MARKS, STRACHAN) (9 KM)

- From the base of The Lions, the well-trodden trail leads to Unnecessary Mountain.
- About 500 m along, roughly equidistant between West Lion and North Unnecessary, you will see Binkert Trail ascending to join Howe Sound Crest Trail.
- Along the ascent to the north peak of Unnecessary there is a narrow notch with a rope where hands are necessary. The rope is optional. There is no exposure.
- Just after the peak of North Unnecessary, you will see Unnecessary Mountain Trail heading down to Lions Bay.
- The trail is generally well marked, occasionally with paint splotches. At times it is narrow. Follow the ridge. At most points, there are spectacular views of Howe Sound.
- Continue your laborious ascent and descent of the three peaks of the aptly named Unnecessary Mountain.
- The trail goes up and down through more second-growth forest before climbing back up, this time to St. Marks Summit.
- At the near end of the short flat section, the trail will not likely be flagged, but you will see a small but clear trail heading east. This trail leads to the actual St. Marks Summit.
- The provincial park sign marked "Saint Marks Summit" is not the true peak, a fact made obvious by looking to the thickly treed slope above and east.
- At the start of a downhill stretch, the trees become denser, the ground less rocky, and the trail less muddy.
- The well-marked path will proceed generally downhill, with the occasional flat or slightly uphill stretch, through second-growth forest.
- After crossing a small bridge, you will reach Strachan Meadows, with scruffy alders to the left (east). Mt. Strachan looms behind.
- Pass the Strachan turnoff and then cross a second bridge. Continue south along HSCT.
- Follow the now-gravel trail down and then up to a map kiosk with a tribute to Paul Binkert, and a fine view of The Lions.

- Follow the switchbacks down. Soon a side trail heading west leads to a great view of Howe Sound: Bowen Lookout. It is well worth the 10-minute detour.
- The trail gives way to a somewhat ugly reclaimed gravel road past a water tower and then begins climbing in gravelly switchbacks.
- You can go directly back to Cypress Mountain Lodge or take a pleasant side trail to Yew Lake and a grove of old-growth trees.
- This south section of the trail is well marked and wide. Follow the Howe Sound Crest Trail signs back to Cypress Mountain Lodge and the downhill ski area parking lot.

SOUTH TO NORTH OVERVIEW OF ENTIRE HOWE SOUND CREST TRAIL

I. CYPRESS BOWL TO WEST LION (STRACHAN, ST. MARKS, UNNECESSARY, NORTH UNNECESSARY) (9 KM)

- This first section of the trail is well marked and wide.
- From Cypress Mountain Lodge, follow the signs to Howe Sound Crest Trail.
- You can go directly, or take a pleasant side trail to Yew Lake and a grove of old-growth trees.
- The first portion is somewhat ugly reclaimed gravel road past a water tower and then climbs in gravelly switchbacks.
- At about 1 km, another side trail, westbound, leads to a great view of Howe Sound: Bowen Lookout. It is well worth the 10-minute detour.
- More switchbacks eventually lead to a map kiosk with a tribute to Paul Binkert and a fine view of The Lions.
- Take the trail down and then up. After crossing a small bridge, you will reach Strachan Meadows, with scruffy alders to the right (east). Mt. Strachan looms behind. Pass the Strachan turnoff and then cross a second bridge. Continue north along HSCT.
- The well-marked path will proceed generally uphill, with the occasional flat or slightly downhill respite, through second-growth forest.
- Eventually, at the end of an uphill stretch, the trees thin out, the ground gets rockier, and the trail becomes flat and at times slightly muddy. At 5.5 km you will see a provincial park signpost reading "Saint Marks Summit."
- Proceed to the end of the short flat section. It will not likely be flagged, but you will see a small but clear trail heading east. This route leads to the actual St. Marks Summit.
- The HSCT descends into more second-growth forest before a laborious 200-m climb to the three peaks of the aptly named Unnecessary Mountain (9 km).
- The trail is generally well marked, occasionally with paint splotches. At times it is narrow. Follow the ridge. At most points, there are spectacular views of Howe Sound.
- Just before the peak of North Unnecessary, you will see the Unnecessary Mountain Trail heading down to Lions Bay.
- Descending from North Unnecessary is a narrow notch with a rope where hands are necessary. The rope is optional. There is no exposure.
- About 500 m along, roughly equidistant between the peak of North Unnecessary

Mountain and West Lion, you will see Binkert Trail ascending to join the HSCT.

- The well-trodden trace from Unnecessary Mountain leads to the porch below West Lion, where many hikers stop to admire West Lion and the humans scampering up it.

II. WEST LION TO MT. HARVEY TRAIL INTERSECTION (WEST LION, THOMAS, JAMES, DAVID) (4 KM)

- From the base of West Lion, cut southeast and downwards. The route is quite steep but obvious. At times, it is marked with a paint splotch or a cairn. On dry or wet days take care: it will be crumbly or slippery. Also take care not to descend too low, onto the scree field below.
- Cut east toward the obvious pass through the two Lions. The trail follows the top of the scree slope and the base of West Lion. At one or two spots you will wish to slow down and use your hands. There is no real exposure, but there is the potential for a fall and injury. The crux is a narrow ledge in the rock face, with a slope down below. It looks scarier than it is. Just take it calm and slow, and only do it in non-wet and non-icy conditions.
- Follow HSCT northeast, up and past a small tarn.
- This leads up to and over Thomas Peak (the bump in between The Lions).
- Descend a scree slope that continues down and east, bypassing an unnamed peak bump between James and Thomas. Then continue north to the base of James.
- At the south base of James there is a viewpoint over Enchantment Lake, with an odd ancient mailbox stuck to a tree.
- Then head down a steep rock face, where hands may be needed, to a rock field and up again, to the steep gap guarding James Peak ridge. A cable and rope across the gap will offer reassurance (although they are not really necessary except in wet or icy conditions).
- Climb up the ridge to James Peak.
- After James Peak the trail descends to a pleasant meadow leading to David Peak. The trail cuts and winds across the turf.
- At the south base of David, the HSCT used to drop down below the mountain, traversing David to the east and nearly reaching Hanging Lake below. That trail is still used, although the newer route, which goes over David, is easier, despite the climbing, and gives better views.
- The south ascent of David is at times a bushwhack due to treefall. A trail should be discernible every few metres at least.
- As you reach the peak of David, the rock is somewhat crumbly. Be careful.
- At the peak of David, there is a small cairn, and a summit logbook, and great views.

III. MT. HARVEY TRAIL INTERSECTION TO BRUNSWICK MOUNTAIN TRAIL INTERSECTION (HARVEY, MAGNESIA, BRUNSWICK) (3 KM)

- From David, descend northeast. The route is obscure at first, but really the only persistent way down. The trail hits trees halfway down. Occasionally you will wish to grasp tree boughs on the steep descent, but there is no exposure.
- Pop out on a small meadow at the far southeast side of the Harvey clear-cut: berry paradise.
- Zigzag up and across the Harvey clear-cut slope. In late summer this area will be

full of thick berry bushes, possibly obscuring the route. Persevere. It may also be full of hungry bears. Be cautious.

- At the top of the ridge, you will pass the Mt. Harvey side trail, and then descend again into the obvious Magnesia Meadows, with its lake and red A-frame shelter. There are fine views of Harvey from the meadows.
- To the east of the shelter is the route to Magnesia Peak, off the HSCT.
- Continue north, and then northwest, through the rocky meadows and then back into forest. The trail is well defined and pleasant, and the trees are large.
- Continue due west. At times the slope is steep, cut across by the trail. At all times, save for the occasional treefall, the track is obvious.
- After a long westward traverse, the route will suddenly turn north and up.
- The intersection with the Brunswick Mountain trail is obvious, with several metallic markers in the trees, some flagging tape, and obvious trails up and down.

IV. BRUNSWICK MOUNTAIN TRAIL INTERSECTION TO DEEKS LAKE (HAT, FAT ASS, WETTIN, HANOVER) (6 KM)

- From the Brunswick-HSCT intersection, head north on the trail, which is at times bounded by steep slope.
- The dirt trail soon gives way to rock underfoot. In summer this stretch is hot.
- The trail ascends to a meadow plateau with several small tarns.
- To the west you will see a small trail ascending sharply through the heather, marked by flagging tape. This is the route to Fat Ass, Hat, and Wettin.
- Past Hat Pass you will see one of the most beautiful sights on Howe Sound Crest Trail: Hat Tarn, with a spectacular view of Hanover in the distance.
- Ascend to the top of the meadow, and see Brunswick Lake, to which you will descend.
- The initial part of the way down is steep, leading to a flatter area with a small creek. Here you will find the side trail to Hanover. There are magnificent views of Hanover, Gotha and Coburg, and the three lakes.
- The trail is first rocky and then dirt, which turns muddy in rain. Here there is a profusion of mushrooms – boletes and amanitas – in the autumn.
- Reach Brunswick Cabin, with fine views of the two-toned Brunswick Lake, and with a hidden bottle of whisky nearby.
- Descend to Brunswick Lake itself. There are various campsites around the lake.
- Cross the log-and-rock bridge that separates the two parts of Brunswick Lake.
- Hike northwest, gradually descending, past a gravelly floodplain area through which Deeks Creek flows, down to a waterfall into Hanover (Middle) Lake, which is a pleasing green (in autumn) or turquoise (in summer).
- Descend steeply alongside the waterfall and down a narrow but well-defined dirt trail.
- Leave the forest and cross a short boulder plain. Cross the creek from the north side to the south. It is easy and safe at most times.
- Follow the creek's west bank. You will see the destination through the trees: Deeks Lake to the north.
- At the lake the trail continues to the west around the lake. This is a dark section marked by a profusion of giant trees and countless varieties of mushrooms.
- The trail follows the lakeshore, about 15 m above it.
- Just short of the opposite point on the shore, you will descend to a log crossing at

the outflow of the lake. The logs are very slippery when wet.

- Ascend, then descend, then ascend again, to meet a campsite and a marked intersection with Deeks Peak Trail and the HSCT. More campsites are found in either direction around the lake.
- Go west and down.

V. DEEKS LAKE TO PORTEAU ROAD TRAILHEAD (COBURG, GOTHA, WINDSOR, DEEKS) (7 KM)

- The descent from Deeks Lake to Porteau Road is as obvious and well marked as it is dull.
- For the first 3 km down from the lake, the trail alternates between reclaimed logging road and rooty trail.
- After 250 m, you will come to the loud and scenic Phi Alpha Falls (named after the UBC chapter of Delta Kappa Epsilon fraternity). The falls themselves stretch in various cataracts for 250 m or so.
- Continue the steep but obvious descent, which flattens briefly at the rocky wash of a landslide. At last visit, flagging marked the route across to rejoin the forest.
- On your left is an old trail down to Deeks Creek. Don't take it.
- Then you will see a valley lookout on your right.
- The trail continues downwards on dull switchbacks, eventually at the 3.7 km marker reaching a small lake and an HSCT signpost at a more road-like portion of the trail.
- Continue down the road, passing several signs. It is a dull trudge.
- On the right see a decent waterfall cascading down a granite face.
- You will see a turnoff to the right for the Deeks Peak hike via Kallahne Lake Trail.
- Go left and downhill on a gravel road past a yellow gate to come to the trailhead and Porteau Road parking lot.

Enjoying salmon berries en route to Coburg

NORTH HSCT: DEEKS LAKE AREA, ACCESS VIA PORTEAU ROAD TRAILHEAD

This section describes the routes to Deeks, Windsor, Gotha, and Coburg.

The northernmost, Deeks Lake portion of Howe Sound Crest Trail provides the most direct route to Deeks, Windsor, Gotha, and Coburg peaks. To reach Deeks Lake, see the description of the first part of Howe Sound Crest Trail, in the introduction to this section.

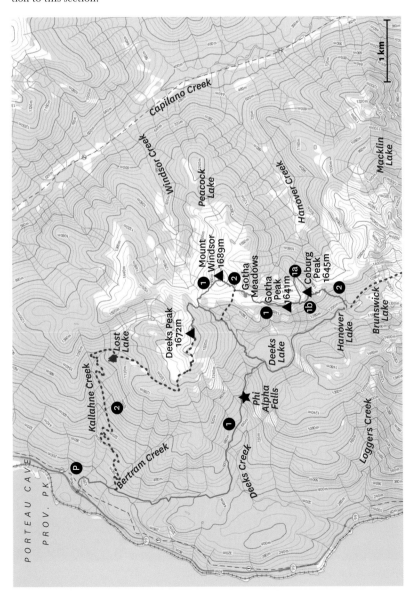

DEEKS LAKE AREA BAGGER TIPS

The summits of Deeks, Windsor, Gotha, and Coburg can be done in a comfortable day trip. There are a number of options, depending on your technical ability and whether or not you prefer loops or "out and backs." They all start from the parking lot at Porteau Road. All these routes are complex, so it is strongly advised that you carry a GPS with tracks loaded before attempting them.

ROUTE 1 (OUT AND BACK; LEAST TECHNICAL)

The most straightforward approach is to take the HSCT to Deeks Lake and from there head east up the trail to Deeks Peak. From Deeks Peak, retrace your steps to the meadow in the Deeks–Windsor col and then head south to Windsor. From Windsor you go cross country in a westerly direction to a large tarn at the base of Gotha in the meadows. This is a nice spot for a swim on a sunny day. From here head straight up Gotha and then over its multi-summit ridge towards the south. There's quite a drop from here as you head towards the col with Coburg. From the col take the North Direct route to the top. With this route you retrace your steps back over Gotha and descend back towards the tarn, from where there is a Windsor bypass trail that joins back with the trail heading down to Deeks Lake.

Round-trip distance: 22.6 km

Time: 11:34

Elevation gain: 2106 m

ROUTE 2 (COBURG–GOTHA TRAVERSE)

This route follows the HSCT to Hanover Lake and then traverses Coburg and Gotha from south to north. From Hanover Lake take the South Direct route to the top of Coburg, then descend via the North Direct route. From the col head up the north ridge of Gotha and traverse the summit plateau, then descend the northeast side to the small tarn below. From the tarn you can hike directly through light bush up Windsor via its west side. Descend the trail to the Deeks–Windsor col and from there locate the poorly marked trail up to Deeks Peak. From the summit retrace your steps to the Deeks–Windsor col and thetn return via the Deeks Lake and HSCT trails.

Round-trip distance: 23 km

Time: 12:20

Elevation gain: 2000 m

ROUTE 3 (GRAND TRAVERSE)

This route is the same as Route 2 all the way to the top of Deeks Peak. However, rather than retracing your steps, descend via Kallahne Lake Trail to the west and north. This takes longer than the Route 2 descent but completes a glorious grand traverse of the entire area. This descent route is only sporadically flagged and hard to follow, so be sure you use a GPS when attempting this for the first time. Going in the wrong direction here will generally lead you to the tops of some very unfriendly cliffs: not somewhere you want to be late in the day.

Round-trip distance: 23 km

Time: 13:15

Elevation gain: 2000 m

DEEKS PEAK
(DEE) (1672 M #6)

A rewarding climb with great views and just the right amount of routefinding.

CAUTION:
Routefinding at times difficult.

PROMINENCE:
207 m.

LATITUDE/LONGITUDE:
N49.52778 W123.20528.

BANG FOR BUCK:
3/5

PEAK VIEW:
4/5. Unobstructed views of surrounding peaks and valleys;

Howe Sound and Mt. Sedgwick; Rainy River Peaks on Sunshine Coast; Sky Pilot.

TRUE SUMMIT LOCATION:
The east peak is slightly higher than the west one.

HEADWATERS:
Some small streams.

BEST VIEWS FROM:
BC Ferries in Howe Sound; Gotha, Hat Pass, Brunswick, Hanover.

TRIP INFORMATION
Round-trip distance: 17 km from HSCT trailhead at Porteau Road.
Elevation gain: 1539 m.
Time: 6–9 hours (6:10) both routes.
Difficulty: 3/5. Sparsely marked trail with some light scrambling.
Snow free: July to October.
Must-see: Deeks Lake.
Scenery: 4/5. Old-growth, second-growth forests. Creeks. Beautiful alpine lakes.
Kids: 2/5. Far.
Dogs: 4/5. Only one spot where a lift is needed.
Runnability: 2/5. Popular lower section of trail offers a good warm-up.
Terrain: Second-growth forest, heath.
Public transit: None.
Cell coverage: Usually present on peak but rare elsewhere.
Sun: 3/5. First 75 per cent tree-covered; final 25 per cent exposed to sun.
Water: Minimal water on access trails above Deeks–Windsor Meadows.
Route links: Windsor, Gotha, Coburg.

HISTORY
Name origin: After John Frederick Deeks (1868 Ontario–1935), whose Deeks Gravel & Rock Co. began working in this area in 1908. Also named for him are Deeks Creek and Deeks Lake.
Name status: Official. Adopted October 4, 1945, on C.3577, as labelled on the Alan John Campbell (1882–1967) 1928 topographic map and on BC map 5B, 1929.
First ascent: Unknown. First BCMC climb May 6, 1962. Likely climbed in the early 20th century by hunters, surveyors, or loggers, and earlier by First Nations.

Deeks Peak is a well-known summit offering decent views of everything from Garibaldi to Howe Sound to Vancouver. Deeks has two peaks, of which the east one is slightly higher. Rumour has it that a bottle of whisky is cached to the east of the summit cairn. There is also a summit register under the cairn.

There are two main routes to Deeks Peak. The traditional one is via Kallahne (Lost) Lake, starting at a side trail from the lower part of Howe Sound Crest Trail. The more popular route is via Deeks Lake. Combine the two and circumnavigate the entire mountain or, for an energetic but achievable day of frenetic and rewarding bagging, do a sweep of Deeks, Windsor, and Gotha.

The peak is named after John Frederick Deeks, who in 1908 began mining sand and gravel from the deposits at what is now Porteau Cove, and shipping it down to Vancouver. A small community of employees lived on site, which had considerable housing, a school, tennis courts, and daily ferry service via the Union Steamship Company. Deeks is not only the namesake of the peak and lake, but he himself enlarged Deeks Lake to its present size by damming it to provide water for his gravel operations around 1910.

Like Windsor, Gotha, and Coburg, Deeks's geology is the same as that of Brunswick and Gambier: Gambier Group, with volcanic andesite, dacite, and rhyolite on top and metamorphic and sedimentary rock at base. As with the Brunswick area, Deeks is an island of these rocks in a sea of granitic and plutonic strata.

ROUTE 1:
FROM WEST VIA DEEKS LAKE

- Drive to the Porteau Cove HSCT trailhead, above.
- Go from the HSCT trailhead at Porteau Road to Deeks Lake, above.
- Pause to soak in the view of surrounding peaks at Deeks Lake.
- From the lakeshore, follow the trail along the northwest side of the lake past a few campsites, then along a moss-cut trail and across a small boulder field to the base of a steep climb. There is a fine view of Brunswick's jagged peak from here.
- The most difficult routefinding moment is at the end of the rock field. Head up and left rather than right and around the lake.
- Nice single-track takes you steeply uphill along stair-like roots through tall trees with minimal undergrowth. After 15 minutes you will see orange flashing on the trees.
- Soon the trail will give you a welcome respite with a gentler climb. Cross two small creeks and approach the distant roar of a larger creek. Head uphill again.
- At publication, there was a messy confluence of deadfall obscuring the path: beware. Go up and then diagonally again.
- At around 1.4 km you will see a shiny red sign indicating Windsor Peak left and Peak 5400 (Gotha) right. Go left and continue uphill.
- After another 15–20 minutes the trail cuts through a band of blueberry bushes and pops out on the lovely, wide, grassy meadow between Deeks and Windsor. Small creeks cut through the heather and pour into small tarns. Birds sing and dragon-flies hum. It is a nice place on a sunny day.

Deeks–Windsor Meadows to Deeks Peak: The trail to the peak is poorly flagged at first. At roughly the midpoint of the meadow, veer left and uphill. Bushwhack through heather and low bushes until you find a narrow trail leading uphill.

- The route is sparsely flagged and barely noticeable except for the occasional boot scuff. It zigs and zags up the slope, with one wide veer to the north. Big trees tower above you, shading out undergrowth. This makes the passage pleasant but the trail tracking at times difficult.
- Eventually you will reach a pleasant granite balcony to the north of the peak. Enjoy the views of the impressive Deeks cliffs to the west.

Deeks Peak: the scuffed path as seen from the balcony above.

- Go left and attain the ridge at the earliest point possible. At last visit, some displaced rocks and a well-scuffed path marked the entry point. Climb upward through the trees.
- Pop out onto another balcony. Descend to a small shoulder above a steep valley to the north (right). Avoid the edge, as grievous injury would result from a fall here.
- Emerge onto yet another balcony, this one with a pair of small tarns. Again climb uphill and left next to the base of the cliff face. Scramble up some boulders, which require minor handholds.
- Continue left on the narrow trail, then to the right and up to the peak on an obvious trail.
- The summit is rocky and marked with a big cairn. Enjoy the splendid views of Howe Sound.

ROUTE 2:

FROM WEST VIA KALLAHNE (LOST) LAKE TRAIL

This route follows an overgrown logging road (deactivated in 1995) to a cabin and lake and then semi-bushwhacks to the peak. While formerly the predominant route to the peak, it has become overgrown recently and fallen out of favour.

- At about 1.5 km from the Porteau Road trailhead, look for an HSCT signpost indicating Deeks Peak via Kallahne Lake. Turn left and go uphill on the trail.

- The road has been taken over by alders, but the route is not hard to follow as it gains elevation.
- Follow Kallahne Creek along the south, steadily climbing. Cross the creek twice. Take care when the water is higher or the weather has been wet, as the rocks are slippery. After about 4 km, you will come to a small A-frame cabin at Kallahne Lake (also known as Lost Lake).
- The next section, from the lake to the peak, is not well marked. Follow the main creekbed south and up, on the west side of the creek. In about 1.5 km you will come to a lovely meadow with beautiful views of Howe Sound on a sunny day.
- Cut east and continue steeply uphill along the ridge. The trail is more discernable here, the orange flagging tape more frequent.
- Pass some small tarns before starting the steepest portion of the climb. Zigzagging up, you'll find the terrain generally rocky underfoot and overgrown to mid-waist.
- Climb over the west subpeak of Deeks, then down, and then up to the main, east peak of Deeks.

Deeks Peak: the crux.

MT. WINDSOR
(WIN) (1689 M #4)

*A seldom visited but rewarding intermediate climb with a pointy peak
and unique views to the northeast*

CAUTION:
No marked trail from either
approach.

PROMINENCE:
264 m.

LATITUDE/LONGITUDE:
N49.52333 W123.19194.

BANG FOR BUCK:
4/5

PEAK VIEW:
4/5. Deeks, Capilano, Hanover,
Brunswick, Lions.

TRUE SUMMIT LOCATION:
Only one peak.

HEADWATERS:
Hanover Creek (into Capilano).

BEST VIEWS FROM:
Gotha, Hat Pass, Brunswick,
Hanover.

TRIP INFORMATION
Round-trip distance: 17 km from HSCT trailhead above Porteau Cove.
Elevation gain: 1554 m.
Time: 5.5–8.5 hours (5:50).
Difficulty: 4/5.
Snow free: Mid-July to early October.
Must-sees: Waterfalls; Deeks Lake.
Scenery: 4/5.
Kids: 2/5.
Dogs: 4/5.
Runnability: 3/5.
Terrain: Second-growth forest.
Public transit: None.
Cell coverage: Inconsistent.
Sun: 2/5. Partial sun on fire road; full sun in alpine.
Water: Plentiful below alpine; snow melt and small tarns above.
Route links: Deeks, Gotha, Coburg.

HISTORY
Name origin: The adopted family name of the present royal family of Britain and Canada. The family's German name of Saxe-Coburg became less popular during the First World War, so they borrowed the name of their castle.
Name status: Official, adopted June 2, 1955. Note: Official name is "Mt. Windsor" rather than Windsor Peak or Windsor Mountain as it is sometimes erroneously called.
First ascent: After 1913.

Opposite page: north to Windsor from north side of Gotha, with headwaters of Hanover Creek below.

Mt. Windsor is a lesser-known gem of a peak. It offers a better alpine experience and more impressive 360° views than does its more popular sister, Deeks. Windsor's pointy peak is unmistakable. It stands like a jewel in the royal crown on a tiara of rock and heather. While remote, it provides a sense of accomplishment without great exhaustion or danger. The scramble looks imposing but is runnable for most of the way. The peak deserves more visitors and love than it receives. On it there is a small rock cairn. Also a whisky cache.

The peak is obvious, although some BCMC trip leaders scouting out Windsor apparently became lost and ascended Deeks instead of Windsor (according to a 1965 BCMC *BC Mountaineer* report). The traditional route (dating back at least to 1965), and the best route, is to climb up to the meadows in the Deeks–Windsor shoulder, and then up to the Windsor Peak. You can, however, go along the rougher route to the meadows in the Windsor–Gotha shoulder.

Whether you are coming from Deeks Peak or Deeks Lake, be sure to pause for a snack at the col. This lovely meadow at the edge of the forest offers vistas of alpine flowers and the opportunity to cool your feet in a seasonal tarn. If you are lucky, you may see a deer or a bear.

Windsor, along with Gotha and Coburg and the area around Deeks Lake, consists of Gambier Group rock, largely of volcanic origin: andesite, dacite, and rhyolite flows. It shares this characteristic with Brunswick, and is thus an outlier among the largely plutonic – granite or hornblende – peaks of the North Shore.

Route 1:

FROM WEST – DEEKS LAKE AND DEEKS–WINDSOR COL

- Drive to Porteau Cove HSCT trailhead, above.
- Go from the HSCT trailhead at Porteau Road to Deeks Lake, above.
- Pause to soak in the view of surrounding peaks at Deeks Lake.
- From the shore of the lake, follow the trail along northwest side of the lake past a few campsites, then along a moss-cut trail and across a small boulder field to base of a steep climb. There is a fine view of Brunswick's jagged peak from here.
- The most difficult routefinding moment is at the end of the rock field. Head up and left rather than right and around the lake.
- Nice single-track takes you steeply uphill along stair-like roots through tall trees with minimal undergrowth. After 15 minutes you will see orange flashing on the trees.
- Soon the trail will give you a most welcome respite with a gentler climb. Cross two small creeks and approach the distant roar of a larger creek. Head uphill again.
- At the time of writing, there was a messy confluence of deadfall obscuring the path: beware. Go up and then diagonally again.
- At around 1.4 km you will see a shiny red sign indicating Windsor Peak left and Peak 5400 (Gotha) right. Go left and continue uphill.
- After another 15–20 minutes, the trail cuts through a band of blueberry bushes and pops out on the lovely wide grassy meadow between Deeks and Windsor. Small creeks cut through the heather and pour into small tarns. Birds sing and dragon-flies hum. It is a nice place on a sunny day.
- **Deeks–Windsor Meadows to Windsor:** From the Deeks–Windsor saddle, avoid the temptation to charge due east and up across the meadow. Instead, go

slightly up (north), to the left of the wooded ridge running down from the peak, to get a view of the rock field and peaks to the north.

- At roughly the middle of the ridge you will see a narrow trail climbing steeply through the heather.
- The trail will eventually top out at the base of a long rock field, with Windsor's peak obvious at the top. Pass a few tarns and rivulets to attain a small balcony covered in heather and grass.
- Head towards the peak, up through a copse of trees and around and east up to a further grassy, heathery balcony.
- The final ascent is up a series of rock slabs. There will always be sufficient hand- and footholds and you should never feel exposed. Avoid the sheer cliffs to the north.
- There is a small rock cairn at the peak. Enjoy splendid views of Sky Pilot and Capilano to the north, Gotha to the south, Deeks to the west, and the rarely visited Peacock Peak in the watershed to the east.

ROUTE 2:

FROM SOUTH – GOTHA MEADOWS

- Read the description for Gotha Meadows below, in reverse.
- There is no trail up to Windsor from Gotha Meadows, but one can go this way.
- Big picture route: Look closely at your map or GPS and follow the most sensible contour line up. It is steep but should never be dangerous. It is safest and most comfortable to follow the vertical tree bands, holding on to branches for stability. The heather and blueberry bushes on the steep slopes outside of the tree copses can be slippery when wet.

GOTHA PEAK
(GOT) (1641 M #11)

A bit of everything, with a spectacular view as a reward.

CAUTION:
No marked route. Some exposed areas near peak.

PROMINENCE:
111 m.

LATITUDE/LONGITUDE:
N49.51278 W123.19917.

BANG FOR BUCK:
3/5

PEAK VIEW:
5/5. Unobstructed views of surrounding peaks and valleys. Brunswick and lakes spectacular.

TRUE SUMMIT LOCATION:
South.

HEADWATERS:
Small streams draining into Deeks Lake.

BEST VIEWS FROM:
Deeks Lake, Windsor, Deeks Peak.

TRIP INFORMATION
Round-trip distance: 17.4 km from HSCT trailhead above Porteau Cove.
Elevation gain: 1508 m.
Time: 7–10 hours (6:54) from Porteau Cove trailhead.
Difficulty: 4/5. Some bushwhacking and light scrambling.
Snow free: Mid-July to early October.
Must-sees: Deeks Lake; boggy meadows between Windsor and Gotha.
Scenery: 4/5. Old-growth, second-growth forests. Creeks. Beautiful alpine lakes.
Kids: 1/5. Far. Some exposure.
Dogs: 4/5. Sharp rocks in alpine.
Runnability: 2/5. Lower section offers a good warm-up. Bushwhacking in the alpine part.
Terrain: Second-growth forest; only occasional flagging.
Public transit: None.
Cell coverage: Inconsistent.
Sun: From Deeks–Windsor col; mostly exposed in the alpine.
Water: Available in Deeks Lake and meadow below.
Route links: Deeks, Windsor, Coburg.

HISTORY
Name origin: Named after the House of Saxe-Coburg and Gotha, the former name of the House of Windsor, the current royal house of the Commonwealth realms: the family of Queen Elizabeth II.
Name status: Unofficial.
Other names: Peak 5400 (with Coburg); LePage Peak (after early BCMC climber Edward LePage, of the Vancouver real estate family).
First ascent: Unknown.

The most impressive feature of beautiful Deeks Lake are the two peaks rising at its east end, with nearly sheer cliffs descending to the cirque lake and rock field below. Gotha is the northern and easier peak; Coburg is the southern and scarier one. Both offer spectacular and quite different views.

Gotha is an exhilarating climb, as it is not attained via a marked trail and is seldom visited, yet the summit is obvious and the views rewarding. Into the wild! It is a long ridge, with two rock knobs for peaks; there is a deceptive cairn at the lower, easier, closer north peak.

The meadows between Gotha and Windsor are well worth a visit. There is a small lake that provides a refreshing dip on a hot day; it provides the headwaters for Hanover Creek, a tributary of the Capilano River. It is surrounded by monoliths and heather and is ridiculously scenic. The rock field climb up to Gotha is also thrilling.

Up Gotha from Deeks Lake and Gotha Meadows.

Geologically, Gotha is marked by interesting geometrical chunks of volcanic rock, cut by nature into square blocks and stairs. Like Deeks, Windsor, and Coburg, its rocks are the same as those of Brunswick and Gambier: Gambier Group strata, combining volcanic andesite, dacite, and rhyolite on top and metamorphic and sedimentary rock at base.

See drive to Porteau Cove Howe Sound Crest Trail trailhead, above.

ROUTE 1:

FROM NORTHWEST VIA HOWE SOUND CREST TRAIL
AND DEEKS LAKE

- Drive to Porteau Cove Howe Sound Crest Trail trailhead, above.
- Go from the HSCT trailhead at Porteau Road to Deeks Lake, above.
- Pause to soak in the view of surrounding peaks at Deeks Lake.
- From the shore of the lake, follow the trail along northwest side of the lake past a few campsites, then along a moss-cut trail and across a small boulder field to base of a steep climb. There is a fine view of Brunswick's jagged peak from here.
- The most difficult routefinding moment in the trail is at the end of the rock field. Head up and left rather than right and around the lake.
- Nice single-track takes you steeply uphill along stair-like roots through tall trees with minimal undergrowth. After 15 minutes you will see orange flashing on the trees.
- Soon the trail will give you a welcome respite with a gentler climb. Cross two small creeks and approach the distant roar of a larger creek. Head uphill again.
- At the time of writing, there was a messy confluence of deadfall obscuring the path: beware. Go up and then diagonally again.
- At around 1.4 km you will see a shiny red sign indicating Windsor Peak left and Peak 5400 (Gotha) right.
- Turn right (east) (left leads to Deeks and Windsor). Cross a small creek.
- Unfortunately this route is no longer a trail. It is merely a rough way up and east through alpine meadows and heath towards the meadowed col between Windsor and Gotha. Use your GPS and head more or less straight towards that destination.
- There are likely few flags. You will see occasional clues of the former trail route through patches of dead heather and moss. It follows the most gentle contour line, running alongside a west–east creek for most of the route. The creek originates in the Windsor–Gotha col meadows.
- You will eventually arrive at Gotha Meadows, an open alpine area in the saddle between Mt. Windsor and Gotha Peak. Boulders and tarns amidst the heather make this a lovely place for a rest. In autumn, massive bolete (porcini) mushrooms abound. Unfortunately the bugs have likely reached the mushrooms before you, and an otherwise glorious meal will be stymied.

From Gotha Meadows to Gotha Peak: Gotha will be visible to your right (south) and a small lake visible straight ahead (east), below you. Cut diagonally and eventually downwards towards the lower middle of the rock field.

- A thick band of trees and a slight drop-off separates you from the rock field, but there are several points where you can get through. Cut through the heather diagonally.
- The rock field is steep but the rocks generally stable and not slippery in decent weather.
- Pop out at the first meadowy balcony at the level of the original Windsor–Gotha Meadows.
- Caution for your return descent at this point: the natural route back to the meadow is split by a set of cliffs and is not recommended.
- There is a good view of Deeks Lake from here.

The route up Gotha from the balcony.

- Uphill from you is a cliff band. Although a gully on the right is climbable, the safer route is to climb up left: easy and safe handholds will bring you up to a second balcony of granite and heather.
- Gentle rock handholds will lead you to the cairned false lower north summit of Gotha, with impressive views of Deeks Lake below. You may wish to stop here, as the true summit is only a few metres higher, with identical views but a somewhat scary approach.
- The true summit of Gotha is 500 m farther along the ridge, to the south, towards Coburg. You will cross over three other sub-summits that are within a few metres' elevation from the actual summit.
- As a general rule, if it looks tricky, head to the right (west, toward Deeks Lake).
- Descend the final bump. At the col, go right and a little down, through a krumholtz, and then up towards the true summit. Be careful, as visibility is not perfect and the exposure and danger are real. The final section is very narrow and potentially dangerous.

Gotha summit, with Deeks Lake below.

Route 2:

FROM NORTH – WINDSOR PEAK

- Follow route to Deeks Lake and Windsor Peak, above.
- There is no trail up to Windsor from Gotha Meadows.
- Big picture route: look closely at your map or GPS and follow the most sensible contour line down. It is steep but should never be dangerous. It is safest and most comfortable to follow the vertical tree bands, holding onto branches for stability. The heather and blueberry bushes on the steep slopes outside of the tree copses can be slippery when wet.
- Follow directions listed above at "From Gotha Meadows to Gotha Peak."

COBURG PEAK
(COB) (1645 M #9)

Very rarely visited, with glorious views but a scary approach.

CAUTION:
Remote! Potentially dangerous!
Exposed sections!

PROMINENCE:
152 m.

LATITUDE/LONGITUDE:
N49.50972 W123.19583.

BANG FOR BUCK:
3/5. Spectacular views but a bit
harrowing.

PEAK VIEW:
5/5. Unobstructed views of
surrounding peaks and valleys.

TRUE SUMMIT LOCATION:
Only one peak.

HEADWATERS:
Minor tributaries of Capilano
River and Hanover Creek
(into Capilano River).

BEST VIEWS FROM:
Deeks Lake, Gotha Peak.

TRIP INFORMATION

Round-trip distance: 19 km from HSCT trailhead above Porteau Cove.

Elevation gain: 1611 m.

Time: 9–13 hours (9:26) from Porteau Cove trailhead.

Difficulty: 5+/5. Some bushwhacking, scrambling, and exposure.

Snow free: Usually June, but no one should attempt before snow wholly gone.

Must-see/hear: Sheer drop to Deeks; echos.

Scenery: 4/5. Old-growth, second-growth forests; creeks; lovely alpine lakes; good views.

Kids: 0/5. Obviously not appropriate.

Dogs: 1/5. Not recommended; sharp rocks in alpine; several very steep sections.

Runnability: 2/5. Popular lower section of trail offers a good warm-up.

Terrain: Several very steep sections; scraggly mountain pines; granite.

Public transit: None.

Cell coverage: Some on peak; inconsistent.

Sun: Mostly exposed.

Water: Scarce after Gotha Meadows.

Route links: Gotha, and Deeks and Windsor accessible on same trip for sturdy runners.

HISTORY

Name origin: Prince Albert (1819–1861), husband of Queen Victoria, was Prince of Saxe-Coburg and Gotha. As such, it is the former family name of Queen Elizabeth II and the House of Windsor, the current royal house of the Commonwealth realms, changed during the First World War, when German names were understandably unpopular.

Name status: Unofficial.

Other names: Peak 5400 (with Gotha); LePage Peak (after early BCMC climber

Edward LePage, of the Vancouver real estate family).

First ascent: Unknown.

Other write-ups: The superb post, with photos, by "RamblingBull" on ClubTread. com is highly recommended: <u>forums.clubtread.com/27-british-columbia/42450-gotha-coburg-exploratory-circuit-29-july-2012-a.html</u>.

You will feel exhilarated on the peak of Coburg, the southern and more remote of the two peaks making up what is also known as Peak 5400. It is not for the faint of heart, and the crux encountered from the Gotha route should be approached with extreme caution. Along with West Lion and Crown N1, this is the most dangerous peak described in this book. Whereas Gotha is trapezoidal in shape, Coburg is a triangle.

While a loop route is tempting for variety, Route 1A, below, climbs up Coburg from the boulder field, and then descends the same way in order to avoid the somewhat scary crux encountered soon after the col between Gotha and Coburg: recommended.

ROUTE 1:

FROM NORTH – GOTHA

- Follow the route to Gotha, above.
- The descent south from the peak of Gotha is relatively easy: a series of balconies leading to a col, with a boulder field to your left. Coburg looms above and to the right.
- There are two approaches, both from the col between Gotha and Coburg.

A. FROM NORTH: BOULDER FIELD ROUTE

- This route is steep and longer than the direct route, but with patient routefinding, and a refusal to poke around would-be routes that go near sheer cliffs, you will make it. If you feel exposed or in cliffy danger, go back and find an alternative route, usually by heading farther east from the peak.
- At the col between Gotha and Coburg, do not climb up Coburg. Instead, descend to the boulder field to the east (left).
- Descend the boulder field, hugging the base of Coburg to your right.
- About 150 m down the rock slope, where the trees end on Coburg, near a persistent sheet of snow on the rock field, it is reasonably easy to climb up a short rock face onto Coburg. You may see a goat trail.
- Generally traverse up left (south), zigging and zagging upwards on Coburg on a series of short rock-climbs to small, heathery balconies. It is possible to traverse and avoid the various cliff bands without much exposure.
- You will reach two primary flat areas overlooking the boulder field below. Continue up the ridge.
- Emerge onto the bouldery peak, for spectacular views.

B. FROM SOUTHWEST: DIRECT ROUTE

<u>Caution:</u> This route is not for the faint of heart or inexperienced. Real exposure.

- Assaulting Coburg head-on from the Gotha–Coburg col entails much grabbing of the short trees and roots and rocks.

- Several metres up, one hits the crux of the route: a cliff rising above you. At first glance it appears impenetrable to the left but if you follow a ledge in that direction you come to the base of a cleft that leads directly up to the crest of the ridge to the right.
- From the top of the cleft, the route roughly follows the crest of the ridge until heading up a bushy treed slope at the top.
- Pay attention to the route you are ascending for the descent. There is some flagging here but avoid descending the west gully which also has some flagging in it.
- After the crux, the peak is swift and easy, albeit steep.
- There are spectacular 360° views, complete with a boulder to stand on and exalt in your triumph.

Route 2:

FROM SOUTH – HSCT NEAR HANOVER LAKE

Caution: This is an unmarked Class 4 climb. Do not attempt a descent of this route unless you are a very seasoned climber with technical experience. It is far easier going up this way than coming down.
- This route is more direct but also more dangerous.
- Follow the HSCT to the north side of Hanover Lake and up the switchbacks next to the waterfall. At the top the trail levels out. From here, N49.50363 W123.19941, the route enters the forest.
- You will soon see a large boulder field. Head for the top left corner of this and then straight up through the trees.
- Eventually it will become obvious you are in a steep gully that at times looks like it is blocked by cliffs but actually continues uninterrupted to the Hanover–Coburg col, at N49.50706 W123.19583.
- The route now heads north directly up the north ridge of Coburg. You come to a spot that appears impassable, with a lone tree to the left above. Stay right here, scrambling up ledges and blocks. This is the beginning of the Class 4 section.
- Stay near the crest of the ridge for about 100 m to reach a ledge system that leads slightly downwards to the right and onto the face of Coburg. The ridge above has large blocks barring the way, so the face is the easiest path.
- Although somewhat intimidating, there are lots of good handholds and footholds in the crack systems up this face. You want to head up the face for a short distance and regain the ridge above its blocky crest.
- Once back on the crest of the ridge, it is a straightforward scramble to the summit.

CENTRAL NORTH HOWE SOUND CREST TRAIL: BRUNSWICK AREA, ACCESS VIA LIONS BAY

This section describes the routes to Hanover, Fat Ass, Hat, Wettin, and Brunswick.

The main access to the central north Howe Sound Crest Trail peaks is the Brunswick trail, from the trailhead at Sunset Drive, in the farthest northeast corner of the town of Lions Bay, about 10 minutes north of Horseshoe Bay off Highway 99. These peaks may also be accessed via Howe Sound Crest Trail from north or south.

1. FROM LIONS BAY TRAILHEAD TO BRUNSWICK TRAIL INTERSECTION WITH HOWE SOUND CREST TRAIL

- You could take your mountain bike for the first part of this hike, to allow for a speedy escape.
- Drive to the Lions Bay exit off Highway 99. Go left on Crosscreek Road, right on Centre Road, left on Bayview Road, left on Mountain Drive, and left onto Sunset Drive.
- Parking is a challenge. There are only about six spots for non-Lions Bay residents at the trailhead, and no legal parking until about 1 km downslope, at Lions Bay Elementary School. Be careful not to park in unauthorized places: the residents in Lions Bay are notoriously protective of their turf, and many cars have been towed, tagged, or vandalized over the years.
- Take the gravel forest service road switchbacks uphill for approximately 3 km. Do not go left onto smaller trails into watershed. Pass by the trail marked "Tunnel Bluffs."
- At the next intersection, Brunswick Trail is marked with a sign.
- Take this trail, which is an ever-narrowing logging road at times thick with vegetation. The way is obvious and well marked the entire way.
- You will make two minor stream crossings and one major one (Magnesia Creek). In early summer, the flow is heavy.
- Eventually, the trail becomes predominantly a dirt track, with a narrow and steep climb some 400 m up the ridge to the HSCT. Keep your eyes peeled for giant trees and, in autumn, mushrooms.
- It will be obvious when you hit the HSCT. You will reach a relatively flat area. A tree to the north (left) has various signs indicating directions and distances).

2. FROM HOWE SOUND CREST TRAIL

- Follow the route of Howe Sound Crest Trail either from Porteau Road (closer) or Cypress Bowl (farther): see above.

BRUNSWICK AREA BAGGER TIPS

The peaks of Wettin, Hat, Fat Ass, Hanover, and Brunswick can be done in a long day trip. Start from Sunset Drive in Lions Bay, then take the Brunswick turnoff and follow it for 1.1 km, taking the left junction that heads for the Tunnel Bluffs–Hat road system. Follow this until it turns into a trail heading up towards Hat from the west. Skirt around the base of Hat, heading for the long, rolling ridge to Wettin.

From Wettin retrace your steps back towards Hat, climbing it on its steep north side. From Hat descend south over Fat Ass Peak and intersect with the HSCT. Cross the trail and go cross-country in a northeasterly direction towards Hanover. Cross the beautiful meadows teeming with glacier-fed streams in a slow descent until you intersect with a major creek flowing into Brunswick Lake. It is best to avoid the HSCT, as it loses considerably more elevation as it heads to Brunswick Lake. From the creek continue uphill, following a creek originating from the side of Hanover, to the left gully leading to the summit with some fixed lines for assistance. From the top of Hanover retrace your steps back to the HSCT and then follow it to the Brunswick summit trail. From the top of Brunswick head back down the main Brunswick trail to Lions Bay. This is another route where carrying a GPS is strongly encouraged.

Round-trip distance:
27.7 km

Time:
13:30

Elevation gain:
2810 m

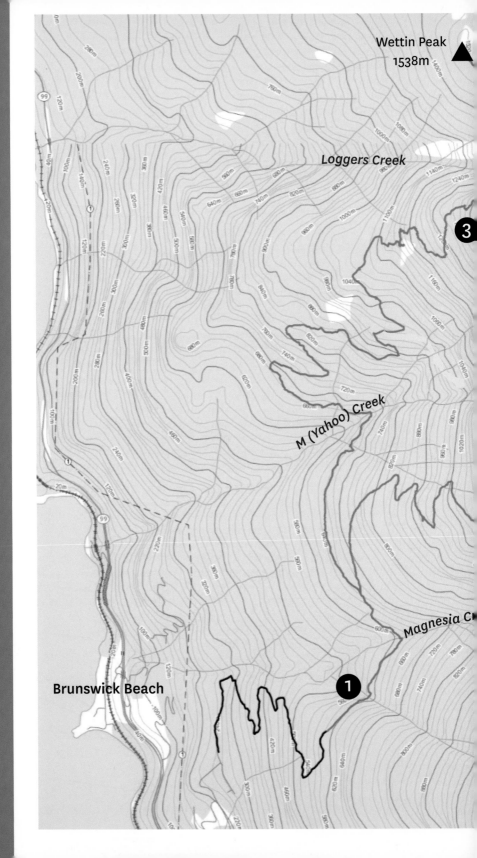

Wettin Peak
1538m

Loggers Creek

M (Yahoo) Creek

Magnesia C

Brunswick Beach

Hanover Lake

HSCT to Deeks Lake & Porteau Road

Mount Hanover 1748m

Brunswick Lake

Hat Mountain 1644m

Fat Ass Peak 1619m

Brunswick Mountain 1788m

Magnesia Peak 1587m

Magnesia Meadows

Hanging Lake

HSCT to Lions and Cypress Bowl Provincial Park

Brunswick Lake with Hanover behind.

MT. HANOVER
(HAN) (1748 M #2)

A grand but at times harrowing scramble across a boulder field and up a chimney.

CAUTION:
Exposure, rockfall, semi-technical climbing, no defined trail.

PROMINENCE:
238 m.

LATITUDE/LONGITUDE:
N49.49917 W123.18389.

BANG FOR BUCK:
3/5

PEAK VIEW:
4/5. Drool-worthy views to S: Lions and Brunswick; N: Garibaldi and northern peaks; E: Judge Howay, Robie Reid, and Howe Sound; and W: Wettin and Hat.

TRUE SUMMIT LOCATION:
The central of three peaks, between the two gullies.

HEADWATERS:
Tributaries of Hanover Creek; Connolly Creek (into Capilano River).

BEST VIEWS FROM:
Brunswick, Hat Meadow tarn, New Brighton Park.

TRIP INFORMATION

Round-trip distance: 19.4 km from Sunset Drive in Lions Bay.
Elevation gain: 2089 m.
Time: 9–11 hours (8:45) from Sunset Drive in Lions Bay.
Difficulty: 5+/5.
Snow free: Usually early June.
Must-sees: The three lakes; pleasing rock field and rock plain.
Scenery: 4/5.
Kids: 0/5. No!
Dogs: 0/5. No!
Runnability: 2/5. Decent until rock-field slope.
Terrain: Alpine meadows, bushwhacking, boulder-hopping, chimney-climbing.
Public transit: None.
Cell coverage: Usually present on peak but not elsewhere.
Sun: Mostly exposed.
Water: None after Brunswick Lake.
Route links: Brunswick or Hat.

HISTORY

Name origin: Royal family of Britain and Canada from George I to Victoria. Name used in 1912 North Vancouver map. Source unknown. There is also a Hanover Mountain near Golden, BC.
Name status: Official. Adopted December 7, 1937.
First ascent: Allegedly by Henry Bell-Irving and Chief Joe Capilano in 1889.

Founding Vancouver archivist Major James Skitt Matthews doubted this and so do we: it would be quite the climb just to shoot a mountain goat. First recorded ascent May 24, 1913, by Don Munday, Ben Hanafin, and Edward LePage, by way of a bushwhack up the Capilano Valley, then up Enchantment and Macklin creeks to Macklin Lake (which they called "Lake Surprise"), and finally going up the eastern slopes. First ascent by a woman was by Phyllis Munday (then Phyllis James), in 1915.
Other write-up: Gunn.

Hanover is the second-highest peak on the North Shore, after Brunswick, which looms to the south. It is, with West Lion, Coburg, and Crown N1, the scariest, most difficult and potentially most dangerous peak on this list. Your arms will be tired from the at times technically challenging climb up a crumbly chimney to the peak. The main risk is the loose rock: the chimney is like a vertical bowling alley, with rocks careening down the gully if dislodged above. It is thus highly recommended that climbers wear helmets for Hanover, and to climb the chimney one-by-one, waiting until the first climber gets to the top before the next person starts. And only do it in perfect weather. If you are tempted to climb it in the snow, first visit the ClubTread item at is.gd/orKbN9 and read the harrowing account of a climber being blasted out of the gully to the rock field 100 m below by an avalanche (he survived). Our friend Ean Jackson read that report, and on a summer bagging trip two years later found that very climber's lost ski pole on the rock field and returned it to him.

Hanover continues the theme of naming peaks after surnames of the British and Canadian royal family, starting with Brunswick (actually one step removed from the royals, named, as it was, after a ship), and then Windsor, and then to Coburg and Gotha. Note that Hanover has a single "n," the British spelling, not the German.

Early climbs of Hanover approached from both the Capilano Valley and Deeks Lake, including efforts in 1915 and 1947. The initial group of Munday, Hanafin, and LePage was racing against another party also seeking to be the first ascenders of Hanover that weekend. That group, approaching from Howe Sound, got socked in by fog, however, and turned back.

In contrast to Brunswick, Mt. Hanover has relatively smooth, curved sides and a rounded top. This exterior is caused by glacial exfoliation: the splitting off of sheets of rock parallel to the weathered exterior. This process is best illustrated by Hanover's granitic cousins in the Yosemite Valley.

You have the choice of two gullies to climb up Hanover. The left is generally considered the easier and less dangerous, although some disagree. We present the left-gully route here. The right gully features a large chockstone with significant exposure. A slip in the left gully will more likely result in broken bones than death.

GETTING THERE
See description, at p. 126, of drive to Sunset Drive trailhead at Lions Bay.

FROM SOUTH – BRUNSWICK MOUNTAIN TRAIL

See the above description of the Brunswick Mountain trail from Sunset Drive trailhead at Lions Bay.

- At the Brunswick Trail–HSCT intersection, continue on HSCT to the left, north.
- The trail is at times bounded by steep slope.
- The dirt trail soon gives way to rock underfoot. In summer this stretch is hot.
- The trail ascends to a meadow plateau with several small tarns.
- To the west you will see a small trail ascending sharply through the heather, marked by flagging tape: the route to Fat Ass, Hat, and Wettin.
- Beyond Hat Pass you will see one of the most beautiful sights on Howe Sound Crest Trail: Hat Tarn, with a spectacular view of Hanover in the distance.
- Ascend to the top of the meadow and see Brunswick Lake, to which you will descend.
- The initial part of the descent is steep, leading to a flatter area with a small creek.

Howe Sound Crest Trail at the Hanover Trail junction.

HSCT to Hanover gullies: The minor but obvious trail to Hanover departs from the HSCT about halfway between the Brunswick Lake hut and the Brunswick Mountain ascent trail. There is a loud creek here.

- After a while the trail peters out but the looming destination is obvious.
- Head north along a boulder field, then down into a soggy creek valley to a stream that feeds into Hanover Lake.
- Cross the creek, and begin the ascent up Hanover.
- The first part is blocked by a dense green patch of short trees.
- You have a choice: bushwhack through the patch or climb a creek on the west side of the patch.
- The creek is usually preferable, if low enough. The creek route is all slippery, with a few dicey bits that can be avoided by holding on to the trees beside the creek. At

one point there is a short side-climb/bushwhack away from the creek, to avoid a large boulder in the main creek.

- Higher up the climb, the creekbed is submerged under large boulders, signalling the second phase of the ascent: fun vertical boulder-hopping on massive white granite boulders.
- Then scramble up steeply on smaller granite boulders (memories of Hanes Valley).

Hanover gullies to peak: This leads up to the base of Hanover peak proper. Two gullies facing southeast are the routes up. They are not visible until the very end of the boulder-hopping.

- Go up the left gully, the easier and safer one. This consists of some five rocky platforms with vast boulders above you. None are more than 3 m high, but most will require careful planning and use of hands and arms to pull yourself up. Each platform presents a mental game: which single combination of hand placements will allow a safe ascent to the next platform? And which will lead to a broken leg or back? There is little real exposure, but a slip could well result in a dire injury. You may encounter several moments of minor fear and hesitation. The climb has sections that are Class 3 and arguably Class 4. At times, there are fixed ropes in the gully, offering some assistance.
- After the final platform there is a gravelly slope leading to the peak (to the right and up).
- Sign the peak register, then gingerly and carefully descend. Make sure you yell down to warn hikers below.

ROUTE 2:

FROM NORTH – ALONG HOWE SOUND CREST TRAIL

See Howe Sound Crest Trail to Deeks Lake, and the description of the Deeks Lake to Brunswick Mountain trail at p 135.

- Cross the log-and-rock bridge that separates the two parts of Brunswick Lake.
- There are several campsites here, with a handsome red-roofed shelter five minutes' climb above the lakes. A whisky cache is nearby.
- Climb up the dirt trail, which turns muddy in rain. Here there is a profusion of mushrooms – boletes and amanitas – in the autumn. At the top there are magnificent views of Hanover, Gotha and Coburg, and the three lakes.
- The minor but obvious trail to Hanover departs from the HSCT about halfway between the Brunswick Lake hut and the Mt. Brunswick ascent trail. It is about 15 minutes above the hut. There is a loud creek here.
- See the description of HSCT to Hanover gullies and to the peak, under Route 1 at p. 133 above.

FAT ASS PEAK

(CFA) (1619 M #12)

An intermediate adventure with great views.

CAUTION:
Not a marked trail (but not difficult to follow).

PROMINENCE:
50 m.

LATITUDE/LONGITUDE:
N49.49272 W123.20679.

BANG FOR BUCK:
3/5

PEAK VIEW:
5/5. Clear views of surrounding peaks and islands of Howe Sound.

TRUE SUMMIT LOCATION:
North; last peak before Hat. Obvious.

HEADWATERS:
M (Yahoo) Creek (into Howe Sound).

BEST VIEWS FROM:
HSCT at Brunswick Mountain junction.

TRIP INFORMATION

Round-trip distance: 15.4 km from Sunset Drive in Lions Bay.
Elevation gain: 1458 m.
Time: 5–8 hours (5:44) from Sunset Drive in Lions Bay.
Difficulty: 3/5.
Snow free: Early June to October.
Must-sees: Grouse and heather and peak views.
Scenery: 4/5. Old and second-growth forests. Creeks. Beautiful alpine lakes. Great views.
Kids: 4/5. Challenging distance, but once there, fine.
Dogs: 5/5. No hands needed.
Runnability: 2/5. Popular lower section of trail offers a good warm-up. Some runnable sections in the alpine.
Terrain: Obvious trail through heather and up rocky slabs.
Public transit: #259 bus; also, #C12 stops in Lions Bay.
Cell coverage: Usually.
Sun: Mostly exposed.
Water: Very little.
Route links: Brunswick, Hat, Wettin. Harvey, and other HSCT peaks are baggable within the same day by a strong runner.

HISTORY

Name origin: See introductory paragraph below.
Name status: Very unofficial and should remain so.
First ascent: Unknown. The first climbers of Hat. Likely climbed by hunters or loggers before 1910 and by Indigenous people before that.

Hat (with tower) and the twin mounds of Fat Ass.

Fat Ass Peak is the second of two bumps on the Brunswick shoulder leading to Hat Mountain. Its rocky orange peak offers fine views of Hat and Brunswick as well as Howe Sound. It was irresponsibly named in 2009 by one of the authors as a consolation prize to several fervent baggers who were trying to summit Hat on the last weekend of the Bagger Challenge but were stopped at Fat Ass Peak by early and unexpected snow and ice. Club Fat Ass is a trail-running and adventuring club founded in 2003 by Ean Jackson and Sibylle Tinsel; the Bagger Challenge was first offered by author David Crerar on the CFA website as a club contest. In ultra running parlance, a "fat ass" is an informal race, usually with no fee or services. The author knew that the name had gained popular knowledge when his massage therapist, an avid hiker, while working on the author's stubborn gluteal injury, said, apropos of nothing, that "there is even a mountain named Fat Ass Peak."

GETTING THERE
See description of drive to Sunset Drive trailhead at Lions Bay, above p. 126.

ROUTE
See description of the HSCT route to Hat Meadows above, pp. 98–101.
- At Hat Meadows, near a series of small tarns, look to the west for a small trail and orange flagging.
- Climb steeply along the narrow but clear trail. At all times the way should be discernible through flagging or boot marks every 5 m or so; if you lose the trail, retrace.
- Attain a small meadow and cut right (north), stepping over a large fallen tree.
- Cut left and up, climbing in logical zigzags up a slope of shattered orange rock giving way to heather. Grouse frequent these slopes.
- Following this trail (which ends at Hat), you will go over Fat Ass Peak en route. A small cairn marks the peak.

HAT MOUNTAIN
(HAT) (1644 M #10)

An underrated scamper up to a radio repeater tower, with fine views of Howe Sound and Brunswick Mountain.

CAUTION:
Some scrambling if approached directly from Lions Bay; no defined trail.

PROMINENCE:
144 m.

LATITUDE/LONGITUDE:
N49.49528 W123.20944.

BANG FOR BUCK:
4/5

PEAK VIEW:
5/5. Clear views of surrounding peaks and islands of Howe Sound; Sky Pilot; Gotha and Coburg.

TRUE SUMMIT LOCATION:
Obvious. Marked by green transmission tower.

HEADWATERS:
M (Yahoo) Creek (into Howe Sound). Loggers Creek (into Howe Sound) is between this peak and Wettin.

Best views from:
Howe Sound, Mt. Gardner, Highway 99 Seascape Drive turnoff sign.

TRIP INFORMATION

Round-trip distance: 16.4 km from Sunset Drive in Lions Bay.

Elevation gain: 1538 m.

Time: 5–8 hours (6:26) from Sunset Drive in Lions Bay.

Difficulty: 3/5. Decent trail that offers a little bit of everything in moderation.

Snow free: Mid-July.

Must-sees: Lovely tarn on HSCT near side trail; Fat Ass Peak.

Scenery: 4/5. Old-growth, second-growth forests. Creeks. Beautiful alpine lakes. Great views.

Kids: 3/5. Far. Once there, fine.

Dogs: 4/5. Some sharp rocks in alpine.

Runnability: 2/5. Popular lower section of trail offers a good warm-up. Some light scrambling in the alpine.

Terrain: Generally well-trodden trail with cairns and the occasional flagging tape.

Public transit: #259 bus; also, #C12 stops in Lions Bay.

Cell coverage: Usually.

Sun: Mostly exposed.

Water: Very little.

Route links: Brunswick, Fat Ass, and Wettin en route or close. Hanover and Harvey and other Howe Sound peaks are baggable within same day by a strong runner.

HISTORY

Name origin: So named because it is a "conspicuous flat-topped peak, shaped like a coolie hat, when viewed from Horseshoe Bay."

Name status: Official. Adopted March 14, 1988. Submitted by Bob C. Harris.

Other names: Mt. Vengeur: the ship *Vengeur du Peuple* was sunk by HMS *Brunswick* on the Glorious First of June. A small glass container on the summit contains a description, dated 1968, of the sinking of the *Vengeur* and refers to the mountain as Mt. Vengeur.

First ascent: Unknown. Likely climbed by hunters or loggers before 1910 and by Indigenous people before that. An old summit register recorded a 1966 ascent by Gerard and Trudi Bloem of the Alpine Club of Canada, but the first ascent must have occurred many years earlier.

Although it is only a side peak of Brunswick, Hat is easily recognizable from both Highway 99 and Howe Sound, with its green radio repeater tower. The tower was installed for the 2010 Olympics and was apparently used for special security communications (keep that classified information under your hat). The peak indeed looks like a hat: a bit like the woven cedar bark Salish hats that the Sea-to-Sky Highway information kiosks are based on. Hat is at times used as a launch site for paragliders.

Final stretch of the Hat ascent, with Harvey behind.

Hat provides a pleasing short destination off the HSCT. Its jutting-out location provides splendid views looking to the south end of Howe Sound, with Bowyer, Bowen, and Passage islands, and to the east the quartzite bands of Brunswick Mountain. Its peak is covered in scrubby, twisted pines. A summit register and a bottle of whisky are hidden on the peak. The register provides an alternative name: Mt. Vengeur, a name encouraged by Terry Taylor from 1968 on into the 1990s but ultimately rejected given the long-standing use of "Hat."

Like Brunswick, Hat (and its shoulder, Fat Ass) are predominantly volcanic, in contrast to the plutonic rock all around. This is evidenced in part by its more shattered rock and its red and orange coloration.

GETTING THERE

See description of the way to Sunset Drive trailhead at Lions Bay, above at p. 126.

Route 1:

FROM NORTH – ALONG HOWE SOUND CREST TRAIL

See description of the HSCT route to Hat Meadows, above at p. 98–101.

- Walk south on the HSCT through Hat Meadows. Near a series of small tarns, look to the west for a small trail and orange flagging.
- Climb steeply along the thin but clear trail. At all times the trail should be discernible through flagging or boot marks every 5 m or so; if you lose the trail, retrace.
- Attain a small meadow and cut right (north), crossing a large fallen tree.
- Cut left and up, climbing in logical zigzags up a slope of shattered orange rock giving way to heather. Grouse frequent these slopes.
- Following this trail (which ends at Hat), you will go over Fat Ass Peak en route. A small cairn marks the summit.
- Look for tape on the western side of Fat Ass and a short scramble down to the saddle.
- The route up to Hat is obvious and well travelled, with occasional flagging. Head towards the tall green cell tower, zigzagging up rocks, at times crumbly, and occasionally through krumholtzes. The trail is never exposed or dangerous.
- Return via same route.

Route 2:

FROM SOUTH – ALONG HSCT

See description of the HSCT route from the intersection of Brunswick Mountain Trail and the HSCT toward Brunswick Lake, above at p. 106.

- About 500 m west of the intersection, near a series of small tarns, watch for small trail and orange flagging to the west. Follow the description above to the peak.

Route 3:

FROM NORTH – LIONS BAY VIA TUNNEL BLUFFS

This is the route used for climbing Hat from Wettin or just from the Tunnel Bluffs trailhead. There is no trail and the going is very steep in places. GPS is strongly recommended.

- Start at the Sunset Drive trailhead.
- At the first fork, take the trail to Brunswick–Tunnel Bluffs.
- After a kilometre you will come to another intersection: take the left, westerly option, the Tunnel Bluffs trail.
- After 2.5 km there is a west turnoff to the Tunnel Bluffs viewpoint. Stay to the right on the former logging road for a further 1.2 km to where you reach another junction with a sign.
- Take the left fork, which is now a well-marked trail heading up to the alpine.
- Eventually you reach a big clearing with the cliffs of Hat looming above. There is a yellow marker in a tree. This is the junction with the route to Wettin. For the direct route to Hat, head straight uphill.
- This route approaches from the northwest side of Hat, then traverses across to the east along grassy ramps and ledges with some pink flagging before finally gaining the summit from its northeast side.

WETTIN PEAK
(WET) (1538 M)

An obscure bump that is somewhat worth the trip.

CAUTION:
No marked trail. Steep approach.

PROMINENCE:
88 m.

LATITUDE/LONGITUDE:
N49.50444 W123.21528.

BANG FOR BUCK:
2/5

PEAK VIEW:
2/5. Mostly treed. Unusual views of Deeks Lake peaks, Hat, Howe Sound, and Anvil and Gambier Islands.

TRUE SUMMIT LOCATION:
Second bump along ridge.

HEADWATERS:
Loggers Creek (into Howe Sound) is directly between this peak and Hat.

BEST VIEWS FROM:
Hat, Hanover, Brunswick.

TRIP INFORMATION

Round-trip distance: 22.2 km from Sunset Drive in Lions Bay.
Elevation gain: 1417 m.
Time: 8–12 hours (8:02) from Sunset Drive in Lions Bay.
Difficulty: 5/5.
Snow free: Mid-July.
Must-see: Pleasant, rolling heather ridge.
Scenery: 2/5.
Kids: 1/5. Steep descent from Hat.
Dogs: 1/5. Steep descent from Hat.
Runnability: 3/5. Apart from the descent down to it, the ridge is pleasantly undulating.
Terrain: Second-growth forest.
Public transit: #259 bus from Horseshoe Bay to Lions Bay.
Cell coverage: Usually present on peak.
Sun: 80 per cent exposed.
Water: Several lakes en route.
Route links: Hat and Fat Ass en route. Brunswick is nearby.

HISTORY

Name origin: From George I to Queen Victoria, the British Royal family was variously called Hanover, Brunswick, and Guelph. In the late 19th century, Queen Victoria charged the College of Heralds in England to determine the correct personal surname of her late husband, Prince Albert of Saxe-Coburg and Gotha, and thus the proper surname of the royal family upon the accession of her son. After extensive research the college concluded that it was Wettin (pronounced "Vettin"), but this name was never used, either by the Queen or by her son or grandson, Edward VII and

George V of the United Kingdom; they were simply called "Saxe-Coburg and Gotha."
Name status: Unofficial. Given by Robin Tivy and bivouac.com.
First ascent: Unknown. Likely climbed by hunters or loggers before 1915.

Wettin is the second significant peak on a ridge below and to the north of Hat Mountain. There is no trail per se to Wettin, although at times one can see a route of sorts along the ridge. Despite its obscurity, Wettin is a pleasant surprise and a pleasant ridgewalk along gentle meadows and heather. Its north end is a steep drop to Deeks Lake.

GETTING THERE
See description to Sunset Drive trailhead at Lions Bay, p. 126.

ROUTE 1:
FROM NORTH – LIONS BAY VIA TUNNEL BLUFFS
- Start at the Sunset Drive trailhead.
- At the first fork, take the trail to Brunswick/Tunnel Bluffs.
- After a kilometre you will come to another intersection: take the left, west, option, the Tunnel Bluffs trail.
- After 2.5 km there is a west turnoff to the Tunnel Bluffs viewpoint. Stay to the right on the road for a further 1.2 km to where you reach another junction with a sign.
- Take the left fork, which is now a well-marked trail heading up to the alpine.
- Eventually you reach a big clearing with the cliffs of Hat looming above. There is a yellow marker in a tree here. Turn left at this marker and head east.
- You will soon reach a boulder field. Descend to the bottom far (northeast) corner of this field.
- Here the route enters a forested section. Keep heading east below a series of steep bluffs, maintaining elevation.
- Eventually you reach a steep gully with a vegetated slope on the right. Head uphill to intersect the top of the gully at the Hat–Wettin col.
- From here the route up Wettin is easy: just follow the contour lines up the ridge.
- You will see human boot routes, but little flagging and no formal trail.
- Most times on the ridge you are bushwhacking, but the bushes are generally low and inoffensive.
- Hit the first (shorter) Wettin ridge peak and dip into a little shoulder.
- Then head up to Wettin's peak proper. There are actually two summits, of which the south one is higher.

ROUTE 2:
FROM HOWE SOUND CREST TRAIL
Caution: This is a difficult and potentially dangerous approach. The approach from Tunnel Bluffs is recommended although this route is commonly followed as part of a larger peakbagging mission.

Follow the route to Hat along the HSCT, above.
- As Wettin is 100 m below Hat, there is a temptation to attempt a traverse of Hat from the Fat Ass Peak–Hat Mountain col. *Despite promising contour lines, various cliffs make this a dubious and dangerous route.*

- Arrive at the peak of Hat, characterized by a tall green cell tower, with 360° views.
- The entrance to the descent route is tricky and precise. There are many cliffs in this area if you get off route. It starts just northeast of the summit tower at N49.49546 W123.20912 in a bushy section. Lower yourself down this bush between some boulders to get access to a grassy ramp.
- The east side of the vegetated ramp/ledge system is at N49.49556 W123.20907. At this point head slightly downhill in a westerly direction. This area has some flagging on it.
- Proceed very slowly and carefully – it is difficult to see what lies below the trees, and often there is a nasty drop. There are cliffs to the northeast to be avoided.
- Pay close attention to your GPS, as the route heads in a generally descending westerly direction across the face of Hat to N49.49575 W123.21108.
- At this point there is a junction with the route that descends to the Tunnel Bluffs trail and the route to Wettin. You now switch direction, dropping down a bushy section before heading easterly across a vegetated ramp and finally slope to gain access to the Hat–Wettin col.
- It is still necessary to grab a lot of heather and many branches to make descent safe. Take care. The heather and undergrowth can be slippery and scary when wet.
- Once you hit the col between Hat and Wettin, the route up Wettin is easy: just follow the contour lines up the ridge.
- You will see human boot routes, but no flagging or formal trail.
- Most times on the ridge you are bushwhacking, but the bushes are generally low and inoffensive.
- Hit the first (shorter) Wettin ridge peak and dip into a little shoulder.
- Then head upward to Wettin's peak proper. There are actually two summits, of which the southern one is higher.
- Both peaks are treed in, with compromised views. Wettin Peak (the southern Wettin spot) offers a good view of glorious Anvil Island.

BRUNSWICK MOUNTAIN
(BRU) (1788 M #1)

The highest peak in the North Shore mountains provides stunning 360° views.

CAUTION:
Some exposure on peak ridge.

PROMINENCE:
1294 m.

LATITUDE/LONGITUDE:
N49.48743 W123.19717.

BANG FOR BUCK:
4/5

PEAK VIEW:
5/5. Clear views of surrounding peaks and islands of Howe Sound.

TRUE SUMMIT LOCATION:
Mid-peak ridge: the peak after (north of) the disused helicopter pad.

HEADWATERS:
Deeks Creek, Brunswick Creek, small streams leading to Brunswick Lake, M (Yahoo) and Magnesia Creeks (into Howe Sound), Connolly Creek (into Capilano Lake).

BEST VIEWS FROM:
Howe Sound, Dam, Highway 99 Seascape Drive turnoff sign, New Brighton Park.

TRIP INFORMATION

Round-trip distance: 15.2 km from Sunset Drive in Lions Bay.

Elevation gain: 1557 m.

Time: 6–9.5 hours (6:14) from Sunset Drive in Lions Bay.

Difficulty: 3.5/5. Some exposure on peak ridge.

Snow free: Mid-July.

Must-sees: Folded granite in cirque to north; chipping granite rock on final ascent.

Scenery: 4/5. Old-growth, second-growth forests. Creeks. Beautiful alpine lakes. Great views.

Kids: 2/5. Long and steep and some exposure.

Dogs: 3/5. Some sharp rocks in alpine. Water scarce in the alpine.

Runnability: 2/5. Too steep on ascent; too crumbly and slippery on descent.

Terrain: Second-growth forest.

Public transit: #259 bus; also, #C12 stops in Lions Bay.

Cell coverage: Sometimes present on peak; poor to non-existent elsewhere.

Sun: First half covered; second half fully exposed.

Water: None.

Route links: Fat Ass, Hat, Wettin, Harvey are relatively close.

HISTORY

Name origin: Named by Captain Richards in 1859–60 after HMS *Brunswick*, which fought at the Glorious First of June in 1794 under Captain John Harvey. Harvey lost a limb during the battle and died of his wounds soon after. The *Brunswick* sank the French ship *Vengeur du Peuple*.

Brunswick, Hanover, and Deeks Lake (S–N) from Brunswick Mountain.

Name status: Official. Adopted March 31, 1924.

Other names: None.

First ascent: Climbed in 1909 by prominent BCMC alpinists Basil Stewart Darling and Bert Armistead. Also climbed in 1909 by BCMC alpinist Charles Chapman, although it is not clear whether that was the same trip. The third ascent was by Billy Gray, Frank Smith, and Don Munday of the BCMC in June 1911. It was claimed, without precision, that the goat-hunting trip by Chief Joe Capilano and Dr. Henry Bell-Irving also climbed Brunswick (plus several other Howe Sound Crest peaks), in July 1889. Major Matthews doubted this, and so do we: why bother making this climb for a goat that one could shoot from below?

Other write-ups: Gunn, Hui.

Brunswick is the highest peak of the North Shore mountains. Its red volcanic rocks, crumbly chipped rock underfoot, quartz streaks, and expansive cirque makes it feel very different from other North Shore peaks, and a grand adventure. The views from the peak are staggering: almost all of Howe Sound and the entire HSCT lie before you, with the city of Vancouver and Mt. Baker looming in the distance. The final ridge climb has real exposure; it is not for the knock-kneed and should never be attempted in icy or rainy conditions. But there is no technical climbing involved, and no need for handholds, although most people will want to grip the plentiful side-rocks for reassurance. Do not be startled by the whoosh of the massive, soaring ravens, which swoop past you out of curiosity rather than, it is hoped, an anticipated meal at the hapless hiker's expense.

Imagine Captain Richards peering up at the two most distinct peaks of the Howe Sound Crest: red, horned Brunswick, with pointy Harvey to the south. The names are directly linked, since Harvey was captain of the *Brunswick*. One can almost see, in the shapes of the peaks, a standing captain watching his massive ship.

A BCMC report of an ascent of Brunswick and Hanover on May 5–6, 1927, gloomily notes a "tedious climb of several thousand feet through fallen and burnt trees." Happily, the forest has bounced back and the trail developed in the past 90 years, making the adventure much more pleasing. The steepness of the ascent is offset by shady, mature second-growth trees as well as mushrooms in the fall. Squirrels and chipmunks chatter at your every step.

Brunswick is one of the more geologically interesting peaks to climb, differing significantly from the granite that typifies most of these profiled peaks. The upper regions of Brunswick consist of mafic volcanic strata and associated sediments of the Upper Jurassic and Lower Cretaceous Gambier Group (approximately 100 million years old). It is a geological island surrounded by peaks predominated by granodiorite, quartz diorite, and other plutonic rocks. Gambier Group rocks also make up Lions Bay and the northern half of Gambier Island. The ridge at 1450 m consists of massive andesite, a volcanic rock. Some outcrops reveal veins containing crystals of black hornblende and yellow-green epidote. At the peak of Brunswick you will see beautifully banded layers of brown sandstone and siltstone, which are sedimentary rocks. The thick white bands are probably recrystallized limestone; an impressive quartz streak running down the cirque is especially visible from Hat. The jagged rock on the peak ridge is due to the abundance of mica, which splits easily. These more readily separated sedimentary rocks account for Brunswick's serrated ridge peak, in contrast to the stolid granite faces of the peaks around it, such as Hanover. Hanover is predominantly plutonic granodiorite, which is more solid and does not split in any particular direction. It erodes not by cracking or splitting, but by exfoliating slabs of granite.

The summit of Brunswick is an example of an arête, a narrow ridge of rock formed when two moving glaciers carved away the sides of a ridge, leaving only a thin line of rock. Other arêtes in the North Shore mountains include Crown Mountain and the Camel.

Brunswick can be approached from Howe Sound Crest Trail (HSCT) from either the north (Porteau exit off Highway 99) or the south (Lions Bay). From the HSCT, the well-marked dogleg to Brunswick climbs steeply uphill through some loose rock sections to a spectacular ridge. There are a series of points along a razor ridge, with the summit located just past a disused helicopter pad.

GETTING THERE
See description to Sunset Drive trailhead at Lions Bay, p. 126.

ROUTE 1:
DIRECT FROM LIONS BAY
See Brunswick Trail from Sunset Drive in Lions Bay on p. 126.

- From the intersection of the HSCT and the Brunswick Mountain access trail, continue straight up, across the HSCT, to Brunswick.
- The first half of the route is a steep but safe climb up through mixed forest.
- Soon the dirt underfoot gives way to crumbly orange rock that can be treacherous and slippery. Use caution and aim for flat surfaces.
- At times, the route is marked with red paint.
- Climb up the open rock field, veering gently to the left. Avoid loose gravel.

- This will lead to some low evergreens and a low shoulder on the peak ridge. You will get your first views of the snow-filled cirque as well as Brunswick, Hanover, and Deeks Lake to the north. The cirque shows uplift rock bands.
- Turn right (east) and follow well-trodden, marked trail steeply uphill along the ridge. There is little marking (occasional paint splotches), but you will see the route through the worn rocks. Continue to watch for loose rock underfoot.
- At the top of the first climb, you will face the first exposed area. Ample legroom and ample opportunities to grip rock offer reassurance.
- A false summit reveals that you have to descend towards another sloping field of loose rock. Do not go all the way down; you can soon climb over the rocky guard-bump. Note that there is a deep chasm falling into the cirque if you cut across too early. It is an easy step down on the other side.
- Climb up to the next bump on the ridge. Here is the crux of the hike. At the crest of this portion of the ridge, there is a narrow shelf to the right (southeast). Take this shelf instead of trying to climb over the bump.
- After the crux you will find some concrete pilings and wooden beams, the remnants of a helicopter pad.
- Make a very short three-step descent and walk 50 m farther to the true summit, marked by a cairn.
- Enjoy the 360° views and vertical drop. Sky Pilot is prominent to the north, as is, closer, Hanover. You will see the three lakes Brunswick, Hanover, and Deeks (south to north).
- Return via same route.

ROUTE 2:

FROM NORTH – ALONG HSCT

See description of Howe Sound Crest Trail. Continue to the intersection with Brunswick Trail, above. Then follow the route to the peak, above.

ROUTE 3:

FROM SOUTH – ALONG HSCT

See the description of Howe Sound Crest Trail. Continue to the intersection with Brunswick Trail, above, and then follow the route to the peak, above.

Brunswick as seen from Hat.

CENTRAL HOWE SOUND CREST TRAIL: LIONS AREA: ACCESS VIA LIONS BAY; BINKERT TRAIL

This section describes the central peaks of HSCT: Magnesia, Harvey, David, James, Enchantment, Thomas, and West Lion.

The most popular trail to this area, Binkert Trail from Lions Bay to The Lions, is described below, under West Lion. Harvey Trail is also a commendable route, described below under Harvey.

LIONS AREA BAGGER TIPS

The peaks of West Lion, Thomas, Enchantment, David, James, Magnesia, and Harvey can be bagged in a long day trip. Start from Sunset Drive in Lions Bay, then take Binkert Trail to the top of West Lion, and from there take the HSCT over Thomas and on to a point just above a large tarn. Drop off the trail here and head over to Enchantment. From Enchantment a more northerly approach can be used to intersect once again with the HSCT. Take this trail over David and James and then on to Magnesia Meadows and its picturesque cabin. From here it's a short side trip up Magnesia before returning to Harvey and summiting via its east ridge trail. From the top of Harvey follow the well-established Mt. Harvey trail back down to Lions Bay. Trail to Lions Bay. This is another route where carrying a GPS is strongly encouraged.

Round-trip distance:
24.3 km

Time:
13:15

Elevation gain:
2547 m

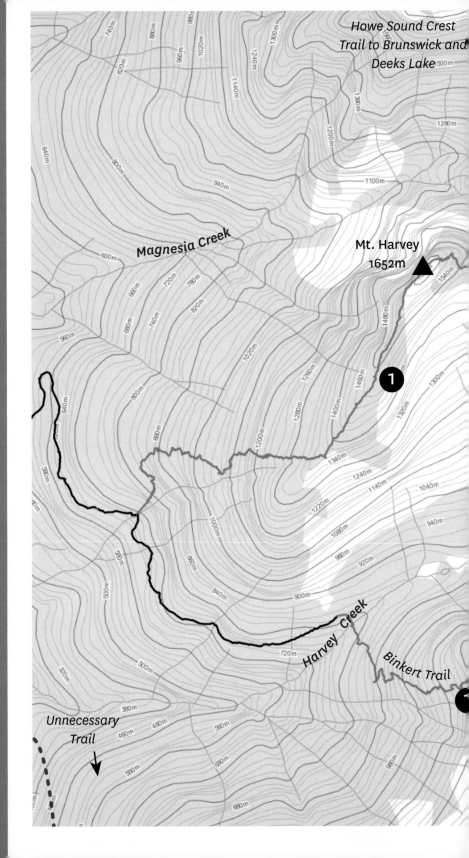

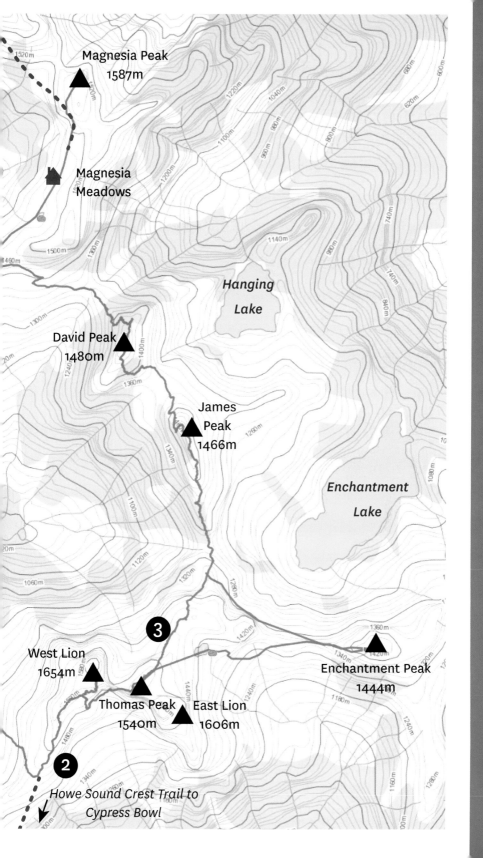

Magnesia Peak
1587m

Magnesia
Meadows

Hanging
Lake

David Peak
1480m

James
Peak
1466m

Enchantment
Lake

3

West Lion
1654m

Enchantment Peak
1444m

Thomas Peak
1540m

East Lion
1606m

2

*Howe Sound Crest Trail to
Cypress Bowl*

MAGNESIA PEAK

(MAG) (1587 M)

A nice scramble above Magnesia Meadows, for unique views of Brunswick, Harvey, and the watershed.

CAUTION:
Sheer drop to north and east.
No trail, marked or otherwise.
Routefinding skills needed.

PROMINENCE:
72 m.

LATITUDE/LONGITUDE:
N49.48370 W123.18751.

BANG FOR BUCK:
4/5

PEAK VIEW:
4/5. Interesting views of Harvey. Also
Cathedral, Sky Pilot, Brunswick, The
Lions, and Hanover.

TRUE SUMMIT LOCATION:
Last peak before chasm at end of
Brunswick Mountain.

HEADWATERS:
Magnesia Creek (into Howe Sound),
Connolly Creek, tributaries of
Enchantment Creek (into Capilano
Lake).

BEST VIEWS FROM:
Magnesia Meadows, Harvey,
Brunswick.

TRIP INFORMATION

Round-trip distance: 19.4 km from Sunset Drive in Lions Bay.

Elevation gain: 1669 m.

Time: 7–11 hours (7:30) from Sunset Drive in Lions Bay.

Difficulty: 3.5/5. Easy but obscure.

Snow free: Mid-July through October.

Must-sees: Red rocks; sheer drop from peak; pointy Witch Mountain.

Scenery: 4/5.

Kids: 3/5 (from Lions Bay route): steep but doable.

Dogs: 4/5.

Runnability: 3/5.

Terrain: Meadow, rock slope, rocky peak.

Public transit: #259 bus; also, #C12 stops in Lions Bay.

Cell coverage: Usually none.

Sun: 90 per cent exposed.

Water: None.

Route links: Short detour off the trail between Brunswick and Harvey. Other nearby peaks include Hat and Fat Ass.

HISTORY

Name origin: From Magnesia Creek (official name, adopted May 7, 1959) and Magnesia Meadows, below. Suggested by Robin Tivy. The origin of "Magnesia Creek" remains uncertain. One account is that early residents found the waters of

the creek to have a laxative effect. The creek is presently a water source for Lions Bay.
Name status: Unofficial.
Other: Legg Peak, after Ken Legg, first winner of the Bagger Challenge.
First ascent: Unknown. Authors David and Harry Crerar popularized it as a destination in 2014, with photographs and as an addition to Bagger Challenge in 2015.

From Magnesia, a view of Harvey and Harvey's Pup and Howe Sound.

Whether as a place to watch the sunset while camping in Magnesia Meadows or as yet another peak to bag from Howe Sound Crest Trail, this rarely visited bump is well worth the short side trip. It offers up-close views of Brunswick's red east slopes, as well as a broad side view of Harvey and Harvey's Pup, with the splendid spread of Howe Sound behind. To the northeast beckons a distant view of the pointy peaks of Macklin and Witch in the watershed.

Magnesia, located between the two Lions Bay HSCT connectors, can be accessed from either one.

GETTING THERE
See description to Sunset Drive trailhead at Lions Bay, p. 126.

ROUTE FROM MAGNESIA MEADOWS

- Ascend to Magnesia Meadows along the HSCT, either along the trail from north or south, or, for a quicker approach, via Harvey or Brunswick trails or Binkert Trail.
- From Magnesia Meadows, climb just upslope of the rockslide/creek valley at the northern end of Magnesia Meadows. This will lead to a shoulder cutting into the ridge above Magnesia Meadows. Other bumps on the ridge lie to your south and north.

Col below Magnesia Peak.

- Bypass the north bump by skirting across to and then up the rock field. Beware of wobbling rocks. This will lead to a thin wall of shrubs, easily bypassed to gain another shoulder.
  - Turn right. You will see the concrete pilings for an abandoned or future helicopter pad up on the rocky base of the peak.
  - Going straight up will require you to thrash through a bushy band guarding the peak while skirting against a sheer cliff to your right. Avoid this route.
  - Instead, veer left and north around the peak knob, towards the meadow. Then corkscrew up and around to the peak. There is a wee cairn. Exult in the views.

MT. HARVEY

(HAR) (1652 M #8)

A superb peak, with two pleasing approaches leading to magnificent views of the HSCT peaks and Howe Sound.

CAUTION:
East approach is a bit steep.

PROMINENCE:
207 m.

LATITUDE/LONGITUDE:
N49.47538 W123.20015.

BANG FOR BUCK:
4/5

PEAK VIEW:
4/5

TRUE SUMMIT LOCATION:
Obvious. Only one.

HEADWATERS:
Harvey Creek, Alberta Creek, tributaries of Magnesia Creek (into Howe Sound).

BEST VIEWS FROM:
Howe Sound, Gardner, Magnesia, Highway 99 Seascape Drive turnoff.

TRIP INFORMATION

Round-trip distance: 13 km from Sunset Drive in Lions Bay.

Elevation gain: 1412 m.

Time: 5–8 hours (5:26).

Difficulty: 3/5 from Lions Bay. 3.5/5 from HSCT.

Snow free: Mid-July.

Must-sees: Spectacular blueberry patches on slopes to the east and heather to southwest.

Scenery: 4/5.

Kids: 4/5 (from Lions Bay route).

Dogs: 4/5 (from Lions Bay route).

Runnability: 4/5 (from Lions Bay route).

Terrain: Second-growth forest, rocky ridge.

Public transit: #259 bus; also, #C12 stops in Lions Bay.

Cell coverage: Generally yes.

Sun: Half covered; half exposed.

Water: None.

Route links: To the north: Brunswick, with a loop return. To the south: a decent and steep loop can be made with Binkert Trail, bagging Harvey, David, James, Thomas, and West Lion.

HISTORY

Name origin: John Harvey, the captain of HMS *Brunswick*, fought at the Glorious First of June in 1794. He died of the wounds he received in the battle, after sinking the French ship *Vengeur du Peuple*. Name used in 1859 Captain Richards map.

Name status: Official. Adopted February 5, 1924, as labelled on British Admiralty

Chart A579, 1860, and on BC map 2B, 1914.

Other names: Brunswick Pinnacle (ca. 1913 by Don Munday; June 1925, BCMC; and in the 1965 and 1969 Dick Culbert guides).

First ascent: Apparently the Squamish Chief Joe Capilano–Dr. Henry Bell-Irving goat hunting trip also climbed Harvey in July 1889 after first ascents of The Lions and Mt. Brunswick. Vancouver archivist and mountain enthusiast Major James Skitt Matthews doubted this.

Other write-up: Hui.

Harvey is a pleasingly pointy peak that is often mistaken for a Lion, from most angles. As such, it is an exhilarating climb, climaxing in relief as you realize that both approaches, while steep, are safe and enormously rewarding. The view from the summit of Howe Sound and the Howe Sound Crest Trail peaks is attractive, and the gently sloped slabs of the peak itself seem designed for a leisurely picnic, libation, or nap.

There are two very pleasing approaches to Harvey: one from Howe Sound Crest Trail (from the east), and one from Lions Bay (from the west). The Lions Bay trail, greatly underestimated in the authors' opinion, is the handiwork of master trail builder Halvor Lunden (1915 Norway – 2008 Vancouver), who blazed it in the 1980s. This trail is less well known and steeper than the Brunswick access trail to the north and The Lions/Binkert access route to the south. That said, we prefer it to the other two because of its splendid views and the fact that, as the middle route, it lends itself well to multi-peak adventures, forming a loop with exit via the other access trails, north or south, or via Howe Sound Crest Trail itself.

Harvey is a particularly pleasing hike in the autumn. The south ridge is a blaze of red and orange and yellow. On the east slopes of Harvey, bolete mushrooms abound.

A shorter pinnacle (by 130 m) to the southwest of Harvey is charmingly named "Harvey's Pup": it was formerly known as "Junior Pinnacle" (Harvey occasionally was called the "Brunswick Pinnacle") and, in a July 1927 *BC Mountaineer*, "Pinnacle Pup." The Pup is for serious climbers only; access is via a trail between the Harvey and Brunswick trails off Binkert Trail. Harvey's Pup was first climbed by a BCMC party on May 20, 1923, coming up from Brunswick Beach. Mountain goats have been sighted on the steep slopes in this area.

Harvey and Harvey's Pup were created when cracks formed in the granitic rock, and seasons of freezing and thawing ice permeated the cracks. Over millennia, huge sheaths of rock exfoliated from the mass, rounding off the peak. The same process created the famous formations in Yosemite National Park such as Half Dome, Sentinel Dome, Lembert Dome, and Pothole Dome. It also created and rounded The Lions.

Harvey Trail follows Alberta Creek and passes a waterfall in a scoured steep valley. On February 11, 1983, heavy rainfall caused logs and boulders to wash down Alberta Creek, destroying five homes and several bridges below in Lions Bay. Two young men were killed: Thomas and David Wade, after whom those peaks opposite Mt. Harvey were named. A similar debris flow occurred in 1981 on M (Yahoo) Creek to the north, killing nine people by destroying the bridge their cars were crossing. Fjordside communities such as Lions Bay are threatened by debris flows because many of them are built on peninsulas created by millennia of such flows (this terrain being the flattest land along these fjords). Several debris dams have been built along Howe Sound creeks to trap sediment and logs in the event of another debris flow.

Harvey's east slope is steep; its west and north faces are sheer. On April 8, 2017, five Korean-Canadian hikers died when a cornice atop Mt. Harvey collapsed. They fell approximately 500 m down the north face.

GETTING THERE

See description to Sunset Drive trailhead at Lions Bay, p. 126.

ROUTE 1:

FROM WEST – HALVOR LUNDEN MT. HARVEY TRAIL FROM LIONS BAY

The first 3 km of the route is reasonably flat and would lend itself well to a cycle approach and descent.

- From the Lions Bay Sunset Drive trailhead, continue up along the gravel road switchbacks for approximately 1.5 km.
- Ignore the first marked left turnoff (to Tunnel Bluffs Trail) and the second marked left (to Brunswick Mountain) and the third, more minor, left turnoff (the Harvey's Pup climbers' trail).

Along Mount Harvey Trail.

- If you hit a major stream or a bridge, you have gone too far.
- After about 3 km total along the gravel road you will see a small and steep but well-trodden trail ascending steeply to the left.
- The trail is marked throughout. Occasionally, there are ropes guiding you away from dangerous gullies. Although the trail is steep at times, there should be no danger if you're careful.
- At 4 km there is a short side trail that leads to a view of Alberta Creek Falls (most spectacular in spring).
- Continuing upward, the trail becomes even steeper. You may need to hold on to trees. Take care not to fall into the Alberta Creek canyon.
- At the top, beside the Alberta Creek canyon, a short side trail leads to an excellent view of Howe Sound, complete with downed tree to serve as bench.
- The trail continues steeply upward.
- Eventually you will see sky through the trees above. The trail punches out onto a heather ridge bench, with views of West Lion (East Lion is hidden). The remnants of trees burned in an accidental fire are seen on the slope.
- Proceed due north, along a ridge, with Howe Sound to your left.
- This is a pleasingly spongy ridge walk leading to a clear view of the objective peak.
- The heather eventually gives way to rocks. You will have to use your hands occasionally, but again there should be no danger if conditions are good.
- To your right (east), in the Harvey amphitheatre, you will see remnants of a forest fire below, giving way to a general clear-cut scree slope now being covered by blueberry bushes.
- The easy slope and obvious trail lead up to the peak of Harvey.

FROM EAST – HOWE SOUND CREST TRAIL

- Go along the HSCT to the high point between Magnesia Meadows to the north and the Harvey berry field to the south. The Harvey side trail heads west, straight towards Harvey from the HSCT.
- The most difficult routefinding is at the start: low, scrubby evergreens obscure the trail. Persevere westwards for about 20 m and the trail becomes obvious.
- Head west towards Harvey. You will start climbing up and then sharply down into a shoulder at Harvey's base. To the north are cliffs.
- Continue up Harvey. Although it seems impossibly sheer, the trail is in most places flagged and obvious as it zigs and zags up the slope. Children and beagles have climbed it. Only in a few places are hands necessary, and there is little exposure. If you ever feel unsafe, retrace your steps: you are off course.
- Eventually the dirt gives way to the rocky peak.

Heading up Harvey Ridge.

DAVID PEAK

(DAV) (1480 M)

Where the HSCT moves from the zone dominated by Brunswick to The Lions,
it provides decent views of the eastern peaks.

CAUTION:
Exposed section, crumbly rock.

PROMINENCE:
130 m.

LATITUDE/LONGITUDE:
N49.47222 W123.18444.

BANG FOR BUCK:
3/5

PEAK VIEW:
4/5. Clear views of surrounding peaks and islands of Howe Sound.

TRUE SUMMIT LOCATION:
North peak.

HEADWATERS:
Harvey Creek (into Howe Sound), tributaries of Enchantment Creek (into Capilano River).

BEST VIEWS FROM:
Harvey, Snug Cove (Bowen Island).

TRIP INFORMATION

Round-trip distance: 17.2 km from Sunset Drive in Lions Bay via Harvey trail.

Elevation gain: 1796 m.

Time: 8–10 hours (8:24) from Sunset Drive in Lions Bay.

Difficulty: 3/5. Challenging trail that offers a little bit of everything.

Snow free: Mid-July

Must-sees: Krumholtzes; Hanging Lake; whisky.

Scenery: 4/5.

Kids: 2/5. Far. Once there, fine.

Dogs: 3/5. Sharp rocks on final ascent.

Runnability: 2/5. Harvey slopes and north descent runnable. Light scrambling in the alpine.

Terrain: Second-growth forest; alpine.

Public transit: #259 bus; also, #C12 stops in Lions Bay.

Cell coverage: Usually good on peak; inconsistent below.

Sun: 80 per cent exposed.

Water: None nearby. Closest is in a small cirque lake to the east of The Lions.

Route links: Harvey, James, and West Lion close. Other HSCT peaks are baggable within same day by a strong runner.

HISTORY

Name origin: After David Michael Wade (1963–1983), of Lions Bay, who was killed at home with his brother, Thomas, while sleeping, by a debris torrent sweeping down Alberta Creek on February 11, 1983.

Name status: Unofficial. Appeared on Cypress Provincial Park maps around 1991.

First ascent: Unknown. Likely climbed by hunters or loggers before 1915 and by Indigenous people before that.

Of the two major peaks between Harvey and The Lions, David is the pointier, more northern one. These two modest bumps in Howe Sound Crest Trail are often conflated: we remember them as "DJ," from north to south. Alternatively, James is closer to The Lions, and "J" is closer to "L" than is David, or "D" (which is closer to Deeks).

The traverse of the two peaks follows the newer, high-elevation routing of Howe Sound Crest Trail as an alternative to the original track, which drops quite far down to the east of the two peaks. While the older route provides an interesting view of Hanging and Enchantment lakes, it is crumblier and overgrown and, counter-intuitively, more tiring than the highland route.

Far below and due east of David (and north of Enchantment Lake) is a lake sometimes referred to as David Lake but more frequently as Hanging Lake. Don't rely on it for water: it would be a distant and arduous bushwhack descent (as would be Enchantment). Mountain goats are occasionally sighted on these slopes.

GETTING THERE

See description of the way to Sunset Drive trailhead at Lions Bay, p. 126.

ROUTE 1:

FROM WEST – LIONS BAY VIA MT. HARVEY

See the descriptions of Mt. Harvey Trail and of the descent from Mt. Harvey to HSCT at pp. 155, 156.

- Go due east. This section of the trail will take you through dense blueberry bushes on the gravelly, dusty slope facing south from Mt. Harvey. This is possibly the densest concentration of mountain blueberry and black huckleberry bushes along the route, perfectly situated with southern exposure and no tree cover. These will be some of the plumpest, sweetest berries you have ever tasted. You might find a bear or two also, especially in September, when they go into a state of manic eating, or hyperphagia, to store up nutrients for hibernation.
- This berry bounty makes it sometimes difficult to follow the trail down Harvey slope to David Peak. The trail switchbacks down a logged slope that will probably be very overgrown with berry bushes. Routefinding is sometimes challenging here, but we have never become lost.
- At the base of that slope, now to the southeast of Harvey, you reach a small grassy area.
- Howe Sound Crest Trail used to drop down below the mountain here, traversing David to the east and nearly reaching a small lake below. That trail is still used, although it always seems more tiring and less rewarding than the new route.
- From the grassy area it is sometimes difficult to find the start of the climb over David and James, due to rapidly growing underbrush. If you head in the obvious direction, south and up and through the shrubs, you will see the path. At all times you should feel as if you are on a trail; if not, go back to the grassy patch and start again.
- The trail climbs steeply and steadily, over and under large tree roots.
- Eventually you pop out of the underbrush to see an obvious trail up the rocks to the summit, which has a cairn and logbook. The rock towards the peak is somewhat crumbly: be careful.

Route 2:

FROM NORTH – PORTEAU COVE, ALONG HOWE SOUND CREST TRAIL

See the description of Howe Sound Crest Trail from north to south, above.

L–R: Harvey berry Slopes, with Harvey, Hat, Brunswick, Hanover and David.

Route 3:

FROM SOUTH – CYPRESS BOWL, ALONG HOWE SOUND CREST TRAIL

See the description of Howe Sound Crest Trail from south to north, above.

- From the base of West Lion, cut southeast and downwards. The route is quite steep but obvious. At times, it is marked with a paint splotch or a cairn. Be careful on dry or wet days: the way will be crumbly or slippery. Also take care not to descend too low, onto the scree field below.
- Cut east toward the obvious pass between the two Lions. The trail follows the top of the scree slope and the base of West Lion. At one or two spots you will wish to slow down and use your hands. There is no real exposure, but there exists the potential for a fall and an injury. The crux is a narrow ledge in the rock face, with a slope down below. It looks scarier than it is. Just take it calm and slow, and only do it in non-wet and non-icy conditions.
- Follow HSCT northeast, up and past a small tarn. This leads up to and over Thomas Peak (the bump in between The Lions).
- Descend a scree slope that continues down and east, bypassing an unnamed peak bump between James and Thomas. Then continue north to the base of James.
- At the south base of James there is a viewpoint over Enchantment Lake, with an odd ancient mailbox stuck to a tree.

- Head down a steep rock face, where hands may be needed, to a rock field and up again, to the steep gap guarding James Peak ridge. A cable and rope across the gap will offer reassurance (although they are not really necessary except when wet or icy).
- Climb up the ridge to James Peak.
- After James Peak, the trail descends to a pleasant meadow leading to David. The trail cuts and winds through the turf.
- At the south base of David, Howe Sound Crest Trail used to drop down below the mountain, traversing David to the east and nearly reaching Hanging Lake below. That trail is still used, although it always seems more tiring and less rewarding than the new route, which goes over David. The newer route is easier, despite the climbing, and gives views.

The south end of David Peak. Note fork of the HSCT: old, lower, east route and the new, upper, west route.

- The south ascent of David is at times a bushwhack due to treefall. A trail should be discernible every few metres at least.
- As you reach the peak of David, the rock is somewhat crumbly: step carefully.
- At the peak of David there is a small cairn and great views.

JAMES PEAK

(JAS) (1466 M)

A good climb with excellent views.

CAUTION:
Rock underfoot is crumbly at times; be careful not to skid while going downhill.

PROMINENCE:
116 m.

LATITUDE/LONGITUDE:
N49.46861 W123.17973.

BANG FOR BUCK:
3/5

PEAK VIEW:
5/5. Clear views of surrounding peaks and islands of Howe Sound.

TRUE SUMMIT LOCATION:
Obvious.

HEADWATERS:
Tributaries of Harvey Creek (into Howe Sound) and Enchantment Creek (into Capilano Lake).

BEST VIEWS FROM:
Harvey.

TRIP INFORMATION

Round-trip distance: 20.2 km from Sunset Drive in Lions Bay via Binkert Trail.
Elevation gain: 1751 m.
Time: 7–10 hours (7:16) from Sunset Drive in Lions Bay.
Difficulty: 3/5. Challenging trail that offers a little bit of everything.
Snow free: Usually early July.
Must-sees: Hidden whisky; cable traverse.
Scenery: 4/5. Creeks. Beautiful alpine lakes. Great views.
Kids: 2/5. Far. Fine once there.
Dogs: 4/5. One tricky bit.
Runnability: 3/5. Popular HSCT section of trail offers a good warm-up.
Terrain: Short alpine forest; alpine rock.
Public transit: #259 bus; also, #C12 stops in Lions Bay.
Cell coverage: Some on peak; inconsistent.
Sun: From neighbouring peaks, half covered, half exposed.
Water: Bring lots; none available nearby.
Route links: The Lions, David, Harvey.

HISTORY

Name origin: Remains a mystery. Located between the two Wade brothers peaks, David and Thomas. Named after 1985. Appeared on Cypress Provincial Park maps around 1991. We like to think it is named after Phyllis Munday's maiden name, "James," but this is unlikely. One theory is that it is named after James Stimpson, the best friend of David and Thomas Wade growing up in Lions Bay.
Name status: Unofficial.
First ascent: Unknown. Likely climbed by hunters or loggers before 1915, and by Indigenous people before that.

James Peak is just off Howe Sound Crest Trail. There are two popular routes to James from the closest trailhead at Lions Bay: from the south via The Lions or from the north via Harvey. Along with David, Thomas, and Unnecessary, it is one of the four mountains Howe Sound Crest Trail passes over.

There are splendid views of Enchantment Lake to the east as well as the rejuvenating former clear-cuts of the Harvey slope to the west. Berries abound. Goats are occasionally seen.

GETTING THERE
See the description of the way to Sunset Drive trailhead at Lions Bay, p. 126.

David (L) and James (R) seen from Harvey. Behind are Brunswick (L) and Hanover (R).

Route 1:

FROM NORTH – FROM DAVID PEAK

See description, above, of Howe Sound Crest Trail to Mt. Harvey and then beyond to David Peak.

- Descend David Peak to the south along a rocky route with some crumbling. Take care not to skid.
- At the south base of David is a pleasing meadow between David and James. The trail cuts and winds across the turf.
- The trail leading to James Peak is sometimes hard to follow but is a logical zigzag up a series of rocky balconies to the peak.

Route 2:

FROM SOUTH – FROM LIONS VIA HSCT

See the description above of Howe Sound Crest Trail or Binkert Trail to West Lion.

- From the base of West Lion, cut southeast and downwards. The route is quite steep but obvious. At times, it is marked with a paint splotch or a cairn. On dry or wet days take care: it will be crumbly or slippery. Also be careful not to descend too low, onto the scree field below.
- Cut east toward the obvious pass through the two Lions. The trail follows the top of the scree slope and the base of West Lion. At one or two spots you will wish to slow down and use your hands. There is no real exposure, but there exists the potential for a fall and an injury. The crux is a narrow ledge in the rock face, with a slope down below. It looks scarier than it is. Just take it calm and slow, and only do it in non-wet and non-icy conditions.
- Follow the HSCT northeast, upward and past a small tarn.
- This leads up to and over Thomas Peak (the bump in between The Lions).
- Descend a scree slope that continues down and east, bypassing an unnamed peak bump between James and Thomas. Then continue north to the base of James.
- At the south base of James there is a viewpoint over Enchantment Lake, with an odd, ancient mailbox stuck to a tree.
- Head down a steep rock face, where hands may be needed, to a rock field, then up again, to the steep gap guarding James Peak ridge. A cable and rope across the gap will offer reassurance (although they are not really necessary except at wet or icy times).
- Climb up the ridge to James Peak.

Enchantment Peak.

ENCHANTMENT PEAK

(ENC) (1444 M)

A fun scramble with a rare close-up view of The Lions from the east.

CAUTION:
No trail, marked or otherwise.
Routefinding skills needed. Cliffs.

PROMINENCE:
114 m.

LATITUDE/LONGITUDE:
N49.45917 W123.16695.

BANG FOR BUCK:
4/5

PEAK VIEW:
4/5. The Lions and
Enchantment Lake.

TRUE SUMMIT LOCATION:
Obvious.

HEADWATERS:
Spuzzum, Enchantment, Hesketh,
Tsileuh Creeks (into Capilano Lake).

BEST VIEWS FROM:
The Lions, James, St. Marks, Harvey.

TRIP INFORMATION

Round-trip distance: 19.7 km from Sunset Drive in Lions Bay via Binkert Trail.

Elevation gain: 1709 m.

Time: 8–11 hours (8:02) from Sunset Drive in Lions Bay.

Difficulty: 4/5. Challenging trail that offers a little bit of everything.

Snow free: Mid- to late July.

Must-see: Small cirque lake northeast of The Lions.

Scenery: 4/5. Cirque and lakes.

Kids: 2/5. Likely too far.

Dogs: 3/5. A few steep sections. Watershed inappropriate for dogs.

Runnability: 4/5.

Terrain: Alpine; heather and rock fields.

Public transit: #259 bus to Lions Bay. None to Cypress Bowl.

Cell coverage: Usually good on peak; inconsistent below.

Sun: Mostly exposed.

Water: Small cirque lake northeast of The Lions.

Route links: The Lions.

HISTORY

Name origin: Named by Edward LePage, along with Enchantment Lake and Creek.

Name status: Unofficial. Enchantment Lake and Creek are official names, adopted December 7, 1937.

First ascent: May 22, 1913, by Edward LePage via a bushwhack up the Capilano Valley en route to Hanover.

<u>Note:</u> This mountain is in the watershed. The authors are not encouraging or condoning trips to the peak. This route description is provided on the basis that people will

nonetheless attempt to travel to the peak, and that describing the route will promote their safety and that of the environment itself.

Enchantment Peak provides rarely seen eastside views of The Lions (including a twin waterfall coming off two icefields at the base of East Lion) and a clear view to Sky Pilot and Black Tusk, not to mention the best vantage point on the tempting but largely inaccessible Enchantment Lake. The lake has intriguing red floats on its surface: perhaps a test site or experiment? Mountain goats are occasionally sighted on the steep slopes of Enchantment Peak.

Do not be tempted to climb to or from Enchantment directly to or from Howe Sound Crest Trail. Viewing contour maps, it would appear possible to slope down from an obvious bump/ridge to the east of the trail, to the col between there and Enchantment. It's a trap, however. The dubious veggie belays, lacerations, and near-deathfall moments make it unwise. Go via The Lions cirque lake, as recommended. As this peak is in the watershed, exercise the utmost restraint and cleanliness.

ROUTE

See description of the way to Sunset Drive trailhead at Lions Bay, p. 126.

- See description above of Howe Sound Crest Trail or Binkert Trail to West Lion.
- Proceed north along the HSCT past The Lions, see description above.
- Access to Enchantment Peak is via the small cirque lake just northeast of The Lions. Carefully descend the scree slopes to the lake.
- From the small lake, resist the temptation to cut straight up to the inviting western ramp heading up Enchantment. This bump ends in thickly wooded cliffs to the east.
- Instead, descend to the northeast before cutting over north to a boulder field (there is a sweet and painless route, but your route may involve bushwhacking).
- Go across the boulder field and ascend via a fallen tree and a modest creekbed.
- Then mild bushwhacking northeast to the rocky patio at the base of Enchantment, leading to the aforementioned ramp straight up to the peak, past a few small tarns.
- Be cautious of the sheer cliff to the north: it's a long and unpleasant tumble into Enchantment Lake.

Refreshing dip in Enchantment meadows tarn still surrounded by snow in July

THOMAS PEAK

(THO) (1540 M)

A pleasant, easy pause between the two Lions, with spectacular up-close views.

CAUTION:
Potential exposure if you
lose the trail.

PROMINENCE:
30 m.

LATITUDE/LONGITUDE:
N49.45722 W123.18306.

BANG FOR BUCK:
4/5

Peak view:
3/5. Unique view of two Lions.

TRUE SUMMIT LOCATION:
Only one; obvious bump
between Lions.

HEADWATERS:
Tributaries of Sisters Creek (into
Capilano Lake) and Harvey Creek
(into Howe Sound).

BEST VIEWS FROM:
Cleveland Dam; James.

TRIP INFORMATION

Round-trip distance: 17 km from Sunset Drive in Lions Bay via Binkert Trail.
Vertical gain: 1459 m.
Time: 5–8 hours from Sunset Drive in Lions Bay.
Difficulty: 3/5. Once you get there, it is not difficult.
Snow free: Usually by mid-July.
Must-see: The Lions.
Scenery: 3/5.
Kids: 3/5. Far but easy. Some potential exposure.
Dogs: 3/5. Some steepness.
Runnability: 1/5.
Terrain: Slabs, climbing, scrubby trees.
Public transit: Lions Bay: #259 bus; also, #C12 stops in Lions Bay.
Cell coverage: Present on peak and usually on bench below peak. Unreliable farther below.
Sun: Wholly exposed.
Water: None on peak. Small, unpalatable tarn towards West Lion. To the east and below, a small cirque lake could provide water in an emergency.
Route links: (North) James, David; (south) West Lion, Strachan, St. Marks, Unnecessary.

HISTORY

Name origin: After Stephen Thomas "Tom" Wade (1964–1983), of Lions Bay, who was killed at home with his brother David, while sleeping, by a debris torrent sweeping down Alberta Creek on February 11, 1983.
Name status: Unofficial. Appeared on Cypress Provincial Park maps around 1991.
Other names: Referred to as the "Third Lion" in 1903. Mount Venus.
First ascent: Likely July 1889, but definitely in 1903. See West Lion, pp. 169–174.

Thomas is the unappreciated bump between the two Lions. It is visible from Vancouver but is more interestingly viewed from the north. It provides in turn spectacular up-close views of The Lions. Howe Sound Crest Trail skirts to the west of the summit, which is a few metres up and off the trail. Take care when approaching from the north: although the trail is well marked, if the rock is wet or if you get off-trail, the fall to the west would likely be fatal.

ROUTE 1:
FROM SOUTH ON HSCT OR FROM LIONS BAY–BINKERT TRAIL
See the description above, from HSCT or Lions Bay–Binkert Trail to West Lion.
• Follow route from Lions north to Thomas.

ROUTE 2:
FROM SOUTH ON HOWE SOUND CREST TRAIL CYPRESS BOWL
See description above, from Cypress Bowl to West Lion, on Howe Sound Crest Trail.

ROUTE 3:
FROM NORTH ON HOWE SOUND CREST TRAIL FROM PORTEAU COVE
See the description of Howe Sound Crest Trail from north to south, to West Lion, above.

West Lion.

WEST LION

(LIO) (1654 M #7)

Epic. But one of the most dangerous of these peaks, with potentially deadly exposure.

CAUTION:
Very exposed! Real risk of death.

PROMINENCE:
369 m.

LATITUDE/LONGITUDE:
N49.45778 W123.18639.

BANG FOR BUCK:
3/5

PEAK VIEW:
5/5. Epic.

TRUE SUMMIT LOCATION:
Only one; obvious.

HEADWATERS:
Tributaries of Sister Creek (into
Capilano Lake) and Harvey Creek
(into Howe Sound).

BEST VIEWS FROM:
Everywhere! BC Ferries, Artaban,
Gardner, New Brighton Park,
Burnaby, Cleveland Dam.

TRIP INFORMATION

Round-trip distance: 16 km from Sunset Drive in Lions Bay via Binkert Trail.
Vertical gain: 1333 m.
Time: 4–7 hours (4:26) from Sunset Drive in Lions Bay.
Difficulty: 5+/5. The most difficult and exposed climb in this book (along with Coburg).
Snow free: Usually by mid-July.
Must-sees: Some giant trees and waterfalls. It's the destination, not the journey.
Scenery: 4/5.
Kids: 0/5. Too exposed.
Dogs: 0/5. Requires handgrips.
Runnability: 0/5.
Terrain: Slabs, climbing, scrubby trees.
Public transit: Lions Bay: #259 bus; also, #C12 stops in Lions Bay.
Cell coverage: Usually good on peak and on bench below peak. Unreliable below that.
Sun: Last 60 per cent exposed.
Water: None on the peak. To the west, nearest is Harvey Creek far below. To the east, a small cirque lake could provide water in an emergency.
Route links: (north) James, David; (south) Strachan, St. Marks, Unnecessary.

HISTORY

Name origin: The Lions were named around 1889 by British Columbia Supreme Court Justice and New Brunswick Father of Confederation John Hamilton Gray (1814 St. George, Bermuda – 1889 Victoria), possibly in reference to the lion statues in Trafalgar Square sculpted by Sir Edward Landseer or to heraldic "lions rampant."

Names status: Official. Adopted December 7, 1937.

First ascent: Perhaps in July 1889, by a group on a goat-hunting trip from Howe Sound. The party was guided by Squamish Chief Joe Capilano and included Dr. Henry Bell-Irving. First recorded climb on August 11, 1903, by Atwell King, George Martin, and Arthur Tinniswood Dalton. See below.

Other names: Known as The Twins, or The Sisters to the Squamish (see below). Also referred to as Sheba's Breasts, Sheba Peaks, The Paps, and Twin Peaks.

Other write-ups: Hanna, Gunn.

The pointy twin peaks of The Lions, earlier known as The Paps, The Sisters, and The Twins, are a defining feature of the Vancouver skyline. They gave their name to the bridge and they are featured on both the crest of the BC Mountaineering Club and the special sesquicentennial $10 bill. By Squamish oral tradition, the area below The Lions, good for hunting mountain goats, was called Ch'ich'iyu'y Elxwiku, sometimes transliterated as Chee-Chee-Yoh-Hee.

Befitting the double prominences, the former name The Sisters or The Twins comes from a Squamish legend that has two variants. In the first (as recounted by Pauline Johnson (Tekahionawake) in *Legends of Vancouver*),[8] twin daughters of a victorious Capilano tyee (chief) persuaded their father to invite their Haida enemies to a feast instead of a battle. Gifts, celebration, and peace followed. For their peacekeeping, the girls were immortalized in the form of the two peaks.

In the second version,[9] the Haida (Stek'in in Squamish), the mortal enemies of the Squamish, travelled down the coast to raid and enslave the Squamish. Among the Haida raiders were young twin brothers who were the son of a Haida chief. The brothers were given the task of guarding the canoes while the elder raiders scouted out the target village. The Haida boys grew restless and climbed up a ridge to view the Squamish village themselves. At sunrise they were surprised to see that the first Squamish villagers up were twin sisters. The Haida raided, killing many Squamish. The twin sisters were spared and given over to the brothers as wives, who returned to the north with them. Among the Haida the Squamish wives were admired but sad. They persuaded their new Haida family to seek peace with the Squamish, which the Squamish accepted. The Creator commemorated their peacekeeping by making them into immortal mountains.

Also befitting the twin peaks and the twin creation stories, there are multiple versions of the first recorded ascent of West Lion. Indeed, the prominence of the peaks made the right to claim the first-ascent a point of public controversy. One version has a group of hunters including Dr. Henry Bell-Irving starting up from Howe Sound, guided by Squamish Chief Joe Capilano. The group was not seeking to climb the peak; they'd ascended to the base of West Lion while pursuing a goat. The next day, Dr. Bell-Irving asked Chief Capilano if one of his younger guides could climb the peak. The guide stripped naked and went up and back down in about 20 minutes. As this climb was not publicized until later, and as the trip was not made to climb peaks at all, the tale was always treated with skepticism. And why would you make a challenging climb just to bag a goat, when goats were plentiful at the time? And why not just shoot it?

The second version is one recently discovered by the authors. Unfortunately there is no contemporaneous record, and it is based solely on Taylor family tradition. In

The Lions as seen from Enchantment Peak.

this version, Joseph Watson Taylor (1869 Coleraine, Ireland – 1932, buried Mountain View Cemetery, Vancouver) canoed from his Keats Island homestead to Brunswick Point and made the first ascent of The Lions in 1888. Taylor trained as a surveyor, and in 1890 served on the International Boundary Commission as assistant to John Brabazon, to explore, survey, and map the mountainous border between British Columbia and Alaska along the Alaskan Panhandle. When the controversy arose in 1903 about the first recorded ascent of The Lions, Taylor was far away, serving in the Boer War in South Africa. He died in 1932 of ailments inflicted by a gas attack in the Second Battle of Ypres.

The first recorded ascent, and the account with more certainty, is the August 11, 1903, ascent by celebrated BCMC climbers Atwell King (1877–1947) (after whom Atwell Peak on Mt. Garibaldi is named), George Martin, and Arthur Tinniswood Dalton (1883–1962) (after whom Dalton Dome is named). They took the Terminal Steamship boat from Vancouver to Hood Point on Bowen Island, and then sailed with the innkeeper across to the east shore of Howe Sound, near present-day Lions Bay. They then commenced what would have been a shredding bushwhack up to West Lion, roped together for safety during much of the ascent. Atwell King reported to the *Vancouver Daily Province* that he had "…been on Crown Mountain and thought the view from there was exceedingly fine, but the prospect from The Lions is infinitely more magnificent."

King, Martin, and Dalton marked their triumph by flying a Union Jack from the summit, which flag was found the next month, on September 7, by the Latta brothers – William (1879 Newton, Ayrshire, Scotland – 1966 Victoria), John (1881 Newton – 1969 Vancouver), and Robert (1886 Scotland – ?) , who proceeded to make the first ascent of East Lion the next day. The Lattas had come from the south, following Capilano River and then Sisters Creek, and then ascending the steep talus slopes to the flat area between the two Lions. Between ascents they watched a herd of about 20 mountain goats clambering on the nearby slopes, likely on the bump immediately to the north – Thomas Peak – or perhaps on Enchantment. John Latta's boots gave out, and he was forced to return to Burrard Inlet from The Lions wearing leather moccasins. John Latta's memoir to commemorate the 50th anniversary of the climb fascinates and humbles: people were made of tougher stuff back then.

The Lions soon became a regular objective for BCMC members and other climbers. Over the 1908 Labour Day weekend, 36 members (including six women) of the Vancouver Mountaineering Club (later BCMC) climbed to The Lions up the Capilano Valley and Sisters Creek, in a party led by Joseph Charles Bishop, Fred Mills, Fred Perry, and William Gray. That same weekend, another 24 people, led by James John Trorey, climbed up from Howe Sound, declaring that route to be the safer and easier. By 1910 the Vancouver Tourist Bureau was advertising The Lions (with Strachan and Crown) as destinations, encouraging alpinists to stay at the Kells Hotel or the Capilano View Hotel, seven miles up the Capilano River (site now under Capilano Lake), before embarking on the trek. The first winter ascent was made in 1922 by Tom Fyles, a modest mail carrier on weekdays and one of the world's premier alpinists on weekends.

Early hikers came from two primary routes. The earlier approach was up the Capilano Valley. The Capilano Timber Company would often serve as hosts to the climbers, allowing them to stay in their camp shacks and serving them breakfast. The Vancouver Water Board would also often facilitate BCMC trips through the watershed to The Lions.

From around 1921 the favoured route was from St. Mark's Camp, located at Lions Bay, the first settlement of sorts in the area now occupied by the village of Lions Bay. The administrator of the camp, St. Mark's Anglican church (then located at Second and Vine in Vancouver), let BCMC members stay in their "fine camp building," thus enabling an early morning start for climbing The Lions after boating up Howe Sound from Vancouver the night before. Climbers of The Lions were still using the beach as a launching pad for trips up The Lions in 1944, 1947, and 1949.

Today the primary and most popular route to The Lions, the 8-km Binkert Trail, was blazed in 1971 by Paul Binkert, a Swiss-born climber who was active in the BCMC. It provided a shorter route to The Lions as a more direct, yet still gruelling, alternative to the route from Cypress Bowl over the peaks of Unnecessary. We are all in his debt.

The East Lion, requiring ropes or a risky veggie-belay scramble, as well as being in the watershed, is not covered in this book. The West Lion, the taller one, is less technical to climb but is not a peak to be treated casually. While it is possible to climb it without ropes, the sheer, near-certain-death drops make the route *not recommended* for casual baggers without climbing experience and psychological fortitude. Many rookie hikers find themselves trapped and frozen on the climb, not realizing the risks and heights involved. It would be crazy to attempt it in anything less than perfect weather: a hint of rain or ice would make the initial ledge traverse harrowing and dangerous. The scariest part of the climb is at the base, where one must traverse east along a series of 75-cm-wide shelves that slope gently towards a near-certain deadly fall on the rock slopes 45 m below. In past decades, there was a fixed steel cable line along this portion. Although it would have been foolish to lean on the line for support, it provided some reassurance. The line was removed in October 2009.

Given the juxtaposition of popularity and risk, it is not surprising there are regular accidents and rescues, including deaths, on The Lions. In September 2006 climber Steve Dirksen fell 100 m to his death when the piece of granite in his hand pulled free of the peak. There have also been near-misses. In August 1999 a female climber slid 40 m down the ridge below The Lions, hitting a tree and fracturing five ribs. In August 2009 a French tourist fell more than 45 m off West Lion but miraculously survived. In April 2012 two hikers slipped and fell several hundred feet while descending from The Lions; both survived. Consider all of these accidents: only climb in perfect conditions and do not rely upon ropes, trees, vegetation, or, indeed, rocks at any point of your ascent.

The Lions are composed of hornblende diorite, some of the oldest igneous rock in this area. They were formed when cracks formed in the rock. Over millennia, erosion and glacial abrasion split off large sheaths of rock, rounding off the peak. The same process created famous domes in Yosemite National Park, such as Half Dome, Sentinel Dome, Lembert Dome, and Pothole Dome. It also created and rounded Hanover, as well as Harvey and Harvey's Pup.

In his write-up of his 1911 climb, Don Munday noted the "strong, clear echo" off the cliffs of the East Lion. They ascended and descended along Sisters Creek and the Capilano river, starting and ending at the Capilano Hotel.

There are two approaches to West Lion: from Lions Bay (west) and from the HSCT (north and south).

Route 1:
FROM WEST VIA LIONS BAY–BINKERT TRAIL
Note: Although this trail is well trodden and well marked, it is one of the most frequent call-out spots for North Shore Rescue and Lions Bay Search and Rescue. It is steep and twisting. It takes just as long to get out as it takes to get in. And there is no water along the route for most of the trip.

- From the Lions Bay trailhead the route is well marked with signs and flagging tape and very well trod.
- The first 5 km is reasonably flat and would lend itself well to a cycle approach and descent.
- From the Lions Bay Sunset Drive trailhead, continue up along the gravel road switchbacks for about 1.5 km.
- Ignore the first marked left turnoff (to Tunnel Bluffs / Hat Trail) and the second marked left (to Brunswick) (there is a colourful sign here pointing the right way to The Lions), and the third, more minor left turnoff (Harvey's Pup climbers trail), and the fourth turnoff (Harvey).
- Cross a landslide area. At about 4 km, cross shallow Alberta Creek on old boards, at times with a waterfall above.
- The old gravel road gives way to a dirt trail.
- Descend briefly down to Harvey Creek, which has a metal bridge across it. On a hot day the water is inviting, off-put somewhat by a sign warning about water quality.
- The hike now become a steep, unrelenting grind up to The Lions. Start the dirt-and-root trudge upwards, giving way to tight switchbacks. Break up the exhaustion by admiring the impressive old-growth trees en route.

- After about 30 minutes, at around 1220 m, pop out of the forest to a grassy bench, with a few campsites and tarns and nice views, especially of your destination: The Lions now loom above you.
- Then continue the steep climb, now on rocks and scree, with no trees above you. Take care as some of the rocks are wobbly or loose. On a sunny day this stretch will be very hot: drink lots of water.
- At least routefinding is easy, with orange paint splotches, cairns, and well-worn rocks. The objective of West Lion is visible above you.
- After about another 30 minutes, at around 1430 m, Binkert/Lions Trail connects to the HSCT about 500 m south and downslope of the West Lion balcony. To the right, the trail goes to Unnecessary. Go left for West Lion. The HSCT is obvious, well worn, and marked with paint splotches and cairns.
- Head north and up, following the well-marked trail and (on a sunny summer day), the crowds. You will usually see several people sitting on the porch to the south of West Lion, picnicking, watching the climbers, and contemplating their mortality. This is where climbers without confidence or experience, or facing wet conditions, should stop.

West Lion ascent: From the porch, proceed towards West Lion. Hidden behind a small copse of trees is (usually) a rope (do not rely on it!) alongside a skinny tree and some roots. The combination of these aids allows you to descend the 4 m to a rocky shelf at the base of West Lion. Cross a short natural bridge to the base proper of West Lion.

- The crux is right at the beginning. You will see a long, narrow shelf heading to the right and up. Follow this ledge slowly and carefully. You will see holes in the rock from bolts which formerly held a wire. On the other side is a sheer drop to near-certain death.
- At the end of the ledge, you will come to a vertical series of stubborn short trees heading up. Follow this line, liberally using their roots for assistance. Avoid looking down.
- Note and remember your route for the descent: although it is well trodden and easy to follow on the way up, one can easily become disoriented on the way back down.
- After several metres of climbing up along the trees, you will go past the treeline and veer rightward along a steep rocky path. This leads to the summit, with its glorious views of the entire HSCT, along with Howe Sound and East Lion.
- Remember to exercise special caution on the descent: most accidents occur climbing down rather than up.

ROUTE 2:
FROM SOUTH VIA HSCT FROM CYPRESS BOWL
See description above of the Howe Sound Crest Trail route from Cypress Bowl to West Lion.

Follow the West Lion ascent, above.

SOUTH HOWE SOUND CREST TRAIL: UNNECESSARY MOUNTAIN ACCESS VIA LIONS BAY, OCEANVIEW ROAD

This section describes the two Unnecessary Mountain peaks on the HSCT, as well as St. Marks Summit to the south. Note that the HSCT continues south to Cypress Bowl: we describe the three peaks in that area (Strachan, Black, and Hollyburn), below, under the "Cypress Group," even though Strachan is popularly visited on the HSCT.

The peaks of Unnecessary and St. Marks Summit are readily accessible from three directions: from The Lions/Binkert trail to the north (see above), from Cypress Bowl via Howe Sound Crest Trail to the south (also above), and from its own trail, which starts at the southeast corner of Lions Bay.

The trail is a steep 5-km climb to Unnecessary Mountain. The authors of *Don't Waste Your Time…* were most unkind to this trail in 1997, giving it a "Don't do" rating: "Only if you're preparing for the Eco-Challenge is this a worthwhile training trail." All other routes, including Binkert Trail, are faster and less strenuous means of reaching Unnecessary. That said, it is, at least at the time of writing, a well-maintained trail that provides a more direct, if steeper, route to Unnecessary, with some pleasant views and impressive old-growth trees.

GETTING THERE 1: FROM CYPRESS BOWL

The first section of the HSCT from Cypress Bowl is well marked and wide.

- From Cypress Mountain Lodge, follow the signs to Howe Sound Crest Trail.
- You can go directly, or take a pleasant side trail to Yew Lake and a grove of old-growth trees.
- The first portion is a somewhat ugly reclaimed gravel road that passes a water tower and then begins climbing in gravelly switchbacks.
- At about 1 km another side trail leads west to a great view of Howe Sound: Bowen Lookout. It is well worth the 10-minute detour.
- More switchbacks lead eventually to a map kiosk with a tribute to Paul Binkert and a fine view of The Lions.
- Go down, then up. After crossing a small bridge you will reach Strachan Meadows, with scruffy alders to the right (east). Mt. Strachan looms behind. Pass the Strachan turnoff and then cross a second bridge. Continue north along HSCT.
- The well-marked path will proceed generally uphill, with the occasional flat or slight downhill stretch, through second-growth forest.
- Eventually, at the end of a uphill stint, the trees thin out, the ground becomes more rocky, and the trail become flat and at times slightly muddy. You will see a provincial parks post reading "Saint Marks Summit" (at 5.5 km).
- Proceed to the end of the short flat section. It will not likely be flagged, but you will see a small but clear trail heading east. This is the way to the actual St. Marks Summit.
- The HSCT descends into more second-growth forest before a laborious 200-m ascent to the three peaks of the aptly named Unnecessary Mountain (9 km).
- The trail is generally well marked, occasionally with paint splotches. At times it is narrow. Follow the ridge. At most points there are spectacular views of Howe Sound.

- Just before the peak of North Unnecessary, you will see the Unnecessary Mountain trail heading down to Lions Bay.

GETTING THERE 2: TO OCEANVIEW TRAILHEAD AT LIONS BAY

- Drive to the Lions Bay exit off Highway 99. Turn right onto Oceanview Road. Stay on Oceanview, passing several turnoffs. At a second switchback, you will encounter a gate.
- There is no parking at the gate and only two spots downslope from it. Between the highway and the gate, parking is sporadic. Be sure to obey parking signs and be considerate of local residents: ticketing, towing, and even vandalism are not uncommon in this area.

Oceanview trailhead to Unnecessary Mountain: Past the gate, Oceanview Road continues, soon turning to gravel. Go past a water tower to the first switchback.

- About 50 m after the switchback, you will see the trailhead on your right, over a ditch, upslope, marked by a sign.
- The trail is narrow and rooty and muddy and bounded by ferns. In places, there will be deadfall obscuring the route. That said, it is well marked with blazes and paint splotches throughout, and you should never feel off trail. If you do, trace back.
- You will pass some giant ancient cedar stumps.
- After a few minutes, come to the intersection with the Lone Tree Creek Trail Loop. There you will find Erin Moore's Enchanted Forest: memorials to a bright and beautiful girl who lost her life at the creek in a random rockslide in December 2014. Her family and friends invite you to pause here, to consider your own loved ones and reflect on the power and the gift of a true and adventuresome spirit. You can read more about the making of this trail and the family's journey at erinkate-moore.weebly.com. The December 19, 2015, entry provides information on how a community rallied together to build this magical and mystical enchanted trail and forest.
- Take the left trail up past some treefall and up a rocky slope.
- You will soon encounter a series of giant Douglas firs and cedars that somehow escaped the loggers' chainsaws.
- You will hit a rocky face, slippery in the rain. There are some thin ropes here, but they should only be used for guidance. Do not commit your weight to them.
- Behind you, you will start to see decent views of Howe Sound.
- Pop out onto a bench. You will have views down into the Lone Tree Creek valley to the south.
- Turn north and head up the steep ridge to Unnecessary.
- The trail emerges onto the HSCT between the two peaks of Unnecessary.

Route 1 (combined HSCT sections IV and V above)

The peaks of Hollyburn, Strachan, St. Marks, Unnecessary, North Unnecessary, and Black can be done as a robust day trip from Cypress Bowl. Park at the downhill area and take the Baden-Powell trail east to its junction with the Hollyburn trail. Take this trail to the top and then descend via the steeper north side trail to its junction with the Strachan trail, next to the Collins ski run. Follow the Strachan trail past the plane wreckage, over the top of Sky Chair, and on to the summit of Strachan. Return to the top of Christmas Gully and descend this to its intersection with the HSCT. Follow the HSCT out over St. Marks, Unnecessary, and North Unnecessary and return the same way but continue following it all the way back to the downhill area. From there it's a short trip up to Black, passing Cabin Lake on the way.

Round-trip distance:
25.8 km

Time:
9:28

Elevation gain:
2030 m

ROUTE 2 (HSCT SECTION IV ONLY)

This variation is shorter, bagging only the peaks of St. Marks, Unnecessary, and North Unnecessary. This is an out-and-back hike along the HSCT. Park at the downhill ski area and take the trail north to St. Marks. Note that the actual summit is slightly above the trail to the east. Descend to the col between St. Marks and Unnecessary and then climb up to the rocky ridge leading to the summit. From here it's a brief descent and ascent to North Unnecessary. Return the same way.

Round-trip distance:
16.4 km

Time:
5:26

Elevation gain:
1150 m

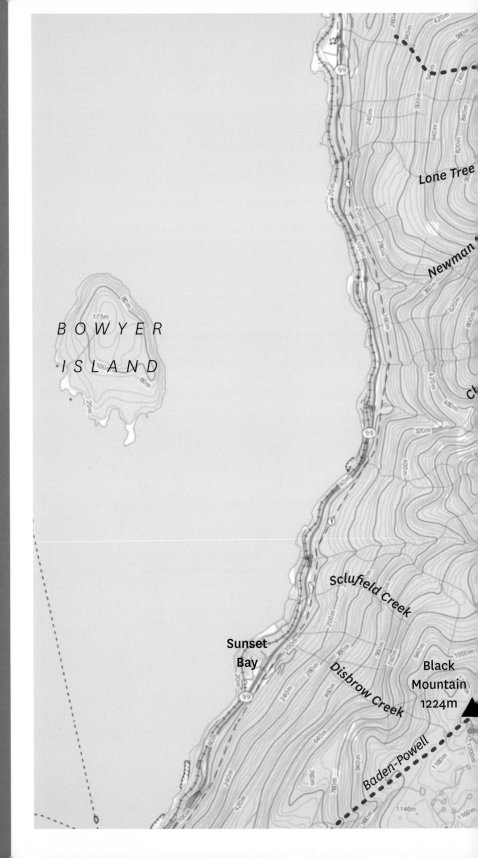

B O W Y E R
I S L A N D

175m

Lone Tree

Newman

Sclufield Creek

Sunset
Bay

Disbrow Creek

Black
Mountain
1224m

Baden-Powell

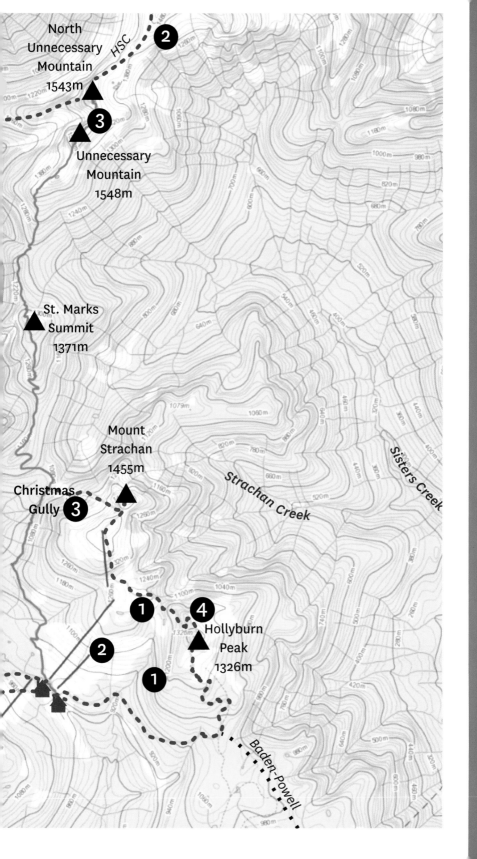

North
Unnecessary
Mountain
1543m

HSC

Unnecessary
Mountain
1548m

St. Marks
Summit
1371m

Mount
Strachan
1455m

Christmas
Gully

Strachan Creek

Sisters Creek

Hollyburn
Peak
1326m

Baden-Powell

NORTH UNNECESSARY MOUNTAIN
(NUN) (1543 M)

No one seeks it out, but it offers splendid views of Howe Sound and The Lions.

CAUTION:
One short rope climb to the north.

PROMINENCE:
53 m.

LATITUDE/LONGITUDE:
N49.44844 W123.19802.

BANG FOR BUCK:
4/5

PEAK VIEW:
4/5

TRUE SUMMIT LOCATION:
There are three peaks, the
northernmost being the true summit.

HEADWATERS:
Newman and Lone Tree Creeks
(into Howe Sound), tributaries of
Sisters and Lembke Creeks
(into Capilano Lake).

BEST VIEWS FROM:
Grouse, Dam, BC Ferries
in Howe Sound.

TRIP INFORMATION
Round-trip distance: About 16 km from Cypress Bowl.
Elevation gain: 1130 m.
Time: 5–8 hours (5:16) from Cypress Bowl.
Difficulty: 2.5/5.
Snow free: Mid-July.
Must-sees: Blueberry patches and views of Howe Sound.
Scenery: 3/5.
Kids: 3/5. For patient and tough kids.
Dogs: 3/5. Good, apart from one difficult spot with rope (if coming from Lions).
Runnability: 4/5. Burning climbs.
Terrain: Second-growth forest approach, leading to exposed alpine ridge.
Public transit: None.
Cell coverage: Usually.
Sun: Approach (80 per cent) covered; remainder largely exposed.
Water: Bring lots; there is none on trail from Cypress Bowl.
Route links: Lions, St. Marks, Strachan, Unnecessary.

HISTORY
Name origin: Unkindly dismissed by earlier mountaineers as an unnecessary obstacle from Cypress Bowl to The Lions.
Name status: Unofficial. "Unnecessary" is official.
Other names: Listed as "Unnecessary North" on bivouac.com. The Unnecessary peaks were also referred to as the "Lion's Back," for obvious reasons.
First ascent: Unknown, but likely before 1900.
Other write-up: Hui.

Unnecessary North is simply the north, slightly shorter, peak of Unnecessary Mountain. It provides a superb view of The Lions, in front of which Unnecessary Mountain provides an arguably unnecessary obstacle. For a fuller description of the Unnecessary peaks, see below, under Unnecessary Mountain.

Howe Sound Crest Trail between West Lion and Unnecessary.

Route 1:

FROM WEST – LIONS BAY ON UNNECESSARY MOUNTAIN TRAIL

See description, above, of drive to Ocean View Trailhead at Lions Bay.

- The trail pops out on the HSCT between the two peaks of Unnecessary. Proceed north.

Route 2:

FROM NORTH – ALONG HOWE SOUND CREST TRAIL FROM LIONS

See description, above, of Howe Sound Crest Trail or Binkert Trail to Lions or to Unnecessary.

Route 3:

FROM SOUTH – ALONG HOWE SOUND CREST TRAIL

See "Getting to Cypress Bowl," above. See description, above, of Howe Sound Crest Trail from Cypress Bowl to Unnecessary.

UNNECESSARY MOUNTAIN

(UNN) (1548 M)

More than an unnecessary bump en route to The Lions, it is a destination in itself,
with hanging views of Howe Sound.

CAUTION:
Very steep cliffs.

PROMINENCE:
123 m.

LATITUDE/LONGITUDE:
N49.44467 W123.20015.

BANG FOR BUCK:
3/5

PEAK VIEW:
5/5. Perfect views of Howe Sound
and The Lions.

TRUE SUMMIT LOCATION:
There are three peaks, the middle
one being slightly the highest.

HEADWATERS:
Newman and Lone Tree Creeks
(into Howe Sound), tributaries
of Sisters and Lembke Creeks
(into Capilano Lake).

BEST VIEWS FROM:
Grouse, Dam, BC Ferries
in Howe Sound.

TRIP INFORMATION

Round-trip distance: About 14.6 km from Cypress Bowl.

Elevation gain: 1030 m.

Time: 4–7 hours (4:38) from Cypress Bowl.

Difficulty: 2.5/5.

Snow free: Mid-July.

Must-sees: Blueberry patches and views of Howe Sound.

Scenery: 3/5.

Kids: 3/5. For patient and tough kids.

Dogs: 3/5. Good, apart from one difficult spot with rope (if coming from Lions).

Runnability: 4/5.

Terrain: Second-growth forest approach, leading to exposed alpine ridge.

Public transit: None.

Cell coverage: Usually.

Sun: Approach (80 per cent) covered; remainder largely exposed.

Water: Bring lots; there is none near trail from Cypress Bowl.

Route links: Lions, St. Marks, Strachan.

HISTORY

Name origin: Unkindly dismissed by earlier mountaineers as an unnecessary obstacle from Cypress Bowl to The Lions.

Name status: Official; adopted March 14, 1988. Used at least as far back as the 1940s.

Other names: Listed as "Unnecessary South" on bivouac.com. Formerly, the name "Mt. St. Mark" was used to refer to Unnecessary rather than St. Marks Summit. The Unnecessary peaks were also referred to as the "Lion's Back," for obvious reasons.

First ascent: Unknown. Likely before 1900.

Other write-up: Hui.

Unnecessary is as indicated by its name: an unloved, double-humped bump standing in the way of The Lions, attained after a seemingly futile descent and climb from St. Marks Summit. But this views it as a glass half-empty. It is the first real relief from the trudging hike from Cypress Bowl, providing the thrill of a narrow but well-defined ridge trail with stunning views of Howe Sound and the leonine destinations. It is a worthy destination unto itself, especially on a sunny day, when it offers a superb view of The Lions and Howe Sound. Unfortunately, unless you get an early start you may have to share it with 50 of your closest friends.

Until Howe Sound Crest Trail was complete, the preferred route to both St. Marks and Unnecessary was from Lions Bay, a route taken at least as early as 1966.

The best view of Unnecessary, and one that conveys its mass, is from the deck of the BC Ferry en route to Bowen Island: the two main and one smaller peak of Unnecessary look like a series of waves heading towards The Lions.

For variety, and to avoid the torture of the double up-and-down return, consider a shuttle pickup from Lions Bay, descending either via the Unnecessary trail or the Binkert–Lions trail.

ROUTE 1:
FROM WEST VIA UNNECESSARY MOUNTAIN TRAIL

See description, above, of drive to Ocean View Trailhead at Lions Bay.
- The trail pops out onto the HSCT between the two peaks of Unnecessary. Proceed south.

ROUTE 2:
FROM NORTH – ALONG HOWE SOUND CREST TRAIL

See description, above, of Howe Sound Crest Trail or Binkert Trail to Lions. See description, above, of Howe Sound Crest Trail or Binkert Trail to Unnecessary.

ROUTE 3:
FROM SOUTH – ALONG HOWE SOUND CREST TRAIL

See "Getting to Cypress Bowl," below. See description, above, of Howe Sound Crest Trail from Cypress Bowl to Unnecessary.

ST. MARKS SUMMIT

(MAR) (1371 M)

A destination for those with insufficient time, stamina, or curiosity to go to The Lions.

CAUTION:
None.

PROMINENCE:
181 m.

LATITUDE/LONGITUDE:
N49.42805 W123.20611.

BANG FOR BUCK:
3/5

PEAK VIEW:
1/5. Treed. Good views from water side of HSCT (see book cover).

TRUE SUMMIT LOCATION:
To east, and above HSCT, via a short side trail.

HEADWATERS:
Charles Creek, Turpin Creek (into Howe Sound), Lembke Creek (into Capilano Lake).

BEST VIEWS FROM:
Grouse, Dam, BC Ferries in Howe Sound.

TRIP INFORMATION

Round-trip distance: 10.4 km from Cypress Bowl.

Elevation gain: 500 m.

Time: 2.5–5.5 hours (2:54) from Cypress Bowl.

Difficulty: 2/5.

Snow free: Mid-July.

Must-sees: Blueberry patches.

Scenery: 2/5.

Kids: 3/5. Safe but dull.

Dogs: 5/5. No obstacles. Dirt trails.

Runnability: 4/5.

Terrain: second-growth forest.

Public transit: None.

Cell coverage: Generally available.

Sun: Mostly covered.

Water: Bring lots of water; there is none near trail from Cypress Bowl.

Route links: Lions, Strachan.

Name origin: St. Mark's Anglican Camp, on the beach at Lions Bay. St. Mark, known as "Mark the Evangelist," was the ascribed (but likely not the actual) author of the second book of the New Testament, reputedly the first gospel written.

Name status: Official. Adopted March 14, 1988. Note that the official name is "St. Marks" (no apostrophe), although the church after which it is named is "St. Mark's."

First ascent: Unknown, but likely before 1900.

Other write-ups: Hanna; Hui.

The summit received its name from St. Mark's Anglican Camp (later known as "Camp Agwatilah"), located at Lions Bay from around 1921. It was the first settlement of sorts in the area now occupied by the village of Lions Bay. The administrator of the camp, St. Mark's Anglican church (then located at Second and Vine in Vancouver), let BCMC members stay in their "fine camp building" in Lions Bay, allowing an early morning start for the steep climb up to The Lions. Climbers of The Lions were still using the beach as a launching pad for trips in 1947 and 1949. It is not hard to imagine a thankful BCMC member calling the nameless peak "St. Mark's." The name "Mount St. Mark" was originally applied to the next peak north (what is now known as Unnecessary Mountain).

Until Howe Sound Crest Trail was completed, the preferred route to both St. Marks and Unnecessary was from Lions Bay, a route taken in 1966.

Note that the signpost on Howe Sound Crest Trail is not the true peak: the slope to the east should have given that away. A short, narrow trail up and to the right leads to the treed summit, which offers views of Enchantment, Wizard, and The Lions.

St. Marks as a destination presents little to be effusive about; it's fine for the under-ambitious or those pressed for time. And it does make a good resting spot en route to Unnecessary or The Lions. The dead white snag is dramatic against the blue sky, with Howe Sound behind. The heather and the blueberries, when blooming and ripe, are dense and pleasing.

But do not underestimate St. Marks. Despite (and perhaps because of) the close proximity of St. Marks to Cypress Bowl, NSR regularly rescues ill-prepared hikers from this area. In one of the more spectacular forehead-slapping incidents, in January 2016, NSR had to rescue seven hikers who ventured to St. Marks to photograph the sunset, only to be surprised that there was insufficient light after the sunset to return to Cypress Bowl (and of course they had no headlamps). The hikers ended up losing the trail and wandering into the Charles Creek valley. The group was also under-equipped for the winter. As NSR said in a blogpost, "Either they had not read our list of [10 Ways to Get Yourself Killed this Winter] or they decided to challenge us on the list."

ROUTE 1:

FROM SOUTH – ALONG HOWE SOUND CREST TRAIL

See "Getting to Cypress Bowl," below. See description, above, of Howe Sound Crest Trail from Cypress Bowl to St. Marks.

- Eventually, at the end of a uphill stretch, the trees thin out, the ground gets rockier, and the trail becomes flat and at times slightly muddy. There will likely be a provincial parks signpost marked "St. Marks Summit."
- This is not the true peak, however, a fact made obvious by looking to the east, and the thickly treed slope above. Instead of bushwhacking up this slope, proceed along the HSCT to the end of the short flat section. It may not be flagged, but you will see a small but clear trail heading east: first up, then down onto a grassy meadow, and then up the back side of the hill. The treed summit, marked with a dead tree, is neither cairned nor obvious nor glorious.
- The entire epic journey to the summit will take all of five minutes.

ROUTE 2:

FROM WEST VIA UNNECESSARY MOUNTAIN TRAIL

See description, above, of drive to Ocean View Trailhead at Lions Bay.

- The trail pops out on the HSCT between the two peaks of Unnecessary. Proceed south.

ROUTE 3:

FROM NORTH – ALONG HOWE SOUND CREST TRAIL

See description, above, of Howe Sound Crest Trail or Binkert Trail to Lions. See description, above, of Howe Sound Crest Trail or Binkert Trail to St. Marks.

Crossing the ledge on the West Lion

CYPRESS AREA
(3 PEAKS)

Cypress Provincial Park contains three peaks near Vancouver as well as all the Howe Sound Crest Trail summits. Black and Hollyburn are the closest things Vancouver has to an actual "Cypress Mountain": contrary to recent ski resort rebranding efforts, there is no such peak. Cypress Bowl is the basin between Black, Hollyburn, and Strachan.

In July 1927 the honorary BCMC president James Porter (who also led the drive to make Garibaldi a park) proposed a provincial park, made up of the slopes of Hollyburn Ridge, Hollyburn Peak, Black Mountain, and Mt. Strachan. Land was set aside for a park in 1944, in part because of concerns about excessive logging on Hollyburn Ridge. In 1969 environmental concerns welled up again, when aerial photographs revealed far more extensive clear-cutting on Black and Strachan than had been anticipated in the mountain plan.

Cypress Provincial Park was created in 1975, with the Howe Sound Crest Trail section added to the park in 1982. The park is a summer and winter playground, with extensive downhill ski runs and mountain trails. Its mixture of preservation and pleasure has been the source of ongoing environmental battles, with old-growth stands of Douglas fir, red cedar, and its namesake, the cypress or yellow cedar, threatened with felling for forestry or additional ski runs. Happily, these giants have been preserved, with the central copse being north of Yew Lake, en route to Howe Sound Crest Trail. Other old-growth stands are found on Black and Hollyburn mountains.

A protected triangle of old-growth trees located to the north of the Quarry Lookout switchback of Cypress Bowl Road will likely become a protected provincial park in the near future. These are popularly referred to as the "Triangle Lands." In 1990 a proposal to build a golf course in the area was defeated by plebiscite later that year, and in 1993 a majority in another plebiscite voted in favour of a permanent park designation for the area. At the time of writing, this vote had still not been acted upon. We hope it will be soon.

The construction of a three-lane paved road from the Upper Levels Highway provided public access to the park in 1973. In 1938 the Heaps Timber Company of Los Angeles had bulldozed a steep logging road as far as the old Nasmyth mill site (just south of the present Parking Lot 5), opening summer access via jeep.

Before those roads, the traditional approach up Hollyburn was up 22nd Street to Forks Trail, beside Rogers and Marr creeks, to First Lake, where Hollyburn Lodge was built in January 1927. The first chairlift was built in 1950, taking skiers up 6,000 feet from the north end of 26th Street, near the present intersection of Chairlift and Skilift roads. The lift was called "Chairway to the Stars," but some hikers and skiers called it the "chairway from nowhere to nowhere," as they still had to hike 20 minutes from the top terminus to the ski lodge. To avoid the hike, Fred Burfield ran a bus in summer and a Bombardier snowcat in winter to take people to his lodge. Both the lift and Hi-View Lodge burned down in June 1965.

In the 1970s the more extensive ski runs currently in use were developed to the western area of the park. Management of the alpine and Nordic ski areas was transferred to private operators in 1984. The Cypress Mountain Resort was a major site of the 2010 Olympics, with slalom ski and ski-jump events, although due to the unusually wet and warm winter, snow had to be trucked in or created on site. The park receives over a million visitors annually, the highest attendance rate for any provincial park in British Columbia.

The lower slopes of the Cypress complex are owned by British Pacific Properties, which developed the British Properties and most of the upper-elevation developments, as well as Lions Gate Bridge. Mulgrave School, at the base of Cypress Bowl Road, is named after the Earl of Mulgrave and Marquess of Normanby, who is a major shareholder in British Pacific Properties.

These slopes were also the birthplace of Hollywood North: in 1970 Robert Altman filmed the superb "anti-western" *McCabe and Mrs. Miller* just above the end of the modern-day location of Woodgreen Drive.

No public transit is available to Cypress Bowl in the summer.

Dogs and other pets must be kept on leash in the Cypress area and are not permitted at all on Yew Lake Interpretive Trail (an alternative path for the south end of Howe Sound Crest Trail).

CYPRESS AREA BAGGER TIPS

The peaks of Hollyburn, Strachan, Black, and St. Marks can be done as a day trip from Cypress Bowl. This is a suitable trip for spring with snowshoes and/or micro spikes or as a summer hike. Park at the downhill area and take the Baden-Powell trail east to its junction with the Hollyburn trail. Take the Hollyburn trail to the top and then descend via the steeper north-side trail to its junction with the Strachan trail next to the Collins ski run. Follow the Strachan trail over the top of Sky Chair and on to the summit of Strachan. Return via Old Strachan Trail.

Round-trip distance:
13.8 km

Time:
5:31

Elevation gain:
1010 m

Strachan Creek

Strip Creek

Montizambert Creek

Howe Sound Crest Trail
to St. Marks and Lions

Mt. Strachan
1454m

Mt. Strachan
(South Peak)

Christmas Gully

HSCT

HSCT

Bowen
Island
Viewpoint

Yew Lake

Cypress Creek

Black
Mountain
1224m

Disbrow Creek

Baden-Powell Trail to
Whyte
Lake

Theagill Lake

Sam Lake

Owen Lake

Baden-Powell Trail

Cypress Creek

P

P

Collins Ski Run

Old Hollyburn Tr.

Hollyburn
Peak 1325m

Heather
Lake

BPT

Nickey Creek

Lookout Lake

Sixth
Lake

500 m

1

2

3

4

1

2

1

2

MT. STRACHAN

(STR) (1454 M)

Nearby and accessible hike offering excellent views and friendly grey jays.

CAUTION:
Steep 200-m cliffs off north end of north peak. Christmas Gully icy in winter.

PROMINENCE:
382 m.

LATITUDE/LONGITUDE:
N49.41306 W123.19334.

BANG FOR BUCK:
4/5

PEAK VIEW:
4/5. Splendid view of Howe Sound,

The Lions, HSCT peaks and Garibaldi peaks to the north, and the city.

TRUE SUMMIT LOCATION:
The north peak is slightly higher.

HEADWATERS:
Strachan Creek East (into Capilano Lake), Strachan Creek West, and Montizambert Creek (into Howe Sound).

BEST VIEWS FROM:
Howe Sound ferry, Gardner, Dam.

TRIP INFORMATION

Round-trip distance: 7.2 km from Cypress Bowl.

Elevation gain: 500 m.

Time: 3–7 hours (3:54).

Difficulty: 2.5/5.

Snow free: Early to mid-July.

Must-sees: South peak boulder field; plane-crash site.

Scenery: 3/5. Good views, old rocky plain.

Kids: 4/5. Grey jays and erratics. But be careful: steep cliffs to north.

Dogs: 4/5. On leash. Dogs are not permitted on Yew Lake Interpretive Trail.

Runnability: 4/5.

Terrain: Well-travelled trails for the most part: flagged but rocky in Christmas Gully and to the north peak.

Public transit: None.

Cell coverage: Usually.

Sun: 60 per cent covered; summit exposed.

Water: Available at Cypress Bowl parking lot.

Route links: Hollyburn and Black.

HISTORY

Name origin: After Admiral Sir Richard John Strachan, 6th Baronet GCB (October 27, 1760 – February 3, 1828). Charted in 1860 by Captain Richards of the Royal Navy as "Mt. Strahan."

Name status: Official. Adopted December 7, 1937.

First ascent: Frequently climbed by BCMC by 1923. Likely climbed before 1895.

Other write-ups: Hanna, Hui.

Mt. Strachan does not derive its name from a hero of the Glorious First but rather after Admiral Sir Richard John Strachan, 6th Baronet GCB, who captured the final four French ships fleeing from the Battle of Trafalgar. He was famed for his ungovernable temper and violent cursing. While Lord Howe was nicknamed "Black Dick," Strachan was called "Mad Dick." A hike up Strachan on a sunny day will make you "Happy Dick": Strachan's location provides spectacular views of The Lions and Garibaldi to the north, with the closest view of the Howe Sound and Vancouver Island peaks.

Grey jays soar overhead and pluck trail mix from your hands and head. In good weather, Strachan is a perfect introduction to slightly off-the-beaten path hikes for children, with the birds, the gentle rock scampering, and the erratic boulders to climb (although it is only suitable for kids with acute self-control: there are sheer cliffs off its north end). It makes a particularly pleasing autumn hike, when the blueberry and other bushes are a blaze of reds and yellows.

Strachan lends itself well to a fine loop route starting at the lodge, ascending via HSCT and the Montizambert Creek Christmas Gully (apparently so called because it was usually ready for skiing by daredevil downhillers by Christmas) and then descending via the conventional trail, or vice versa (we prefer climbing up Christmas Gully to going down: more stable and easy on the knees). It can be linked to Hollyburn through the now disused but still decent traditional trail. And those who run out of time or energy can beat a retreat via gravel roads back down to Cypress Lodge.

The peak name is properly pronounced "Strawn" or "Stru-an," not "Strack-an." The predominant British Columbian pronunciation is "Strack-an," perhaps influenced by 1980s Social Credit cabinet minister Bruce Strachan, while transplanted Ontarians pronounce it "Strawn," perhaps influenced by Bishop John Strachan, founder of Trinity College at the University of Toronto. Even in the surname's Scottish homeland, both pronunciations are used. That said, the peak's namesake, Sir Richard, did pronounce his name as "Strawn." Early Vancouverites also pronounced it that way. The 1860 Captain Richards chart, the 1906 O.F. LeRoy mineral survey map, the 1912 C.J. Heaney map, and the 1915 water map, as well as hiking maps from the *Daily Province* in 1925 and from BC Electric Railway Ltd. in 1935 and 1946, refer to Black Mountain and "Mt. Strahan" (no "c"); the name was not officially corrected to its present spelling until February 1924. During the tourist heyday of the 1920s there was a Mt. Strahan Lodge (again no "c") on Bowen Island, later named the Terminal Hotel.

The namesake is not the only military history associated with the peak. On November 23, 1963, a Royal Canadian Navy T-33 jet on a naval training flight crashed in heavy forest, killing both Royal Canadian Navy crew members Lt. Norman Ogden and Lt. Donald Clark, both from Victoria. In 2014 a plaque was unveiled near the crash site, memorializing these men. The crash site is just off the ski run now named T-33, leading up to the south peak of Strachan: twisted aluminum fuselage and engine parts are gathered in three main clusters. Please respect the site. People died here.

Despite Strachan's proximity to ski runs and the first section of Howe Sound Crest Trail, death has visited it many times, particularly among those skiing out of bounds on the mountain's eastern side into the Strachan Creek drainage gullies. The waterfalls, steep slopes, cliffs, narrowing canyons, and avalanche hazards here have taken their toll. On the south branch of Strachan Creek, closer to Hollyburn than to Strachan, is Tony Baker Gully, named after the 14-year-old boy who died there in February 1987 in a skiing accident. Snowboarder Danny Epp was found dead there in January 2006. Central Strachan Creek, located on the east side of the col separating North and South Strachan, opposite Christmas Gully, is referred to as Australian Gully, after the provenance of a skier who, fortunately, survived his ordeal there. William Leboe, aged 34, was not so fortunate. He and his friend Earl Kurz, 31, skied off Strachan on December 19, 1992. Kurz managed to walk out to the top of the gully, but Leboe was not found until the next spring, after the snow had melted. In March 2000 two teenaged snowboarders died here.

The west side of Strachan is also dangerous. The Montizambert Creek drainage has claimed many lives. One was that of a young girl who skied down it and hit a log in 1993. In November 2013, British tourist Tom Billings disappeared. His remains were found below Strachan Meadows, near Montizambert Creek, in May 2016.

The traditional route up Strachan is described below as Route 1 or 3: BCMC members and other hikers would often continue to Strachan after a Hollyburn climb. That trail dates back to at least 1923.

Route 1, the Old Strachan Trail, will take you past an enormous yellow cedar called the "Hollyburn Giant." With a diameter of 3.2 m, it is one of the largest known yellow cedars in British Columbia. Despite its broken top and ancient appearance, the tree is still alive and estimated to be over 1,000 years old. Several metres upslope from the Hollyburn Giant is the largest known mountain hemlock in Canada, with a diameter of 1.9 m.

In 1987 a rickety chairlift to the peak of Mt. Strachan was constructed. Around the same time, reprised in 1997, there was a scheme, happily suppressed, to build a restaurant and chalet on the peak. This and other proposals also threatened old-growth trees in the area.

Strachan is a rich climb geologically as well. While the lower slopes are ancient hornblende diorite (a plutonic rock), the upper slopes contain banded amphibolite (a metamorphic rock) and metasedimentary rocks. In the meadows towards the top of the Strachan chairlift are 3- to 4-m dark, chlorite-rich layers with narrow brown bands separating them. The green-coloured bands were likely basaltic, metamorphosed to a finer size. The original dark minerals (mostly hornblende and pyroxene) metamorphosed to green chlorite. On the south peak of Strachan is a large bare area of banded chloritic (green) and beige to black schist that has metamorphosed. The layers might represent sediments. The meadows are strewn with erratics (large boulders deposited by retreating glaciers) and covered in striation (scratches caused by glaciers dragging rock against rock). Between the south and north peaks, the schist and sedimentary rocks are cut vertically, creating a natural staircase. The north peak itself consists primarily of leftover sedimentary rock: siltstone and sandstone, with green, brown, and black stripes.

GETTING THERE

From Lions Gate Bridge, drive west on Highway 1 and take the Cypress Bowl exit, #8. Drive until the end of the road, at the downhill skiing parking lot. Free parking.

Route 1:

FROM SOUTH – CYPRESS MOUNTAIN LODGE VIA OLD STRACHAN TRAIL

This was the traditional route up Strachan from around 1900. In the 1990s it was rediscovered by Halvor Lunden (1915 Norway – 2008 Vancouver) and rehabilitated by Lunden and BCMC members.

- From the parking lot, go north past a small service building and up the ski run for a few minutes to join Baden-Powell Trail descending into the woods to the right (east). This is perhaps counterintuitive, as Strachan is due north.
- Baden-Powell Trail is well marked as it continues east over a series of small creeks. After the second more substantial stream (about 15–25 minutes into the hike), leave Baden-Powell Trail and take a lesser but obvious track to the left heading uphill.
- The trail climbs, following the creek valley to the left. It is generally obvious and well trodden. You will see several ancient trees, including the Hollyburn Giant.
- Eventually the trail hits a meadow plateau and heads west. You will see a small pond (Emily Lake) to your right and the Strachan service road to your left.
- The trail starts a steep ascent and passes the 1963 T-33 crash site. At most times, the Sky Chair and the ski run are visible through the trees to your west (left). In wet weather you may prefer to hike the gravel road under the ski run, as the roots and rocks on the trail can be slippery.
- After 15–20 minutes the trail emerges from the forest and follows the Sky Chair to the end.
- The track through the alpine meadows is generally obvious, cutting a path through grass and heather. At times, paint splotches mark the route.
- Past the end of the chair lift you enter the slabby granite paradise of the south peak, with many odd erratics atop the granite plane. Kids love to scramble up these beasts.
- At the north end of the south peak a narrow but obvious trail cuts down through the heather to the col between the two peaks.
- Cross over to the obvious and short trail up to the north peak of Strachan. Some gentle rock-scrambling past blueberries and heather takes you to a gentle slope leading up to the peak.

Route 2:

FROM SOUTH – CYPRESS MOUNTAIN LODGE VIA ACCESS ROAD

This is a duller version of Route 1, largely up service roads.

- From the parking lot, go north, past a small service building. Follow the gravel road heading up the far right (east) side of the ski area.
- The road curves up and around the ski slope to connect with the Strachan trail (Route 1) just below the plane-crash site.
- Alternatively you can continue up along the road, which does five switchbacks to the top of the Strachan chairlift.

ROUTE 3:

FROM WEST VIA HSCT AND CHRISTMAS GULLY

<u>Caution:</u> This route should only be attempted after snow and ice have vanished and when conditions are generally dry. In winter, avalanches are not uncommon, and there have been deaths at this site.

- From Cypress Mountain Lodge, hike north on Howe Sound Crest Trail for approximately 3 km.
- After crossing a small bridge, you will reach Strachan Meadows, with scruffy alders to the right (east). Mt. Strachan looms behind and above. *If you hit a second bridge in the meadows, you've gone too far.*
- Head towards an obvious stream (the headwaters of Montizambert Creek) and gully leading up between the two peaks of Mt. Strachan: Christmas Gully.
- The route continues up along the creek, on the left side of the gully. The trail occasionally scrambles over rocks and sometimes retreats into the trees to the left (north). It is generally easy to follow and sporadically flagged. At times, hands are needed to climb up helpful roots and boughs in the forest. There are occasional ropes, but do not trust them. At no point should you feel exposed or in danger.
- About three-quarters of the way up, the trail widens for a viewpoint of The Lions.
- The trail then heads back towards the rocks of the gully.
- Towards the top, the rock becomes less secure, and the way less obvious: stay safe.
- Head up towards the obvious destination: the grassy shoulder between the two peaks of Strachan.
- Turn left (north) and make the short and obvious climb past heather and over rock to the summit of Strachan.
- Return by same route, or make a loop, descending on Route 1 or 2.

ROUTE 4:

FROM EAST – FROM HOLLYBURN

<u>Note:</u> This route is muddy and slippery when wet and much rougher than the other three.

- On the north-northwest point of the peak of Hollyburn, you will see a trail cutting into the blueberry bushes and heather and a sign saying the trail is closed.
- The trail proceeds downhill, occasionally past and around eroded muddy patches and fallen trees.
- After the valley floor, you will start a steep climb up.
- The trail joins the main trail (Route 1) about 500 m below the south peak.

BLACK MOUNTAIN
(BLA) (1224 M)

A good hike for kids. Salamanders in the lake. The bald south peak is a great place to camp and watch the sunset.

CAUTION:
None.

PROMINENCE:
296 m.

LATITUDE/LONGITUDE:
N49.39444 W123.21861.

BANG FOR BUCK:
4/5

PEAK VIEW:
3/5. Partial views of Lions, Brunswick, and surrounding peaks, and islands of Howe Sound.

TRUE SUMMIT LOCATION:
Two peaks of almost identical height: one south and one north of Cabin Lake. The north summit is slightly higher: the pointy slab at the Yew Lake viewpoint (1224 m).

HEADWATERS:
Disbrow, Sclufield (into Howe Sound); Whyte, Nelson, Dick/Eagle, Cypress, and Godman Creeks (into Burrard Inlet).

BEST VIEWS FROM:
Howe Sound ferry, Gardner, English Bay.

TRIP INFORMATION

Round-trip distance: 4.2 km from Cypress Bowl.

Elevation gain: 300 m.

Time: 1–3 hours (1:20).

Difficulty: 1/5. Well-marked trail. Steep and a bit crumbly in places.

Snow free: Early to mid-July.

Must-sees: Cabin Lake and its salamanders.

Scenery: 4/5. Mostly second-growth forests. Ocean views. Small lake with salamanders in it.

Kids: 5/5. Child-friendly.

Dogs: 5/5. On leash. Dogs are not permitted on Yew Lake Interpretive Trail.

Runnability: 4/5. The popular Baden-Powell Trail offers many opportunities to run.

Terrain: Well-marked and well-groomed trail alongside ski run for most of way.

Public transit: None.

Cell coverage: Usually.

Sun: 90 per cent covered; peak exposed.

Water: Available at Cypress Bowl parking lot washroom; also from Cabin Lake if needed.

Route links: Hollyburn and Strachan.

HISTORY

Name origin: Charted in 1860 by Captain George Henry Richards of the Royal Navy and presumably named by him (Crown was the only other Burrard Inlet North Shore peak named on the chart). In the 1850s the mountain was ravaged by a forest fire which left many charred stumps, giving a black appearance that is still evident in places.

Name status: Official. Adopted December 7, 1937.

Other names: Occasionally called "Cypress Mountain," as in a May 3, 1925, Pollough Pogue article in *The Province*, "Haunted Trails of Hollyburn," and in current branding efforts.

First ascent: Unknown but likely before 1890. Likely climbed long before by Indigenous people, hunters, or prospectors.

Other write-ups: Hanna, Hui.

Poor Black Mountain gets little respect. In the 1850s and again in 1884 it was ravaged by forest fires (the latter one having blazed from Eagle Harbour over Black Mountain all the way to Hollyburn), leading to its name. Widely forested again by 1899, the mountain was ravaged again in the 1970s by the ski slopes cut into its southeastern flanks. Black Mountain definitely deserves more love. The place is a fine day hike for the whole family. A summer day rewards a hiker with glorious views as well as a swim in Cabin Lake. These pleasures make up for the at times steep, dull, rocky, and dusty climb up from the downhill ski parking lot via the Yew Lake trailhead. The trail was put in for the 2010 Olympics, diverting the existing Baden-Powell Trail, at a significant cost. Efforts to minimize intrusions onto the ski run and the forest resulted in an overly steep and crumbly trail.

There are two peaks, almost of equal height. The popular south peak (1210 m), is a bald slab of rock just off Baden-Powell Trail, a pleasant spot for feeding the grey jays, watching boats in English Bay, munching a sandwich, or watching the stars. The actual summit is the slightly higher (1224-m) pointy slab at the Yew Lake viewpoint, to the north, with excellent vistas of The Lions and Howe Sound. Between the two summits is the charming Cabin Lake, where salamanders are often seen swimming. As mentioned earlier, it is also a great place for human swimmers on a hot day. On the north side of Black Mountain, below Cabin Lake, is one of the largest known amabilis firs in the world, with a diameter of 2.33 m.

From Cabin Lake, a well-marked kilometre-long loop past Owen, Theagill, and Sam lakes is well worth the trip, particularly in the early morning or evening, and especially when the blueberries are out. For a longer addition, about an hour west past several pleasant small lakes, Baden-Powell Trail leads to Eagle Bluffs, with a spectacular view of Eagle (Dick) Lake (the 1929 Water Map calls it "Duck Lake") and Eagle Harbour to the south, Vancouver to the southeast, and Howe Sound to the west.

On July 11–14, 1912, Professor John Davidson of the BCMC and the Vancouver Natural History Society carried out a botanical survey of Black Mountain and area. It was on this trip that he gave Hollyburn Ridge its name.

In 1913 the typical route was up Cypress Creek, past the falls, then northwest to Eagle Lake and up to the plateau. A better trail was blazed to the Black summit from Whyte Lake in June 1926 by the delightfully named BCMC member Frederic Alan "Brick" Spouse (1905 West Hartlepool, Durham, England – 1996; so nicknamed because of his red hair). Spouse's route was close to the present Baden-Powell Trail up Eagle Bluffs. The BCMC's *BC Mountaineer* was pretty impressed with it: "Gone is the terror of Black Mountain! No longer will the haggard-faced party come staggering back to the lake with tattered shirts and bleeding arms, to be welcomed as returning tropical explorers!"

Another intensive BCMC trail-blazing occurred in September 1961, clearing a route that continued to Black via Donut Rock.

In April 1966 five Grade 8 students from Gladstone High School survived the night after getting lost on a hike on what the newspaper called "rugged Black Mountain."

GETTING THERE
- From Lions Gate Bridge, drive west on Highway 1 and take Cypress Bowl exit (#8).
- Drive to the end of the road, at the downhill skiing parking lot. Free parking.

ROUTE 1:
FROM EAST – BEGINNING AT CYPRESS BOWL PARKING LOT
Black is on the west side of the Cypress Bowl ski area, along Baden-Powell Trail.
- Take Howe Sound Crest Trail past the lodge.
- The Baden-Powell forks left and uphill. Wide dirt and gravel trail parallels the ski lifts, switchbacking up to the alpine.
- As you approach the alpine, the trail becomes smoother and gravelly.
- Take a sharp, easily overlooked right (otherwise you will miss Cabin Lake and wind up at Sam Lake).
- The path leads to a signposted junction. Keep going straight, to Cabin Lake.
- Left (south) leads up to the south peak of Black, through a muddy patch.
- Turning right (north) to the Yew Lake viewpoint leads up to the true summit.

ROUTE 2:
FROM WEST VIA BADEN-POWELL TRAIL FROM NELSON CREEK PARKING LOT
The trail is steep but well marked throughout, following Baden-Powell Trail for the most part.
- From Highway 1 take Exit 4 (Woodgreen). From either direction, the road is circuitous; check a map beforehand. The road winds under the highway. There is a parking lot off Westport Road, up against the highway, separated by a fence.
- From the signboard at end of parking lot, walk along well-established trail that curves under the highway bridge over Nelson Creek.
- Pass a water tower and ascend a steep gravel slope.
- After 500 m from the trailhead, a well-marked trail ascends into the forest to the right, just short of another water tower.
- Pass some signboards telling of plants and animals.
- After about 1 km total, the trail forks: take the left fork, which goes to Whyte Lake. (Straight would take you east along the Trans-Canada Trail towards Dick (Eagle) Lake, which is the wrong way.)
- A well-defined and pleasant trail leads to Whyte Lake about 1.5 km farther. The most beautiful outhouse in the world is seen in the southwest corner.
- At the outhouse, continue west and down a short reclaimed gravel road to the main Baden-Powell trail, heading right (north) and upwards.
- The path will alternate between reclaimed gravel road and single-track and rock. The trail is well defined throughout, with regular triangular orange Baden-Powell Trail markers on trees.

- The route will then become more forested. Keep heading north and up.
- Climb up a short rock field and then a larger one. The larger rock field will usually have flagging or cairns. Look for worn rocks denuded of moss. This is the trickiest place to keep your bearings. Look back for your first spectacular view of Howe Sound.
- Re-enter the forest for some very steep and tiring bits.
- Eventually you will hit the rock base of Eagle Bluffs. Again the route is well marked by boot erosion and the occasional flag, cairn, or paint splotch. You will have to use your hands occasionally, but you should never feel exposed.
- At the top of Eagle Bluffs, exult in the views of Vancouver Island, Vancouver, Horseshoe Bay, English Bay, and Howe Sound.
- Continue north into forest again for an undulating trail through second-growth forest.
- Reach a plateau with a series of small lakes, the Cougar Lakes, and the headwaters of Dick (Eagle) Creek. This area is muddy when the snow is melting. Continuing along, you will see another small lake, Owen Lake, on your right.
- At the fork stay left, past Theagill Lake and up. Do not take the right-hand fork, Cabin Lake Trail.
- Continue up through forest to the bald south peak of Black.
- The trail continues to the north, descending to Cabin Lake.
- The north, true, summit is via the small Yew Lake viewpoint trail.

HOLLYBURN MOUNTAIN

(HOL) (1325 M)

A gentle climb for the whole family, with excellent views.

CAUTION:
None.

PROMINENCE:
161 m.

LATITUDE/LONGITUDE:
N49.40055 W123.18306.

BANG FOR BUCK:
5/5

PEAK VIEW:
5/5. Vancouver, Howe Sound, Garibaldi, Lions, Crown, Baker, Judge Howay, Mamquam.

TRUE SUMMIT LOCATION:
Obvious.

HEADWATERS:
McCallum (into Cypress Creek), Cypress, Brothers, Lawson, McDonald, Marr, Rodgers, Westmount, Hadden (into Burrard Inlet), Sowerby, Eureka, Nickey, Lorenzetta Creeks, tributaries of Strachan Creek (into Capilano River).

BEST VIEWS FROM:
Grouse, Dam, downtown Vancouver, New Brighton Park.

TRIP INFORMATION

Round-trip distance: 8.2 km from Cypress Bowl cross-country ski area.
Elevation gain: 410 m.
Time: 2–4 hours.
Difficulty: 1/5. Well-marked trail.
Snow free: Early July.
Must-sees: Blueberries, grey jays, tarns.
Scenery: 4/5.
Kids: 5/5. Child-friendly.
Dogs: 5/5. Only on leash.
Runnability: 5/5. Popular Baden-Powell Trail offers many opportunities.
Terrain: Well-marked trail through forest and meadows.
Public transit: None.
Cell coverage: At base and on peak; otherwise, surprisingly scarce.
Sun: 50 per cent exposed.
Water: Bring lots; none drinkable along route.
Route links: St. Marks, Black, and Strachan are close. Several other Howe Sound peaks are baggable within the same day by a strong runner.

HISTORY

Name origin: See narrative text below. Name used in 1912 North Vancouver map.
Name status: "Mt. Hollyburn" adopted December 7, 1937. Confirmed May 3, 1951, on 92G. Form of name changed to Hollyburn Mountain June 7, 1951, on 92G. Hollyburn Ridge adopted May 7, 1959, on 92G/SW.

Other names: Mt. Vaughan. Until 1912 Hollyburn was generally considered a subpeak of Strachan.

First ascent: First climbed by BCMC in 1908 and frequently climbed by BCMC members and others from that date onwards. Likely climbed much earlier by Indigenous people, trappers, and hunters.

Other write-ups: Hui, Hanna.

Kids love Hollyburn.

Hollyburn is the perfect peak for novice hikers, children, out-of-town visitors, or for a first date. It is neither long nor steep, and has a well-marked and well-groomed trail. Most of the hike is through a 4-km-long fruit basket teeming with delicious mountain blueberries. In July and August, blueberry hunting and the energy from their juices will keep kids hiking along this longest stretch of the adventure. The meadows below the peak are one of our favourite spots in the North Shore mountains; their heather and tarns and rocky slabs are beautiful, and whisper that the peak is near. Some call this area "Heather Meadows" and its tarns, the "Heather Lakes." The peak itself is a playground for kids, with squat, slabby peaks for frolicking on, a large tarn with a rocky peninsula, spectacular views of Sky Pilot and The Lions, and an avian air force of grey jays eager to land on hands and heads and gobble trail mix or birdseed in exchange for photo opportunities.

In contrast to most of the peaks in the book, Hollyburn also makes a splendid winter destination on snowshoes or skis. It is a more direct route than the hiking trail, and makes a fun, fast descent. Pack a headlamp and some hot chocolate and gaze at the city and the stars.

The peak was originally named Mt. Vaughan. On July 11–14, 1912, botany professor John F. Davidson (1878–1970), of the BCMC and the Vancouver Natural History Society, carried out a botanical survey of Black Mountain. It was on this trip that he gave Hollyburn Ridge its name. The name Hollyburn Ridge was generally used by the BCMC for the entire area until references to "Hollyburn Peak" first occurred around 1926. The name Mt. Hollyburn was officially adopted in 1937. It was not named from any feature on the peak, but rather from the grove of holly bushes growing beside the creek (or "burn" as they say in Scotland) at the Ambleside home of West Vancouver pioneer John Lawson (1869–1954) and his family, on the shore at 17th Street. The Lawsons had arrived in West Vancouver from Ontario in 1887. John Lawson developed an early ferry service to West Vancouver, established the first school, and served as the settlement's first postmaster and telephone agent.

The peak has long been a popular destination. A *BC Mountaineer* report of a June 10, 1928, club trip to Hollyburn Ridge and Peak noted: "This was the first trip under the leadership of the lady members of the club and we hope that in future these trips will form a permanent part of our climbing schedule."

The sight of fresh snow on Hollyburn Ridge, with early morning blue skies above, or illumination by rosy-fingered dawn, is sublime.

In contrast to the hornblende granodiorite plutonic strata of many of the surrounding peaks, Hollyburn is topped with banded amphibolite and metasedimentary rock of the same kind found on Mt. Gardner. These younger strata originated as ocean or river sediments and were then pressurized into metamorphic rock. Chlorite schist is exposed on various outcrops here. Narrow quartz veins cut across, having poured into fractures while the material was still hot and fluid. Outcrops are also cut by several foot-wide hornblende diorite dikes – streaks of sedimentary rock torn from the wall during intrusion.

At the junction of Connector Trail (from Baden-Powell Trail) and Old Strachan Trail is a giant yellow cedar called the "Hollyburn Giant." With a diameter of 3.2 m, it is one of the largest known yellow cedars in British Columbia. Despite its broken top and ancient appearance, the tree is still alive, estimated to be over 1,000 years old. Several metres upslope from the Hollyburn Giant is the largest known mountain hemlock in Canada, with a 1.9 m diameter.

GETTING THERE
From Lions Gate Bridge, drive west on Highway 1 and take Cypress Bowl exit (#8). Drive to Cypress Mountain Provincial Park. Turn right at the cross-country ski area. *Do not go to the downhill ski area unless you are taking Route 2.* Free parking at the trailhead.

ROUTE 1:
FROM SOUTH – FROM CROSS-COUNTRY SKI AREA
The trailhead is on the left side of parking lot, just before you reach the cross-country ski rental area.
- One option is to go up the dull powerline gravel road.
- The more interesting choice is to turn east (right) onto the Sitzmark cross-country ski trail bounded by blueberry bushes. Continue to Baden-Powell Trail (Wells Gray cross-country trail). Turn left (north) and climb up the most rocky and least groomed section of the trail.
- The trail pops out onto Powerline Trail. Cross under the powerlines and go past the warming hut. You will find a well-established and -marked single-track trail

here. Note on the ground the old water pipes made of hollowed-out cedar logs held together with thick wire binding.

- Walk past pleasant Fourth Lake. There is a nice spot for a break here, in the shade.
- The well-defined trail continues north and up, following the route of the Pacific cross-country ski trail. For most of the remainder of the hike, the foliage is 90 per cent blueberry bushes, so watch out for hungry but happy bears, particularly at dusk and dawn.
- You'll see another small lake to the right.
- Eventually the trail hugs the left side of the slope. You will see a signpost marking the continuation of Baden-Powell Trail towards the Cypress downhill ski area. Do not take this; continue climbing up and north. The sign indicates 2.2 km back to parking, 1.8 km to the summit.
- Eventually you will come to three pleasant photo opportunities and welcome rest spots for kids: a giant "giraffe tree" with space in its crook for five children to sit and pose; a bench with a good view of the Grouse–Crown range; and the giant root ball of an overturned tree.
- Eventually, the somewhat too long blueberry switchbacks end and you will pop out into a pleasant slabby meadow of twisted trees and mossy tarns (sometimes called the "Heather Lakes"). Water striders scurry over the ponds. Boletes abound here in the autumn. A mysterious rope marks the southern boundary. Hollyburn Peak is right above you to the north.
- Continue north and up. The trail turns into a series of safe climbing walls that will delight kids.
- You will soon come to the citadel of the peak proper. The trail snakes up and to the right. There are a few narrow steps on rock walls with a 2- to 3-m potential fall. At this point, hold the hands of any small children.
- Punch through the trees to see the final low peak, which is also a fun and safe climb for kids.

Alternative route: If you are feeling tired or it is getting dark on the descent, you can take Powerline Trail from the warming hut at Fourth Lake back down to the parking lot.

ROUTE 2:

FROM WEST – DOWNHILL SKI AREA

Take Baden-Powell Trail east. The trail entrance is between the parking lot and the ski slope on north side and is well marked.

- The narrow, well-travelled single-track is eroded and rooty in places.
- Cross two creeks before coming to a wide, open cross-country ski trail that is covered in blueberry bushes. You will see a signpost saying it is 2.2 km back to the parking lot and 1.8 km to the summit.
- Go left and uphill along the well-marked trail to the top.

ROUTE 3:

FROM WEST – STRACHAN

Note: This route is muddy and slippery when wet; also much rougher than the others.

- Follow the trail down from Strachan. The way through the alpine meadows is generally obvious, cutting a path through grass and heather. At times, paint splotches mark the route.

- The trail soon becomes denser in the heather and then cuts into the forest. Follow this steep section. The roots and rocks here are slippery when wet. At most times, the Sky Chair and the ski run are visible through the trees to your west (right).
- The trail passes the T-33 plane-crash site.
- Eventually, the trail hits a plateau and heads east. You will see a small pond (Emily Lake) to your left and the Strachan service road to your right.
- After the valley floor you will start a steep climb up.
- The trail proceeds uphill, occasionally past and around eroded muddy patches and fallen trees.
- The route pops out on the north-northwest point of the peak of Hollyburn.

GROUSE MOUNTAIN AREA

(9 PEAKS)

Grouse Mountain, an all-season playground and ski resort, is the gateway not only to several rewarding peaks of incremental challenge but also the route to a pleasing but tough loop connecting Grouse with Lynn Canyon via the Hanes Valley. Do not be deceived by the tourists, the tidy signposts, the groomed trails, and the gentle front peaks of Grouse, Dam, and Little Goat. Many hikers get lured onto these trails unprepared, with inadequate equipment or experience, and pay for their error through a chilly night or worse.

On the summit in the second ascent of Grouse, October 1894, were Sidney Williams, Mr. Knox, R. Parkinson, and Ernest Cleveland.

To reach the peaks of Grouse, you will pass the chalet (with theatre, restaurants, and gift shops), the ice rink, the lumberjack show, the BeaverTails kiosk, the grizzly bear pen, the raptor show site, and most of the resort's 26 ski runs.

As the closest peak to downtown Vancouver, Grouse received the first attention for recreation. In 1906 Rochfort Henry Sperling, the general manager of the British Columbia Electric Railway Company, in the process of installing what would become three tramway lines in North Vancouver, envisioned the extension of the Lonsdale line to the top of Grouse Mountain: "...and the summit being covered with snow all the year round it may at a future period become a popular tourist resort." In 1911 a plan was advanced to build an inclined railway from near Clements Avenue and Capilano Road to the top of the peak. The development would include a hotel, sport facilities, and what would be the world's most powerful telescope, built by astronomer Thomas Shearman and financed by Edward Mahon, the owner of the Capilano suspension bridge. Some money was raised and a groundbreaking ceremony was held, but the project was abandoned due to the First World War.

Grouse was first developed as a ski area by Scandinavian Vancouverites in the 1920s and rapidly grew in popularity. Resort plans rekindled afresh. In October 1926 the Grouse Mountain Highway was opened, and a toll charged, by the Alpine Scenic Highway Company, headed by A.S. Williamson and William Curtis Shelley.

Grouse Mountain Chalet, circa 1930.

In November 1926 the Grouse Mountain chalet was built on the site currently occupied by the rental shop. A 1927 map of the Grouse Mountain plateau shows an extensive network of trails, with exotic-sounding faux-Chinook placenames. Some of these remain in popular use – Thunderbird Ridge, Flint and Feather – while others have vanished in the mist of time: Mowitch Ridge (Little Goat Mountain) and Smanet Ridge (Goat Ridge). Again a resort was planned, and even the plan for Shearman's observatory was resurrected. The development was then struck by three disasters. In 1928 the Williamson–Shelley business went into receivership. In 1929 the Great Depression hit. In 1930 the Second Narrows Bridge was struck by a barge and was not rebuilt until 1934. In 1935 the property reverted to the District of North Vancouver for non-payment of taxes. The District operated the ski facilities until the formation in 1964 of the private Grouse Mountain Resort, chaired by Andrew Saxton Sr. The ambitious plans continued: unfulfilled 1968 development plans for the Grouse plateau included a multi-storey hotel, convention centre, shops, apartments, a swimming pool, and curling and skating rinks.

In the interim, people continued to flock to the Grouse Mountain area for recreation. By the 1930s a village of some 100 cabins had sprung up at the base of the ski run called The Cut. Even today, ruined huts, along with bedsprings, bottles, pots and pans, and various cabin detritus, can be found there. In 1949 a double chairlift, one of the first in North America, was built, allowing skiing down The Cut from the top of the ridge. In 1951 the Village Chair was opened, constructed of wooden towers and running from the top of Skyline Drive. Both of these lifts were removed in the early 1970s. The chalet itself burned down in 1962.

There are seven main front access routes to the Grouse plateau (as well as a mess of other trails of varying consistency). We list them from west to east. The easiest and most popular is the Grouse Mountain Skyride, at the top of Nancy Greene Way, commemorating the Canadian ski slalom gold medallist in the 1968 Olympics. The Skyride, costing $44.95 per adult at time of writing, will give you expansive views of Vancouver and UBC, Stanley Park and Lions Gate Bridge, North Vancouver, Capilano Lake, and The Lions. The first such skyride – the blue one, used now for service and overflow – was opened on December 15, 1966, by W.A.C. Bennett; the present, larger, red skyride, was installed in 1976.

To the immediate east of the Skyride parking lot, along Baden-Powell Trail, is the ever- and over-popular Grouse Grind (usually open April–November). The Grouse Grind was created in the early 1980s by renowned trail blazers Don McPherson and Phil Severy, who must have had no idea what a conga line it would become, with over 150,000 people hiking the trail annually. Climbing 2,830 stairs, gaining 853 m of elevation over the course of 2.9 km up the mountainside, with an average grade of 17 per cent (and short, steeper sections of up to 30 per cent), it is nicknamed "Nature's Stairmaster." With its perpetual scents of sunscreen, tobacco, perfume, and cologne, it is far from natural, though. Watch climbers toting sandals, high heels, baby carriers, excess fat, and other inappropriate gear as they keel over, halfway up, and beg for mercy.

Off the Grind is Flint and Feather Trail, named after a 1912 book of poetry by Pauline Johnson (the trail dates back to at least the 1920s). This more robust route up between the BCMC and the Grouse Grind at times requires the use of hands but is rewarded by good views. To access the Flint and Feather, start upward on the Grind. At the bridge, turn right off the Grind. Go east and up. Then cross a dry creekbed west and up, and climb. Unmarked but obvious.

To the east of the Grind trailhead is BCMC Trail, carved out by the British Columbia Mountaineering Club, first in 1908 to the east of its present route ("Old BCMC Trail"), and then, in its current form, in 1923. Once an un-Grind-like, peaceful climb, it is now almost as crowded, but at least features a less rocky and more sylvan trail. About 350 m up BCMC Trail a side route to the west connects to the Grouse Grind, crossing the west branch of Mackay Creek (pronounced "Mac-eye" and the "K" is lower-case).

To the east of BCMC Trail, about 1.6 km along Baden-Powell Trail, are two minor tracks that will take you to the base of The Cut ski run: Larsen Trail (blazed in 1910) and Mackay Creek Trail, to the west and east respectively from the west branch of Mackay Creek. These routes are sketchier but rarely hiked, so if you're seeking solitude, they're your best bet.

At the top of Skyline Drive runs Skyline Trail, a steep and slippery route that follows the path of the old Grouse Mountain Village chair. The bases of the towers are still visible. Much farther east, the north end of Mountain Highway morphs into the former Grouse Mountain Highway, running about 10 km through 14 switchbacks and ending near the Grouse Mountain chalet. Dodge the mountain bikers.

In April 2017 Metro Vancouver announced the creation of a new regional park that will encompass most of the trails and territory set out above.

GETTING THERE

From Lions Gate Bridge, drive east to Capilano Road. Drive north up Capilano Road, which turns into Nancy Green Way. Arrive at Grouse Mountain Skyride. Pay parking is available in paved and gravel lots.

Note: The route lengths and times listed here are measured from Grouse Mountain Chalet. If you are hiking up to the chalet from the parking lots at the foot of Grouse (rather than taking the Skyride up), don't forget to add the length of whichever trail you'll take: the Grind is 2.9 km, the BCMC slightly longer. Similarly add your Grind/BCMC time: the average is 90 minutes, though co-author Bill Maurer once did the Grind in 55 minutes and BCMC in an hour. Please note also that all times and distances we give describe the round trip.

This entire area can be done as one long day trip but it is more commonly split into two shorter ones. The peaks of Fromme, Little Goat, Dam, and Grouse are quite accessible early in the season while there is still snow on the ground. That leaves West Crown, Crown, Goat, Goat Ridge, and Forks for the warmer period.

ROUTE 1 (GROUSE AREA)

From the Grouse parking lot take the BCMC trail to a fork at 890 m where a minor path heads east to the base of the Screaming Eagle chair. Continue traversing across the bottom of the ski run to a gravel road leading northeast to Mountain Highway. This does a switchback where it crosses Mosquito Creek and then heads southeast to the base of the Fromme trail. Follow this to Fromme and then descend via the north side trail, which passes a small lake as you descend. At 935 m you will hit another junction with the Pipeline (Eric the Red) trail. Turn to the right here and notice the remnants of the old wooden water pipe as you head up this infrequently used route behind Grouse which takes you to the Alpine trail. Turn right again here and head up Little Goat via Ridge Trail. Now turn around and follow Ridge Trail over Dam and on to Grouse. The final section takes you back to the chalet and down BCMC Trail.

Round-trip distance:
14.8 km

Time:
8:03

Elevation gain:
1484 m

ROUTE 2 (CROWN AREA)

From the Grouse parking lot take the Grouse Grind trail to the chalet. From there take the Alpine trail around Dam and Little Goat to the junction with the route heading to Crown Pass on the left. Descend to the pass and continue uphill to Crown. From the top you can see West Crown to the southwest. Return to the ridge and follow it to West Crown. There is a faint trail with some flagging here. There is a small rock cairn on the east side of the main Crown trail where West Crown Trail heads west. From the top of West Crown head back to Crown Pass along the route you came. Then back up to the junction with the Alpine trail. Turn left at this junction and follow the trail north to Goat. From Goat you can see Goat Ridge Peak in the distance to the east. Follow the Goat Ridge trail to get there, passing by a couple of very swimmable tarns en route. A dogleg to the north takes you to Forks. Return the way you came, bypassing Goat on its north side, and head back to the chalet via the Alpine trail. Descend to the parking lot via BCMC Trail.

Round-trip distance:
20.1 km

Time:
11:01

Elevation gain:
2097 m

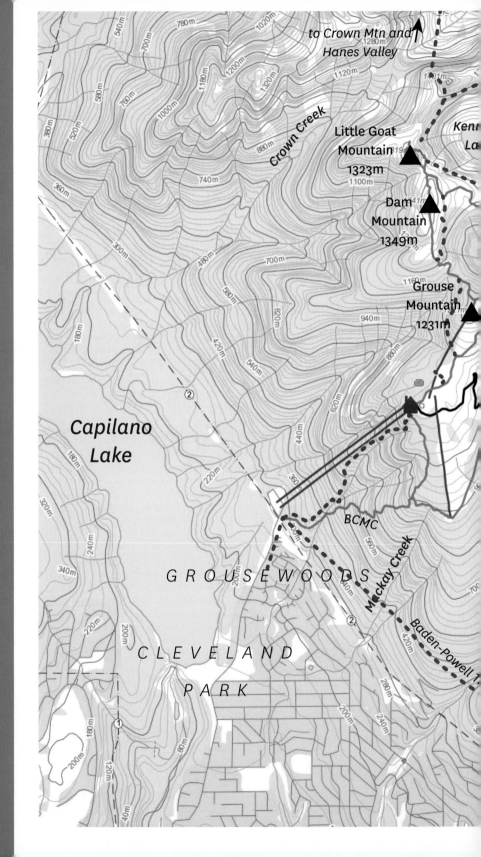

to Crown Mtn and
Hanes Valley

Crown Creek

Little Goat
Mountain
1323m

Dam
Mountain
1349m

Grouse
Mountain
1231m

Kenr
La

Capilano
Lake

BCMC

GROUSEWOODS

Mackay Creek

Baden-Powell Tr

CLEVELAND

PARK

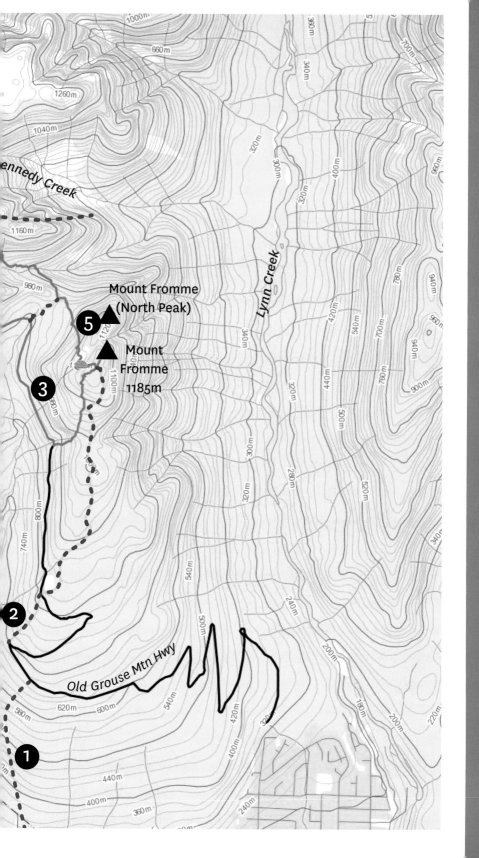

Mount Fromme
(North Peak)

Mount
Fromme
1185m

Kennedy Creek

Lynn Creek

Old Grouse Mtn Hwy

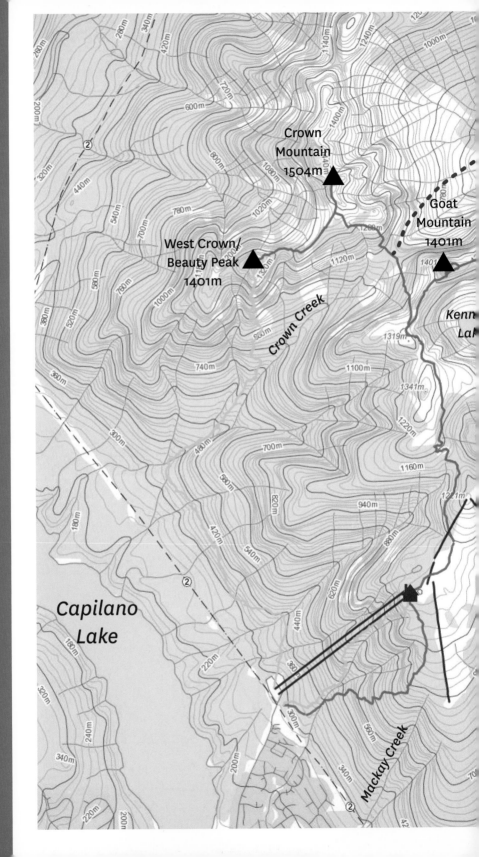

to Lynn
Lake

Forks Peak
1160m

Goat Ridge
Peak 1269m

Wickenden Creek

Kennedy Creek

Lynn Creek

1171m.

GROUSE MOUNTAIN

(GRO) (1231 M)

Take the Skyride up the North Shore's most painless and visited peak.

CAUTION:
Surprisingly slippery gravel on Heaven's Sake ski run trail on east side of peak.

PROMINENCE:
86 m.

LATITUDE/LONGITUDE:
N49.38611 W123.07639.

BANG FOR BUCK:
2/5

PEAK VIEW:
3/5. Good view of Vancouver. And paragliders.

TRUE SUMMIT LOCATION:
Under Olympic Express chairlift (not in use in the summer).

HEADWATERS:
Eighteen Mile (into Capilano River), Mosquito, and Mackay Creeks (into Burrard Inlet).

BEST VIEWS FROM:
Lonsdale, Spanish Banks, downtown Vancouver, Burnaby.

TRIP INFORMATION

Round-trip distance: 1 km round trip from chalet.

Elevation gain: 140 m.

Time: 0.5–1 hour from chalet (0:50).

Difficulty: 2/5 Grouse Grind / BCMC, 0/5 if using chairlift, 1/5 if walking.

Snow free: Mid-June.

Must-sees: Lumberjacks, grizzly bears, wood sculptures, ziplines, beer gardens, and beavertails.

Scenery: 2/5. City views, the Eye of the Wind, and tourists galore.

Kids: 5/5. Easy, with many other things to see. Not to mention ready access to snacks.

Dogs: 5/5. Must be on leash.

Runnability: 4/5. Dodge the tourists.

Terrain: Gravel road.

Public transit: #232 bus from Phibbs Exchange or #236 from Lonsdale Quay.

Cell coverage: On peak.

Sun: Mostly exposed.

Water: Available at lodge.

Route links: Sweep with Dam, Little Goat, Goat, and Crown. West Crown may be ambitious.

HISTORY

Name origin: Named on October 12, 1894, after the blue grouse shot by a hiking party that included Sydney Williams (and Ernest Albert Cleveland, later chief commissioner of the Greater Vancouver Water District, after whom Cleveland Dam is named). Name used in 1912 North Vancouver map. A 1926 proposal to rename Grouse as "Mount Vancouver" failed to gain traction.

Name status: Official. Adopted December 7, 1937.

First ascent: October 5, 1894, climbed by Sydney "Sid" Williams and Captain Phil Thompson. The first female ascent was by Mrs. Roger Casement in 1894 or (more likely) 1897. Climbed by local First Nations people years before.

Grouse Mountain is Vancouver's most-visited tourist attraction, with attendance of some 1.2 million each year. It is the most accessible of all of the peaks, and can be summited with little physical effort via the Skyride and the Peak chairlift.

That said, Grouse is worth the trip, beyond just ticking off a bag list. There are splendid views of Vancouver. If you are lucky, you will see paragliders launching from the summit. Just below the peak is the Eye of the Wind, a 1.5 MW wind turbine, completed in 2010. The plan was for the windmill to supply 25 per cent of the resort's electricity, although it rarely seems to be moving. It is the first wind turbine built in North America in an extreme high-altitude location. Its observation deck offers excellent views of the North Shore peaks, even offering a view of the obscure Echo Peak/Mt. Perrault.

In her 1911 story "The Lost Island," Pauline Johnson (Tekahionwake) tells of a shaman cursed and obsessed with visions of the coming Europeans and their future city:

> Only this haunting dream of the coming white man's camp he could not drive away; it was the only thing in life he had tried to kill and failed. It drove him from the feasting, drove him from the pleasant lodges, the fires, the dancing, the story-telling of his people in their camp by the water's edge, where the salmon thronged and the deer came down to drink of the mountain-streams. He left the Indian village, chanting his wild songs as he went. Up through the mighty forests he climbed, through the trailless deep mosses and matted vines, up to the summit of what the white men call Grouse Mountain. For many days he camped there. He ate no food, he drank no water, but sat and sang his medicine-songs through the dark hours and through the day. Before him – far beneath his feet – lay the narrow strip of land between the two salt waters. Then the Sagalie Tyee gave him the power to see far into the future. He looked across a hundred years, just as he looked across what you call the Inlet, and he saw mighty lodges built close together, hundreds and thousands of them – lodges of stone and wood, and long straight trails to divide them. He saw these trails thronging with Pale-faces; he heard the sound of the white man's paddle-dip on the waters, for it is not silent like the Indian's; he saw the white man's trading posts, saw the fishing-nets, heard his speech. Then the vision faded as gradually as it came. The narrow strip of land was his own forest once more.[10]

The shaman's Grouse Mountain vision inspired him to tell his people to travel up the North (Indian) Arm in quest of a lost island which, when found, would restore his people to greatness.

The first recorded European climb of Grouse (and possibly Dam and Goat) is recounted by Neal Carter and G.B. Warren:

> In the fall of 1894 a party including Rev. L. Norman Tucker, Messrs. W. Skene and Burnett attempted to ascend some local mountain (the bluffs of Grouse or Dam from Capilano according to one account, and The Lions from Howe sound according to another) but because of the heavy brush and some bluffs, reported such ascents were "not feasible." A Mr. Sydney Williams, who had a shack about 400 feet up the hill from the present foot of Lonsdale Avenue in North Vancouver, and a Capt. Phil Thompson disagreed with the above opinion, so on or about October 5, 1894, they climbed Grouse Mountain from the shack to prove their contention. This party may have gone farther, possibly as far as Dam or Goat.

Fired by success, Williams led a party back up to Grouse the next weekend (October 12, 1894), blazing a trail up Mosquito Creek. The party consisted of Williams, George W. Edwards (a photographer), Ernest Cleveland (later of the Vancouver Water Board, and namesake of the dam), R. Parkinson (a surveyor), and a Mr. Knox (of Duncan, British Columbia, secretary to the lieutenant-governor). It took four and a half hours to reach the peak of Grouse from the Lonsdale shack. On Grouse they shot a blue grouse. They then continued on to Dam and Goat Mountains.

In 1953, noted BCMC mountaineer Arthur Tinniswood Dalton described the route of the early climbs up Grouse:

> Trythall's Clearing, North Vancouver, 1902: I started to climb Grouse Mountain about 1895. A very poor trail led up what is now Lonsdale Ave.; you were considered quite skillful if you could keep on it; we called it "Pig Alley"; some Chinamen kept pigs. It took us a day to get to "Trythall's Gash"; another day to the top, and a third day to come down, – three days. Trythall had slashed about two acres, and built a poor log cabin; no door; we often stayed there a day to rest. It was about two or three hundred feet under "Trythall's Creek," now called "Mosquito Creek."

> ...It was about two acres of slashed timber and a poor log cabin sunk in a great wilderness of primeval forest which covered all North Vancouver. Land cost one dollar per acre. A poor trail led up what is now Lonsdale Ave. to 13th, swung west, followed roughly Mahon Ave.; was quite close to Mosquito Creek on Lot 32, D.L. 883. It adjoined what in 1953 is known as "Canyon Heights." The ascent of Grouse Mountain took three days: one to Trythall's, one to the top, and one down again to the ferry. The clearing was just below where the Grouse Mountain Ski Lift aerial tramway starts. William J. Trythall reached Vancouver from England 21 June 1888. He founded Trythall & Son, printers, and printed the first Vancouver directory, 1888.[11]

Put in terms of modern geography, early hikers would arrive by ferry to the base of Lonsdale Road, hike up Lonsdale to Lonsdale Trail, which veered along 13th Street towards the modern-day Mahon Avenue and to Mosquito Creek. From there it proceeded to the top of what is now Prospect Drive, and then across the creek and up Grouse Mountain Trail. On the typical two-day trek, many hikers would stop or stay at a cabin built by William John Trythall, a printer and bookbinder, who would leave the door unlocked for guests.

In 1902 all of Vancouver was enraptured by the sight of a bonfire on top of Grouse lit by climbers; newspapers had provided prior publicity for the climb and illumination. Today, of course, we take the sight of glowing lights on our peaks for granted, but in 1902 Vancouverites turned off the lights in their homes to be able to see this miraculous sight.

By 1910, thanks to streetcars and the improvement of trails up Grouse, the gruelling trek described by Dalton was reduced to three or so hours: approximately 11,000 persons climbed it that year. Most treks started at Carisbrooke Park, on Upper Lonsdale near the old terminus of the Lonsdale streetcar. They would then hike uphill, cross Mosquito Creek, and climb up the Old BCMC and later other trails.

In 1906 the BCMC constructed its "Red Shack" on the lower slopes of Grouse Mountain at around 833 m, off Old BCMC Trail. It served as the staging grounds for forays up the Grouse Mountain peaks. It was soon replaced with a larger cabin in 1910, then another in 1926. In addition to trip planning and rest, these cabins hosted annual Christmas and New Year's Eve dinners, including roast turkey and oyster soup.

On September 2, 1929, Winston Churchill, Britain's chancellor of the exchequer at the time, visited Grouse Mountain and dined in the original chalet. He proclaimed the view from Grouse to be "the finest sight [he had] ever been privileged to see." He immediately took out his paints and canvas and sketched the view of the city, with the Olympic Mountains in the background.

On February 12, 1954, Lt. Lamar J. Barlow of the US Air Force crashed his F-86 Sabre jet, armed with 24 rockets, beside the old chairlift at 800 m. His speed was estimated at 760 miles per hour. The cause was a "ghost" radar signal that apparently made him believe he was near Tacoma rather than North Vancouver. The wreckage of the plane's engine is still visible at the site, just off the steep Skyline Trail leading up to the "Cut."

Most of Grouse Mountain is granodiorite, a plutonic rock of which Plymouth Rock and the Rosetta Stone are composed. As with Mt. Seymour, the main Grouse ski run sloping toward Vancouver is built on a relict of the peneplain, the ancient flat surface before uplift. While this surface has been eroded at lower elevations, it survives in these two areas, to the recreational advantage of skiers.

In recent years Grouse's peak has been guarded by an aggressive namesake bird known to attack hikers. Perhaps it was avenging the death of its ancestor murdered by the Williams party, or maybe it was just a lone and lonely male, bereft of a mate. Some have called it Grotius the Grumpy Grouse. Beware.

Route 1:

VIA SKYRIDE

Easy, lazy route up: take the Skyride. From the Skyride, walk past the hideously disproportionate wood sculptures, following the grizzly bear footprints on the pavement, to the Peak chairlift. Jump on and go up.

- The disembarkation platform is the high point of the peak, but the true summit is probably at the site of the Olympic Express chairlift (not in use in the summer).

Route 2:

FROM GROUSE MOUNTAIN PARKING LOT

If you prefer to hike from the ski area parking lot, proceed east on the popular Baden-Powell Trail.

- Two popular (some would say "too popular") trails climb the mountain off Baden-Powell Trail, as well as the more minor routes described in the introduction.
- The Grouse Grind, the first, westernmost trail, is very well marked, both by signs as well as the perfume-and-sunscreen-scented throngs of pilgrims snaking up the trail.
- The less beaten (but still popular) route is about 250 m to the east along Baden-Powell Trail: the BCMC (British Columbia Mountaineering Club) trail.
- About 350 m up the BCMC trail a side path to the west connects to the Grouse Grind, crossing the west branch of Mackay (pronounced "Mac-eye") Creek. It also leads to the Flint and Feather Trail, a more robust route up between the BCMC and the Grouse Grind that at times requires the use of hands; you are rewarded by good views.
- The Grouse Grind and BCMC Trail are well marked; both lead to Grouse Mountain Chalet.
- Wherever your destination, it is prudent to load up on water at the chalet.
- **Grouse Mountain plateau:** Proceed uphill past the lumberjack show and the grizzly bear pen. At the base of the peak, take the road to the right up to the windmill.
- Take care: although the route is a gravel road, it is often slippery with pebbles or water in warm or wet weather.
- The disembarkation platform is the highest point of the peak, but the true summit is the loading area of the Olympic Express chairlift (not in use in the summer).

Route 3:

FROM NORTHWEST, OFF START OF DAM MOUNTAIN TRAIL

Note: This route is an unofficial "back door" that provides a forested way up Grouse.

- Walk to and past the grizzly bear pen.
- Take the gravel road at the start of the Dam Mountain trail, curving around the base of Grouse.
- Where that road turns left (west) to become a scree-ish trail up, do not follow it. Instead, turn right (east) and go up a duffy, pebbly slope. Aim straight for the windmill.
- Take care not to go up a false trail slightly to the north; it leads to steep cliffs.
- You will see the occasional flagging tape as a narrow but clear and consistent trail winds up the west slope of Grouse over heather and fallen trees.
- The trail pops out just north and down the road from the chairlift disembarkation platform, near where the Grouse Mountain road turns right (east) towards the windmill.

DAM MOUNTAIN
(DAM) (1349 M)

Stunning views of Crown and the Camel for gentle effort.

CAUTION:
Cliffs to the west.

PROMINENCE:
99 m.

LATITUDE/LONGITUDE:
N49.39417 W123.08111.

BANG FOR BUCK:
4/5

PEAK VIEW:
3/5. Views of Crown and the Camel.

TRUE SUMMIT LOCATION:
Obvious pointy peak.

HEADWATERS:
Kennedy Creek, many tributary creeks of Hanes Creek (into Lynn Creek); Crown Creek, Ferguson Creek (into Capilano River); Kennedy Creek (into Lynn Creek).

BEST VIEWS FROM:
Grouse Mountain Skyride, Crown, Hollyburn.

TRIP INFORMATION

Round-trip distance: 4 km from chalet.
Elevation gain: 269 m.
Time: 1–3 hours (1:00).
Difficulty: 1/5.
Snow free: Usually early to mid-June.
Must-sees: Thunderbird Ridge; summit slide.
Scenery: 3/5.
Kids: 5/5. Children will feel like heroes and love sliding down the rocky peak to the trail.
Dogs: 4/5.
Runnability: 4/5.
Terrain: Well-marked trail through second-growth forest.
Public transit: #232 bus from Phibbs Exchange or #236 from Lonsdale Quay.
Cell coverage: Good on peak; inconsistent on east side.
Sun: Tree cover for hike. Exposed from Skyride to trailhead and on peak.
Water: Load up at Chalet/Skyride.
Route links: Sweep with Crown, Goat, and/or Little Goat Mountains.

HISTORY

Name origin: On October 12, 1894, Sydney Williams, Captain Phil Thompson, Ernest Cleveland, R. Parkinson (a surveyor), and a Mr. Knox of Duncan were shooting in this area; from the top of this mountain they could see the old waterworks dam on the Capilano River, hence the name "Dam Mountain." The name is not connected to the Cleveland Dam, which was not built until 1954.
Name status: Official. Adopted December 7, 1937, on 92G/6, as labelled on Alan

Base of Dam–Grouse connector trail.

John Campbell's 1927 map, and on BC map 5B, 1929. Used in 1910.

Other names: The 1912 C.J. Heaney map referred to it as "Dam Peak."

First ascent: October 12, 1894, by a party including Ernest Albert Cleveland (see Grouse). The Williams–Thompson party may have reached Dam (again see Grouse) on October 5, 1894. Likely climbed long before by Indigenous people, hunters, or prospectors.

Other write-up: Hui.

Dam should be one of everyone's first climbs: nicely signposted and not too far. It opens one's eyes to the glories of North Shore peakbagging, with close-up views of Crown and the Camel. Its summit slab provides a fun slide for kids (have them wear old pants).

Hikers today approach Dam via the same trails that have been used for a hundred years. The 1927 Grouse Mountain brochure map shows the trail wrapping around the west side of Grouse Mountain, in its present path; the steep chasm to the southwest is called "Royal Chasm." Where the trail ceases to be a gravel road and turns left and up, it was referred to as "Whistler Pass" after the (now vanished) marmots who also gave their name to our most famous local ski resort. At Whistler Pass the now vanished Illahie Trail (Chinook for "dirt") led down and east into the valley between Grouse and Thunderbird Ridge.

On October 12, 1894, Sydney Williams led a party up to Grouse via Mosquito Creek and on to Goat Mountain. The group consisted of Williams, George W. Edwards (a photographer), Ernest Cleveland (later of the Vancouver Water Board, and namesake of the dam), R. Parkinson (a surveyor), and a Mr. Knox (of Duncan, BC, secretary to the Lieutenant-Governor). After bagging a peak and a grouse on Grouse, they continued to Dam, which, it was noticed, provided a view of the dam across the Capilano River below. Built in 1889 by the Vancouver Waterworks Co., the dam became a public utility in 1891. It was located several kilometres north of the present-day Cleveland Dam, and its site is now submerged beneath the upper third of Capilano Lake. As an April 16, 1910, *Province* article puckishly noted: "… [Dam Mountain]… was not named in commemoration of any particular brand of language used by the first climbers when they stubbed their toes or stirred up wasps' nests during the ascent…"

It was on a shoulder of Dam that famed mountaineer Don Munday (1890–1950) built his cabin, Evenglow, in 1918. It was constructed of cedar gathered and split on site, with a fireplace of river rock hauled up the mountain on his back in a sling. He and Phyllis Munday (1894–1990) honeymooned here in February 1920.

ROUTE

Grouse Mountain Chalet to Ridge Trail fork: From Grouse Mountain Chalet, hike on the road heading up the hill. You should pass the first chairlift, the lumberjack show, and the grizzly bear pen.

- Hike to the bottom of the Peak chair (as this is the only chair operating during the summer, it should be easy to spot). A gravel road winds to the left across the base of the peak of Grouse. You will see a large sign with a registration book. Sign in at the map kiosk, then take this gravel road. It eventually turns left (west) up into a narrower and steeper trail.

- You will soon meet a pile of creosote beams supporting a pipe bringing water from Kennedy Lake (which you will later see) for use at the Grouse Mountain resort.
- After a small meadow the trail soon forks. Take Ridge Trail on the left (the trail on the right, Alpine Trail, traverses Dam and meets up with Ridge Trail at the Little Goat–Goat col).

Alpine–Ridge trail fork to Dam Peak: At times the trail is a bit steep and rooty, but always manageable. When very dry or very wet, it may be a little slippery.

At the junction of Ridge Trail and Alpine Trail.

- Emerge into a small meadow with more signage. Keep climbing up.
- Enter an even larger, heather meadow, where there is a helicopter pad built of a grid of cedar beams that kids love to march along.
- The trail leaves this area to the right (east). The final ascent to the peak comes from the east and then twists to the west, to a moderately sloped granite ramp leading up to the summit. Kids of all ages will enjoy practising rock climbing up and bum-sliding back down this slab.
- Enjoy the butterflies and dragonflies buzzing around the peak.
- If Dam is your final destination, do not stop at the peak. Go north just a few metres to enjoy a hitherto obscured view of West Crown, Crown, and the Camel.
- For a descent, you can return down Ridge Trail, or, for variety and a less steep route, go north to join Alpine Trail, which you can then take south to hug the east slope of Dam back to the start of the trail.

LITTLE GOAT MOUNTAIN
(LIL) (1323 M)

Pleasant hike to modest mountain with reasonable views.

CAUTION:
South trail down is sometimes slippery.

PROMINENCE:
58 m.

LATITUDE/LONGITUDE:
N49.39806 W123.08334.

BANG FOR BUCK:
4/5

PEAK VIEW:
2/5

TRUE SUMMIT LOCATION:
Well-trodden knoll in centre of peak plateau.

HEADWATERS:
Small streams.

BEST VIEWS FROM:
Crown, Dam.

TRIP INFORMATION
Round-trip distance: 5.2 km from the chalet.
Elevation gain: 243 m.
Time: 1.5–3 hours (1:30).
Difficulty: 2/5. Easy side trip from Dam or Goat Mountains.
Snow free: Mid-June.
Must-sees: View of Crown and Camel; heather.
Scenery: 3/5.
Kids: 5/5. Easy bag for children.
Dogs: 5/5.
Runnability: 5/5. A gentle hill workout as part of a superb run from the Skyride.
Terrain: Well-established trails through second-growth forest to heather-covered peak.
Public transit: #232 bus from Phibbs Exchange or #236 from Lonsdale Quay.
Cell coverage: Yes.
Sun: Sufficient shade. Even peak has trees for shade.
Water: None.
Route links: Good sweep with all peaks between Crown and Grouse Mountain.

HISTORY
Name origin: So named because it is the next small peak from Goat Mountain, not because it resembles a diminutive ruminant.
Name status: Official. Adopted December 7, 1937. It was used at least as early as 1926.
First ascent: October 12, 1894, by party including Ernest Albert Cleveland (see Grouse). The Williams–Thompson party may have reached Little Goat (again see Grouse) on October 5, 1894.
Other names: The 1927 Grouse Mountain brochure map referred to it as "Mowitch Ridge" (Chinook for "deer" or "wild animal").
Other write-ups: Hanna, routes to Goat Mountain and Hanes Valley travel via Little Goat; Hui.

Think of Little Goat as a bonus peak, a pleasant side-excursion between Dam and Goat. Although it was once obscure, the trail is now well trodden and the powers that operate Grouse Mountain have recently erected guideposts and signs making Little Goat part of both Ridge Trail and Alpine Trail running from Grouse over Dam to Goat (we like to think the Bagger Challenge contributed to this revitalized interest in Little Goat). The flat peak is covered in heather, and its rocky outcrops with their fine views of Crown and Goat make for a splendid picnic site.

There are two approaches to Little Goat off the trail, both marked: one from the south, at the north foot of Dam (somewhat steep and often dusty or muddy), the other from the north, just above Goat Mountain junction, and after you have traversed around Little Goat along the trail. The north approach is better established and gentler. It takes you to a heather-covered peak plateau. The peak is an obvious knoll, shaded by a large tree with some axe marks. Here you can take foolish pictures of your children with stuffed goat animals and plastic toys, and relax as they scamper up and down the knoll with little risk of harm.

In the 1920s, Edmund Atholl Agur (1895 Winnipeg – 1927 Kennedy Lake), a friend of the Mundays, had a cabin on Little Goat which was often visited on BCMC trips. On February 19, 1927, Agur was swept 800 feet to his death by an avalanche collapsing into the Kennedy Lake cirque. His body was not found until July of that year. He is remembered in Mt. Agur, located beside Mt. Munday in the Waddington Range.

ROUTE
Follow the trail description from Grouse Mountain Chalet to Alpine Trail–Ridge Trail fork.
- For the easier route to Little Goat, go to the right to traverse Dam. (Alternatively, climb up and over Dam via Ridge Trail and rejoin Alpine Trail on the north side of Dam.)

Alpine Trail fork to Little Goat fork: Alpine Trail has a few rooty sections but is well marked and not difficult.
- After a short while you will rise and have a decent view east, of the Needles and Coliseum, and Cathedral, as well as the turnoff to Thunderbird Ridge.
- Continue north to the north base of Dam.
- Continue down to a broad section of trail where there is a signpost for the first (the south) turnoff to Little Goat Mountain. Hike up the trail, which is a little eroded and at times slippery.
- Alternatively, continue along Alpine Trail to the north base of Little Goat, where a more solid and better-marked trail leads back up to the peak.
- The peak, while treed, is obvious: a rocky slab surrounded by several solid trees. Excellent views of Goat and Crown.

GOAT MOUNTAIN

(GOA) (1401 M)

Nice hike and adventure-playground ascent to a granite dome peak with fine views.

CAUTION:
Although the trail is well established, there are some sheer drops toward the end.

PROMINENCE:
336 m.

LATITUDE/LONGITUDE:
N49.40361 W123.07889.

BANG FOR BUCK:
5/5

PEAK VIEW:
4/5. N: Crown, Sky Pilot; E: Echo, Cathedral, Coliseum, Needles, Seymour, Robie Reid and Judge Howay; S: Little Goat.

TRUE SUMMIT LOCATION:
South end of peak, covered in paint splotches.

HEADWATERS:
Kennedy Creek (into Lynn Creek).

BEST VIEWS FROM:
Hollyburn, Crown.

TRIP INFORMATION

Round-trip distance: 7 km from the chalet.

Elevation gain: 321 m.

Time: 2–4 hours (2:30).

Difficulty: 2/5. Well-marked trail.

Snow free: Usually early to mid-June.

Must-sees: Splendid views; beautiful Goat Ridge; slab approach.

Scenery: 4/5.

Kids: 4/5. For hardy children; excellent first adventure to push them.

Dogs: 4/5.

Runnability: 4/5. Excellent run from Skyride, to steep final slog.

Terrain: Second-growth forest.

Public transit: #232 bus from Phibbs Exchange or #236 from Lonsdale Quay.

Cell coverage: Usually.

Sun: Sufficient shade until totally exposed peak.

Water: *None except for a few seasonal tarns on the peak.*

Route links: Good sweep with all peaks between Crown and Grouse Mountain.

HISTORY

Name origin: After the poor mountain goat shot by hunters here in 1894.

Name status: Official. Adopted December 7, 1937.

Other names: The 1912 C.J. Heaney map referred to it as "Goat Peak."

First ascent: October 12, 1894, by a party including Ernest Albert Cleveland (see Grouse). The Williams–Thompson party may have reached Goat (see Grouse) on October 5, 1894.

Other write-ups: Hanna, Hui.

Goat Mountain is a superb introduction for the hiker who would like to venture beyond the obvious routes in the front country to a semi-backcountry experience, all in the safe bosom of Grouse Mountain's well-marked and well-maintained trails. The views at the end – you can practically seize the Crown and pet the Camel – are highly rewarding, and the trail and distance will make any novice hiker feel proud and full of adventure. It is an excellent hike for a sturdy child with a sufficient sense of self-control. When they gaze at the 360° views stretching to Whistler and the Tantalus Range, to Vancouver, to Mt. Baker, to Vancouver Island, and the Olympic Mountains, and as they bound over and scamper up the rocky playground on the peak, they will feel like monarchs of the world. That said, be careful of the north edge, which is a sheer drop down to Hanes Valley. In the tarn you will see round water bugs, called "backswimmers" due to their tendency to, well, swim on their backs.

While a pleasing and relatively safe summer adventure, Goat Mountain is particularly risky in the winter. Weather can turn the snow to slippery ice, with no protection from the nearly sheer cliffs down to Kennedy Lake. In March 2002 a snowshoer fell 200 m down the face of Goat to the rocks above Kennedy Lake. He was killed on impact.

There is a good view down to a pretty cirque, Kennedy Lake, named after Thomas Leslie Kennedy (1866–1958), a North Vancouver councillor who proposed setting aside Kennedy Lake as a reservoir. Referred to earlier (as in 1916 and 1927) as "Goat Lake," the lake still serves as a reservoir for Grouse Mountain Resort and feeds the pleasing Kennedy Falls far below near Lynn Creek. To the west the slope drops sharply into Capilano Lake. The 1927 Grouse Mountain map refers to the sharp valley to the southwest of Dam as "Big Horn Canyon" and the creek to its northwest as "Mowitch Creek."

On October 12, 1894, Sydney Williams led a party up to Grouse via Mosquito Creek. The party consisted of Williams, George W. Edwards (a photographer), Ernest Cleveland (later of the Vancouver Water Board, and namesake of the dam), R. Parkinson (a surveyor), and a Mr. Knox (of Duncan, British Columbia: secretary to the lieutenant-governor). After bagging a peak and a grouse on Grouse, they continued to Dam, and then Goat Mountain, where they shot two goats on the summit, "one of which was secured while the other took a tumble over the cliffs above Crown Pass after being wounded."

Prominent BCMC member Charles Chapman and his new wife Millie spent their 1913 honeymoon on the peak.

ROUTE

Follow the trail description above from Grouse Mountain Chalet to the Alpine–Ridge trail fork.

- Follow the trail description above from the Alpine–Ridge fork to Little Goat fork.
  - Continue past the turnoff to Little Goat Mountain.
  - The dominant trail again traverses eastward, this time avoiding the peak of Little Goat Mountain.
  - Ascend to a trail marker that will send you back to Little Goat (Ridge Trail).

Goat Mountain Trail: Continue north, descending to a signpost clearly marking the Goat Mountain turnoff. Less than a kilometre remains to the summit.

- Continue north along a well-marked path, past small tarns, a helicopter pad, a raised North Shore Rescue barrel shelter and storage tower, and several sections of smooth rock.
- After a short rise there is a hidden sheer drop on the left (west), marked with a rope.
- A final descent to a boulder section and then a climb towards the peak.
- Soon you will hit a rocky cliff. Resist the temptation to climb up roots; instead, traverse to the left.
- The trail leads to a set of chains up a face of rock and roots. The chains are more for comfort than necessity; children will find them fun rather than scary.
- A sign marks the difficult, shorter, and steeper route (straight and up) or a more gradual route to the right. The steeper way is not terrifying.
- Both routes lead to a rocky wall at the east side of the Goat summit plateau. Look closely and you will see a natural staircase leading up the rock face to the left.
- This route takes you straight towards the true summit, to the south. Unfortunately it has been sprayed with yellow paint for inexplicable reasons. Superb views of Vancouver and Mt. Baker and Kennedy Lake below. Just south, there is a small tree offering some shade.

Goat Mountain.

GOAT RIDGE PEAK

(GRP) (1269 M)

*Very rewarding and scenic scamper to end of Goat Ridge, for grand views
of Norvan Valley and surrounding peaks.*

CAUTION:
In winter, acute risk of deadly fall
down sheer cliffs to south.

PROMINENCE:
59 m.

LATITUDE/LONGITUDE:
N49.40240 W123.06063.

BANG FOR BUCK:
5/5

PEAK VIEW:
3/5. Needles, Coliseum,
Burwell, Hanes Valley, Cathedral.

TRUE SUMMIT LOCATION:
Obvious rocky knoll just before
the end of the ridge.

HEADWATERS:
Kennedy Creek, Wickenden Creek
(into Lynn Creek).

BEST VIEWS FROM:
Goat, Grouse, Crown N1, North
Needle.

TRIP INFORMATION

Round-trip distance: 10.2 km from the Grouse base parking lot.
Elevation gain: 371 m.
Time: 3–6 hours (3:00).
Difficulty: 2/5.
Snow free: Late June.
Must-sees: Beautiful ridge; tarns.
Scenery: 4.5/5.
Kids: 4/5. Fun mixture of terrain.
Dogs: 5/5.
Runnability: 5/5. A gentle hill workout as part of a superb run from the Skyride.
Terrain: Well-established trails through second-growth forest to heather-covered peak.
Public transit: #232 bus from Phibbs Exchange or #236 from Lonsdale Quay.
Cell coverage: Generally yes.
Sun: Sufficient shade until nearly shadeless ridge.
Water: From tarns if necessary.
Route links: Good sweep with all peaks between Crown and Grouse Mountain.

HISTORY

Name origin: The small peak at the end of the ridge running east of Goat Mountain.
Name status: Unofficial.
First ascent: Frequently climbed well before 1923. First ascent likely soon after 1894.
Other write-up: Hanna, under Goat Mountain.

Goat Ridge Peak is one of the nicest trips in this entire book, and a very pleasant surprise. The gently rolling ridge walk snakes past low spruce and cedar and over granite slabs and heather meadows. Towards the end of the ridge, below the peak and cradled in a granite amphitheatre, are two ponds. The eastern one, smaller and shallower, called Tadpole Tarn, isn't quite deep enough for swimming. The slightly larger pond to the west, though, is about 10 feet deep and offers a refreshing dip, skinny or otherwise, on a hot day. It has been proposed to be named "Spouse Tarn," after Lt. John Spouse, CE (born 1875 at Eyemouth, Berwickshire, Scotland and killed in the First World War), who hiked here with his son Brick. The entire trip offers so-close-you-can-almost-touch-them views of Kennedy Lake (a former reservoir for Vancouver and the present source of all water for the Grouse Mountain resort). Also visible are the Needles and Lynn; Coliseum, Burwell, and Cathedral; Echo, Crown N1, and the back side of Crown.

What is usually referred to as Goat Ridge is really East Goat Ridge: BCMC traditionally referred to the ridge to the west (including the present trail from Little Goat to Goat) as "Goat Ridge." BCMC trips went to the East Ridge of Goat Mountain, via Goat Ridge and Goat Mountain, at least as early as 1924. The 1927 Grouse Mountain brochure map referred to it as "Smanet Plateau." The ridge has also been called "Raven Ridge."

Spouse (Apostrophe) Tarn on East Goat Ridge.

ROUTE 1:

FROM GROUSE MOUNTAIN CHALET TO GOAT RIDGE, BYPASSING GOAT MOUNTAIN

Follow the trail description above from Grouse Mountain Chalet to Alpine Trail–Ridge Trail fork.

- Follow the trail description above from Alpine–Ridge fork to Little Goat fork.
- Continue past the turnoff to Little Goat Mountain.
- The dominant trail again traverses east, this time avoiding the peak of Little Goat Mountain.
- Ascend to a trail marker that will send you back to Little Goat (Ridge Trail).

Goat Mountain Trail: Continue north, descending to a signpost clearly marking the Goat Mountain turnoff. Less than a kilometre remains to the summit.

- Continue north along a well-marked path, past small tarns, a helicopter pad, a raised NSR barrel shelter and storage tower, and several sections of smooth rock.
- After a short rise there is a hidden sheer drop on the left (west), barred with a rope.
- Make a final descent to a boulder section, then climb towards the summit.
- Soon you will hit a rocky cliff. Resist the temptation to climb up roots; instead, traverse to the left.
- The trail leads to a set of chains up a face of rocks and roots. The chains are more for comfort than necessity; children will find them fun rather than scary.
- A sign marks the difficult, shorter, and steeper route (straight and up) to Goat Mountain or a more gradual option to the right. Take the gradual way to the right to go straight to Goat Ridge and the summit and bypass Goat Mountain.

Goat Ridge Trail: The ridge is a pleasant and easy ramble over rocks and heather and past tarns to the modest summit of Goat Ridge Peak, a rocky knoll at the end, surrounded by cliffs. The trail perambulates over the ridge. Occasionally you may lose the track over granite slabs. If in doubt, veer left (north).

- At the meadow east of and below the Goat Mountain citadel ("Goat Mountain Meadow"), you will see a sign for Goat Ridge (1.6 km round trip).
- The trail wends through the meadow along an easily negotiable and well-trodden path through the heather. The trail leads to a large, mossy granite slab sloping east and seems to vanish. No fear: go to the north end of the slab and regain the trail on your right.
- Continue along until you reach a seeming cliff. Happily, the trail heads north over a few fallen bleached logs and then down a steep section assisted by a set of chains.
- Veer left (north) for a large grassy meadow and an up-close view of Palisade Ridge (also called Echo Ridge) to the north. To the south you will see Spouse Tarn, with Tadpole Tarn just to the east. It is easy to access both tarns without molesting the heather or moss, by walking down a seasonal streambed and across granite.
- A few more, smaller seasonal tarns are seen down the main trail. Veer left (north) along a narrow sandy trail through the heather to another meadow with a seasonal tarn. Go over a small granite slab and then again left (north) to hook around to the final meadow, also lovely, with another seasonal tarn.
- After this last meadow, the trail becomes slim, snaking upwards through the heather and around the rocky knoll to the right (south).
- This is the peak proper. Resist the urge to climb straight up the short bluff, through

trees. The easier final climb is found at the back side (near a tarn) or from the northeast side. Both of these final climbs are trail-free, 20-m bushwhacks. There is a cairn on top.

- Make sure to hike the additional 40 m to the final bump (slightly shorter than the true summit, the penultimate bump) at the end of the ridge, separated from the peak by a trio of small seasonal tarns. There are fine, unimpeded views of Norvan Valley, the back side of Crown, the peaks of Echo/Palisade Ridge, various Grouse area peaks, and to the east the Needles, Coliseum, Burwell, and Cathedral. The views are similar to those from North Needle, with much less exertion.

ROUTE 2:
TO GOAT RIDGE FROM GOAT MOUNTAIN PEAK

- At the immediate base east of the Goat Mountain citadel, you will see a sign for Goat Ridge (1.6 km round trip). The well-trodden and occasionally flagged trail descends steeply. Take care, especially if the dryness makes the dirt slippery. There are occasional granite chunks to serve as steps.
- This chute leads to Goat Mountain Meadow and the trail sign referred to above. Follow that trail description.

East Goat Ridge Peak: Spouse (Apostrophe) and Tadpole Tarns.

FORKS PEAK

(FOR) (1160 M)

Short but exciting peak looming over Hanes Valley. Not for beginners.

CAUTION:
No trail; minimal flagging; many cliffs. Slippery in rain or snow.

PROMINENCE:
172 m.

LATITUDE/LONGITUDE:
N49.41101 W123.05921.

BANG FOR BUCK:
3/5

PEAK VIEW:
4/5. Needles, Coliseum, Burwell, Hanes Valley.

TRUE SUMMIT LOCATION:
The highest peak south of Hanes Creek and north of East Goat Ridge.

HEADWATERS:
Kennedy Creek, Wickenden Creek (into Lynn Creek).

BEST VIEWS FROM:
Third Debris Chute (Cedars Mill Trail), Goat, Crown N1, North Needle.

TRIP INFORMATION

Round-trip distance: 12.2 km from Grouse Mountain parking; 16 km from Lynn Headwaters parking.

Elevation gain: 781 m.

Time: 6–9 hours.

Difficulty: 4/5.

Snow free: Late June.

Must-sees: Lynn Creek; beautiful East Goat Ridge; tarns.

Scenery: 4/5.

Kids: 0/5. Cliffs.

Dogs: 1/5. Need hands.

Runnability: 3/5. Good on Cedars Mill Trail; good to Goat Ridge; rest bad.

Terrain: Well-established trails to steep bushwhacking.

Public transit: #232 bus from Phibbs Exchange or #236 from Lonsdale Quay.

Cell coverage: Present on Goat Ridge and Goat Peak but not at Lynn Headwaters.

Sun: Sufficient shade until nearly shadeless ridge and peak.

Water: Tarns.

Route links: East Goat Ridge and Goat back to Grouse Mountain. The very ambitious could link Echo or Crown N1.

HISTORY

Name origin: Above BCMC Forks camp at confluence of Lynn, Hanes, and Norvan Creek.

Name status: Unofficial.

First ascent: Likely around 1910. Frequently climbed between 1925 and 1939.

Forks Peak is the eastern and taller of two steep bumps off the northeast end of East Goat Ridge (1160 m and 1000 m respectively). It offers a spectacular panorama from high in the middle of the Hanes Valley, looking as if you could reach out and touch the Lynn Peaks, the Needles, Coliseum and Cathedral, Crown and Goat. The June 1929 BCMC Forks trip report (via Draycott Gully) refers to "the pass that divides Forks Peak from Goat," and endorses the route: "the comparative low altitude of this mountain and its accessibility make it an easy trip and gives one time to breathe the air, take in the scenery, and have a leisurely lunch." It is neither safe nor easy today; be careful.

The best route is Route 1, up Wickenden Creek. More-adventurous souls can make a loop by climbing up to East Goat Ridge via Route 2 and then to the Grouse Mountain Skyride.

Forks made its debut in the BCMC Summer Program for 1925: "May 31 – Forks Peak The climb of a new peak, at the extreme end of Goat Ridge, above the camp at Lynn Forks." The BCMC kept a regular camp near where Lynn Creek meets what is now called Norvan Creek, at that time called the East Fork of Lynn Creek. (Hanes Creek was called the West Fork, with Lynn Creek proper running due north to its source at Lynn Lake.) From this camp, BCMC groups would conquer Burwell, Cathedral, and, closer, Forks and the North Peaks of Crown. BCMC reports refer to the pool and water-falls (likely Norvan Falls) and cave (location unknown) at Forks. This peak would have loomed above the camp, especially where the area had just been logged.

To conquer Forks, hikers would cross Lynn Creek a little more than a kilometre above the cedars mill site (now marked with a sign along Cedars Mill Trail, which is named after it). Their crossing was likely at a spot near the outflow of Kennedy Creek, which can be forded when Lynn is low (and which links to a trail to a giant cedar, Kennedy Falls, and the Old Grouse Mountain Highway, on the west side of Lynn). They would then hike to the junction of Draycott Creek and Lynn Creek. Draycott Creek is likely the unnamed creek just upstream from where Norvan flows into Lynn, closer to the location of Forks Camp (it may also be what is now called Wickenden Creek). Climbers would go up the bed of Draycott Creek and then up the Draycott gully (of which there were two) to an amphitheatre from where a steep climb would take them up to Forks. They would then climb farther up to the east end of Goat Ridge. Return to civilization was via the Grouse Mountain chalet. As an alternative exit, a March 1928 issue of the Vancouver ACC's *Avalanche Echoes* reported that "the climax of the day came with a thrilling 1,300-foot slide into Crown Pass."

Descriptions of BCMC trips to Forks Peak in May 1928 and June 1929 are consistent with the theory that Forks is the 1160-m peak. Two undated maps in the North

Vancouver archives provide clues. One, in the Macaree fonds (the archived files of the authors of *103 Hikes*), shows a way to this very peak off East Goat Ridge, which we've called Route 2 below. The other map, in the Alpine Club of Canada fonds (which also contains a Macaree file), shows a loop route accessing Forks Peak from East Goat Ridge and descending via a steep creek valley heading northwest down to Hanes Valley (Route 4 below).

By April 1939 Forks Peak was stated to be in the watershed; hikers were required to have a blood-test certificate to preserve the water purity. And thereafter, Forks seemed to vanish from BCMC trip lists and from the collective knowledge and memory of Vancouver hikers.

While the rock field descent north, down to Hanes Valley Trail, appears promising, the thick clusters of salmonberry bushes will shred your shins. Footing is unsteady as well. That said, the salmonberries here are the finest we've ever tasted: purple and red and juicy.

Forks Peak, in middle, as seen from North Needle.

ROUTE 1:

WICKENDEN CREEK FROM EAST SIDE OF LYNN CREEK

Caution: Only take this route in late summer, when the creek is low.

- Start at the Lynn Headwaters Regional Park parking lot. Continue north on Cedars Mill Trail. After you come to the Third Debris Chute, the trail continues northward but is now named Lynn Headwaters Trail.
- Continue north for about 1 km.
- Note the location of Wickenden Creek on your map or GPS. Bushwhack down to Lynn Creek. Ford Lynn Creek, over several sandbars, to the mouth of Wickenden Creek.
- Climb up the rocky Wickenden Creek gully. It is usually dry by August. There are

a few boulders, but generally this is an easy climb. Stay on the obvious main creek, ignoring side gullies. At most times your destination is in view: the col between Goat Ridge and Forks Peak.

- About two-thirds of the way up, the rocky creek valley curves to the left (west) towards East Goat Ridge. *Do not* follow it. Instead, continue straight up, following a minor tributary creek gully.
- After some short, steep bushwhacking, you will come to the col at the base of Forks Peak.
- From the col, climb up the obvious (but still very steep) contour line, often using hands. A steep 180-m climb leads up to Forks Peak. There is some flagging.

ROUTE 2:
FROM GROUSE MOUNTAIN CHALET TO GOAT RIDGE, BYPASSING GOAT MOUNTAIN

Caution: This route is steep and hazardous. Only attempt it if you are an experienced hiker with bushwhacking and routefinding skills and armed with a GPS.

- Follow the trail description given above at Goat Mountain from Grouse Mountain Chalet to the Alpine Trail–Ridge Trail fork.
- Follow the trail description above from Alpine–Ridge fork to Little Goat fork.
- Continue past the turnoff to Little Goat Mountain.
- The dominant trail again traverses east, this time avoiding the peak of Little Goat.
- Rise to a trail marker sending you back to Little Goat (Ridge Trail).

Goat Mountain Trail: Continue north, descending to a signpost clearly marking the Goat Mountain turnoff. Less than a kilometre remains to the peak.

- Continue north along a well-marked path, past small tarns, a helicopter pad, a raised NSR barrel shelter and storage tower, and several sections of smooth rock.
- After a short rise there is a hidden sheer drop on the left (west), barred by a rope.
- Make a final descent to a boulder section and then a climb towards the summit.
- Soon you will hit a rocky cliff. Resist the temptation to climb up roots; instead, traverse to the left.
- The trail leads to a set of chains up a face of rocks and roots. The chains are more for comfort than necessity; children will find them fun rather than scary.
- A sign marks the difficult, shorter and steeper route (straight and up) to Goat Mountain or a more gradual route to the right. Take the gradual route to the right to go straight to Goat Ridge and the peak and bypass Goat Mountain.

Goat Ridge Trail: The ridge is a pleasant and easy ramble over rocks and heather and past tarns, to the modest "summit" of Goat Ridge Peak, a rocky knoll at the end, surrounded by cliffs. The trail perambulates over the ridge. Occasionally you may lose the trail over granite slabs. If in doubt, veer left (north).

- At the meadow east and below the Goat Mountain citadel ("Goat Mountain Meadow"), you will see a sign for Goat Ridge (1.6 km round trip).
- The trail wends through the meadow along an easily negotiable and well-trodden path through the heather. The trail leads to a large, mossy granite slab sloping east and seems to vanish. No fear: go to the north end of the slab and regain the trail to the right.
- Continue along until you reach a seeming cliff. Happily, the trail heads north over a few fallen bleached logs and then down a steep section assisted by a set of chains.

- Veer left (north) for a large, grassy meadow and an up-close view of Palisade Ridge to the north. To the south you will see Spouse Tarn, with Tadpole Tarn just to the east. It is easy to access both tarns without molesting the heather or moss, by walking down a seasonal streambed and across granite.
- A few more, smaller seasonal tarns are seen down the main trail. Veer left (north) along a narrow, sandy trail through the heather to another meadow with a seasonal tarn.

Goat Ridge to Forks: At the widest point of East Goat Ridge, a steep ridge extends north and down, directly towards Forks.

- Descend 100 m to a rocky viewpoint and balcony. A steep and slippery gully with ample handholds leads down.
- There are sheer, dangerous cliffs to the west. Descend northeast to bypass them.
- Veer right (east) to avoid further cliff bands. A series of gullies will allow you to descend.
- The rightmost gully ends in a waterfall. Scamper up and west and then descend, using hands throughout. As you approach the col, it gets easier.
- From the col, climb up the obvious (but still very steep) contour line, often using hands. A steep 180-m climb leads up to Forks Peak. There is some flagging.

Route 3:

LIKELY DRAYCOTT CREEK FROM EAST SIDE OF LYNN CREEK

Caution: This route is untested and speculative. It will certainly be steep and hazardous. Only attempt if you are an experienced hiker with bushwhacking and routefinding skills and equipped with a GPS.

- Start at the Lynn Headwaters Regional Park parking lot. Continue north on Cedars Mill Trail. Come to the debris chute, after which the trail continues north but is called Lynn Headwaters Trail.
- At the Norvan Falls sign, follow that creek downstream, bushwhacking down to its confluence with Lynn Creek.
- Ford Lynn Creek.
- Locate the only significant creek, which heads steeply upward. Climb it all the way to Forks Peak.

Route 4:

FROM NORTH – UNNAMED CREEK TO HANES VALLEY

Caution: Due to the thick clusters of prickly salmonberry bushes and the unsteady rock field footing, this route is not recommended.

- From the col at the base of Forks Peak, head downward (northwest), following the optimal contour lines. There are steep portions; be cautious.
- Carefully cross the rock field to rejoin Hanes Valley Trail.

CROWN MOUNTAIN

(CRO) (1504 M)

Rewarding and robust hike to glorious views, all feeling pretty close to home.

CAUTION:
Exposure on peak and in various rocky areas. Slippery and dangerous when wet. Only do in perfect weather.

PROMINENCE:
519 m.

LATITUDE/LONGITUDE:
N49.40995 W123.09193.

BANG FOR BUCK:
3.5/5

PEAK VIEW:
5/5. Superb, unobstructed 360° views from Garibaldi to Olympics.

TRUE SUMMIT LOCATION:
Obvious diamond-shaped peak.

HEADWATERS:
Hanes (into Lynn Creek); Dean and Fellowes creeks, tributaries of Crown Creek (into Capilano River).

BEST VIEWS FROM:
Everywhere! Lions Gate Bridge, downtown Vancouver, Spanish Banks, UBC.

TRIP INFORMATION

Round-trip distance: 9 km from the chalet.

Elevation gain: 780 m.

Time: 4–7 hours (4:08).

Difficulty: 3/5. Steep descent into and out of Crown Pass.

Snow free: Early July.

Must-sees: View down Hanes Valley; heather; slabs.

Scenery: 3/5.

Kids: 3/5. Only for robust, safe children above age 11 in good conditions and under proper supervision.

Dogs: 3/5. Unable to reach proper peak.

Runnability: 2/5. Too steep in places (but Hanes Valley and Lynn Headwaters approach trails are 5/5).

Terrain: Well-marked trail through second-growth forest and over rocky traverses.

Public transit: #232 bus from Phibbs Exchange or #236 from Lonsdale Quay.

Cell coverage: Good on peak; inconsistent below.

Sun: Sufficient shade. Exposed peak.

Water: Little available. Crown Creek and a few small streams on the climb up to Crown plateau.

Route links: A sweep of all Grouse Mountain area peaks.

Vancouver and Capilano Lake from Crown Peak.

Name origin: Resembles a crown. Charted in 1860 by Captain Richards of the Royal Navy and presumably named by him as "Mt. Crown" (Black was the only other Burrard Inlet-facing North Shore peak named on the chart). "Sleeping Beauty" is an old term for the entire Crown massif (Crown proper, the Camel, and Crown west and north peaks as seen from Vancouver). The west peak of Crown was sometimes called "the Knees" (of the Sleeping Beauty). The main peak of Crown (as well as West Crown) have both been called "the Pyramid".

Name status: Official. Adopted December 7, 1937. Marked (as Mt. Crown) on Sir Sandford Fleming's 1877 CPR map; in 1899 on North Vancouver map; and on Alan John Campbell's 1927 topographic survey, and on BC map 5B (south), 1929.

First ascent: June 1895, by Messrs. Edwards, Parkinson, and Knox, the first claimed conquerors of Grouse, Dam, and Goat, from Grouse. The first female ascent is disputed. A 1904 group accompanied by a chaperone claimed the title, but a July 30, 1902, *Vancouver Daily Province* article headlined "In the Region of the Clouds: Mountain climbing fad now counts its devotees among both sexes," claims Mrs. J.A. Green and her two daughters, aged 15 and 17, were the first women, guided by two unnamed men. The youngest-ever person to summit Crown was Edith Munday, daughter of

Don and Phyllis Munday, who was carried up Crown at the age of 11 weeks in 1921 (note to new parents: please don't ever do this) the Camel's hump was first climbed by Fred Mills, Franklin Walter Hewton, Thomas Lyttleton, and Herbert Miskin on August 4, 1908, and the Camel's head on October 5, 1908, by Hewton. Miss L.A. Debeck climbed the Camel in 1909.

Other write-up: Gunn.

The first ascent of Crown by women, 1904.

Crown is one of our favourite peaks: accessible from the Grouse Mountain Skyride yet truly epic. If you brave the pyramid-shaped peak saddle, looking back and to the side at sheer cliffs, and south to downtown Vancouver, you will feel like the monarch of the world.

There are three main parts of Crown Mountain: the peak itself; West Crown (also known as Sleeping Beauty or Beauty or Pyramid Peak: see below), with a rock face – the Crown Buttress – below to the west and the Camel (a rock form to the east of the peak, quite compellingly resembling a camel, and only for roped and experienced climbers, with all routes Class 5 or above). Just before the final push to the peak, a classic triangular prism, one comes to a shoulder of exposed gabbro rock with a heart-stopping view of the cliffs and slopes to the north. This edge and the slopes below are traditionally referred to as "the Crater," although of course the origin is not volcanic: the dramatic view is caused by glacial scraping and scouring. In 1914 Don Munday suggested that a better name would be "the Hopper." The summit of Crown Mountain is an example of an arête, a narrow ridge of rock left behind after two moving glaciers carved the sides of a ridge. The summit of Mt. Brunswick is also an arête.

Despite its accessibility via the Dam–Goat–Hanes Valley trail corridor, it is a physically exhausting hike, for sturdy legs not fearing extended up-and-down stretches. Do not underestimate the time of the out-and-back hike. Many hikers do, to their regret, and many North Shore Rescue calls have occurred here. On the weekend of March 2–3, 2015, NSR was called in three times for Crown alone.

In particular, the risks posed by the slanted rocky slabs leading up from Crown Pass to the base of the peak must not be underestimated. This hike should only be climbed in perfect weather, and in such conditions the slabs are a fun and fairly safe scramble for the reasonably prudent adventurer. When covered in ice, snow, or rain, though, they become the world's least rewarding and deadliest tobogganing hill, where a slip would lead to death or grievous injury. On Father's Day 2012, NSR extracted a fallen climber on Crown Mountain who had a serious fracture of the leg. The hiker had slid off the rock slabs 80 m above, falling on steep snow and rock. He came to rest in a gap between a steep snow slope and a creek. But for this arrest, he would have fallen many hundreds of metres more and likely died.

Crown has seen several deaths, particularly on its more technical approaches. The Widowmaker route (not profiled here), a 5.7/5.8 ascent from the Hanes Valley, claimed the life of a climber who fell about 75 m, in September 2017. His partner suffered third-degree burns in an attempt to stop the fall. The Widowmaker route acquired its name when legendary climber and founding president of the International Triathlon Union Les McDonald, CM (April 30, 1933 – September 4, 2017) made the first ascent on his honeymoon.

Crown was recognized early on as a most picturesque and enticing peak to the mountaineer. The first recorded climb was in June 1895, by Messrs. Edwards, Parkinson, and Knox, the first claimed conquerors of Grouse, Dam, and Goat (see Grouse). They followed their 1894 route up to Goat, where they camped overnight. As recounted by Neal Carter and G.B. Warren:

> Early next morning, undaunted by snow seen sliding off the faces of the mountain ahead of them, they set off down into Crown Pass. The route chosen up Crown was the same as that now usually used. It was a lovely day, and an hour and a half was spent on the summit admiring the view and theorizing as to what and where the various peaks seen might be. On the return, a second night was spent on Goat Peak.

By 1908 hikers were taking roughly the same way as the predominant route today: up Grouse and then over the shoulders of Dam and Goat before descending into the Crown Creek valley and ascending Crown. This way was considered less toilsome than the traditional one up Capilano Road, around the bump known as Burnt Mountain above the Capilano River to the west flank of Crown and making the steep climb up Crown Creek, a route first taken in July 1898 by James John Trorey, J.S. Tait, and a Mr. Jones. Their campfire on the top of Crown attracted considerable attention, from both the public and media, in Vancouver far below.

The 1927 Grouse Mountain brochure indicates that visitors to the Grouse Mountain Chalet could take a pony on the trail to Crown Pass, along roughly the same trail as today.

In the 1920s BCMC members had a casual contest to see who could make the first ascent of Crown in the new year. On New Year's Eve in 1924 a group led by Ted Taylor and Frederic Alan "Brick" Spouse started off via Crown Creek wearing "bug lights" (carbide headlamps). After a miserable, soggy ascent, they attained the peak, bitterly cold with 30–40 m.p.h. winds, at 11:45 a.m. on New Year's Day. For good measure they made a complete traverse, descending via Hanes Valley and out by way of what is now Lynn Headwaters Regional Park.

In 1904 Charles Mee made the remarkable proposal of a chalet, restaurant, and cottages near the peak of Crown. Luckily, the plan did not progress.

In an August 1904 ascent, Arthur Tinniswood Dalton saw both a mountain goat and a deer high up Crown. Both species are still seen in the area, albeit very rarely.

A September 1940 BCMC report notes that the spectre of the Brocken is often seen on Crown Mountain. Named for a peak in the Harz mountains in Germany, the Brocken spectre is an optical phenomenon where the shadow of the observer is magnified onto a cloudbank when the sun is low, its head often haloed in multicoloured bands.

A dilapidated plaque near the summit commemorates two persons named Murison (or Morison), referring to the Second World War. The first names are obliterated and there is no record of local casualties with those surnames.

Crown is the only one of these peaks to host the Stanley Cup. In the summer of 2010 Andrew Ladd (born in Maple Ridge) of the champion Chicago Blackhawks, had the trophy with him as he watched the sunrise atop the mountain.

Crown is primarily composed of hornblende diorite: one of the oldest forms of plutonic rock in the North Shore mountains, and the primary rock making up The Lions.

ROUTE 1:
FROM GROUSE MOUNTAIN CHALET AND SKYRIDE
Follow the route from Grouse Mountain Chalet to Goat Mountain trail fork.
- Continue past the Goat turnoff. This is the last fork in the trail.

Goat Mountain to Crown Meadows: The trail steeply descends Crown Pass into the Crown Creek Valley. There are a few very steep sections with chains and ropes, but no exposure. At the valley floor you cross a rockslide. Look up and behind for an interesting view of Goat.
- You will see a sign for Crown Pass and the Hanes Valley trail to the east. Don't take it. Go left and up.

Crown Pass to Crown Meadows: Start the steep climb, alternating between forest and exposed slanted slabs. The slabby sections are fun in good weather but treacherous in wet or icy conditions.
- A route is marked with paint splotches. On the way up you will be rewarded with some gasp-worthy views down into the Hanes Valley.
- Come to a creek and climb up to a heather plateau.

Crown Meadows to Crown Peak: Head north. Cross a rock field. Veer to the left and climb up. The route heads right, to the rim of the crater and the base of the Camel. Go up and west. If you fear heights, do not look down at this point.

- The final route is a bit rough and gravelly but should be obvious. If in doubt, go left (west).
- After a minor rock scramble and a traverse of the Camel, you reach a small flat area below a narrow ridge of rock.
- The ridge of rock is obviously the true peak, but it is very exposed and an acrophobe's nightmare. Straddle it slowly and carefully. Or, if that is not your thing, stop at the balcony below the true summit and admire the views.

ROUTE 2:

FROM LYNN HEADWATERS AND HANES VALLEY TRAIL

This is a long route, to be attempted only in perfect summer conditions by experienced hikers in prime shape. It makes a glorious but tiring loop from Lynn Headwaters to the Grouse Mountain Skyride.

- Follow the route from the Lynn Headwaters parking lot and Hanes Valley Trail to Crown Pass, below, under "Hanes Valley Peaks."
- Climb Crown, following the Crown Pass to Crown Peak route described above.

Slab-hopping up to Crown.

WEST CROWN (BEAUTY) PEAK
(WCR) (1401 M)

Glorious and close-up views of Vancouver: you will likely have it all to yourself.

CAUTION:
Trail difficult to follow in places.
Well off beaten path. Watershed.

PROMINENCE:
110 m.

LATITUDE/LONGITUDE:
N49.40400 W123.10122.

BANG FOR BUCK:
3/5

PEAK VIEW:
5/5. Superb view of Vancouver,
and beyond.

TRUE SUMMIT LOCATION:
Obvious flat peak at end.

HEADWATERS:
Deneau and Fellowes creeks,
other tributaries of Capilano Lake
(into Capilano River).

BEST VIEWS FROM:
British Properties, Capilano
Road, Lions Gate Bridge, downtown
Vancouver, Jericho Beach.

TRIP INFORMATION

Round-trip distance: 10.4 km from the chalet.

Elevation gain: 680 m.

Time: 4–8 hours (4:52).

Difficulty: 3.5/5.

Snow free: Usually late June.

Must-sees: Unique city views; slabby approach.

Scenery: 3/5. Some pleasant tarns and rock faces.

Kids: 2/5. Only for robust, safe children above age 11 in perfect weather.

Dogs: 3/5. Two roped sections requiring a boost. Watershed inappropriate for dogs.

Runnability: 2/5. Too steep in areas.

Terrain: Some routefinding through heather and over rocky, sloping surfaces.

Public transit: #232 bus from Phibbs Exchange or #236 from Lonsdale Quay.

Cell coverage: Yes.

Sun: Sufficient shade for beginning. Some exposure en route. Exposed peak.

Water: Small, muddy tarn.

Route links: Could do a sweep with Crown and all Grouse Mountain peaks.

HISTORY

Name origin: It is located to the west of Crown.

Name status: Unofficial.

Other names: "Sleeping Beauty" is an old term for the entire Crown massif (Crown proper, the Camel, west peak, north peaks as seen from Vancouver); used as far back as 1908. The west peak of Crown was sometimes called "the Knees" in reference to its anatomical position in the inclined Sleeping Beauty figure. It was also sometimes called Capelano or Capilano peak (1902 and 1950). West Crown has also been called "Fairview." BCMC leader Tom Fyles referred to it as "West Crown" in his 1920 album.

First ascent: Before 1929, likely soon after 1895.

<u>Note:</u> This mountain is in the watershed. The authors are not encouraging or condoning trips to it. This route description is provided based on the fact that people will attempt to travel to the peak nonetheless, and that the route description will promote the safety of those individuals and the environment itself.

West Crown Peak is in some ways more spectacular than Crown itself: from the Stanley Park Causeway it is a pyramid perfectly framed by Lions Gate Bridge. It is 100 m shorter than its parent, but from this angle it looks to be the dominant peak. Although every Vancouverite has seen it, almost no one would be able to name it. The author's shame at not knowing its name, and his surprise at the difficulty in discovering its name, in part led to the writing of this book and the start of the Bagger's Challenge.

As set out above, West Crown's pleasing shape had prompted many different names to be attached to it. It is also sometimes referred to as "Crown Buttress," although this refers to the rocky west face of the peak, where an alternative route, entirely through the watershed, beloved yet illegal, climbs to West Crown.

The amount of traversing through heather and up a long rocky slab make this much more suitable for a dry day than a wet one, the difference between a relatively easy hike and a dangerous one. It makes a marvellous place to camp, so close to the city but so far away. Revel in your solitude. The summit provides a balcony seemingly hanging over Capilano Lake, providing unimpeded views of the entire metropolis of Vancouver and, on a clear day, Vancouver Island.

En route to the peak you will see a small tarn which on August 9, 1902, celebrated mountaineers Arthur Tinniswood Dalton and Atwell King facetiously named "Alexandra Lake":

West Crown and Crown as seen from Dam.

The joke was, as they sat around that little lake that 9th August 1902 coronation day [of] King Edward VI and Queen Alexandra, that… "they were 'Crown'ing the King in England, and 'King'ing (Atwell D. King) the 'Crown' in Vancouver."

The striking and central peak prompted artistic tributes. Lieutenant Willis of HMS *Ganges* depicted it in a painting in 1861. As an adult in 1949, James Allan Ward Bell, the first European child born on the North Shore, wrote a poem to the peak:

THE SLEEPING BEAUTY

Upthrown from a place primeval
By the thrust of a giant hand
With an eagle's nest on its highest crest
The mighty mountain stands.

Couch of the sleeping beauty,
Rock-ribbed, massive and strong,
By the Lion's Gate where the vessels wait,
Where the sons of the sea belong.

Asleep on top of the mountain
With her face upturned to the skies,
The rounded breast where the snowflake rests
And the seal of God on her eyes.

Asleep, yet guarding the city
And the people by the sea,
Calm and serene as in a dream
She sleeps for eternity.

West Crown was the site of two early local mountaineering casualties when David Spencer and Arthur Willis fell to their deaths on February 10, 1924. BCMC and Alpine Club of Canada members assisted with the recovery. Articles about the search suggested that it would be appropriate to organize a more permanent search and rescue organization for the North Shore mountains.

ROUTE

Follow the route from Grouse Mountain Chalet to Goat Mountain trail fork.
- Follow the route from Goat Mountain to Crown Meadows.
- Punch out from between a few large trees (one with a yellow trail marker) to a relatively flat stretch among heather (see photo).
- The West Crown side trail is found about 10 m past the marker tree, heading into the heather directly in the direction of West Crown. *If you reach the short final rock field below the main Crown peak area, you have overshot the turnoff by about 50 m.* There is a small rock cairn adjacent to (on the right) the trail junction.

- The trail will likely be overgrown in places, especially at the start. No fear: so long as you generally head towards West Crown, you will find your way.
- The trail takes you up and over a minor knob before descending consistently downward to the col at the base of West Crown. A short section is aided by a couple of rope segments, neither of them very high or dangerous.
- Arrive at a col that is shaded by large cedar trees.
- Continue west towards the peak of West Crown.
- The route is generally obvious, continuing up two exposed rock surfaces that are easy to travel on in good weather but would be slick when wet.
- Continue up, up, up along any path you choose.
- There is a minor cliff band protecting the summit, but a rooty tree in the middle of the rock face provides an easy scramble up.
- Reward yourself with splendid views of Vancouver: you will feel as if you are suspended over the whole metropolis.

Climbing the Crown Buttress route

Summit of West Crown

MT. FROMME

(FRO) (1185 M)

A well-travelled trail through second-growth forest to this prominent dome on the Vancouver skyline.

CAUTION:
A rabbit warren of trails (some steep) to and from the peak may get you lost.

PROMINENCE:
235 m.

LATITUDE/LONGITUDE:
N49.38333 W123.05611.

BANG FOR BUCK:
3/5

PEAK VIEW:
3/5. Close-up views of the Grouse peaks; to the east are Cathedral, Coliseum, the Needles.

TRUE SUMMIT LOCATION:
South. The north, shorter summit is called "Senate Peak" for reasons unknown.

HEADWATERS:
Grainger Creek, Hastings Creek (into Lynn Creek); Mosquito Creek.

GOOD VIEW OF PEAK FROM:
downtown Vancouver, Grouse Mountain.

TRIP INFORMATION

Round-trip distance: 11.6 km from Grouse parking lot.

Elevation gain: 1011 m.

Time: 2–5 hours from St. Mary's Avenue via Peer Gynt Trail (4–6 from Grouse Mountain parking lot).

Difficulty: 2.5/5. Easy to get lost on the many trails.

Snow free: Mid-June.

Must-sees: Some ancient forestry cables and equipment; some impressive modern-day mountain-bike infrastructure.

Scenery: 2/5. Second-growth forest.

Kids: 3/5. Safe but a bit long.

Dogs: 5/5.

Runnability: 3/5 up; 5/5 down.

Terrain: Gravel road; second-growth forest; rocks.

Public transit: #232 bus from Phibbs Exchange or #236 from Lonsdale Quay.

Cell coverage: Usually good.

Sun: Mostly covered except peak.

Water: Little water above Grouse Mountain Highway.

Route links: Grouse, Dam, and the Goats.

Name origin: Named in 1928 by Ernest Albert Cleveland, chief commissioner of Greater Vancouver Water District, after Julius Martin Fromme (1858–1941), the "Father of Lynn Valley," the lumber camp foreman who in 1899 built the first house in the valley. From 1924 to 1929 he served as reeve (mayor) of North Vancouver. Ironically, his company, Lynn Valley Lumber, owned the timber rights on the mountain and wholly clear-cut it. Note that the name of the man and the mountain rhymes with "home," not with "hum" or "aplomb."

Name status: Official. Adopted December 7, 1937. First named around 1928. Used in the 1946 BC Electric Railway Ltd. hiking map.

First ascent: In 1891 a mining claim was staked at the top of Fromme by Arthur Sullivan and his brother. Likely climbed long before by Indigenous people, hunters, or prospectors.

Other names: Formerly known as Dome Mountain (1908 BCMC; 1912 C.J. Heaney map; 1915, 1920, 1922, 1923, 1938, and 1946 BCMC; 1941 and 1946 ACC Vancouver section; 1927 Varsity Outdoor Club; Alan John Campbell's 1927 topographic survey; 1927 Grouse Mountain brochure; 1936 L. Frank photographic survey of North Shore Peaks), as well as Timber Mountain. In 1912 the name "Mount Diplock" was proposed, after A.B. Diplock, managing director of the Western Corporation, which was logging there at the time, but the name never caught on.

Other write-up: Hui.

Despite being in the middle of the North Shore peak panorama, and the mountain that creates the slope of Lonsdale Avenue, poor Mt. Fromme, in past and present, garners little respect. The authors of *Don't Waste Your Time...* call it "the Rodney Dangerfield of mountains." The 1913 BCMC journal *The Northern Cordilleran* sniffed: "To the east of the plateau, on the other side of the deep ravine of Mosquito Creek, is a rounded eminence known as The Dome. This is seldom visited, as it presents no difficulties to the mountaineer, and the view from the top is neither beautiful nor extensive." Although on the front range of peaks, and visible from all of the Lower Mainland, its name is unknown to most Vancouverites, save for mountain bikers, who venerate its lower slopes as a world-renowned mecca of their sport: ambitious trails, jumps, and apparatuses are found throughout its slopes.

The slabby summit offers unique views of the vista from Crown to Garibaldi to Cathedral to Golden Ears. There is a small tarn. Apart from the main mountain, there is a lower north summit called "Senate Peak." It is rocky and makes a good lunch spot. It has direct and close views of the Grouse Mountain Eye of the Wind and Blueberry Bowl runs, and provides a good sense of Fromme's proximity to Grouse in a way the true peak does not. A rough but obvious trail leads from the south summit to the north one. Another track leads down west to a small pond nicknamed "Meech Lake."

Mt. Fromme's name has shifted over the years. It has sometimes been referred to as Timber Mountain, owing to the prime timber once found on its slopes. A 1953 newspaper article referred to "Timber Mountain" as "the local name for Fromme Mountain." The clear-cutting by Julius Fromme's company perhaps accentuated the mountain's physical profile, leading to its being labelled as "The Dome" on Alan

John Campbell's 1927 topographic survey. The 1915 Water Map, the 1918 BCMC summer program, a 1925 *Daily Province* and the 1935 and 1939 BC Electric Railway Ltd. hiking maps, and a 1941 newspaper story all called it "Dome Mountain." In 1928 it gained the name of Mt. Fromme, after the local lumber baron whose company had sheared its mighty timber. Even then, the name "Fromme" took a while to take hold. As late as 1946 the BCMC *BC Mountaineer* was still referring to it as "Dome," with reference to a misspelled "Frome" as an alternative name.

The mountain has a fiery history. In 1912 its mill burned down, and in 1914 its south side was consumed by a forest fire.

The quarry just off the Old Grouse Mountain Highway that Route 1 passes has been in operation since around 1900, as reported on by Walter Draycott in his *Lynn Valley: From the Wilds of Nature to Civilization* (1919). Granite from the quarry was used for roads.

ROUTE 1:
FROM SOUTH – ST. MARY'S AVENUE VIA PEER GYNT TRAIL, OLD MOUNTAIN HIGHWAY, AND BILL'S TRAIL

- Take Exit 19 off Highway 1. Travel north (up) Lonsdale to Braemar. Turn right. Left on St. George's. Right onto St. Mary's. Go to the end of St. Mary's.
- Go through the gates at the end of St. Mary's and turn left. Take the signposted St. George's Trail up.
- St. George's soon intersects Baden-Powell Trail near a bench with a limited view of the city.
- Continue up St. George's Trail, across Baden-Powell Trail. The way is steep but obvious.
- Soon you will pop out onto the old Grouse Mountain highway, a gravel road frequented by mountain bikers. Turn left and proceed to the switchback. At the elbow of the switchback you will find a trail ascending into the forest: Peer Gynt Trail, named after the Henrik Ibsen play about a wastrel who meets mountain trolls. Take it.
- The trail feels similar to St. George's Trail but is steeper and shorter.
- Again pop out onto the old Grouse Mountain highway. The route (here called "Bill's Trail" or "Mt. Fromme Trail") continues across the road and ditch, where it continues to climb, skirting an old quarry.
- The route continues steadily but gently upwards through second-growth forest, topping a knoll, then briefly descending, and then climbing again. You will come to a marked four-way intersection.
- Take the north trail up a few more steps to the summit of Fromme.

ROUTE 2:
FROM SOUTH – UPPER PEER GYNT TRAIL FROM OLD GROUSE MOUNTAIN HIGHWAY TO SUMMIT

- From Lions Gate Bridge, drive east to Capilano Road.
- Drive north up Capilano Road, which turns into Nancy Green Way.
- Arrive at Grouse Mountain Skyride, where there is pay parking in paved and gravel lots.

- This route, usually marked with a sign at the base of the summit plateau, provides a steeper and more direct route between the summit and the old Grouse Mountain highway.
- It runs to the west of the main Fromme trail (Route 1), connecting with the old Grouse Mountain highway about 1.5 km north of a gravel pit and about 1.5 km south of the final switchback, described in Route 3 below. Although rooty and rocky, it is generally well flagged and blazed.

ROUTE 3:
FROM WEST – GROUSE MOUNTAIN
- From Highway 1, take Exit 21 to Lynn Valley. Drive up and to the end of Mountain Highway. Go through a gate and drive up the gravel road for about 500 m. Park in the gravel lot.
- From the top of the Grouse Mountain Skyride, head east past the chalet. You will see the start of the old Grouse Mountain highway.
- Proceed downhill along five switchbacks.
- After the longest stretch, you will see a dead-end side road leading back and to the right. Ignore it.
- A few paces later you will come to a flat area with a pond. An obvious trail leads northeast along some old shinglebolt road. You will see some ancient log water pipes, remnants of a pipeline from Kennedy Lake. The route joins with Erik the Red Trail and heads south and up.
- After several minutes of relatively gentle grade, turn southeast and start climbing on the obvious, if narrower, trail. There should be regular flagging. This is perilous when muddy, especially downhill. Make liberal use of your hands.

ROUTE 4:
FROM BCMC TRAIL AND BASE OF GROUSE MOUNTAIN SKYRIDE
- From the Grouse parking lot take the BCMC trail to a fork at 890 m where a minor trail heads east to the base of the Screaming Eagle chair.
- Continue traversing across the bottom of the ski run to a gravel road leading northeast to Mountain Highway.
- This trail does a switchback where it crosses Mosquito Creek and then heads southeast to the base of the route up to Fromme.
- Follow this to the summit of Fromme.

ROUTE 5:
FROM DAM MOUNTAIN VIA ERIK THE RED TRAIL
- The route from Grouse to Fromme takes you to a seldom visited land of the lost, a world of mist, huge trees, boulder fields, and some nifty technical single-track. There are spectacular bushes teeming with the best-tasting black huckleberries and mountain blueberries you will encounter. Flocks and flocks of chickens of the woods and lemon boletes.
- From Dam Mountain Trail, at the widened viewpoint, head east over some logs down the Thunderbird Ridge trail.
- Soon, turn right and proceed down to Barrier Creek.

- At times, the trail is overgrown. Winter storms will usually leave it with some blowdown.
- The trail ends at the base of Fromme, at Pipeline Pass, near the headwaters of Mosquito Creek.
- After several minutes of relatively gentle grade, start climbing on the obvious if thinner trail. There should be regular flagging. This is perilous when muddy, especially if proceeding downhill. Make liberal use of your hands.

HANES VALLEY PEAKS

(3 PEAKS)

The three most remote and arguably most hazardous peaks in this book are usually gained from Hanes Valley Trail, a 5-km route joining the Grouse Mountain peaks (connecting with them at Crown Pass, at the base of Crown) with the Lynn Headwaters trails (linking to them at Norvan Creek). Of course, it is much longer than a 5-km hike: the full Lynn Headwaters to Grouse Chalet loop is 18 km, and much farther than that psychologically and physically. As set out in the Echo Peak profile below, Hanes Valley Trail had its origin in a trail to the zinc mine explorations on what we will refer to as Palisade Ridge (also called Echo Ridge), the east–west ridge to the north of the Hanes Valley. BCMC led expeditions to both Echo and the north peaks of Crown (including Crown N1) via this route, usually after camping at the BCMC site near the confluence of Hanes Creek, Lynn Creek, and Norvan Creek. It is an area of giant trees, spectacular mushrooms, bears, waterfalls, archaeological finds, and grand views. It is also, for the ill-prepared or badly timed, a place of danger and at times death.

A SPECIAL WARNING ABOUT THE HANES VALLEY TRAIL

In perfect summer conditions, the Hanes Valley is a splendid adventure, offering a loop from Lynn Headwater Regional Park to the Grouse Mountain peaks. A fit hiker can do the loop in a single long summer day. But in anything short of perfect conditions, it is potentially deadly. It is one of the most frequent spots for fatalities, serious injuries, and North Shore Rescue call-outs. In November 2011 Brian Safari Mbaruk went missing in the area. His body was found near Norvan Falls the following May. In December 2014 hiker Liang Jin went missing. In February 2015 his body was found in Hanes Valley, huddled under a boulder for shelter.

Several factors combine to make Hanes Valley Trail especially perilous. Both approaches (from Grouse Mountain or Lynn Headwaters) lead the hiker, via gentle trails and friendly signposts, from areas swarming with casual hikers to much more inhospitable, unsignposted realms. The numerous streams between Norvan Creek and the rock field, while sleepy rock-hops in late summer and autumn, are raging torrents at other times, requiring crossings over slick rocks and logs. The rock field at the west end of the trail is a slippery death trap in rain and a postholing ordeal in deep snow. In the spring and early summer, the rock field becomes a vertical ice rink: a slip will blast you at high velocity to death or grievous injury on the rocks below. Even in the summer you will hit wobbly rocks that can slice, crush,

---

or break legs. In the winter the valley is prone to vertical avalanches. In the spring (and at any time) there can be rockslides from the sheer cliffs on all sides. Routefinding on the rock field is tricky at the best of times: challenging in good weather and impossible in the fog to which the valley is very prone. There are bears and cougars. And there is no cell coverage if anything goes wrong. Have we convinced you that this terrain should not be underestimated? Only enter this area during perfect conditions, with sufficient fitness and experience, with the Ten Essentials, and with at least one other person.

GETTING THERE

- From Ironworkers Memorial (Second Narrows) Bridge, take Highway 1 to the Mountain Highway exit right (up).
- Continue to Lynn Valley Road. Turn right.
- Continue to the end of Lynn Valley Road, past End of the Line General Store, and through the yellow gate into Lynn Headwaters Regional Park. There is rare premium parking at the end of the road, near the bridge and three overflow parking lots farther back towards the gate.

Note that the gate gets locked at sundown, which could trap your car and possibly triggering NSR if you have not left a message.

HANES VALLEY BAGGER TIPS

These three peaks can be done together in one trip. Be prepared for lots of bush. This is a very remote area, so experience is required. The way follows Route 1 for Echo Peak below and then crosses the ridge to the base of Crown N1. From there it's a slabby scramble to the top. Rather than retracing your steps, descend directly down into the Hanes Valley and return via the Lynn Headwaters trail. This loop can also be done in the reverse direction with no change in difficulty.

Round-trip distance:
35.2 km

Time:
15:35

Elevation gain:
1830 m

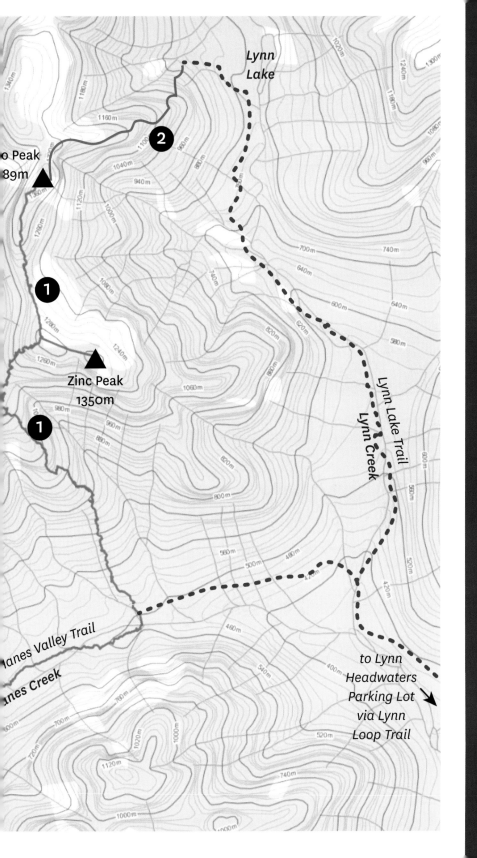

Lynn Lake

o Peak
89m ▲

Zinc Peak
1350m

Lynn Lake Trail

Lynn Creek

Hanes Valley Trail

Hanes Creek

to Lynn
Headwaters
Parking Lot
via Lynn
Loop Trail

CROWN N1
(CN1) (1408 M)

Stunning view of the back side of the Camel from a rarely summited peak.

CAUTION:
Remote! No trail! Steep!
Exposure! Dangerous!

PROMINENCE:
158 m.

LATITUDE/LONGITUDE:
N49.42167 W123.08972.

BANG FOR BUCK:
2/5

PEAK VIEW:
3/5. Unusual view of Crown back side
and Capilano Reservoir Road.

TRUE SUMMIT LOCATION:
Obvious: at west end of ridge.

HEADWATERS:
Tributary creeks of Hanes Creek
(into Lynn Creek).

BEST VIEWS FROM:
Crown, Fromme, Echo.

TRIP INFORMATION

Round-trip distance: 30.2 km via Hanes Valley.

Elevation gain: 1232 m.

Time: 13–16 hours (13:32 from Lynn Headwaters parking lot).

Difficulty: 5+/5. Far; bushwhacking; no marked trail.

Snow-free: Usually mid-June.

Must-see: Industrial archaeology on top of Palisade Ridge.

Scenery: 3/5.

Kids: 0/5. Do not bring children.

Dogs: 1/5. Only if the dog has been bad.

Runnability: 1/5 (but Hanes Valley and Lynn Headwaters approach trails are 5/5).

Terrain: From west: boulder fields and some rocky scrambling. From east: bushwhacking up steep terrain through first-growth forest and berry bushes while dodging cliff bands.

Public transit: #228 bus from Lonsdale Quay or #210 from Phibbs Exchange.

Cell coverage: Some on peak; inconsistent below.

Sun: Sufficient shade for beginning. Some exposure en route. Exposed peak.

Water: After Hanes Creek, only a few manky tarns.

Route links: Zinc, Echo, Forks.

HISTORY

Name origin: Naming convention for an unnamed peak; next major peak north of Crown.

Name status: Unofficial.

First ascent: Unknown. Climbed regularly by BCMC members in the 1930s.

Other names: The BCMC *BC Mountaineer* throughout the 1920s and '30s refers to Crown N1 and the surrounding bumps as the North Peaks of Crown, with Crown N1 singled out as *the* "North Peak of Crown" (1922). Bivouac.com calls it "Godmother Peak" (named by Fred Touche), riffing on the Charles Perrault–Sleeping Beauty theme. See also Echo (Perrault) Peak.

Crown N1 from Palisade Ridge.

Crown N1 is in fact the second bump north of Crown Mountain: located where the ridge running from Crown turns from north–south to west–east. A pointier, more exposed peak between it and Crown has been called "Spindle Peak." Spindle isn't profiled in this book, because of its exposure. Crown N1 almost didn't make the cut either, because the potential for injury is great and there is no established trail. This climb should not be attempted in less than perfect conditions; otherwise, those rocks would be a slippery death trap. It should also only be attempted during the long days of summer. You will have plenty of false starts, the going will be slow, and this is no place to routefind in less than good conditions.

That said, you will almost certainly be the only ones on the peak and you will be rewarded with waterfalls, fat blueberries, and some perhaps too-exhilarating hand-climbing through shrubbery. On the peak, you will be rewarded by unique and magnificent views of the back side of the Camel and Crown, along with the Howe Sound Crest Trail peaks, the watershed road, Capilano Lake, Sky Pilot, the Garibaldi peaks, and the entire Hanes Valley.

The BCMC regularly led trips to the North Peaks of Crown, including Crown N1, in the 1920s and 1930s. The North Peaks were approached predominantly from Grouse and Crown Pass, but also (as in a July 1927 trip) from Lynn Valley via Lynn Forks camp and what was then Zinc Mines Trail, essentially Route 1 below. Some of the North Peaks trips involved very exposed and technical climbs up the back side of Crown, an admirable feat in hobnailed boots.

ROUTE 1:

FROM SOUTH – LYNN HEADWATERS, HANES VALLEY TRAIL, AND UP PALISADE RIDGE

<u>Caution:</u> This is a remote route, with no trail. Only attempt it if you are very experienced with routefinding and with climbing exposed pitches, and are armed with a map and GPS.

Lynn Headwaters to east base of Palisade Ridge: Start at the Lynn Headwaters parking lot. Go along Cedars Mill Trail and Lynn Headwaters Trail to Norvan Creek. Cross Norvan Creek suspension bridge.

- Go west along Hanes Valley Trail. Go past the Lynn Lake junction. Cross a large creek on a log. Go about 2.5 km west on Hanes Valley Trail.
- Start the ascent by hiking up one of two creekbeds (dry in August). The larger, east creek (shown on most maps as having three tributaries) dead-ends at a waterfall, at which point you will want to scamper up to the ridge on your left and start the long bushwhack straight up. The narrower, west creek may be flagged with three strips of bright-green tape on a tree in the middle of the creek. (*If on the Hanes Valley Trail approach you hit the western rock-slide area leading up to Crown Pass, you've overshot these creeks by about a kilometre.*)

East base of Palisade Ridge to the ridgecrest: On whichever creek you choose, trundle up until you tire of creek climbing. Then trundle up some more to the ridge between the two creeks and go up, up, up.

- Again there is no trail, so it is a game of follow the best contour lines.
- You will climb past a series of spectacularly huge old-growth cedars and Douglas firs.
- After a long while you hit a less steep section. Here (and elsewhere on this trip) you will likely see copious bear scat. There is also, intriguingly, a pile of mining core samples and, nearby, the ruins of a long-term campsite, with cast-iron stove, wash bowls, a hand mixer, and metal barrels galore. In the autumn you may spot a dead tree covered with countless chicken-of-the-woods fungi practically glowing orange.
- From here, one can traverse the slope to the right, leading up to the ridge (and a nasty hanging valley on the right). Alas, it is a thickly vegetated ridge, so one has little sense of being on a ridge, and there is no view.

Top of Palisade Ridge westward along ridge: Instead of heading east, head west along the ridge.

- At the top of Palisade Ridge, you will see a grassy area with various boards, perhaps covering materials from the old zinc campsite located here in the early 1950s.
- Head west (left) and up, staying generally in the middle of the ridge.
- **Stay on the ridge. DO NOT** traverse any of the three subpeak bumps on the ridge in an attempt to save time. To the south, it is oppressively bushy and steep. To the north, there are sheer drops.
- Between each bump is a pleasant low area of heather and grass, with shallow, muddy tarns.
- At the final bump, you will see a view of Crown N1 across the col. It does not look promising: a seemingly sheer wall of trees.
- Descend to the shoulder: not a steep descent.

Ascent of Crown N1: Zigzag your way up the wall of trees. You will have to use your hands for most of the climb, but you should never feel exposed, despite the steepness.

You will frequently duck under the evergreens and, just as frequently, cuss. If in doubt, veer left (south).

- This leads to a balcony in front of a near-cliff on south face of Crown N1. At this point, veer right again, into shrubbery. And then head out onto a long rock slab resembling those on the ascent of Crown. Up and around to a false summit, and then the base of the peak itself.

Crown N1 with Cathedral and Coliseum behind.

- The peak proper is claimed from the right/east, up to a false summit, and then hiking as far up and west as you can.

ROUTE 2:

FROM SOUTH – LYNN HEADWATERS, HANES VALLEY TRAIL, AND DIRECTLY UP TO CROWN N1

Lynn Headwaters to base of Hanes rock field: Go along Cedars Mill Trail and Lynn Headwaters Trail to Norvan Creek. Cross the suspension bridge.

- Go west along Hanes Valley Trail. Go past the Lynn Lake junction. Cross a large creek on a log. Go about 1.5 km west on Hanes Valley Trail.
- Travel to the Hanes Valley boulder field either from Grouse Mountain (see Crown Mountain route description) or from Lynn Valley (see Echo Peak description).
- At the base of the boulder field, where the forest largely thins out, cut north and straight up towards the right side of Crown N1, generally following the most pleasing contour line.

Note: Resist the temptation to gain height on the Hanes Valley boulder field. A traverse will put you through the thickest alder patch known to humans, interspersed with devil's club, followed by a snow field and a gravelly valley.

- Aim to the northwest: the white band, with a creek, below the Crown N1 peak.

Up Crown N1 north rock field to base of Crown N1: The route starts as a bushwhack. Then it goes over a rock and boulder field, then creekbeds, then foliage patches. At times it will be very steep. Generally head straight up along the gentlest path.

- You will then require a few careful hand-climbs up a few short rock faces. If in doubt, veer right.

Slabs leading up to Crown N1, in foreground.

- This leads to a balcony in front of a near-cliff on the south face of Crown N1. At this point, veer right again, into shrubbery. Then head out onto a long rock slab resembling those on the ascent of Crown. Go up and around to the base of the peak itself.
- The peak proper is claimed from the right/east, up to a false summit, and then hiking as far up and west as you can.

ROUTE 3:
FROM WEST, FROM CROWN PASS
Follow the route from Grouse Mountain Chalet to Crown Pass described above.
- From Crown Pass, descend the rock field to its base.
- Follow Route 2 up to Crown N1.

ZINC PEAK

(ZIN) (1350 M)

Steep bushwhacking alleviated by industrial archaeology, massive old-growth giants, and a fine view of the Hanes Valley.

CAUTION:
Remote! No trail! Steep!
Some exposure! Bears!

PROMINENCE:
130 m.

LATITUDE/LONGITUDE:
N49.429677 W123.066485.

BANG FOR BUCK:
1/5

PEAK VIEW:
3/5. Unusual views of Echo,

Cathedral, Burwell, Hanes Valley, Crown, Crown N1, Forks, and Goat.

TRUE SUMMIT LOCATION:
Both peaks identical height.

HEADWATERS:
Tributary creeks of Hanes Creek (into Lynn Creek); Lynn Creek.

BEST VIEWS FROM:
Forks, Goat, Coliseum, North Needle.

TRIP INFORMATION

Round-trip distance: 28 km via Hanes Valley.

Elevation gain: 1263 m.

Time: 9–13 hours (9:08 from Lynn Headwaters parking lot).

Difficulty: 5/5. Far, bushwhacking, very little marked trail.

Snow-free: Usually mid-June.

Must-sees: Logging camps; old-growth trees.

Scenery: 3/5.

Kids: 0/5. Do not bring children.

Dogs: 1/5. Only if the dog has been bad.

Runnability: 1/5 (but Hanes Valley and Lynn Headwaters approach trails are 5/5).

Terrain: Bushwhacking up steep terrain through first-growth forest and berry bushes while dodging cliff bands.

Public transit: #228 bus from Lonsdale Quay or #210 from Phibbs Exchange.

Cell coverage: Only on peak.

Sun: Sufficient shade for the beginning. Some exposure en route. Exposed peak.

Water: After Hanes Creek, only a few manky tarns.

Route links: Echo, Crown N1, Forks.

HISTORY

Name origin: From the exploratory zinc mines in area.

Name status: Unofficial.

Other names: South Perrault / South Echo. Don Munday recounted that it was called "Cat Scat Peak" after a cat owned by the zinc mine manager, Mr. Emmons. followed its owner up the peak on the ascent.

First ascent: Before 1910 by Mr. Emmons of the zinc mine and his cat.

Other write-ups: Much of the information on zinc exploration in this area came from remarkable on-foot research that culminated in an amazing mash-up by Craig Williams superimposing historical mine stake maps onto Google Earth. See ClubTread.com at is.gd/08Hf53

Zinc Peaks are at the southeastern corner of Palisade Ridge, which runs northeast from Crown along Hanes Valley and then north to Echo Peak, following Lynn Creek Valley, before joining Burwell above Lynn Lake. "Zinc Mountain" is shown on an early, undated City of North Vancouver Engineering Department map of the Lynn Creek watershed. The rocks on the peak are crumbling, red-black and slatey, seeming more like Brunswick than the surrounding granitic peaks.

West and East Zinc Peaks are separated by a gentle and short col that is easily negotiated. East Zinc Peak has a ruined helicopter pad and the apparent start of a new helicopter pad.

The history of zinc mining and exploration in this far-off area of the North Shore peaks is almost unknown to modern Vancouverites. Claims were staked on both sides of Hanes Creek and Lynn Creek, from Norvan Creek to approximately 2 km west of the creek (roughly where the Hanes Valley trail starts to climb up the rock field to Crown Pass). The claims ran all the way up to the top of Palisade Ridge. As you hike through thick forests and pass by old-growth trees, be thankful that these mining ventures never reached fruition. The first claim staked was Kemptville, in 1893. By 1914 additional claims had been filed: Evening Star, Jersey, Angel, The Cascades, Fleming, Pretty Bess, Banker, Mountain Lions, and Lucky Star. By 1912 most claims had been consolidated in Lynn Creek Zinc Mines Ltd., and considerable exploratory work was carried out. In 1915 nine men were employed, digging 220 feet of a 5x7 foot tunnel, with an additional 250 feet of prospecting tunnels and 330 feet of diamond drilling. At this time a camp, with two offices, a bunkhouse, a cookhouse, a storehouse, a powder house and a blacksmith shop, was built on site. A trail, approximating the route of Cedars Mill Trail, Lynn Creek Trail, and the east end of Hanes Valley Trail was built to the mine, and is shown on the 1936 trail map. The project lay dormant for a time and was briefly revitalized in 1924 but was not activated. A drop in zinc prices and the closure of the Upper Lynn for water intake in 1929 dampened efforts at revitalization. In 1951 and 1952 Graham Bousquet Gold Mines of Toronto optioned the holdings of Lynn Creek Zinc Mines Ltd. Employees were helicoptered in, right to the top of the ridge. Most of the industrial remnants you will find on this adventure date from that effort. Tunnels and camp detritus such as bedsprings can be found just upslope of Hanes Valley Trail, along with a signposted warning – which should be heeded – about the danger of exploring abandoned mine shafts. As you reach the top of the first climb up the Palisade Ridge, you will likely see much evidence of their presence, in the form of core samples, cast-iron stoves, pipes, shovels, bottles, and crockery.

Bousquet received permission to build a road into the area along the route of the existing Cedars Mill / Lynn Headwaters trails but never proceeded. Remarkably, as late as 1985, a mining syndicate sought to revitalize the mine and cut a road from Lynn Valley Road to the site. In a presentation to the district council, the company cited a 1918 report that estimated 700,000 tonnes of zinc, worth about $70-million in 1985, to be under the mountain. By that time, Lynn Headwaters Regional Park was well under way to approval, and the mining proposal was rejected. That said, the claim area, on the slopes of Palisade Ridge, remains a postage-stamp carve-out in the regional park.

The climb up to Palisade Ridge, described below as Route 1, will take you, successively climbing, through the Jersey, Kemptville, Evening Star, and August Fraction claims. You will see the most remnants at the lowest and highest sections of the slope.

Route 1:
FROM SOUTH – LYNN HEADWATERS AND HANES VALLEY TRAIL
Caution: There is no formal trail for most of this route. Steep. Easy to get lost. You must be experienced and have good routefinding skills to climb this peak.

Lynn Headwaters to base of Palisade Ridge: Start at the Lynn Headwaters parking lot. Go along Cedars Mill Trail and Lynn Headwaters Trail to Norvan Creek (8 km). Cross the suspension bridge.

- Go west along Hanes Valley Trail past the Lynn Lake junction. Cross a large creek on a log.

To top of Palisade Ridge: At around 1.5 km west on Hanes Valley Trail, start the ascent by hiking up one of two creekbeds (dry in August).

1. The larger, east creek, which Hanes Valley Trail clearly dips up and down into (shown on most maps as having three tributaries), dead-ends at a waterfall, at which point you will want to scamper up to the ridge on your left and start the long bushwhack straight up.

2. The narrower, flatter, west creek is the preferable approach. Hanes Valley Trail does not dip much as it goes over this smaller creek (which may be flagged). Head about 10 m up and then cut into the forest on the right. *(If on the Hanes Valley Trail approach you hit the western rock slide area leading up to Crown Pass, you've overshot the creeks by about a kilometre.)*

- On either approach creek, trundle up until you tire of creek climbing, and then amble up to the ridge between the two creeks. Then go up, up, up.
- Again there is no trail, so it is a game of follow the contour lines.
- You will climb past a series of spectacularly huge old-growth cedars and Douglas firs.
- After a long while you hit a less steep section. Here there is copious bear scat (as there was on much of the hike). There is also, intriguingly, a pile of mining core samples and, nearby, the ruins of a long-term campsite, with cast-iron stove, wash bowls, a hand mixer, and metal barrels galore. Such industrial archaeology is found across a wide swath of the upper ridge. In autumn, you may spot a dead tree covered with countless chicken-of-the-woods fungi, practically glowing orange.
- From here one can traverse the slope to the right, leading up to the ridge (and a nasty hanging valley on the right). Alas, it is thickly vegetated up there, so one has little sense of being on a ridge, and there is no view.

West Palisade Ridge to North Palisade Ridge: Turn left, traversing the left slopes of West Zinc Peak. The contour lines would indicate that this west traverse is fairly wide and flat, but it is for the most part a cliffhanger (sore arms again).

- Eventually you come to a rocky landslide area. One can scamper up it, veering left, to a heather meadow.
- Then hook right (south) for an easy ascent up West Zinc Peak.
- West and East Zinc peaks are separated by a gentle and shallow col that is easily negotiated.
- East Zinc has a ruined helicopter pad and the apparent beginnings of a new helicopter pad.

ROUTE 2:
FROM NORTH – LYNN LAKE AND ECHO PEAK
Follow the description to Echo Peak, below. Continue south on the ridge. Descend via either this route or Route 1.

ECHO PEAK

(ECO) (1389 M)

Steep bushwhacking alleviated by industrial archaeology, massive old-growth giants, and a visit to the most obscure North Shore peak.

CAUTION:
Remote! No trail! Steep! Some exposure! Bears!

PROMINENCE:
259 m.

LATITUDE/LONGITUDE:
N49.43655 W123.06483.

BANG FOR BUCK:
1/5

PEAK VIEW:
3/5. Unusual view of Crown back side and Needles, with Sky Pilot

Group, Ben Lomond, and Red, Garibaldi, Bagpipe, and Haggis Peak to the north.

TRUE SUMMIT LOCATION:
Of the three peaks, the southern one on the ridge is the highest.

HEADWATERS:
Healmond Creek (into Capilano River), tributary creeks of Hanes Creek (into Lynn Creek); Lynn Creek.

BEST VIEWS FROM:
Grouse Mountain Eye of the Wind; Crown N1; Cathedral.

TRIP INFORMATION

Round-trip distance: 30.4 km via Hanes Valley.

Elevation gain: 1302 m.

Time: 9–13 hours (9:08 from Lynn Headwaters parking lot).

Difficulty: 5/5. Far, bushwhacking, very little marked trail.

Snow-free: Usually early June.

Must-sees: Logging camps; old-growth trees.

Scenery: 3/5.

Kids: 0/5. Do not bring children.

Dogs: 1/5. Only if the dog has been bad.

Runnability: 1/5 (but Hanes Valley and Lynn Headwaters approach trails are 5/5).

Terrain: Bushwhacking up steep terrain through first-growth forest and berry bushes while dodging cliff bands.

Public transit: #228 bus from Lonsdale Quay or #210 from Phibbs Exchange.

Cell coverage: Only on peak.

Sun: Sufficient shade for beginning. Some exposure en route. Exposed peak.

Water: After Hanes Creek, only a few manky tarns.

Route links: Crown N1. Forks. Could do a sweep with Crown and Grouse Mountain, but Echo is a long haul.

Name origin: Known as Echo Peak from the 1910s to the 1940s, because of its echo, the peak was renamed Mt. Perrault by Robin Tivy of bivouac.com, after Charles Perrault, he widely published 17th-century popularizer of early European folktales.

Name status: Unofficial.

Other names: Don Munday and hiking companions called Echo Peak "Mt. Noname" on their first ascent.

First ascent: Likely September 16–17, 1910, by BCMC members, probably consisting of Don Munday and six other hikers approaching up Lynn Creek.

Little Red Riding Hood, one of the most primally terrifying stories of all time, was first published by Charles Perrault as *Le Petit Chaperon rouge* in 1697. Author David Crerar's first ascent of Perrault's namesake North Shore peak some years later, however, transcended that tale in terms of gruelling horror. Its superlatives abounded: densest concentration of devil's club on a bagging hike; worst-lacerated legs from underbrush; loudest scream when entering bathtub; thickest concentration of pine needles left in tub.

Giant cedar below Zinc Peak.   Evidence of black bears below Zinc Peak.

This description is unfair and reflects the poor weather and unhappy route chosen at that time. Echo Peak does have some very pleasant features. On a clear day it provides interesting views of the back side of Crown Mountain, and one gets to bag probably the most obscure and remote North Shore peak. The steep hike up to the initial ridge offers a spectacular parade of old-growth Douglas fir and cedar trees. There is a bounty of plump blueberries of all varieties.

You will see ample evidence of the little-known history of zinc mining on the North Shore. And you may see evidence – in the form of tufts of white fur, or even the creature itself – of that rarest of North Shore sights, a mountain goat, as Crerar and Ean Jackson did during their initial ascent. The goat was as shocked as they were.

Echo is located on a bushy ridge of peaks extending east and northeast from Crown Mountain. It was given the name "Perrault" in the 1990s. The name refers to the nickname for West Crown, in the opposite direction, which is also known as Sleeping Beauty, after another tale popularized by Perrault. The appearances of the name "Echo Peak" up into the 1940s occur in BCMC reports from that time. BCMC trips in 1918, 1923, 1924, 1925, and 1928 went to Lynn Lake and then Echo Peak by

Another big cedar, up Palisade Ridge from Hanes Valley.

travelling up a gully before descending back down via Zinc Mine Trail (see Zinc Peak above). According to these reports, and confirmed by the authors, the namesake echo can indeed be heard from the peak, bouncing off the bluff on the nearly as tall bump to the north. Echo is curved, dramatic, and pointy when viewed from the east, north, and west, but slabby when viewed from the south. Writing of his first ascent, in September 1910, Don Munday remarked that it "…is an odd, conical peak possessing a certain amount of individuality…" He noted that the summit wreaked havoc on their compasses, and he supposed it might possess strong magnetic properties. Munday also recorded that they spent three hours on the top, "most of it debating suitable (and unsuitable) names, finally compromising on Mt. Noname, and as such it is known." This silly name was soon supplanted by "Echo," the name chosen by later BCMC members.

Significant caution should be exercised on this adventure. There is no trail: it is a long exercise of bushwhacking and routefinding. Don't even think of doing this hike unless you have ample experience, good routefinding skills, a powerful GPS or comprehensive map, and exceptional stamina and patience. Long pants, shirt, and gloves are heartily recommended: this is primo West Coast bushwhacking.

ROUTE 1:
FROM SOUTH – LYNN HEADWATERS AND HANES VALLEY TRAIL

<u>Caution:</u> No formal trail exists for most of this route. Steep. Easy to get lost. You must be experienced and have good routefinding skills to climb this peak.

- Follow Route 1 for Zinc Peak described above, from Lynn Headwaters to the base of Palisade Ridge to the top of Palisade Ridge.

West Palisade Ridge to North Palisade Ridge: turn left, traversing the left slopes of Zinc Peaks, and continue on to the south side of Echo. The contour lines would indicate that this west traverse is fairly wide and flat, but it is for the most part a cliffhanger (sore arms again).

- At around 1215 m, you come to a rocky avalanche path. One can scamper up it, veering to the left toward a heather meadow, then down and to the right a bit, into the saddle between the peaks, before climbing again to start on the long, slow ridge leading up to Echo proper.
- This nasty, heavily vegetated bushwhack is alleviated by a few heather and snow fields, but it also requires multiple vertical frontal assaults on ramparts of blueberry bushes.
- Eventually there is more rock underfoot and a scamper up a crumbly, rocky knoll. Continue north and down along the ridge, now pleasantly covered with heather and short pines.
- Look up at the peak to see a notch in the trees. Head straight up towards it. If you keep this bearing, the bushwhack up the final ridge will be less unpleasant.
- Pop out of the trees, and a final, easy climb up rocks leads to the heather-dotted peak, marked with a very, very small cairn. To the northwest across a deep valley is the Echo subpeak, mere metres shorter.

ROUTE 2:

FROM EAST – LYNN HEADWATERS AND LYNN LAKE TRAIL

<u>Warning:</u> This track is even rougher than the one described just above. Strongly recommended to be done only in late summer, when the snow has melted and the water flow has abated. This is a remote trek, with some exposure at the top.

- Start at the Lynn Headwaters parking lot. Go along Cedars Mill Trail and Lynn Headwaters Trail to Norvan Creek. Cross a suspension bridge.
- Go west along Hanes Valley Trail to the Lynn Lake junction. Take the trail north to Lynn Lake.
- The route goes up, then down, and then generally follows Lynn Creek. You will literally be rock-hopping for most of this, so do not attempt it in anything but dry weather: these rocks are slick.
- The creek runs straight north for the bulk of the route. At about three-quarters of the way, be sure not to miss the tricky turn of the creek (and the trail) to the right (north) at a bluff. The natural (and incorrect) inclination is to continue along the seemingly more dominant creekbed toward the northwest, which is wider and more open.
- At the narrow Lynn Lake, head west and up towards Echo, following a creek that forks at 880 m. Take the south (left) fork up.
- The gully route is increasingly steep.
- Continue climbing up the gully. You will pop out onto a col below Echo Peak, to your left. Cross a narrow ridge. Head to a narrow ledge which leads to an obvious place to pull yourself up. You will have to use your hands and vegetation frequently. *There is real exposure on this route. Be careful.*

Up the final ridge to Echo.

LYNN PEAKS

(5 PEAKS)

Given its proximity to both Lynn Headwaters Regional Park and the Lower Seymour Conservation Reserve (LSCR), and the bustling and expanding (too fast) neighbourhood of Lynn Valley, it is not surprising that Lynn Peaks is one of the more popular hiking areas in the Lower Mainland. It probably should not be: the trail up to Rice and Lynn is surprisingly crumbly and has many twisted ankles notched in its belt. The perceived summit, a rocky viewpoint over the Lower Seymour Conservation Reserve, is not in fact the top. The actual peaks are viewless and joyless copses of third-growth forest. The classic Bruce Fairley climbing guidebook described them as "entirely forested... neither difficult nor interesting."

That said, in the past decade, the expansion of the trail to the Needles has invigorated what would be a dull climb for any single peak into a pleasing multi-bag adventure, tying into Hydraulic Creek Trail and down to the LSCR, or as an out-and-back. It is a decent trail run. Hydraulic Creek marks the division between the southern Lynn Peaks and the northern Needles.

The three (actually five) summits north of the Lynn peaks are known as "the Needles." Although somewhat deserving of this name when viewed from Lynn Peak, from anywhere else they are merely a series of low, lumpy bumps with almost nothing needley about them. That said, they offer a baby step into a more backwoods experience: always reasonably close to civilization, with a half-decent trail, but you will probably be the only one there. And the riches of berry bushes, waterfalls, and the occasional old-growth tree provide surprises.

There are two primary access points to the Lynn area: Lynn Headwaters Regional Park (from the southwest, at the end of Lynn Valley Road) and the Lower Seymour Conservation Reserve (from the southeast, at the end of Lillooet Road). Both have a reasonable amount of parking. These two areas are linked by a pipeline bridge at the end of Rice Lake Road, opposite End of the Line General Store, as well as a trail running from the Cedars Mill Trailhead at the Lynn Headwaters parking lot, past Rice Lake, to the start of the LSCR–Seymour Valley Trail.

Easy access to this wilderness playground is relatively recent. On the east side, the Seymour Demonstration Forest, with its 12-km paved Seymour Valley Trailway, opened in 1987. This area was also at one time off-limits as being watershed; the first plan for it was to demonstrate renewable forestry methods. Its ecological and recreational aspects were emphasized by its renaming in 2000 as the Lower Seymour Conservation Reserve. This reserve stretches from the gazebo and parking at the south end of the trailway, to the Seymour Dam (built in 1928, creating the artificial Seymour Lake) and a fish hatchery at the north end. You'll find an abundance of side trails here, including some old-growth trees that somehow escaped the forester's chainsaw in this heavily and repeatedly clear-cut area.

On the west side, the Lynn Headwaters was North Vancouver's water supply from 1883 to 1981 and off-limits from 1929. From at least 1923 to 1940, those seeking access to Lynn Peaks, along with Mt. Seymour, Cathedral, North Peaks of Crown, Echo Peak and others then in the watershed, were required to carry a blood-test certificate confirming they had no diseases that would endanger the purity of the drinking water. When storms damaged the water intake (visible from the bridge just north of the Lynn Headwaters picnic area) over the 1981 Thanksgiving weekend, North Vancouver stopped relying on the Lynn watershed. The area was reopened to the public, and Lynn Headwaters Regional Park made its debut in 1985. Thanksgiving, indeed!

The primary artery on the Lynn Valley side is Cedars Mill–Lynn Headwaters Trail, stretching from the LSCR parking lot to past Norvan Falls, soon after which it forks. The north fork heads to the actual Lynn headwaters, at Lynn Lake. The west fork heads to Hanes Valley Trail. The Cedars Mill–Lynn Headwaters trail is gentle gravel for the first 3 km or so, and then becomes dirt, rocks, and roots. Unbeknownst to most Vancouverites, this trail to natural adventure and scenery has industrial origins. The initial road went to Cedars Mill, located roughly at the midpoint between the Cedars Mill Trail–Upper Lynn Loop Trail connector and the large debris flow marking the end of Cedars Mill Trail. Cedars Mill was a substantial undertaking, with several buildings, including a school. It operated from 1917 to 1929. The trail was extended in the years after the First World War, to support zinc exploration at the east end of what is now Hanes Valley Trail, around Norvan Creek (see Zinc Peak above for the history of those operations). The lower western slopes of the Lynn Peaks and the Needles were also explored for minerals, including gold, silver, and zinc, but primarily copper. Explorations at the Mountain Lion and Copper Duke Mine sites, located on the east side of Lynn Creek, roughly opposite the mouth of Wickenden Creek, bored five tunnels some 400 feet long and erected several buildings. In 1902, on a fishing trip to Lynn Lake, Mr. and Mrs. G.E. McDonald (the latter the first European woman to visit the lake) "saw several new mines on which development work was being done, and valuable copper deposits being opened up."

Space does not permit a survey of Lynn Valley's rich history. Logging began early there, in the 1860s. The Spicer Shingle Company laid extensive trails and flumes throughout the valley to transport trees and shingles. In 1897 its interests were purchased by Hastings Shingle and Manufacturing, whose foreman was J.M. Fromme. A decade later, Fromme would start his own enterprise, the Lynn Valley Lumber Co. Marvel and weep when you contemplate that some of the largest trees in the world grew, and were felled, here. One of the tallest Douglas firs in history was cut down in 1902 in Lynn Valley at Argyle Road and Mountain Highway, on the property of Alfred John Nye. The tree apparently measured 415 feet (126.5 m) tall, with a diameter of 14 feet 4 inches (4.3 m), with bark 13.5 inches (34 cm) thick. It took three days to cut down. Granted, we probably would not be living in North Vancouver or hiking these peaks were it not for the Edwardian-era lure of these magnificent forests. What has been lost is commemorated in the persistently remaining massive cedar stumps, scarred with plank-notches for cutting, seen throughout Lynn Valley.

Note that both Lynn Headwaters and the LSCR–Seymour Valley Trailway have gates that are locked at sundown. If you are parked there and come back late, you will be trapped. Worse yet, this may trigger a search and rescue operation or inconvenience police and park officials by having to make vehicle searches and inquiries to your loved ones. If you anticipate a late return, consider a bike approach or a drop-off or parking outside the gate. In a worst-case scenario, at least leave a note in your car.

Lynn Headwaters generally requires dogs to be on leash, except for the Cedars Mill–Lynn Headwaters Trail (until Norvan Falls): see map at metrovancouver.org/ services/parks/ParksPublications/LYN_dogtrailmap_Jan2013_web.pdf.

Dogs are not permitted on Seymour Valley Trailway, Fisherman's Trail (north of the Homestead Trail junction), or Rice Lake Loop Trail.

GETTING THERE

Route 1: West to Lynn Headwaters Regional Park

- From Ironworkers Memorial (Second Narrows) Bridge, drive Highway 1 to the Mountain Highway exit to the right (up).
- Continue to Lynn Valley Road and turn right.
- Go to the end of Lynn Valley Road, past End of the Line General Store and through the yellow gate into Lynn Headwaters Regional Park. There is rare premium parking at the end of the road, near the bridge, plus three overflow parking lots farther back towards the gate.
- Again note that the gate gets locked at sundown, which would trap your car inside and possibly trigger NSR if you have not left a message.

Route 2: East to Lower Seymour Conservation Reserve and Seymour Valley Trail

- From Ironworkers Memorial (Second Narrows) Bridge, drive Highway 1 to Exit 22A to the right. Then turn left up Lillooet Road.
- You will pass a horse stable, Capilano University, the North Vancouver cemetery, a prominent gate, and then (after several kilometres) the Seymour–Capilano water treatment plant. The road ends at a large gravel parking lot.
- The path starts next to the outhouses and map kiosk. Follow the trail leading to the west. This brings you to a gazebo and a paved road, where your journey begins.
- Again note that the gate (near the cemetery) gets locked at sundown, which could trap your car inside and possibly trigger NSR if you have not left a message.

The Lynn and Needle peaks can be done as a
traverse from north to south. Begin in the Lynn
Headwaters by heading up the trail towards Norvan
Falls and Coliseum. From the Coliseum–Needles
col you cross a ridge which takes you to the base of
North Needle. It's a bushy scramble from here but
then a nice traverse as you head southward over
the North, Middle, and South Needles. These three
summits are in the alpine but their more southerly
siblings of Lynn and Rice peak are treed summits.

Round-trip distance:
18.5 km

Time:
8:48

Elevation gain:
1830 m

South Lynn Peak: The Enchanted Forest

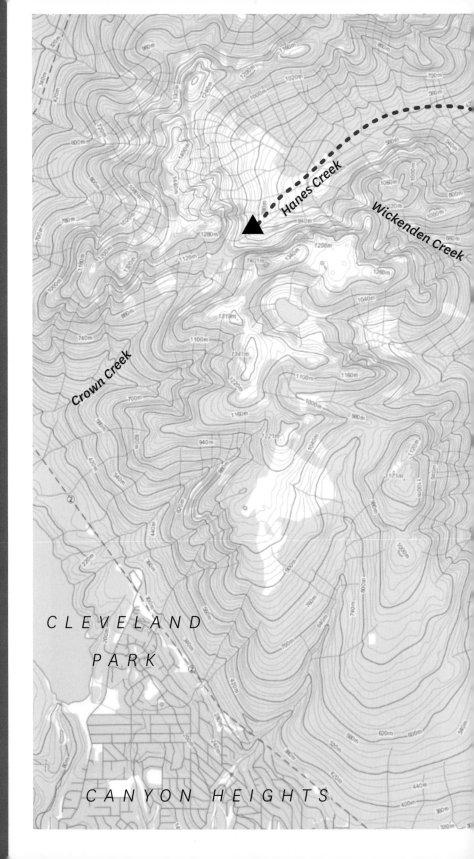

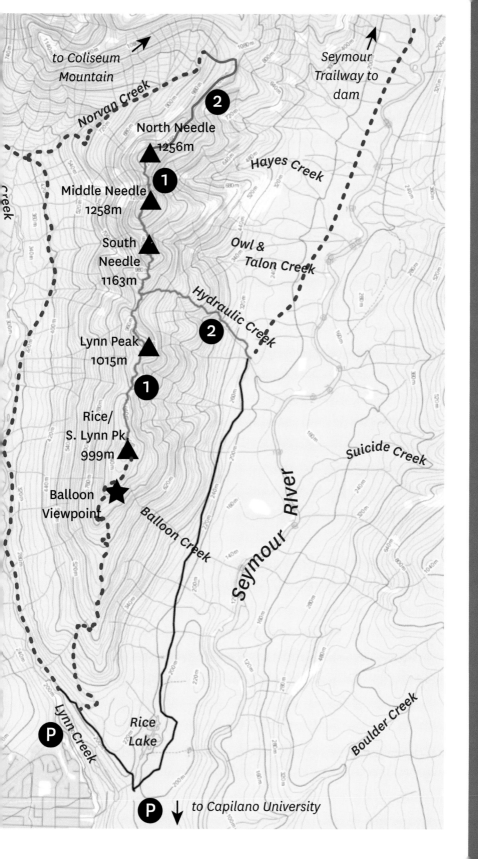

to Coliseum
Mountain

Norvan Creek

2

North Needle
1256m

1

Middle Needle
1258m

South
Needle
1163m

Seymour
Trailway to
dam

Hayes Creek

Owl &
Talon Creek

Hydraulic Creek

2

Lynn Peak
1015m

1

Rice/
S. Lynn Pk
999m

Balloon
Viewpoint

Balloon Creek

Seymour River

Suicide Creek

Boulder Creek

P

Lynn Creek

Rice
Lake

P ↓ to Capilano University

RICE (SOUTH LYNN) PEAK

(SLY) (999 M)

A dull, forested peak a little past the Balloon Lookout where most day-hikers stop.

CAUTION:
None.

PROMINENCE:
109 m.

LATITUDE/LONGITUDE:
N49.38500 W123.01778.

BANG FOR BUCK:
3/5

PEAK VIEW:
1/5. None.

TRUE SUMMIT LOCATION:
Treed knob about 1 km north
of Lynn Viewpoint.

HEADWATERS:
Rice Creek, Gin Pole Creek
(into Seymour River).

BEST VIEWS FROM:
Mt. Seymour, Burnaby,
Downtown and East Vancouver,
Ironworkers Bridge.

TRIP INFORMATION

Round-trip distance: 8.8 km from Lynn Headwaters.

Elevation gain: 801 m.

Time: 1.5–4 hours (2:10).

Difficulty: 2/5.

Snow free: Early June.

Must-sees: The viewpoint across to Seymour; old-growth red cedar and Douglas fir; giant cedar stumps.

Scenery: 2/5.

Kids: 3/5.

Dogs: 5/5. Leash required.

Runnability: 4/5.

Terrain: Forested trail up groomed paths, then well-defined trails.

Public transit: #209 bus from Phibbs Exchange to Lynn Headwaters Park; none to Mt. Seymour.

Cell coverage: Usually.

Sun: 100 per cent shaded.

Water: Nearby corner store; faucet at Lynn Headwaters Park; a few small creeks en route.

Route links: Needles Sweep or Needles Loop via Hydraulic Creek Trail.

HISTORY

Name origin: In its clear-cut state, one could see Rice Lake from the peak. The origin of the name "Rice Lake" is surprisingly elusive; Lynn Valley pioneer and historian Walter Draycott does not provide it. One theory is that a form of wild rice grew around its swampy edges, although there is no record of *Zizania* growing there (including in the botanical inventories of Rice Lake by Draycott, an enthusiastic botanist) and wild rice is not native to British Columbia. In the 1890s there was a log mill beside Rice Lake operated by Japanese workers. Almost certainly they would have eaten rice and perhaps grew it there as well, which may be the origin of the name.

Name status: Unofficial. Used on the 1936 L. Frank photographic survey of North Shore peaks; in November and December 1937 BCMC trip reports ("Rice Peak" and "Rice Mountain" respectively); a 1945 ACC Vancouver section trip; and in Dick Culbert guides (1965 and 1969). A March 1928 ACC *Avalanche Echoes* referred to the entire Lynn–Needles Ridge as the "Lynn Peaks." A 1929 map referred to the entire ridge as "The Needles," with no mention of Lynn or Rice.

Other names: The 1912 C.J. Heaney map referred to the Lynn Peaks and the Needles as "Lynn Peaks."

First ascent: August 23, 1908, by a BCMC party (Fred Mills, Fred Perry, and Charles Chapman) attempting to climb White Mountain (Burwell–Coliseum). Climbed May 2, 1909, by a BCMC party led by Mills, which is when the peak was named.

Confusion surrounds the various mountains named Lynn Peak. What most people (and the regional park signs) refer to as "Lynn Peak" is really not a peak at all, but a viewpoint over the Seymour Valley with a pleasant balcony. The place has a little-known history: Lynn and the Needles were the site of experimental balloon logging by the Balloon Transport Company from 1967 to remove timber knocked down by Hurricane Freda in 1962. The viewpoint was the docking station. The helium-filled balloon was 137 feet long by 52 feet wide and could lift up to 8.5 tons of logs. It cost approximately $100,000. After three days of operation, the balloon tore loose and drifted to Grouse Mountain, where it became impaled on a snag. Operations recommenced a few months later with a smaller balloon, but the experiment was not a success. Balloon Creek, below the tether site, commemorates this short-lived experiment.

Rice Peak, also known as South Lynn Peak, is surrounded by trees, about 300 m north and up from the viewpoint. It was named Rice Peak when the clear-cut slopes allowed a clear view down to Rice Lake, which at that time was a reservoir for North Vancouver. In 1918 and again in 1950 Rice Lake was drained from its natural size, first to serve as a reservoir, and then to lay pipe.

The true Lynn Peak (see next route description), the higher of the two Lynn summits, is a valley and a climb beyond, along the trail en route to the Needles. It is closer to Hydraulic Creek than it is to the Lynn balloon viewpoint.

The bump was named Rice Mountain on May 2, 1909, by BCMC president Joseph Charles Bishop, after a climb by a club party of 25 led by Roland Manfred "Fred" Mills. In those days, such a feat warranted a newspaper story, and the *Daily Province* reported that "tangled masses of fallen timber were the main obstacles encountered, and at one spot in particular on an exposed bluff, the trees appeared to have been in the path of a violent hurricane, and fell like corn before the reaper." A peak photograph from the period shows Rice Lake clearly visible through the clear-cut slopes. It is no longer so visible. It was referred to as Rice Peak or Rice Mountain in BCMC reports until the Second World War.

The hike to Rice Peak is a gently sloped 2.9-km slog. The entire route provides a decent jog or power-hike workout, and is runnable at both bottom and top. It is a well-travelled route, especially in the summer, giving comfort for those anxious about remote hikes.

ROUTE

Start at Lynn Headwaters Regional Park. Go over the bridge over Lynn Creek.

- This will take you to a map board, with Cedars Mill Trail proceeding straight. Take the right-hand trail, which is a well-graded, wide path that leads east towards Rice Lake and Seymour Valley Trailway.
- Before those two destinations, halfway along the road, you will come to the Lynn Loop–Lynn Headwaters Trail turnoff, going left and up. This too is a well-graded path, which continues uphill at a gradual rate.
- After about 1 km turn right at the well-marked junction with Lynn Peak Trail.
- Lynn Peak Trail is well marked and defined, although rougher and rockier than Lynn Loop. The ascent is a steady but gradual climb. At times the rocks underfoot can be precarious.
- After about 2 km you will come to a series of openings in the tree cover, with partial views east over Seymour Valley Trailway.
- At a flat stretch, there are some large boulder erratics that are fun climbing for kids.
- A few minutes later the trail becomes more gradual and then more open. Old-growth Douglas fir and cedars are visible to the left in a grove called the "Enchanted Forest."
- At around 2.5 km there is a rocky outcrop (the balloon docking station) with views of the LSCR and the Fannin Range across the Seymour Valley. Most people stop here and mistakenly think it is the peak. It is not.
- The first (south) peak of Lynn is another 500 m along. The trail continues just to the right of the sign falsely marked "Lynn Peak." Continue in the same northerly direction as the main Lynn Peak Trail. The trail narrows considerably after the viewpoint but remains well trodden and well marked.
- South Lynn Peak, a.k.a. Rice Peak, is a short jaunt left (west) when you reach the upturned root ball of a giant tree. Go left and past the fallen trunk of the tree, up a gradual hill to find an unspectacular wooded peak, with a rock and a tree with flagging around its diameter, confusingly labelled "Lynn Peak."

LYNN PEAK

(LYN) (1015 M)

Somewhat dull true peak of the Lynn Ridge, with a fun approach route.

CAUTION:
None.

PROMINENCE:
114 m.

LATITUDE/LONGITUDE:
N49.39528 W123.01472.

BANG FOR BUCK:
3/5

PEAK VIEW:
2/5

TRUE SUMMIT LOCATION:
Fourth bump on Lynn Ridge from Lynn balloon viewpoint. Southern, partly exposed, bump on that bump.

HEADWATERS:
McKenzie Creek, Hydraulic Creek (into Seymour River).

BEST VIEWS FROM:
Mt. Seymour, Burnaby, Downtown and East Vancouver, Ironworkers Bridge.

TRIP INFORMATION

Round-trip distance: From Lynn Headwaters, 11.6 km. From gazebo at start of LSCR trail, roughly 13 km return via paved trail.

Elevation gain: 1001 m.

Time: 3–6 hours return (3:12).

Difficulty: 2/5.

Snow free: Usually early or mid-June.

Must-see: Traditional "Lynn Peak balloon" viewpoint.

Scenery: 2/5. Old-growth, second-growth forests. Rivers.

Kids: 3/5.

Dogs: 4/5. Leash required.

Runnability: 4/5.

Terrain: Second-growth forest.

Public transit: #209 bus from Phibbs Exchange to Lynn Headwaters Park; none to Mt. Seymour.

Cell coverage: Usually good.

Sun: Sufficient shade throughout.

Water: Several small seasonal streams.

Route links: South Lynn and Needles.

HISTORY

Name origin: After John Linn (1821 Edinburgh – 1876 Lynn Valley), a British Royal Engineer and early North Vancouver settler. Linn came to BC in 1859 after participating in the Fraser River gold rush. In 1869 he moved his family from the barracks at New Westminster (Sapperton) to a cottage he built on the north shore of Burrard Inlet just east of what is now Lynn Creek. He obtained a free grant of the land, Lot

204, under the government plan for rewarding soldier settlers. His son Hugh was later convicted of murdering two men on Savary Island and hanged.

Name status: Official. Adopted May 6, 1924.

Other names: The 1912 C.J. Heaney map referred to the Lynn Peaks and the Needles as "Lynn Peaks"

First ascent: August 23, 1908, by a BCMC party (Fred Mills, Fred Perry, and Charles Chapman) attempting to climb White Mountain (Burwell).

Other write-ups: Hanna, Hui.

The true Lynn Peak, the higher of the two Lynn summits, is a valley and a climb beyond South Lynn Peak, along the trail en route to the Needles. It is closer to Hydraulic Creek than it is to the Lynn balloon viewpoint.

Although the Lynn/Needles trail route is easier, the Hydraulic Creek trail is the more direct and fun approach, taking a vertiginous but glorious way up the steep Hydraulic Valley from Seymour Valley Trailway, passing en route old-growth trees and waterfalls. We can thank trailbuilder Gabriel Mazoret for this delightful trek. Hydraulic Creek separates the Needles (north) from the two Lynn Peaks (south), and this route provides enjoyable access to both. It also allows for a pleasing loop, starting at Lynn Headwaters, climbing up and over the two Lynn Peaks, and descending down to Seymour Valley Trailway for a 5-km jog back to the LSCR parking lot or a 7-km one back to the Lynn Headwaters parking lot.

The Group of Seven artist Frederick Horsman Varley (1881–1969), who rented a home at the end of Rice Lake Road (near the present pipeline bridge), and after whom Varley Trail running alongside Lynn Creek is named, called Lynn Peak "The Dumpling," presumably reflecting its modest, bulbous shape. Luckily for the dignity of the peak, this name gained no traction. Ironically, in 1974, a director of the National Gallery of Canada wrote to suggest that the peak be renamed after Varley.

ROUTE 1:
FROM LYNN HEADWATERS

Follow the above route from Lynn Headwaters parking lot to South Lynn Peak.

- South Lynn / Rice Peak is a short jaunt left (west) from the upturned root ball of a giant tree. Go straight, through the footprint of the fallen tree. This will lead to Needles Trail, which was a nasty route until around 2008 when the NSR improved it.
- The trail is a duffy but runnable delight. It is not densely flagged, but the route is almost always obvious. Descents can be slippery even when dry. Dig your heels in.
- Descend into the col after South Lynn. The trail then goes up and down two bumps, neither of them terribly deep, and then rises again to the true Lynn Peak.
- The final bump plateau is about 220 m long, with knobs at the north (on trail) and south (about 30 m off trail to the west). The south mound is 1 m higher than the north one.
- For the true peak, do a mini-bushwhack up to an exposed granite knoll. On a granite balcony facing southwest there is a boulder with a small cairn.
- Continue north to the north bump, just before the descent to the Hydraulic Creek trail, the dividing line between the Lynn and the Needle groups of peaks. This knob has an interesting view of the Needles, looking north. They actually look pretty epic from here.

ROUTE 2:

FROM LSCR, UP HYDRAULIC CREEK TRAIL

From the LSCR parking lot, run, bike, or skateboard 5.5 km along Seymour Valley Trailway to Hydraulic Creek.

- The trailhead is to the right of the creek, opposite the picnic area. At twilight, barred owls may be seen here.
- The trail may be difficult to see, but it is likely flagged and will be obvious once you punch into the foliage and your eyes adjust.
- The trail was clearly a labour of love. If you are lucky, you will find, attached to trees at the top and bottom of the route, trail descriptions protected by zip-lock bags.
- The trail is a constantly steep climb, always close to Hydraulic Creek to your left (west).
- The way takes you past gentle series of burbling cascades on the creek, as well as old-growth giants.
- Underfoot the trail is spongy with centuries of soft cedar rot. It makes for an enjoyable, very runnable, slalom-esque descent.
- The trail ends at the col between Lynn Peak and South Needle. Go left (south) towards Lynn Peak.

1935 Hiking Guide to the North Shore (BC Electric Car Railway Ltd.). Note "Strahan," "Dome," and Zinc Mines.

SOUTH NEEDLE

(SNE) (1163 M)

Fun, unusual views from the easiest and shortest of the Needles.

CAUTION:
A little remote.

PROMINENCE:
70 m.

LATITUDE/LONGITUDE:
N49.40554 W123.01431.

BANG FOR BUCK:
3/5

PEAK VIEW:
3/5. Unusual view south

back on Lynn Range to Vancouver and Baker beyond.

TRUE SUMMIT LOCATION:
Obvious.

HEADWATERS:
Hydraulic and Owl & Talon creeks (into Seymour River).

BEST VIEW FROM:
Downtown or East Vancouver, Burnaby, Mt. Fromme, Dam Mountain, Lynn Peak.

TRIP INFORMATION

Round-trip distance: 14.4 km from Lynn Headwaters parking lot.

Elevation gain: 1381 m.

Time: 5–9 hours return (4:49) via Hydraulic Creek.

Difficulty: 3/5.

Snow free: Usually mid- to late June.

Must-sees: Giant trees and waterfalls on Hydraulic Creek Trail.

Scenery: 3/5.

Kids: 3/5. A bit far.

Dogs: 4/5.

Runnability: 4/5.

Terrain: Second-growth forest.

Public transit: #209 bus from Phibbs Exchange to Lynn Headwaters Park, or #228 to LSCR and Hydraulic Creek.

Cell coverage: Inconsistent en route; generally good on peak.

Sun: Sufficient shade for beginning. Some exposure en route. Exposed peak.

Water: None except puddles.

Route links: Lynn Ridge and/or Needles.

HISTORY

Name origin: A series of needles, although the peaks themselves are not particularly pointy or needle-like except when viewed from true Lynn Peak.

Name status: "The Needles" official. Adopted December 7, 1937.

Other names: The Needles were known as the Mountain Lion Group, Cougar Peaks, Lynn Peaks (the 1912 C.J. Heaney map referred to the Lynn Peaks and the Needles as "Lynn Peaks"; also 1920s and '30s BCMC trip reports), and the Three

Maids (Don Munday, ca. 1913). A March 1928 ACC Vancouver *Avalanche Echoes* referred to the entire Lynn–Needles Ridge as the "Lynn Peaks." A 1929 map referred to the entire ridge as "The Needles." "Lynn Peaks" was used on a 1936 L. Frank photographic survey of North Shore Peaks, and as an alternative name in the Dick Culbert guides (1965 and 1969).

First ascent: August 23, 1908, by a BCMC party (Fred Mills, Fred Perry, and Charles Chapman) attempting to climb White Mountain (Burwell).

Other write-up: Hui.

Formerly in the watershed, the three peaks known as the Needles are now all open to climbing. The trail to South Needle from Hydraulic Creek continues the superb Lynn–Needles Trail put in by NSR and others, running north from the Lynn balloon docking station viewpoint. The trail to South Needle is a tough workout (four significant ups and downs) but is well flagged, with excellent but subtle pruning and foot-notching on fallen logs. The summit rewards you with glorious and unique views of Crown to the west, Coliseum, Burwell, and Cathedral to the north, and Seymour and the Fannin Range to the east.

You may travel to South Needle via either the Lynn Ridge trail (see South Lynn above) or the LSCR–Hydraulic Creek trail (see Lynn above). Both are fun trails that are spongy underfoot and generally runnable.

As with the Lynn Peaks, the lower slopes of the Needles were explored extensively for minerals, particularly copper, and some short tunnels were dug. Bears and deer are frequently seen on the Needles and their slopes. Even mountain goats have been spotted on the flanks of the Needles, from both the Norvan Creek and the Seymour Valley Trailway sides.

ROUTE 1:

FROM LYNN HEADWATERS AND LYNN PEAK, ALONG LYNN/ NEEDLES RIDGE

Follow the route described above from Lynn Headwaters parking lot to Lynn Peak.

- From Lynn Peak continue north. The trail is narrow but generally obvious and occasionally flagged. If you encounter deadfall, which is frequent in this area, the trail is probably under the deadfall. You are generally proceeding along the middle of the obvious spine of the trail.
- In the col between South Needle and Lynn, you will find the junction with the Hydraulic Creek trail, which plunges down to the LSCR in a very steep but beautiful track with duffy soil, old-growth trees, and waterfalls. It is more pleasant to go down than up.
- Continue north. You will go up and down over four minor hills.
- Eventually you will hit some small and non-threatening bands of rock. The rock can be slick in the rain but it is quite straightforward.
- Keep ascending, through increasing blueberry bushes. Pop out onto the obvious rocky summit and exult in the unique views of Lynn Peak, Burnaby, and Vancouver.

FROM LSCR, UP HYDRAULIC CREEK TRAIL

Follow the route described above, up Seymour Valley Trailway to Hydraulic Creek Trail and then up Hydraulic Creek Trail.

- The trail ends at the col between South Needle and Lynn Peak. Go left (south) towards Lynn Peak.
- You will pop out at the junction with the Needles trail in the col between South Needle and South Lynn. Turn right (north).
- You will go up and down four minor hills.
- Eventually you will hit some small and non-threatening bands of rock. The rock can be slick in the rain, but it is straightforward. Climb up to the summit.

The jog west, descending north from South Needle.

MIDDLE NEEDLE

(MNE) (1258 M)

The true summit of the Needles, with unusual and interesting views of everything. And delicious blueberries too.

CAUTION:
Minor cliffs and exposure on descent from South Needle to col, and on ascent up Middle Needle. Trail remote and sometimes obscure; real danger and exposure if you get lost; only do in perfect weather. No water.

PROMINENCE:
260 m.

LONGITUDE/LATITUDE:
N49.40972 W123.01417.

BANG FOR BUCK:
3/5

PEAK VIEW:
4/5

TRUE SUMMIT LOCATION:
Obvious.

HEADWATERS:
O'Hayes Creek, Clear Creek
(into Seymour River).

BEST VIEWS FROM:
Fromme, Dam.

TRIP INFORMATION

Round-trip distance: 16.6 km from Lynn Headwaters.
Elevation gain: 1641 m.
Time: 7–9 hours return (6:43) via Hydraulic Creek.
Difficulty: 3.5/5.
Snow free: Usually mid- to late June.
Must-sees: Blueberries and view of Seymour.
Scenery: 3/5. Pleasant peak ridge.
Kids: 1/5. Remote; minor exposure.
Dogs: 2/5. Two rocky cruxes requiring hands.
Runnability: 3/5. Steep and bushwhacky.
Terrain: Second-growth forest.
Public transit: #228 Lynn Valley bus from Lonsdale Quay or #210 Upper Lynn Valley from Phibbs Exchange.
Cell coverage: Unlikely in trees; sporadic on peak.
Sun: Sufficient shade for beginning. Some exposure en route. Exposed peak.
Water: None.
Route links: Other Needles and the Lynn Peaks.

HISTORY

Name origin: A series of needles, although the peaks themselves are not particularly pointy or needle-like.
Name status: "The Needles" official. Adopted December 7, 1937.
Other names: The Needles were known as the Mountain Lion Group, Cougar Peaks, Lynn Peaks (1930s, and as an alternative name in the 1965 and 1969 Dick

Culbert guides), and the Three Maids (Don Munday, ca. 1913).

First ascent: August 23, 1908, by a BCMC party (Fred Mills, Fred Perry, and Charles Chapman) attempting to climb White Mountain (Burwell).

Middle Needle is the true peak of the Needles, although it is only taller than its northern neighbour by a few metres. You will earn the climb, however. The route from South Needle to Middle Needle is considerably more challenging and risky than the route to South Needle. You will see the occasional downed flag on the ground, but there is no marking or even, for that matter, any trail to speak of. Happily, the route is relatively clear of underbrush.

The descent to the col between South and Middle Needle is not at all obvious looking down from South Needle. Although it looks steep, it is less so than the sheer drops to the west and east. It is essentially a slow descent along a series of ledges. Hold tight to the scraggly pines and blueberry bushes and gingerly lower yourself down ledge by ledge. It is mossy and slippery and you could do yourself real harm without care. Towards the bottom the terrain changes to a mere slope, and then you bushwhack down through blueberry bushes to the base of the col.

The major redeeming feature of this area is the plentiful supply of massive blueberries: wild berries the size of domesticated ones, growing in clusters of three. The bushes actually sag with the weight of the fruit. In autumn the ridgecrest is a pleasing red heath of blueberry bushes.

In August 2012 two climbers were rescued from a rock face below Middle Needle. They had been travelling along the ridge to Burwell when, their plans foiled by terrible weather, they decided to try to rappel into the Seymour Valley.

ROUTE: FROM SOUTH NEEDLE

Follow the route to South Needle, either from Lynn Headwaters parking lot to Lynn Peak and South Needle or from LSCR to Hydraulic Creek Trail to South Needle.

- The route from South Needle to Middle Needle is the nastiest of the Lynn–Needle ridge. You should never feel exposed; if you do, you are likely off-route and should return to the centre of the ridge.
- From the South Needle summit, go to the end of the summit plateau and veer to your left (northwest). Using hands and feet and at times gripping vegetation ("veggie belays") should make for a fairly easy descent, the first 10 m of it on the left (west) side of the cliff face.
- Then zag to the right (east) side of the face and complete the descent to a smooth slab that comes down across the base of this pitch and runs approximately 6 m. The key is to traverse downward from right to left (east to west), gingerly moving your feet along a crack ledge that runs diagonally down the entire slab. Hold on to vegetation and rocks (there are lots of both), leading to the col.
- At the col, veer to the far right (east) for a sharp vista down a sheer rocky gully to Seymour Valley Trailway. A little trail work here, clearing deadwood and opening views, would make this a most spectacular lookout.
- The ascent to Middle Needle is a steep bushwhack; happily the shrubbery underfoot is not dense.
- Halfway up you hit a cliff band that stretches the entire length of the Middle Needle

face. Although one can ascend at various points using cedar handholds, the best way is to cut across to the far west (left) side, where one can avoid most of the cliff and stick to a dirt ascent.

- Above the cliff band the steep bushwhacking continues. But nowhere is the blueberry and other undergrowth, or the steepness, particularly brutal.
- Punch out of the foliage onto a rocky false summit. Across a deep gully, which appears to run the width of the ridge, is the true peak of Middle Needle.
- Jog to the right, however, and you will find an easy traverse down and then up a rocky face to the true summit.

Krumholtz to Middle Needle (under white tree on left).

NORTH NEEDLE
(NNE) (1256 M)

The most remote Needle, with spectacular views of all the North Shore peaks.

CAUTION:
Hidden drop-offs on descent
from Middle Needle to col.
Remote; real danger and exposure
if you get lost; only do in perfect
weather. Little or no water.

PROMINENCE:
72 m.

LATITUDE/LONGITUDE:
N49.41417 W123.01444.

BANG FOR BUCK:
2/5

PEAK VIEW:
4/5. N: Coliseum and Cathedral;
S: Needles; W: Echo, Forks, Goat,
and Crown; E: Bishop.

TRUE SUMMIT LOCATION:
Obvious cairn.

HEADWATERS:
Norvan Creek (into Lynn Creek);
Clear Creek (into Seymour River).

BEST VIEWS FROM:
Coliseum, Middle Needle, Crown,
Goat, Norvan Meadows.

TRIP INFORMATION

Round-trip distance: 18 km from Lynn Headwaters.
Elevation gain: 1841 m.
Time: 5–10 hours (8:03) via Hydraulic Creek.
Difficulty: 4/5. Remote and rough.
Snow free: Mid-June.
Must-see: Blueberry patches.
Scenery: 3/5.
Kids: 2/5. Too remote.
Dogs: 1/5. Access via Middle Needle requires hand grips.
Runnability: 3/5.
Terrain: Second-growth alpine trees; rocks.
Public transit: #228 Lynn Valley bus from Lonsdale Quay or #210 Upper Lynn Valley from Phibbs Exchange.
Cell coverage: Sporadic on peak; rare on col.
Sun: Sufficient shade for beginning. Some exposure en route. Exposed peak.
Water: Small tarns.
Route links: Needles sweep; Lynn–Needles sweep.

HISTORY

Name origin: See South Needle.
Name status: "The Needles" official. Adopted December 7, 1937.
Other names: The Needles were known as the Mountain Lion Group, Cougar Peaks, Lynn Peaks (1930s), as an alternative name in the Dick Culbert guides (1965 and 1969), and as the Three Maids (Don Munday, ca. 1913).

First ascent: Likely August 23, 1908, by a BCMC party (Fred Mills, Fred Perry, and Charles Chapman) attempting to climb White Mountain (Burwell).

It is exhilarating standing on the northernmost Needle and seeing such odd and otherwise unattainable views. You will feel like you can reach out and touch Coliseum, Burwell, and Cathedral to the northeast, and Echo and Crown to the northwest, with the Howe Sound Crest Trail peaks behind. To the south you survey the entire Lynn–Needles ridge, with the city beyond.

As with the other Needles, this is a good hike in the autumn, when the blueberry bushes turn a blazing red. It is an even better hike in July, when the blueberries themselves grow thick and fat.

The trail and flagging are thinnest here. There are a few hidden cliffs. Be very careful.

ROUTE 1:
FROM MIDDLE NEEDLE

Follow the route to Middle Needle, either from Lynn Headwaters parking lot to Lynn Peak and South Needle or from LSCR to Hydraulic Creek Trail to South Needle.

- From Middle Needle go north, veering slightly to the east to bypass a slabby stretch by hugging the right. Then comes a flat patch followed by a steep section that is easily climbed using hands and rocks and vegetation.
- Descending into the col, veer to the right of a smooth slab. This will take you along a metre-wide ramp with a nasty drop to your right (northeast) hidden by a cedar tree, leading down to a heather-strewn slab. Keep heading straight down towards the col.
- From the col, a faintly trodden path leads up what at first seems to be a steep and bushy climb, but if you follow the path, it turns out to be relatively easy with sufficient handholds.
- The rocky peak is obvious; travel through the heather up to it.

ROUTE 2:
FROM NORTH – COLISEUM TRAIL

It is possible but *not at all recommended or pleasant* to approach North Needle from the north, from Norvan Meadows on the Coliseum Mountain trail, which branches off from Lynn Headwaters Trail just east of Norvan Falls.

- Follow the most gentle (but still steep!) contour lines on the map. It will take you partly up a creek gully and partly up a rock-slide face. At no point will you feel comfortable, but you should not feel very exposed either.
- The hardest point is at the very top, which is particularly crumbly, with a high lip up the peak ridge.
- Once on the peak ridge, it is an easy climb up through the heather, southwest to the peak.

CATHEDRAL PEAKS

(4 PEAKS)

Although it would take a very ambitious (or foolhardy) hiker to link the Needles with Coliseum and Burwell (the back side of the North Needle is climbable but nasty), the two sections are situated in a straight line, in a mini-range. Coliseum (and its shoulder peak of Paton Peak) serve as a threshold of sorts for the higher peak of Burwell. Together, they are a granite playground of slabs and tarns, and together or individually, they make grand adventures. And towering over them, and over most of the North Shore peaks, is the organ-pipe-like Cathedral Mountain, with its mysterious radio towers. Its remoteness and scarce trail should deter all but the most experienced, hardy, and swift adventurer. As only a masochist would attempt to link the two areas, we shall consider them separately.

The lofty, symmetrical peak of Cathedral and the gleaming white granite of Coliseum have attracted hikers since the foundation of the BCMC. For most of the 20th century these peaks were off-limits, and Cathedral remains so. This area is best approached via Seymour Valley Trailway, with a bike saving you some 8 km of northward trooping. Alternatively you can take the traditional route to this area, via the Lynn Headwaters trails to just short of Norvan Falls, and then by way of Coliseum Mountain Trail. Either way, it is a long day's adventure for Coliseum and Burwell, and likely an overnight adventure for Cathedral.

GETTING THERE

Route 1: West to Lynn Headwaters Regional Park
- From Ironworkers Memorial (Second Narrows) Bridge, take Highway 1 to the Mountain Highway exit, to the right and up.
- Continue to Lynn Valley Road and turn right.
- Continue to the end of Lynn Valley Road, past End of the Line General Store and through the yellow gate into Lynn Headwaters Regional Park. There is rare premium parking at the end of the road, near the bridge, with three overflow parking lots farther back towards the gate.
- Note that the gate gets locked at sundown, which could trap your car inside and possibly trigger NSR if you have not left a message.

Route 2: East to Lower Seymour Conservation Reserve and Seymour Valley Trail
- From Ironworkers Memorial (Second Narrows) Bridge, take Highway 1 to Exit 22A right and then turn left up Lillooet Road.
- You will pass a horse stable, Capilano University, the North Vancouver cemetery, a prominent gate, and then (after several kilometres' drive) the Seymour–Capilano water treatment plant. The road ends at a large gravel parking lot.
- The path starts next to the outhouses and map kiosk. Follow the path leading to the west. This brings you to a gazebo and a paved road, where your journey begins.
- Note that the gate (near the cemetery) gets locked at sundown, which could trap your car and possibly trigger NSR if you have not left a message.

CATHEDRAL BAGGER TIPS

The peaks of Paton, Coliseum, Burwell, and Cathedral can be linked together in a very long day. This is an out-and-back hike with plenty of elevation changes in both directions. The preferred approach is to take the LSCR pathway by bike to the Paton trailhead at 9.5 km as described below. Be mindful that the gate is closed from dusk to dawn if you are attempting this in the shoulder season. There are parking spots immediately outside the gate if you want to avoid any possible call-out to the RCMP/North Shore Rescue by LSCR staff. It adds 2 km to get from the gate to the LSCR parking lot.

Round-trip distance:
23.8 km (from trailhead)

Time:
12:04

Elevation gain:
2317 m

Bike from gate to trailhead:
22.0 km 1:00 (round trip)

bears on Coliseum col

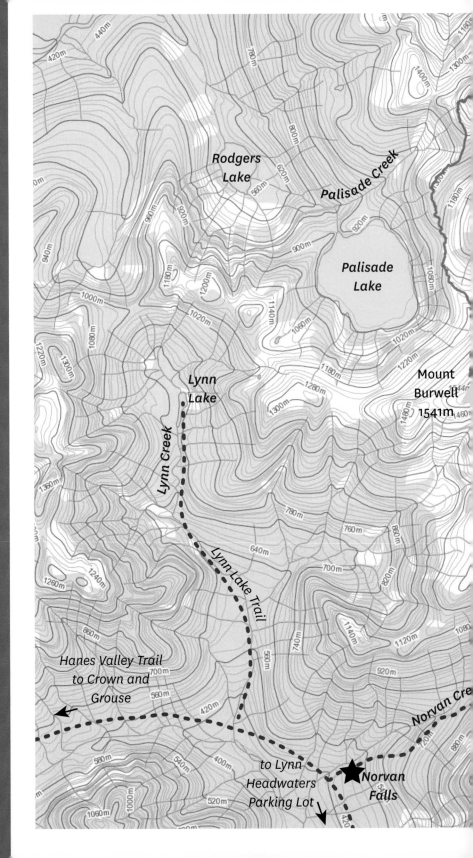

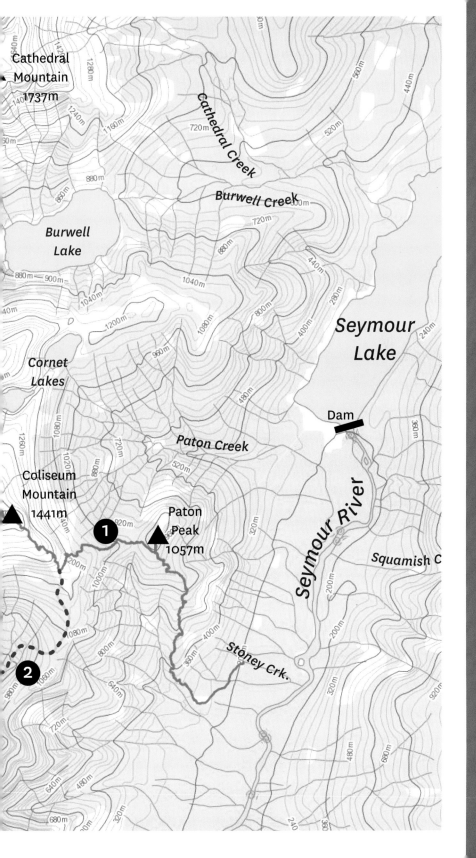

Cathedral
Mountain
1737m

1280m

Cathedral Creek

Burwell Creek

720m

Burwell
Lake

Cornet
Lakes

Seymour
Lake

Dam

Coliseum
Mountain
1441m

Paton Creek

Paton
Peak
1057m

Seymour River

Squamish C

Stoney Crk.

1

2

The steep start of the trail up Paton

PATON PEAK

(PAT) (1057 M)

A steep but pleasant climb to glorious views of Coliseum, Cathedral,
Meslilloet Mountain, and the Seymour Valley.

CAUTION:
Sheer cliffs not far from the trail.
Needles can be slippery, especially
when dry. Some roped rocky faces.

PROMINENCE:
90 m.

LATITUDE/LONGITUDE:
N49.43235 W122.98952.

BANG FOR BUCK:
5/5

PEAK VIEW:
4/5. Grand views of Coliseum,
Cathedral, the Needles,
LSCR, Seymour Lake, the Fannin
Range, and Meslilloet.

TRUE SUMMIT LOCATION:
An obvious rock pile at the south
end of the summit.

HEADWATERS:
Paton Creek, Stoney Creek,
Cougar Creek
(into Seymour River).

BEST VIEWS FROM:
Seymour Valley Trailway,
Bear Island Bridge, Elsay.

TRIP INFORMATION

Round-trip distance: 5.8 km from Seymour Valley Trailway to Stoney Creek trailhead; 25.4 km from LSCR parking lot.

Elevation gain: 841 m.

Time: 2.5–5 hours (2:44) from Seymour Valley Trailway.

Difficulty: 3/5.

Snow free: Mid-June.

Must-sees: Fun Seymour Valley Trailway; some big trees.

Scenery: 4/5.

Kids: 2/5. Steep but a great triumph for a kid.

Dogs: 3/5.

Runnability: 1/5 up, 4/5 down.

Terrain: Spongy through steep single-track leading to slabby granite peak.

Public transit: #228 Lynn Valley bus from Lonsdale Quay or #210 Upper Lynn Valley from Phibbs Exchange.

Cell coverage: Generally decent from Paton to Coliseum to Burwell.

Sun: Entirely in shade until near wholly exposed summit.

Water: None.

Route links: A nice stop en route to Coliseum and beyond.

Name origin: Paton Creek was named in 1928 for James Alexander Paton (1886 Beamsville, Ont. – 1946 Vancouver), a Vancouver alderman. In 1906 he came to Eburne (Marpole) in Vancouver, where he worked as a stationer and publisher, printing the *Point Grey Gazette* (which later became the *Vancouver Courier*). In 1925 Paton and others were charged for alleged involvement in the kidnapping and torture of Wong Foon Sing, accused of having killed Janet Smith (one of the province's most notorious unsolved murders), but Paton was acquitted. Paton was a member of the Vancouver Water Board 1926–27, and represented Vancouver–Point Grey in the BC legislature from 1937 to 1946 as a Conservative. He died in office. Paton was responsible for suggesting the name of Mt. Robie Reid, a striking peak north of the Fraser Valley, in 1944.

Name status: Unofficial. Paton Creek is an official name, adopted July 4, 1957.

First ascent: Unknown.

Other names: Seymour Valley Lookout, Paton Lookout.

Paton Peak.

Most people call this a lookout rather than a peak, although it has decent prominence from its taller neighbour, Coliseum. It is a fun adventure, best approached as a bike-and-hike from Seymour Valley Trailway to the trailhead at Stoney Creek. Finding the trailhead is the hardest part, although it is now well flagged and well trodden. The route up is steep but the views provide ample reward. The Paton promontory offers amazing vistas of the valley. Be sure to venture to the north end of the summit plateau for a splendid look at the Seymour dam and lake.

ROUTE

- Start at the Seymour Valley Trailway parking lot. Bike, skateboard, run, or hike 9.5 km along the trailway, over the Stoney Creek bridge and past the 9-km marker on the left.
- Continue along the trailway for another 250 m to a hard-to-see gravel road to the left that cuts back upslope from the trailway. Go up this. There are several places to hide and lock your bike. (If you arrive at the intersection of the trailway and the closed to the public Seymour Dam road, you've gone too far.)
- At the end of the short gravel road (less than 1 km), and at the edge of Stoney Creek, you will find the trailhead, which should be marked with a series of cairns and tape flagging. The trailhead is to the right, across a ditch. Punch into the dark forest.
- Proceed up an initial steep patch past some giant cedar trees on a narrow but well-trodden trail. Bask in the dappled sunlight along this section if the weather is nice.
- As the trail ascends, you'll see a sheer cliff down to Seymour Trailway on your right and the sharp hanging valley of Stoney Creek on your left.
- At 580 m you will start seeing pleasant views out over the Seymour Valley. Also straight down, so be careful.
- At 620 m, use your hands to climb up along an exposed slab of rock. The well-defined trail continues, with good views looking south to the Needles ridge.
- At 775 m, come to a welcome flat bench that traverses the east side of a rocky knob. There is a candy-cane-twisted cedar tree here.
- At around 800 m, there is a fine view of the sheer cliffs below Paton.
- After a short and rooty rise to the right of a rocky knob, take care not to continue too far rightward, as the trail does an easily missed dog's leg to the left, back into the knob proper.
- After ascending the rocky bluff, punch out to another flat bench with a pleasing view to the north over the Seymour Valley. Then come to a gentle and twisting climb with boulders emerging from the rooty duff. The flagging continues as the trail climbs.
- At 997 m there is a rocky patch where the trail splits. Take the right-hand path, up to Paton Lookout (the left trail goes straight across towards the trail up to Coliseum). The going here is steep and rocky and hands are occasionally needed, but there is no exposure.
- Be sure to walk to the northeast end of the flat Paton Peak for fine views of Seymour Lake.

COLISEUM MOUNTAIN

(COL) (1441 M)

A white slabby granite playground and paradise.

CAUTION:
Slippery and muddy ascent;
many bears.

PROMINENCE:
51 m.

LATITUDE/LONGITUDE:
N49.43389 W123.00667.

BANG FOR BUCK:
4/5

PEAK VIEW:
3/5. W: West Lion, Crown;

S: Vancouver, Lynn Peaks;
N: Burwell, Cathedral;
E: Seymour, Baker.

TRUE SUMMIT LOCATION:
Obvious, with cairn.

HEADWATERS:
Norvan Creek, Coliseum Creek
(into Lynn Creek).

BEST VIEWS FROM:
Richmond, Burnaby, Goat,
Seymour, Bishop.

TRIP INFORMATION

Round-trip distance: 11 km via Stoney Creek; 25 km via Norvan Falls; 30 km from LSCR parking lot.

Elevation gain: 1237 m via Stoney Creek; 1245 m via Norvan Falls.

Time: 4–7 hours (4:46) from Seymour Valley Trailway–Stoney Creek trailhead. About 1–3 hours longer from Lynn Headwaters; 1–2 hours from Paton Peak.

Difficulty: 3/5.

Snow free: Early July.

Must-sees: Beautiful tarn; big trees; blueberries.

Scenery: 3/5.

Kids: 4/5. Far but rewarding. A giant granite playground. Would make a good overnight hike.

Dogs: 5/5. Far but rewarding.

Runnability: 4/5. At times steep and rocky but generally runnable.

Terrain: Second-growth forest leading to a slabby granite playground paradise.

Public transit: #228 Lynn Valley bus from Lonsdale Quay or #210 Upper Lynn Valley from Phibbs Exchange.

Cell coverage: Good on peak; generally decent from Paton to Coliseum to Burwell.

Sun: Sufficient shade for beginning. Some exposure en route. Wholly exposed peak.

Water: Ample along Lynn Headwaters route; *minimal* on Paton Peak route until last part.

Route links: Paton, Burwell, Cathedral.

HISTORY

Name origin: Because the bleached granite superficially resembles ancient Roman ruins such as the Colosseum. Named around 1911 by William J. ("Billy") Gray, a geology student and legendary mountaineer, who drowned in the Kootenay River in 1927 on an expedition. Gray used to talk about this "natural amphitheatre," and after his death Alan John Campbell incorporated the name on his topographical map of North Vancouver watersheds.

Name status: Official. Adopted December 7, 1937.

Other names: White Mountain referred to Burwell and Coliseum. In 1908 and 1911 Coliseum was referred to as "Moose Peak" of White Mountain. "Coliseum" was used in the 1912 North Vancouver water map. The 1929 water map gives Burwell and Coliseum as separate names.

First ascent: October 11, 1908, by a BCMC party including Bert Armistead, Fred Smith, Fred Mills, Charles Chapman, Billy Gray, Herbert Miskin, Charles J. Heaney, Franklin Walter Hewton, Basil S. Darling, Basil G. Hawkins, and Wilfred Henry Tassell.

Other write-ups: Gunn (route to Burwell travels via Coliseum); Hui.

In late summer, Coliseum is a blindingly white granite-slab playground, distinctive from afar and enormously fun up close. Of all of these peaks, this one has the widest swath of exposed granite, and it is not a stretch to imagine it as a ruined Roman forum. Its wide white amphitheatres also reinforce the name.

White (Coliseum & Burwell), ca. 1910.

Coliseum is a flattish mountain that is really just a subpeak of the more distant Burwell. Early visitors referred to them together as "White Mountain," with the lower Coliseum bestowing its shine on the overall peak. The 1915 Water Map, the 1918 BCMC summer program, a 1925 *Daily Province* article and the 1935 BC Electric Railway Ltd. hiking map all lumped Burwell and Coliseum together as "White Mountain." Coliseum was also distinguished by the name "Moose Peak" of White

Mountain, although it seems unlikely that a moose would have been seen in the area (perhaps an elk?) and there is nothing moose-like about the peak. Needless to say, the name of the mountain has nothing to do with the Pacific Coliseum (built in 1968), although each is visible from the other. To add to the dazzling geology, Coliseum has many quartz dikes on the south side and wide, green intrusion dikes (where basaltic or andesitic magma oozed into the granite) on its west side.

The view of the eastern slopes of Coliseum and Burwell as one climbs up Berkley Road gives the name to that neighbourhood: Blueridge.

Coliseum Tarn.

Coliseum makes for an excellent long-day or overnight adventure, offering a wide variety of sights and terrain on the hike up, with stunning peak views of the city and the adjoining peaks, rivers, and lakes. On a clear summer day the brilliant blue of Coliseum's tarn, contrasting with the white of the granite, is worth the hike in itself. To the north are the twin suspended Cornett Lakes (formerly known as Cougar Lakes), also crisp and blue against the rock. Although camping is technically not allowed, Coliseum makes a lovely overnight trip.

ROUTE 1:
FROM LSCR SEYMOUR VALLEY TRAILWAY AND PATON PEAK
This is our favourite route, via bike.
• Follow the route to Paton Peak described above.
• From Paton Peak one can backtrack to the Y junction or continue north along the slabs of Paton Peak, following the occasional cairn and path through the moss to rejoin the forest trail.

- Descend a steep valley into the shoulder between Paton and Coliseum. Soon the route starts to climb sharply up to Coliseum at a similar angle on similar territory on a narrow but well-travelled trail over very pleasant, duffy soil. It makes for a delightful descent, slaloming among the boulders and trees.
- At 1160 m, traverse right and north for a spectacular view of Meslilloet Mountain up the Seymour Valley.
- You will soon reach a rock slide area. The rocks are slippery when wet, which is most of the time. On the other side of the slide, enter a more open, steep meadow at the base of a towering cliff. This area tends to be muddy, even in dry summers.
- The trail continues to be fairly obvious and well marked, climbing steadily upwards.
- When you come to a broad boulder field, climb steadily upwards, generally along the south edge of the field.
- Be sure to look back and to the north for a beautiful eye-level view of one of the Cornett Lakes, seemingly suspended.
- Eventually, you top out at a grassy crossroads. To the left (south) is the trail to Norvan Falls and Lynn Headwaters. To the right (north) is the way to Coliseum. From here the peak is about 30 minutes away.
- Go right (north) up to Coliseum. This will take some climbing, at times using your hands to ascend tree roots.
- Come to a granite balcony with views of the Needles looking all needle-y.
- Then down and up again to another granite balcony with a head-on view of the Needles, the Seymour River, and Vancouver.
- Arrive at a rocky bowl. Although the trail heads rightward to a view, the main trail goes left over a low bump and then descends into a wide granite bowl.
- There are occasional cairns, but generally head straight up the centre of the slope, choosing the gentlest route.
- Over the top you will see the summit cairn. There is rumoured to be a bottle of Sambuca nearby.

ROUTE 2:
FROM LYNN HEADWATERS, AND UP COLISEUM MOUNTAIN TRAIL
- From the parking lot at the entrance to Lynn Headwaters Regional Park, take Cedars Mill Trail and then Lynn Headwaters Trail towards Norvan Falls (7 km).
- Just before Norvan Falls, note the obvious sign for Coliseum Mountain: go right and up.
- Continue northward, gaining elevation. The first part is the steepest and slipperiest, due to trail erosion. Throughout, the trail is very well marked and well trodden, though it can be slippery when wet.
- Go up and down three unpleasant bumps where the trail again is eroded.
- Continue north into the forest. Norvan Creek is generally to your left.
- After a while you will hear Norvan Creek more loudly, and the valley opens up. Through the trees you can see a series of cascades above Norvan Falls.
- Where the trail dips into a small gully, you can follow the gully down to Norvan Creek in low flow, leading to a charming waterfall and pool. Some have called it "David's Pool."

- Soon after, come to a grove of impressive trees. Nearby is the Norvan Giant (a.k.a. the Norvan Castle), the largest western hemlock in British Columbia, with a circumference of 9.58 m. The tree was discovered by famed tree-hunter Randy Stoltmann in the 1990s.
- You will cross Norvan Creek and some of its minor tributaries several times.
- Pass through Norvan Meadows, noting the remnants of a massive 1998 rockslide. There are several large fallen trees. A small, faint trail leads to North Needle from here.
- After about 5 km, the trail starts climbing sharply up to Coliseum Pass. You will see several more huge and ancient trees and cross over Norvan Creek a few more times.
- Ascend a rooty quasi-stairway. Come to a small tarn on the right. You are almost there.
- To your right you will meet the alternative route up to Coliseum, from the LSCR and Paton Peak. *Do not follow it down!* Instead, keep going straight and up.
- Continue north up to Coliseum, at times using your hands to ascend tree roots.
- Arrive at a rocky bowl. Although the trail branches to the right, to a view, the main trail goes left, over a low bump, and then descends into a wide granite bowl.
- There are occasional cairns but generally head straight up the centre of the slope, choosing the gentlest route.
- At the top, you will see the summit cairn.

MT. BURWELL

(BUR) (1541 M)

A great day adventure or overnighter, with pleasing views of Cornett Lakes and the watershed.

CAUTION:
Trail at times unclear.

PROMINENCE:
369 m.

LATITUDE/LONGITUDE:
N49.44250 W123.01528.

BANG FOR BUCK:
4/5

PEAK VIEW:
4/5. Coliseum, Cathedral,

Cornett and Palisade lakes;
E: Peneplain and Robie Reid.

TRUE SUMMIT LOCATION:
Central, closest peak to Coliseum.

HEADWATERS:
Burwell Lake, Burwell Creek,
Paton Creek (into Seymour River).

BEST VIEWS FROM:
Coliseum, New Brighton Park.

TRIP INFORMATION

Round-trip distance: 14 km from Stoney Creek trailhead; 33 km from LSCR parking lot.

Elevation gain: 1377 m.

Time: 5–9.5 hours (5:54) from Seymour Valley Trailway Stoney Creek trailhead; about 1–2 hours longer from Lynn Headwaters.

Difficulty: 3/5.

Snow free: Early July.

Must-sees: Cornett Lakes; Rodgers Lake; Coliseum granite; tarns.

Scenery: 4/5.

Kids: 2/5. Far but rewarding; a great overnight adventure for a sturdy kid.

Dogs: 4/5. Far but a good adventure for a sturdy dog.

Runnability: 4/5. Far but generally runnable.

Terrain: 4/5. Well-marked trail to Coliseum. Route is fairly obvious to Burwell despite no trail.

Public transit: #228 Lynn Valley bus from Lonsdale Quay or #210 Upper Lynn Valley from Phibbs Exchange.

Cell coverage: Generally decent from Paton to Coliseum to Burwell.

Sun: Sufficient shade for beginning. Wholly exposed from before Coliseum to Burwell.

Water: Cornett Lakes, but no creeks or streams from Coliseum to Burwell.

Route links: Paton Peak, Coliseum Mountain, Cathedral Mountain.

Name origin: Named by Greater Vancouver Water Board after Herbert Mahlon Burwell (1862 London, Ont. – July 30, 1925 Vancouver), a surveyor who had come to Vancouver in 1887. In the spring of 1906 Burwell's firm was engaged by the City to build the intake and settling basins for a new joint water main on Capilano Creek, from the intake to First Narrows. In 1913 Burwell retired from Hermon & Burwell but continued to practise as a consulting engineer until his death at age 62. A great lover of the outdoors, Burwell wrote many articles about fishing on the streams and lakes of BC; he was an authority on that sport.

Name status: Official. Adopted December 7, 1937. Name used in 1912 North Vancouver map. Labelled on 1926 topographic survey by Alan John Campbell in association with Burwell Creek and Lake.

Other names: From 1908 even into the 1950s, Burwell and Coliseum were commonly referred to as White Mountain. The name was last used in a BCMC journal in 1941.

First ascent: October 11, 1908, by a BCMC party including Bert Armistead, Fred Smith, Fred Mills, Charles Chapman, Billy Gray, Herbert Miskin, Charles Heaney, Franklin Walter Hewton, Basil S. Darling, Basil G. Hawkins, and Wilfred Henry Tassell, leaving from the BCMC camp at the forks of Lynn Creek (where Hanes Creek meets Lynn).

Other write-ups: Gunn, Hui.

Mt. Burwell is a fine day or overnight adventure, combining the tree and granite views of Coliseum. The granite slab-hopping from Coliseum to Burwell is fun and fast: usually less than an hour. You will be rewarded with a vista of lake views: the tiny twin Cornett Lakes to the east, with larger Burwell Lake to the northeast, and Palisade Lake to the west, deep in the Capilano watershed. Burwell and Palisade are large mirror glacial cirques separated by the narrow ridge between Burwell and Cathedral. Celebrate your day of happily impersonating a mountain goat with a bracing dip in a Cornett Lake below. On a sunny day there are few more glorious places to be.

Burwell has an interesting west ridge and peak that warrant exploration. To the north, on the west and east of the ridge respectively, are Palisade Lake (and the smaller, farther Rodgers Lake) and Burwell (formerly Stoney) Lake.

The 1915 Water Map, the 1918 BCMC Summer Program, a 1925 *Daily Province* article and a 1935 BC Electric Railway Ltd. hiking map called Burwell and Coliseum together "White Mountain." BCMC was still referring to Burwell as "White" as late as September 1941. The 1929 water map gives Burwell and Coliseum separate names.

The *Daily Province* of October 14, 1908, reported on the first ascent, from the west up Lynn Creek:

Herbert Mahlon Burwell (1863–1925).

There are three peaks and many acres of rocky slopes all around them, scarred and bleached by snow and sun, resembling in places a gigantic rock slide, and again rising terrace after terrace, like the layers of a vast amphitheatre. The rock is white granite and it was decided that the peak should go down in the club records as White Mountain.

GETTING THERE

From either Lynn Headwaters Park or LSCR; see the descriptions for Coliseum and Paton above.

ROUTE

Follow the route to Coliseum Mountain described above, via either LSCR and Paton or Lynn Headwaters Trail and Coliseum Trail.

- From the Coliseum cairn the peak of Burwell is obvious. It only takes about 30–60 minutes to travel about 1.5 km along the equally obvious ridge up to Burwell's summit.
- There is little trail to speak of: the route largely consists of slabby granite that is enormously fun to hop across in dry weather (and not at all fun in slippery weather).
- Fix your sights on Mt. Burwell and head straight there. You will have to go up and down the occasional treed bump. Resist the temptation to stick entirely to the granite; do not swerve to the right in an attempt to traverse the bumps. You should never feel exposed on this hike.
- At times you may lose the path, but look to clues such as paths through the lichen, scuffed dirt, and the occasional flag.
- You start by passing a beautiful tarn (well, at least in early summer when it is a crystalline blue; it becomes murkier as the summer progresses). The contrast between white and blue makes this one of the most beautiful places in the North Shore mountains.
- Go down. You will see the first bump to ascend. There should be cairns leading you on a rough but obvious path leftward, straight up into the trees. *Do not* swerve right into the granite bowl or towards the lakes.
- Go down again, to a flat mini-valley. Then head left and straight up to the treed bump and follow the trail.
- The final push starts with a gravelly slope looking up at the peak. There should be cairns. Head straight up, but watch your footing.
- The peak gives grand views of Palisade Lake and the smaller Rodgers Lake to the west, the Causeway leading to Cathedral below, and Cathedral itself, looking close enough to touch.
- Be sure to head north and picnic on the gleaming granite boulders for a view of Burwell Lake, with its small dam, to the northeast.

CATHEDRAL MOUNTAIN

(CAT) (1737 M #3)

A grand, remote bushwhack that is not as difficult and steep as it seems from afar.

CAUTION:
Very remote. No consistent trail.
Some exposure. Out of bounds
because wholly within a watershed.

PROMINENCE:
832 m.

LATITUDE/LONGITUDE:
N49.46667 W123.00861.

BANG FOR BUCK:
3/5

PEAK VIEW:
4/5. Unique views of Coliseum;
unimpeded views north;

N: Mamquam; S: Baker.

TRUE SUMMIT LOCATION:
Obvious: final peak on trail
after a few false summits.
At transmitter tower.

HEADWATERS:
Burwell Lake, Burwell Creek,
Cathedral Creek
(into Seymour River); Palisade
Creek (into Capilano River).

BEST VIEWS FROM:
Paton Peak, Burwell Peak,
North Needle.

TRIP INFORMATION

Round-trip distance: 23.8 km from Stoney Creek trailhead; 43.6 km from LSCR parking lot.

Elevation gain: 2317 m.

Time: 11 hours to 2 days (12:04).

Difficulty: 5/5.

Snow free: Mid-July.

Must-sees: Slabby stairs on back side of Burwell; alien space towers on peak.

Scenery: 4/5.

Kids: 0/5. Not suitable: too far.

Dogs: 1/5. Hands required at times; far; watershed inappropriate for dogs.

Runnability: 3/5. Not so much on Cathedral itself.

Terrain: After Burwell, only a route with occasional flagging: much rock-hopping, bushwhacking, and use of hands.

Public transit: #228 Lynn Valley bus from Lonsdale Quay or #210 Upper Lynn Valley from Phibbs Exchange.

Cell coverage: Usually good on peak; scarce elsewhere.

Sun: Beginning and ending mostly exposed. The climbs up Coliseum and from the col between Burwell and Cathedral are forested.

Water: Some small creeks; *little water in late summer.*

Route links: By necessity, Coliseum and Burwell. Also Paton.

HISTORY

Name origin: A grand and majestic mountain, like a Cathedral. Used in 1910. Name used on 1912 North Vancouver map.

Name status: Official. Adopted May 6, 1924.

First ascent: October 11, 1908. Basil Stewart Darling and Franklin Walter Hewton, two of the BCMC group climbing Burwell (White) for the first time, split from the main group to climb Cathedral as well.

Note: This mountain is in a watershed. The authors are not encouraging or condoning trips to it. This route description is provided based on the fact that people will nonetheless attempt to travel to this peak, and that describing the route here will promote the safety of those individuals and of the environment itself.

Cathedral Mountain.

In delightful understatement, a 1918 BCMC report called Cathedral Mountain "a fine trip of a rather strenuous character." Cathedral is the tallest peak overlooking Vancouver. From most vantage points, it looks like a very daunting and steep climb. It should only be contemplated by the hardiest adventurers, as it is very remote, with no trail, and ample opportunity to get lost or shredded in bushwhacking. A single-day trip is a near-impossibility. The mountain is also off-limits, located wholly in the watershed.

That said, the route, which descends from Burwell down into the col and then zigs to the northwest before zagging back to attain the summit from the west, is, if tackled correctly, no more than a Class 2 scramble. If you ever feel exposed or excessively shredded by vegetation, you are not going the right way: backtrack! In contrast to the looming south face, the west approach is a natural, even fun, ramp up to the summit of Cathedral, with its three mysterious green towers (some say they are mundane radio repeater towers but another theory is that they were placed there by aliens) and its glorious 360° views. The distance from Burwell to Cathedral is about 5.3 km.

There are also fine views en route to the peak. The slabs down to the ridge between Burwell and Cathedral offer a jumbo-sized staircase with views of Burwell and Palisade Lakes: large mirror glacial cirques separated by a narrow ridge. Below the summit look for "Cougar Rock," an outcrop looking north that makes a good "diving board" photograph.

The BCMC led trips to Cathedral most years in the 1920s, '30s, and '40s. The usual route was up Lynn Creek to Lynn Lake and then up to the saddle between Burwell (then called White) and Cathedral. In the 1910s BCMC members called this saddle "The Causeway" and, in a letter to the Chief Geographer in Victoria, suggested that what would become Burwell Lake and Creek be called Causeway Lake and Creek. The suggestion was not followed.

It was on a solo ascent of Cathedral on June 27, 1915, that Don Munday decided to enlist for the First World War:

> As I stood on the snowy summit of Cathedral Mountain I found it hard to renew my resolve to enlist, until a strange coldness crept down over the mountains, as though their aspect declared, 'Unless you are worthy to make this sacrifice, you are unworthy to frequent our shrines.[12]

GETTING THERE

From either Lynn Headwaters Park or from LSCR: see the descriptions to Coliseum and Paton, above.

ROUTE FROM COLISEUM AND BURWELL

Follow the route to Coliseum Mountain and then to Burwell described above, via either LSCR and Paton or Lynn Headwaters Trail and Coliseum Trail.

- From Burwell follow the ridge down the logical route toward the visible long point in the col (The Causeway) between Burwell and Cathedral.
- The route down is a series of giant steps. At no time should you feel exposed. If so, veer left or right and choose an easier route down. If in doubt, head left.
- Cross a creek and reach an obvious ledge that brings you down to the col.
- When you hit the base of the col, it becomes shrubby and dense. At last visit, there was also thick blowdown, making the faint route a challenge to find.
- From the col continue in roughly a straight line towards the ridge rising ahead. A GPS is very useful here, as the trees are thick.
- If you aim towards the centre of the ridge, the ascent should never be too steep or bushy. At times, you will be walking through pleasant heather.
- If you cut right towards Cathedral and traverse too soon, however, you will face a very nasty and thick bushwhack. Resist this temptation!
- Soon you will meet a boulder field among the trees. Regain the ridge and follow it for some distance. Cathedral's west slopes, to your right, will appear to be too steep, and they are. Keep walking north until you can climb them readily.
- Eventually an obvious bench leads left towards a rock field.
- Climb up and left across the rock field. Keep climbing up the rock field, as high as you can go, until you hit trees. There is some flagging here.

Cathedral: The Gully of Doom.

- If you go too far left, you will come to a deep and steep gully nicknamed "The Gully of Doom." This is the most difficult part of the climb, but the crossing place is obvious, and if conditions are good and you take care, there should be little risk.
- Either way, climb through and up some shrubby krumholtzes.
- Continue climbing, heading left rather than tackling Cathedral head-on.
- After a while, look for an obvious point to turn and head up a wet rocky spot towards Cathedral's summit.
- You will come out onto a grassy ledge. Head left. The ledge narrows but ultimately leads to another ledge above. Take care to remember this section (which was marked with flagging and some cairns on last visit), as it is the key point of the route and easily missed on the descent, with potentially disastrous results.
- Keep climbing, occasionally pulling yourself up on non-exposed sections. You will then start ascending a more obvious and wide ridge again, with the peak in view. The ridge is generally easy and non-exposed. If in doubt, veer right.
- After a short dip, you will reach a false summit. Above this false summit, you will have to use your hands and climb through a section of krumholtz tunnels.
- You will then see the mysterious green towers on the peak. It is an easy scramble up.
- There is a helipad and, at last visit, a mysterious toilet seat. Bask in the views to the north.
- As you return past Burwell, take care to head toward Coliseum rather than the also slabby, bald side peak of Burwell to the West. The fatigued mind could readily make this error.
- Also resist the temptation to traverse Burwell to the west, thinking it will save time and elevation; the southwest slope has cliffs and thick vegetation that would block your passage to Coliseum.
- You will sleep well that evening.

FANNIN RANGE

(14 PEAKS)

Located between the Seymour River on the west and Indian Arm and Indian River to the east, the Fannin Range runs the gamut from the immensely popular front country of Mt. Seymour Provincial Park, with its readily accessible trails and peaks, to the very remote Mt. Dickens and beyond, north to the rarely visited Haggis and Bagpipe peaks (due east of Furry Creek as the crow flies). At 1657 m, Bagpipe is the highest peak in the range. We have not included Haggis and Bagpipe in this book, due to their remoteness. The southern peaks – mere bumps – are Dog Mountain and Dinkey Peak, which lack the prominence to make the cut for this book. The tallest summits in the range barely emerge above the treeline, and the trees themselves are generally second-growth, having been razed by early loggers.

The range is named after naturalist John Fannin (1837–1904), who in 1886 was the first curator of the British Columbia Provincial Museum (now the Royal British Columbia Museum). Born in Kemptville, Ont., Fannin came to BC with the Overlanders, hardy gold-seekers from Manitoba who eschewed the easier gold-rush route by sea and river. Fannin also worked as a shoemaker, hunting guide, and taxidermist. Several other British Columbia features are named after Fannin, including a creek and a lake in this range, as well as Mt. Fannin (near Quatsino, on Vancouver Island).

The best-known peak, Mt. Seymour, is named for Frederick Seymour, governor of British Columbia from 1864 to 1869. Various other landmarks are also named after him. Seymour opposed Confederation, perhaps because it would diminish his status. He was apparently unpopular and died on a trip to Bella Coola, reputedly of either alcoholism or syphilis, or perhaps a combination of both. Other Seymour landmarks (such as Seymour Narrows, off Vancouver Island) are named after a different Seymour: Rear Admiral George Francis Seymour, commander of the British fleet in the Pacific from 1844 to 1847 and eventually promoted to Admiral of the Fleet in 1866.

In a common pattern, hunters and lumbermen arrived at Seymour before the hikers, with logging starting in the 1880s. The west side of the mountain was logged by the Hastings Mill Co. in the 1920s, the east side by the Buck Logging Co. (also known as Deep Cove Lumber Co., operated until 1926). The (now old) Buck Logging Trail, built in the early 1920s, offered relatively easy access all the way up to the treeline from the water. Logging was short-lived on the east side, as a fire swept through the region in 1922. Two flumes carried logs down the mountain, to the Seymour River on the west and to Deep Cove (then called Deepwater) in the east. Modern exploration of the lower reaches of Seymour on the seldom visited west side reveals extensive remnants of corduroy logging roads and campsites full of broken bottles and crockery. The crockery is often inscribed with Chinese or Japanese characters, reflecting the origins of those loggers.

Although the first recorded climb of Mt. Seymour occurred in 1908, the recreational opportunities of the area were not recognized for another two decades. The process was no doubt hastened by the erection of a bridge at the Second Narrows in 1925 (standing only four years before being knocked out by a ship; the Depression delayed its rebuilding until 1934). In 1929 the Alpine Club of Canada conducted the first significant ski tour of the Mt. Seymour area. The tour was apparently a success, as the next year the ACC applied for a 21-year lease for skiing in the area and in 1931 built a cabin. In 1933 the BCMC built its first cabin on Mt. Seymour, marking the event with a venison feast; a larger cabin was built in 1938. In the 1930s many private recreational cabins appeared as well, the remnants of which can primarily be found on the seldom visited western slopes between the historic Mushroom Parking Lot and Boulder Creek. By 1941 there were approximately 80 cabins on the mountain.

Mt. Seymour Provincial Park was opened in 1936, with a total of 274 hectares. Half of this land was purchased by Harold Enquist to develop a ski area. The road to the ski hill was built from 1938 to 1942, to bring skiers halfway up the mountain to the Mushroom Parking Lot. The present road, to the ski-lift parking lot, was officially opened on December 9, 1950. In 1949 the provincial government purchased Enquist's ski operations and hired him to run it. This was followed by the first chairlift and rope tow. In 1984 the Controlled Recreation Area and its facilities was awarded to Mt. Seymour Resorts Ltd. under a park use permit.

The park itself is presently 3650 hectares in size. Camping is permitted north of Brockton Point, although there are no designated campgrounds, and campfires are not permitted. Sometimes a snack bar is open at Seymour in the summer. Washrooms are usually open. Both are located on the east side of the parking lot.

Well-established and generally well-marked trails lead to the peaks at the south end of the park. The main Mt. Seymour trail brings you near or to the three peaks of Mt. Seymour: Pump, Tim Jones, and the Seymour summit. Just before the final climb up the main peak of Seymour, Indian Arm Trail splits west off the main trail. Indian Arm Trail serves as the artery to Runner, Elsay, the Episcopal Peaks of Rector/Curate/Vicar, down to Vicar Lakes, up to Bishop, then north to the Bishop subpeaks of Jarrett (Deacon) and Clementine (Presbyter), and beyond to Fannin Lake and Mt. Dickens, and beyond that to Bearclaw Ridge, across the Indian River to the east side of Indian Arm, back up to Eagle Ridge, to finish at Buntzen Lake. Built by legendary trail builder and City of Vancouver engineer Don McPherson (b. 1943, Yerrington, Nev.) in the late 1990s and early 2000s, and first hiked through in 2003, the trail proved too remote to attract enough boots to keep the salal, blueberries, and evergreens from reclaiming nature's domain. That said, recent interest in the peaks north of Seymour, thanks in part to the Bagger Challenge, has retrodden and reblazed Indian Arm Trail to the use it deserves.

Despite this being one of the most popular hiking areas in Canada, it is easy to find oneself in remote, dangerous, and uncharted territory very swiftly in Mt. Seymour Provincial Park and the Fannin Range. As set out in this chapter, the area has seen many rescues and fatalities. In separate incidents, in 1996 and 2007 respectively, Stephen Gander and Christopher Morley slid off the east side of the Seymour hike and only miraculously survived. In 1999 experienced hiker Debra White suffered a similar slip but died. In 1980 Michael Rempel, an inexperienced 21-year-old hiker, died after falling 300 m down the gully between Tim Jones Peak and Mount Seymour while en route to Mt. Elsay. In 1982 Charlie Muso went for a hike in the Seymour backcountry and disappeared without a trace. In 1991 Steven Ebbey went on a solo hike towards Mt. Elsay. His headless body was discovered the next spring in a drainage system above Indian Arm.

All of the peaks profiled, with the exception of Dickens, are in Seymour Provincial Park. Under park regulations, pets must be on leash at all times and are not allowed in park buildings.

All of the peaks in the Fannin Range are accessible via the Mt. Seymour parking lot.

The Mt. Seymour area has often been used in Hollywood films, including *Hot Tub Time Machine*; *Superman: Man of Steel*; *The Twilight Saga: Eclipse*; *Star Trek Beyond*; and various *X-Files* episodes.

GETTING THERE

Route 1: via Mt. Seymour parking lot
- From Ironworkers Memorial (Second Narrows) Bridge, take Highway 1 to Exit 22B to turn right, onto Mt. Seymour Parkway, avoiding Lillooet Road.
- After 4.3 km, turn left onto Mt. Seymour Road.
- Follow Mt. Seymour Road up to the Mt. Seymour ski resort.

That said, the peaks north of Vicar Lakes are in most cases better approached via the LSCR Seymour Valley Trailway, with a bike trip to the trailhead of the steep Vicar Lakes Trail, on the east side of the Seymour River. This is also an option for an energetic loop trip back to the Seymour parking lot, although you will have to return later to the LSCR to retrieve your bicycle.

Route 2: via LSCR and Seymour Valley Trailway
- From Ironworkers Memorial (Second Narrows) Bridge, take Highway 1 to Exit 22A right and then turn left up Lillooet Road.
- You will pass a horse stable, Capilano University, the North Vancouver cemetery, a prominent gate, and then (after several kilometres' drive) the Seymour–Capilano water treatment plant. The road ends at a large gravel parking lot.
- The path starts next to the outhouses and map kiosk. Follow the path leading to the west. This brings you to a gazebo and a paved road, where your journey begins.
- Note that the gate (near the cemetery) gets locked at sundown, which would trap your car and possibly trigger NSR if you have not left a message.

Mt. Dickens is also accessible, and interestingly so, by boat, sailing to the end of Indian Arm, likely from Deep Cove. See Mt. Dickens for that description.

SOUTH FANNIN RANGE: SEYMOUR AREA ACCESS VIA MT. SEYMOUR PARKING LOT

(5 PEAKS)

Towards Pump Peak (Seymour First Peak) in the dawn's early light

SEYMOUR AREA BAGGER TIPS

Suicide Bluffs, de Pencier Bluffs, Pump, Tim Jones, and Seymour can be done as a day trip from the Mt. Seymour parking lot. This is a suitable trip for spring with snowshoes and/or micro spikes or as a summer hike. Park at the ski area and start by taking the Mystery Lake trail to de Pencier Bluffs. From there get back onto the main Seymour trail and traverse over Pump and Tim Jones to finally reach Mt. Seymour. Pick up de Pencier Bluffs on the way back to the parking lot as an out and back from the Seymour trail.

Round-trip distance:
9.9 km

Time:
4:52

Elevation gain:
640 m

to Runne
Elsay and
Vicar lake

Intake Creek

Suicide Bluffs
1167m

Dog
Mountain

First
Lake

Dog Mtn. Trail

1

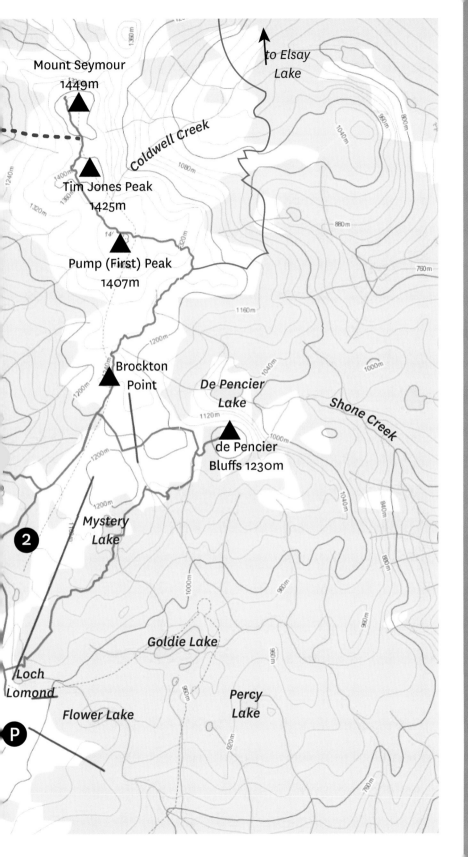

Mount Seymour
1449m

to Elsay
Lake

Coldwell Creek

Tim Jones Peak
1425m

Pump (First) Peak
1407m

Brockton
Point

De Pencier
Lake

Shone Creek

de Pencier
Bluffs 1230m

Mystery
Lake

2

Goldie Lake

Loch
Lomond

Percy
Lake

Flower Lake

P

SUICIDE BLUFFS

(SUI) (1167 M)

Pleasant, shorter perambulation of lower Seymour plateau.

CAUTION:
Some cliffs.

PROMINENCE:
57 m.

LATITUDE/LONGITUDE:
N49.37833 W122.95695.

BANG FOR BUCK:
3/5

PEAK VIEW:
2/5.

TRUE SUMMIT LOCATION:
North of Second Lake.

HEADWATERS:
Semlin Creek, Boulder Creek,
Suicide Creek
(all into Seymour River).

BEST VIEWS FROM:
South Lynn Peak Balloon Lookout.

TRIP INFORMATION

Round-trip distance: 4 km.
Elevation gain: 160 m.
Time: 1.5–3 hours (1:30).
Difficulty: 3/5.
Snow free: Usually mid- to late June.
Must-sees: Small lakes, large trees.
Scenery: 2/5.
Kids: 3/5. A relatively easy and safe hike, but some kids may be intimidated by the steep sections and cliffs.
Dogs: 5/5. Must be on leash.
Runnability: 5/5.
Terrain: Second-growth forest; some old-growth cedars and Douglas fir.
Public transit: #C15 bus to base of Mt. Seymour Road. It is a long climb to the ski area/trailhead.
Cell coverage: Good throughout.
Sun: 40 per cent exposed.
Water: Seasonal creeks and tarns.
Route links: de Pencier Bluffs, Mt. Seymour.

HISTORY

Name origin: The sheer cliffs down to Suicide Creek would provide a good realization of the name; unsure if it is a reference to a specific sad instance.
Name status: Unofficial. Used at least as early as 1959.
Other name: Suicide Bluff.
First ascent: Unknown but first recorded ascent likely circa 1910, and likely years before that by First Nations.

View from Suicide Bluffs at sunset.

Although not marked on official Mt. Seymour Trail signposts, and cautioned on various maps as an "undeveloped route," the way is easy to find. Suicide Bluffs is located at the north end of the plateau that contains Dog Mountain (not included in this book because of its modest size). There is a 200-m cliff and a hazardous gully to the north, hence the name. The southern approach is a gentle hike from the Second Lake plateau. Suicide Bluffs is the second peak, immediately north of Second Lake.

The route makes a good loop with the "official" Dog Mountain trail. The quick and dirty approach is an out-and-back via the Seymour main trail. The longer and more satisfying climb goes via Dog Mountain past pleasant views of Vancouver, the Seymour River valley, Cathedral, Grouse, and other peaks, multiple small murky lakes, bolete mushrooms, and some impressive old-growth cedars and hemlocks.

Suicide Bluffs is not an easy climb for children, but our smaller hiking companions, aged 8 to 12, survived with minimal grumbles and with pride and joy at the viewpoints. There are fearsome cliffs at the north side of the peak, into the Suicide Creek Valley, that children should not approach.

ROUTE 1:

FROM SOUTH VIA DOG MOUNTAIN TRAIL

- From Seymour parking lot, take the Dog Mountain trail. At the bluff at the end, go north on a less developed trail. Instead of turning left and up to Dog, turn onto the trail on the right. Several metres along, a tree is marked with a metal tag as "Suicide Bluffs Trail."
- There is an immediate climb. It is generally a clear trail. Pass five tarns, some of which may be empty on the driest summer days, then climb steeply up to a viewpoint on some bluffs. This is not the peak, although it has best view. (The true summit, to the east, is obviously the higher from this angle.)
- Descend. After passing one more tarn, the trail climbs steeply again. Two plastic cable ropes are provided but are usually not necessary.
- The trail leads to an obvious, wide, bare-granite summit. There are good views of the Seymour River and Seymour Valley Trailway. To the north a sheer cliff and valley separate Suicide Bluffs from the looming Seymour massif.

The steepest part of the Suicide Bluffs trail.

- Find the trail eastward, snaking through the heather. Descend. When you reach a fork near a tarn, go left (the right fork simply ends at the tarn).
- Take a minor ascent to a third bluff summit before descending and passing just above Hidden Lake. You will see the rope placed along the Mount Seymour boundary by staff to mark its location in the winter. The trail ends in a boggy area at Mt. Seymour Trail, 1 km north of the parking lot. Turn right to complete the loop and return. You will pass the Dinkey Peak Nature Trail marker, a memorial to NSR leader Tim Jones, and the turnoff to First Lake.

Route 2:

FROM EAST – OUT AND BACK VIA SEYMOUR MAIN TRAIL

- Start at the Seymour parking lot. Pass the Dog Mountain Trail and First Lake Trail signposts.
- The first 1.5 km is a dull drudge up a ski run/gravel road. An alternative rougher but greener trail parallels the road, to the west.
- You will pass the Dinkey Peak Nature Trail marker and the turnoff to First Lake.
- The Suicide Bluffs trail starts in a boggy area about 1 km north of the parking lot.

DE PENCIER BLUFFS

(DEP) (1230 M)

Pleasant short perambulation of lower Seymour plateau leading
to a lovely view of Indian Arm.

CAUTION:
Some cliffs.

PROMINENCE:
50 m.

LATITUDE/LONGITUDE:
N49.37889 W122.93361.

BANG FOR BUCK:
5/5

PEAK VIEW:
2/5. Great views of city and
mountains. Partially obscured.

TRUE SUMMIT LOCATION:
On obvious knoll,
covered in tight alpine trees;
small cairn.

HEADWATERS:
de Pencier Lake,
Shone Creek,
Percy Creek
(into Indian Arm).

BEST VIEWS FROM:
Hike to Pump Peak,
Brockton Point.

TRIP INFORMATION

Round-trip distance: 3.6 km round trip from parking lot.

Elevation gain: 200 m.

Time: 1.5–3 hours (1:30).

Difficulty: 2/5. Easy trail. Relatively short distance.

Snow free: June.

Must-sees: Autumn leaves; small tarns; inukshuks on slabby bluff.

Scenery: 3/5. Good variety of mountains views, lakes, and woods.

Kids: 5/5. Safe and easy.

Dogs: 5/5. No hands needed. Must be leashed.

Runnability: 4/5. Mostly runnable. Some eroded, rooty bits.

Terrain: Second-growth forest; some old-growth cedars and Douglas fir.

Public transit: #C15 bus to base of Mt. Seymour Road.

Cell coverage: Generally good throughout.

Sun: Generally covered. Some exposure on peak.

Water: Seasonal creeks and tarns.

Route links: Suicide Bluffs, Mt. Seymour.

HISTORY

Name origin: The Most Reverend Adam de Pencier, OBE, DD (1866–1949), Bishop of New Westminster and later the second Archbishop and Metropolitan of British Columbia, 1910–1940. The bishop spelled his name with a small "d" and a space and you should too.

Name status: Unofficial. De Pencier Lake, near the peak, is an official name, adopted February 27, 1976. There are two versions of when the lake was named and by whom: in 1910 by James Theodore Underhill of Vancouver (who first mapped the area) "after meeting the bishop deer hunting near the lake, when he shot his first goat"; and around 1915 by the bishop's friend W. Chester Smith of the Water Rights Branch, who placed it on the 1915 Water Map.

Other names: De Pencier Bluff. Sometimes mistakenly referred to as "Mystery Peak," which is the summit where the Mystery chairlift is located.

First ascent: Unknown, but first BCMC climb likely around 1910, and before that by Indigenous people.

De Pencier Bluffs is a very pleasant adventure for the younger bagger and the bagging trail runner alike. The east side of Seymour, with lakes, tarns, bluffs, and blueberries and a rabbit warren of runnable trails, is not often explored but is well worth it. In autumn its peak becomes a red blaze of blueberry leaves, a pleasing contrast to the grey of the rock and the city. It makes for a very agreeable post-work bag, ideally on a sunny day. De Pencier Bluffs is the easternmost peak in the Seymour area, due east of the Brockton chairlift and due south of De Pencier Lake. The peak provides an unusual view of Indian Arm and Buntzen Lake, as well as fine vistas of Mt. Baker, Vancouver, De Pencier Lake, Mt. Seymour, and Brockton Peak. You can make it a loop by heading back to the main trail and then continuing northwest to the bottom of the Brockton chairlift and beyond to the Mt. Seymour main trail.

ROUTE

Avoid the typical boring approach up Seymour via the gravel road. Instead, start just to the right, in the trees, on a well-marked single-track path up to Mystery Lake. You will pass a sign for the Unicorn ski run.

- At Mystery Lake, say hello to the salamanders, venture forth on Salamander Island, and eat some blueberries before continuing northeast around the lakeshore on a thin but clear trail that goes up and down a small rocky bluff to the east.
- The trail heads down to the first of two flat areas of small fairy tarns. In autumn you will likely see an abundance of *Amanita muscaria* (fly amanita): the charming but poisonous red-and-white-capped toadstools from fairy tales.
- Down and up and then down the slope, along well-marked trail.
- A tricky turnoff occurs when you are hiking along a small creek. You will see the Brockton chairlift up ahead to the left along the dominant trail. *Do not continue up.* Instead, veer sharp right, down a faint trail towards a small creek.
- Easily cross the creek and climb up.
- Continue upward on a clear but rough trail. You will see flagging and a small sign indicating de Pencier Bluffs.
- Up and down to another fairyland tarn.
- Then upwards again and another tricky turnoff. The dominant trail heads north, toward a trail leading to Brockton Point. Just before the crest, however, there is a marked lesser trail heading up and right. Take it. At the time of writing, there was a small sign.

- This leads to a rocky-slab open area with a few boulders to the right. Resist the temptation to go that way, but rather head up and leftwards. The trail continues up, faint but obvious. Come to a series of low, swampy areas alternating with rocky-slab faces with easy routes up.
- Then come to a flattish area, with a table-like rock likely covered with a small inukshuk or two.
- Climb to the pleasant, flat, tarned summit. The peak is in a tight cluster of pines. Views of Indian Arm, Mt. Baker, Burrard Inlet, and De Pencier Lake.

The de Pencier turnoff.

PUM P PEAK

(PUM) (SEYMOUR FIRST PEAK) (1407 M)

Delivers much of the adventure and views of Mt. Seymour at half the distance.

CAUTION:
Cliffs to south: watch children.

PROMINENCE:
60 m.

LATITUDE/LONGITUDE:
N49.38718 W122.94130.

BANG FOR BUCK:
5/5

PEAK VIEW:
5/5. Interesting views of Indian Arm,
Mt. Seymour, and Mt. Baker. Alex

Fraser Bridge, Fraser Valley peaks.
Tim Jones and Mt. Seymour.

TRUE SUMMIT LOCATION:
Small and obvious.

HEADWATERS:
Suicide Creek, Baxter Creek,
Intake Creek (into Seymour River),
Gopher Lake, Caldwell Creek
(into Indian Arm).

BEST VIEWS FROM:
Mt. Seymour.

TRIP INFORMATION

Round-trip distance: 5 km.

Elevation gain: 400 m.

Time: 1.5–3 hours (2:10).

Difficulty: 1/5. Well-marked trail.

Snow free: June.

Must-sees: Increasingly impressive views.

Scenery: 5/5. Lovely tarns and granite.

Kids: 5/5.

Dogs: 5/5. Must be leashed.

Runnability: 4/5. Very runnable except for the middle.

Terrain: Dull gravel ski run to pleasant forest to slabby paradise.

Public transit: #C15 bus to base of Mt. Seymour Road. It is a long climb to the ski area/trailhead.

Cell coverage: Usually but sometimes surprisingly absent.

Sun: Approach 80 per cent shaded; peak 100 per cent exposed.

Water: Some creeks and tarns in spring; plenty of water at trailhead.

Route links: Sweep from Seymour to Vicar, or full Fannin Sweep, or Elsay Lake Loop.

HISTORY

Name origin: From Frank Smith's remark that a wizened stump near the summit of Pump Peak looked like a pump.

Name status: Official: Adopted January 2, 1987.

First ascent: Mountain probably climbed by early hunters. First recorded ascent August 16, 1908, by BCMC party: William Gray, Fred Mills, George Harrower, Frank Harold Smith.

Other names: "First Pump Peak"; "Third Seymour Peak" (circa 1908; so called because the initial approaches were from the north, after climbing the main and second peaks).

Other write-ups: Hanna, hike to Seymour travels via Pump Peak; Hui.

The first peak of Mt. Seymour overlooks the first granite tarns of Seymour. The peak or those tarns make a pleasant lunch spot or a destination unto themselves. The views are spectacular and a child or neophyte hiker will feel like the monarch of the world. The bleached granite slabs surrounding the peak are at the perfect angle to make a grand adventure for children. You will receive a fine view of the Fraser River with the Port Mann and Golden Ears bridges, as well as Mt. Baker. On clear winter days you can even see Mt. Rainier.

An account by Charles Chapman in the August 29, 1908, *BC Saturday Sunset* recounts how the peak received its odd name. The party, which consisted of legendary BCMC alpinists Billy Gray, Fred Mills, George Harrower, Frank Smith, Basil Darling, and Charles Chapman, started their climb from the Seymour River (considered a creek back then). At alpine they observed several mountain goats on the bluffs. They emerged between the now named Tim Jones Peak and Mt. Seymour and climbed them. They then proceeded south towards Pump Peak, where "a peculiar formation of trees on the southern peak caught the notice of Frank Smith (known as Smithy). To Smithy these trees looked like an old pump…." In the 50th Anniversary publication of the BCMC, Frank H. Smith noted that the name "remains an awful example of how a casual remark may perpetuate a name as unsuitable and mystifying as that above referred to."

In 1908 the gully leading up from the Pump Peak amphitheatre toward what is now Tim Jones Peak was called "Roy Howard Gully." Roy Howard (born 1899), an automotive mechanic and insurance appraiser who had come to Vancouver in 1909, was president of the BCMC in 1934–35 and still active in 1937.

In January 2007 Christopher Morley, an experienced hiker on a snowshoeing trip back from Runner Peak, slid down the icy east side of this hike. He fell more than 100 m into Theta Lake. His hiking partner, Simon Chesterton, attempted to rescue him, at considerable personal risk. Tim Jones and Gord Ferguson of North Shore Rescue, along with pilot Peter Murray of Talon Helicopters, led the rescue, in which some 85 people assisted. Morley had to spend two nights with his rescuers in a snow shelter before the snowstorm cleared enough to permit rescue.

The gentle south-facing ski slopes on Seymour and Grouse are remnants of peneplain: gently rolling hills that characterized the Lower Mainland before uplift. While this surface has eroded at lower elevations, it remains in these two places. While the main peak of Mt. Seymour consists largely of granodiorite, the terrain near the ski parking lot for Pump Peak consists of pre-Jurassic Gambier Group volcanic rocks of breccia and andesite. The area south of the parking lot and between Pump and Tim Jones peaks is scored with minor east–west fault lines.

ROUTE

See the description at p. 328 of the Seymour parking lot to Pump Peak amphitheatre route.

- Climb and emerge from the forested portion of the trail.
- Turn west and enter a gateway leading to a great view of Pump Peak, with a permanent snow patch and a pleasing tarn at the base of a mini-cirque.
- The main Seymour trail heads north, up a rocky staircase. Instead, travel west, past the tarn.
- Veer left, then right on an obvious scree channel. In truth, though, most of the cirque face is readily climbable. You can make your own route.
- At the top of the first climb, you will enter a mini-valley between the peak on the right and a low bump on the left. Go westward along this valley for a few seconds.
- Just before the end of the valley, you'll see the path snake right and uphill. Look up and you'll spot the summit post. Zig right and up, then zag left and up, and – presto – you are on the peak with its wooden summit post.
- To rejoin the Seymour trail proper, you can retrace your steps. The better and swifter route, however, is to rock-hop, carefully, northward off the peak. At no point should you need to jump too far to regain the main Seymour trail, which is visible and obvious from Pump Peak.

TIM JONES PEAK

(TIM) (1425 M)

Delivers much of the adventure and views of Seymour, with less distance and effort.

CAUTION:
Cliffs to the east.

PROMINENCE:
45 m.

LATITUDE/LONGITUDE:
N49.39056 W122.94334.

BANG FOR BUCK:
5/5

PEAK VIEW:
5/5. Interesting views of
Indian Arm and Mt. Seymour.

TRUE SUMMIT LOCATION:
Small and obvious.

HEADWATERS:
Suicide Creek, Baxter Creek,
Intake Creek (into Seymour River),
Gopher Lake, Caldwell Creek
(into Indian Arm).

BEST VIEWS FROM:
Mt. Seymour.

TRIP INFORMATION

Round-trip distance: 6 km.
Elevation gain: 500 m.
Time: 2–4 hours (2:50).
Difficulty: 1/5. Well-marked trail.
Snow free: Early July.
Must-sees: Increasingly impressive views.
Scenery: 5/5.
Kids: 5/5.
Dogs: 5/5. Must be leashed.
Runnability: 4/5.
Terrain: Dull gravel ski run to pleasant forest to slabby paradise.
Public transit: #C15 bus to base of Mt. Seymour Road. It is a long climb to the ski area/trailhead.
Cell coverage: Usually.
Sun: Approach 80 per cent shaded; peak 100 per cent exposed.
Water: Some creeks and tarns in spring; plenty of water at trailhead.
Route links: Sweep from Seymour to Vicar, or full Fannin Sweep, or Elsay Lake Loop.

HISTORY

Name origin: Tim Jones, head of NSR, who with his team saved hundreds of lives before being felled by a heart attack, at too young an age, while hiking down from the NSR cabin near Dinkey Peak on January 19, 2014.
Name status: Official. January 20, 2017.
First ascent: Mountain probably climbed by early hunters. First recorded ascent

August 16, 1908, by BCMC party: William Gray, Fred Mills, George Harrower, Frank Harold Smith.

Other names: Commonly (and erroneously) called "Second Pump Peak" before 2014. The proper name was Centre Peak (as used in 1951, for example) or Second Seymour Peak.

Other write-ups: Hanna and Hui routes to Seymour travel via Tim Jones Peak.

Tim Jones.

The second peak of Mt. Seymour was sometimes erroneously called "Second Pump Peak," after Seymour's first peak, the true "Pump Peak." It has recently gained the popular name of Tim Jones Peak, named after the leader of North Shore Rescue, who died of a heart attack at age 57 on January 19, 2014, while hiking down from NSR's cabin on Mt. Seymour, near Dinkey Peak. Jones was a North Vancouver native and paramedic who was instrumental in developing NSR as a professional and well-equipped force, with advanced communications systems. He assisted in over 1,600 rescues. In 2014 the federal government recognized Jones in its budget by dedicating a national search-and-rescue volunteer tax credit in his name. Among his many honours, he received the Order of British Columbia as well as an Honorary Doctor of Laws from Capilano University. Thousands of emergency services personnel and members of the community marched in a parade up Lonsdale Avenue to his memorial ceremony.

The day after Tim Jones's death, author David Crerar suggested on ClubTread.com that a peak be named after Jones, proposing Runner Peak or Crown N1. Simon Chesterton proposed West Crown but it was Drew Brayshaw's suggestion of Seymour's Second Peak that won the day. Mick Bailey set up a Facebook page with 3,069 members. Mel Turner filed the formal request. The peak was officially named on January 20, 2017, announced by Premier Christy Clark at the North Shore Rescue headquarters.

In 1996 Tim Jones and the NSR team rescued a scout, Phillip Gander, who had fallen 300 m into the Gopher Lake drainage below. He woke up after 19 days of life support. Gander went on to gain a Ph.D. specializing in head injury trauma recovery.

The east side of the peak features the scabrously named "Tim's Crack," which was named before his death.

ROUTE

See the route description for Seymour parking lot to Pump Peak amphitheatre, at p. 328. See the route description for the Pump Peak amphitheatre to Tim Jones Peak, at p. 329.

MT. SEYMOUR

(SEY) (1449 M)

Very satisfying half-day hike to excellent 360° views and a fun rocky peak.

CAUTION:
Some cliffs and steep sections north of Tim Jones Peak.

PROMINENCE:
453 m.

LATITUDE/LONGITUDE:
N49.39333 W122.94444.

BANG FOR BUCK:
5/5

PEAK VIEW:
5/5. Elsay, Bishop, Garibaldi, Meslilloet, Baker, Golden Ears, Robie Reid, Judge Howay.

TRUE SUMMIT LOCATION:
Obvious peak at edge of ridge.

HEADWATERS:
Suicide Creek, Baxter Creek, Intake Creek (into Seymour River), Rolf Creek, Gopher Lake, Caldwell Creek (into Indian Arm).

BEST VIEWS FROM:
Mt. Elsay, Cambie Street Bridge, Simon Fraser University.

TRIP INFORMATION

Round-trip distance: 6.8 km.

Elevation gain: 660 m.

Time: 2.5–5 hours (3:38).

Difficulty: 1/5. Well-marked trail.

Snow free: Early July.

Must-sees: Salamanders in Mystery Lake; rocky slabs at Pump Peak; glorious views.

Scenery: 5/5.

Kids: 5/5.

Dogs: 5/5. Must be leashed.

Runnability: 4/5.

Terrain: Dull gravel ski run to pleasant forest to slabby paradise.

Public transit: #C15 bus to base of Mt. Seymour Road. It is a long climb to the ski area/trailhead.

Cell coverage: Usually good on peak; inconsistent below.

Sun: Approach 90 per cent shaded; peak 100 per cent exposed.

Water: Some creeks and tarns in spring; plenty of water at trailhead.

Route links: Sweep from Seymour to Vicar, or full Fannin Sweep, or Elsay Lake Loop.

HISTORY

Name origin: After Frederick Seymour (1820 Belfast, Ireland – 1869 Bella Coola, BC), second governor of the colony of British Columbia, from 1864 to 1866, and the first governor of British Columbia after unification of the colonies of British Columbia and Vancouver Island, from 1866 to 1869.

Name status: Official. Adopted in the 1930 *BC Gazetteer*, as labelled on BC map 2B,

1914. Used in 1910. Name used in 1912 North Vancouver map.

First ascent: First recorded ascent August 9, 1908, by BCMC party: William Gray, Fred Mills, George Harrower, Frank Harold Smith, Charles Chapman, Basil Darling.

Other names: Third Peak, Third Pump Peak.

Other write-ups: Hanna, Hui.

Seymour is one of the most popular, accessible, and rewarding hikes in the North Shore mountains. It offers tarns, forest, granite slabs, and bald peaks, flat sections and steep sections, and pleasing nearby and far-off views. It is also the most flexible of hikes: for parties who get tired or encounter a change in weather, the trip can be cut short at either of the two subpeaks of Seymour – Pump (the first one) or Tim Jones (the second) – and yet still have an excellent outing.

Despite its popularity and ample signage, Seymour can be hazardous, particularly in the stretch between Tim Jones and the Seymour summit, and particularly in late May and June. Hikers venture up onto the hardened, icy snow wearing improper footwear. They don't think about what might happen if they slip on the hard snow. This has led to deaths and many serious injuries, as it is nearly impossible to stop sliding on these very steep slopes until a rough collision with a tree or a final ride off a cliff. *Do not blindly read the "beginner appropriate" rating of this peak. That score is based on perfect weather, with clear visibility and no slippery freezing rain. Seymour often has late-lingering snow, particularly on its north and east faces. Its kid-friendly rating assumes the child is sturdy and possesses good judgment and self-control.*

Many have died on Seymour. One fatality that received significant media coverage was that of Gordon McFarlane in October 1956. He and two hiking companions, Alick Patterson and Robert Duncan, all recently arrived from Scotland, embarked on what they anticipated would be a three-hour hike. They became lost in fog, and instead of returning down the Mt. Seymour trail, they descended below Suicide Bluffs. A snow-storm struck and they sought shelter in a cave. After spending two nights without food, McFarlane set out on his own over the objections of his companions. Patterson grew very weak, and when the weather cleared the next day, Duncan set out for help. He soon found McFarlane's body in a creek. He stumbled down the mountain, and before being taken to hospital he directed authorities to the approximate location of Patterson. The ensuing search and rescue operation was one of the largest in British Columbia history to that time. The helicopter extraction of McFarlane's body – and the rescue of Patterson, who had survived nights in the snow before being found on the edge of a waterfall – was the first ever in Canada. The rescue led to the formation of the Mountain Rescue Group, a joint enterprise of the Vancouver section of the Alpine Club of Canada and the BCMC. The tale is told in the book *Cloud Walkers*, by climber Paddy Sherman, who assisted in the rescue. Sherman, a journalist, later became publisher of the *Vancouver Province*.

Seymour was first climbed on August 15–16, 1908, by a BCMC party of early British Columbia mountaineering legends: William Gray, Fred Mills, George Harrower, Frank Harold Smith, Charles Chapman, and Basil Stewart Darling. They took the ferry to North Vancouver and hiked up the old Lillooet cattle trail before ascending to the Seymour plateau from the west. Towards Seymour Peak, several mountain goats were seen, as were many bear tracks. They delighted in the views from the peak and watched pieces of rock smash to bits as they hurled them off the peak (*note to modern readers:* please do not do this). They then enjoyed a swim in a tarn, presumably at the base of Pump Peak. (See **Appendix 19** for the article on this climb.) Charles "Chappy" Chapman took extensive photographs of the trip.

To mark the 100th anniversary of the climb, to the day, Chapman's grandchildren Lid Hawkins and Hugh Kellas climbed up Seymour; Hawkins learned later that she had rested in the very spot where the tree that gave Pump Peak its name formerly grew.

Before the road was laid down, the traditional Seymour route was an arduous affair, following the Lillooet trail to the water intake site (near the present-day Spur Bridge, below the Mid-valley picnic site) and then climbing the gully up to the col between the second (Tim Jones) and the main peaks of Seymour, popping out at the trailhead of the route north to Runner and Elsay. It roughly followed what is now known as Intake Creek. In winter this route is marked by a long, snowy-white line prominent on the northern skyline.

In 1952 lawyer Roderick Pilkington, BCMC's president at the time, wrote a Swiftian poem that still rings true:

SPRING COMES TO SEYMOUR MOUNTAIN

When roses have replaced the daffodils,
Spring leaves the valley and ascends the hills.
And through the frozen forest's lifeless hush
Rings the reveille of the varied thrush,
And in the echoes yellow violets wake,
As reborn waters from their prison break.
And as the snow from meadows disappears,
Emerge the putrid middens of the skiers.
Where Spring's warm breath has set the snowbanks shrinking
Garbage lies stinking.

The summit of Seymour largely consists of plutonic granodiorite. It is less perfectly granitized than the more purely granitic rock that makes up Pump Peak and areas to the south. The rock around Seymour peak is referred to as migmatite, or a mixture of metamorphic and igneous rock. Small cavities containing small, light-purple quartz crystals can also be found: these were created when the rock cooled under lower pressure near the surface. At the north end of the peak is an outcrop of Gambier Group volcanic rocks.

Route 1:
VIA MYSTERY LAKE
The more scenic and interesting route up Seymour involves a side trip to Mystery Lake. This avoids the somewhat boring approach up Seymour via the gravel road, with only modest additional difficulty, steepness, and duration.
- Go up the gravel road to just past the base of the chairlift. A gravel side path veers right, to an obvious trail ascending up over rocks to the trees. The route is a well-marked single-track path.

- At Mystery Lake, say hello to the salamanders, venture forth on Salamander Island, and eat some blueberries before continuing northeast along the lakeshore on a thin but clear trail that goes up and down a small rocky bluff to the east.
- The trail heads down to the first of two flat areas of small fairy tarns. In autumn you will likely see an abundance of *Amanita muscaria* (fly amanita): the charming but poisonous red-and-white-capped toadstools from fairy tales.
- Down and up and then down again, along well-marked trail.
- You will see the Brockton chairlift up ahead to the left, along the dominant trail.
- Proceed under and to the right of the chair, heading up to join the main Seymour trail. Alternatively, take the dull gravel road to the northwest, towards a squat building. Either way you will see a signpost directing you north on the main Seymour trail at Brockton Point.
- Continue north from Brockton Point on the main Seymour trail, described below.

Route 2:

MOST DIRECT, TO BROCKTON POINT AND BEYOND

Seymour parking lot to Brockton Point: start at the Seymour parking lot.
- The first 1.5 km is a dull drudge upward beside Manning ski run, on a gravel road running to the west of the run. An alternative, rougher but greener trail runs parallel to the road, to the west of it.
- At a flat stretch in the road (which continues up and to the right) veer left down towards a small tarn, sometimes referred to as the "Sugar Bowl." This is the headwaters of Suicide Creek.
- The path is visible climbing out of the hollow on the far side. This well-defined trail will take you up towards Brockton Point, a bald promontory just to the left (west) of the trail.
- There are fine views of the peaks behind Grouse Mountain to the west, as well as Pump Peak, rising here to the north.

Brockton Point to Pump Peak Amphitheatre: Continue east and downwards on rocks. You will soon come to a rocky granite platform with the best viewpoint of de Pencier Bluffs.
- Continue downward along the trail, coming to a meadow and some small tarns. The trail heads right (east) to skirt the base of Pump Peak.
- Begin a steady rise again along rocks interspersed by large trees, snaking northeast on a boulder field at the base of Pump Peak. You may get chattered at by pikas. Look up for birds catching the updrafts around Pump Peak.
- You will see a signpost and a suspended warning sign marking the turnoff to the Elsay Lake Trail to the east. Do not take this trail. Instead head straight, north and upwards into a steep stretch of the hike.
- The trail soon turns into a climb over big rocks and slabs. At its easternmost point there is a nice large boulder with an amazing view of the peaks of the Fraser Valley to the east. In the early morning light, one can see row upon row of mountain ranges, each in a different shade of blue and green.
- Turn west and enter a gateway leading to a great view of Pump Peak, with a permanent snow patch and a pleasing tarn at the base of a mini-cirque. The views of the eastern peaks continue to impress.

- Make the 10-minute scamper up to Pump Peak or bypass it by staying on the dominant trail to the northwest.

Pump Peak Amphitheatre to Tim Jones Peak: Continue along the steep, rocky path up and northwestward.

- Behind (northwest of) Pump Peak, the trail turns into a slabby playland, with a spectacular view of downtown Vancouver to the southwest. Occasional paint splotches and cairns mark your route. If snow lingers, however, the route may be difficult to find. Head towards the far hills!
- Then descend to a small col before climbing again to Tim Jones Peak.
- Ascend up a longish rock staircase to the Tim Jones Peak turnoff. Pop out to the base of Tim Jones for an impressive view of the Needles, Coliseum, and Cathedral to the west

Tim Jones Peak to Mt. Seymour: The next section is the most hazardous, especially with ice or rain. There is a steep descent, and some cliffs to the west.

- From Tim Jones Peak the trail narrows and descends into a valley with a permanent snowfield that marks the turnoff for the trail to Mt. Elsay and points beyond.
- With the assistance of the roots of the "octopus tree", descend before doing the final push up Seymour via a slabby face. Children (and adults) will find this a fun adventure playground of scrambling and gentle rock climbing.
- After a false summit, dip again into the final push up Seymour along slabs and finally along a narrow, rocky trail.
- The peak is an obvious high point with a small cairn up top. Enjoy the stunning 360° views of Mt. Baker, downtown Vancouver, the Tantalus Range, Garibaldi Plateau, and peaks to the east.

The octopus tree on Mount Seymour.

Up the final slab on Seymour.

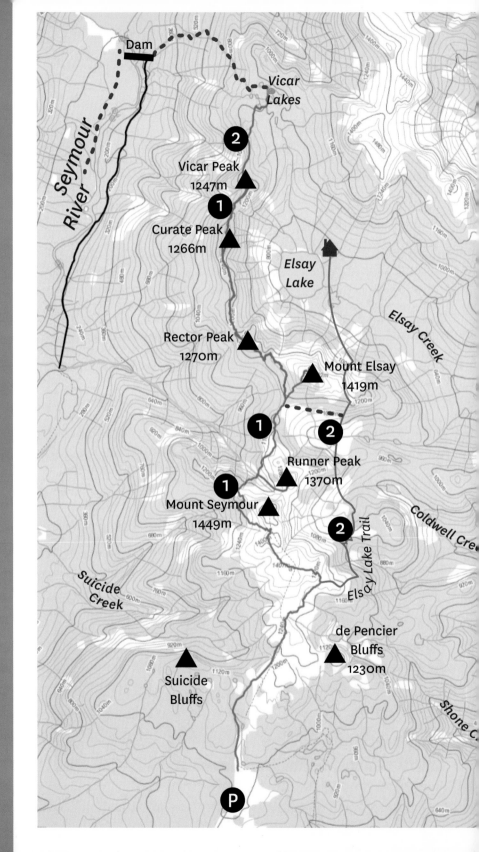

Dam

Vicar Lakes

Seymour River

2

Vicar Peak
1247m

1

Curate Peak
1266m

Elsay Lake

Rector Peak
1270m

Mount Elsay
1419m

Elsay Creek

1

2

Runner Peak
1370m

1

Mount Seymour
1449m

2

Coldwell Creek

Elsay Lake Trail

Suicide Creek

de Pencier Bluffs
1230m

Shone C.

Suicide Bluffs

P

CENTRAL FANNIN RANGE: ELSAY AREA ACCESS VIA MT. SEYMOUR PARKING LOT

(5 PEAKS)

ELSAY LAKE, VICAR LAKES

It is also possible to link Elsay Lake with Vicar Lakes, allowing for a lollipop route from the Seymour parking lot over the Episcopal Bumps to Vicar Lakes, down to Elsay Lake, and back to the parking lot: a tough but glorious adventure if the weather is good. It is easier to proceed down from Vicar Lakes to Elsay Lake. From the largest Vicar lake, follow occasional ribbons on a route heading west. Climb the minor divide. Then follow ribbons southward beside Elsay Creek. The trail passes the southernmost Vicar lake (which drains into Elsay Lake). Descend on the west side of Upper Elsay Creek, following occasional flagging. It is more of a route than a trail, and steep at times. There is some beautiful old growth and mushrooms. As you approach Elsay Lake the trail peters out and you will likely find yourself gently bushwhacking to the cabin.

ELSAY AREA BAGGER TIPS

The peaks of Runner, Elsay, Curate, Rector, and Vicar can be done as a long day trip from the Mt. Seymour parking lot. Take the Mt. Seymour trail to the low point between Tim Jones Peak and Mt. Seymour and pick up the trail that flanks the west side of Seymour to approach Runner Peak. This is a long out-and-back which crosses the bushy ridge of the Episcopal Bumps.

Round-trip distance:
24.9 km

Time:
10:50

Elevation gain:
1396 m

Runner Peak

RUNNER PEAK

(RUN) (1370 M)

A step beyond the comfort level for some sketchy boulder-field scrambling.

CAUTION:
Exposed slope with risk of death;
Class 3 scrambling.

PROMINENCE:
120 m.

LONGITUDE/LATITUDE:
N49.39611 W122.94111.

BANG FOR BUCK:
3/5

PEAK VIEW:
3/5. Interesting views of Indian Arm
and Mt. Seymour.

TRUE SUMMIT LOCATION:
Obvious.

HEADWATERS:
Elsay Creek (into Seymour River).

BEST VIEWS FROM:
Mt. Seymour, Mt. Elsay, LSCR
mid-valley viewpoint.

TRIP INFORMATION

Round-trip distance: 13 km.

Elevation gain: 696 m.

Time: 4–7 hours (4:42).

Difficulty: 3.5/5.

Snow free: Early July.

Must-sees: Meadow on Seymour back side; permanent snowfield.

Scenery: 4/5.

Kids: 1/5. Exposed.

Dogs: 3/5. Must be leashed.

Runnability: 2/5.

Terrain: Up wobbly boulder field to granite-slab scrambling.

Public transit: #228 Lynn Valley bus from Lonsdale Quay or #210 Upper Lynn Valley from Phibbs Exchange; #C12 to foot of Mt. Seymour Road, but a long climb.

Cell coverage: Sporadic.

Sun: Rock valley shaded; peak 100 per cent exposed.

Water: Some creeks in spring.

Route links: Sweep from Seymour to Vicar, or full Fannin Sweep, or Elsay Lake Loop.

HISTORY

Name origin: Referred to as "Runner Peak" in 1920 by Tom Fyles and in 1923 and 1926 editions of the BCMC newsletter. Name origin persistently unknown.

Name status: Official. Adopted January 2, 1987, on 92G/07, as submitted by Glenn Woodsworth.

First ascent: May 5–6, 1923, by a BCMC party led by Tom Fyles.

Runner Peak was a popular club climbing trip for members of the BCMC and ACC in the 1930s and '40s, but with the improvement of roads to other destinations it became less visited. From the main Mt. Seymour trail, Runner is visible as the lower bump to the right and east of the peak of Seymour. To reach Runner, follow Indian Arm Trail, which takes you to Mt. Elsay and beyond. Although the peak is low, the trail has several potential dangers. The first half of the ascent climbs up a rocky field that can be icy in early summer and wobbly in late summer. The second half climbs up a granite ramp with minimal hand- and footholds. Runner should only be climbed in perfect conditions, when it should not be terribly difficult or dangerous. In wet or icy weather, Runner Peak is very dangerous, with opportunities for death either on the cliffs to the east or the icefield to the west.

Runner's name remains a stubborn mystery. It certainly predates the rise of trail running or the use of that term for a type of footwear. Nothing about its appearance suggests speed or flight. Perhaps it comes from some long-forgotten tale of an early hiker fleeing a bear. Or perhaps a family surname: there were Runner families in Vancouver in the early 1900s, although they were not known to be mountaineers. Or perhaps its pointy shape, next to the long, narrow valley, resembled a foundry runner to an engineer climber? Or a plant shoot or runner (growing off larger Seymour), to a gardener climber?

The first part of the trail to Runner, at the gully just before the final ascent of Seymour, follows the traditional route up to Seymour from the old water-intake dam on the Seymour River.

ROUTE 1:

FROM SEYMOUR PARKING LOT TO BASE OF RUNNER VALLEY AND UP

Follow the route described (pp. 328–329) from the Seymour parking lot to Tim Jones Peak.
Base of Seymour to Runner Valley: The trail starts in the "octopus tree" gully (the northernmost of two gullies) just before the large slab at the base of Mt. Seymour proper.

- Look left down the gully to spot the faint but certain path, which at the time of writing was marked with a piece of flagging tape.
- This is where the Mt. Elsay–Indian Arm trail diverts from the main Mt. Seymour trail. Indian Arm Trail (stretching beyond Mt. Elsay to Mt. Bishop and around Indian Arm) is the creation of master trail builder Don McPherson in the 1990s.
- From there a thin but clear trail leads left (west) along the base of the rock, before descending sharply down a similarly thin but clear track, with occasional flagging, through the heather and bushes and grass at the base of Seymour proper.
- Sections of the trail follow a streambed that is slippery even in dry weather.
- After descending about 250 m the trail turns right and begins a still steep north traverse of the Seymour summit. The traverse takes you past and down some potentially dangerous steep bits, with the occasional rotten old rope attached to trees. Use with caution.
- The trail then climbs first a duffy and then a bouldery slope leading to the path between Seymour and Elsay. At the top of the slope, punch out into a pleasant heather meadow with Seymour towering to your right, Runner Peak to the north-east, and Mt. Elsay straight ahead.

- To the right you will see a large rock field with a permanent ice patch.
- The natural tendency is to head straight towards Runner. Do not do so, but go up and left over a bump and down the other side, following the occasional flagging tape. Enjoy the views west to Crown.
- At this point you can continue to follow the trail down and north (see the description below at *** for an alternative direct and rocky route).
- Descend a steep and in places mossy boulder field. Just before the boulder field gets impossibly steep, look to your right (directly at Runner Peak) to spot a trail usually marked by a cairn.
- Continue down the path through the heather and grass towards the clearly visible white boulder field below.
- If you take this trail in the autumn, you will start seeing many mushrooms growing on the north face. The first colony is purple russula lane.
- Be careful of the next stretch. It has loose dirt and loose stones which go careening down to the large rock field below.
- The trail opens out onto the Runner Peak boulder valley rising up to your right (east).

Snowfield up to Runner (on left).

Up Runner Valley to Runner Peak: Gingerly head up the boulder field. Boulder-hop up to the left (north) of the icefield.

- The boulder field narrows near the top, hemmed in by trees. Proceed to the top of the shoulder. Climb over a large fallen tree. (This is where the alternative route, described below, rejoins the main route: ###.)
- Turn left and go straight up towards Runner Peak. Veer to the left at the bluff, ducking under a krumholtz and climbing up some grass, dirt, duff, and rocks. There is some sparse flagging and some evidence of bootsteps.
- Reach a heathery balcony below the final ascent to Runner Peak. You face what seems to be a scary smooth rock face that ascends at a 55° angle. In fact, it is not a daunting climb. You will see a long diagonal gutter running up to the left. Follow this halfway up, to a cluster of berry bushes. At that point, a walkable dirt path leads up and north in the opposite direction, to a pair of trees and some flags. Then the peak is an easy climb up.

ROUTE 2:

DIRECT AND ROCKY ROUTE FROM ABOVE RUNNER VALLEY

The following is a route rather than a trail, with considerably greater risk of rockfall or person-fall. Do not take it if wobbly boulders or slippery grit make you nervous, or if conditions are less than perfect. We prefer the route above, as it is more stable and less stompy on plants.

- Follow the route above to the *** mark on p. 335.
- From the bump, head straight towards the head of the Runner Peak boulder valley (sharp right and east of the trail). You will see some faint bootmarks and cairns.
- Climb halfway down towards the boulder valley until you are roughly in line with two-thirds of the height of the valley. Cut east towards the head of the valley, traversing alternating lines of maidenhair ferns and foliage, and rocks and gravel. Take care on the rocks and steep portions: the ground is unsteady. If in doubt, go higher.
- Eventually your route will connect you with the boulder field valley, near the top.
- Resume the trip description at the ### mark in Route 1 above.

MT. ELSAY

(ELS) (1419 M)

Fun rocky slab for an adventure into the not-too-far backcountry

CAUTION:
Semi-remote.

PROMINENCE:
254 m.

LONGITUDE/LATITUDE:
N49.40964 W122.93723.

BANG FOR BUCK:
4/5

PEAK VIEW:
4/5. Superb views of Elsay Lake and Bishop and the Episcopal Bumps, as well as Indian Arm, Tantalus Range, and Garibaldi Plateau.

TRUE SUMMIT LOCATION:
Well-cairned knob to east of trail.

HEADWATERS:
Rolf Creek (into Seymour River), Elsay Creek East (into Indian Arm), Elsay Creek West (into Seymour River).

BEST VIEWS FROM:
Mt. Seymour, LSCR mid-valley viewpoint, Barnet Highway.

TRIP INFORMATION

Round-trip distance: 13.4 km.

Elevation gain: 726 m.

Time: 4–9 hours (5:02).

Difficulty: 3/5. Not steep, but remote and entails some bushwhacking.

Snow free: Early July.

Must-see: Spectacular view of Elsay Lake and back to Seymour.

Scenery: 4/5.

Kids: 3/5. Too remote.

Dogs: 5/5. Must be leashed.

Runnability: 3/5. Several good stretches.

Terrain: Decent trail across forest, rock fields, and heather meadows.

Public transit: #209 bus from Phibbs Exchange to Lynn Headwaters Park; #228 Lynn Valley from Lonsdale Quay or #210 Upper Lynn Valley from Phibbs Exchange for LSCR; #C12 to foot of Mt. Seymour Road, but a long climb.

Cell coverage: Occasional. Do not rely on it.

Sun: 80 per cent shaded; peak 100 per cent exposed.

Water: Some tarns on peak and approach.

Route links: Sweep from Seymour to Vicar, or full Fannin Sweep, or Elsay Lake Loop.

HISTORY

Name origin: Named after Elsay Lake below, which was apparently named by "a Scotch settler, probably after a place of same name in Scotland." (November 20, 1914, list of names submitted to William F. Robertson, BC's representative on the Geographic Board of Canada, by a joint committee of Vancouver's mountaineering clubs – copy in Chief Geographer's file). There is an Elsay Broch (Bronze Age hut circle) in Caithness, Scotland. "Elsay" may be a misspelling of Ailsa Craig, a volcanic island off Ayrshire, Scotland. Other versions have the namer or the namesake as a prospector. Name used on 1912 North Vancouver map.

Name status: Official. Adopted August 4, 1955, on C. 3435, as identified on 1926 topographic map by Alan John "A.J." Campbell (1882–1967), and on BC map 5C, Howe Sound, 1929 (file H.1.29). Don Munday scribbled "Mt. Elsay" in reference to the peak, in his notes on Mt. Seymour, likely around April 1914. Tom Fyles referred to Mt. Elsay in his 1920 album.

Other names: A repeated error is that Mt. Elsay was originally named Mt. Jarrett, after George Jarrett, a founding member of the BCMC. The authors have discovered that the mountain named Mt. Jarrett by the BCMC was what bivouac.com calls Deacon Peak, and not Elsay. See Mt. Jarrett.

First ascent: May 5–6, 1923, by a BCMC group of 29 hikers led by the legendary BCMC director Tom Fyles (England 1887–1979; Mount Fyles near Bella Coola is named in his honour), coming from Seymour and past Runner.

Other write-up: Hui.

Elsay is a good first excursion for hikers interested in exploring beyond the front range and expanding their routefinding skills. But it is not at all a hike to be underestimated. There is a clear and consistent trail, but there are also many opportunities to get lost on animal tracks and false starts. Hike with someone who has been there before, and pack your GPS. This trail should generally not be attempted except in perfect weather.

Mount Elsay summit.

The intermediate hiker will get the tingle of exploring new terrain that is slightly outside their comfort zone. The trail leads to a gully climb that is just challenging enough and to a domish peak of pleasingly bleached granite. There is a tall summit cairn and droolworthy views of Elsay Lake and, across the water, of Bishop. On the west side of the peak is a picturesque hanging tarn.

It is possible to do a loop of the Seymour peaks and Elsay with Elsay Lake Trail and Indian Arm Trail (the two routes described below). It is recommended that you go out via the more difficult Elsay Lake Trail, to tackle this portion while your legs are fresh; climbing Wes's Staircase is soul-destroying at the end of a long day. A mega-loop for an endurance athlete could take you to Elsay Lake, then up the rough route to Vicar Lakes, then back over the Episcopal Bumps to Elsay, then back to the parking lot (see Bagger Tips at p. 331. (II. Central Fannin Range). We did this on a bluebird day and it was a spectacular adventure.

On April 28, 1947, Trans-Canada flight 3, from Lethbridge to Vancouver, crashed on the mid-slopes of Mt. Elsay, killing 15. The site was not discovered until September 1994, when two hikers found it by chance and casually mentioned a plane crash to a Greater Vancouver Regional District employee who happened to be aware of the history of its disappearance. The crash site is near the north arm of Elsay Creek, at around 1020 m. It is far from the trail and should not be visited. There are memorials to the dead at the site and at Rice Lake.

The rocks of Elsay are a purer hornblende granite, closer in composition to Pump Peak than Seymour summit.

ROUTE 1:

FROM SOUTH – INDIAN ARM TRAIL FROM MT. SEYMOUR PARKING LOT
Follow the description from Seymour parking lot to Tim Jones Peak, pp. 328–329.
• Follow the description for the base of Seymour to Runner Valley, p. 334.
Runner Valley to Elsay Trail Junction: To proceed to Mt. Elsay, cross the rock field. You are aiming for a point almost exactly opposite the trail whence you came. Cairns on the rock will mark the route. On the other side, a well-defined and well-flagged path quickly ascends, passing a grove of mature hemlock. The climb takes you to the base of the shorter, unnamed peak north of Runner Peak (Jogger Peak?), and then descends slightly to traverse it.
• Soon after the ascent ends, there is a short descent into the much narrower and milder boulder field at the base of Runner Peak.
• The trail picks up to the north slightly downslope of the trail on the south side. At last visit, there were cairns and flags, at times difficult to see leading across the rock field.
• You will soon reach a very pleasant meadowed promontory with a fine view of Bishop, Coliseum, and Cathedral.
• The next stretch of trail is one of the most pleasing in the hike, with a narrow but well-defined path ambling at gentle angles through heather. Between here and the Elsay trail the occasional tree blowdown will from time to time hide and animal tracks will occasionally lure you away from the proper trail. Be patient and retrace if necessary: the proper trail should always be clear.

Mt. Elsay junction to Mt. Elsay: The pleasant, spongy trail continues down until a giant boulder field is seen to the right (east) descending towards Indian Arm. Here the trail meets the connector that links to Elsay Lake Trail (which starts from just below Pump Peak).

- Continue north. At approximately 1240 m a sign marks the junction between Vicar Lakes Trail (the Indian Arm Trail route) and the Mt. Elsay climb. Note that the junction is after (not below) the sign and not immediately visible: somewhat counter-intuitive.
- From here it is about 500 m to the peak. Go generally straight up along the pleasant but at times slippery and needley duff. About halfway up, zig left towards the rock face, then back rightward to the final approach to the summit.
- The route zags to the left through a narrow gap before reaching a 45° granite face with lots of little ledges and handholds. Proceed upward. The peak is on your right.
- When the slab gets a little steep, veer to your left and follow a narrow path through the heather to the fun, slabby peak complex. Exult as you hop from one white granite slab to the next to reach the summit.
- The peak is the bump with the prominent cairn on it. Another bump to the east is in fact about 30 cm lower.
- An impressive view of Bishop, with the Garibaldi Peaks as backdrop, is your reward. Most striking, however, is the fierce blue circle of Elsay Lake below you, bounded to the west by the Episcopal Bumps of Rector, Curate, and Vicar.

ROUTE 2:

FROM SOUTH – ELSAY LAKE TRAIL FROM MT. SEYMOUR PARKING

Follow the description for the Seymour parking lot to Brockton Point route, p. 328.

- Continue downwards on rocks. You will soon come to a rocky granite platform with the best viewpoint of de Pencier Bluffs.
- Continue down along the trail, coming to some small tarns. The trail heads right (east) to skirt the base of Pump Peak.
- The trail soon begins a steady rise again along rocks interspersed with large trees, snaking northeast to the Seymour plateau on a boulder field at the base of Pump Peak. You may get chattered at by pikas. Look up for birds catching the updrafts around the peak.
- You will see a signpost and a suspended warning sign marking the turnoff to Elsay Lake Trail to the east. Take it.
- The trail descends steadily, and at times steeply, through boulders and occasional trees, down "Wes's Staircase." Fear the return by this route; it is endless and exhausting.
- The trail flattens out and traverses the steep peaks to your left (west). You march along the accumulated rockfall of the ages, with boulders and scree all around and the occasional creek and fern. Cross Coldwell Creek.
- Continue northeast for about 1 km until you come to a wide, flat spot that is the low point of the hike (physical, not emotional). *If you hit a tarn and a creek, you've gone too far.*
- Look up and to your left to see a wide slope of boulders and scree. Runner is to the left (south), Elsay to the right (north). You will see lightened rocks, boot prints, cairns, and a rough trail. Head upward on this slope.

- After a long (more than a kilometre), rocky, and increasingly steep climb, you will pop onto a forested col and join Indian Arm Trail, described above. You will likely see flagging tape. Turn right.
- Follow the route from the Mt. Elsay junction to Mt. Elsay as described above.

Descent from Elsay.

RECTOR PEAK
(REC) (1270 M)

Southernmost of the three Episcopal Bumps, with a pleasant porch of a peak.

CAUTION:
Remote bushwhacking from
Mt. Elsay. Trail faint at times.

PROMINENCE:
60 m.

LATITUDE/LONGITUDE:
N49.40998 W122.94753.

BANG FOR BUCK:
2/5

PEAK VIEW:
3/5

TRUE SUMMIT LOCATION:
Large balcony overlooking
Elsay Lake.

HEADWATERS:
Elsay Lake (into Indian Arm),
Rolf Creek (into Seymour River).

Best views from:
Mt. Elsay.

TRIP INFORMATION

Round-trip distance: 17.6 km.
Elevation gain: 526 m.
Time: 5–9 hours (6:06).
Difficulty: 3.5/5. Not steep but remote bushwhacking.
Snow free: Early July.
Must-sees: Elsay Lake; twisted trees.
Scenery: 2/5.
Kids: 2/5. Too remote.
Dogs: 4/5. Must be leashed.
Runnability: 3/5.
Terrain: Bushwhacking through low forest cover.
Public transit: #209 bus from Phibbs Exchange to Lynn Headwaters Park; #228 Lynn Valley from Lonsdale Quay or #210 Upper Lynn Valley from Phibbs Exchange for LSCR; #C12 to foot of Mt. Seymour Road, but a long climb.
Cell coverage: Rare to non-existent.
Sun: 50 per cent shaded.
Water: Some murky tarns.
Route links: Sweep from Seymour to Vicar, or full Fannin Sweep, or Elsay Lake Loop.

HISTORY

Name origin: After Mt. Bishop was named after the president of the BCMC (not after a priestly office), these nearby mountains were named after other members of the clergy. A rector is one type of parish priest. Traditionally, a rector directly received both the greater and lesser tithes of his parish, while a vicar received only the lesser tithes. A rector as priest usually also had glebe lands attached to the parish.
Name status: Unofficial but popular.
First ascent: Unknown.

The western ridge separating Elsay Lake from the Seymour Valley has three (actually six) bumps endowed with non-official names riffing on the misassociation of nearby Mt. Bishop (a toponym based on a surname, not on an ecclesiastical title) with episcopal ranks in the Anglican Church. In contrast to the lofty peak of Bishop, the three peaks of this ridge are named after the three orders of parish priests: Rector, Curate, and Vicar (from south to north).

The route follows Indian Arm Trail, constructed in the late 1990s by renowned trail builder Don McPherson. The trail is faint at times, but you should not travel more than 10 m or so without the reassurance of a trail or flagging tape. Keep your eyes on the next bump on the ridge.

The peak of Rector is an open, flat slab that makes a good spot for a picnic or to put Band-Aids on your bleeding legs.

ROUTE

Follow the route description for Seymour parking lot to Tim Jones Peak, pp. 328–329.
- Follow the route described at pp. 334–335 for the base of Seymour to Runner Valley.
- Follow the route described at p. 341 for Runner Valley to the Mt. Elsay Trail junction.

Mt. Elsay Trail junction to Rector: At last visit, the path up Mt. Elsay was marked with a series of handsome orange flags. The turnoff to Vicar Lakes and Mt. Bishop was marked with a series of handsome blue flags.
- Heading northwest, the trail quality immediately becomes more tenuous; the Episcopal Bumps receive far less traffic than Elsay does.
- Do not panic if you lose the trail. Keep traversing northward below the west side of Elsay. Soon you will hit a rock field that covers the entire west side. Head towards a pair of large hemlocks, each with marks on their bark and one with a faded orange marker. The trail passes between these trees and a rocky bluff.
- This is the most discouraging part of the entire trail: overgrown and difficult to follow. If you persevere, you will see occasional blazes and flags.
- Past a weathered old rope, veer left (west) over a pleasantly gradual shoulder of Elsay, leading to another pleasing rocky promontory, your gateway to the Episcopal Bumps.
- Keep heading northwest, directly towards Rector. You will feel as if you are running out of land, but peer over the west edge to see the route to Rector quite clearly.
- Descend a cliffy bit to a bench above the Rector col. Using hands and legs, you will always find a safe route down here.
- The descent into the Rector col is not pleasant or well marked. Generally stick to the centre-right.
- The path is heavily overgrown and requires routefinding and bushwhacking. Happily, there are the occasional pieces of flagging tape and orange blazes, and the undergrowth is not thick. The trail at Rector proceeds generally along the middle of the ridge. Persevere and you will find a well-trodden route through the heather, with occasional flagging.
- The peak at Rector has a pleasant flat balcony with views of Bishop and Elsay Lake.

CURATE PEAK

(CUR) (1266 M)

The middle, and tallest, of the three Episcopal Bumps.

CAUTION:
Trail thin in places; narrow, exposed col between Curate and Vicar.

PROMINENCE:
76 m.

LATITUDE/LONGITUDE:
N49.41986 W122.95084.

BANG FOR BUCK:
2/5

PEAK VIEW:
3/5

TRUE SUMMIT LOCATION:
Second-to-northernmost of four peaks.

HEADWATERS:
Elsay Lake
(into Indian Arm),
Squamish Creek
(into Seymour River).

BEST VIEWS FROM:
Mt. Elsay.

TRIP INFORMATION

Round-trip distance: 20.4 km.

Elevation gain: 646 m.

Time: 6–10 hours (7:42).

Difficulty: 3.5/5. Not steep, but remote and with bushwhacking.

Snow free: Early July.

Must-sees: Elsay Lake; twisted trees.

Scenery: 2/5.

Kids: 2/5. Too remote.

Dogs: 4/5. Must be leashed.

Runnability: 3/5.

Terrain: Bushwhacking through low forest cover.

Public transit: #209 bus from Phibbs Exchange to Lynn Headwaters Park; #228 Lynn Valley from Lonsdale Quay or #210 Upper Lynn Valley from Phibbs Exchange for LSCR; #C12 to foot of Mt. Seymour Road, but a long climb.

Cell coverage: Rare to non-existent.

Sun: 50 per cent shaded.

Water: Some murky tarns.

Route links: Sweep from Seymour to Vicar, or full Fannin Sweep, or Elsay Lake Loop.

Name origin: After Mt. Bishop was named after the president of the BCMC (not after a churchly office), these nearby mountains were named after other members of the clergy. A curate is a parish priest, but the word is colloquially used to refer to assistant clergy to the parish priest. He or she is trusted with the care or "cure" (from the Latin *cura*) of souls of a parish.

Name status: Unofficial but popular.

First ascent: Unknown.

Curate is the central and tallest peak on the ridge above and to the west of Elsay Lake. Like the other Episcopal Bumps, it is on Indian Arm Trail, created in the 1990s by master trail designer Don McPherson. Like Rector, its peak provides a flat spot suitable for a nap or a picnic. The true summit is marked by a tight tangle of scrubby trees. In July there are ample blueberries; in the autumn these turn a pleasing red.

ROUTE

Follow the description of the route from the Seymour parking lot to Tim Jones Peak, pp. 328–329.

- Follow the description of the route from the base of Seymour to Runner Valley, p. 334.
- Follow the description of the route from Runner Valley to the Mt. Elsay Trail junction, p. 339.
- Follow the description of the route from the Mt. Elsay Trail junction to Rector, p. 343.

Rector Peak to Curate Peak: The descent from Rector Peak to the Curate col is to the west of the peak. From a shallow tarn a faint but persistent trail can be followed, generally veering left and down towards the col. If you do not see a path through the heather, retrace your steps. You will glimpse the occasional scrap of tape. If in doubt, veer left (west).

- A final stretch into the col is dicey. You will find a few ropes and plenty of small trees to provide some reassurance as you make the steep descent.
- The col between Rector and Curate is quite narrow, crowned by a beautiful old Douglas fir.
- The trail becomes inconsistent, but just before the summit, veer right past a tarn and around a rocky bulb to ascend through heather and berry bushes to the summit.
- There are several bumps on Curate. The first false summit is marked by a set of gnarled Douglas firs.
- A brief down and then up to a second false summit in the middle of the ridge. Keep going.
- It is the third and tallest peak that is the true summit of Curate. Happily, the trail between the second and third bumps is the easiest to follow.
- Curate Peak is an inauspicious bump covered in blueberry bushes that turn a striking red in autumn.

Vicar Lake and Mount Bishop.

VICAR PEAK

(VIC) (1247 M)

Northernmost of the three Episcopal Bumps, with the best views.

CAUTION:
Steep cliffs on col between
Curate and Vicar; very faint trail,
especially north of Vicar Peak to
Vicar Lakes; remote bushwhacking.

PROMINENCE:
57 m.

LATITUDE/LONGITUDE:
N49.42611 W122.94808.

BANG FOR BUCK:
2/5

PEAK VIEW:
3/5

TRUE SUMMIT LOCATION:
West knob on ridge.

HEADWATERS:
Elsay Lake
(into Indian Arm),
Squamish Creek (into
Seymour River).

BEST VIEWS FROM:
Elsay, Bishop.

TRIP INFORMATION

Round-trip distance: 22.2 km.

Elevation gain: 766 m.

Time: 5–9 hours from Seymour (8:50); 3–6 hours from Vicar Lakes trailhead off Spur 4 Road.

Difficulty: 3.5/5. Not steep, but remote and with bushwhacking.

Snow free: Early July.

Must-sees: Vicar Lakes; blueberries.

Scenery: 2/5.

Kids: 2/5. Too remote.

Dogs: 4/5. Must be leashed.

Runnability: 3/5.

Terrain: Bushwhacking through low forest cover.

Public transit: #209 bus from Phibbs Exchange to Lynn Headwaters Park; #228 Lynn Valley from Lonsdale Quay or #210 Upper Lynn Valley from Phibbs Exchange for LSCR; #C12 to foot of Mt. Seymour Road, but a long climb.

Cell coverage: Rare to non-existent.

Sun: 40 per cent shaded.

Water: Some murky tarns.

Route links: Sweep from Seymour to Vicar, or full Fannin Sweep, or Elsay Lake Loop.

HISTORY

Name origin: As with other peaks in the area, the use of clerical ranks for toponyms became a false theme after Mt. Bishop was named after the president of the BCMC. GeoBC notes that "presumably the name resulted from misinterpretation of the significance of nearby Mount Bishop, or else a play on that name." A vicar is a parish priest. In modern-day Anglicanism, the roles of rector and vicar are essentially the same, and which of those titles a given parish priest may hold is a matter of local tradition. Some parishes have a rector, others a vicar.

Name status: Unofficial but popular. Vicar Lakes is an official name, adopted August 4, 1955, on C.3435, as identified in the 1953 *BC Gazetteer* (the 1929 Water Map gives "Bishop Lakes" as an alternative name). "Vicar Lakes" also appears on the 1940 BC Forest Service Map.

First ascent: Unknown.

Vicar Peak, like Rector and Curate, is an unremarkable bump on the ridge surrounding Elsay Lake. The most striking things about Vicar Peak are its brilliant red blueberry foliage in the autumn and the poor condition of the trail down to Vicar Lakes. The latter is a shame: whether linked with the Vicar Lakes trail down to the LSCR or with the Vicar–Elsay ramp down to Elsay Lake, these are strenuous but glorious loops.

Route 1:

FROM SOUTH – FROM MT. SEYMOUR PARKING LOT AND RECTOR PEAK

- Follow the description of the route from the Seymour parking lot to Tim Jones Peak, pp. 328–329.
- Follow the description of the route from base of Seymour to Runner Valley, p. 336.
- Follow the description of the route from Runner Valley to the Mt. Elsay Trail junction, p. 339.
- Follow the description of the route from the Mt. Elsay Trail junction to Rector, p. 343.
- Follow the description of the route from Rector Peak to Curate Peak, p. 345.

Curate Peak to Vicar Peak: Continue along the ridge towards the final Episcopal Bump, Vicar Peak. The trail cuts through a tarn and up the centre of the ridge to a fourth false summit. The trail is faint but generally easy to follow. There is one dangerous patch that is steep and concealed in branches, but you can use the branches for reassuring handholds.

- The col between Curate and Vicar is a somewhat dangerous knife edge. The good news is that there is clearly only one way to go: down a steep, narrow slope towards a large tree. Berry bushes offer some comforting handholds. Take it very steady at this point, because a slip here would only give you a choice between two different plummeting deaths.
- Melodrama aside, in good weather this section poses little danger for the cautious.
- From the col the path is narrow but well flagged. Traverse one false summit by proceeding to the left. Then the route makes a final dip down before rising up again for the true summit, to the northeast.
- Attain the peak from the east past two small tarns. Vicar Peak is a side-hook to the west, off the main trail. The peak is generally bald with a gnarled old tree.

TRAIL NORTH, DOWN TO VICAR LAKES
(if you wish to continue)

- The trail connecting Vicar Peak with Vicar Lakes is very difficult to discern. In general, veer left (west) off the peak. Do *not* go right (east). Although that way looks promising at first, it soon turns into a harrowing vertical bushwhack as you descend. Be sure to orient yourself with the trail before descending, as it is narrow and difficult to follow at the best of times.

- You will pass by a large Douglas fir that appears ready to topple.
- Continue down along the ridge. The trail is at times overgrown by blueberry bushes and other brush. If you lose your bearings, be sure not to veer off the ridgeline. The bushwhacking should never get too unbearable.
- Eventually you will see through the trees the welcome blue jewels of the Vicar Lakes, a collection of some 20 ponds suspended in spongy sphagnum moss and ranging in size from a pothole to a small playing field.
- In order to link to the trail descending to Seymour Valley Trailway, bushwhack through the low berry bushes towards the westernmost set of ponds (you will occasionally see flagging among these thick bushes, but the trail is far from consistent). The final two ponds are bisected by a narrow bridge of sphagnum over which the trail passes. Look up to see a sign on a tree indicating the descending trail.

Vicar Lakes Trail to Seymour Valley Trailway: Vicar Lakes Trail down to Seymour Valley Trailway is long, technical, and steep, but well marked. There are about 10 sets of ropes along it for ease of access, but none are utterly necessary to use except when the trail is wet.

- Vicar Lakes Trail emerges on the Spur 4 gravel road that runs along the east side of the Seymour River. About 250 m to the north is the well-marked connector trail leading down to the new Bear Island bridge, eventually reaching Seymour Dam, Seymour Fish Hatchery, and, to the west, Seymour Valley Trailway.
- If the Bear Island bridge is locked (which it is at times), you can gain access to Seymour Valley Trailway over the Spur 4 bridge, about 7 km south.

Vicar Lake and Mount Bishop.

Route 2:

FROM NORTH, FROM LSCR AND SEYMOUR VALLEY TRAILWAY

- Follow the route from the LSCR parking lot to the end of Seymour Valley Trailway, as described at p. 358 under Bishop.
- Follow the route from Vicar Lakes Trail to Vicar Lakes, as described at p. 358 under Bishop.
- Eventually you will see through the trees the welcome blue jewels of Vicar Lakes, a collection of some 20 ponds suspended in spongy sphagnum moss, and ranging in size from a double tennis court to a pothole.
- At the largest Vicar Lake head due south over a faint trail, toward Episcopal Ridge.
- Climb up the ridge and try to find the trail, which is in poor shape through this stretch. The way is at times overgrown with blueberry bushes and other brush. If you lose your bearings, be sure not to veer off the ridgeline. The bushwhacking should never get too unbearable.
- You will pass by a large Douglas fir that appears ready to topple.
- Pop out to the heath-covered peak of Vicar.

Vicar in a tutu

NORTH FANNIN RANGE: BISHOP AREA ACCESS VIA VICAR LAKES TRAIL

(3 PEAKS)

BISHOP AREA BAGGER TIPS

The peaks of Bishop, Jarrett, Clementine, and Dickens can all be done as a day trip from Vicar Lakes Trail. In fact, if Dickens is your objective, the other three peaks only add an hour of moving time to your day. If you skip Dickens, the round-trip time is reduced by half to under six hours, though you'll also be missing Fannin Lake, which is one of the more spectacular remote lakes in this book. Do not leave your car at the LSCR parking lot if attempting Dickens or it will be locked in. Park just outside the gate a couple of kilometres down the road. Also make sure you are prepared to travel in the dark, with a headlamp and spare batteries. This is the most remote area covered by this book, so you need to be self-sufficient and well prepared with the Ten Essentials if attempting Dickens.

Round-trip hiking distance:
23.6 km

Time:
12:48

Elevation gain:
2494 m

Cycle approach from LSCR gate:
31.8 km 1:52 (round trip)

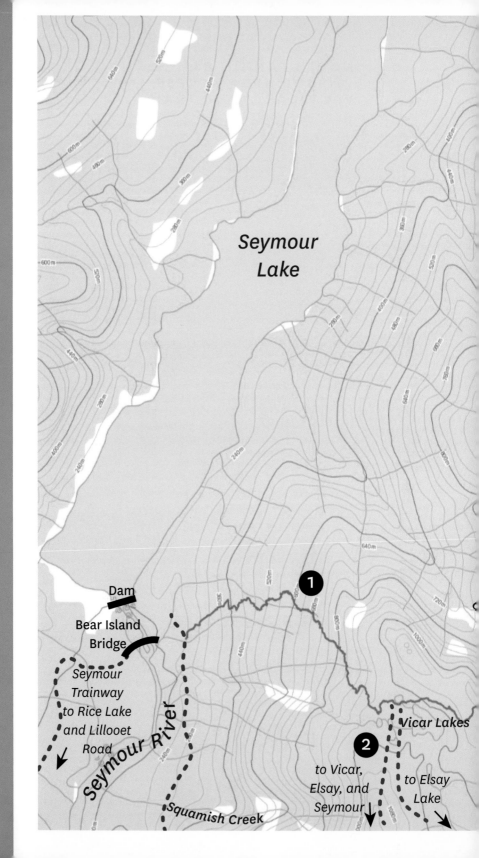

Seymour Lake

Dam

Bear Island Bridge

Seymour Trainway to Rice Lake and Lillooet Road

Seymour River

Squamish Creek

Vicar Lakes

to Vicar, Elsay, and Seymour

to Elsay Lake

1

2

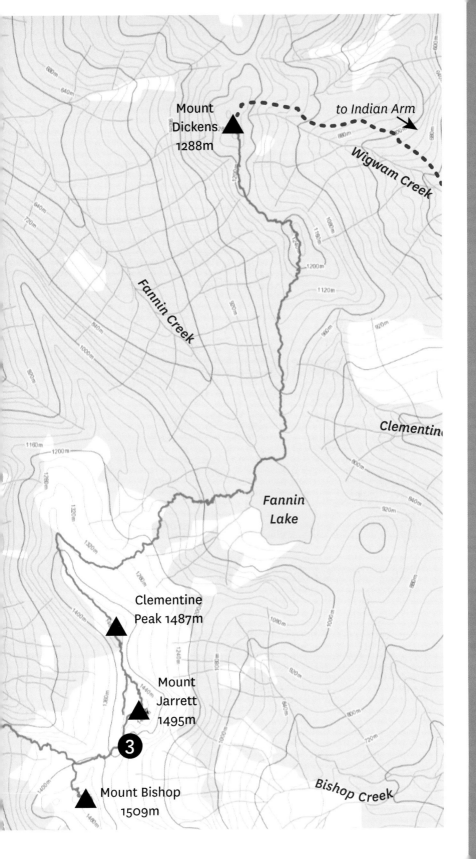

Mount
Dickens
1288m

to Indian Arm

Wigwam Creek

Fannin Creek

Clementine

Fannin
Lake

Clementine
Peak 1487m

Mount
Jarrett
1495m

3

Mount Bishop
1509m

Bishop Creek

Heading up Mount Bishop.

MT. BISHOP
(BIS) (1509 M)

A worthy adventure to a seldom visited peak, with stunning views and a swim at the end.

CAUTION:
Vicar Lakes Trail up from LSCR
is steep, rooty, and remote.

PROMINENCE:
613 m.

LATITUDE/LONGITUDE:
N49.43028 W122.92722.

BANG FOR BUCK:
3/5

PEAK VIEW:
4/5

TRUE SUMMIT LOCATION:
North summit slightly taller
than other bump 20 m away.

HEADWATERS:
Gibbens Creek
(into Seymour River),
Bishop Creek, tributaries
of Elsay Creek
(into Indian Arm).

BEST VIEWS FROM:
Elsay, Seymour.

TRIP INFORMATION

Round-trip distance: 9.8 km from bottom of Vicar Lake Trail.

Elevation gain: 1285 m.

Time: 4–8 hours from base of Vicar Lake trailhead (5:04).

Difficulty: 4/5. Remote; routefinding required.

Snow free: Late July.

Must-sees: Vicar Lakes fairyland; giant trees.

Scenery: 5/5.

Kids: 2/5. Probably too remote and steep.

Dogs: 3/5. Steep. Must be leashed.

Runnability: 3/5. First half very steep.

Terrain: Low forest cover.

Public transit: #209 bus from Phibbs Exchange to Lynn Headwaters Park; #228 Lynn Valley from Lonsdale Quay or #210 Upper Lynn Valley from Phibbs Exchange for LSCR; #C12 to foot of Mt. Seymour Road, but a long climb.

Cell coverage: Good on peak and halfway up Vicar Lake Trail; rare elsewhere; none at lakes.

Sun: 80 per cent shaded.

Water: Vicar Lake. Past that, some tarns and creeks usually until midsummer.

Route links: Sweep from Seymour to Vicar, or full Fannin Sweep, or Elsay Lake Loop.

HISTORY

Name origin: After Joseph Charles Bishop (1851–1913), of Bishop and Christie, Vancouver photographers. A leading mountaineer and a founder and the first president of the BC Mountaineering Club (1907–1910), Bishop was killed in a fall into a crevasse on Mt. Baker on July 21, 1913. He is buried in Mountain View Cemetery, Vancouver.

Name status: "Bishop Mountain" was adopted in the 1930 *BC Gazetteer*, as labelled on BC map 5B, 1929; changed to "Mt. Bishop" May 3, 1951, on 92G, as had been labelled on BC map 2B, 1914. Name used on 1912 North Vancouver and BCMC maps.

Other names: Labelled "Godfrey Mtn." on 1915 and 1929 watershed maps and a 1946 municipal map (long after Bishop was officially named), but never submitted or considered for adoption, and the identity of Godfrey is unknown. Apparently also called "Goat Mountain" by early Vancouverites, after the mountain goats on the peak, and possibly a translation of its Downriver Halkomelem name used by the Musqueam and other Indigenous peoples.

First ascent: August 9, 1908, BCMC party of 19, led by Fred Mills, from Indian Arm. Participants were George Jarrett, Fred Mills, Charles Chapman, George Harrower, J.C. MacKenzie, H.B. Rowe, Bert Armistead, Robert J. Cromie, William J. Gray, Ernest Burns, Luke Edmond Seney, Fred Perry, F.J. Stevens, Basil Stewart Darling, E.B. Batstone, H.A. Peters, Charles Dickens, Roy Willoughby Trythall, and George McQueen.

While remote and arduous, Mt. Bishop is closer than you think and well worth the trip for its stunning and unimpeded 360° views. On descent you can enjoy a refreshing swim in the relatively warm waters of Vicar Lake, which is a beautiful destination in itself. The air hums with bluebottles, dragonflies, bees, and hummingbirds.

It is a grand, multi-stage adventure. Start with a 10-km bike ride along and to the end of Seymour Valley Trailway. Cross the Bear Island bridge and bike up to Spur 4 Road. Scamper up the steep adventure playground that is Vicar Lake Trail, often gripping ropes and roots. It feels like an extended ropes adventure course, or perhaps a 1980s video game: you are never in grave peril, but negotiating the various granite and root walls with your hands and feet is a fun and continuous contest.

Pop out at the fairyland Vicar Lake landscape of myriad ponds and lakes of various sizes suspended in sphagnum moss. Ascend through another band of forest to emerge into a granitic alpine bowl headed by the peaks of Bishop, Jarrett/Deacon, and Clementine/Presbyter, the trio of which makes a worthy destination for a long day or overnight adventure.

Bishop was first climbed on August 9, 1908, by a BCMC party embarking from Berg's Landing beach, near Croker Island on Indian Arm (then called "North Arm," its name until 1921, when it was changed to avoid confusion with the North Arm of the Fraser River). They bushwhacked up beside Bishop Creek, viewing blueberries and old-growth cedars. They explored the peaks of Bishop, which they then named for their president, Joseph Charles Bishop. Nine of the hikers then proceeded to the peak north of Bishop (which bivouac.com today calls "Deacon") following the crest of a long, snow-covered ridge, a trip they reported to have taken half an hour. The peak was named Mt. Jarrett, after the BCMC secretary. The two parties shouted greetings to each other before returning to the main group. On the descent, five mountain goats were spotted on the cliffs. Fifty years later, one of the climbers, Charles Dickens, recounted: "That was the first time I saw mountain goats in their native habitat. They were going up an appalling cliff face, leaping and balancing from narrow ledges." In his newspaper report of the climb in 1908 (see "New Peaks Named by Mountaineering Club" in **Appendix 19**), Dickens remarked that Mt. Bishop "will probably be referred to very often as 'Papa's Mountain,' as Mr. Bishop is affectionately known among his fellow climbers as 'papa.'"

Despite its remoteness, Bishop became a favourite destination of early BCMC climbers. They would boat up Indian Arm to Bishop's Beach (now generally referred to as Berg's Landing, where Bishop Creek flows into Indian Arm opposite Croker Island). They would then follow a log chute (1923), and later a logging road (1945), along Bishop Creek, either ascending to the col between Jarrett and Clementine (the usual route), or to the south up a gully from the large glacial amphitheatre to the east of the Bishop peak. They would then descend in an exhilarating 750-m glissade back down into the snowy amphitheatre facing Indian Arm. This eastern approach was still being used in 1949 and 1953.

The construction of the Vicar Lake–Mt. Bishop trail and Indian Arm Trail in the 1990s changed the usual approach from the east to the west and increased visits to Bishop. Vicar Lake Trail was blazed primarily by Denis Blair, Jim Sedor, and Moe Lamothe in 2000. It was improved by Don McPherson and currently is maintained by North Shore Rescue as an evacuation route. The trail is sometimes nicknamed "Gerry's Escape" after Gerry Chicalo, who used it to exit Indian Arm Trail after an injury. The steepness of the trail is impressive: 1268 m over 3.25 km, in contrast to the Grouse Grind, which covers a piddly 890 m over 2.9 km. The distance from the bottom of Vicar Lake Trail to Vicar Lake is roughly the same as the distance from Vicar Lakes to the summit of Mt. Bishop.

Tsleil-Waututh legends describe mountain-goat hunting around Mt. Bishop, and as the first BCMC climbers noted, goats abounded there in 1908. There are still rumoured sightings.

Mt. Bishop illustrates the naming convention of placing a "Mount" in front of a peak named after a person. The peak is not named after the religious office (in which case it would be called "Bishop Mountain"), but rather honours a person. Nonetheless, the name prompted both unofficial and official naming of the neighbouring peaks after episcopal and other clerical offices. (For more on place naming, see **Appendix 15**.)

As for Vicar Lakes, which is also an official toponym, it is unclear whether it was a play on the already named Mt. Bishop, or a mistaken reference in its own right to "bishop" as a religious office, or after an actual person, whether spelled Vicar or Vicker.

GETTING THERE

From Ironworkers Memorial (Second Narrows) Bridge, take Highway 1 to Exit 22B. Turn right onto Mt. Seymour Parkway and continue straight, onto Lillooet Road.

- Continue up Lillooet Road. You will pass a horse stable, Capilano University, the North Vancouver Cemetery, a prominent gate, and then (after several kilometres' drive) the Seymour–Capilano water treatment plant. The road ends at a large gravel parking lot.
- The path starts next to the outhouses and the map kiosk. Follow the path leading to the west. This brings you to a gazebo and a paved road, where your journey begins.

Note that the gate (near the cemetery) gets locked at sundown, which would trap your car and possibly trigger NSR if you have not left a message.

ROUTE 1:

FROM LSCR AND VICAR LAKES TRAIL

LSCR parking lot and Seymour Valley Trailway: From the LSCR parking lot, run or bike along the trailway.

- After about 11 km, you will see Seymour Dam.
- The road changes from pavement to gravel. The dominant path slopes and curves down to the right. You will see the fish hatchery. Before the hatchery, veer left, towards the Bear Island bridge, a repurposed structure built in 1912 that formerly spanned the Coquitlam Dam spillway and was moved here in 1999.
- After crossing the two parts of the bridge, the trail ascends a couple of steep switchbacks before ending at another gravel road. This is the route marked "Spur 4" on LSCR maps. Go down to the right for about 100 m (if you go the wrong way – left, north – you'll soon hit the end of the road, blocked by a chain-link fence).
- Vicar Lakes Trail is on the left (east) side of this road, between the first and second culvert (the culverts are marked with orange tape). The trail is opposite the SLOW sign. It can be hard to spot due to foliage but careful eyes will note a few ribbons and blazes on the trees.
- If you cycled here, stash your bike in a secluded spot in the forest to your right before embarking on Vicar Lakes Trail.

Vicar Lakes Trail to Vicar Lakes: Follow Vicar Lakes Trail up, up, up for 3 km. The route starts out as a gentle slope but soon becomes steep. It is generally well trodden and well marked with flagging and orange and silver blazes. If you ever feel like you are off-trail for more than 20 seconds, you probably are. There are ropes in the steepest areas, and you will be using your hands for about 10 per cent of the climb. The trail will take between 1 and 3 hours to ascend. Given its steepness, and your likely fatigue, the descent is not markedly quicker: probably about 75 per cent of your ascent time. The track is much better and safer when dry than wet. Avoid the latter at all costs, as the trail becomes a rooty, slippery nightmare, an ersatz streambed.

- About 5 minutes in you will reach a group of giant trees. The main one, a cedar, is nicknamed "The General." Nearby giants are the "General's Wife" and "The Twins."
- Soon thereafter you'll hit your first of many ropes. Remember not to rely on the ropes too much, and never put your full weight on them. You never know how old they are or whether sunlight or goat nibbles have attacked their integrity.
- After 20 minutes or so, glimpse Coliseum and then Cathedral through the trees across the valley.
- After a half-hour there is a short descent into a mini-pocket of blowdown. The trail is obvious as it continues under fallen trees.
- After a rope-assisted climb up a granite face, you will come across another giant tree, at a precarious angle. See it while you still can!
- Next you encounter a steep dirt-and-root wall. Climb the roots and ropes, then do a rope climb and traverse combo up a short granite face. As with other granite slabs on this hike, the ropes are largely superfluous in dry weather and utterly indispensable in wet weather.
- About 45 minutes up, you come to a green bench and maybe a sudden burst of sunlight. Then another bench as you hop over the granite remnants of a rockfall. Continue under a series of large fallen logs and over a creekbed that is dry in summer.

Taking a break en route to Bishop, with Seymour Lake below.

- Looking up, you will see tantalizing glimpses of sky, but the open area of Vicar Lakes is still a ways up and off.
- Turn left and up to cross another dry creek.
- Now up again, into a band of berry bushes humming with bees. You're almost there!

Vicar Lakes: The trail ends at these beautiful lakes. Punch out of the bushes to encounter the first small Vicar Lake ponds. The trail continues between them. You will feel a spring in your step as you hike along the bouncy sphagnum.

- A larger lake is on the next rise. Take a series of logs along the right (south) side to a short wall of blueberry bushes. The main Vicar Lake is on the final rise. Lily pads and flowers coat the surface, where bees, bluebottles, and dragonflies buzz. On the right (south) side are several inviting swimming spots off granite patios. The water is shallow and thus of a generally perfect temperature for a post-hike dip. Above preside Bishop (right, south) and Jarrett (left, north).
- Vicar Lake is likely the only water (besides a few nasty, murky puddles) on the trail. Load up or regret it, particularly in the heat of summer.

Vicar Lakes to Mt. Bishop: Head to the north shoreline of Vicar Lake. A trail, likely bushy and uncertain, leads between the lake and a small tarn, through the berry bushes and into the woods. Once you hit the forest, however, the trail is obvious, with a decent tread and regular flagging and blazes. Again, if you feel like you are off trail for more than 20 seconds, you probably are, so retrace your steps.

- The trail starts as a gentle slope heading east. Blowdown and the occasional false trail heading steeply northward may fool you. Look for blazes and continue along the same contour band for about 1 km.
- You will see several giant yellow cedars. One, the Bishop Giant, is more than 2 m in diameter and over 800 years old.
- The trail will then twist north and more sharply up at the site of a trio of a large cedar, Douglas fir, and hemlock. Underfoot the trail is duffy and needley, and can be slippery in dry weather. Although it gets steeper, it remains clear in both trail markers and boot tracks.
- Soon you will get a view of the steep, open gully to the north leading down from

Clementine/Presbyter and Jarrett/Deacon.

- The trail will then snake to face south, and you will see Vicar Peak through the trees. The way then twists again for a pleasing view of Coliseum and Cathedral and increasingly fine views of the peaks toward Garibaldi.
- After a rope, and increasingly visible skies through the trees, pop out from the forest into a heather meadow and more magnificent views. A granite slab offers a pleasant patio to enjoy the views to the peaks west and north. Clementine/Presbyter (left) (with an odd white spot below its peak) and Jarrett/Deacon (centre) are fully visible, with the peak of Bishop still hiding to the south (right).
- The trail is increasingly marked by boot tracks through dead heather.
- You will come to a small tarn about 5 m in circumference that usually remains wet until late summer. For emergency (and filtered) drinking only.
- Soon you will pop out of the trail into the amphitheatre of crumbly granite at the base of Bishop.

Bishop amphitheatre to Mt. Bishop summit: There are many ways to ascend, none of them terribly steep. The wetness of the rock may affect your choices. Avoid walking on the semi-arctic undergrowth.

- At a position approximately 2 o'clock on the cirque (with the peak at noon) there is a long cleft running towards the peak. This is a useful route, taking you to a bench at the base of the final granite slabs below Bishop. Take care, as it is slippery when wet.
- From this bench be sure to look southwest for a splendid view of the Vicar Lakes and ponds shimmering below.
- Again there is no single route. We found it useful to go a few steps south of the centre of the ridge and granite-hop up through a few tree clusters. You will see some footprints where people have come before.
- The summit is obvious and marked by a cairn. The sharpish, rampy peak some 20 m south is about 2 m lower.
- Bishop's summit gives spectacular 360° views of Indian Arm and all of the North Shore and Fraser Valley peaks, as well as Mt. Baker, the Garibaldi massif, and Sky Pilot. Be sure to stroll over to the south side of the summit platform, past the short trees, for a splendid view of Elsay Lake and Mt. Elsay.
- Return the way you came (take care not to slip on the needles and duff, especially in dry weather), or take a short side trip to summit Jarrett/Deacon and Clementine/Presbyter to the north.

ROUTE 2:

FROM SOUTH – SEYMOUR ALONG INDIAN ARM TRAIL

An ambitious hiker could come down from Vicar Peak to Vicar Lakes and back up to Bishop: see the Vicar Peak description above. This follows the route of the largely overgrown Indian Arm Trail, built by the legendary Don McPherson (who also created the Grouse Grind) in the 1990s. It will be a very tiring day or days.

ROUTE 3:

FROM NORTH – MT. DICKENS ALONG INDIAN ARM TRAIL

One could also approach from Dickens in the north, down to Fannin Lake, and up to Clementine/Presbyter. See the description of Dickens below and do the route in reverse.

MT. JARRETT (DEACON PEAK)

(JAR) (1495 M)

A shoulder of Bishop, with similar views; a worthwhile side trip.

CAUTION:
Steep route up from LSCR;
trail at times faint; remote.

PROMINENCE:
105 m.

LATITUDE/LONGITUDE:
N49.43472 W122.92278.

BANG FOR BUCK:
3/5

PEAK VIEW:
4/5

TRUE SUMMIT LOCATION:
Obvious.

HEADWATERS:
Gibbens Creek
(into Seymour River).

BEST VIEWS FROM:
Elsay, Seymour.

TRIP INFORMATION

Round-trip distance: 10.2 km.

Elevation gain: 1296 m.

Time: 4.5–8.5 hours from Vicar Lake trailhead on Spur 4 Road (5:00).

Difficulty: 4/5. Remote; routefinding required.

Snow free: Late July.

Must-sees: Vicar Lakes fairyland; gleaming rock field; ferns.

Scenery: 3/5.

Kids: 2/5. Too remote.

Dogs: 4/5. Must be on leash.

Runnability: 3/5.

Terrain: Rock field, low forest cover.

Public transit: #209 bus from Phibbs Exchange to Lynn Headwaters Park; #228 Lynn Valley from Lonsdale Quay or #210 Upper Lynn Valley from Phibbs Exchange for LSCR; #C12 to foot of Mt. Seymour Road, but a long climb.

Cell coverage: Rare to non-existent.

Sun: Mostly exposed. 20 per cent shaded.

Water: A usually nasty and muddy tarn just to the north of and below the peak.

Route links: Sweep from Seymour to Vicar, or full Fannin Sweep, or Elsay Lake Loop.

HISTORY

Name origin: Named "Mount Jarrett" after the first secretary of the BCMC, George Jarrett (January 9, 1878, Penshurst, Kent, England – November 14, 1952, Vancouver). Jarrett was a veteran of the second Boer War who came to Vancouver with fellow veteran H.B. Rowe. Jarrett convened the founding meeting of the BCMC (initially named the Vancouver Mountaineering Club) in October 1907. His wife, Mary May Creech, was also a founding BCMC member and was on the first ascent of Bishop.

Jarrett worked at the Hastings sawmill before moving to Santa Ana, California, in the 1920s. He is buried in Mountain View Cemetery, Vancouver.

Name status: Both unofficial.

First ascent: August 9, 1908, by a BCMC party led by Fred Mills.

Other names: Deacon Peak. After Mt. Bishop, bivouac.com named the nearby peaks for other ranks of the Anglican clergy. Deacons are the lowest order. Although they are ordained (they wear clerical collars and are styled "Reverend"), they are not permitted to preside at the Eucharist, bless people, or absolve sins.

Jarrett is a shoulder of Bishop, more impressive from afar than close up. Its views are very similar to those of Bishop. That said, it offers impressive views of Bishop's eastern cliffs and pointy Clementine/Presbyter to the north. From the Bishop cirque Jarrett takes about half an hour to climb.

Jarrett/Deacon was first climbed on August 9, 1908, by a BCMC party embarking from Berg's Landing beach, near Croker Island on Indian Arm (called "North Arm" at the time; its name was changed in 1921 to avoid confusion with the North Arm of the Fraser River). They bushwhacked up beside Bishop Creek, viewing old-growth cedars and blueberries. They explored the peaks of Bishop, the main one of which they named for their president, Joseph Charles Bishop. Nine of the hikers then proceeded to Jarrett/Deacon along a long snow-covered ridge, a trip they reported as having taken half an hour. The peak was named Mt. Jarrett, after the BCMC secretary, who was present on the trip. The two parties shouted greetings to each other before returning to the main group. On the descent, five mountain goats were spotted on the cliffs. One of the climbers, Charles Dickens, described the trip in a newspaper article (see "New Peaks Named by Mountaineering Club" in **Appendix 19**):

> … Away below to the left was Seymour Creek Valley and in some of the higher valleys three or four beautiful lakes lay deep and dark, almost hidden from the light of the sun by the hills piled high above them.
>
> Greetings were exchanged from peak to peak, for the voices of the two parties easily carried across the distance, although when seen with the naked eye the men seemed more the size of ants than human beings. … the descent was commenced along a vast snow field. It really needed one leg longer than the other to make the going comfortable, but the slope and ridge were finally crossed and the two parties reunited.

It is a mystery why Bishop's name persisted and that of poor Jarrett was neglected. Despite its then recent baptism, Mt. Jarrett does not receive a name on the 1912 map in the BCMC *Northern Cordilleran* (Mt. Bishop is the only named peak north of Seymour; there is no mention of Runner, Elsay, Clementine or Dickens either). Neither is Mt. Jarrett mentioned in later reports of trips to Mt. Bishop; the only subsequent BCMC reference appears to be a May 1923 *BC Mountaineer* inclusion of it in a list of peaks given as an example of mountain naming conventions: Bishop, Jarrett, Clementine, and Dickens (listed in that order, from south to north, fortifying the locations and identities of Jarrett and Clementine peaks).

By some theories, including one sent to the BC Geographic Office, Mt. Elsay was the other peak climbed by the BCMC party, and the name Mt. Jarrett was an earlier name for Mt. Elsay. This is incorrect. The photograph in the Charles Dickens article shows Jarrett/Deacon, not Elsay. The article says the hikers went from Bishop to Jarrett in half an hour. Such a time would be impossible heading south to Elsay (about 4 km on a bushy, undulating ridge with a necessary deep descent into Vicar Lakes, which themselves are not mentioned in the article), but very plausible north to Deacon (less than 1 km). The article describes the Seymour Valley and Vicar Lakes to the left (consistent with going north rather than south). The article says the climbers went via a ridge and returned to Bishop by way of a vast snowfield: more consistent with the topography to the north, between Deacon and Bishop. The article says Jarrett is higher than Bishop by several hundred feet: neither Elsay nor Deacon is higher than Bishop, but Deacon is almost the same height as Bishop and Elsay is shorter by about a hundred feet.

ROUTE

Follow the route described on p. 359 from Vicar Lakes to Mt. Bishop Amphitheatre.

Mt. Bishop Amphitheatre to Mt. Jarrett: Go to the middle of the Mt. Bishop granite rock field and amphitheatre. Look east. You will see to your right the steep north cliffs of Bishop rising up, and on the other side a fairly steep slope descending into the valley. There is a lone tree about the same level as the trail down to Vicar Lakes. It is marked with a blaze. Head towards it, following a rough path marked by trampled heather boughs. This could be very slippery if wet. Be careful.

- The trail then descends shortly and steeply to the boulder field at the base of Jarrett/Deacon. It is well trodden, clear, and probably flagged. Use your hands for a safe descent.
- The rock field is small. Travel upward, generally aiming for the peak. Climb the granite slabs. There are pretty maidenhair ferns along the way. Continue a bit to the east, imagining and following a straight line up the ridge from Bishop to Jarrett. You will climb through a group of trees, along a faint trail marked on rocks and heather by past boots.
- After a few steps on the right (east) of the ridge, the trail returns to the middle of it and up to the bald granite peak.
- You will be rewarded with slightly different views of Indian Arm and all the views that Bishop provided. The most imposing is that of Clementine/Presbyter, rising to the north, seemingly steeply.

CLEMENTINE (PRESBYTER) PEAK
(CLE) (1487 M)

Enjoyable one-day hike from the LSCR road up decent trails to a seldom visited peak

CAUTION:
Steep trail up from LSCR; trail faint at times; remote.

PROMINENCE:
77 m.

LATITUDE/LONGITUDE:
N49.43889 W122.92500.

Bang for buck:
3/5

PEAK VIEW:
4/5. Fannin Lake, Dickens, Indian Arm.

TRUE SUMMIT LOCATION:
Obvious.

HEADWATERS:
Gibbens Creek (into Seymour River).

BEST VIEWS FROM:
Mt. Elsay, Mt. Seymour.

TRIP INFORMATION
Round-trip distance: 11.6 km.
Elevation gain: 1396 m.
Time: 5.5–10 hours from Vicar Lake trailhead on Spur 4 Road (5:48).
Difficulty: 4/5. Remote; routefinding required.
Snow free: Late July.
Must-sees: Vicar Lakes fairyland.
Scenery: 3/5.
Kids: 2/5. Too remote.
Dogs: 4/5.
Runnability: 3/5.
Terrain: Low forest cover.
Public transit: #209 bus from Phibbs Exchange to Lynn Headwaters Park; #228 Lynn Valley from Lonsdale Quay or #210 Upper Lynn Valley from Phibbs Exchange for LSCR; #C12 to foot of Mt. Seymour Road, but a long climb.
Cell coverage: Rare to non-existent.
Sun: Mostly exposed; 20 per cent shaded.
Water: Some tarns and creeks.
Route links: Sweep from Seymour to Vicar, or full Fannin Sweep, or Elsay Lake Loop.

HISTORY
Name origin: See below.
Name status: Unofficial.
First ascent: August 9, 1908, by BCMC party also making first ascents of Bishop and Jarrett.
Other names: North Peak of Bishop. Bivouac.com calls it "Electric Railway Presbyter," following on from the Bishop name and their naming of nearby mountains after other ranks of Anglican clergy. "Presbyter" means "priest" (and is the

etymological origin of that English word). In some Protestant denominations, such as Presbyterianism, however, presbyters are non-priest elders who govern the church.

Like Jarrett/Deacon, Clementine/Presbyter is really just a secondary peak of Bishop. From Jarrett it takes only 30 minutes or so more to also bag Clementine, less than 1 km away. Although Clementine is lower than Jarrett, its views are superior, with a clear view of Fannin Lake below and the bumps of Mt. Dickens to the north. There is also a view of the clear-cut on the Clementine Creek slope.

There are several stories as to the origin of the name Clementine, all or none of which may be true. Clementine Creek runs down the Dickens side of Fannin Lake, flowing into Indian Arm roughly in line with the north end of Croker Island. A property through which the creek flows was apparently at one time owned by the family of famous mountaineer Arthur Tinniswood Dalton (or by a neighbour of the Daltons); the property was named "Clementine" after a board bearing the name "Clementine" was seen on a float owned by a local logger. In 1942 former BCMC president Charles Chapman recounted (in a note now held in the Vancouver Archives) how Clementine Peak received its name, likely on August 9, 1908, on the first ascent of Bishop and Jarrett:

> I was on the first trip to Mount Bishop. "Pa" Bishop, he was old – or we youngsters looked upon him as old – and we started off in a motor launch of sorts, and there were nineteen of us, and before long someone said the boat was filling with water it was so crowded. However, we fixed the leak, and the first creek we came to was called Bishop Creek to please "Pa" Bishop. Then we started to climb; there are three peaks, and the big one we called Mt. Bishop, and then someone said to name the other "Jarrett" (not Janet) after George Jarrett of the Hastings Sawmill; he's in Santa Ana, Cal., now. And then we were all joking and laughing and singing, and you know how we used to sing "Oh my darling, oh my darling, oh my darling Clementine," the song, so we named the third peak "Clementine." Both names are forgotten now, but Mt. Bishop has been officially named. It was either 1909 or 1910; I think 1909.

Although Dalton was not one of the first baggers of Bishop/Jarrett/Clementine, the property and possibly the creek names would likely have been known by his climbing friends, so it's plausible the name Clementine would have been on their minds. In June 1910 Basil Stewart Darling referred to Clementine in an article titled "The Passion for Mountain Climbing," published in the very manly *Man-to-Man Magazine* (see **Appendix 22**). Clementine is mentioned in a later BCMC article on naming peaks, along with Bishop, Jarrett, and Dickens as four peaks of the same complex. The name was still in use in a July 1927 trip report but seems to have vanished after that.

ROUTE:

JARRETT TO CLEMENTINE

- Follow the route from Vicar Lakes to the Mt. Bishop amphitheatre described at p. 359.
- Follow the route from the Mt. Bishop amphitheatre to Mt. Jarrett, also described p. 363.

Mt. Jarrett to Clementine Peak: From Jarrett you can look down at the narrow col crossing over to Clementine. Head more or less towards it, hopping down a series of granite shelves and over heather. It should never be excessively steep or sheer or dangerous or obscured. If it is, retrace your steps and try again. If anything, torque a little left and down.

The col to Clementine from Jarrett.

- At the col, there are reassuring bootsteps marking an obvious path.
- The climb up Clementine will require use of your hands, but the path is generally clear and safe and occasionally flagged. Follow the dead heather and blueberry boughs.
- The trail veers to the east side of the ridge, where it is a bit steep. This is the trickiest part of the climb. Note the place where you climb up and out onto a flat balcony of granite and heather, as it is easy to get lost here on the descent. At this spot when returning back down, take care to veer left (east) from this balcony; although it appears steep, it is much less so than following false paths straight south down the ridge bluff.
- The summit is obvious.

Descent back to the base of Bishop: It is not necessary to reclimb Jarrett to return to the base of Bishop. Just above the Clementine–Jarrett col, on the Jarrett side, there is a small tarn to the right (southwest) at roughly the same height as the rock field at the base of Jarrett, visible through the trees. From here it is possible to traverse Jarrett, through blueberry bushes and krumholtz, back to the rock field. Navigate slightly up or down to find a comfortable traverse route. Take care if the going is wet: the grass will be slippery and there are steep and potentially dangerous patches.

MT. DICKENS (DIC) (1288 M)

Enjoyable one-day hike from the LSCR road up decent trails to a seldom visited peak, or one can take a boat to head of Indian Arm and bushwhack up from there.

CAUTION:
Steep trail up from LSCR;
trail faint at times; remote.

PROMINENCE:
143 m.

LATITUDE/LONGITUDE:
N49.46389 W122.91583.

BANG FOR BUCK:
3/5

PEAK VIEW:
4/5

TRUE SUMMIT LOCATION:
From the south,
the second peak, due west of
Wigwam Inn, at the beginning
of Wigwam Creek.

HEADWATERS:
Wigwam Creek and
Spray of Pearls Falls
(into Indian Arm).

BEST VIEWS FROM:
Mt. Elsay, Mt. Seymour.

TRIP INFORMATION

Round-trip distance: 22.6 km.

Elevation gain: 2350 m.

Time: 11–20 hours (12:00) from Vicar Lakes trailhead; 4–8 hours from Wigwam Creek outflow on Indian Arm.

Difficulty: 4.5/5. Remote; routefinding required.

Snow free: Late July.

Must-sees: Vicar Lakes fairyland and Fannin Lake (from Seymour Trailway); Spray of Pearls Falls and Seymour Lake (from Indian Arm).

Scenery: 3/5.

Kids: 2/5. Too remote.

Dogs: 2/5.

Runnability: 3/5.

Terrain: Low forest cover.

Public transit: #209 bus from Phibbs Exchange to Lynn Headwaters Park; #228 Lynn Valley from Lonsdale Quay or #210 Upper Lynn Valley from Phibbs Exchange for LSCR; #C12 to foot of Mt. Seymour Road, but a long climb.

Cell coverage: Rare to non-existent.

Sun: 90 per cent shaded.

Water: Some tarns on peak ridge and creeks on climb up.

Route links: Sweep from Seymour to Vicar, or full Fannin Sweep, or Elsay Lake Loop.

Name origin: Likely named on July 14, 1908, by James John Trorey and others after Benjamin Franklin Dickens (1860 Belleville, Ont. – 1952 Vancouver), the original owner of the Wigwam Inn.

Name status: Official. Adopted March 10, 1975.

First ascent: On July 26, 1908, the summit was reached by a BCMC group led by Fred Mills: Elizabeth B. Fowler, Mary May Creech (who would later marry club secretary George Jarrett), Miss Wickwire, Joseph Charles Bishop, Harry Extence, George Jarrett, J.S. Stevens, George Harrower, James Porter, Mr. A.H. Fleisch, Mr. A.B. Patterson, Miss L.E. Martin, Charles Dickens, Charles Chapman, Wilfred Henry Tassell, and Bert Armistead. Mills had led a group including Benjamin Franklin Dickens, Joseph Charles Bishop, and James John Trorey close to the peak on October 8, 1906 (see below).

Other names: A 1936 brochure for the Wigwam Inn and Indian River Park referred to Mt. Dickens as "Pearl Mountain."

Mt. Dickens is a relatively low, four-peaked mountain located at the head of Indian Arm, above the Wigwam Inn. It is the most remote peak that would normally be approached from the North Shore. There are three bumps along Indian Arm Trail (and a fourth to the north, beyond the trail) of more or less equal height, as well as a lower duckbill ridge or bench that juts out towards Indian Arm. This latter, duckbill bump is often marked on maps as being the peak although it is considerably lower than the main ridge. When Vancouver archivist Major James Skitt Matthews submitted his application in July 1937 for official recognition of the name, he described the mountain as being "due west of Wigwam Inn, and approached by Wigwam Creek. It is not the highest elevation." The official name now, however, designates the high point on the ridge.

There are two main approaches: by land from Bishop/Jarrett/Clementine from the south along Indian Arm Trail (about 6 km); and by sea from just north of the Wigwam Inn. Both routes have commendable aspects. By land you pass the enchanting Fannin Lake; by sea, the enchanting Spray of Pearls Falls. Whichever way you take, this adventure is likely an overnight affair or a gruelling single-day trail run or power hike. And either way, a GPS with extra batteries is highly recommended; this is not at all an adventure for beginners.

Just to the north of the Wigwam Inn, the Indian River estuary teems with soaring bald eagles, sunning seals, and, in odd-numbered years, spawning pink salmon. The Tsleil-Waututh call this area Inlailawatash. At high tide it is possible to canoe about a kilometre up the Indian River.

Dickens is due west and directly above the Wigwam Inn. At night, the lights of the inn are visible from the peak (one of the authors of this book can personally attest to this, based on an unplanned overnight stay on Mt. Dickens). The inn was opened in June 1910 by Prussian-born financier Alvo von Alvensleben and Benjamin Franklin "Benny" Dickens (1861–1952) (a businessman and a journalist with the Vancouver *Daily Province*), after whom the peak is named. Dickens described himself as "distant" cousin or nephew of the novelist, and had come to Vancouver from Belleville, Ont., in 1898. He was also the uncle of Charles Dickens, who was a prominent early Vancouver mountaineer (see **Appendix 19**). Guests of the Wigwam Inn included magnates John

D. Rockefeller and John Jacob Astor (the same year he died on the *Titanic*), comedian W.C. Fields, and Nazi leader Joachim von Ribbentrop. Over the years, the inn served as a saloon and brothel. It is presently owned by the Royal Vancouver Yacht Club; respect the private property and do not trespass.

The differing definitions of the peak – is it the high point or the lower, duckbill bench? – contribute to the differing stories of when the peak was first climbed and named. A July 1908 *Vancouver Daily World* story, for example, reported that the party stopped at the bench and christened the peak anyway, using a Union Jack provided to them by B.F. Dickens:

> Mr. James Glover volunteered to climb a tall tree right on the edge of the mountain and make a place to fly the red ensign. This was a ticklish position to be in. With the trees swaying violently and a straight drop below for thousands of feet, his work of cutting away the branches and securing the flag was a serious undertaking. After this he and Mr. Trorey mounted a stump, the rest of the party grouped themselves around, and the flood of eloquence was let loose. With a bottle of champagne held aloft, Mr. Trorey christened the mountain with the following words: "In the name of Benjamin Franklin Dickens, of the governor-general and of His Majesty King Edward VII, I christen thee Mount Dickens."[13]

They may have imbibed too much champagne, as they lost their way on the descent, resulting in arrival at camp after dark.

Two weeks later, on July 26, 1908, the summit was reached by a BCMC group led by charter member Roland Manfred "Fred" Mills (1883–1966); the group included three women. It took the group two-and-a-half hours to reach the bench, and another hour-and-a-half to the summit. At the bench, they found the Trorey expedition Union Jack. The August 1, 1908, *Saturday Sunset* reported that "the party was especially well pleased as this is the first time on record that the actual top of the peak was reached." After spending four hours on the peak, the party returned to the shore, where they "gave three cheers for Mr. Fred Mills, who guided them so unerringly to the top and back again." In 1937 Benjamin F. Dickens, and later, in 1957, his son Charles Dickens, had similar recollections.

The article also stated that Fred Mills had twice in 1906 led hunting trips that approached but did not summit the peak. In 1957 Fred Mills recalled it slightly differently: that he had summited the peak in 1906 and named it in 1909. By this version, Benjamin Dickens had asked him, as well as Joseph Bishop (the first president of the BCMC), and James John Trorey (a founding member of the club), as well as an Australian artist and a Vancouver photographer to accompany him to Indian River at Thanksgiving weekend 1906. Mr. Dickens had stated that he planned to build a "first class inn or hotel" at Indian River, and that he wanted to choose the site. A month later Mills returned again, along with Walter Green of the Vancouver *Daily Province* and Vince Easthope, climbed the mountain, and "got a splendid Billy [i.e., mountain goat] just below the snow that had fallen since my trip previously." These differing accounts likely arise, again, from confusion as to whether Dickens is considered the highest point on the ridge or the protruding bench.

The route up to Dickens from Indian Arm follows Wigwam Creek, which Dickens had called Cathedral Creek, in part because the high walls of the creek valley and the wall over which the falls tumble reminded him of a cathedral and, no doubt, because it sounded good on a tourist brochure. The trail up to the falls and the peak was called "Cathedral Trail." Spray of Pearls Falls cascades down the steep valley over several cataracts and offers spectacular views. At least at the time of the 1955 tourist brochure, the trails up to Spray of Pearls Falls and Mt. Dickens were still marked with posts (although no sign of them remains today).

Note that Indian Arm Trail, contrary to intuition, does not descend near the Wigwam Inn in order to cross the Indian River; instead it continues some 7 km north of Dickens. The north peak of Dickens has been referred to, reputedly by persons caught overnight on the long trail, as "Brokeback Mountain" for reasons unknown.

ROUTE 1:

BY LAND – FROM LSCR / SEYMOUR VALLEY TRAILWAY AND VICAR LAKES VIA INDIAN ARM TRAIL

Caution: This route is remote and requires routefinding skills. There is likely no cell-phone coverage.

- Follow route from LSCR parking lot to Vicar Lakes trail, p. 358.
- Follow route from Vicar Lakes to the Mt. Bishop amphitheatre, p. 359.
- Follow route from the Mt. Bishop amphitheatre to Mt. Jarrett, p. 363.
- Follow route from Mt. Jarrett to Clementine Peak, p. 366.
- It takes between 2 and 3 hours to travel from Clementine to Fannin Lake, and another hour or so up to Dickens.
- From Clementine, descend to the north along a series of heathery slabs. You should never feel in danger; if so, trace back.
- Continue down towards a heathery bowl, veering slightly right (east) of the ridge down.
- Watch the trail carefully. The natural inclination is to descend down the middle of the slope, across a pleasant meadow, towards the thickening forest, which is what one of the authors did on his first descent. It led to a nasty steep bushwhack, an unexpected overnight stay, and physical and emotional scarring. Don't go this way!
- In fact the trail sharply doglegs to the southeast, hugging the cliff at the northeast base of Clementine and proceeding down a treed ramp.
- Cross some boulders and occasionally steep shrubbery. You'll find occasional flagging and cairns as the trail descends into the bowl and then via a small gully into the forest. Keep your eyes peeled for tape and blazes here, and don't hesitate to backtrack if you feel you've gone off trail.
- Although the trail is narrow and rarely trodden at this point, you should always feel confident you are on the route. If not, retrace your steps and try again.
- After about 20 minutes you will encounter some ropes and climbs down roots and duff, along with some large old-growth cedars. It is at times steep and cliffy, but there are always sufficient handholds. Do not endanger yourself. Occasionally you will see original metal trail markers on trees.

High above Fannin Lake.

- After about 40 minutes the trail exits to the lovely and seldom visited Fannin

Lake, suspended above Indian Arm by spongy moss and bounded by granite cliffs to the south.

- The trail leads left (north) alongside a charming, burbling creek that reminds one of Scotland.
- At the north end of the lake, at approximately 1 o'clock (if north is noon), ascend back into the forest. Head straight up the ridge on the natural route.
- At this point, somewhat surprisingly, the orange flashes on the trees become more regular and the trail becomes more trodden. Climb up, using the occasional rope.
- Dickens has four peaks of more or less equal height on its ridge, separated by several cols interspersed with tarns. The true peak is, from the south, the second one, due west of Wigwam Inn, at the beginning of Wigwam Creek. As of writing, it was uncairned.

ROUTE 2:
BY WATER – VIA INDIAN ARM

This is the shorter route, attainable in a half-day (not counting boat time), and approximates the original route of the first climb up Dickens from the Wigwam Inn site.

- On Indian Arm (at the end of Burrard Inlet), Cates Park is a good place to launch a powerboat. Kayaks are available for rent at Deep Cove Kayaks (604-929-2268; 2156 Banbury Road), although kayaking adds about a day to this trip.
- Boat up Indian Arm to the Wigwam Creek washout plain at the head of the arm, just north of the Wigwam Inn property boundary.
- Walk up along the creek (an alder-strewn but flat path on the south side of the creek) until just before the creek becomes more boxlike and canyonish. At that point, cut over the creek and into the forest north of the creek.

- Head up the steep but readily climbable terrain. Flagging is minimal, but for most of the way the route (as a faint trail) is clear.
- Generally travel up the gentlest contour line, with Wigwam Creek on your left (south). Follow Wigwam Creek up to the promontory and then head left (south) to the true peak.
- You can readily avoid cliffs and vegetation for most of the journey up, and even follow a clear but rarely trodden trail running parallel to the creek and past the double set of cascades making up the Spray of Pearls Falls.
- At times, you can veer towards the falls for a better view. Beware of steep portions obscured by undergrowth. That said, there are several places where you can scramble down to the base of the various falls for lovely views, refreshment, and water. Below the two cascades are pools that would be pleasant on a hot day (as would some of the pools in the lower part of Wigwam Creek).
- About three-quarters of the way up, the trail becomes more obscure and the bushwhacking starts.
- As you approach the ridge the trail becomes more vegetal but is still a relatively gentle bushwhack. After the brief bushwhack, you pop out of the underbrush onto a promontory overlooking Indian Arm through the trees. Some maps mark Mt. Dickens as this promontory instead of the peak above.
- To attain the true summit of Dickens, turn left (southwest) and up.
- At this point the hike does get a bit nasty and woolly, although there are also plenty of stretches of clear undergrowth.
- The blueberry bushes abate as you punch out to the very clearly marked Indian Arm Trail. The flagging is reassuring after your semi-bushwhack.
- From there, head south and up along Indian Arm Trail to the peaks of Mt. Dickens.

Wigwam Creek just below the start of the forest trail route.

APPENDICES

DIFFICULTY: EASIEST TO HARDEST

Based on difficulty of terrain, proximity to trailheads, and how well established the trail is, if any. We strongly recommend not trying any peak that is more challenging until you have mastered the technical and routefinding skills required for your present level. And remember:

> The difficulty ratings are on a relative scale. A 1/5 score does not mean it is an easy stroll. Seymour, for example, is rated 1/5 but is nevertheless past the fitness level and wilderness competence of most Canadians.

> Difficulty is based on perfect conditions: blue skies, perfect visibility, no lingering snow, no rain, no clouds. If the weather is doubtful, do not test your limitations!

BEGINNER
Well marked with well-established trails. No significant danger if blessed with good conditions, decent health, and common sense.

1. Grouse
2. Hollyburn
3. Dam
4. Black
5. Pump Peak
6. Tim Jones
7. Seymour

EXPERIENCED BEGINNER
At times, routefinding may be necessary.

8. Little Goat
9. Rice (South Lynn)
10. Goat
11. Goat Ridge
12. Gardner
13. Lynn
14. Suicide Bluffs
15. Artaban
16. Strachan
17. de Pencier Bluffs
18. Fromme
19. St.. Marks
20. Collins
21. Unnecessary
22. North Unnecessary
23. Killam

INTERMEDIATE
Some challenging sections, in effort and climbing. Signage rare or non-existent. At times, routefinding may be necessary.

24. Paton
25. Coliseum
26. Burwell
27. David
28. James
29. Thomas
30. South Needle
31. Fat Ass
32. Hat
33. Leading
34. Crown
35. Elsay
36. Deeks Peak
37. Harvey
38. Burts
39. Apodaca

INTERMEDIATE TO ADVANCED
Some challenging sections, in effort and climbing. No signage. Routefinding necessary. Some moderate exposure.

40. Magnesia
41. Brunswick
42. Runner
43. Middle Needle
44. West Crown
45. Rector
46. Curate
47. Vicar

ADVANCED

Potential exposure and danger. At times difficult climbing and routefinding. No signage. Flagging inconsistent. Trails inconsistent. Remote.

48. Bishop	51. Gambier	54. Gotha	57. Clementine/
49. Enchantment	52. Liddell	55. Dickens	Presbyter
50. North Needle	53. Windsor	56. Jarrett/Deacon	58. Capilano

EXPERIENCED ONLY

Very remote. Significant exposure. Real chance of becoming lost or dying if unprepared or inexperienced. Flagging inconsistent.

59. Zinc	62. Cathedral	65. Forks
60. Wettin	63. Echo	66. Coburg
61. West Lion	64. Hanover	67. Crown N1

EASIEST TO NAVIGATE

Guideposts and well-established trails for those worried about getting lost.

1. Grouse	5. Seymour	9. Hollyburn	13. South Lynn
2. Black	6. Dam	10. St. Marks	14. Goat Ridge Peak
3. Tim Jones	7. Little Goat	11. Unnecessary	15. Lynn
4. Pump	8. Goat	12. North Unnecessary	

TIME: SHORTEST TO LONGEST

Times are round-trip, from Route 1 for each peak unless otherwise noted.

1. Grouse: 0.5–1 hr.
2. Collins: 0.75–2.5 hrs.
3. Suicide: 1–3 hrs.
4. Dam: 1–3 hrs.
5. Black: 1–3 hrs.
6. Apodaca: 1–3 hrs.
7. de Pencier: 1.5–3 hrs.
8. Little Goat: 1.5–3 hrs.
9. Pump: 1.5–3 hrs.
10. Rice (South Lynn): 1.5–4 hrs.
11. Hollyburn: 2–4 hrs.
12. Tim Jones: 2–4 hrs.
13. Artaban: 2–4 hrs.
14. Burts: 2–4 hrs.
15. Goat: 2–4 hrs.
16. Fromme via Peer Gynt: 2–5 hrs.
17. Seymour: 2.5–5 hrs.
18. St. Marks via Cypress Bowl: 2.5–5 hrs.
19. Killam: 2.5–5 hrs.
20. Paton: 3–5 hrs. via LSCR.
21. Goat Ridge Peak: 3–6 hrs.
22. Gardner: 3–6 hrs.
23. Lynn: 3–6 hrs.
24. Leading: 3–6 hrs.
25. Vicar via Vicar Lakes: 3–6 hrs.
26. Strachan from Cypress Bowl: 3–7 hrs.
27. Fromme via Grouse parking lot: 4–6 hrs.
28. Crown: 4–7 hrs.
29. Runner: 4–7 hrs.
30. Coliseum via Stoney Creek: 4–7 hrs.
31. West Lion: 4–7 hrs.
32. Unnecessary via Cypress Bowl: 4–7 hrs.
33. West Crown: 4–8 hrs.
34. Dickens via Indian Arm: 4–8 hrs.
35. Bishop via Vicar Lakes: 4–8 hrs.
36. Liddell: 4–9 hrs.
37. Gambier: 4–9 hrs.
38. Elsay: 4–9 hrs.
39. Jarrett via Vicar Lakes: 4.5–8.5 hrs.
40. North Unnecessary via Cypress Bowl: 5–8 hrs.
41. Harvey via Lions Bay: 5–8 hrs.
42. Fat Ass via Lions Bay: 5–8 hrs.
43. Thomas via Lions Bay: 5–8 hrs.
44. Hat via Lions Bay: 5–8 hrs.
45. South Needle via Hydraulic Creek: 5–9 hrs.
46. Rector: 5–9 hrs.
47. Vicar via Seymour: 5–9 hrs.
48. Middle Needle: 5–10 hrs.
49. North Needle via Hydraulic Creek: 5–10 hrs.
50. Burwell via Stoney Creek: 5–9.5 hrs.
51. Windsor via Porteau: 5.5–8.5 hrs.
52. Clementine via Vicar Lakes: 5.5–10 hrs.
53. Deeks via Porteau: 6–9 hrs.
54. Forks: 6–9 hrs.
55. Curate: 6–10 hrs.
56. Capilano: 6–12 hrs.
57. Gotha via Porteau: 7–10 hrs.
58. James via Lions Bay: 7–10 hrs.
59. Magnesia via Lions Bay: 7–11 hrs.
60. David via Lions Bay: 8–10 hrs.
61. Enchantment via Lions Bay: 8–11 hrs.
62. Brunswick via Porteau: 8–11 hrs.
63. Wettin via Lions Bay: 8–12 hrs.
64. Hanover via Lions Bay: 9–11 hrs.
65. Echo via Hanes Valley: 9–13 hrs.
66. Coburg via Porteau: 9–13 hrs.
67. Crown N1 via Hanes Valley: 13–16 hrs.
68. Dickens via Vicar Lakes: 11–20 hrs.
69. Cathedral via Stoney Creek: 11 hrs. to 2 days

ELEVATION: HEIGHT AND PROMINENCE

HIGHEST

1. Brunswick Mountain (1788 m)
2. Mt. Hanover (1748 m)
3. Cathedral Mountain (1737 m)
4. Mt. Windsor (1689 m)
5. Capilano Mountain (1685 m)
6. Deeks Peak (1672 m)
7. West Lion (1654 m)
8. Mt. Harvey (1652 m)
9. Coburg Peak (1645 m)
10. Hat Mountain (1644 m)
11. Gotha Peak (1641 m)
12. Fat Ass Peak (1619 m)

MOST PROMINENT

Prominence measures the distinctiveness and individuality of a peak as considered on its own rather than as just one of several bumps. It measures the distance one must descend from one summit before starting to climb up to the next. More precisely, prominence ("p") is the vertical distance between the summit of the particular peak and the lowest contour line that encircles the base of that peak without including any part of a higher neighbouring mountain.

1. Brunswick Mountain (1788 m) (p: 1294 m)
2. Gambier Peak (Gambier Island) (904 m) (p: 904 m)
3. Cathedral Mountain (1737 m) (p: 832 m)
4. Leading Peak (Anvil Island) (765 m) (p: 765 m)
5. Mt. Gardner (Bowen Island) (727 m) (p: 727 m)
6. Mt. Bishop (1509 m) (p: 613 m)
7. Capilano Mountain (1685 m) (p: 603 m)
8. Mt. Artaban (Gambier Island) (615 m) (p: 592 m)
9. Crown Mountain (1504 m) (p: 519 m)
10. Mt. Seymour (1449 m) (p: 453 m)
11. West Lion (1654 m) (p: 369 m)
12. Mt. Strachan (1454 m) (p: 382 m)
13. Mt. Collins (Bowen Island) (413 m) (p: 358 m)
14. Goat Mountain (1401 m) (p: 336 m)
15. Black Mountain (1217 m) (p: 296 m)
16. Windsor Peak (1689 m) (p: 264 m)
17. Middle Needle (1258 m) (p: 260 m)
18. Mt. Elsay (1419 m) (p: 254 m)
19. Mt. Hanover (1748 m) (p: 238 m)
20. Mt. Fromme (1185 m) (p: 235 m)

APPEARANCE: MOST BEAUTIFUL SHAPE AND COMPOSITION

1. Lions
2. Cathedral
3. West Crown
4. Crown
5. Leading
6. Harvey
7. Hanover
8. Gotha/Coburg
9. Seymour
10. Bishop
11. Brunswick
12. Coliseum/Burwell

BEST ADVENTURES

Based on all factors, but predominantly peak views, scenery on the way, reward for amount of effort, and sheer epicness of the trip.

FIRST-RATE

1. Brunswick
2. Cathedral
3. Bishop
4. Leading
5. Crown
6. Capilano
7. Seymour
8. Hollyburn
9. Strachan
10. Coliseum
11. Burwell

EXCELLENT

12. Tim Jones
13. Goat Ridge
14. Windsor
15. Clementine/ Presbyter
16. Goat
17. Runner
18. Elsay
19. Paton
20. Harvey
21. South Needle
22. Magnesia
23. West Lion
24. West Crown
25. Suicide Bluffs
26. de Pencier Bluffs
27. Pump
28. Hat
29. Hanover

GOOD

30. Enchantment
31. Gotha
32. Black
33. Artaban
34. Lynn
35. Deeks Peak
36. Burts
37. Fat Ass
38. Gardner
39. Fromme
40. St. Marks
41. Killam
42. Unnecessary
43. North Unnecessary
44. Echo
45. Zinc
46. Dam
47. Little Goat
48. Rice
49. Collins
50. Middle Needle
51. North Needle
52. Dickens
53. Jarrett
54. Coburg
55. Crown N1
56. Rector
57. Curate
58. Vicar
59. David
60. James
61. Thomas
62. Wettin
63. Forks

ONLY DO TO CHECK OFF THE LIST

64. Grouse
65. Gambier
66. Liddell
67. Apodaca

MOST BANG FOR YOUR BUCK

Best views and other perquisites in relation to difficulty.

1. Pump
2. Hollyburn
3. Seymour
4. Goat
5. Little Goat
6. Black
7. de Pencier
8. Tim Jones
9. Gardner
10. Strachan

Coliseum tarn.

BEST MOUNTAIN ADVENTURES WITH KIDS

Combining views, sense of adventure, other highlights (lakes, tarns, berries), safety, reasonable distance, steepness, and variety. Trail-tested by a kindergartener.

1. Dam	4. Black	7. Goat Ridge	10. Gardner
2. Hollyburn	5. Seymour	8. Strachan	11. Artaban
3. Little Goat	6. Goat	9. de Pencier	12. Grouse

MOST MASOCHISTIC CLIMBS AND ADVENTURES

1. Crown N1	5. Forks	9. Hanover	13. Coliseum
2. Echo	6. Leading	10. Gambier/Liddell	14. Unnecessary
3. Cathedral	7. Capilano	11. Brunswick	15. West Lion
4. Gotha/Coburg	8. Dickens	12. Burwell	16. Apodaca

MOST RUNNABLE BAGGING ADVENTURES

Based on overall adventure: up and down. Some of these ascents will be run only by masochists.

1. Collins	11. South Needle	21. Paton
2. Goat Ridge	12. Capilano	22. Dickens
3. Seymour	13. de Pencier	23. Deeks
4. Hollyburn	14. Strachan	
5. Dam	15. Crown	
6. Gardner	16. Lynn	
7. Goat	17. Coliseum	
8. St. Marks	18. Burwell	
9. Fromme	19. Leading	
10. Black	20. Windsor	

BEST SLALOM RUN DESCENTS

There is nothing more glorious than returning from a triumphant bagging adventure down a steep slope that is a bit technical but not too much so, on a surface that consists primarily not of rocks and roots but of wonderful, duffy, decayed cedar. Gravity and duff combine to emulate a slalom descent. Only in good conditions, though, never when icy!

1. South Needle: down to Hydraulic Creek connector trail and thence to Seymour Valley Trailway.
2. Leading: down Nighthawk Trail.
3. Fromme: down south face to Old Mountain Highway.
4. Paton: approach from Coliseum and thence down to Seymour Valley Trailway.
5. Dickens: back down to Fannin Lake.
6. Deeks: down to Deeks Lake.
7. Harvey: down the southwest face to Lions Bay.
8. de Pencier or Suicide: down Magic Kingdom Trail, then Cambodia.
9. Strachan: down Christmas Gully.

BEST MULTI-PEAK ROUTES

For vigorous adventurers who wish to bag several peaks in a day or make a pleasing loop of hikes.

1. Grouse–Dam–Little Goat–Goat–Goat Ridge–Crown–West Crown (and Fromme via Thunderbird Ridge and Erik the Red Trail)
2. Seymour–Runner–Elsay–Rector–Curate–Vicar
3. Pump–Tim–Seymour
4. Suicide–Pump–Tim–Seymour–de Pencier
5. Bishop–Jarrett–Clementine
6. Hollyburn–Strachan–Black
7. Harvey–Magnesia–David–James–Lions
8. Brunswick–Hat–CFA–Magnesia–Harvey
9. Wettin–Hat–Fat Ass–Brunswick–Magnesia–Harvey
10. Collins–Gardner–Apodaca
11. St. Marks–Unnecessary–Lions
12. Deeks–Windsor–Gotha–Coburg
13. Killam–Liddell–Gambier
14. Artaban–Burts

BEST BIKE-AND-BAG ADVENTURES

A few of these peaks lend themselves well to a cycling approach: glorious and saves time.

1. South Needle (via Seymour Valley Trailway and up Hydraulic Creek Trail)
2. Paton–Coliseum–Burwell (via Seymour Valley Trailway)
3. Vicar–Bishop (via Seymour Valley Trailway and Spur 4 Road on east side of Seymour River)
4. Lynn–South Lynn
5. Seymour
6. Black
7. Grouse
8. Lions–Harvey–Brunswick from Lions Bay

BEST WATERBAGS

For purists: a climb from the ocean to the peak, on one's own propulsion.

1. Leading
2. Gardner
3. Dickens
4. Killam
5. Artaban
6. Burts

BEST RAINY-DAY BAGS

Where you're twitchy for a climb and views don't really matter.

1. Rice (South Lynn)
2. Lynn
3. Grouse
4. Hollyburn
5. Dam
6. Black
7. Pump
8. Tim Jones
9. Suicide Bluffs
10. de Pencier Bluffs
11. Fromme
12. St. Marks
13. Gardner
14. Killam
15. Burts
16. Collins
17. Apodaca
18. Leading

BEST SNOWSHOE TRIPS

This is not a winter alpine guide, and easy peaks in summer can be deadly dangerous in winter (see Goat). Always check the avalanche conditions (avalanche.ca) before heading out (and donate to this worthy organization: it's good karma!).

1. Thunderbird Ridge
2. Hollyburn
3. Pump
4. Little Goat
5. Tim Jones
6. Suicide Bluffs
7. Black (including all the way to Eagle Bluffs)
8. Seymour
9. Fromme
10. St. Marks

BEST HIKES FOR AUTUMN COLOURS

1. de Pencier
2. Hollyburn
3. Dam–
   Thunderbird Ridge
4. Strachan
5. Middle Needle
6. Black
7. Paton
8. Suicide Bluffs
9. Seymour
10. Goat
11. Fromme
12. Windsor
13. St. Marks
14. Capilano

BEST PEAKS FOR CAMPING ON OR NEAR

1. Coliseum
2. Black
3. Magnesia Meadows,
   between Harvey and
   Brunswick, and near
   Magnesia
4. Capilano
5. Fromme
6. West Crown
7. Bishop
8. Goat Ridge
9. Goat
10. Deeks Lake

MOST ROMANTIC BAGGING ADVENTURES

Either because you and your loved one are likely to be the only people there, and/or because the sunrise or sunset or views may stir romance and other feelings of nature.

1. Capilano
2. West Crown
3. Goat Ridge
4. Coliseum
5. Black
6. Elsay
7. Bishop
8. Seymour

BEST GRANITE SLABBY PLAYGROUNDS

The Coast Mountains have some of the most extensive and most pleasing granite vistas on the planet, perfect for rock-hopping, trail-running, and climbing – but only in perfect dry weather.

1. Coliseum
2. Capilano
3. Burwell
4. Elsay
5. Pump
6. Seymour
7. Goat
8. Bishop
9. Hollyburn
10. Paton
11. Black
12. Cathedral

BEST WATERFALLS

1. Dickens via Indian Arm
   (Spray of Pearls Falls)
2. Deeks
   (Phi Alpha Falls)
3. Middle Needle
   (via Hydraulic Creek Trail)
4. Hanover–Brunswick
   (Hanover Lake Falls)
5. Enchantment Peak
   (falls off East Lion icefield)
6. Coliseum (via Norvan Falls)
7. Harvey
   (Alberta Falls via Harvey Trail
8. West Lion
   (via Binkert Trail: several falls en route,
   including Alberta Creek)
9. Crown N1
10. Capilano

BEST PEAK ROUTES FOR OLD-GROWTH AND GIANT TREES

Some of the largest trees that have ever lived on our planet grew in Lynn Valley. If early loggers' reports are to be believed, one of the tallest trees ever recorded stood at what is now the intersection of Mountain Highway and Argyll Road; it was chopped down in 1902. Despite the wholesale logging of the North Shore mountains, there still survive some massive trees visible en route to peaks. Ironically, they were usually spared because they were misshapen or knotted. Others perhaps owe their survival to a broken saw, a broken foot, or a hungry stomach calling it a day.

1. Echo (Perrault)–Zinc
2. Middle Needle (via Hydraulic Creek Trail)
3. Bishop (via Vicar Lakes Trail)
4. Coliseum (via Norvan Creek Trail)
5. St. Marks (via Yew Lake Old-growth Tree Loop)
6. Black (northwest slope)
7. Hollyburn (especially via Brother's Creek Trail and Old Strachan Trail)
8. Clementine – Dickens
9. South Lynn
10. Paton Peak
11. Unnecessary (via Unnecessary Trail)
12. Capilano
13. Elsay
14. Lions via Binkert Trail
15. Deeks–Windsor via Howe Sound Crest Trail

Blacktail deer, Bowen Island.

BEST MOUNTAIN BLUEBERRY/HUCKLEBERRY ABUNDANCE

Usually at their juiciest and fruitiest in early August. Beware: bears like them even more than you do.

1. Middle Needle
2. Capilano
3. Crown
4. Paton
5. Fromme
6. Hollyburn
7. Strachan
8. Bishop
9. Elsay
10. West Crown
11. Goat
12. Windsor
13. Gotha
14. Vicar
15. Cathedral
16. Brunswick

BEST MUSHROOM ABUNDANCE

Rainy Septembers and Octobers are the best months for mountain mushrooms.

1. Howe Sound Crest Trail between Deeks Lake and Brunswick Lake
2. Capilano
3. Deeks and Windsor
4. Fromme
5. Liddell (Gambier Island)
6. The Needles
7. Vicar
8. de Pencier Bluffs
9. Bishop (especially via Elsay Lake Trail)
10. Echo
11. Hollyburn

BEST HEATHER BURNS

Robbie Burns loved to hike and do other physical activities "Amang the blooming heather" and so do we.

1. Hollyburn
2. Goat Ridge
3. Capilano
4. Vicar
5. Rector
6. Curate
7. Deeks
8. Clementine
9. Dickens
10. St. Marks
11. Harvey

BEST PEAKS FOR WILDLIFE

We are constantly worried about the lack of wildlife that we see, even in the remotest corners of the North Shore. That said, we have had some wonderful encounters and sightings. We do not count the Grouse Mountain tourist grizzlies or wolves.

1. between Harvey and David (bears)
2. between Harvey and Brunswick (bears, mountain goats)
3. Capilano (deer, bears)
4. Coliseum (bears)
5. Fromme (deer)
6. Echo (mountain goats, bears)
7. Dickens (seals, deer, bears)
8. Bishop and Vicar Lake (bears)
9. Needles (owls, bears, mountain goats)
10. Gambier (salamanders)
11. Black (salamanders)
12. Seymour (salamanders)
13. Grouse (deer)

BEST MOUNTAINS FOR HISTORICAL ARTIFACTS

Despite the impermanence of wooden structures left by Indigenous and European forebears, and the relatively recent history of industry and settlement, the North Shore has a rich archaeological heritage for those who know where to find it.

1. Dickens: Indigenous petroglyphs on west side of Indian Arm, near Lion's Nose, while paddling up
2. Zinc–Echo: zinc mines and camps; many old camps on and near Hanes Valley Trail
3. Strachan: plane crash
4. Grouse (below the Cut): plane crash, old ski-lift pilings, old cabins
5. Grouse (Mackay Creek Trail): remnants of cabins and outhouses
6. Gambier: corduroy logging roads from Lost Lake to Gambier Lake
7. Seymour: logging roads and camps on lower slopes
8. Hollyburn: logging roads, Shields log dam, old incline railway on lower slopes
9. Lynn: old dam and cedar mill remnants on lower slopes.

BEST POST-BAG SWIMMING HOLES

No finer way to celebrate a hot summer adventure than an outdoor swim. As none are glacially fed, most are swimmable without too much freezing and/or male humiliation. The list below favours warm, shallow water and swims surrounded by gleaming white granite.

1. Vicar–Bishop: Vicar Lakes
2. Liddell–Gambier: Gambier Lake
3. Goat Ridge: Spouse and Tadpole tarns
4. Enchantment–Lions: unnamed cirque tarn northeast of Lions
5. Coliseum tarn
6. Capilano: Gordan Lake and tarns, Beth Lake
7. Burwell–Coliseum: Cornett Lakes
8. Brunswick–Hanover: Brunswick and Hanover lakes
9. Elsay: Elsay Lake if via Elsay Lake Trail
10. Windsor–Gotha: lake to east of and below Gotha Meadows
11. Deeks–Windsor: Deeks Lake
12. Seymour: Mystery Lake
13. Black: Cabin Lake

BEST POST-BAG FOOD AND DRINK

1. **The Snug on Bowen:** 445 Bowen Island Trunk Road. Coffee and salads.
2. **Rustique Bistro** (Bowen): 433 Bowen Island Trunk Road: French.
3. **Shika Provisions** (Bowen): 400 Bowen Island Trunk Road. Delicious Japanese takeout.
4. **Tuscany Pizza** (Bowen): 451 Bowen Island Trunk Rd.
5. **Artisan Eats** (Bowen): 539 Artisan Lane. Salads, sandwiches, beer, wine.
6. **Backcountry Brewing** (Squamish): 405–1201 Commercial Way. The newest, and the best food and beer on this list.

7. **The Crabapple Café** (Squamish): 41701 Government Rd., Brackendale.

8. **Howe Sound Brew Pub** (Squamish): 37801 Cleveland Ave., Squamish. Pub.

9. **Shady Tree** (Squamish)**:** 40456 Government Rd., Garibaldi Highlands. Pub.

10. **Mountain Woman** (Capilano, Deeks Peak, HSCT): off Hwy. 99 at Britannia Beach. Burgers and fish & chips. No beer.

11. **Lions Bay General Store and Café** (HSCT): 350 Centre Road, Lions Bay. No beer.

12. **Crazy Raven** (Cypress Bowl): Cypress Mountain Lodge, Cypress Bowl. Shorter hours in summer.

13. **Altitudes Bistro** (Grouse): Grouse Mountain Chalet.

14. **Capilano Pizza** (Grouse): 4370 Capilano Road. Pizza. No beer.

15. **The Observatory** (Grouse). Finer dining at Grouse Mountain Chalet.

16. **Sushi Mori** (Grouse): 4740 Capilano Rd., North Vancouver. Sushi.

17. **Black Bear Pub** (Lynn Valley peaks): 1177 Lynn Valley Rd., North Vancouver. Pub.

18. **End of the Line General Store** (Lynn Valley peaks): Lynn Valley Rd. & Dempsey, North Vancouver. Convenience store. Coffee and muffins. No beer.

19. **Queen's Cross Pub** (Lynn Valley peaks): 2989 Lonsdale Ave., North Vancouver. Pub.

20. **Bean around the World** (Seymour): Parkgate Mall, 1151 Mount Seymour Road, North Vancouver. Amazing coffee and muffins. No beer.

21. **Raven Pub** (Seymour): 1052 Deep Cove Road, North Vancouver. Pub. Lots of beer and pizza.

BEST PEAKBAGGING SONGS

1. Boney M: Brown Girl in the Ring

2. Pink Floyd: Fearless

3. Bob Dylan: A Hard Rain's A-Gonna Fall

4. Bob Dylan: Series of Dreams

5. Bob Dylan: Percy's Song

6. Kate Bush: Running Up that Hill

7. Tangerine Kitty: Dumb Ways to Die

8. Robbie Burns: Yon Wild Mossy Mountains

9. The Corries and others: Wild Mountain Thyme

10. William Blake / Sir Hubert Parry: Jerusalem

11. Moby: Extreme Ways

12. First Aid Kit: Lion's Roar

13. Tom Waits: We're All Mad Here

14. Moby: God Moving Over the Face of Waters

15. Sigur Ros: Staralfur

16. Of Monsters and Men: Mountain Sound

17. The Sound of Music: Climb Ev'ry Mountain

18. Bruce Cockburn: Wondering Where the Lions Are

19. Neutral Milk Hotel: In The Aeroplane Over the Sea

20. Neutral Milk Hotel: Communist Daughter

21. David Bowie or Nina Simone: Wild Is the Wind

22. William Shakespeare: The Wind and the Rain

BEST PEAKBAGGING POEMS

1. Earle Birney: David
2. Samuel Taylor Coleridge: Hymn before Sun-rise, in the Vale of Chamouni
3. William Wordsworth: Lines Composed a Few Miles above Tintern Abbey
4. Robbie Burns: Song Composed in August/Now Westlin Winds
5. Robbie Burns: Yon Wild Mossy Mountains
6. Robbie Burns: My Heart's in the Highlands
7. Samuel Taylor Coleridge: Frost at Midnight
8. William Blake: Jerusalem
9. Emily Dickinson: Ah, Teneriffe!
10. Marianne Moore: An Octopus
11. Gary Snyder: Beneath My Hand and Eye the Distant Hills, Your Body
12. Li Bai: Green Mountain
13. George Sterling: Night on the Mountain
14. Carolyn Crosby Wilson: Attainment
15. William Wordsworth: Descriptive Sketches Taken during a Pedestrian Tour among the Alps
16. George Sterling: From the Mountain
17. Liu Hong-ping: Geladandong Mountain
18. Lew Sarett: The Granite Mountain
19. Alcman: The Mountain Summits Sleep
20. Marjorie Allen Seiffert: Mountain Trails

The round lake in the lower right corner lies in the bottom of a cirque. Note the bowl-shaped cliffs above it.

APPENDIX 2:
HIKING AND CLIMBING TERMINOLOGY

GENERAL GLOSSARY

alpine start: Starting a climb very early in the morning so as to use as much daylight as possible.

alpine zone, alpine tundra: Terrain above the treeline. Characterized by stunted trees (krumholz) and clear lakes.

arête: A narrow ridge. Usually found on a ridge between two glacier-carved valleys.

bagging or peakbagging: The action of climbing mountains, usually as part of a list of peaks.

belay: To lower oneself down a cliff or slope on a rope.

bench: A flat area in steep terrain.

bivy (or bivvy): Abbreviation of the French "bivouac." Camping overnight with no tent, usually on a rock ledge.

bivy-bag: A sac or light article of clothing offering protection in an emergency

bushwhack: To hike where there is no trail. An essential skill in the North Shore mountains.

buttress: A column of rock that juts out from a mountain.

cairn: A pile of stones placed to mark a summit or a trail. A large one can be found on Elsay.

chimney: A near-vertical gully with walls close enough to climb. One can be found on Hanover.

cirque: A depression in the mountains carved by a glacier. These sometimes contain lakes. Examples are Kennedy Lake, Elsay Lake, Burwell Lake, and Palisades Lake.

cirque glacier: A glacier in a cirque.

Class 5 terrain: Technical climbing terrain. Rope required by most climbers.

col: The low point on the ridge between two peaks. See also **saddle**.

cornice: Snow hanging over the edge of a ridge. Dangerous.

couloir: A narrow gully. Often surrounded by cliff walls. From the French word for passage or corridor.

crampons: Metal spikes that attach to one's boot. Increases grip on snowy and icy sections. Not needed on most of these North Shore mountains in the summer.

crevasse: A crack in a glacier, usually with almost-vertical walls.

cross-ditch: A ditch carrying water from one side of a road or trail to the other.

crux: The hardest part of a hike or climb.

culvert: A pipe underneath a road or trail carrying water across without inconveniencing traffic.

cutblock: A clear-cut patch of forest.

drumlin: A ridge or hill formed from rock left by retreating glaciers. From the Gaelic word for ridge.

erratic or glacial erratic: A large anomalous rock carried and deposited by a glacier. Examples are found on the Lynn Peak trail and on the south summit of Strachan.

exposure: An area where a fall will cause death or serious injury.

false summit: A point on a ridge that appears from lower down to be the summit but is not.

gendarme: A rock tower or pinnacle.

glacier window: The hole at the bottom of a glacier where meltwater drains out.

glissade: Sliding down a steep slope of snow.

krumholz (also **krummholz**): Stunted and windswept trees found in the alpine. From the German "twisted wood." Many on Gotha and Cathedral.

moraine, ground: The rocky debris extending out from the terminus of a glacier.

moraine, lateral: A ridge of rock formed at the side of a glacier.

moraine, medial: A ridge of debris in the middle of a glacier. Also formed when two glaciers come together or as a glacier moves around a central peak.

moraine, terminal: A ridge of debris formed at the end of a glacier.

post-holing: Stepping on seemingly safe snow, only to have your foot sink.

saddle: Like a col (which see above), but larger; the low point between two peaks.

scramble: A type of climbing somewhere between hiking and graded rock climbing.

scree: Small broken loose rock. Usually found at the base of a cliff. Also a slope covered in scree. Scree is smaller than talus.

snow bridge: a bridge of snow with no structural foundation underneath. Usually not fatal, but may drop you into a freezing creek, or armpit-deep in snow.

talus: Like scree, but larger and often less loose.

tarn: A small alpine lake.

technical climbing: Climbing requiring rope and some sort of protection (as opposed to scrambling).

traverse: To proceed in a horizontal direction along a route.

veggie belay: To climb or descend a slope holding onto shrubs, trees, vines, and foliage of varying strength and solidity. Not recommended.

Yosemite Decimal System: A system used to rate the difficulty of hikes, scrambles, and climbs, used primarily in North America. 1 = hiking; 2 = scrambling; 3 = some use of hands but no ropes required; 4 = most parties will rope together or use belay stations; 5 and above = rock climbing part of the scale.

2WD: Two-wheel drive

4WD: Four-wheel drive.

BAGGING GLOSSARY

Can generally be used as nouns or verbs. Thanks to Craig Moore for some of these silly terms.

bag: To climb a peak.

waterbag: An ascent up a peak from sea level to the summit. Can only brag of one peak per sea level ascent, e.g., dip toe in ocean at Ambleside Beach; run up Capilano Trails, Nancy Greene Way, and Grouse Grind; summit Grouse, Goat, and Crown = one waterbag, not three.

sandbag: Excessively downplaying one's level of fatigue or skills in order to fool one's bagmates.

speedbag: Fastest known ascent/descent.

friendly bag: Two or more of you did it.

free bag: Local equivalent of "naked munroing."

fun bags: Topless peakbagging.

true bag: Climb at least halfway and back under your own steam, nothing motorized near the top.

ultra bag: Bag at least one peak during a run longer than a marathon.

seasonal bag: A series of bags in one season of the year such as winter.

snowbag: A winter climb.

pure bag: A single peak, starting from sea level to the peak and back.

round bag: Continuous unsupported completion of all peaks on foot. There is room for interpretation here such as the method of traversing between mountain ranges.

pure round bag: (See pure bag, above.)

doggy bag: Accompanied by your canine friend.

laundry bag: A mud-soaked adventure.

garbage bag: Not worth doing.

trash bag: Saint-like toting out of garbage left behind by scumbag hikers.

scumbag (a.k.a. d*bag): A hiker littering, playing music, or not cleaning up after their dog.

bag man/bag lady: Gender-specific baggers.

bag bomb: A climb marred by your companion's gastric troubles.

unibag: To climb one peak on an adventure.

duobag: To climb two peaks on an adventure.

tribag: To climb three peaks on an adventure.

quadbag: To climb four peaks on an adventure.

quintbag: To climb five peaks on an adventure.

sextibag: To climb six peaks on an adventure.

septibag: To climb seven peaks on an adventure.

octobag: To climb eight peaks on an adventure.

nonobag: To climb nine peaks on an adventure.

decibag: To climb ten peaks on an adventure.

unodecibag: To climb eleven peaks on an adventure.

duodecibag: To climb twelve peaks on an adventure.

This chapter was prepared with the substantial assistance of Paul Geddes (ACC) and Glenn Woodsworth (BCMC), to whom the authors express their gratitude.

Since the early 1900s, both the Alpine Club of Canada (ACC) and the British Columbia Mountaineering Club (BCMC) have been dedicated to mountain climbing and other outdoor recreation in the Vancouver area. The mountains north of Vancouver had been a destination for adventurers since the city's founding. There was no real organized mountain climbing or systematic exploration of the North Shore peaks, however, until these clubs formed and began to attract new members. Many famous British Columbian mountaineers, such as Don Munday, Phyllis Munday, James John Trorey, Tom Fyles, Neal Carter, Beverley Cochrane Cayley, Frank Smith, and later John Clarke were active in both the BCMC and the ACC.

The two clubs grew as the peaks of the North Shore became easier to access. Members also climbed loftier and more-distant peaks. Mt. Waddington, the highest peak in British Columbia, was discovered by Don and Phyllis Munday, members of both the BCMC and ACC, who led many early attempts to climb it, starting in 1926.

BC MOUNTAINEERING CLUB

On October 28, 1907, the BCMC held its first meeting at the Vancouver Tourist office on Granville at Dunsmuir. The organization was first called the Vancouver Mountaineering Club, and renamed the BC Mountaineering Club on March 29, 1909. Joseph Charles "Pa" Bishop was the first president with vice-presidents Miss L. Laverock and George Edwards. George Jarrett was the secretary, Atwell King the treasurer. Other charter members were James Porter, Miss Mitchell, Arthur Tinniswood Dalton, W. Nicholson-Lailey, Roland Manfred "Fred" Mills, A.G. Ross, H.B. Rowe, R.S. Sherman, Wilfred Henry Tassell, James John Trorey, and W.T. Willett. Trips led by the BCMC climbed many iconic Vancouver mountains for the first time, such as Mt. Seymour (1908) and the Camel (also 1908). The club also ascended many great peaks in the Garibaldi area (Black Tusk was first climbed in 1912 by a party led by Billy Gray) and northern Washington State.

From its start, the BCMC was a very democratic society. In his 1957 article "Early Days of the BCMC," Fred Mills noted that the BCMC mixed a wide variety of professions and all levels of income from lawyers, land surveyors, bankers to nurses, stenographers, a cigar maker, a piano tuner, and real estate men, "all gentlemen and gentlewomen." There were many women members, and the charter members elected a woman as vice-president. Two women have served as president. As evident from early club photographs, climbers often married each other; the club was nicknamed the "Matrimonial Club" and alpinist newlyweds often honeymooned on local peaks.

The early journals of the BCMC, chronicling the regularly scheduled mountaineering trips, are an important source of information about the first ascents of many of the local peaks and a vivid perspective on early mountaineering in British Columbia. The 1913 *Northern*

Cordilleran provides a useful snapshot of mountaineering at the time. In March 1923 the club started a monthly newsletter, the *BC Mountaineer*, announcing and recounting club trips, and discussing nature, geology, and climbing tales; the journal has continued, in various forms, to this day.

In 1906–07, hikers who would later form the BCMC constructed the "Red Shack" on the lower slopes of Grouse Mountain. It served as the staging grounds for club forays up the Grouse Mountain peaks. In his *Memoirs*, Fred Mills wrote about the first cabin:

> In the late summer of 1906 we decided to continue our exploring through the coming fall and winter, also to make a base for hunting the large amount of big game which we had seen during our trips. For this purpose a cabin was built. This cabin was located in the midst of a fine stand of primeval forest (since logged off), to the right of the Grouse Mountain trail, elevation about 2,500 feet. We named it "The Red Shack," and from this base all of our hunting and other trips to Grouse, Dome, Dam, Goat and Crown Mountains were made during a period of some four years. What tales this cabin could have told, what feasts it saw. W.J. Grey and Tommy Lyttleton (of Littleton Bros. Jewellers), ran a loose tongue up and down the scale of a mouth organ. Fred Perry, Dave Connor, Pa Bishop and banker A.G. Ross made a heart throbbing quartet and Charles Chapman (of Chapman and Warwick), of all things recited from Shakespeare. As for my share, the best I could do was blow the head off a skunk that had stolen in under our stove. This skunk never knew what hit him and had no time to let loose. The hunting was mostly left to me anyway, except the mouse catching, which was Fred Perry's sideline, along with the cooking.

The Red Shack was soon replaced with a larger cabin in 1910, a few hundred yards upslope and to the west, with separate bunking quarters for men and women. Another clubhouse was built in 1926. In addition to trip-planning and rest, these cabins hosted annual Christmas and New Year's dinners, including roast turkey, oyster soup, mince pie, cigars, and whisky. Two cabins were built on Mt. Seymour, in 1933 and 1940. Further cabins were built in the Lucky Four Group (Chilliwack Valley), near Singing Pass and Wedgemount Lake (Garibaldi Park), at Mountain Lake (above Britannia Beach), near Tellot Glacier (Mt. Waddington area), and the North Creek Valley.

Today the BCMC has approximately 900 members. The club executive and membership continue to do much good work in training aspiring climbers and participating in access and conservation issues.

Another important and venerable organization promoting mountaineering and exploration in British Columbia is the Alpine Club of Canada (ACC), established in 1906 in Winnipeg. Several Vancouver climbers travelled to Winnipeg for the original meetings and were therefore among its Charter Members. As of 2016 the ACC is divided into 22 local sections from coast to coast and manages a system of 30 mountain huts throughout British Columbia and Alberta. The national ACC currently has over 10,000 members and the Vancouver section membership is approximately 1000 members. Other sections in BC include Whistler, Vancouver Island, Okanagan and Prince George. There is also a section in Whitehorse, Yukon and members south of the border.

In 1910 the Vancouver section was the first to form and soon other sections started to appear. A.L. Kendall was the first chairperson of the Vancouver section, and C.H. Gillis volunteered as secretary. An annual banquet celebrating the anniversary of the founding of the ACC is held in downtown Vancouver. It was customary for the president of the BCMC to attend.

The club led the first ski exploration of the Seymour area, sparking a wave of outdoor enthusiasts skiing, hiking, and building cabins. The club has erected and maintained several cabins throughout its history, including those at Seymour (1931), Whistler, Meslilloet, Burwell Lake, and three cabins in the Tantalus Range: the Tantalus Hut at Lake Lovely Water (1961), the F.J. Green Shelter (Red Tit Hut 1968–2008), and the Jim Haberl Hut on the Serratus–Dione col (2006). The Whistler Section operates the Wendy Thompson Hut north of Pemberton.

The activities of many ACC members focused on trips farther afield than the local mountains, such as to the Canadian Rockies and the Selkirks. The Alpine Club of Canada has since its founding 1906, with its first camp in Yoho Pass, held a General Mountaineering Camp (GMC) each summer. The GMC was the focal point of many Vancouver section members in the early years of the club. Local exploration was also important to many members with camps often held in the Garibaldi area. In the 1920s and '30s trips by the section included peaks in the Chilliwack Valley and the Lillooet Icecap. Exploration on skis in the 1950s and '60s continued with Howard Rode, Fips Broda, Paddy Sherman, and Scipio Merler into the Homathko and Mount Monarch areas.

In 1967, to celebrate Canada's Centennial the Yukon Alpine Centennial Expedition (YACE) was held in the St. Elias Mountains in Yukon. Well-known Vancouver section member Eric Brooks was on the national organizing committee. Norman Pursell, Gertrude Smith, Fips Broda, Paddy Sherman, and Ralph Hutchinson were climbing leaders of various Centennial Range peaks.

Starting in 1927 the Vancouver section issued a monthly newsletter, *Avalanche Echoes* (now in electronic format). Its members contributed significantly to the accurate survey of parts of the Coast Mountains, and significant exploits are recorded in the *Canadian Alpine Journal*, published annually since 1907. Other important writing by ACC Vancouver section members included the *Waddington Guide*, by Don Serl (2003), and Bruce Fairley's *Canadian Mountaineering Anthology* (1994), a selected history of climbing from the Coast Mountains to the Canadian Rockies going back to 1888. Paddy Sherman was known for his mountain writing, including *Cloud Walkers* (1965). In that book Paddy describes the joint ACC/BCMC (second) ascent of Mount Fairweather in honour of British Columbia's centennial in 1958. Perhaps the ACC's best-known chronicler is Chic Scott: his *Pushing the Limits* (RMB, 2000) is truly the story of Canadian mountaineering and includes a chapter on the Coast Mountains.

The Vancouver section's first botanist, Mrs. Julia Henshaw, wrote a thorough guide to the wildflowers of Canada's mountains titled *Mountain Wild Flowers in Canada*, first published in 1906. The 1980 publication *In The Western Mountains*, compiled and edited by Susan Leslie, contains two chapters dedicated to early mountaineering in the British Columbia Coast Mountains.

JOINT ACTIVITIES BY BCMC AND ACC

ACCESS AND CONSERVATION

One mission shared by both clubs is to promote outdoor recreation while protecting wilderness. This is made possible through an affiliation with the Federation of Mountain Clubs of BC. Areas of wilderness preserved in part through the efforts of the BCMC/ACC include the campaign to preserve the Garibaldi area as a provincial park, a goal it achieved in 1926. Neal Carter's two maps to the park are in the Vancouver section's archives. Don Munday wrote a guide in 1922 entitled *Mt. Garibaldi Park: Vancouver's Alpine Playground*.

In July 1927 honorary BCMC president James Porter proposed a provincial park made up of the slopes of Hollyburn Ridge, Hollyburn Peak, Black Mountain, and Mt. Strachan, a goal achieved in 1944 and 1975. More recently the ACC has been involved in the government planning process to protect areas of the Sea-to-Sky, Tantalus Range, Upper Elaho, Chilko Lake in Tsylos Provincial Park, and South Chilcotin Provincial Park.

The BCMC has also built and repaired many trails across the North Shore mountains, including the eponymous BCMC Trail and Binkert Trail to The Lions. Members of the ACC monitor trails in Cypress Provincial Park.

Both the BCMC (bcmc.ca) and ACC Vancouver section (accvancouver.ca) are still very active in organizing trips to North Shore mountains as well as providing outdoor education and training. Both welcome visitors to their meetings and trips to assist in deciding whether to join (some trips are joint). Do consider joining these clubs and exploring these peaks in the comfort of experienced and like-minded individuals: it is safer and more enriching. Those interested in hiking only might also consider the North Shore Hikers, another well-organized club that holds monthly meetings.

SEARCH AND RESCUE

The first search-and-rescue team on the North Shore mountains – called the B.C. Safety Climbers Association – was established through the joint efforts of the ACC and the BCMC. The committee's first meeting was held on February 2, 1929. Don Munday and H.J. Graves represented the ACC and F.W. Johnson and L.G. Colman the BCMC.

NATURAL HISTORY

A subgroup of the BCMC and ACC dedicated to natural history became the Vancouver Natural History Society in 1918. That club has contributed greatly to the knowledge of the geology, flora, and fauna of the province.

SPEARHEAD HUTS

The exciting news received early in 2016 was the signing of an agreement with BC Parks to allow the construction of three huts along the Spearhead Traverse between Blackcomb and Whistler in Garibaldi Provincial Park. The success of this project is largely due to the efforts of both the ACC and BCMC.

ARCHIVES

The main archives of both clubs reside at the North Vancouver Museum and Archives. Other collections on Coast Mountain climbing can be found in the ACC archive at the Whyte Museum in Banff, the Vancouver Archives, and the British Columbia Archives in Victoria. Full online copies of the *Canadian Alpine Journal* can now be found at library.alpineclubofcanada.ca.

BCMC PRESIDENTS

Joseph Charles Bishop	1907–1910**
Edward Wesley Bridgman	1910–1912
William J. "Billy" Gray	1912–1914**
Charles "Chappy" Chapman	1914–1919**
Charles Heaney	1919–1922**
Les Ford	1922–1924
Frank Johnson	1924–1932
Les Ford	1932–1933
Herbert Christie	1933–1934
Roy Howard	1934–1935
F.W. Dobson	1935–1937
Elliott Henderson	1937–1939**
W. Williams	1939–1942
E. Smith	1942–1944
Clare Willis	1944–1946
J. Irving	1946–1948
George Rose	1948–1950
John Booth	1950–1952
Jim Addie	1952–1954
Rod A. Pilkington	1954–1956**
Fred H. Smith	1956–1958
Roy Mason	1958–1960
Dick Chambers	1960–1962
Frank Dawe	1962–1963
Don MacLaurin	1963–1964
John Harris	1964–1965
Martin Kafer	1965–1967
Jim Woodfield	1967–1968
Brendan Moss	1968–1970
Dave Boyd	1970–1972
Jack Bachrich	1972–1973
Esther Kafer	1973–1975
Paul Starr	1975–1976

Jim Craig	1976–1977
Glenn Woodsworth	1977–1980
Rick Sheppard	1980–1982
Mark Force	1982–1983
Theo Mosterman	1983–1985
Brian Gavin	1985–1989
Paul Kubik	1989–1992
Andrew Wilkinson	1992–1994
Anders Ourom	1994–1998
David Hughes	1998–2002
Kit Griffin	2002–2005
David Hughes	2005–2007
Todd Ponzini	2007–2009
David Scanlon	2009–2011
Alena Dzukova	2011–2012
Francis St. Pierre	2012–2015
David Scanlon	2015–2017
Wilson Edgar	2017–

BCMC HONORARY PRESIDENTS

Joseph Charles Bishop**
James Porter**
Les Ford
Charles Chapman   (1884–1960)**
Paul Binkert**
Esther & Martin Kafer

** BCMC presidents and honorary presidents who have had mountains or other features officially named for them.

ACC AWARDS TO VANCOUVER SECTION MEMBERS

The Alpine Club of Canada is proud to recognize members and others who have made valuable contributions to the club. The following have contributed greatly to the Vancouver section.

A.O. WHEELER LEGACY AWARD (1995)

"For outstanding and varied contributions to the Alpine Club of Canada over many years"

1995	F.C. Bell
1995	Eric Brooks
1995	Phyllis Munday
2006	David Toole

HONORARY MEMBERSHIP (1906)

"For contributions in Canadian mountaineering"

1931	Julia Henshaw
1938	Phyllis Munday
1969	Eric Brooks
1974	Neal Carter
1983	Fred Beckey
1987	Dick Culbert
1987	John Clarke
2006	John Wheeler
2009	Don Serl
2011	Michael Feller

PRESIDENT'S AWARD (1987)

"Presented to individuals deserving recognition for extraordinary service towards the activities of the ACC"

1998	Brad Harrison

SILVER ROPE AWARD FOR LEADERSHIP (1933)

"A mountaineering and ski mountaineering award for excellence in leadership and technical ability"

1934	W.W. Foster
1934	D.N. McTravis
1934	W. Don Munday
1937	Eric Brooks
1938	Tom Fyles
1948	Phyllis Munday
1961	Scipio Merler
1970	Phil Dowling
1971	Gertrude Smith
1978	Klaus Haring
1978	Murray Foubister
2001	Don Serl
2001	Mike Thompson
2002	Howard Rode
2011	Fips Broda
2013	Bruce Fairley
2014	Paul Geddes

DISTINGUISHED SERVICE AWARD (1970)

"An award for distinguished service to the club in matters other than mountaineering"

1970	Phyllis Munday
1971	Elizabeth Walker
1973	Phil Dowling
1977	Moira Irvine
1978	John Wheeler

1981	Andrew Gruft
1985	Fips Broda
1985	Norman Pursell
1985	Gertrude Smith
1987	Scipio Merler
1988	Doug Herchmer
1990	Bruce Fairley
1991	Brad Harrison
1994	Doug Fox
2001	Irene Goldstone
2001	Jay MacArthur
2001	Ron Royston
2001	David Toole
2002	Helen Habgood
2003	Paul Geddes
2003	Liz Scremin
2003	Manrico Scremin
2004	Mary Rode
2005	Fern Hietkamp
2007	Rob Brusse
2009	Tony Knight

ERIC BROOKS LEADER AWARD (2000)

"A mountaineering and ski mountaineering award for strong commitment to learning and applying technical and leader skills"

2003	Peter Woodsworth
2005	Margaret Hanson
2009	Dustin Hines

DON FOREST SERVICE AWARD (2000)

"An award for significant service to the ACC"

2005	Colin Boyd
2002	Tami Knight
2005	Ian Bruce
2005	Peter Taylor
2009	Martin Naroznik
2009	Richard Keltie

Author David Crerar thought of the Bagger Challenge while running a 95-mile race in Scotland in 2009, after having bagged a few Munros around Loch Tay, the home of his ancestors. The event took off with a furious four-way race for the victor of the first Munro Quaich, or whisky-cup, with many other participants discovering the joys of local mountains. The first Munro quaich, ordered from a Scottish supplier, was run over by a Royal Mail or Canada Post truck, arriving quite squashed: the squashed quaich became the "Twisted Quaich," awarded for spirit, enthusiasm, getting others involved and/or insanity in the field. The first-place finisher for the gender opposite the winner receives the Pippa Quaich, named after Philippa Crerar, Crerar's eldest daughter (this was usually awarded to the first-place female finisher, until 2014, when Doris Leong won first overall and Avery Gottfried became the first male Pippa Quaich winner). The youth division quaich is named the Harry Quaich, after Crerar's eldest son. The canine division winner receives an engraved silver doggy bowl, named the Tundra Quaich, after Ken Legg's gentle, loyal, sturdy husky–Alsatian cross, who was the first canine compleatist. As of 2017 about 425 people had joined in this fun celebration of adventure, athleticism, and nature.

QUAICHES

Munro Quaich for Overall Bagger Champion
Pippa Quaich for Bagger Champion of gender opposite to the overall Bagger Champion
Harry Quaich for Bagger Champion younger than 16
Tundra Quaich for canine-division Bagger Champion
Twisted Quaich for spirit, enthusiasm, getting others involved, and/or insanity

2017 BAGGER CHAMPIONS
Munro Quaich: Steve White: 69 peaks
Pippa Quaich: Katie Longworth: 37 peaks
Harry Quaich: Darien Day: 10 peaks
Tundra Quaich: Bella, Queen of the Mountain!: 30 peaks
Twisted Quaich: Mike Wardas

2016 BAGGER CHAMPIONS
Munro Quaich: Laurent Schoenacker: 67 peaks
Pippa Quaich: Karen Hadley: 67 peaks
Harry Quaich: Harry Crerar: 14 peaks
Tundra Quaich: Bella the Great: 36 peaks
Twisted Quaich: River Jones

2015 BAGGER CHAMPIONS
Munro Quaich: Michael Kay: 64 peaks
Pippa Quaich: Christine Moric: 64 peaks
Harry Quaich: Harry Crerar: 19 peaks
Tundra Quaich: The Mighty Bella: 35 peaks
Twisted Quaich: Bill Maurer

2014 BAGGER CHAMPIONS
Munro Quaich: Doris Leong: 60 peaks
Pippa Quaich: Avery Gottfried: 60 peaks
Harry Quaich: Harry Crerar: 10 peaks
Tundra Quaich: Nanik: 24 peaks
Twisted Quaich: Mike Kuiack

2013 BAGGER CHAMPIONS
Munro Quaich: Bill Maurer: 51 peaks
Pippa Quaich: Carolyn King: 31 peaks
Harry Quaich: Harry Crerar: 9 peaks
Tundra Quaich: Stetson the Mountain Hound: 7 peaks
Twisted Quaich: Dave Berg

2012 BAGGER CHAMPIONS
Munro Quaich: Bill Maurer: 57 peaks
Pippa Quaich: Carolyn King: 21 peaks
Harry Quaich: Harry Crerar: 15 peaks
Tundra Quaich: Tundra the Ultra Dog: 18 peaks
Twisted Quaich: Team Dagg and Team Healey-Thorpe

2011 BAGGER CHAMPIONS
Munro Quaich: Bill Maurer: 50 peaks
Pippa Quaich: Carolyn King: 33 peaks
Harry Quaich: Harry Crerar: 10 peaks
Tundra Quaich: Tundra the Ultra Dog: 22 peaks
Twisted Quaich: Ken Legg

2010 BAGGER CHAMPIONS
Munro Quaich: Ean Jackson: 48 peaks
Pippa Quaich: Carolyn King: 24 peaks
Harry Quaich: Harry Crerar: 10 peaks
Tundra Quaich: Tundra the Ultra Dog: 16 peaks
Twisted Quaich: Neil Ambrose and Craig Moore

Munro Quaich: Ken Legg: 42 peaks
Pippa Quaich: Carolyn King: 16 peaks
Harry Quaich: Harry Crerar: 5 peaks
Tundra Quaich: Tundra the Ultra Dog: 32 peaks
Twisted Quaich: Ean Jackson

COMPLEATISTS: RECIPIENTS OF THE BAGGER CHALLENGE BEARS

Those who have compleated (the traditional spelling of the term for climbing all peaks in an area or range) all of the peaks in the Bagger Challenge have received a limited-edition bear statuette. Those marked with "!!" astonishingly climbed all of the peaks in a single season.

Ken Legg	2010
David Crerar	2011
Ean Jackson	2012
Bill Maurer	2013 !!
Dave Berg	2013
Neil Ambrose	2013
Carolyn King	2014
Doris Leong	2014 !!
Avery Gottfried	2014 !!
Christine Moric	2015 !!
Craig Moore	2015
Michael Kay	2015 !!
Laurent Schoenacker	2016 !!
Karen Hadley	2016 !!
Steve White	2016 !!
Ran Katzman	2017

Anvil Island and Leading Peak, with McNabb Lions on Sunshine Coast behind.

APPENDIX 5:
TOUR DE HOWE SOUND

Conceived in 2009 by Ken Legg, this annual invitation-only adventure sails waters, bags peaks, drinks whisky, and eats steak. It is modelled on the UK Three Peaks Yacht Race (founded 1977): five-person teams (three sailors and two runners), sail from Barmouth on the coast of Wales to Caernarfon, where the runners run up Mt. Snowdon and back; then sail to Whitehaven on the northwest coast of England, where the runners cycle to the foot of Scafell Pike and then run to the top and back; and finally they sail to Fort William in Scotland, where the runners climb Ben Nevis and return to the yacht. The race was conceived of by legendary mountaineer and sail explorer Major Harold William "Bill" Tilman, CBE, DSO, MC (February 14, 1898–1977), and founded by his doctor after Tilman's death at sea. A similar race, the Scottish Islands Peaks Race (founded 1983), sends teams of combined fell runners and sailors from Oban to the Scottish islands and peaks of Mull (Ben More), Jura (The Paps), Arran (Goat Fell), and then to Troon. The Howe Sound version starts at Bowen Island, with a run up Gardner and a protein- and carbohydrate-loading meal at Snug Cove. Then to Keats, with a run up the colossal 200-m Lookout Peak, usually without oxygen. Then to Gambier and up Killam and/or Liddell, depending on the energy, enthusiasm, and alcohol content of the group. Beer may be pilfered from cabins owned by the participants. Then to Anvil Island and up Leading Peak. There may be dances with dolphins. Joy is guaranteed.

Found a whisky cache!

APPENDIX 6:
WHISKY BAGGING

There is whisky in the hills. The caching and stashing of invigorating beverages in the mountains has long been a tradition, partly for survival, partly for conviviality. And not just conviviality for the drink-stashing climber: all later-comer climbers raise a bottle to the climbers who came before, and to those who will come after, to celebrate the good fortune to be alive with the beauty of the peaks. And the choice of whisky as beverage, quaffed among our blooming heather, salutes Sir Hugh Munro, the progenitor of peakbagging.

The first known concentrated effort to cache whisky on the local peaks was by brothers Al and Dave Martin, along Howe Sound Crest Trail. Authors David and Harry Crerar added a few more in the area in 2015. Others have followed.

Known whisky caches on or near peaks, with the kind of whisky at time of publication:
- Leading: Glenlivet (Speyside)
- Deeks: Glendullan (Speyside)
- Windsor: Finlarig (Islay)
- Gotha: Glencadam (Angus)
- Hat: Robbie Burns (Arran)
- Wettin: McLennands (Highland)
- Brunswick Mountain: Glenlivet (Speyside)
- Brunswick Lake: Ardbeg (Islay), near shelter
- Magnesia Meadows: Johnnie Walker Gold, near shelter
- Harvey: (unknown distillery) five minutes south of peak, on Lions Bay Trail
- James: Auchentoshan (Lowland)
- Enchantment: Glenlivet (Speyside)
- Lions: Highland Park (Orkney), near small tarn between the East and West Lions.
- St. Marks: Auchentoshan (Lowland)
- Fromme: Glenfiddich (Speyside)
- Forks: The Macallan (Highland)
- Echo: Glenlivet (Speyside)
- North Needle: Canadian Club
- Cathedral: (unknown distillery)

Enjoy finding and modestly sampling the water of life and leave a few notes of your visit (most bottles are stored with logbooks). If you wish, please refill or replace a bottle (preferably single malt), and place new stashes for others to find.

Please keep the specific locations secret, or share them very discreetly with your friends. They are not obvious, but relatively easy to find. If you feel as if your life is in danger or if you have lost the peak or other natural feature referenced, you have gone too far.

We encourage all to be environmentally responsible in hunting for these treasures, and in caching more.

Sláinte!

APPENDIX 7:
GEOCACHING

Geocaching involves the hunting of caches via GPS coordinates and clues. A geocache usually consists of a watertight container (such as Tupperware, a pipe, or an ammunition box) with a logbook and pencil for people to record their finds. Some caches have trinkets and toys: a person finding the cache can take a treat and leave a treat for the next geocacher. The first documented placement of a GPS-located cache took place on May 3, 2000, by Dave Ulmer of Beavercreek, Oregon.

While folks of all ages will have enormous fun with geocaching, this giant easter-egg hunt appeals especially to children, and provides a great incentive and introduction to hiking and adventuring to younger baggers.

There are several websites listing geocaches, as well as several excellent apps for your smartphone. The most popular site is geocaching.com. The geocaching.com app allows you to track your visited caches.

Trackables are small objects, such as dog tags, with a code on them. Geocaching.com users can monitor the trackable as it travels around the world. Trackables can be purchased at geocaching.com.

All of the front-row North Shore peaks have multiple caches on them. Bill Dagg gets credit for having placed many new caches in the past few years, including at Lynn, Little Goat, Goat, Goat Ridge, Suicide Bluffs, de Pencier, and Dam. Register geocaches at geocaching.com.

When hunting for or placing geocaches, take great care not to disturb the natural environment, either through tromping across moss or undergrowth, or lifting up foliage. Take care in hunting for geocaches on peaks: around the globe, there have been several deaths and injuries of frenetic geocachers whose attention was distracted from cliffs, traffic, etc. by the hunt at hand.

Several geocaches on or near peaks are listed below, although this is by no means a complete list and we have not visited every cache on the list. Keep in mind that old caches may be destroyed by animals, the weather, and humans, and new ones are occasionally added. The caches are located on or very near the summit unless otherwise noted.

- (GAR) Love Is Like a Rock: N49.22348 W123.23839
  - Located near the Gardner viewpoint, not the true Gardner peak.
- (CAP) Capilano Mountain Summit: N49.33390 W123.08146
- (BRU) Brunswick Mountain Summit: N49.29242 W123.11839
- (LIO) The West Lion Cache: N49.27472 W123.11195
  - Located on the summit of West Lion
- (STR) Mt. Strachan North Peak: N49.24789 W123.11618
- (GRO) Turbine Stump: N49.23209 W123.04526
  - Hidden near the base of the Eye of the Wind turbine
- (LIL) Peak Bagger: Little Goat: N49.23892 W123.04998
- (GOA) Goat Mountain: N49.24223 W123.04741
- (CRO) Almost There: N49.24584 W123.05522
  - Located on Crown ridge before Crown proper, covered with some rocks
- (FRO) Mt. Fromme Cache: N49.22993 W123.03366
- (SNE) South Needle: N49.24337 W123.00852
- (COL) Coliseum Mountain: N49.26031 W123.00400
- (TIM) Tim Jones: N49.3903333 W122.9436333
- (SEY) Third Pump (Mount Seymour Summit): N49.23591 W122.56676
- (DEP) Peak Bagger: de Pencier: N49.22726 W122.56026

APPENDIX 8:
PEAK CAIRNS AND SUMMIT LOGS

Since the dawn of mountain climbing as a pursuit, climbers have placed cairns on peaks to mark a true peak and to provide guidance to fellow hikers: part of the universal siblinghood of climbers. They exist from the dawn of time, to mark peaks as a means of navigation. Cairns are found on all of these peaks. Appropriately, the word *cairn* comes from the Scottish Gaelic *càrn*. A Scottish Gaelic blessing is *Cuiridh mi clach air do chàrn*, "I'll put a stone on your cairn." Before they fought in a battle, each Highland warrior would place a stone in a pile. Those who survived the battle would return and remove a stone from the pile. The remaining stones were built into a cairn to honour the dead. The cairn is not, however, a uniquely European creation: ancient examples are the Inuit inukshuk and the Hawaiian ahu.

In or near some cairns, you will find summit logs, often protected in sealed pipes or ammunition boxes or Tupperware.

When King, Dalton, and Martin made their celebrated first ascent of West Lion, a minor controversy flared, including letters to the editor and newspaper stories, when other alpinists disputed their claim. But the Latta climb the next month confirmed the earlier ascent in part through the cairn left by the trio. As asserted soon afterwards in a Vancouver newspaper:

> It is both astonishing and disgraceful that the plain statement of the party of Mountaineers, who climbed one of the "Lions" a short time ago, should have been doubted in the public press by a person or persons with apparently no substantial reasons to advance.
>
> Of course, Mr. Atwell King can now afford to smile at the whole matter, since his second ascent of the much-discussed peak, but that is not the question; there is a principle involved, and unless the public promptly frowns down such unwarrantable conduct, we shall soon hear it questioned: "Did Whymper climb Mount Collie?" "Did Outram climb Assiniboine?"
>
> Fortunately, the silent "stone man" on the summit never lies.[14]

Respect cairns and summit logs. Revel in their history. If a summit log is full, alert the BCMC or ClubTread.com and add a new one on your next visit. For those sad, forlorn peaks lacking logs, won't you please lend a hand and add one?

APPENDIX 9:
RADIO REPEATER TOWERS

The peaks of Gardner, Hat, and Cathedral (and many other peaks in southwest British Columbia) sport odd, green, rocket-shaped towers: perhaps left there by visiting extraterrestrials? In fact, they are radio repeater towers.

Radio waves function in a similar manner to other waves such as ripples on a pond. Ripples diminish in intensity as they travel farther from the epicentre (a rock thrown in a pond, or a radio transmitter). They may also be blocked by obstacles (an island in a pond, mountains in the way). To avoid this, radio repeater towers receive radio waves at one frequency and retransmit them at another. The repeaters are located at high elevations to extend their range.

The green aluminum structures housing the repeaters on Hat, Gardner, and Cathedral are known as "comshells": short for "communications shelters." They provide excellent protection from the elements. They also usually house emergency and other supplies. Most repeaters are shared between North Shore Rescue and another agency or government.

Of the three towers on Cathedral, one is owned by Metro Vancouver (formerly called GVRD, the Greater Vancouver Regional District), one by NSR and one by the provincial Ministry of Forests. The tower on Hat is owned by the provincial government; among other uses, it functioned as a high-frequency listening post during the 2010 Olympics. On Gardner, NSR and a telecommunications company share the repeater.

There are also repeaters at Mt. Seymour (shared between NSR and BC Ambulance) and Cypress Mountain (NSR and the ski resort), as well as several located within the city. These repeaters, however, are not housed in comshells and are less alien-looking.

APPENDIX 10:
FLORA AND FAUNA OF THE NORTH SHORE MOUNTAINS

Note: This is not meant to be a guide to every single animal, plant, and mushroom found on the North Shore. Several such guides are described in the bibliography, **Appendix 22.**

ANIMALS

MAMMALS
BLACK BEAR *(URSUS AMERICANUS)*

Black bears are the only bears living on the North Shore mountains (grizzlies were extermi- nated in the Vancouver area in the early 1900s; the closest are found in the Squamish Valley). The best sightings are when blueberries are ripe.

Do not let the prospect of bears paralyze you with fear; bear sightings are not common. That said, in our thousands of hours in the North Shore mountains, the authors have encoun- tered many bears up close. At no time have we felt in danger. A calm approach is best. The best way to avoid a bear is to stay vigilant and to make your presence known on the trail. If bears know that you are there, they will likely avoid you.

Never approach a bear cub. If you see one, or a recent kill, move away swiftly. These are the most likely times for a bear attack. *If you spot a bear, do not run.* Even if you are Usain Bolt, the bear will always outrun you. Running may trigger an instinctive attack. Bears are also excellent tree-climbers, so that escape manoeuvre will not help. Use the same tactics as with a cougar: collect children and slowly back away. Make yourself large and wave a stick. Do not look them in the eye; they may feel challenged by that and attack. Note: The best way to escape a grizzly bear (playing dead) is a terrible tactic with black bears. Black bears are scavengers, and when presented with a seemingly dead animal, will often begin to eat it. In the highly unlikely event you are attacked by a black bear, fight back.

BLACK-TAILED DEER *(ODOCOILEUS HEMIONUS COLUMBIANUS)*

Black-tailed deer are the most common species of deer in the Lower Mainland. While rare on the steeper slopes of the mainland, they are very common on most of the Howe Sound Islands. They are often found on the edge of the forest, grazing.

COUGAR *(FELIS CONCOLOR)*

Cougars are rarely seen in the North Shore mountains, but inhabit all of the areas described in this book. You have likely been watched by a cougar. None of the authors, however, have ever seen one in tens of thousands of hours in these parts. *If you see a cougar, do not run.* Make yourself large and wave a stick. Make no sudden movements or noises. Keep children close, slowly back away (giving the cougar room to escape), and never turn your back on the cougar.

If attacked, fight back, cover your stomach, and aim for the cat's nose and eyes. Also called puma, catamount, mountain lion.

COYOTE (CANIS LATRANS)
Coyotes reside both in our forests and cities. You may mistake a coyote for a dog. They generally avoid humans. Attacks are rare, and are usually limited to a bite. That said, they are potentially dangerous and rabid. If you see one or a pack of coyotes, keep children and dogs close.

HARBOUR SEAL (PHOCA VITULINA)
Although very rarely seen on mountain peaks, you will almost certainly see a harbour seal on your way to a marine ascent of Dickens via Indian Arm or an ascent of the peaks of the Howe Sound Islands. These seals are often found lolling on exposed rocks or logs. They are especially abundant in Indian Arm in the autumn of odd-numbered years, feasting on pink salmon returning to the Indian River to spawn.

MOUNTAIN GOAT (OREAMNOS AMERICANUS)
The mountain goat was once a common animal in the North Shore mountains: Goat Mountain was named after an unlucky goat killed by hunters, and the first ascent of West Lion was reportedly made by a group pursuing a goat. They have been hunted almost to extinction here. We have only seen one, on an ascent of remote Echo Peak. Other hikers have spotted goats on Deeks, Gotha, Crown, Goat, Enchantment, David, Harvey, the Needles, and Bishop in recent years.

PACIFIC WHITE-SIDED DOLPHIN (LAGENORHYNCHUS OBLIQUIDENS)
Although absent from Vancouver waters for most of the 20th century, dolphins have returned thanks to water quality improvements due to pollution control and treatment of the pollutants released by the abandoned Britannia Mine. Dolphins can now be seen in Howe Sound. Pacific white-sided dolphins are slightly longer than an adult human, with a grey backs, white faces and sides, and black noses.

BIRDS
BALD EAGLE (HALIÆTUS LEUCOCEPHALUS)
Eagles are commonly found near rivers, lakes, and the sea during salmon season (July to November), where food is plentiful. Although bald eagles are the national bird of the USA, there are actually more bald eagles in Canada (mostly in British Columbia).

BLUE GROUSE *(DENDRAGAPUS OBSCURUS)*, **RUFFED GROUSE** *(BONASA UMBELLUS)*

The blue grouse and its cousin the ruffed grouse are common in subalpine forests. On multiple occasions, the authors have been surprised by a previously hidden grouse jumping out of the underbrush (they are not smart birds). This is usually followed by loud swearing and a desire to wring the grouse's neck, bring it home, cook it, and eat it for dinner (we have not actually tried this). Grouse Mountain was named after a grouse shot and killed near its peak in the 1890s. The grouse makes that strange low "whump-whump-whump" sound heard throughout these mountains.

COMMON RAVEN *(CORVUS CORAX)*

Ravens are distinguished from crows by their larger size, larger beak, and lower call. An important character in Indigenous legends across North America, ravens are common in the North Shore mountains. They are clever, and occasionally steal food. As the sun sets, you may find that you are being closely followed by a raven on your hike. We are sure they are just being friendly rather than anticipating your death and a tasty meal. Really.

GREY JAY *(PERISOREUS CANADENSIS)*

The grey jay (a.k.a. whisky jack, Canada jay, meatbird, camp robber, moosebird) was named as Canada's national bird by the Royal Canadian Geographic Society in November 2016. They are commonly found at high altitudes. They are one of the tamest birds in the province and often approach hikers for food. The authors often bring a small bag of birdseed to Hollyburn or Strachan, where many whisky jacks can be found. Do not feed them anything other than birdseed or berries; our metabolisms are different from theirs, and food (such as most granola bars and fruit leather) that is harmless to us will hurt them. In particular, chocolate is poisonous to birds.

STELLER'S JAY *(CYANOCITTA STELLERI)*

The Steller's jay, the provincial bird of British Columbia, is often found close to civilization. It is blue with a black head and crest.

AMPHIBIANS

NORTHWESTERN SALAMANDER *(AMBYSTOMA GRACILE)*, **LONG-TOED SALAMANDER** *(AMBYSTOMA MACRODACTYLUM)*, **ROUGHSKIN NEWT** *(TARICHA GRANULOSA)*

Like frogs, salamanders lay their eggs in water, live in water as tadpoles, then live their adult life on land. Salamanders can be found in Cabin Lake (Black Mountain) and in Damsoon and Gambier lakes (Gambier Island), and Mystery Lake (Seymour area). The Northwestern salamander is greyish-brown in colour and very blocky in shape. The long-toed salamander is darker and narrower. The roughskin newt is grey and covered in granules (hence the name). If you see an adult salamander (or frog), do not touch it: salamanders breathe through their skin through osmosis. Roughskin newts also secrete a poisonous substance through their skin, the same poison that is found in pufferfish. In 1979 a drunken Oregonian died after eating one of these newts on a dare.

GASTROPODS

BANANA SLUG (ARIOLIMAX COLUMBIANUS)

Banana slugs are often found on the forest floor. They are black, olive-green, or yellow in colour, usually dotted with black spots. Banana slugs are usually the size of a finger. Also called leopard slug (with black spots).

PLANTS

DEVIL'S CLUB (OPLOPANAX HORRIDUS)

The bane of hikers across the Pacific Northwest, devil's club is distinguished by its massive leaves, clusters of red poisonous berries, and nasty thorns. The thorns, found all over the plant, break easily and can become embedded in skin. To add insult to injury, a rash usually develops. Consider avoiding. It is usually found in depressions but can be found on slopes as well. It is related to American ginseng, and its roots have been harvested for this reason. Also called Alaskan ginseng, devil's walking stick.

ENGLISH IVY (HEDERA HELIX)

English ivy is the nastiest invasive species in British Columbia. Many North Shore parks have been completely smothered by ivy: there are many North Shore-based organizations dedicated to its eradication. Like holly, it even threatens mountain slopes. If you see it, pull it out!

EUROPEAN HOLLY (ILEX AQUIFOLIUM)

European holly, along with ivy, is one of the nastiest invasive species in British Columbia. It is easily identifiable by its prickly green leaves and red berries. It is commonly found in North Shore parks as an escapee from gardens. If you see it, pull it out! Also called English holly, Christmas holly.

PINK MOUNTAIN HEATHER (PHYLLODOCE EMPETRIFORMIS)

Heather is very common in alpine meadows and flat areas such as the upper slopes of Deeks Peak. It is a small bushy green plant with grey flowers. It resembles rosemary to some degree.

ROUND-LEAVED SUNDEW (DROSERA ROTUNDIFOLIA)

The sundew is one of the strangest plants on the North Shore, and the only common carnivorous plant. Small hairs radiate from the leaves. A droplet of clear fluid is found at the end of the hairs. Sundews are found in bogs, such as the bog surrounding Damsoon Lake on Gambier Island.

STINGING NETTLE (URTICA DIOICA)

Although more common in Europe and on the Gulf Islands, stinging nettles can be found on the North Shore. They are small, with leaves branching from a straight stem. They are somewhat distinctive, often forming clusters. Small hairs are present on top of and below leaves, producing a stinging sensation and numbness when touched; although painful, this is not poisonous.

TWISTED STALK *(STREPTOPUS AMPEXIFOLIUS)*

Large, oval, teardrop-shaped leaves branch off from a thin, twisted stalk. The red berries that grow below the leaves are poisonous, so avoid them.

WESTERN SKUNK CABBAGE *(LYSICHITON AMERICANUS)*

Skunk cabbage is a very common sight in muddy areas of the Lower Mainland. It is distinguished by a skunky smell and a large yellow flower. Although bears eat it and First Nations cooked and ate the root during times of famine, it is poisonous for humans and can occasionally result in death. Note that this species differs from the "skunk cabbage" of the eastern USA.

BERRIES

BLACKBERRIES AND RELATIVES (RUBUS)

HIMALAYAN BLACKBERRY *(RUBUS ARMENIACUS)*

The most common blackberry species in British Columbia, and the blackberry you are likely to find in stores, is not native at all, but was introduced from either Armenia or Iran. It grows extremely well in our climate, causing many impenetrable (and prickly) thickets. It is often found in disturbed areas and along roads and streams. Massive bushes ensure that, unless a bear or other berrypicker has reached it before you, it is easy to pick a large amount of berries in a short time. Also called Armenian blackberry. Season: late summer.

PACIFIC BLACKBERRY *(RUBUS URSINUS)*

The native Pacific blackberry is uncommon nowadays, having been largely replaced by the Himalayan blackberry, but it can still be found. Its stems and berries are smaller than the Himalayan, and the berry itself is sweeter and has been said to taste better. Also called Californian blackberry, California dewberry, douglasberry, trailing blackberry, Pacific dewberry. Season: late summer.

SALMONBERRY *(RUBUS SPECTABILIS)*

Closely related to blackberries and raspberries, salmonberries are often found lining the trails of North Shore parks. The thorned stems are far thinner and woodier than blackberries, and the berry is orange or yellow instead of black. Salmonberries have a much milder and less sweet flavour than blackberries, but some find it too bitter. Season: mid-May, June to late June.

THIMBLEBERRY *(RUBUS PARVIFLORUS)*

The most fragile, rarest, and (according to some) tastiest berries found on the North Shore are thimbleberries. These resemble flat raspberries and are found at lower elevations. Unlike blackberries and salmonberries, thimbleberries have no thorns and the leaves are fuzzy to the touch. Thimbleberries are ready to harvest when the berry is red and it falls easily off the stem. Note that another *Rubus*, *Rubus occidentalis*, is known as thimbleberry in eastern North America but does not occur naturally in BC. The leaves make excellent toilet paper in an emergency. Also called salmonberry, snow bramble. Season: mid- to late summer.

WILD RASPBERRY *(RUBUS SPP.)*

Several wild raspberries are found in British Columbia, the most common being blackcap (*Rubus leucodermis*) and European raspberry (*Rubus idaeus*). They are rare compared to blackberries and salmonberries and non-existent in the alpine.

BLUEBERRIES AND HUCKLEBERRIES (VACCINIUM)

The most common berries on these hikes are of the genus *Vaccinium*. These healthy and delicious berries share the same etymology as the word "vaccine" and were staples of Indigenous medicine and sustenance. The Hollyburn hike is perhaps the best display of the different *Vaccinium* species. On high-altitude routes such as Gotha and Echo, bushwhacking through blueberry bushes is an essential skill. In the steepest areas, you will be ascending slopes with blueberries as your only handhold: useful for veggie belays.

ALASKA BLUEBERRY *(VACCINIUM ALASKENSIS)*

Resembles the supermarket blueberry but has more flavour and tang. The berries have no white sheen; leaves are green and oval.

BLACK HUCKLEBERRY *(VACCINIUM MEMBRANACEUM)*

The prime varietal has dark black skin and rich red juice. Its reddish leaves turn a brilliant and beautiful red in the autumn. It is full of flavour, tasting like plums and grapes, with a metallic hint.

MOUNTAIN BLUEBERRIES *(VACCINIUM SPP.)*

Several *Vaccinium* species grow in the mountains of British Columbia, and (with the exception of the red huckleberry) they are hard to tell apart. All are more delicious than their supermarket cousins (domesticated *Vaccinium corymbosum*, or northern highbush blueberries, not found in BC), but the richer the colour of the leaves and juice, the richer the taste.

OVAL-LEAFED BLUEBERRY *(VACCINIUM OVALIFOLIUM)*

Sometimes has a cloudy white sheen, and its leaves are sometimes dusty and mottled green, with a hint of red and grey. It has a somewhat lemony taste. It is the most common blueberry in the area.

RED HUCKLEBERRY *(VACCINIUM PARVIFOLIUM)*

Red huckleberries, like salmonberries, are commonly found in North Shore parks but are rare at higher altitudes. The berries resemble tiny apples. The berries are edible: the riper the berry and the more sunlight it has received, the less sour it will taste.

OTHER:

BUNCHBERRY *(CORNUS CANADENSIS)*

Small, six-leaved plants. A small white flower reminiscent of thimbleberry and blackberry flowers becomes a cluster of small red berries. The berries are edible but not really worth eating. The seed at the centre is poisonous.

FALSE SOLOMON'S SEAL *(MAIANTHEMUM SPP.)*

False solomon's seal is a small plant with large, kayak-shaped leaves. The berries are red in colour and edible.

OREGON GRAPE *(MAHONIA AQUIFOLIUM)*

Oregon grape resembles holly, but the leaves are less sharp and the berries are blue. Unlike holly, oregon grape is native to British Columbia. Its berries are quite sour but can be used to make jam. Other name: Oregon grape-holly.

SALAL *(GAULTHERIA SHALLON)*

Very common near sea level, salal is distinguished by its rough green oval-shaped leaves, purple bell-shaped flowers, and hairy blueberries. The berries are edible, but mealy, and an important food for local First Nations. Also called shallon, gaultheria.

TREES

ARBUTUS *(ARBUTUS MENZIESII)*

Arbutus trees are common in rocky coastal areas such as Lighthouse Park. Some are found on lower Black Mountain. They are distinguished by their paper-thin bark, which peels off in the autumn.

Leaves: Green and elliptical, unlike many British Columbia trees.

Other name: Madrone.

BIGLEAF MAPLE *(ACER MACROPHYLLUM)*

Bigleaf maple is often seen in disturbed areas and second-growth forest, being one of the first species to return after a clear-cut. It is often buried in moss, which sometimes grows so thick that roots grow through it. Unlike the sugar maple of Ontario and Quebec, bigleaf maple is not used to make maple syrup (while technically possible, it takes a large amount of bigleaf maple sap to make inevitably mediocre maple syrup).

Leaves: Maple-shaped; see the Canadian flag.

Other name: Oregon maple.

DOUGLAS FIR *(PSEUDOTSUGA MENZIESII)*

The Douglas fir is the most common fir in the Lower Mainland. It is distinguished by its extremely rough, gnarled and thick bark. Its cones start as green but become brown when mature. They are slightly bigger than an adult's thumb. An old legend explains that the seeds sticking out of the pinecone are mice fleeing a fire.

The bright green new growth needles are edible.

Leaves: Thick, flat needles.

Look-alikes: Other firs are sometimes found in the Lower Mainland but they are rare and hard to tell apart.

SITKA SPRUCE *(PICEA STICHENSIS)*

Found at lower elevations. Has thin, flat bark. Sitka spruce is often confused with hemlock: the easiest way to tell the two apart is that hemlock leaves only grow on two sides of the branch (like Douglas firs) while spruce needles grow everywhere (looking something like a hedgehog).

The bright green new growth needles of fir, spruce, and both hemlocks are edible and full of vitamin C: they taste like a cross between kale and beer hops, with a touch of citrus.

Leaves: Four-sided needles growing on all sides of the branch.

Look-alike: Engelmann spruce (rare in BC).

WESTERN HEMLOCK (*TSUGA HETEROPHYLLA*), MOUNTAIN HEMLOCK (*TSUGA MERTENSIANA*)

Western hemlock and mountain hemlock resemble Douglas fir but with thinner and less gnarly bark: smaller Douglas firs and hemlock are often confused.

Western hemlock and mountain hemlock are also very similar. As one might expect, mountain hemlock is found at higher altitudes while western hemlock is found lower down mountains. Western hemlock is also taller and its cones are smaller (mountain hemlock cones are purple and about the size of a Douglas fir cones).

Hemlock the tree is not related to hemlock the poison, the stuff that killed the philosopher Socrates. The bright-green new-growth needles are edible.

Leaves: Flat. In spring the last inch or so of branches are bright green and soft to the touch.

WESTERN RED CEDAR (*THUJA PLICATA*)

Many Pacific Northwest tribes called the cedar the tree of life. It provided material for their houses, canoes, clothes, tools, and almost everything else. It is British Columbia's provincial tree. It is distinguished by its bark: the bark is easy to peel off in strips, and those strips were in fact used by First Nations. When cut, cedar has a distinctive and pleasing smell.

Leaves: Scale-like. Unlike any other British Columbia tree.

FERNS AND LICHENS

FERNS

Ferns are some of the oldest plants found on the North Shore. Millions of years more ancient than dinosaurs, ferns have not evolved seeds and still reproduce through spores. Some ferns are eaten when young, as fiddleheads (usually the ostrich fern, which does not grow in British Columbia).

BRACKEN FERN (*PTERIDIUM AQUILINIUM*)

These ferns are found all over the world. They are characterized by a thin, tough stem from which slender fronds sprout. Bracken ferns are the tallest ferns in the Lower Mainland, growing up to 2.5 m tall. This tenacity makes them especially common in disturbed areas such as clear-cuts, roadsides, and burnt areas. Although parts of this fern were eaten by desperate Indigenous people, some evidence indicates that this fern is toxic.

DEER FERN (*BLECHNUM SPICANT*)

Deer ferns resemble sword ferns. They are distinguished by the base of the leaflets, which are attached to the stem, in contrast to the leaflets of sword ferns, which are attached to a stalk. Sometimes a stalk rises from the centre of the fern.

LADY FERN (ATHYRIUM FILIX-FEMINA)

Lady fern is relatively common in the Lower Mainland. It is distinguished by jagged leaflets.

MAIDENHAIR FERN (ADIANTUM PEDANTUM)

Maidenhair, the most delicate North Shore fern, is found in very wet areas. It resembles a smaller deer fern but with a black stem. It is uncommon.

SWORD FERN (POLYSTICHUM MUNITUM)

Sword ferns are the most common type of fern on the North Shore. At their largest, they grow to 1.5 m tall from a centre the size of a hand. They are distinguished by their shaggy thick stem (resembling a rope) and the leaves, which taper to a point before connecting to the main stem. Apparently, the young ferns can be eaten as fiddleheads.

LICHEN

Lichens consist of an algae or cyanobacteria living in the filaments of a fungus. There are many lichen species found in the North Shore mountains, ranging from scraggly old man's beard to splashes of colour on rocks.

OLD MAN'S BEARD (USNEA SPP.)

Scraggly, green-grey, hairlike lichen seen hanging from tree branches everywhere in the North Shore mountains. Some specimens are over 150 years old. Traditionally used by First Nations for diapers and feminine protection. It is edible in an emergency but tastes dry and horrible. An easy indicator that one is about to reach the alpine is the proliferation of old man's beard on the trunks of trees, instead of the moss found at lower elevations.

MUSHROOMS

Caution and disclaimer: Many edible mushrooms have poisonous lookalikes. Only eat mushrooms if you are 100 per cent sure what they are. Consult an expert first. If in doubt, throw it out. People have died after misidentifying mushrooms! Heed the old adage "every mushroom is edible once."

Coastal British Columbia's extremely wet climate creates a mushroomer's paradise. The northern end of Howe Sound Crest Trail is a veritable zoo of mushrooms, overflowing with variety and numbers. Capilano Mountain is also an excellent mushroom hunting ground.

This short guide describes only the most common, deadliest, and tastiest mushrooms in the Lower Mainland. More complete guides can be found in **Appendix 22**. We particularly like David Arora's *All That the Rain Promises and More.*

With a little research and study, you will have the happy epiphany that the most delicious mushrooms (chanterelles, oysters, morels, boletes, hedgehogs, chicken of the woods, bear's head, lion's mane, and cauliflower) are very distinct, with few or no poisonous lookalikes. There are other edible mushroom that have too many dangerous lookalikes to make them worth eating (e.g., all amanitas, agaricus, lactarius, and russula mushrooms) for anyone but an expert mycologist. The highly prized matsutake, or pine mushroom, is in a class of its own. While delicious, it has several highly poisonous lookalikes.

We have noted their edibility: poisonous; inedible; mediocre (edible but why bother?); edible; and delicious.

GILLED MUSHROOMS

These mushrooms are what most people think of when they think of mushrooms. A (usually) round cap rests on a stalk. Gills are found on the underside of the cap.

ANGEL WINGS (PLEUROCYBELLA PORRIGENS) *(Edible)*

Angel wings are small, white, shelf-like mushrooms, usually found on dead conifers. They resemble oyster mushrooms; in our opinion, they are distinctive enough to break the "no eating white mushrooms" rule. They have been described as a poor man's oyster mushroom due to their taste, which is not quite as good.

Spores: White.

CHANTERELLE (CANTHARELLUS CIBARIUS) *(Delicious)*

Chanterelle

The chanterelle is recognized as one of the tastiest mushrooms in the world, fetching prices of $33–$55 the kilo. While more common in the drier Fraser Valley, they have been found on local mountains (we won't tell you where). Chanterelles are distinguished by the gills running all the way down the stalk to the base of the mushroom: beware mushrooms that look like chanterelles but do not share this characteristic.

DEATH CAP (AMANITA PHALLOIDES) *(Poisonous)*

Closely related to the fly amanita and the destroying angel, the death cap is a dull olive-green in colour. Like the destroying angel, it has caused several deaths.

DESTROYING ANGEL (AMANITA OCREATA) *(Poisonous)*

The destroying angel is an excellent reason to stay away from small white mushrooms in the wild. As a young mushroom, it resembles the white button mushrooms found in stores. As one might expect from a mushroom called the destroying angel, it is deadly. The destroying angel and the death cap are the most poisonous mushrooms known, and many deaths have occurred.

FLY AMANITA (AMANITA MUSCARIA) *(poisonous)*

The toadstool of fable, found in temperate climates all over the world, with a red (or sometimes yellow) cap and white gills. White warts are found on top of the cap: the remnants of the veil it wears while emergent. Younger specimens resemble white eggs. This mushroom is poisonous and, while beautiful, should be avoided. It has been used as a hallucinogen, although is usually accompanied by gastric explosions and discomfort.

Also called fly agaric.

Other species of amanita, such as the panther amanita, resemble the fly amanita but possess different-coloured caps. They too are poisonous.

OYSTER *(PLEUROTUS OSTREATUS)* *(Delicious)*

Oyster mushrooms are found growing shelf-like on the sides of dead or dying logs, trees, and stumps. They are grey with white gills. They are also considered an excellent mushroom and are often found in stores.

PURPLE CORT *(CORTINARIUS VIOLACEUS)* *(Mediocre)*

This mushroom is one of the most distinctive gilled mushrooms in British Columbia because of its deep beautiful purple colour. It is edible but not worth the trouble.

Also called edible cort, violet cort.

RUSSULA *(RUSSULA SPP.)* *(Poisonous/Inedible/Mediocre/Edible)*

Russulas add a touch of colour to our woods. They are very variable in color, but the most common varieties have red or purple caps, white gills, and white to purple stalks. Some are edible and some are not. Exercise caution.

POLYPORES

Polypores are the woody mushrooms growing on the side of dead trees. They resemble shelves. Gills are absent. Most are too woody to eat, with the exception of the delicious chicken of the woods.

ARTIST'S CONK *(GANODERMA APPLANATUM)* *(Inedible)*

The artist's conk resembles the western varnished conk, with one exception: any scratches made on the bottom of the conk turn brown and stay brown for the rest of the mushroom's life. Intricate works of art have been created this way.

CHICKEN OF THE WOODS
(LAETIPORUS SULPHUREUS) *(Delicious)*

The chicken of the woods is a bright orange and yellow spongy polypore. It really does taste like chicken and is sometimes used in vegan and vegetarian cuisine as a chicken substitute. Older chickens of the woods are tough, ragged, and stringy and should be avoided. Some strains of this species are rumoured to cause mild gastrointestinal distress, so eat with caution.

Also called sulfur shelf.

Chicken of the woods along Howe Sound Crest Trail.

RED-BELTED CONK *(FOMITOPSIS PINICOLA)* *(Inedible)*

The red-belted conk, along with the western varnished conk, is common. Too woody to eat.

TURKEY TAIL *(TRAMETES VERSICOLOR)* *(Mediocre)*

A small polypore that commonly grows on hardwoods. It is too woody to eat, although *All the Rain Promises and More* suggests using it as a natural chewing gum. Turkey tail tea is sometimes brewed by people who claim it is effective against cancer. According to the American Cancer Society, the mushroom by itself is not effective, but some substances found in it may warrant further study.

WESTERN VARNISHED CONK *(GANODERMA OREGONENSE)* *(Inedible)*

The western varnished conk differs from the red-belted conk in its lack of a red belt. It is also shiny on the top, unlike the red-belted conk.

BOLETES

Boletes resemble gilled mushrooms. They differ in that they have a spongy mass beneath their caps instead of gills. Most of them are edible.

BLUE-STAINING BOLETES *(Poisonous/Inedible/Mediocre/Edible)*

Several boletes growing in the Lower Mainland resemble the king bolete, but their pores turn blue after a few seconds if poked or cut. None of these are as tasty as the king bolete, and some may be poisonous. Beware of red boletes that stain blue: many of these are poisonous, and none are worth eating.

KING BOLETE *(BOLETUS EDULIS)* *(Delicious)*

Debate rages on about whether king boletes or chanterelles are the tastiest wild mushroom: fortunately for Lower Mainland residents, both are commonly found in this area. King boletes are distinguished from other boletes by their massive size and their lack of a blue stain when the spongy pores are cut or prodded. They are commonly found in sheltered areas along the HSCT, where they are more noticeable, but can be found in other places too. Make sure that the mushroom is maggot-free and does not stain blue before picking it.

Also called cep, porcini, steinpilz.

LEMON BOLETE *(BOLETUS MIRABILIS)* *(Edible)*

The lemon bolete is the most common bolete in the Lower Mainland. It has a purple cap and stem, and yellowish-green pores. It has a faint lemon flavour, which gives it its name. It is tasty but not as good as the king bolete. A similar bolete is Zeller's bolete *(Boletus zelleri)*, which resembles the lemon bolete except for its red stalk and (sometimes) blue-staining spores. It is also edible but lacks the lemony taste.

Also called admirable bolete.

Lemon bolete.

OTHER

Any mushroom that does not fall into any of the categories above.

BEAR'S HEAD *(HERICIUM ABIETIS)* AND LION'S MANE *(HERICIUM ERINACEUS)* *(Delicious)*

Bear's head grows on the side of trees. It resembles a deformed coral mushroom (see below): the fungus forms many branches and spines hang like icicles from the ends of branches. Lion's mane resembles a cotton ball, or a pompom, or the top of a truffula tree from *The Lorax*. At their best, they taste like seafood, with a similar texture. Bear's head and lion's mane are sometimes sold in high-end French restaurants under the name of *pom pom du blanc*. They are also used in Chinese vegetarian cuisine as a substitute for pork or lamb.

Also called *pom pom du blanc*, old man's beard, *Yamabushitake*, *hóu tóu gū* (猴头菇).

CAULIFLOWER MUSHROOM *(SPARASSIS CRISPA)* *(Delicious)*

The cauliflower mushroom resembles a brain coral or a bowl of linguine. Specimens have weighed as much as 50 pounds, but most are 1–5 pounds. If cleaned well (the mushroom's shape makes it notoriously difficult to clean) and cooked, it is delicious. We have spotted some near Capilano Mountain.

CORAL MUSHROOM *(RAMARIA SPP.)* *(Mediocre)*

Coral mushrooms are very common in the Lower Mainland. Many species look very similar and are hard to tell apart. Some are edible and some are not.

Coral mushroom.

HEDGEHOG *(HYDNUM REPANDUM)* *(Delicious)*

The hedgehog mushroom resembles a flattened chanterelle with teeth instead of gills. Like the chanterelle, it is more common in the Fraser Valley but has been found on the North Shore. Some prefer it to chanterelles.

WITCH'S BUTTER *(TREMELLEA MESENTERICA)* *(Mediocre)*

Witch's butter resembles orange Jell-O. It is very common in the Lower Mainland and elsewhere. It is edible but has no taste.

APPENDIX 11:
GEOLOGY OF THE NORTH SHORE MOUNTAINS

This section is largely based on two excellent books about our geologically fascinating region. *Vancouver, City on the Edge*, by John Clague and Bob Turner, is an amazing book that not only provides a geological overview but is an exercise in effective teaching through inspired presentation. Jack E. Armstrong's *Vancouver Geology* is more technical, describing interesting geological features found on North Shore mountain hikes. The book also contains a splendid map of the base geological regions of the North Shore.

Vancouver is one of the most beautiful cities in the world. It owes this beauty, and the mountains, to the various geologic forces that have shaped the terrain into what it is today.

These forces operate on a timescale so vast as to be beyond our comprehension. A popular way to visualize geologic time is to imagine Earth's history as a single year, with the planet forming on January 1 and the present day being December 31. On this scale, the average Canadian lifespan (80 years) lasts less than a quarter of a second. A week on this scale represents about 80 million years, a day roughly 12 million years.

Earth forms on January 1 (4.6 billion years ago). For the first two months, it is a molten ball of fire. It starts to cool in early March; the oldest surviving rocks (located in Australia and the Canadian Shield) date from the second week of March. Oceans form soon after, and the earliest life appears in late April (according to scientists' best guesses; some sources say it happened around the beginning of April).

It takes life eight months to evolve beyond bacteria. Around November 19 an sudden flourishing of life called the Cambrian explosion occurs in the oceans. Life diversifies and we see the first invertebrates with shells, for example. By December 1 life has spread to the land. The first dinosaurs appear on December 13 and are killed off by an asteroid on the 27th. The oldest common rocks in the Vancouver area, the Gambier Group (found on northern Gambier Island and the summit of Brunswick), form sometime around December 23.

All human history lies within the last four hours of the day. The first modern humans appear in East Africa at 8 p.m. on December 31. An hour-and-a-half later the Ice Age starts, eventually covering almost all of Canada with glaciers. The ice sheets reach their greatest extent at 11:56:30 and have left the Vancouver area by 11:58:36. Around this time, Mt. Garibaldi erupts for the last time.

The first human inhabitants of Vancouver reach the place at 11:59:01, as part of a larger migration from Siberia to Chile enabled by the vanishing ice sheets. Around 11:59:22, the climate warms and enough plants arrive for Vancouver's climate to become the temperate rainforest it is today. The first large civilizations and the invention of writing also arise around this time in Egypt and Mesopotamia. All of recorded history, therefore, falls within the last 30 seconds of this timescale.

At 11:59:58 (specifically, 9 p.m. on January 26, 1700), the latest of many massive earthquakes strikes the British Columbia coast, devastating Aboriginal villages. Vancouver is shielded from the full force of the earthquake by Vancouver Island, but great damage is still done. First Nations oral histories record this event and pass the story down through generations. Captain James Cook becomes the first European to visit the British Columbia coast at 11:59:59 (specifically, 1778).

THE ROCKS

There are three types of rocks: igneous, metamorphic, and sedimentary.

Sedimentary rocks are formed when sediments, such as mud and sand, are compressed into rock. These rocks tend to be softer and grainier than igneous rocks. The rocks that form the Grand Canyon, with the exception of the schist at the very bottom of the canyon, are sedimentary. Fossils are most frequently found in sedimentary rocks.

The peak of Brunswick. Note that the volcanic rock on Brunswick is much redder and flakier than the granitic rock on Hanover behind.

In the North Shore mountains, erosion has removed sedimentary rocks from all but the very highest peaks (including Brunswick and Strachan) and Gambier Island. Such isolated patches of sedimentary rock are called roof pendants. The Brunswick–Gambier sedimentary rock, called the "Gambier Group" by geologists, is composed of sandstone and siltstone deposited roughly 110 million years ago (December 23 on our single-year timeline). In contrast, downtown Vancouver is mostly built on newer sedimentary rocks deposited between 70 and 40 million years ago (December 26 to 29).

The second most common type of rock in the North Shore mountains is metamorphic rock. Metamorphic rocks are igneous or sedimentary rocks that were compressed and heated deep inside the Earth, then brought back to the surface. An example is the peak of Strachan.

Igneous rocks, the most common type of rock in the North Shore mountains, are pieces of former magma (lava) that cooled into solid rock. There are two types of igneous rock: volcanic and plutonic. Volcanic rocks solidify above the ground, after they are blasted out by eruptions. Plutonic rocks are magma that cooled and solidified underground, later being exposed through uplift or erosion. Examples of volcanic rocks are those of the Hawaiian Islands and

Mt. St. Helens, formed in volcanic eruptions and cooled when exposed to air. Examples of plutonic rocks are the granite domes of Yosemite National Park and Stawamus Chief.

Most of the igneous rocks found in the North Shore mountains are plutonic. The granite in the Coast Mountains, called the Coast Plutonic Complex, once formed the magma chambers of ancient, long-vanished volcanoes. After millions of years of inactivity, the volcanoes' magma chambers cooled, and continental drift and erosion then pushed the solid granites to the surface. Most of the granites were formed between 150 (December 22) and 80 million years ago (December 26) deep underground, but some are older or younger than that. The mountains themselves are younger than the granite, perhaps 20 million years old or less.

While we associate the North Shore mountains with granite, that rock, made up of light-coloured minerals such as feldspar, quartz, mica, and amphibole, is actually relatively rare. More common plutonic rocks are granodiorite, diorite, and quartz diorite, which are darker than granite. Gabbro, a dark rock sometimes referred to as "black granite," is rarer but can be found on The Lions, Crown, and other peaks.

The Lions are the most striking examples of igneous rock. They are composed of hornblende diorite, one of the oldest plutonic rocks in this part of the world.

Some volcanic igneous rocks can be found around Vancouver. Lava rose along cracks in the earth (called faults) and then cooled. This process creates a line of white or black volcanic rock in the bedrock, called dikes. Dikes can be found at the shore at Lighthouse and Caulfield Parks in West Vancouver, Siwash Rock in Stanley Park, Coliseum Mountain, and Mt. Seymour. Larger outcroppings of andesitic volcanic rock, called sills, include Sentinel Hill and Queen Elizabeth Park.

PLATES AND TERRANES

Why is the North Shore mountainous instead of being a flat plain? The answer is plate tectonics.

Earth's crust is composed of several large tectonic plates that float on the mantle. Most plates correspond to continents or oceans (but not all of them; for example, the North American plate includes North America to southern Mexico, Greenland, and part of Kamchatka in Russia). Convection in the mantle moves these plates (in the same way as bubbles in boiling water push other water away from them).

Some 70 million years ago (December 26), the eastern half of the Pacific Ocean was occupied by two plates: Kula in the north, and Farallon in the south. The motion of the Pacific plate pushed these two plates northeastward, where they sank under the less dense North American plate. This type of plate boundary, where one plate sinks below another, is called a subduction zone.

Today, the only traces of the Farallon and Kula plates are the Cocos and Nazca plates off Central and South America, fragments off the Alaskan coast, and the Juan de Fuca plate off the coast of British Columbia, Washington, Oregon, and extreme northern California. The boundary between the Juan de Fuca plate and the North American plate is located roughly 200 km off the coast of Vancouver Island.

The close proximity to a fault means that volcanoes and earthquakes pose a threat to Vancouver. Molten lava from the Juan de Fuca plate rose to the surface through vents, creating the Cascades, a chain of volcanoes extending from Lassen Peak in northern California to Mt. Silverthrone halfway between Vancouver and the tip of the Alaska Panhandle. Mt. St.

Helens is the latest volcano in this range to erupt. Mt. Baker is the closest active volcano to Vancouver, and that which poses the greatest threat. Mounts Meager and Cayley, northwest of Whistler, are often seen as the most likely candidates for the next eruption. Mt. Garibaldi near Squamish has not erupted in thousands of years; geologists are wary of declaring it extinct but will admit it is not the greatest threat facing Vancouver today. Far older volcanoes pose no threat. Their magma chambers have cooled into the plutonic igneous rocks which form the backbone of the North Shore mountains.

As it slowly works its way beneath the North American plate, the Juan de Fuca plate sometimes gets stuck and its sudden release causes earthquakes. The latest major quake here has been dated to January 26, 1700 (December 31 at 11:59:58), from Japanese records. The earthquake caused a tsunami that wiped out many First Nations villages on the West Coast and dealt significant damage to Polynesia and Japan. Most geologists agree we are overdue for another catastrophic earthquake.

Plate tectonics is also responsible for the formation of almost all natural features in the Lower Mainland. Islands and seamounts located on the Farallon, Kula, and Pacific plates were scraped off by subduction and migrated to the North American plates. Such wandering rocks are called terranes. Geologists have determined that all regions of British Columbia, except for the Rockies and the northeastern plains, are partly composed of terranes. Vancouver Island and Haida Gwaii, for example, are mostly terranes.

The motion of the Juan de Fuca plate warped the North American plate. Ground was pushed upwards and folded, creating the Coast Mountains, the Gulf Islands, and most mountains on Vancouver Island. Farther to the east, the Rockies rose. These mountains continue to rise, with the Coast Mountains and the Rockies growing by a millimetre or two each year.

A modern-day Vancouverite transported to the Vancouver of 70 million years ago (Boxing Day) may have vaguely recognized it. The land would look like a rough sketch of today's Vancouver. Small rolling hills, not the mighty mountains of today's Vancouver, rose to the north. Vancouver Island and some of the Gulf Islands would have existed, albeit in less mountainous form. A prototype of the Squamish River would have fed into the Pacific in a small bay, a sort of proto-Howe Sound. A giant bay would have existed where the city of Vancouver and the Fraser Valley exists now. This bay would have extended as far east as present-day Harrison Lake. Indian Arm, Pitt Lake, and Harrison Lake would have been minor arms of this bay, if they existed at all.

Because the Vancouver area back then was farther south than it is now, it had a tropical climate. Imagine a swamp or Louisiana bayou populated by dinosaurs. *Tyrannosaurus rex* would have roamed the Vancouver hills, possibly preying on herbivores such as *Parasaurolophus*. The precise ranges of plants at this time are uncertain, and so it is harder to determine what these herbivores may have eaten. Trees and ferns had existed for over a hundred million years by this time, so there were certainly trees there. Flowering plants had also existed for many years by this time.

Over the next few million years, sediment from the Fraser River (which was at that time a smaller coastal river comparable to today's Squamish River) filled in the Vancouver bay and created the eastern Fraser Valley. The rocks beneath Stanley Park and downtown Vancouver were also created during this time. In the last 20 million years (since December 30), plate tectonics pushed the North Shore mountains to a height closer to today's mountains, although in a more jagged shape.

A U-shaped valley carved by glaciers, viewed from Golden Ears.

THE ICE AGE

The penultimate chapter in the history of Vancouver began two million years ago (December 31 at 9:30 p.m.). Vancouver was no longer the tropical swamp it had been when the dinosaurs roamed, having moved to almost its current latitude. The climate cooled across the world. Four massive ice sheets covered almost all of Canada. At the ice sheets' greatest extent, roughly 16,000 years ago (December 31 at 11:56:30), British Columbia and the southern Alaska coast were covered in a massive ice sheet known as the Cordilleran ice sheet. East of the Rockies, the rest of Canada and the northern United States were covered in the larger Laurentide ice sheet. Ellesmere Island, located in extreme northern Nunavut, was covered in the Innutian ice sheet. Greenland was covered in its own ice sheet. Most of present-day USA and, surprisingly, northern Yukon and Alaska were never glaciated.

The Vancouver area was buried in up to 2 km of ice. All mountains (except for the very highest) were engulfed by the white sea.

Today, a rare weather pattern called a thermal inversion gives Vancouverites a glimpse of this past. Fog sinks into the Lower Mainland basin and no clouds are found above a certain elevation. Viewed from the top of a mountain, the buildings and trees of the city are buried beneath hundreds of metres of fog. The effect is eerie.

The glaciers profoundly altered the landscape of the Lower Mainland. Glacial erosion changed the direction of a large northeastward-flowing river, which likely drained into the present-day Peace River. This river now drained into the Fraser, vastly increasing the amount of water that the latter carried. Expanding and retreating glaciers carved out what had previously been small valleys into larger fjords such as Howe Sound, giving British Columbia a coastline to rival Norway and New Zealand. The glaciers stopped, and thus the fjords stop, around Puget Sound in Washington. The Howe Sound Islands are the remnants of small mountains abraded by the Howe Sound glacier. Formerly V-shaped valleys became U-shaped as rock was carved out: in such valleys it is often easy to tell the height of the glacier that carved it. Above the glacier the unglaciated summits (called nunataks) of the tallest mountains retained their jagged form; Hanover, parts of Brunswick, and The Lions are nunataks. But the contrast between nunatak and glacial valley is easier to see in the taller Tantalus Range as one drives north toward Whistler. Round basins called cirques were scooped out by glaciers: Kennedy Lake lies at the bottom of one. Narrow ridges called arêtes were formed as two glaciers pushed past both sides of a ridge. Examples include Brunswick Mountain, Crown Mountain, and the Camel. Erratics – boulders, often huge – were carried by glaciers kilometres away from their origin. Examples are found on the Lynn Peak trail and on the south summit of Strachan. Glaciers also deposited sediments from the mountains, representing the predominant soil of the Fraser Valley and the lower areas of the North Shore.

PAST, PRESENT, AND FUTURE

By around 10,000 BCE, the last of the Fraser Valley ice had melted, and by 8000 BCE (December 31 at 11:58:40 p.m.), the glaciers had retreated to the north of the Lower Mainland. Glacial sediments had filled in most of the Vancouver bay. The coastline to the north of what is today the North Arm of the Fraser River was in roughly the same location as it is today (with the exception of the Pitt River, which was a small oceanic channel connecting what is now Pitt Lake to the Fraser; it was comparable to today's Burrard Inlet).

South of the Fraser, the coastline extended to just before what is now New Westminster, with a small bay extending inland roughly along the course of the Serpentine and Nicomekl Rivers. Point Roberts was a small island, composed of glacial deposits left behind after the Ice Age. Richmond, Sea Island, and Delta had yet to be created.

Plants and animals gradually colonized this newly scoured land from the refuges of Alaska and the USA. Between 4700 and 1500 BCE, the climate was drier and about 1–1.5 degree warmer. By 1000 BCE (December 31 at 11:59:25), the climate was close to today's.

From 10,000 to 2000 BCE, sediment from the Fraser filled in the Pitt River area, Richmond, Delta, Tsawwassen, and Sea Island. This process still continues today, although it has been somewhat slowed by regular dredging of the Fraser. Left unimpeded, Vancouver Island could become a peninsula, connected to the mainland by the Gulf Islands and the Fraser Delta.

No longer weighed down by the ice sheet, the terrain at Vancouver began to regain elevation, in a phenomenon called isostatic rebound. Between 11,000 and 6000 BCE, the land rose by about 4 cm a year. After the glaciers had fully retreated, the land was lifting at the astonishing rate of 10 cm a year, so quickly that the first humans in the area would have noticed the changes year by year. Modern-day evidence of this rapidly shifting shore can be seen in the remnants of sandy beach benches at various levels of the Capilano highlands, such as the Pemberton Heights bluff and sections of the Capilano Canyon trails. Off Highway 99, the Magnesia Creek gravel quarry showcases the remnants of the ancient Magnesia Creek delta, now 150 m above sea level. Before this land rise, the sea had reached as high as the 175-m contour, about the elevation of Prospect Avenue or Cross Creek Road.

It is uncertain what Vancouver will look like a million years from now. Technically, the Ice Age never ended: we are merely experiencing a warm fluctuation in the geological cycle.

Earlier models predicted a return to the colder temperatures of 20,000 years ago. Greenhouse gases emitted by humans, however, could change all this, bringing the world out of the Ice Age for good. Sea level is predicted to rise several metres by the end of this century, a major threat to coastal Vancouver. Worsening the problem is the threat of an earthquake: the 1700 earthquake lowered the local sea level by several metres and caused a tsunami that inundated the Fraser delta. Such a tsunami, amplified by climate change, would be one of the deadliest natural disasters in history. It could wreak havoc on the third-largest city in Canada and on a major American city as well as on the capital of British Columbia.

Further in the future, plate tectonics will render Vancouver unrecognizable. The last fragments of the Juan de Fuca plate will disappear beneath North America. The Pacific Ocean is shrinking as the Atlantic Ocean expands. The San Andreas Fault is splitting California in two: in millions of years, Los Angeles and San Francisco will become California's version of Vancouver Island (although formed differently). That island will eventually move past the British Columbia coast on its way to Alaska.

Some 250 million years from now, North America, South America, Africa, and Eurasia are predicted to merge into a new continent called Pangea Ultima. Antarctica and Australia will be another continent located to the south, with the centre located roughly where Mauritius is today.

It is impossible to predict the climate of the Vancouver area this far in the future. Maybe it will be a desert, maybe a swamp. It will likely be located on the western coast of Pangea Ultima at a latitude comparable to today's Taiwan or Cuba. Vancouver Island will have merged with the coast. One thing is certain: it will look nothing like today's Vancouver.

The forces of nature that drive the motion and erosion of the continents have transformed the surface of the Earth since it began and will do so until the planet's core cools and all life freezes. We happen to live in an era where a city we call Vancouver, built on rock transported thousands of kilometres along a short-lived river we've called the Fraser, is silhouetted against a backdrop of mountains created by the motion of the continents. Geology has blessed this city with clean water, abundant timber, a seaport to trade with the rest of the world, and a mild climate where food can be grown. Yet at the same time, the threat of a catastrophic volcano or earthquake looms over our heads like the sword of Damocles.

APPENDIX 12:
NORTH SHORE WATERSHEDS

There are eight main creeks and rivers descending from the North Shore peaks to Burrard Inlet. From west to east these are Cypress, Brothers, Capilano, MacKay, Mosquito, Hastings, Lynn, and Seymour. All are salmon-bearing. The watersheds, in order of size are:

1. Seymour 176 km² (19 km long below dam; over 50 km long total)
2. Capilano 172 km² (36 km long)
3. Lynn 55.2 km² (18 km long)
4. Mosquito 14.5 km² (8.5 km long)
5. Cypress 13.3 km² (9 km long)
6. Mackay 7.8 km² (8.1 km long)
7. Hastings 7.1 km² (7.5 km long)
8. Brothers 5.63 km² (6.9 km long)
9. Nelson 5.1 km² (4.94 km long)
10. McCartney 4.6 km² (2.2 km long)
11. McDonald 3.74 km² (5.99 km long)
12. Vinson 3.74 km² (4 km long)

The steep slopes of the Howe Sound Crest mountains do not create sizeable rivers, but rather a series of very steep creeks that at peak flow can descend violently, with destructive results below. The watersheds, in order of size are:

1. Furry 54.3 km² (12.4 km long)
2. Deeks 11.5 km² (8 km long)
3. Harvey 6.71 km² (4.9 km long)
4. Magnesia 4.78 km² (4.55 km long)
5. Montizambert 3.92 km² (3.9 km long)
6. Kallahne 3.60 km² (4.75 km long)
7. M/Yahoo 3.25 km² (3.25 km long)
8. Loggers 2.91 km² (3.1 km long)
9. Newman 2 km² (2.4 km long)
10. Bertram 1.91 km² (3.50 km long)
11. Charles 1.7 km² (2.55 km long)
12. Lone Tree 1.44 km² (3.15 km long)

FLOWING INTO HOWE SOUND (NORTH TO SOUTH)

- **Middle Creek** (Squamish name Slhewlháwt').
- **Furry Creek** (Squamish name Énwilh Spalhxn): from Chanter Peak. Named in the 1870s after early prospector and settler Oliver Furry (1863 Ontario – 1905 New Westminster, BC). Logged 1950–1977. Average gradient 7.7°. Tributary:
  ○ **Phyllis Creek**: from Phyllis and Marion lakes (formerly named Fripp and Mackay lakes, after Harry Mackay and Robert Mackay Fripp: see Capilano River below).
- **South Creek** (Squamish name Wékw'wekw'm).
- **24.2 Kilometre Creek**

- **Kallahne Creek** (Squamish name Xwáẁchayay): after Robert Kallahne (b. ca. 1869 Germany; later moved to Bethel, Kitsap County, Washington). Flows from Deeks Peak to Howe Sound. Logged before 1968. Average gradient 19.2°. Official.
- **Bertram Creek** (Squamish name Lhk'etksn): Average gradient 25.2°. Official.
- **Bosco Creek**
- **Brunswick Point Creek**: Logged 1954–1955. Average gradient 22.7°.
- **Deeks Creek** (Squamish name Stl'álkem Stakw or Smàẏlilh-staq or Smalqm-staq: "supernatural water" or "monster creek"): carries water from Deeks Lake to Howe Sound. Logged 1954–1955. Average gradient 12.4°. Official.
- **Loggers Creek** (Squamish name Nínich Kw'litkm): adopted 1983. Logged 1952–1957 and 1960–1965. Average gradient 28.0°. Official.
- **Dry Gulch Creek**
- **M (Yahoo) Creek** (Squamish name Kw'pel): flows from Brunswick and Hat to Howe Sound (to the north of Brunswick Beach). Both names official. Origin of "Yahoo" unknown. "M" so named because it is the 13th creek along the highway. Logged 1960–1965. Average gradient 27.9°. Official.
- **Magnesia Creek** (Squamish name Kél'etstn): drains Magnesia Meadows. Named because early explorers believed the waters had a slight laxative effect, similar to milk of magnesia. Logged before 1957 and 1960–1965. Average gradient 21.1°.
- **Alberta Creek** (Squamish name P'ap'k'): drains slopes of Mt. Harvey. The trail from Lions Bay to Mount Harvey gives one a view of this creek. Named at the same time as nearby Alberta Bay in 1903 by William Allan, a surveyor. Origin of "Alberta" not known. In 1983 a debris flow in this creek killed two Lions Bay brothers (see HAR, JAS, and THO). Logged in the 1950s. Average gradient 27.1°. Official.
- **Harvey Creek**: drains James, David, and Lions area. Enters Alberta Bay to the south of Lions Bay. After Mt. Harvey. Logged 1966–1970. Average gradient 18.6°. Official.
- **Rundle Creek**: average gradient 24.8°. Official.
- **Lone Tree Creek**: drains Unnecessary area. Average gradient 25.8°. Official.
- **Cosmo Creek**
- **Newman Creek**: drains area between St. Marks and Unnecessary. Named after W.J. Newman, who staked a claim on the creek in 1922. Logged in 1966. Average gradient 31.0°. Official.
- **Turpin Creek**: after Thomas K. Turpin, who owned land in the area in 1909. Drains lower slopes of St. Marks Summit. Enters Howe Sound to the north of Strachan Creek. Formerly known as "Strachan Creek No. 1." Logged 1966–1968. It is the steepest creek, with an average gradient of 35.5°. Official.
- **Charles Creek**: after Charles McCarroll Smith, who applied for water rights on this creek in 1951. Drains ridge to the south of St. Marks. Enters Howe Sound. Sometimes referred to as "Strachan Creek" (or "Strachan Creek No. 2"), although its official name has been Charles since 1959. Average gradient 28.2°. Official.

- **Strip Creek**: drains area to the north of Black. Enters Howe Sound. The second-steepest creek, with an average gradient of 33.1°. Official.
- **Montizambert Creek**: after Lt.-Col. H. St. John Montizambert, who owned part of the creek. Montizambert was granted his land in 1909. Flows into Howe Sound to the north of Sunset Beach. Communities on the eastern side of Howe Sound receive some of their water from this creek. Logged 1968–1969. Average gradient 20.1°. Official.
- **Sclufield Creek**: after Edith Sclufield, an early landowner. Enters Howe Sound to the south of Sunset Beach. Average gradient 31.3°. Official.
- **Sunset Creek**: enters Howe Sound at Sunset Beach.
- **Disbrow Creek**: after Caroline Brydon-Jack (née Disbrow). Her son William Disbrow Brydon-Jack was a Vancouver surgeon (and coroner from 1923 to 1935). Enters Howe Sound to the south of Sunset Beach. Average gradient 25.3°. Official.
- **Larsen Creek** (Squamish name Temlh: "ochre-gathering place"): after pioneer and North Vancouver hotelier Peter Larsen, who owned the land at the mouth of the creek. Originates on Arbutus Plateau on the southwest side of Black Mountain. Flows through Gleneagles golf course and the site of Peter Larsen's ranch, to Larsen Bay. Formerly labelled "Dodds Creek."
- **Nelson Creek**: after August Nelson (Neilson), at one time the owner of Eagle Island, and a framer at Hastings Mill. Flows into Fisherman's Cove. Official. Tributary:
  - **Whyte Creek**: after Colonel Albert Whyte, early West Vancouverite. Flows from Whyte Lake to Nelson Creek.
- **Eagle Creek**: named after the abundance of eagles during salmon spawning season (July–November; best salmon around September–October). Sometimes called an extension of Dick Creek rather than a creek in its own right. Flows from Dick Lake to Eagle Harbour. Tributary:
  - **Dick Creek**: after William James Dick, an early North Vancouver alderman. Dick discovered Dick Lake (the source of Dick Creek) while searching for potential water sources for the growing city. Flows from the slopes of Black Mountain into Dick (Eagle) Lake.
- **Wood Creek**: after Jack A. Wood, municipal forest ranger of West Vancouver from the 1940s to the 1970s. Enters Eagle Creek just before the latter enters Eagle Harbour.

FLOWING INTO BURRARD INLET (FROM POINT ATKINSON, WEST TO EAST)
- **Caulfeild Creek**: after pioneer Francis Caulfeild. Not to be confused with Caulfields Creek (now named Willow Creek).
- **Piccadilly Creek**: originally called Claymore Creek. Named after North Piccadilly area of West Vancouver, which it drains. Flows from Upper Caulfeild to English Bay at the western end of Ross Crescent.
- **Willow Creek**: originally named Caulfields Creek after Francis Caulfeild, who dammed it (at roughly 85 m above sea level) to provide water. Caulfeild then built another dam 210 m up Cypress Creek. Name later changed to Willow Creek for reasons unknown. Enters Burrard Inlet at Cypress Park.
- **Cypress Creek** (Squamish name S-tq'-il, meaning "bad flatulence smell"): after stands of yellow cedar (often called cypress) near its source. In 1870 Vancouver businessman (and founder of Moodyville) Sewell Prescott Moody tried to float yellow cedar down the creek as part of a new logging operation, but the venture failed. Area near mouth settled in 1886 by Walter Irwin, the Point Atkinson lightkeeper. In the late 19th century there was a logging

flume from Cypress Creek at 366 m to Eyremount Mill at 304 m. Originates on east Black Mountain plateau, Mount Strachan, and Hollyburn Mountain in Cypress Provincial Park. Drains Strachan and Yew Lakes. Discharges near Pilot Cove. It has over 25 tributaries in the upper watershed, mostly unnamed. Named tributaries:

- o **Black Creek**: flows from lakes near the top of Black Mountain to Cypress Creek.
- o **McCallum Creek**: name origin unknown. Name unofficial.
- **Godman Creek**: after Richard T. Godman, a British industrialist who planned to build a sawmill along the creek in 1907. Originates on Hollyburn Ridge near Eagle Lake Road and enters Burrard Inlet at the east end of Sandy Cove. Also called "Sandy Cove Creek" in 1976.
- **Turner Creek**: named after a blacksmith named Turner. Enters Burrard Inlet at West Bay (Patterson Cove).
- **Cave Creek**: after Guy N. Cave, who in 1918 settled in the West Bay area. At some point the Pacific Great Eastern Railway used water from this creek for their steam engines. Enters Burrard Inlet at West Bay.
- **Westmount Creek**: originates on the south flank of Hollyburn Ridge. Enters Burrard Inlet between Radcliffe and Travers avenues. Named after the Westmount neighbourhood it passes through.
- **Pipe Creek**: flows into Burrard Inlet to the east of 31st Street. Name origin obscure. In the summers of 1914 and 1915, the Municipality of West Vancouver drew water from this creek to meet demand. Perhaps a pipe was involved in this operation. Called "Gisby Creek" in 1976.
- **Rodgers Creek**: after Bill J. Rodgers, who took water from this creek. Enters Burrard Inlet to the west of 28th Street.
- **Marr Creek**: after George Marr, operator of an early logging camp from 1903 to 1909. Originates on the south flank of Hollyburn Ridge. Flows into Burrard Inlet 100 m east of 25th Street, at Dundarave Park.
- **McDonald Creek** (Squamish name Ch'tl'am Swa7lt): likely named after Angus McDonald, who owned land bordered by the creek. This creek was also known as Spencer Creek because it crossed the property of a man named Spencer. Has three main branches. Originates on the south flank of Hollyburn Ridge. Flows into Burrard Inlet below 19th Street. Called "McGowan Creek" in 1976.
- **Lawson Creek** (Squamish name Smelákw'a Swa7lt): after John Lawson, the father of West Vancouver. Formerly known as Hollyburn Creek or Capilano Creek.
- **Vinson Creek**: after Valient Vivian Vinson, West Vancouver reeve from 1918–1920, 1922, and 1927–1929. Originates on the south flank of Hollyburn Ridge. Enters Burrard Inlet at the base of 13th Street. Mistakenly called "Vincent Creek" in 1976.
- **Swy-Wee Creek**: runs through Ambleside Park to Duck Pond, which is the remnant of a slough connected to Burrard Inlet. Squamish burial parties used to paddle their canoes up the slough to reach their cemetery, located above what is now Park Royal.
- **Capilano River** (Squamish name Homulcheson or Xwemélch'stn Stakw): after Chief Kiapalano. For more on Kiapalano, see the Mt. Capilano route description. The mouth of the Capilano was formerly a wide estuary with outflow to both west and east of the present Lions Gate bridge. Much of the landmass including the present Capilano Reserve #5 was reclaimed when the river was channelled to the west of the bridge; the ghost of the former estuary is still obvious to the east. Capilano was officially elevated from "Creek" to "River" on May 6, 1947. There is debate about the first European expedition to discover its

headwaters: both claimants were accompanied by Chief Capilano. One version has Phillip Oben (1855–1933) and Chief Joe Capilano (1870 Yakw'ts near Squamish – 1910 North Vancouver) crossing from the First Narrows to Howe Sound in June 1892. In the other, Amedee Percy "A.P." Horne (1867 London – 1967 Vancouver); Harry Hadfield Mackay (1879 Inverness – 1895 Vancouver), son of George Grant Mackay (1827 Inverness – 1893 Vancouver), the owner of the Capilano Suspension Bridge; and Robert Mackay Fripp (1858 St. Pancras, London – 1917 Vancouver), an architect; with Chief Joe Capilano and his nephew, also named Joe Capilano, crossed from Howe Sound to the First Narrows on May 21–28, 1890. Tributaries listed from north to south, with the direction from which they enter the river:

- west: **Windsor Creek**, after Mt. Windsor.
- east: **Andrews Creek**, after Mt. Andrews.
- west: **Hanover Creek**, after Hanover Mountain.
- east: **Daniels Creek**, after Mt. Daniels.
- west: **Connolly Creek**
- west: **Macklin Creek**, flows from Macklin (Surprise) Lake.
- west: **Enchantment Creek**
- west: **Hesketh Creek**
- east: **Eastcap Creek**, from "East Capilano". Headwaters at Little Eastcap Lake. Tributary:
  - » **Palisade Creek**: headwaters at Palisade Lake.
- east: **Healmond Creek,** after H.E. Almond, who represented Vancouver on the Greater Vancouver Water District Board in the 1920s (for a similar play on a GVWDB name, see Mount Eldee below in **Appendix 20**.
- east: **Dean Creek**, after E.W. Dean, member of the Greater Vancouver Water District Board 1927–28. Formerly "West Crown Creek." A traditional route up Crown Mountain.
- west: **Sisters Creek**, after the legendary name for The Lions. Tributaries:
  - » **Lembke Creek**
  - » **Strachan Creek**: after Mt. Strachan. Flows from Mt. Strachan to Sisters Creek, a tributary of the Capilano River before Capilano Lake.
- west: **Nickey Creek**: after Addison B. Nickey, of the Capilano Timber Company, which logged the nearby slopes. Originates on eastern Hollyburn Ridge.
- east: **Fellowes Creek**: after Frederick Lyon Fellowes (1860–1941), Vancouver city engineer from 1911 to 1924. Originally named Johnston Creek. Flows into upper Capilano Lake.
- east: **Crown Creek**: after Crown Mountain.
- east: **Colwood Creek**: into Capilano Lake.
- east: **Lions Creek**: into Capilano Lake.
- east: **Windsor Creek**: into Capilano Lake.
- east: **Drifter Creek**: into Capilano Lake.
- east: **Grouse Creek**: into Capilano Lake.
- west: **Houlgate Creek**: after R. Kerr Houlgate, the builder of the first log flume in the Capilano valley. Remnants of the flume can still be seen on the ground near Houlgate Creek Park.
- west: **Brothers Creek**: originally named Sisters Creek by workmen in the Mathers

Avenue area encountering three creeks close to one another. Name changed to Brothers due to other Sisters Creek. Drains Elveden Lake in British Properties, West Lake, and Lost Lake. Enters the Capilano River near eastern Clyde Avenue, just north of the Marine Drive Bridge.

> » **Hadden Creek**: after Harvey Haddon, a textile merchant from Nottingham, England. Haddon bought 160 acres in West Vancouver (in what is now the British Properties) in 1903. He built a mansion on this property; the clubhouse of the Capilano Golf and Country Club stands on the site today. The creek was also known as Meglaughlin Creek after I.T. Meglaughlin, who owned land nearby.

- **Mackay Creek** (pronounced "Mac-eye," not "Mac-Kaye") (Squamish name Tl'alhmá7elkw Swa7lt, "salt water creek") after Mackay Road, which was named after George Grant Mackay (1827 Inverness – January 1, 1893), who in 1889 had built the first iteration of the Capilano Suspension Bridge, and who owned extensive property in the area. He was also a founder of Vernon and a pioneer in developing the Okanagan. Originates at around 853 m near the top on the southwest slope of Grouse Mountain. Tributaries:
  - ○ **Salal Creek**: from west, running parallel to Blue Skyride.
  - ○ **Sokalie Creek:** northeast headwaters of Mackay (on 1927 Grouse Map).
  - ○ **Emsley Creek**: named in 1986 after Albert and Ruth Emsley, who lived near and cared for the creek, after a request from their neighbours.
- **Mosquito Creek** (Squamish name Eslha7án Swa7lt or Melawahna, meaning "sweet wind"): formerly known as Trythall's Creek (1902). Known as Mosquito Creek by 1910. Likely named by Sid Williams, the first known ascender of Grouse. The creek had a large estuary that no longer exists: the estuary between Fell and Bewicke was filled and extended 500 m into the inlet for industrial use (1912–1915) and the eastern part of the estuary was filled in 1960. Tributaries:
  - ○ **Wolverine Creek**: from west, from Grouse Plateau (on 1927 Grouse Map).
  - ○ **Tumwata Creek:** from east, from Fromme slopes (on 1927 Grouse Map) ("waterfall" in Chinook).
  - ○ **Mission Creek**: after the Squamish Mission Indian Reserve, through which it passes. The settlement originated as an early mission, St. Paul's Catholic church (a national historic site) being the oldest surviving church in British Columbia. Also known as Ustlawn (Eslá7an). Tributary:
    - » **Thain Creek**: after Captain Murray N. Thain (1839 Saint John, NB – 1907), Moodyville pioneer and first harbourmaster.
  - ○ **Wagg Creek**: after George Wagg, who owned a lot between 29th and Queens, in the North Lonsdale area. Tributary:
    - » **St. Martin's Creek**: after St. Martin's Anglican church on Windsor Road.
- **Lynn Creek** (Kwa-hul-cha or Xá7elcha Swa7lt): formerly known as "Fred's Creek" after Frederick Howson, who was granted land in 1863. A survey made by J.B. Launders in 1869 showed Lynn Creek as "Freds Creek." From 1877 to 1900 the creek appeared without a name on maps, and then was labelled Lynn Creek. The spelling is probably a drafting error, based on the name of John Linn, an early settler (see LYN for more on the life of John Linn). Tributaries, from south to north:
  - ○ west: **Keith Creek**

- ○ east: **Morton Creek**
- ○ west: **Hastings Creek** (into Lynn): after the Hastings Shingle and Manufacturing Company, which started logging the area in 1897. Tributaries, from west to east:
  - » **Transformer Creek**: from the nearby powerline.
  - » **Dunell Creek**: possibly named after a Dunell family that lived in North Vancouver in the 1930s.
  - » **Dyer Creek**: starts on the east side of Grouse Mountain. Possibly named after Dr. Harold Dyer (1875 England – 1963) who immigrated to Canada in 1905 and became health officer for the District of North Vancouver. He became coroner in 1923 and retired in 1961.
  - » **Kilmer Creek**: starts on the east side of Grouse Mountain. Possibly after J.H. Kilmer, civil engineer, ca. 1910.
  - » **Thames Creek**: after the River Thames in England. Tributary:
    - – **Coleman Creek**
  - » **Pierard Creek**: after Leander and Helen Pierard (ca. 1973), of Belgium, neighbours of Walter Draycott.
  - » **Hoskins Creek**
- ○ west: **Barrier Creek**, flows into Kennedy Creek.
- ○ west: **Kennedy Creek**, after Thomas Leslie Kennedy (1866–1958), a North Vancouver councillor who proposed setting aside the lake as a reservoir. The 1927 Grouse Mountain map names the lake and its creek "Goat."
  - » **Whistler Creek**: flows into Kennedy Creek, with headwaters between Grouse and Dam. The col between these two mountains was formerly referred to as "Whistler Pass."
- ○ west: **Wickenden Creek**, after Charles Osborne Wickenden (1849 – 1934), District of North Vancouver reeve (1901–1902) and architect responsible for the design of many early Vancouver buildings including Christ Church Cathedral. Also referred to as Neve Creek.
- ○ west: **Draycott Creek**, after Walter MacKay Draycott (February 24, 1883, Belgrave, Leicestershire, England – 1985), Lynn Valley pioneer, geologist, historian, naturalist. Draycott Creek and Gully lead up to Forks Peak.
- ○ east: **Norvan Creek**, formerly White Creek and East Fork of Lynn Creek. A contraction of "North Vancouver." Has several falls: Norvan Falls, Fairy Falls, Paisley Falls, downstream to upstream respectively.
- ○ west: **Hanes Creek**, after George S. Hanes, mayor of North Vancouver (1913; 1915–16) and Vancouver city engineer for many years. Formerly known as "West Fork of Lynn Creek."
- **Seymour River** (Tsleil-Waututh name Ch'ich'elxwi7kw Stakw, meaning "narrow"): officially promoted from "creek" to "river" on May 6, 1947. Tributaries, from south to north:
  - ○ west: **Maplewood Creek**, originates above Mount Seymour Parkway. Upslope groundwater discharged through springs and seepages creates wetlands below which form the headwaters of Maplewood Creek.
  - ○ east: **Canyon Creek**
  - ○ east: **Mystery Creek**, after Mystery Lake, which it drains.
  - ○ east: **Boulder Creek**, likely after boulders in the creek.
  - ○ east: **Semlin Creek**
  - ○ west: **Rice Creek**, name origin unknown. See Rice Peak for more.

- west: **Balloon** or **Ginpole Creek**, after the balloon logging above on South Lynn Peak: see that peak.
- east: **Suicide Creek**, name origin unknown. See Suicide Bluffs.
- west: **McKenzie Creek**
- west: **Hydraulic Creek**, after the 1911 hydraulic works on a zinc claim above and upstream.
- east: **Intake Creek**, from former water intake dam site.
- east: **Jessie Creek**
- east: **Baxter Creek**
- west: **Owl & Talon Creek**
- west: **O'Hayes Creek**
- east: **West Elsay Creek**, after Mt. Elsay.
- east: **Rolf Creek**, from Rolf (Lost) Lake; named by E.A. Cleveland but origin of "Rolf" unknown.
- east: **Wyssen Creek**, probably after the Wyssen logging cableway systems used in logging the Seymour area: a still-active Swiss company founded in 1926 by Jakob Wyssen.
- west: **Clear Creek**
- west: **Stoney Creek**
- east: **Squamish Creek**, after Squamish First Nation.
- west: **Fir Creek**, likely after the Douglas firs growing near the creek.
- east: **Crossen Creek**, possibly after Eric Congdon Crossin (1923 Winnipeg – 2013 North Vancouver), a forester integral to the development of the Seymour Demonstration Forest and to recording the forest history of North Shore forests. He donated his extensive collection of maps and aerial photographs of the North Shore to the North Vancouver Museum and Archives.
- west: **Paton Creek**, after James Alexander Paton, an early Vancouver alderman and member of the water board. Named by E.A. Cleveland. See Paton Peak. Formerly called Cougar Creek.
- west: **Burwell Creek**, into Seymour Lake), into which flows:
  - » west: **Cathedral Creek**
- east: **Gibbens Creek**, into Seymour Lake
- east: **Fannin Creek**, into Seymour Lake. After John Fannin (1837 Kemptville, Upper Canada – 1904 Victoria), shoemaker, office holder, guide, taxidermist, natural historian, and founder of the Royal British Columbia Museum.
- **McCartney Creek**, after Alan Edward McCartney (1852–1901), Vancouver civil engineer and North Vancouver councillor, who owned land adjoining the creek. It is the main freshwater source for the Maplewood estuary at Maplewood Flats Conservation Area. Tributaries, from west to east:
  - **Blueridge Creek**: after the appearance of the blue ridge on the lower slopes of Seymour.
  - **Trillium Creek**
  - **Woods Creek**
  - **Mountain Creek**
- **Range Creek**: after nearby Blair Rifle Range.
- **Thomas Creek**
- **Taylor Creek**
- **Roche Point Creek**, after nearby Roche Point, and in turn after Lt. Richard Roche of the Royal Navy.

FLOWING INTO INDIAN ARM (SOUTH TO NORTH)

The names of most of these creeks are unofficial.

- **Hegel Creek**
- **Parkside Creek**
- **Mackeras Creek**
- **Gallant Creek**, after Gallant Drive, in turn after Edward Gallant (1887 Halifax – 1959 Deep Cove), a local chiropractor.
- **Hunter Creek**
- **Panorama Creek**
- **Kai Creek**
- **Matthews Brook**
- **Gavles Creek**
- **Cove Creek**, after Deep Cove.
- **Cleopatra Creek**
- **Francis Creek**: (official), name origin unknown.
- **Ward Creek**, after John Eades Ward (1878–1940), a realtor and Woodlands owner; son-in-law of the Reverend Hugh Wood, the brother and heir of Alexander Myddleton Wood.
- **Ostler Creek**, after Thomas Alfred Ostler (1864 England – 1936 Vancouver), a settler in Woodlands who worked for the owner, Boer War veteran Alexander Myddleton Wood (1873 – 1906 Vancouver), after whom Woodlands was named.
- **Allan Creek** (official), possibly after Alan Edward McCartney (see McCartney Creek).
- **Gardner Creek**: see Gardner Brook below.
- **Sunshine Creek**, after Sunshine resort or beach, north of Woodlands. Flows into Indian Arm via a small waterfall.
- **Cayley Creek**, possibly named after Beverley Cochrane Cayley (1898 Rossland – 1928 Vancouver), a young lawyer, early BCMC member, and namesake of Mt. Cayley.
- **Scott-Goldie Creek** (official), after the Scott-Goldie company that operated a quarry on the west side of Indian Arm opposite Twin Islands from 1912.
- **Buddeny Creek**
- **Percy Creek** (official), likely after Major Percy Ward (1882–1964), a South Woodlands owner. He was the brother of J.E. Ward, above, and a Boer War veteran who served as a North Vancouver alderman intermittently between 1912 and 1921.
- **Vapour Creek**
- **Gardner Brook**, likely after Bill Gardner, who lived at Brighton Beach from the 1940s to the 1970s.
- **Shone Creek** (official)
- **Underhill Creek** (official), after the Underhill family, who had a cottage at Frame's Landing. See **Appendix 20** at "Unknown peaks."
- **Ragland Creek**
- **Holmden Creek** (official)
- **Coldwell Creek** (official), named after Charles A. Coldwell (1844 Saint John, NB – 1897 Vancouver), a realtor and one of the ten aldermen on Vancouver's first city council (1886).
- **Friar Creek**
- **Elsay Creek** (and Silver Falls) (official), after Mount Elsay, its source.
- **Clegg Creek**: flows from Clegg Lake (named by E.A. Cleveland, chief commissioner of the Greater Vancouver Water District, after Albert H. Clegg, a draftsman with the District). Includes Rainbow Falls.

- **Bishop Creek** (official): see Mt. Bishop.
- **Clementine Creek** (official): see Clementine Peak.
- **Wigwam Creek** (and Spray of Pearls Falls): (both official), formerly Cathedral Creek. Falls named by Jack P. McConnell, editor of the *BC Saturday Sunset* newspaper.

APPENDIX 13:
NAME HISTORY FROM THE GLORIOUS FIRST OF JUNE

In naming peaks and other geographic landmarks in and around Howe Sound in 1859, Captain George Henry Richards, aboard HMS *Plumper*, drew inspiration from the historic naval battle in which English forces defeated the French on June 1, 1794, continuing the theme set down by Captain Vancouver, who had named Howe Sound after the (future) commander of the Royal Navy in that battle. These later names include the mountains Gambier, Harvey, Gardner, Strachan, Brunswick, and (across the sound) Elphinstone; the islands Pasley, Bowyer, Hutt, and Keats; Defence Islet (between Gambier and Anvil Island); the channels Montagu (between Anvil Island and the east side of Howe Sound) and Ramillies (between Anvil Island and Gambier), and Collingwood (between Bowen and Keats); the passages Latona (between Woolridge Island and Gambier), Barfleur (between Keats and Pasley Island), and Thornborough (between Gambier and the west side of Howe Sound); the points Cotton (Keats), Hood (Bowen), Hope and Ekins (Gambier), Irby and Domett (Anvil); Port Graves (Gambier); and Cape Roger Curtis (Bowen).

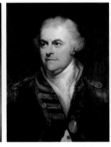

Captain James Bowen (1751–1835).

Captain John Harvey (1740–1794).

Vice-Admiral Lord Alan Gardner (1742–1809).

Admiral of the Fleet James Gambier, 1st Baron Gambier GCB (1756–1833).

LORD HOWE'S FLEET ON THE GLORIOUS FIRST OF JUNE

HMS *Caesar*	Captain Anthony Molloy; third rate*; 80 guns.
HMS *Bellerophon*	Rear Admiral Thomas Pasley; Captain William Johnstone Hope; third rate; 74 guns; extensive damage to masts and rigging.
HMS *Leviathan*	Captain Lord Hugh Seymour; third rate; 74 guns.
HMS *Russell*	Captain John Willett Payne; third rate; 74 guns.
HMS *Royal Sovereign*	Vice-Admiral Thomas Graves; Captain Henry Nicholls; first rate; 100 guns; damage to masts and rigging.
HMS *Marlborough*	Captain George Cranfield-Berkeley; third rate; 74 guns; totally dismasted.

HMS *Defence*	Captain James Gambier; third rate; 74 guns; totally dismasted.
HMS *Impregnable*	Rear Admiral Benjamin Caldwell; Captain George Blagdon Westcott; second rate; 98 guns; damage to masts and rigging.
HMS *Tremendous*	Captain James Pigott; third rate; 74 guns.
HMS *Barfleur*	Rear Admiral George Bowyer; Captain Cuthbert Collingwood; second rate; 98 guns.
HMS *Invincible*	Captain Thomas Pakenham; third rate; 74 guns.
HMS *Culloden*	Captain Isaac Schomberg; third rate; 74 guns.
HMS *Gibraltar*	Captain Thomas Mackenzie; third rate; 80 guns.
HMS *Queen Charlotte*	Admiral Lord Howe; Captain Sir Roger Curtis; Captain Sir Andrew Snape Douglas; Master (later Rear Admiral) James Bowen; first rate; 100 guns; extensive damage to masts and rigging.
HMS *Brunswick*	Captain John Harvey†; Lieutenant William Edward Cracraft; third rate; 74 guns; lost mizzenmast, extensive damage to remaining masts and rigging.
HMS *Valiant*	Captain Thomas Pringle; third rate; 74 guns.
HMS *Orion*	Captain John Thomas Duckworth; third rate; 74 guns; minor damage to masts and rigging.
HMS *Queen*	Rear Admiral Alan Gardner; second rate; 98 guns; lost main-mast, damage to remaining masts and rigging.
HMS *Ramillies*	Captain Henry Harvey (and Lieutenant, later Admiral Sir, Richard Keats); third rate; 74 guns.
HMS *Alfred*	Captain John Bazley; third rate; 74 guns.
HMS *Montagu*	Captain James Montagu†; third rate; 74 guns.
HMS *Royal George*	Vice-admiral Sir Alexander Hood; Captain William Domett; first rate; 100 guns; lost foremast, damage to remaining masts and rigging.
HMS *Majestic*	Captain Charles Cotton; third rate; 74 guns.
HMS *Glory*	Captain John Elphinstone; second rate; 98 guns; severe damage to masts and rigging.
HMS *Thunderer*	Captain Albemarle Bertie; third rate; 74 guns.

SUPPORT VESSELS

HMS *Phaeton*	Captain William Bentinck; fifth rate; 38 guns.
HMS *Latona*	Captain Edward Thornbrough; fifth rate; 38 guns.
HMS *Niger*	Captain Arthur Kaye Legge; fifth rate; 36 guns.
HMS *Southampton*	Captain Robert Forbes; fifth rate; 36 guns.
HMS *Venus*	Captain William Brown; fifth rate; 36 guns.
HMS *Aquilon*	Captain Robert Stopford; fifth rate; 36 guns.
HMS *Pegasus*	Captain Robert Barlow; sixth rate; 28 guns.

HMS *Charon*	Captain George Countess; hospital ship.
HMS *Comet*	Commander William Bradley; fireship; 14 guns.
HMS *Incendiary*	Commander John Cooke; fireship; 14 guns.
HMS *Kingfisher*	Captain Thomas Le Marchant Gosselyn; sloop; 18 guns.
HMS *Rattler*	Lieutenant John Winne; cutter; 16 guns.
HMS *Ranger*	Lieutenant Charles Cotgrave; cutter; 16 guns.

ADMIRAL MONTAGU'S ATTACHED SQUADRON

HMS *Hector*	Rear Admiral George Montagu; Captain Lawrence Halstead; third rate; 74 guns.
HMS *Alexander*	Captain Richard Rodney Bligh; third rate; 74 guns.
HMS *Ganges*	Captain William Truscott; third rate; 74 guns.
HMS *Colossus*	Captain Charles Pole; third rate; 74 guns.
HMS *Bellona*	Captain George Wilson; third rate; 74 guns.
HMS *Theseus*	Captain Robert Calder; third rate; 74 guns.
HMS *Arrogant*	Captain Richard Lucas; third rate; 74 guns.
HMS *Minotaur*	Captain Thomas Louis; third rate; 74 guns.
HMS *Ruby*	Captain Sir Richard Bickerton; third rate; 64 guns.
HMS *Pallas*	Captain Henry Curzon; fifth rate; 32 guns.
HMS *Concorde*	Captain Sir Richard Strachan; fifth rate; 36 guns.

CAPTAIN RAINIER'S CONVOY ESCORT

HMS *Suffolk*	Captain Peter Rainier; third rate; 74 guns.

Total casualties: 953, of which 229 killed, 724 wounded

† = killed in battle

* The Royal Navy rated its warships according to the size of their crews and later the number of their carriage-mounted guns.

APPENDIX 14: NAME HISTORY OF THE HOUSE OF WETTIN–SAXE-COBURG–WINDSOR

The Stuart King James II (1633–1701), feared to be planning the return of Britain to absolutist Catholic rule, fled the country after the birth of a son, James Francis Edward Stuart (1688–1766) (later known as the "Old Pretender," in contrast to his son, Charles, a.k.a. the "Young Pretender," or "Bonnie Prince Charlie" (1720–1788)): the Glorious Revolution of 1688. James's Protestant daughter, Mary II (1662–1694), became co-regent with her husband (and cousin) William III of Orange (1650–1702). Mary died in 1694. William was loath to remarry and died without an heir. The next in line to the throne was Mary's sister Anne. In 1700 Anne's only surviving child, Prince William, Duke of Gloucester, died. It appeared that the House of Orange would soon meet an abrupt end, leading to the risk that the Catholic James or his son would be reinstated.

Accordingly the English Parliament, in the Act of Settlement, 1701, declared that in the default of legitimate issue from Anne or William III, the Crown was to settle upon the Protestant Princess Sophia of the Palatinate, Electress of Hanover (1630–1714). Sophia was a granddaughter of James I of England. Her husband was Prince Ernest Augustus of Brunswick–Lüneburg (1629–1698), a younger son of the duke of that duchy. Sophia died less than two months before she would have become queen, and her eldest son, George Louis, Elector of Hanover (1660–1727), ascended the throne as George I on August 1, 1714, upon the death of Queen Anne. This created a union between the British Crown and the Electorate of Hanover which lasted until 1837 at the death of William IV without a male heir. Under Salic law Victoria could not inherit the Kingdom of Hanover and the duchies unless the entire male line became extinct; thus those possessions passed to the next eligible male heir, Victoria's uncle Ernest Augustus I of Hanover, Duke of Cumberland and Teviotdale, the fifth son of George III.

Queen Victoria was the last British monarch of the House of Hanover. She married Albert (1819–1861), of the House of Saxe-Coburg and Gotha. The son of Victoria and Albert became King Edward VII. As such, he became the first British monarch of the House of Saxe-Coburg and Gotha. After Albert's death, Queen Victoria had consulted the College of Heralds in England to determine the correct personal surname of her late husband and thus the proper surname of the royal family upon the accession of her son. The college concluded that the proper surname was "Wettin," after the royal house that ruled territories of the present-day German states of Saxony and Thuringia from the 10th century to the end of the First World War and from which Albert was descended. But this name was never used, either by the Queen or by her son and grandson, King Edward VII and King George V; they used the surname "Saxe-Coburg and Gotha."

Anti-German sentiment during the war prompted the royal family to change their very Germanic surname in 1917. "Wettin" and "Wipper" (after a river flowing through the Wettin territory of Saxony) were both considered but both were mercifully rejected as "unsuitably comic." In the end, the British royal family adopted the name of the castle where George V spent his boyhood – Windsor – as it remains today.

The present King Philippe of Belgium is a Saxe-Coburg and Gotha descendant. The heir to the former House of Hanover is Prince Ernest Augustus of Hanover (born 1954), husband of Princess Caroline of Monaco.

The House of Hanover is a younger branch of the House of Welf (otherwise known as the House of "Guelph" after which the Ontario city is named), which in turn is the senior branch of the House of Este. These, along with "Saxe," provide other potential names for peaks in the Howe Sound Crest Trail area.

APPENDIX 15: NAMING PEAKS

Some of the names of peaks in the book are official; others are unofficial, developed either through recent popular use (e.g., Thomas) or a return to historic use (e.g., Gambier, Echo, Rice, Jarrett, Clementine). The process to become an official name in modern times is stringent.

The provincial Geographical Names Office, Heritage Branch, Ministry of Forests, Lands, Natural Resource Operations and Rural Development is the final arbiter of names of mountains that lie wholly within British Columbia (peaks in national parks, or straddling provincial or international borders are the joint responsibility of the provincial and federal governments). The office maintains a six-page document (pdf at is.gd/xuZbb3) that sets out its broad policy, philosophy, and ambitions:

> Geographical names are more than labels on maps and road signs; they convey aspects of the history and promise of an area that might otherwise be overlooked or forgotten by visitors and later generations. Whether preserved on maps, in texts, or through an oral tradition, they reveal patterns of settlement, exploration and migration, and mirror outside influences to our history. … The application of names to geographical features is a public trust, carried out for the benefit of present and future generations. Underlying the naming process is the recognition that not all features need a name at this time; to preserve and enhance the aesthetic appeal of wilderness areas in the province….

> The policy sets out the principles for naming peaks:
> A. The principles of openness and administrative fairness are followed;
> B. Proposals for new geographical names or changes to existing names may be submitted by any interested individual or group;
> C. Office itself does not initiate new names or changes to existing names for geographical features;
> D. A geographical name, or the right to name a geographical feature, cannot be bought or sold, raffled or otherwise conferred through contest or auction;
> E. Names of facilities established by postal authorities, railway companies and major public utilities will be accepted as official place names, if they conform to the other policies;
> F. The Geographical Names Office will, upon request, advise any group concerned with the selection of geographical names regarding the suitability and spelling of such names;
> G. Official adoption of submitted geographical names is based on conformity with the Geographical Naming Policies and is not subject to the wish of a dominant interest group or persons;
> H. Ownership of land does not confer the right or entitlement to name a geographical feature. Application of a name does not prejudice legitimate claims to the land;

I. Company or commercial product names are not acceptable as geographical names unless there is long-standing local usage of the name by the general public. Proposals for new names or changes to existing names that are intended to promote or enhance a commercial venture will not be considered;

J. Geographical names should be recognizable words or acceptable combinations of words, and should be in good taste. Discriminatory or derogatory names will not be considered.

APPENDIX 16:
INDIGENOUS PEOPLES
AND THE NORTH SHORE MOUNTAINS

The two First Nations communities that live in the areas covered by this book are the Squamish (traditionally pronounced "Sqw-HO-o-meesh," rendered in phonetic symbols as Skwx̱wú7mesh, with the "7" representing a glottal stop as found in the expression "uh-oh"), in the west and north, and the Tsleil-Waututh (formerly called "Burrard"; pronounced "tSLAY-wah-tooth"), in the east. Both peoples are Coast Salish and speak a dialect of what is referred to as the Downriver Halkomelem language. The two groups are ethnically and culturally close but politically separate.

The Tsleil-Waututh, known as the "people of the inlet," had villages at the site of their present Burrard reserve, located between Maplewood Flats and Deep Cove (Tsleil-Waututh), as well as Cates Park (Whey-ah-wichen) and Cove Cliff (Say-umiton). Their population numbers around 500, of whom about half live on the reserve.

The Squamish were centred on Howe Sound but had villages on the North Shore at present-day Horseshoe Bay (Ch'axa'y, referring to the sizzling sound of the herring as they spawned in the bay); Ambleside and the Capilano Reserve at First Narrows (Homulcheson or Xwemelch'stn), to the east of the Capilano River; the site of the Mission Reserve (Siha7an' or Esla7an or Ustlawn), on Wagg and Mosquito creeks; and the Seymour Creek Reserve (Ch'ich'elxwi7kw or Jol-gul-hook), near the mouth of the Seymour River at the Second Narrows. The Squamish Nation is comprised of descendants of the Coast Salish peoples who lived in the present-day Greater Vancouver area, Gibson's Landing, and the Squamish River watershed. On July 23, 1923, 16 Squamish-speaking tribes amalgamated to form the Squamish Band. The nation's population is scattered among nine communities stretching from North Vancouver to northern Howe Sound. Approximately 2,200 of the 4,100 Squamish Nation members live on-reserve.

The Indigenous population on the North Shore is the subject of conjecture and debate. By the time of Contact, in 1792, much of the population had been killed by a series of smallpox and influenza epidemics sweeping north from Mexico. Captain Vancouver notes the number of deserted villages he saw. These waves of disease continued from the 1770s to 1860s. By the 1830s the population had been reduced to a few hundred. The 1862 smallpox epidemic was particularly devastating, annihilating entire villages and reducing the population by two-thirds: the Squamish to around 300, the Tsleil-Waututh to just 41.

Local First Nations hunted game and gathered plants and rocks on the slopes of the North Shore mountains. Deer and elk were hunted on the slopes of the mountains on Bowen, Gambier, and Anvil islands. From North Shore mountain valleys, Indigenous peoples gathered stone (mainly dacites and andesites) for arrows, spears, and tools. Residue from iron deposits gathered on mountains was used for blue pigmentation. As the snow melted, groups would erect temporary camps on mountain slopes for this hunting and gathering of resources. The mountains also played a role in spiritual and ceremonial practices. According to Rudy Reimer's "Alpine Archaeology and Oral Traditions of the Squamish," a person training to become a shaman would live in the mountains for a decade before returning to the village with their acquired skills of healing and prophecy.

Blueberries, as well as mountain goats, a valued prey for their fur (used to knit sweaters favoured by Tsleil-Waututh elites), hides, and horns (carved into spoons), were the primary draws to the mountain slopes. The blueberries were dried, like raisins, and then pressed into cakes and then into blocks. Both blueberries (presently) and mountain goats (before active hunting in the last century) were found at relatively low elevations (in the summer, goats migrated downslope, close to the ocean), so these would not necessarily have taken the local peoples to or near the summits of these mountains.

The earliest European climbers of local peaks were at times accompanied by local Indigenous guides: Chief Capilano led the Bell-Irving hunting party up The Lions, for example. That said, there does not appear to be a tradition of peak climbing or extensive upper alpine use among local Aboriginal groups. This is understandable, given the abundance of resources close to the water, where their villages were located; as berries, game, and wood were plentiful nearby, there was no need to shred feet and flesh bushwhacking to precarious and far climes to hunt and gather these resources.

What's more, peaks were often associated with legends and gods, further dissuading climbing. The mountains were home to the Smàylilh (Wild People) who could change their shape, appearing as humans, dogs, or trees. They kept pet wolves. The Wild People lived high in the mountains, away from Squamish villages. People had to take care when travelling in the mountains or deep forest, or near waterfalls, lakes, and other areas of strong spiritual power. Reimer's "Alpine Archaeology" paper reports that the Squamish forbade most of their people to travel to the highest elevations; only doctors, seers, and ritualists, with proper spiritual training and integrity, were permitted.

Only one higher-elevation archaeological site has been identified in the North Shore mountains, and even then, that site is a considerable distance below treeline and below the peak: a rock shelter located near the "Big Boulders" point of interest on the Lynn Loop Trail in Lynn Headwaters [DiRs-4]. That said, no focused search for such sites has ever been conducted; more high-elevation sites may well be found, as have been found in the Squamish Valley and Garibaldi Provincial Park, with greater search. There is some evidence of Indigenous peoples venturing to higher elevations. Culturally modified trees, with cedar bark stripped off for clothing, baskets, and other handicrafts, have been discovered in the Cypress Provincial Park area, indicating likely local Aboriginal use as far back as 350 to 400 years ago. A chipped-stone point, likely an arrowhead, was found on the Grouse plateau by H.B. Rowe, an early member of the BCMC.

With the exception of The Lions, referred to as Chee-Chee-Yoh-Hee ("The Twins"), traditional names for these peaks are also scarce. Modern Squamish and Tsleil-Waututh maps only mention The Lions. The Squamish Nation's Xay Temixw *(Sacred Sites) Land Use Plan* (2001) contains no traditional peak names. Nor does the comprehensive recent study *Tsleil-Waututh's History, Culture and Aboriginal Interests in Eastern Burrard Inlet* (May 2015) [Morin]; nor the extensive Tsleil-Waututh *Land Use and Occupancy Research Maps* [Tobias]. The J.S. Matthews 1937 maps of Indigenous names for the Vancouver area (1936) and the Squamish

Territories (1937), based on interviews with many elders, feature many names of creeks and villages, but only Chee-Chee-Yoh-Hee among the mountains. In the archivist's 515-page *Conversations with Khahtsahlano, 1932–1954*, based on hundreds of interviews with Indigenous elders, only that one mountain is mentioned among the North Shore peaks. It may be that mountain names have not survived the passage of time. It may also reflect that most of these North Shore peaks are not readily visible from the main Squamish and Tsleil-Waututh settlements, with the exception of villages on Howe Sound islands.

The Squamish claim all of the land surveyed in this book. The Tsleil-Waututh claim everything except for the Howe Sound Islands and the northern Britannia Range. The Musqueam (centred in south Vancouver) claim all of the land surveyed of this book, except for Gambier and Anvil, and the northern Britannia Range.

<u>Note:</u> The above information, including mountain names, reflects an extensive review of academic and popular literature concerning Indigenous history in the Vancouver area, as well as the results of communications with Indigenous scholars and communities. We were surprised by how little had been written about the relationship between local Indigenous peoples and the mountains, and in particular the lack of material on Indigenous names for local peaks, which must have figured prominently in their lives and their legends. It is hoped that the future will bring more study and writing on this important topic.

APPENDIX 17: CAPTAIN VANCOUVER VISITS BURRARD INLET AND HOWE SOUND

Captain George Vancouver explored Burrard Inlet (which in the 1801 revised edition of his book was called Burrard's "Channel") and Howe Sound (which he called Howe's Sound) from June 13–15, 1792. From his *Journals*:[15]

The shores of this channel, which, after Sir Harry Burrard of the navy, I have distinguished by the name of BURRARD'S CHANNEL, may be considered, on the southern side, of a moderate height, and though rocky, well covered with trees of large growth, principally of the pine tribe. On the northern side, the rugged snowy barrier, whose base we had now nearly approached, rose very abruptly, and was only protected from the wash of the sea by a very narrow border of low land. By seven o'clock we had reached the N.W. point of the channel, which forms also the south point of the main branch of the sound: this also, after another particular friend, I called POINT ATKINSON, situated north from point Grey, about a league distant. Here the opposite point of entrance into the sound bore by compass west, at the distance of about three miles; and nearly in the centre between these two points, is a low rocky island producing some trees, to which the name of PASSAGE ISLAND was given. We passed in an uninterrupted channel to the east of it, with the appearance of an equally good one on the other side.

Quitting point Atkinson, and proceeding up the sound, we passed on the western shore some detached rocks, with some sunken ones amongst them, that extend about two miles, but are not so far from the shore as to impede the navigation of the sound; up which we made a rapid progress, by the assistance of a fresh southerly gale, attended with dark gloomy weather, that greatly added to the dreary prospect of the surrounding country. The low fertile shores we had been accustomed to see, though lately with some interruption, here no longer existed; their place was now occupied by the base of the stupendous snowy barrier, thinly wooded, and rising from the sea abruptly to the clouds; from whose frigid summit, the dissolving snow in foaming torrents rushed down the sides and chasms of its rugged surface, exhibiting altogether a sublime, though gloomy spectacle, which animated nature seemed to have deserted. Not a bird, nor living creature was to be seen, and the roaring of the falling cataracts in every direction precluded their being heard, had any been in our neighbourhood.

Towards noon I considered that we had advanced some miles within the western boundary of the snowy barrier, as some of its rugged lofty mountains were now behind, and to the southward of us. This filled my mind with the pleasing hopes of finding our way to its eastern side. The sun shining at this time for a few minutes afforded an opportunity of ascertaining the latitude of the east point of an island which, from the shape of the mountain that composes it, obtained the name of ANVIL ISLAND, to be 49° 30′, its longitude 237° 3′. We passed an island the forenoon of Friday the 15th, lying on the eastern shore, opposite to an opening on the western, which evidently led into the gulph nearly in a s.w. direction, through a numerous assemblage of rocky islands and rocks, as also another opening to the westward of this island, that seemed to take a similar direction. Between Anvil island and the north point of the first opening, which lies from hence s. by w. five miles distance, are three white rocky islets, lying about a mile from the western shore. The width of this branch of the sound is about a league; but northward from Anvil island it soon narrows to half that breadth, taking a direction to the N.N.E. as far as latitude 49° 39′, longitude 237° 9′, where all our expectations vanished, in finding it to terminate in a round basin, encompassed on every side by the dreary country already described. At its head, and on the upper part of the eastern shore, a narrow margin of low land runs from the foot of the barrier mountains to the waterside, which produced a few dwarf pine trees, with some little variety of underwood. The water of the sound was here nearly fresh, and in color a few shades darker than milk; this I attributed to the melting of the snow, and its water passing rapidly over a chalky surface, which appeared probable by the white aspect of some of the chasms that seemed formerly to have been the course of water-falls, but were now become dry.

The gap we had entered in the snowy barrier seemed of little importance, as through the vallies caused by the irregularity of the mountain's tops, other mountains more distant, and apparently more elevated, were seen, rearing their lofty heads in various directions. In this dreary and comfortless region, it was no inconsiderable piece of good fortune to find a little cove in which we could take shelter, and a small spot of level land on which we could erect our tent; as we had scarcely finished our examination when the wind became excessively boisterous from the southward, attended with heavy squalls and torrents of rain, which continuing until noon the following day, …, occasioned a very unpleasant detention. But for this circumstance we might too hastily have concluded, that this part of the gulf was uninhabited. In the morning we were visited by near forty of the natives, on whose approach, from the very material alteration that had now taken place in the face of the country, we expected to find some difference in their general character. This conjecture was however premature, as they varied in no respect whatever, but in possessing a more ardent desire for commercial transactions; into the spirit of which they entered with infinitely more avidity than any of our former acquaintances, not only in bartering amongst themselves the different valuables they had obtained from us, but when that trade became slack, in exchanging those articles again with our people; in which traffic they always took care to gain some advantage, and would frequently exult on the occasion. Some fish, their garments, spears, bows and arrows, to which these people wisely added their copper ornaments, comprised their general stock in trade. Iron, in all its forms, they judiciously preferred to any other article we had to offer.

The weather permitting us to proceed, we directed our route along the continental or western shore of the sound, passing within two small islands and the main land, into the opening before mentioned, stretching to the westward from Anvil island. At the distance of an hundred yards from the shore, the bottom could not be reached with 60 fathoms of line, nor had we been able to gain soundings in many places since we had quitted point Atkinson with 80 and 100 fathoms, though it was frequently attempted; excepting in the basin at the head of the sound, where the depth suddenly decreased from sixty fathoms to two. We had advanced a short distance only in this branch, before the colour of the water changed from being nearly milk white, and almost fresh, to that of oceanic and perfectly salt. By sun-set we had passed the channel which had been observed to lead into the gulf, to the southward of Anvil island; and about nine o'clock landed for the night, near the west point of entrance into the sound, which I distinguished by the name of HOWE'S SOUND, in honor of Admiral Earl Howe; and this point, situated in latitude 49° 23′ longitude 236° 51′, POINT GOWER; between which and point Atkinson, up to Anvil island, is an extensive group of islands of various sizes. The shores of these, like the adjacent coast, are composed principally of rocks rising perpendicularly from an unfathomable sea; they are tolerably well covered with trees, chiefly of the pine tribe, though few are of a luxuriant growth.

APPENDIX 18: CAPTAIN RICHARDS SURVEYS BURRARD INLET AND HOWE SOUND

While Captain G.H. Richards left a fascinating and genial journal of his survey of Vancouver Island (see Dorricott and Cullon's *The Private Journal of Captain G.H. Richards*), he left only notes of his early survey of Howe Sound, Burrard Inlet, and North Arm (now referred to as Indian Arm).[16] The passage below is from the 1864 Admiralty Office publication *The Vancouver Island Pilot: Containing sailing directions for the coasts of Vancouver Island, and part of British Columbia; compiled from the surveys made by Captain George Henry Richards, R.N., in H.M. ships* Plumper *and* Hecate, *between the years 1858 and 1864, based in part on the notes of E.P. Bedwell, Master, R.N.*[17]

[106] ... In coming from the northward, Passage Island, at the entrance of Howe sound, kept on or just open of a remarkable peak on Anvil island within the sound, bearing N. by W. ¾ W., will clear the edge of the Sturgeon bank until the bearings just given are brought on for entering ...

[108–109] BURRARD INLET is the first great harbour which indents the shores of British Columbia north of the 49th parallel. Its entrance, which is between Grey point on the south and Atkinson point on the north, is 14 miles N.N.W. from the Sand heads of Fraser river, 20 miles N. by E. from Portier pass, and 21 miles N.E. ¾ E. from Entrance island of Nanaimo. Howe sound immediately adjoins it on the north, Atkinson point, the northern entrance point of the inlet, being the eastern limit of the sound.

The entrance of the inlet is well marked; Grey point, a long wooded promontory terminating in a rounded bluff, is very conspicuous from the southward, while Bowen island, which lies at the entrance of Howe sound, and may also be said to form the northern boundary of the inlet, is very remarkable; its high round and almost bare summit, mount Gardner, reaching an elevation of 2,479 feet, is easily recognized from any point of view. Passage island, small but prominent, lies in the eastern passage of Howe sound, midway between Bowen island and Atkinson point, and is an excellent mark from the southward; as before observed ..., Anvil peak, on with or just open westward of this island bearing N. by W. ¾ W., clears the edge of the Sturgeon bank.

Burrard inlet differs from most of the great sounds of this coast in being extremely easy of access to vessels of any size or class, and in the convenient depth of water for anchorage which may be found in almost every part of it; its close proximity to Fraser river, with the great facilities for constructing roads between the two places, likewise adds considerably to its importance. It is divided into three distinct harbours, viz., English bay or the outer anchorage, Coal harbour above the first narrows, and Port Moody at the head of the eastern arm of the inlet. ...

[111–112] NORTH ARM, just before reaching port Moody, and 3 miles above the Second narrows, branches off from the main inlet, and runs in a general northerly direction for 11 miles. It is entirely different in its character from other portions of the inlet. The depth of water varies from 50 to 110 fathoms, and it is enclosed on both sides by rugged mountains rising from 2,000 to 5,000 feet almost perpendicularly, and down the steep sides of which the melting snow in summer forces its way in foaming cascades, rendering the surface water in the inlet below all but fresh.

Croker Island lies within a mile of the head of the arm, and on either side of it there is a deep but narrow channel; that to the eastward is the widest. The head terminates in a delta of swampy rushes, through which some rapid streams find their way into the inlet from a deep and narrow gorge in a N.N.W. direction. There is scarcely sufficient level land in this arm to pitch a tent, nor is there any anchorage except in a narrow creek 2 miles within the entrance, on the eastern shore, named Bedwell bay, where from 7 to 9 fathoms may be found near its head. The breadth of the North arm at the entrance is nearly a mile; a mile within it is contracted to a little over 2 cables, when it shortly opens out again, and maintains an average breadth of two-thirds of a mile to Croker island near the head.

[132] HOWE SOUND, immediately adjoining Burrard inlet … on the north is an extensive though probably useless sheet of water, the general depth being very great, while there are but few anchorages. It is almost entirely hemmed in by rugged and precipitous mountains rising abruptly from the water's edge to elevations of from 4,000 to 6,000 feet; there is no available land for the settler, and although a river of considerable size, the Squawmisht, navigable for boats, falls into its head, it leads by no useful or even practicable route into the interior of the country…

[133] Anvil Island is oval-shaped, and 3 miles long, and its summit, Leading peak, 2,746 feet high and very remarkable, resembles the horn of an anvil pointed upwards. From almost all parts of the strait of Georgia this peak appears as a most prominent object; it is mentioned…as an excellent leading mark to clear the shoals off the Fraser River by being kept just open westward of Passage island, on a N. by W. ¾ W. bearing…

[136] GAMBIER ISLAND, lying in the centre of the sound, immediately northward of Bowen island, is almost square shaped, and 6 miles in extent either way. On its western side are two very remarkable cone-shaped mountains over 3,000 feet in elevation; the southern face of the island is indented by three very deep bays or inlets, in the easternmost of which only is convenient anchorage found. Close off the south-west point of the island are the Twins, two small islets; they are the only part of its coast which may not be approached very close …

MOUNT DICKENS IS CHRISTENED SUNDAY: VANCOUVER
ATHLETIC CLUB MOUNTAINEERS, TWENTY STRONG,
CONDUCT INTERESTING CEREMONY AT PEAK

Vancouver Daily Province, July 14, 1908

The Vancouver Athletic Club Mountaineering Club had the most successful outing and climb of the year on Sunday. Twenty club members and their
friends gathered at the boat on Saturday, at 2 p.m. going to the end of the
North Arm, which is better known as Indian River. There the party camped
and made its headquarters until this morning when the early boat brought back
a cheerful, happy but so sleepy group of mountaineers.

It was through the kindness of Mr. and Mrs. B.F. Dickens, who own property including the rugged mountain which the party climbed that the club was able to have such
a delightful time. The afternoon was spent in rowing, fishing and swimming.

On Mr. Dickens' property, better known as Indian River Park, is a most beautiful water
fall 150 feet high. The club had a delightful time exploring the woods and crevices in
the canyon formed here. During the evening the party were invited for a moonlight sail
on a large motor boat. Mere words cannot describe the beauty of that part of the North
Arm on a calm peaceful night, with a full moon shining upon the mountains and water.
It was a fine preparation for the strenuous work of the next day.

Bright and early Sunday morning 4:30 to be exact, Mr. J.J. Trorey, president of the club,
aroused the party. He had a difficult contract on his hands, but finally succeeded. After
a hasty breakfast the start for the mountain was made. Headed by a Jap boy, Omura by
name, though he was promptly nicknamed Togo, and Mr. Trorey, who, by the way, is
one of the oldest mountain climbers in the city, the ascent was begun. For the first 500
or 600 feet the going was easy, being along a logger's trail. Soon the climbing became
steeper, the underbrush thicker, and the path more rugged. After the first 1000 feet, there
was no trail or guide of any kind. With great difficulty the leaders picked a way. In many
places the entire party had to assist one another, for every phase of mountain climbing
was experienced. This mountain seemed to have a special liking for deep canyons, and
desperate climbing. Large boulders, would suddenly loom up ahead causing dismay
to the valiant workers, for they were certainly working hard.

Realize the pathetic heart rendering sighs which would escape, when, after accomplish-
ing an especially difficult piece of ascent, the party would come up short against a wall of
a precipice hundreds of feet high. This only meant retracing the slope so courageously

gained and climbing up again in another non-accessible locality. This continued until the peak was reached. Here occurred the grand act of the day. Namely, the christening of the mountain with its official name. Mr. Dickens had invited the Vancouver Athletic Club to perform this most important ceremony. The first feature was when Mr. Jas. Glover took the Red Ensign and climbed the tallest tree on the peak. After much difficulty he gained the top. Although the tree was swinging to and fro in a nerve-racking way he cut away a number of branches and fastened the flag securely. After regaining the ground he and Mr. Trorey mounted a stump, the rest of the party grouped around and the speeches began. Mr. Trorey with a bottle of champagne did the proper stunt with these words: "In the name of Benjamin Franklin Dickens, the Governor General and His Majesty King Edward VII, I christen thee Mount Dickens."

A very pleasing response was made by Master Chas. Dickens, the son of the owner. In a few well chosen words he thanked Mr. Trorey on behalf of his father. After the usual posing for pictures the descent was started.

If one has any regard for the feelings of those happy but soon to be unhappy people, the advice is offered not to talk too much about that descent. If the ascent was a leg breaker the descent was heart-breaker. About half way down, the trail was lost and so were the trailers. The wanderings to and fro, up and down, back and forth for several hours, caused many a weary limb. Talks of camping all night on the mountain side was freely heard. Suggestions were offered right and left bringing forth more "would be" backwoodsmanship than could be used in a large volume on Pathfinding. Is there anything more depressing to one's feeling than when tired, thirsty and hungry one is hustling down a mountain side and one suddenly comes to an abrupt stop on the edge of a canyon several hundred feet deep? Ask one of the party and hear the tale of woe.

But like all things, there must be an end somewhere, so the descent was finally accomplished. At 9 o'clock after fourteen hours of hard work the camp was reached. A swim, supper and bed and the day was over. Early this morning amid cheers and sincere words of gratitude for the most hospitable hosts, Mr. and Mrs. B.F. Dickens and their beautiful Indian River Park, the Vancouver Athletic Club Mountaineering Club left behind the glories of conquest and headed for the busy life of a busy city.

First ascent of Mount Bishop.

NEW PEAKS NAMED BY MOUNTAINEERING CLUB

by Charles Dickens
BC Saturday Sunset, August 15, 1908

The most successful trip that the Vancouver Mountaineering Club has yet made took place on Saturday and Sunday. Nineteen of the club members made the ascent of two peaks about three miles south of Indian River Park and west of the southern end Croker Island. These were easily the highest in that vicinity, their tops being just above the timber line and their upper slopes well covered with snow.

The party left Hastings Mill wharf on Saturday afternoon on the launch *Adelaide*, which conveyed them to the camping ground opposite Crocker [Croker] Island. Supper was cooked and eaten and brush gathered for beds before darkness fell upon the scene and then around a blazing campfire songs were sung and stories told until the time for turning in. The night was warm and the busy gnats made rest and sleep almost impossible, so that the call to rise at 3:30 a.m. was more welcome than usual. The last stars were just fading as breakfast was cooked, and hot coffee and bacon did much to brace up every would-be climber. The road at the start was up a steep long log chute for some distance, then through magnificent groves of cedar and fir which thinned out higher up and gave place to blueberry bushes, which made strong handholds but required considerable trouble to penetrate. The line of travel was up a steep hogs-back which bordered a mountain torrent. Near the top of this three benches were traversed, two of which were thickly scattered with glacier worn rocks. A sharp descent had to be made to reach the slope of the final peak. The last 700 feet was easy climbing over smooth rock and the actual top of peak No. 1 was reached at 9:30 a.m. Here a halt was called and lunch eaten, after which for half an hour everyone sat and drank in the beauty of the scene, a beauty enhanced by the vast cloud mass that blanketed all valleys below and reached half way up the slopes of the mountains. Rolling clouds of vapour surged up against the rocky walls exactly like the surf against a sea cliff. Every mountain top, however, was perfectly clear and bathed in warm sunlight, making a wonderful contrast to the gloom below. A precipice deeper and wider than the crater on Mt. Crown dropped sheer away from the utmost ridge. The efforts of the climbers were rewarded by seeing mountain ranges hitherto not seen in any of their other trips. A tremendous rampart of ice and snow crests lay to the north-east, and Mt. Garibaldi could be picked out high above his fellows in the north-west. All the well known peaks seen from the city were noted, such as Crown, Grouse and The Lions, as well as Goat Mountain.

Named Peak Mt. Bishop

The club having conquered a new peak, decided that it should be given a name, so with due ceremony it was named Mt. Bishop in honour of Mr. J.C. Bishop, president of the club. It will probably be referred to very often as "Papa's Mountain," as Mr. Bishop is affectionately known among his fellow climbers as "papa."

After the christening ceremony nine of the party started for the sister peak opposite Mt. Bishop. A long snow-covered ridge was crossed the ascent of the rocky dome and made up through a narrow crevice of chimney. The top of this mountain was only a half hour's climb from Mt. Bishop, but it is several hundred feet higher and a different view was unfolded to the eyes of the small party who reached its summit. Away below to the left was Seymour Creek Valley and in some of the higher valleys three or four beautiful lakes lay deep and dark almost hidden from the light of the sun by the hills piled high above them.

Greetings were exchanged from peak to peak, for the voices of the two parties easily carried across the distance, although when seen with the naked eye the men seemed more the size of ants than human beings. It was decided to call this second peak Mt. Jarrett, in honor of Mr. George Jarrett, secretary of the club. Photographs were taken and then the descent was commenced along a vast snow field. It really needed one leg longer than the other to make the going comfortable, but the slope and ridge were finally crossed and the two parties reunited. By this time the clouds had begun to disperse and the shore line of the North Arm came into view. There was Crocker Island and Lake Buntzen and the Power House, from which the sound of the humming turbines plainly reached the ears.

At 1 o'clock the descent was commenced, following the course of the water draining from the snow. This route proved to have a number of sharp rock descents which required steady nerves to negotiate. The traveling then led down across a tremendous moraine into what was probably at one time a glacier basin. The party traversed nearly a mile of huge blocks of granite and came at last into the big timber where the going was easy and fast. On this trip, up and down no less than five goats were seen and all of them seemed perfectly at home in places all but inaccessible. The mountaineers "dropped" back into camp at 4:15 p.m., a pretty tired lot but with appetites that made short work of the remaining grub. Mr. Fred Mills, who by the way did most of the leading, said that the trip was the most successful the club has yet made, they having reached a height within a few feet of the 6000' mark in one day without any mishap whatever.

The boat cast off at 6 o'clock filled with a tired and sleepy crowd, but happy and strong with the health and strength that the hills and the woods alone can give.

Those who made the trip were George Jarrett, Fred Mills, C. Chapman, Geo. Harrower, J.C. MacKenzie, H.B. Rowe, Bert Armistead, R.J. Cromie, W.J. Grey, E. Burns, L.E. Seney, F. Perry, F. Stevens, B.S. Darling, E.B. Batstone, H.A. Peters, Charles Dickens, R.W. Trythall, George McQueen.

TRAILS THAT LEAD TO TOP OF SEYMOUR MOUNTAIN

by Charles Chapman
BC Saturday Sunset, August 29, 1908

Since its formation, less than a year ago, the Vancouver Mountaineering Club has made remarkable progress, and is now firmly established as the premier organization of its kind in British Columbia. Under the able presidency of Mr. J.C. Bishop, assisted by an energetic secretary and committee, its membership has rapidly increased until it is considerably over a hundred. Its weekend outings have been most successfully carried out and a great deal of pleasure and healthy exercise have been derived by the members generally. The club has been the means of bringing together many kindred spirits who have collectively reached many points which would have been practically unattainable individually. In addition to the regular program, small parties occasionally make special trips, endeavouring to acquire further knowledge of the location of various peaks and the best method of ascent, information which is essential before conducting a large party to the summit.

Six members of the club, Messrs. W. Gray, F. Mills, G. Harrower, F. Smith, B.S. Darling and C. Chapman, crossed to North Vancouver by the 2:15 ferry on Saturday afternoon, August 15th, with the intention of finding a way up the Seymour Mountain from Seymour Creek. Under the leadership of Mr. Gray the long tramp on the Lillooet trail commenced, and before Lynn Creek was reached, every pack felt considerably heavier. The few people who were passing gazed with mirthful eyes at the uncouth specimens of humanity trudging along the dusty road under a burning sun, and seemed to be thinking "He sweats to death. And lards the lean earth as he walks along. Were 't not for laughing, I should pity him."

About 4:30 the new city waterworks dam on Seymour Creek was reached. Just above the dam the creek is spanned by a wooden pipe number, the party made the welkin ring with the usual sing-song around the fire. "Lights out" was given at 9:30, and as the flies had evidently not yet returned from the camping ground of the previous week's trip, where they were massed in battalions a good night's sleep was anticipated. But, no! The beds were made on an incline and showed a persistent resolve to move a little farther down, with the result that a small rock or root was touching a tender spot and stopped all desire to sleep for the time being. Still, even without sleep, there is great charms in lying under the trees on a clear night, the stars peeping through the branches, the murmur of the mountain torrents, the gentle breeze swaying the canopy of leaves, and the soft furry caterpilline supported by a cable, and as this promised to save fording, the other side was reached by performing the Blondin-like act of walking the pipe.

With unerring judgment Mr. Gray had struck the mouth of a large mountain stream, and traveling along its course was easy and rapid, no hush work being encountered. At

5:30 camp was made at an altitude of a thousand feet and all immediately proceeded to refresh themselves by a plunge into the icy water of a large pool in the creekbed. Soon the camp fire was burning brightly and bacon was grilling in time-honored fashion, a rasher being impaled on a pointed stick and held over the flames till cooked. A taste of smoke merely gave further zest to the meal, and from appearances one would think that "appetite increased with what it fed on."

After supper, beds were made in the bush, and then, although small in lars clinging lovingly to the locks of the would-be sleeper, all combining to produce a pleasurable sensation of novelty which is one of the delights of mountaineering.

There were no sluggards in the morning at four o'clock when the leader's call aroused everyone. Breakfast was soon over, although the attempt to fry eggs on a flat stone was a slow and unsatisfactory experiment, and at 5:15 the party started on their climb to the summit by way of the creek, which ran in an almost straight line northeast and at an angle approaching 45 degrees. Many recent rock slides had taken place and enormous boulders were passed, some of which required only a touch to send them thundering down the creek. Several goats were observed on neighboring bluffs and bear tracks were frequently found. Great speed was made up the creekbed and all were agreeably surprised to find that it was quite free from "drop-offs" and ran clear above the timber line. The crystal stream of water flowing amongst the rocks was a source of great comfort to the thirsty toilers, and although lost at times, it could be heard on the bedrock below murmuring at its confinement in subterranean channels.

Shortly before reaching the top, a most beautiful scene was encountered. Two rugged peaks of massive and sombre-looking rock rose on either side of a small divide through which the sun was peeping and flooding with a rosy glow a river of snow which the climbers had just reached. In a glacier-like formation it stretched down from the peak in a narrow lane which the snows of ages have worn in the solid rock, and in place its depth was at least twelve feet. The snowy crystals glittered in the long lines of light from the morning sun and it seemed a fitting place for Apollo to appear with his golden chariot. 'Twas a sight for the gods.

When the passage over the snow had been safely negotiated the party made for the highest peak, which lies to the northwest. A rocky rise of about a hundred and fifty feet was easily scaled and the summit was conquered by seven o'clock, the ascent occupying less than two hours.

A heavy haze hung around the mountains and in the valleys, and thick banks of cloud hid the North Arm of the Burrard Inlet from view, but as the sun's strength increased, the mists were dispelled and a magnificent panorama was before the admiring eyes of the mountaineers. Range after range of snow-clad peaks stretched away to the north as far as the eye could see, towering one above the other in ever-increasing majesty until the culminating point was reached in the mighty bulk of Garibaldi, which seemed to pierce the skies like a gigantic iceberg. Glaciers and snowfields, many acres in extent, glittered and sparkled as they reflected the sun's warm rays, and formed a delightful contrast to the heavily timbered slopes and valleys, dotted here and there with beautiful little lakes. The aesthetic sense of the climbers was satisfied to the utmost as they drank in the wonderful glory and splendor of this vision of Nature. It was an intoxication of delight.

Cathedral Mountain raised its precipitous sides a few miles away to the northwest, and Mounts Jarrett and Bishop were quite close on the north-east side. The peaks in the immediate vicinity of Vancouver were easily recognizable, one peak of The Lions being visible.

After a little recreation had been obtained by dropping rocks over a precipice and watching them shatter into a thousand fragments as they awoke the echoes, a start was made for the southern peak about half a mile distant. The center peak drops sheer away on the northeastern side, but was easily rounded, and a tramp across the snow in the exhilarating mountain air brought the sextette to the end of the trip.

On finding a large pool of water among the rocks everyone must have a swim, and it was much enjoyed, although the heat the water derived from the sun was tempered by an icy stream which flowed into it from the melting snows above. No towels being obtainable, the sun did duty as in the days of boyhood, an the grotesque spectacle of six hardy mountaineers pirouetting on a snow bank, clad in a costume which rivalled the kilt for simplicity and elegance, would have startled a casual observer.

The descent was commenced at two o'clock by way of the creek, and was rough, rocky and rapid. Camp was reached, shortly before four o'clock, and all were thoroughly satisfied with their climb of well over 5,000 feet, and convinced that it was the best mountain in all respects that had been climbed this year. Supper over, packs were made up, and the long tramp for the city began. Seymour Creek was easily crossed in the same manner as before, and notwithstanding tired feet and aching eyes, good speed was made to the carline and connection made with the 8:45 ferry, bringing to an end a most delightful and eventful trip.

APPENDIX 20:
OTHER PEAKS AND BUMPS

The named peaks listed below are not profiled in this book, either because their hazards require sufficient technical skills (marked **), or because they lack height or prominence, or because they are deep within the watershed. Most of them are listed on bivouac.com. ["p:" = prominence.]

HOWE SOUND (NORTH TO SOUTH)

- **Night Hawk Peak** (NHP) (640 m): N49.53069 W123.30885 (p: 40 m). Small bump to the south of Leading.
- **Carmichael Peak** (CAR) (240 m): N49.403611 W123.448889 (p: 100 m). The tallest peak on Keats Island. Named after Duncan Carmichael (1853 Glasgow – 1932 Vancouver) and his son William McMillan Carmichael (1880 Glasgow – 1947 Vancouver). The Carmichaels came to Keats Island in the 1910s and were known as the honorary mayors of Keats Island. Name official; adopted in 2005.
- **Stony Hill/Highest Peak** (HPK) (215 m): N49.399166 W123.465556 (p: 60 m). Confusingly, the hill known to Keats Island residents and campers as "Highest Peak" is not the highest on the island. It does, however, offer a better view. The official name is Stony Hill.

WATERSHED (NORTH TO SOUTH)

- **Sheba** (SHE) (1398 m): N49.55785 W123.07840 (p: 188 m). Small peak due east of Capilano. Name unofficial; called Sheba after nearby Sheba Creek.
- **Drone** (DRO) (1529 m): N49.55167 W123.10000 (p: 236 m). Located to the southeast of CAP and southwest of SHE. Name unofficial; named by Robin Tivy after the "Bagpipe" theme of the nearby Bagpipe massif. Bagpipes have several drone pipes.
- **Peacock** (PEA) (1283 m): N49.52732 W123.16573 (p: 93 m). Forested knob to the south of Mt. Windsor, above Peacock Lake. Name unofficial; named after Peacock Lake below the peak, an official name.
- **Appian** (APP) (1586 m): N49.52500 W123.10694 (p: 497 m). The tallest and westernmost of three peaks to the south of Drone and Capilano. Name official, adopted May 3, 1951. First used in A.J. Campbell's map; he thought it resembled Italy's Via Appia, or Appian Way.
- **Daniels** (DAN) (1545 m): N49.52889, W123.09111 (p: 61 m). The middle peak of the Appian–Daniels–Eastcap massif. Name unofficial. Named after nearby Daniels Creek, a tributary of the Capilano River.
- **Eastcap** (EAS) (1523 m): N49.52922 W123.07793 (p: 93 m). The easternmost peak in the Appian massif. Treed. Name unofficial. Named after nearby Eastcap Creek.
- **Macklin** (MAC) (1419 m): N49.50083 W123.15389 (p: 289 m). Cliffy peak located on the lower slopes of Hanover, above Macklin Lake. Name unofficial. Named after Macklin Lake.
- **Cardinal** (CAR) (1456 m): N49.49083 W123.06973 (p: 226 m). Located to the south of Eastcap and west of Brunswick. Not to be confused with Pontiff: Cardinal is farther from the HSCT. Name unofficial. Named by Robin Tivy after Cathedral/Bishop theme.
- **Pontiff** (PON) (1446 m): N49.48556 W123.09000 (p: 256 m). Steep treed peak to the

southwest of Cardinal and due west of Magnesia. Not to be confused with Cardinal. Name unofficial. Named by Robin Tivy after Cathedral/Bishop theme.

- **Witch** (WIT) (1322 m): N49.47306 W123.14584 (p: 152 m). Located off the east end of the Enchantment ridge. Name unofficial. Named by Robin Tivy after Enchantment/Sleeping Beauty theme.
- ****East Lion** (ELI) (1606 m): N49.45611 W123.18111 (p: 121 m). Name unofficial (Squamish: *Elxwikn*). First climbed on September 8, 1903, by William, John, and Robert Latta. The Latta brothers had come from the south, following the Capilano River and then Sisters Creek, and then ascending the steep talus slopes to the flat area between the two Lions. Between ascents they watched a herd of about 20 mountain goats clambering on the nearby slopes, likely on the bump immediately to the north of Thomas Peak, or on Enchantment. John Latta's boots gave out and he was forced to return to Burrard Inlet from The Lions wearing leather moccasins. John Latta's memoir to commemorate the 50th anniversary of the climb fascinates and humbles: they were made of tougher stuff back then.
- **Wizard/Sisters** (SIS) (1295 m): N49.44695 W123.14528 (p: 245 m). Located south, across the Hesketh Creek amphitheatre from Enchantment. True peak on far east of ridge after a series of false summits. Name unofficial. Named by Robin Tivy after Enchantment/Sleeping Beauty theme. Early BCMCers referred to it as "Sisters Peak" after nearby Sisters Creek (not to be confused with Brothers Creek, formerly named Sisters), in turn a reference to The Lions. A photo in the BC Archives shows The Lions as viewed from this peak.
- **Magic** (MGC) (1230 m): N49.43687 W123.14176 (p: 275 m). Located to the south of Wizard. Name unofficial. Named by Robin Tivy after the Enchantment/Sleeping Beauty theme.
- **Burnt** (BNT) (490 m): N49.402023 W123.131633 (p: 90 m). A low bump at the north end of Capilano Lake, between East Capilano River and West Crown Mountain, and separated from West Crown slopes by the powerline and road. The traditional route up Crown passed up this valley.

WEST OF HSCT/CYPRESS AREA

- **Deeks Bluff** (DBL) (473 m): N49.52905 W123.24918 (p: 63 m). Small bluff on the western slopes of Deeks. Name unofficial.
- ****Harvey's Pup** (PUP) (1512 m): N49.47460 W123.20351 (p: 47 m). Small pinnacle below Harvey. Requires ropes to climb. Name unofficial. It was formerly known as "Junior Pinnacle" (Harvey occasionally was called "Brunswick Pinnacle") and, in the July 1927 issue of *BC Mountaineer*, "Pinnacle Pup." Access is via a trail between the Harvey and Brunswick trails off Binkert Trail. Harvey's Pup was first climbed by a BCMC party on May 20, 1923, climbing up from Brunswick Beach. A goat was spotted on the Pup in 2002.

CYPRESS PROVINCIAL PARK AREA

- **Hillstrom Peak** (HIL) (1158 m): N49.391312 W123.169205 (p: 25 m). On southeast slopes of Hollyburn, south of Sisters Creek and north of Nickey Creek, at the end of the cross-country ski area. Featured on a 1962 map of Hollyburn ski trails. Called "Hollyburn Knob" on a 1925 *Daily Province* hiking map. Named after Uno Hillstrom who in January 1925, with R.J. Verne and Eilif Haxthow, set up a ski lodge and rental shop in the bunkhouses at the abandoned Nasmyth Mill on lower Hollyburn Ridge. Name unofficial.

- **Bald Mountain** (BAL) (780 m): N49.364321 W123.210211 (p: 30 m). Name unofficial. To the north of the Quarry picnic site switchback on the Cypress Bowl road; traversed by Antagonizer mountain bike trail. Shown on a 1925 *Daily Province* hiking map. Now fully retreed.
- **Sentinel Hill** (SEN) (145 m): N49.333820 W123.140259 (p: 50 m). Also called Baby Mountain or Ambleside Mountain. A volcanic outcrop. Official name.

GROUSE AREA
- **Senate Peak** (SEN) (1170 m): N49.385409 W123.056741 (p: 40 m). The north, lower, steeper and rockier peak of Fromme facing Grouse. Name unofficial.
- ****The Camel** (CML) (1475 m): N49.41029 W123.09090 (p: 25 m). Just southeast of Crown. Visible from Vancouver. Unlike many peaks with animal names, it actually looks like a camel. Name unofficial but widely used since the 1900s. First ascent in 1907.
- ****Spindle Peak** (SPI) (1498 m): N49.41242 W123.09368 (p: 46 m). Due north of Crown Mountain. Sharp gaps between it and Crown, and it and CN1. Name unofficial. Likely named by Robin Tivy after Enchantment/Sleeping Beauty theme. Called, with CN1, "North Peaks of Crown" by early BCMC climbers.

SEYMOUR AREA (SOUTH TO NORTH)
- **Devil's Thumb or Peak** (DEV) (620 m): N49.36301 W122.98650 (p: 20 m). A promontory off the west side of Seymour, most visible from the Ironworkers Memorial Bridge when fog or snow accentuates the valleys. Name unofficial.
- **Dinkey Peak** (DIN) (1117 m): N49.37139 W122.95167 (p: 40 m). Trail off main Seymour trail and First Lake Trail. Name official, adopted February 3, 1988, on 92G/7, as identified on BC Parks's Mount Seymour Provincial Park pamphlet, 1974: "Small but distinct, hence the name Dinkey" (February 1975 letter from BC Parks, file L.1.56).
- **Dog Mountain** (DOG) (1050 m): N49.37378 W122.97038 (p: 29 m). Trail off main Seymour trail. Described by Robin Tivy as "one of the least technically difficult summits in BC, if not the world." Name official: adopted February 8, 1988, on 92G/7. On BC Electric Railway Company March 1927 hiking map. Earlier named "Dogshead Mountain; so named from the outline of a St. Bernard dog appearing after a light snowfall."
- **Mystery Peak** (MYS) (1230 m): N49.37667 W122.94222 (p: 40 m). North of Mystery Lake, at the top of the chairlift. Name official, adopted February 3, 1988, on 92G/7, as labelled on Mount Seymour Park pamphlet; named after the lake.
- **Brockton Point** (BRO) (1258 m): N49.38139 W122.94194 (p: 35 m). Lookout on the main Mt. Seymour trail. Name official, recorded February 21, 1975, on 92G/7, as labelled on Parks Branch pamphlet 1974 et seq. Probably named by the first climbing party in 1908, in association with Brockton Point in Stanley Park.
- **Hastings (Holmden) Peak** (HAS) (957 m): N49.38511W122.91359 (p: 87 m). Above Hastings Lake; named after nearby Hastings Lake or Holmden Creek; may well be Underhill Peak (which see below).
- **Theta Peak** (THE) (1092 m): N49.39196 W122.92538 (p: 80 m). East of Elsay Lake trail; named after nearby Theta Lake.
- **Clegg/Klegg Peak** (KLE) (ca. 1400 m): N49.42489 W122.91511 (p: 80 m). off east shoulder of Bishop. Named after nearby Clegg Lake (by Water District chief commissioner E.A. Cleveland after District draftsman Albert H. Clegg) and first Bagger Challenge champion Ken Legg.

- **Bishop Bump** (BBU) (ca. 1250 m): N49.42061 W122.90728 (p: 50 m). Last, east bump along ridge, opposite KLE, with both overlooking Clegg Lake.

FANNIN RANGE NORTH OF DICKENS (SOUTH TO NORTH)

- **Dickens Ridge** (DRI) (960 m): N49.465466 W122.904434 (p: 0 m). When Vancouver archivist Maj. James Skitt Matthews submitted his application on July 13, 1937, for official recognition of the name Mt. Dickens, he described it as "due west of Wigwam Inn, and approached by Wigwam Creek. It is not the highest elevation." The official name now, however, designates the high point in the ridge. DRI is the original Dickens.
- **Brokeback Mountain** (BRK) (1240 m) N49.472586 W122.911262 (p: 60 m). North peak of Dickens, along Indian Arm Trail. Unofficially named by Ean Jackson.
- **Eldee SE3** (LD3) (1319 m): N49.49640 W122.93030 (p: 354 m). Due west of Mt. Felix, across the Indian River. Located above the spot where the Seymour River becomes Seymour Lake. Unofficially named after nearby Eldee.
- **Eldee** (ELD) (1432 m): N49.51694 W122.95556 (p: 282 m). Extremely obscure peak located to the north of upper Seymour Lake. Name official, adopted 1930. Originally named by Alan John Campbell after L.D. Taylor, mayor of Vancouver, in 1928. "LD" became "Eldee."
- **Bivouac** (BIV) (1485 m): N49.53170 W122.97920 (p: 103 m). Located to the east of Eastcap and north of Eldee. Name official, adopted October 3, 1969. First used by A.J. Campbell but was a "well-established local name" for years before that.

UNKNOWN PEAKS

- **Underhill** (UND): In his *North Vancouver 1891–1907: Saga of a Municipality in Its Formative Days*, J. Rodger Burnes refers to an Underhill Mountain: "Grouse, Crown, Sleepy [sic] Beauty [i.e., West Crown], Lions, Fromme, and, farther north, Underhill and Burwell." Underhill is not an official name, or even a generally used name. Underhill Creek, flowing into Orlomah Beach on Indian Arm, may provide a clue: there is a 940-m bump that is visible from Indian Arm, to the north of Underhill Creek. Dr. F.T. Underhill's family had a cottage at Frame's Landing (also called Thwaytes Landing), north of Orlomah Beach. The counter-theory is that the Indian Arm bump certainly wouldn't be considered in the same breath as those other, well-established peaks listed above, all very visible from Vancouver. Another possibility, given its reference to Burwell, is that Underhill is the west peak of Burwell. The peak is likely named either after Dr. Frederic Theodore Underhill (1859–1936), appointed in 1904 as the first municipal health officer for Vancouver, who was instrumental in protecting the Vancouver water supply. Alternatively, it may be named for one of Dr. Underhill's sons, Frederic Clare Underhill or James Theodore "Jim" Underhill, founders of Underhill & Underhill, which was involved in surveying the area between North Vancouver and Britannia Mines.

APPENDIX 21:
BEST ROBBIE BURNS PEAKBAGGING SONGS AND POEMS

SONG COMPOSED IN AUGUST ("NOW WESTLIN WINDS")

Now westlin' winds and slaught'ring guns
Bring Autumn's pleasant weather;
The moorcock springs on whirring wings
Amang the blooming heather:
Now waving grain, wide o'er the plain,
Delights the weary farmer;
And the moon shines bright, when I rove at night,
To muse upon my charmer.

The partridge loves the fruitful fells,
The plover loves the mountains;
The woodcock haunts the lonely dells,
The soaring hern the fountains:
Thro' lofty groves the cushat roves,
The path of man to shun it;
The hazel bush o'erhangs the thrush,
The spreading thorn the linnet.

Thus ev'ry kind their pleasure find,
The savage and the tender;
Some social join, and leagues combine,
Some solitary wander:
Avaunt, away! the cruel sway,
Tyrannic man's dominion;
The sportsman's joy, the murd'ring cry,
The flutt'ring, gory pinion!

But, Peggy dear, the ev'ning's clear,
Thick flies the skimming swallow,
The sky is blue, the fields in view,
All fading-green and yellow:
Come let us stray our gladsome way,
And view the charms of Nature;
The rustling corn, the fruited thorn,
And ev'ry happy creature.

We'll gently walk, and sweetly talk,
Till the silent moon shine clearly;
I'll grasp thy waist, and, fondly prest,

Swear how I love thee dearly:
Not vernal show'rs to budding flow'rs,
Not Autumn to the farmer,
So dear can be as thou to me,
My fair, my lovely charmer!

Yon Wild Mossy Mountains

Yon wild mossy mountains sae lofty and wide,
That nurse in their bosom the youth o' the Clyde,
Where the grouse lead their coveys thro' the heather to feed,
And the shepherd tends his flock as he pipes on his reed.

Not Gowrie's rich valley, nor Forth's sunny shores,
To me hae the charms o'yon wild, mossy moors;
For there, by a lanely, sequestered stream,
Besides a sweet lassie, my thought and my dream.

Amang thae wild mountains shall still be my path,
Ilk stream foaming down its ain green, narrow strath;
For there, wi' my lassie, the day lang I rove,
While o'er us unheeded flie the swift hours o'love.

She is not the fairest, altho' she is fair;
O' nice education but sma' is her share;
Her parentage humble as humble can be;
But I lo'e the dear lassie because she lo'es me.

To Beauty what man but maun yield him a prize,
In her armour of glances, and blushes, and sighs?
And when wit and refinement hae polish'd her darts,
They dazzle our een, as they flie to our hearts.

But kindness, sweet kindness, in the fond-sparkling e'e,
Has lustre outshining the diamond to me;
And the heart beating love as I'm clasp'd in her arms,
O, these are my lassie's all-conquering charms!

MY HEART'S IN THE HIGHLANDS

Farewell to the Highlands, farewell to the North,
The birth-place of Valour, the country of Worth;
Wherever I wander, wherever I rove,
The hills of the Highlands for ever I love.

My heart's in the Highlands, my heart is not here,
My heart's in the Highlands, a-chasing the deer;
Chasing the wild-deer, and following the roe,
My heart's in the Highlands, wherever I go.

Farewell to the mountains, high-cover'd with snow,
Farewell to the straths and green vallies below;
Farewell to the forests and wild-hanging woods,
Farewell to the torrents and loud-pouring floods.

My heart's in the Highlands, &c.

APPENDIX 22:
BIBLIOGRAPHIES AND FURTHER RESOURCES, ANNOTATED

---

1. NORTH SHORE MOUNTAINS CLIMBING AND HIKING

PAPER

Bourdon, Marc. *Squamish Hiking: Hiking Trails from Horseshoe Bay to the Callaghan Valley.* Squamish, BC: Quickdraw Publications, 2017.

Bryceland, Jack, and Mary & David Macaree. *103 Hikes in Southwestern British Columbia.* 6th ed. Vancouver: Greystone Books, 2008. Latest edition of the classic text.

Copeland, Kathy, and Craig Copeland. *Don't Waste Your Time in the BC Coast Mountains: An Opinionated Hiking Guide to Help You Get the Most from this Magnificent Wilderness.* Riondel, BC: Voice in the Wilderness Press, 1997. As the title implies, a fun guide.

Culbert, Dick. *A Climber's Guide to the Coastal Ranges of British Columbia.* 2nd ed. Vancouver: Alpine Club of Canada, 1969. The classic book by a bagger of over 250 first ascents. *Nanos gigantum humeris insidentes.*

Fairley, Bruce. *A Guide to Climbing & Hiking In Southwestern British Columbia.* West Vancouver: Gordon Soules Book Publishers, 1986. The worthy successor to Culbert's book.

Freeman, Roger, and Ethel Freeman. *Exploring Vancouver's North Shore Mountains.* Vancouver: Federation of Mountain Clubs of BC, 1985. Interesting snapshot of the newly opened Lynn Headwaters.

Gunn, Matt. *Scrambles in Southwest British Columbia.* Vancouver: Cairn Publishing, 2005. Detailed guide to local scrambles, including a few local peaks, with excellent route drawings.

Hanna, Dawn. *Best Hikes & Walks of Southwestern British Columbia.* Edmonton: Lone Pine, 2006. Beautiful full-colour guide focusing on some of the easier North Shore peaks and on lower-elevation hikes.

Hui, Stephen. *105 Hikes in and around Southwestern British Columbia.* With a foreword by T'uy't'tanat – Cease Wyss. Vancouver: Greystone Books, 2018. The successor to *103 Hikes*, featuring many more destinations and trails.

Macaree, Mary, David Macaree, Alice Purdey, and John Halliday. *109 Walks in British Columbia's Lower Mainland.* 7th ed. Vancouver: Greystone Books, 2014. A classic guide, updated.

Munday, Don. *Mt. Garibaldi Park, Vancouver's Alpine Playground.* Vancouver: Cowan & Brookhouse, 1922.

Serl, Don. *The Waddington Guide: Alpine Climbs in One of the World's Great Ranges.* Squamish, BC: Elaho, 2003.

Watt, Norman D. *Off the Beaten Path: A Hiking Guide to Vancouver's North Shore.* Madeira

Park, BC: Harbour Publishing, 2014. Engaging guide touching on some of the peaks covered in the present book.

Wheater, Rich. *Vancouver Trail Running: The Good, the Bad and the Gnarly*. Squamish, BC: Quickdraw, 2011. Engaging book with innovative design and beautiful photographs covering running routes, including some of the peaks covered in the present book.

ONLINE

ashikaparsad.com/trip-planning-links. A cornucopia of resources, including weather reports, webcams, trail conditions, etc., compiled by Ashika Parsad and Ryan Morasiewicz.

baggerbook.ca; facebook.com/baggerbook. The authors' websites and host sites for this book.

bctreehunter.wordpress.com. Mick Bailey's fascinating blog about explorations of the North Shore and beyond.

bivouac.com. Robin Tivy's masterful and definitive international encyclopedia of peaks, with a comprehensive focus on southwestern British Columbia. Comprehensive peak statistics as well as photographs, trip reports, photographs, and maps.

clubtread.com. The best discussion forum for hiking in southwestern British Columbia, with coverage of adventures all around the world. Extensive discussion of peak routes, conditions, and secrets.

facebook.com/groups/baggerchallenge. Facebook page for the Bagger Challenge.

peakery.com. A useful and fun means of recording peakbags around the world. Plots your conquests on an international map. Extensive collection of photographs, with growing archive of trip reports and routes.

peakfinder.org. Plug in a peak name or latitude/longitude at this amazing site and it will generate a rotatable 360° rendering of the visible peaks, with names, sun or moon trajectories for any day of any year, plus several measuring tools. Smartphone versions use your actual GIS position to overlay coordinates onto photos taken with your device.

MAPS

District of North Vancouver Geoweb 3.0. District of North Vancouver, 2014. Accessed 2017-11-01 at geoweb.dnv.org/index.html. This municipal website is a treasure trove of thematic maps and data resources, including cycling and bus route maps, a hydrology map with streams and lakes, and an interactive map showing historical events in the district. Prepare to spend an afternoon browsing. See, for example, two detailed topographic maps with trails and roads for front-row peaks:

geoweb.dnv.org/products/maps/singles/24x36_Topo_GrouseArea.pdf;
geoweb.dnv.org/products/maps/singles/24x36_Topo_SeymourArea.pdf.

District of West Vancouver Map. District of West Vancouver, 2014. Accessed 2017-12-01 (pdf) at is.gd/JnLQgl. 1:17,500 scale, showing contour lines, trails, roads etc.

District of West Vancouver WestMap (GIS). District of West Vancouver, 2017. Accessed 2017-11-01 at maps.westvancouver.ca/westmap2017/map.htm. More interactive but a little slow and clunky, this map features skins of creeks, topography, buildings and more.

Google Earth. Mountain View, Calif.: Alphabet Inc., 2017. Accessed 2017-11-01 at google.com/earth. Also invaluable for route planning as well as projecting GPS data to display your routes.

Google Maps. Mountain View, Calif.: Alphabet Inc., 2017. Accessed 2017-11-01 at google.ca/maps. Everyone knows and loves this amazing resource. Peak enthusiasts can activate the enormously useful terrain feature, with contour lines, slope shadowing, and more names of topographical features, by clicking on the "stacked" menu button at the top left of the map and choosing "terrain" view. Invaluable for route planning.

North Shore Trail Map. 2nd ed. updated, 1:20,000. Vancouver: Trail Ventures BC, 2017. Description accessed 2017-11-01 at trailventuresbc.com/north-shore-map-info. Our favourite map.

OpenStreetMap. Sutton Coldfield, West Midlands, UK: Openstreetmap Foundation, 2017. Description accessed 2017-11-01 at openstreetmap.org/about. An open-source street and trail map with a great selection of established and obscure North Shore trails and peaks. Zoom in on the North Shore region from openstreetmap.org/#map=11/49.4101/-122.9257.

Vancouver's Northshore Hiking Trails. 6th ed., 1:40,000/1:250,000. Richmond, BC: ITMB Publishing, 2011. Description accessed 2017-11-01 at is.gd/9eXB9p. Another good local map.

2. FLORA, FAUNA, AND GEOLOGY

Acorn, John, and Ian Sheldon. *Bugs of British Columbia.* Edmonton: Lone Pine, 2001. Another excellent guide, with beautiful illustrations and perfect degree of detail.

Arora, David. *All That the Rain Promises and More: A Hip Pocket Guide to Western Mushrooms.* Berkeley: Ten Speed Press, 1991. Fun and user-friendly introduction to mushrooms, with a focus on the West Coast.

——— *Mushrooms Demystified: A Comprehensive Guide to the Fleshy Fungi.* 2nd ed. Berkeley: Ten Speed Press, 1986. A comprehensive, phonebook-sized guide.

Armstrong, John E. *Vancouver Geology.* Edited by Charlie Roots and Chris Staargaard. Vancouver: Geological Association of Canada – Cordilleran Section, 1990. With useful illustrations based on North Shore hiking; a technical but accessible guide, with useful hiking and mountain context. Scanned original pages accessed 2017-11-05 at gac-cs.ca/publications/VancouverGeology.pdf.

BC Big Tree Registry. UBC Faculty of Forestry website. Accessed 2017-11-01 at <u>bigtrees. forestry.ubc.ca/bc-bigtree-registry</u>.

Burwash, Edward Moore Jackson. *The Geology of Vancouver and Vicinity*. Chicago: University of Chicago Press, 1918. Searchable scans of original pages accessed 2017-12-05 at <u>is.gd/tttfL6</u>.

Clague, John, and Bob Turner. *Vancouver, City on the Edge: Living with a Dynamic Geological Landscape*. West Vancouver: Tricouni Press, 2003. An amazing book that not only gives a fascinating overview of the geology of the city, but also is an exercise in teaching through inspired presentation.

Hamersley Chambers, Fiona. *Wild Berries of British Columbia*. Edmonton: Lone Pine, 2011. A useful guide to our local berries.

Henshaw, Julia W. *Mountain Wild Flowers of Canada: A Simple and Popular Guide to the Names and Descriptions of the Flowers That Bloom Above the Clouds*. Toronto: William Briggs, 1906. Searchable scans of original pages accessed 2017-12-30 at <u>archive.org/details/ mountainwildflo01hensgoog</u>.

Invasive Species Council of British Columbia. *Grow Me Instead*. Accessed 2017-12-01 (pdf) at <u>bcinvasives.ca/documents/GMI-Booklet_2013_WEB.pdf</u>. A fine guide to invasive species and planting alternatives.

Jones, Bill. *The Deerholme Mushroom Book: From Foraging to Feasting*. Victoria: TouchWood Editions, 2013. Mushrooms and recipes.

Kavanagh, James. *Nature BC: An Illustrated Guide to Common Plants and Animals*. Illustrated by Raymond Leung, Linda Dunn, Horst H. Krause, and Marianne Nakaska. Edmonton: Lone Pine, 1993. High-quality guide to flora and fauna.

Pacific Streamkeepers Federation. "Watershed Profiles" webpage. North Vancouver, 2017. Accessed 2017-12-01 (pdf) at <u>www.pskf.ca/ecology/watershed/index.html</u>. Excellent historical and ecological profiles of major North Shore creek watersheds.

Pojar, Jim, and Andy MacKinnon. *Plants of Coastal British Columbia*. Rev. ed. Vancouver: Lone Pine, 2016. A detailed and comprehensive guide.

Schalkwijk-Barendsen, Helene M.E. *Mushrooms of Western Canada*. Edmonton: Lone Pine, 1991. Colourful photographs.

St. John, Alan. *Reptiles of the Northwest*. Edmonton: Lone Pine, 2002. An excellent guide.

Turner, Nancy J. *Food Plants of Coastal First Peoples*. 2nd ed. Victoria: Royal BC Museum, 1995, reprinted 2010. A guide to local plants, with detailed descriptions of First Nations uses.

Underhill, J.E. *Northwestern Wild Berries*. 2nd ed. Surrey, BC, and Blaine, Wash.: Hancock House, 1994. Inviting photographs.

Varner, Collin. *Plants of Vancouver and the Lower Mainland*. Vancouver: Raincoast, 2002. Part of the Raincoast Pocket Guides series. An excellent field resource.

Vitt, Dale, Janet E. Marsh, and Robin B. Bovey. *Mosses, Lichens and Ferns of Northwest North America*. Edmonton: Lone Pine, 1988. A more technical guide.

PAPER

Akrigg, G.P.V., and Helen B. Akrigg. *British Columbia Place Names*. 3rd ed. Vancouver: UBC Press, 1997.

Alpine Club of Canada, Vancouver Section. *Avalanche Echoes*. (Newsletter published continuously since 1927.) Issues from September 1999 to November/December 2013 are accessible in pdf from accvancouver.org/newsletters.asp.

Armitage, Doreen. *Around the Sound*. Madeira Park, BC: Harbour Publishing, 1997, 2001.

Bradbury, Elspeth. *West Vancouver: A View through the Trees*. West Vancouver, BC: District of West Vancouver, 2007.

Bridge, Kathryn. *A Passion for Mountains: The Lives of Don and Phyllis Munday*. Calgary: Rocky Mountain Books, 2006.

——— *Phyllis Munday: Mountaineer*. Montréal: XYZ Publishing, 2002.

British Columbia Geographical Names Office. "British Columbia's Geographical Naming Principles, Policy and Procedures." Victoria: Ministry of Forests, Lands, Natural Resource Operations and Rural Development. Policy rev. 2000, ministry name rev. 2017. Accessed 2017-11-01 (pdf) at is.gd/yMJ7dj. A searchable place names database with interactive relief map is at apps.gov.bc.ca/pub/bcgnws.

British Columbia Mountaineering Club. *The BC Mountaineer*. Vancouver: BCMC newsletter published since 1923. Availability info accessed 2017-12-01 at bcmc.ca/m/book/home.

——— *The Northern Cordilleran*. Vancouver: BCMC, 1913. Accessed 2017-12-01 (microform) at is.gd/gfHBm6.

Burnes, John Rodger. *North Vancouver, 1891–1907: Saga of a Municipality in its Formative Days*. North Vancouver: [s.n.], 1972.

Chapman, Charles. "Trails that Lead to Top of Seymour Mountain." *BC Saturday Sunset*, August 29, 1908. See Appendix 19.

Cox, Tony, and Lions Bay Historical Society. *The Village of Lions Bay: Historical Passages from the 1790s to the Present*. Lions Bay, BC: Lions Bay Historical Society, 2001.

Crerar, David, Anders Ourom, and Harry Crerar. "Let the Sky Fall: Lawyers in the History of British Columbia Mountaineering." Pts. 1, 2. *The Advocate* 75, nos. 1, 3 (January and May 2017).

Darling, Basil S. "The Passion for Mountain Climbing." *Man to Man* [formerly *Westward Ho!*] 6, no. 6 (June 1910): 325–332. Searchable scans of original pages accessed 2017-12-01 at is.gd/iBzFqG.

Davis, Chuck, ed. *The Greater Vancouver Book: An Urban Encyclopaedia*. Surrey, BC: Linkman Press, 1997.

Dickens, Charles. "New Peaks Named by Mountaineering Club." *BC Saturday Sunset*, August 15, 1908: 9. Searchable scan of original page accessed 2017-12-30 at newspapers.lib.sfu.ca/bcss-5/bc-saturday-sunset. See also Appendix 19.

Dorricott, Linda, and Deidre Cullon, eds. *The Private Journal of Captain G.H. Richards: The Vancouver Island Survey (1860–1862)*. Vancouver: Ronsdale Press, 2012.

Draycott, Walter MacKay. *Early Days in Lynn Valley*. North Vancouver: North Shore Times, 1978.

———— *Lynn Valley, from the Wilds of Nature to Civilization: A Short History of Its Resources, Natural Beauty and Development; Also Its Part in the Great War*. North Vancouver: North Shore Press, 1919.

Drew, Ralph. *Ferries & Fjord: The History of Indian Arm*. Belcarra, BC: Ralph Drew, 2015.

Fairley, Bruce. *The Canadian Mountaineering Anthology*. Vancouver: Lone Pine, 1994.

Francis, Daniel. *Where Mountains Meet the Sea: An Illustrated History of the District of North Vancouver*. Madeira Park, BC: Harbour Publishing, 2016.

Fripp, Robert Mackay. "A Short Expedition in British Columbia." In J.S. Matthews, ed. *Capilano Creek: Discovery of Source, 1890*, 7–19. Vancouver: City of Vancouver Archives, 1952.

Heal, S.C. *The Romance of Historic Names*. Vancouver: Cordillera Books, 2006.

Hill-Tout, Charles. *The Salish People, vol. II: The Squamish and the Lillooet*. Edited with an introduction by Ralph Maud. Vancouver: Talonbooks, 1978.

Hopwood, Doug. *Mount Artaban Nature Reserve Management Plan*. Victoria: Islands Trust Fund, June 2009. Accessed 2017-11-01 (pdf) at islandstrustfund.bc.ca/media/10352/itfmgmtplanartaban.pdf.

Howard, Irene. *Bowen Island 1872–1972*. Bowen Island, BC: Bowen Island Historians, 1973.

Humphreys, Pam, and Steven Wong. *The History of Wigwam Inn*. Vancouver: Perfect Printers, 1982.

Jessiman, Mary. "An Indian Map of Vancouver." Illustrated sketchmap (ink, pencil, gouache), 1936. City of Vancouver Archives technical and cartographic drawing collection, AM1594: Map 51. Accessed 2017-12-01 (jpg) from searcharchives.vancouver.ca/indian-map-of-vancouver.

Johnson, Pauline (Tekahionawake). *Legends of Vancouver*. Toronto: McClelland, Goodchild & Stewart, 1911. Searchable scans of original pages accessed 2017-12-30 at is.gd/oQBnmi.

Khahtsahlano, August Jack, with Major J.S. Matthews. *Conversations with Khahtsahlano 1932–1954*. Compiled by Major J.S. Matthews; typing and index by Alera Way. With hand sketches by Khahtsahlano and archival photographs. Vancouver: City Archives, 1955. Complete scanned book accessed 2017-11-01 at is.gd/ad6hkd.

Latta, John F. *The Ascent of The Lions, 1903*. Vancouver: City Archives, 1953.

Leslie, Susan. *In the Western Mountains: Early Mountaineering in British Colombia*. Sound Heritage Series vol. 8, no. 4. Victoria: Provincial Archives Aural History Program, 1980.

Lil'wat, Musqueam, Squamish, and Tsleil-Waututh Peoples. *People of the Land: Legends of the Four Host First Nations*. Penticton, BC: Theytus Books, 2009.

Mansbridge, Francis. *Cottages to Community: The Story of West Vancouver's Neighbourhoods*. West Vancouver: West Vancouver Historical Society, 2011.

———— *Hollyburn: The Mountain & The City.* With research associate Lois Enns. Vancouver: Ronsdale Press, 2008.

Marshall, Lt. John. *Royal Naval Biography* [&c.]. Vol. 2. London: Longman, 1824. Searchable scans of original pages accessed 2017-12-05 at is.gd/PImalO.

Matthews, Major J.S. *Conversations with Khahtsahlano 1932–1954.* See Khahtsahlano, August Jack.

———— *Early Vancouver: Narratives of Pioneers of Vancouver, BC, Collected between 1931 and 1956.* 7 vols. Vancouver: City of Vancouver Archives, 1959, 2011. Searchable scans of original pages accessed 2017-12-30 at is.gd/O6KIG5.

Morin, Jesse. *Tsleil-Waututh Nation's History, Culture and Aboriginal Interests in Eastern Burrard Inlet.* Redacted, public version of expert's report prepared for Gowling, Lafleur, Henderson LLP on behalf of Tsleil-Waututh Nation in relation to the Trans Mountain [Pipeline] Expansion Project. May 2015. Accessed 2017-11-01 (pdf) at twnsacredtrust.ca/wp-content/uploads/2015/05/Morin-Expert-Report-PUBLIC-VERSION-sm.pdf.

Morrow, Pat. "Peak Bagging." In *Voices from the Summit: The World's Great Mountaineers on the Future of Climbing,* edited by Bernadette McDonald and John Amatt, 59–65. Banff: Banff Centre for Mountain Culture, and Washington, DC: National Geographic Society, 2000. Accessed 2017-11-01 (pdf scan) at is.gd/iiMdCz. A meditative essay on peakbagging by one of Canada's greatest mountain climbers.

"Mount Dickens Christening Ceremony Performed on Summit." *Vancouver Daily World,* July 15, 1908, 10. Accessed 2017-12-01 at newspapers.com/newspage/64534152.

"Mount Dickens Is Christened Sunday: Vancouver Athletic Club Mountaineers, Twenty Strong, Conduct Interesting Ceremony at Peak." *Vancouver Daily Province,* July 14, 1908. See also Appendix 19.

O'Donnell, Brendan. *Indian and Non-native Use of the Capilano River: An Historical Perspective.* Department of Fisheries and Oceans, Native Affairs Division, Policy and Program Planning Series, issue 5. Ottawa: Fisheries & Oceans Canada, 1988? Scanned original pages (pdf) accessed 2017-03-05 at dfo-mpo.gc.ca/library/112596.pdf.

———— *Indian and Non-native Use of the Seymour River: An Historical Perspective.* Department of Fisheries and Oceans, Native Affairs Division, Policy and Program Planning Series, issue 6. Ottawa: Fisheries & Oceans Canada, 1988? Scanned original pages (pdf) accessed 2017-03-05 at dfo-mpo.gc.ca/library/112597.pdf.

———— *Indian and Non-native Use of the Squamish and Cheakamus Rivers: An Historical Perspective.* Department of Fisheries and Oceans, Native Affairs Division, Policy and Program Planning Series, issue 4. Ottawa: Fisheries & Oceans Canada, 1988? Scanned original pages (pdf) accessed 2017-03-05 at dfo-mpo.gc.ca/library/112594.pdf.

Proctor, Sharon. "Early Hike to the Top of Grouse." North Vancouver Museum & Archives *Express* 26, no. 2 (June 2017): 2. Accessed 2017-12-01 (pdf) at nvma.ca/wp-content/uploads/2017/07/Express-June-2017.pdf.

Reimer, Rudy. "Alpine Archaeology and Oral Traditions of the Squamish." In *Archaeology of Coastal British Columbia: Essays in Honour of Professor Philip M. Hobler,* edited by Roy L. Carlson, c. 5. Publication no. 30. Burnaby, BC: Simon Fraser University Department of Archaeology, 2003. Accessed 2017-11-01 (pdf) from archpress.lib.sfu.ca/index.php/archpress/catalog/book/41.

——— *The Mountains and Rocks Are Forever: Lithics and Landscapes of* Sḵwxwú7mesh Uxwumixw. Ph.D. thesis, McMaster University, December 2011. Accessed 2017-11-01 (pdf) at macsphere.mcmaster.ca/handle/11375/11794.

Richards, Captain G.H. *The Private Journal of Captain G.H. Richards: The Vancouver Island Survey (1860–1862)*. Edited by Linda Dorricott and Deidre Cullon. Vancouver: Ronsdale Press, 2012.

——— *The Vancouver Island Pilot: Containing Sailing Directions for the Coasts of Vancouver Island and Part of British Columbia: Compiled from the Surveys Made by Captain George Henry Richards, R.N, in HM Ships* Plumper *and* Hecate *between the years 1858 and 1864*. London: Hydrographic Office, Admiralty, 1864. Searchable scans of original pages accessed 2017-11-05 from catalog.hathitrust.org/Record/100266523/Home.

Scott, Andrew. *The Encyclopedia of Raincoast Place Names: A Complete Reference to Coastal British Columbia*. Madeira Park, BC: Harbour Publishing, 2009.

Scott, Chic. *Pushing the Limits: The Story of Canadian Mountaineering*. Calgary: Rocky Mountain Books, 2000.

Sherman, Paddy. *Cloud Walkers: Six Climbs on Major Canadian Peaks*. Toronto and New York: Macmillan, 1965.

Snyders, Tom. *Namely Vancouver: The Hidden History of Vancouver Place Names*. Vancouver: Arsenal Pulp Press, 2001.

Sparks, Dawn, and Martha Border. *Echoes Across the Inlet*. Edited by Damian Inwood. North Vancouver: Deep Cove and Area Heritage Association, 1989.

Squamish Nation. *Xay Temixw (Sacred Land) Land Use Plan: For the Forests and Wilderness of the Squamish Nation Traditional Territory*. First draft May 2001. Accessed 2017-12-01 (pdf) at is.gd/VlZxbv. Summary accessed 2017-12-01 at is.gd/sgF2VO.

Tekahionawake. See Johnson, Pauline.

Threndyle, Steven. "Natural Skyline." In *The Greater Vancouver Book: An Urban Encyclopaedia*, edited by Chuck Davis. Surrey, BC: Linkman Press, 1997.

Tobias, Terry. *Living Proof: The Essential Data-Collection Guide for Indigenous Use-and-Occupancy Map Surveys*. Vancouver: Union of BC Indian Chiefs and Ecotrust Canada, 2009.

Vancouver, Captain George. *A Voyage of Discovery to the North Pacific Ocean* [&c.]. Vol. 1. London: G.G. & J. Robinson and J. Edwards, 1798. Searchable scans of original pages accessed 2017-12-05 at is.gd/jxLECe.

——— *A Voyage of Discovery to the North Pacific Ocean* [&c.]. New edition with corrections. Vol. 2. London: John Stockdale, 1801. Searchable scans of original pages accessed 2017-12-05 at is.gd/ALdIrF.

van Dyke, Henry. *The Story of the Other Wise Man*. New York: Harper & Brothers, 1895. Searchable scans of original pages accessed 2017-12-05 at is.gd/quzMKJ.

Walbran, Captain John T. *British Columbia Coast Names: Their Origin and History.*
Vancouver: Douglas & McIntyre, 1971, 1991. First published 1909 by Geographic
Board of Canada.

ONLINE

Alpine Club of Canada. *Canadian Alpine Journal.* Searchable archive of some 6,500 articles accessed 2017-12-21 at library.alpineclubofcanada.ca/?search_field=all_fields.

Alpine Sandwiches. Blog. Accessed 2017-11-01 at alpinesandwiches.com. A brilliant collection of photographs and videos of, well, sandwiches in alpine terrain, shot mostly on
southwestern British Columbia peaks.

BC Geographical Names. Database. Accessed 2017-11-01 at at apps.gov.bc.ca/pub/
bcgnws. Administered by GeoBC, a division of the Ministry of Forests, Lands,
Natural Resource Operations and Rural Development, this is a database of all officially named geographic features in British Columbia, including mountains.

BC Ministry of Forests, Lands, Natural Resource Operations and Rural Development.
"British Columbia's Geographical Naming Principles, Policy and Procedures."
Victoria: Government of BC, 2017. Accessed 2017-12-01 (pdf) at is.gd/yMJ7dj.

BCMC. *Passion for Mountains.* Video, 37:43. Accessed 2017-11-01 at youtube.com/
watch?v=bo2686Q0Tls. Produced for the centennial of the BC Mountaineering Club.

BCTreehunter. Blog. Accessed 2017-11-01 at bctreehunter.wordpress.com. Mick Bailey's
adventures in and celebrations of obscure corners of the North Shore wilderness.
Brilliant photographs and ruminations focusing on ancient trees.

Canadian Geographical Names Data Base. Accessed 2017-11-01 at www4.rncan.gc.ca/
search-place-names/search?lang=en. Maintained by Natural Resources Canada, this
comprehensive, searchable resource delivers geographical coordinates; a zoom-
able, pannable map segment; the NTS map number; a permanent link for the name
searched; even the date the name became official.

City of Vancouver Archives. Accessed 2017-11-01 at searcharchives.vancouver.ca.
Extensive collection of historical climbing photographs, audiovisual materials, and
other information, with excellent search capability.

Hollyburn Heritage Society. Archive. Accessed 2017-11-01 at hollyburnheritage.ca.
A rich collection of maps and articles, particularly on the Hollyburn and Cypress
Provincial Park area.

Montgomery, Charles. "The Blazer." Blogpost about Don McPherson [n.d.]. Accessed
2017-12-01 at charlesmontgomery.ca/the-blazer.

Mount Seymour History Project. Website. Accessed 2017-12-01 at mtseymourhistory.ca.

North Vancouver Museum & Archives. General search page accessed 2017-12-01 at
is.gd/SzjclY.

——— *Climbing to the Clouds: A People's History of BC Mountaineering.* Extensive online
collection of historical climbing photographs and information. Accessed 2017-12-22 at
nvma.ca/climb2cloud.

——— *Mountain Light: Photos from the BCM Collection.* An online selection of images taken by photographers from the British Columbia Mountaineering Club since the founding of the club in 1907. Accessed 2017-12-22 at nvma.ca/virtual-exhibits/mountain.

APPENDIX 23:
UNSOLVED MYSTERIES

Despite our research efforts, there remain some mysteries about these peaks. Any leads would be most welcome as to:

1. first ascents of:
   A. Gardner, Leading, Liddell, Killam
   B. Peak 5400 (Coburg–Gotha), Windsor, Deeks, ridge between Harvey and Lions (David, James, Thomas)
   C. Strachan, Black, Hollyburn, St. Marks, Unnecessary
   D. Paton Peak
   E. Suicide Bluffs, Runner Peak
2. name origins for:
   A. Unnecessary Mountain
   B. Runner Peak
   C. James Peak
   D. Mt. Elsay
   E. Godfrey Mountain (Bishop)
   F. Mt. Vaughan (Hollyburn)
   G. Burt's Bluff
   H. Rice Lake
   I. Bill's Trail
   J. Christmas Gully
   K. Vicar Lakes
   L. all North Shore creeks
3. Mt. Underhill: see "Unknown peaks" in **Appendix 20** above.
4. Indigenous names for all peaks and creeks.
5. any early copies of *Avalanche Echoes* from 1927–1939, published by the Alpine Club of *Canada's Vancouver Section*; almost none exist today, even in archives.

APPENDIX 24:
PANORAMA PHOTOGRAPHS WITH PEAK NAMES

Cypress Provincial Park peaks from Coal Harbour.

Central peaks from Coal Harbour.

Central peaks from Coal Harbour.

Central peaks from Coal Harbour.

Fannin Range peaks from Coal Harbour.

Liddell and Killam.

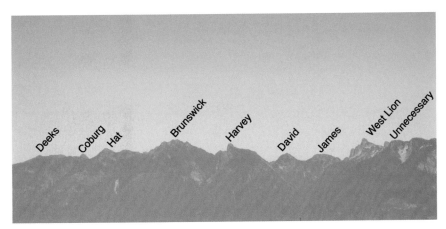

Howe Sound Crest peaks from Gardner.

Howe Sound Crest Peaks from Gardner.

Howe Sound Crest peaks from Gardner.

Deeks Lake peaks from near Hat.

Deeks Lake peaks from near Hat.

Hanover from Hat Meadows Tarn.

Hat and Wettin from Hanover.

Howe Sound Crest peaks from Mt. Strachan.

E from Crown.

E from Goat.

Needles and the Fannin Range from Goat.

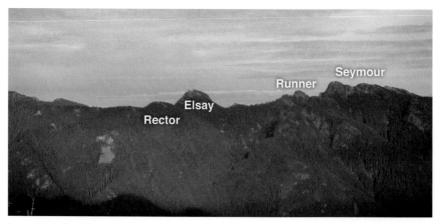

Fannin Range from Fromme.

Fannin Range from Fromme.

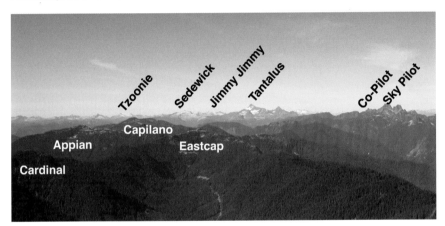

WNW from Cathedral.

NW from Cathedral.

N from Cathedral.

NE from Cathedral.

NE from Cathedral: Fraser Valley.

E from Cathedral: Fraser Valley.

View from from Elsay.

Vicar and Bishop seen from Elsay.

Howe Sound Crest peaks from Strachan.

PHOTO CREDITS

Photography by David Crerar unless otherwise noted.

Harry Crerar: pages 52, 59, 68, 98, 100, 112, 130, 136, 144, 146, 151, 152, 155, 156, 162, 200, 227, 315, 388, 418, 419, 422, 425

City of Vancouver Archives: pages 14, 204, 237, 304, 453

Tim Jones photograph (page 324 courtesy of North Shore Rescue)

ENDNOTES

1 Captain Harvey of HMS *Brunswick* and Captain Hutt of HMS *Queen* both lost a limb in the Battle of the Glorious First of June (June 1, 1794), and both died June 30. They are remembered by the same monument in Westminster Abbey, and, to complete the coincidence, before leaving England the two officers had driven down together in the same post-chaise to join their respective ships. Mt. Harvey, close southward of Brunswick Mountain, is named after the unfortunate Harvey, and Hutt Island after the equally unfortunate captain of the *Queen*. See Capt. John T. Walbran, *British Columbia Coast Names 1592–1906* (Vancouver: Douglas & McIntyre, 1971), 69 (first published 1909).

2 George Vancouver, *A Voyage of Discovery to the North Pacific Ocean* [&c.], new edition with corrections, vol. 2 (London: John Stockdale, 1801), 194–95.

3 Capt. G.H. Richards, *The Vancouver Island Pilot* (London: Hydrographic Office, Admiralty, 1864), 132.

4 Lt. John Marshall, *Royal Naval Biography*, vol. 2 (London: Longman, 1824), 96 at unnumbered note.

5 Richards, *The Vancouver Island Pilot*, 136.

6 Richards, *The Vancouver Island Pilot*, 106, 133.

7 Richards, *The Vancouver Island Pilot*, 106.

8 (Toronto: McClelland, Goodchild & Stewart, 1911), 1–10. Searchable scans of original pages accessed 2017-12-30 at is.gd/1eMkiS.

9 Lil'wat, Musqueam, Squamish, and Tsleil-Waututh, Peoples, *People of the Land: Legends of the Four Host First Nations* (Penticton, BC: Theytus Books, 2009).

10 *Legends of Vancouver*, 75–76.

11 Major J.S. Matthews, *Early Vancouver*, vol. 7 (Vancouver: City of Vancouver, 1956, 2011), 335, 336. Searchable scan of original pages accessed 2017-12-30 at is.gd/o5dWTq.

12 Kathryn Bridge, *Phyllis Munday: Mountaineer* (Montréal: XYZ Publishing, 2002), 48.

13 "Mount Dickens Christening Ceremony Performed on Summit," *Vancouver Daily World*, July 15, 1908, 10. See also the *Vancouver Province's* version, "Mount Dickens Is Christened Sunday," in **Appendix 19**.

14 From an undated typescript note in the Vancouver Archives, signed by archivist J.S.

Matthews, which briefly recounts the controversy and labels the text reproduced here as a "copy of a newspaper clipping (preserved in the A.T. Dalton, FRGS, docket, City Archives) from some old Vancouver newspaper, either *Province*, *World*, or *News-Advertiser...*"

15 George Vancouver, *A Voyage of Discovery to the North Pacific Ocean* [&c.], new edition with corrections, vol. 2 (London: John Stockdale, 1801), 193–199.

16 Captain Richards named this fjord "North Arm," which remained its name on many maps and charts well after it was officially changed in November 1921. The rationale was that Indian Arm received the outflow of Indian River, and that the North Arm of Burrard Inlet would be confused with the North Arm of the Fraser. There was also a suspicion that the change was in part encouraged by the Wigwam Inn resort, with its Indian River Park and its faux Indian themes. Vancouver archivist Major J.S. Matthews was particularly irked about this change: "Another of those crazy changes made by some thoughtless official who came from Ottawa, and, being ignorant of local history, imagined he could change it for no other reason than 'keeping his records straight,' and quite unmindful that his messing has caused tremendous confusion."

17 Searchable scans of original pages accessed 2017-11-05 from catalog.hathitrust.org/Record/100266523/Home.

INDEX

DAVID CRERAR

David grew up on the lower slopes of Mt. Seymour and now lives on the lower slopes of Grouse. In 2009 he created the Bagger Challenge, a contest to see who could climb the most North Shore peaks in a season; since then over 400 people have participated and that project led to this book. David is a partner in the commercial litigation group of the Vancouver office of Borden Ladner Gervais LLP. Since 2004 David has served as an adjunct professor at the University of British Columbia Faculty of Law, lecturing in civil procedure. He is the author of *Mareva and Anton Piller Preservation Orders: A Practical Guide* (Irwin Law, 2017). He is also the co-editor and a co-author of *British Columbia Business Disputes*, as well as the leading Canadian text on civil procedure, *The Civil Litigation Process*. He serves on the boards of the Vancouver International Marathon and the Canadian Media Lawyers' Association and is a member of the BC Mountaineering Club and the Alpine Club of Canada. David is an outdoors fanatic, and especially loves adventures with his four children on trails, lakes, oceans, and rivers. He has completed more than 170 marathons and ultra-marathons, on road and trail. He aspires to visit every national park in North America with each of his children.

HARRY CRERAR

Harry attends Mulgrave School in West Vancouver and has climbed most of these North Shore peaks. He loves travel and the outdoors: hiking, skiing, kayaking, and canoeing. He has adventured in many US and Canadian national parks. With his father (and co-author) and the rest of their family, Harry lives on the lower slopes of Grouse Mountain, with views of Hollyburn, Mount Fromme, and Mount Seymour from the backyard.

BILL MAURER

Bill grew up in East Vancouver and began climbing in his late teens. He quickly established a reputation as a peakbagger, earning the nickname "do it in a day Maurer," making day trips of what once were considered weekend club excursions. Since moving to the North Shore in 1993 he has been extensively exploring the trails, swimming the lakes, and bagging the peaks in his backyard. In 2011 he discovered the Bagger Challenge, a competition to see who can climb the most North Shore peaks in one season. There was no turning back: he won the challenge three years in a row and in 2012 climbed all of these peaks in a single season, in 18 outings. Bill's love of outdoor adventure sports and travelling has involved him in trail running, packrafting, paragliding, backcountry skiing, cycling, and high-altitude climbing. In 2015 he scaled the three Washington volcanoes – Mt. Hood, Mt. Adams, and Mt. St. Helens – on three consecutive days with his daughter, and traversed the Hikers Haute Route in the Alps with his son. He has also summited McKinley, Huascaran, Chopicalqui, Matterhorn, Mont Blanc, Mt. Baker, Mt. Rainier, and Mt. Whitney. Bill is a life member of the BC Mountaineering Club.

WEBSITE AND UPDATES

Check out the book websites for updates and additional information:
baggerbook.ca and facebook.com/baggerbook.

FEEDBACK WELCOME!

Trails and conditions change all the time. The authors are already hard at work on the second edition of this book and we welcome your ideas, corrections, and suggestions. Drop us a note at baggerbook@gmail.com. Thanks and credit will be given in the next edition!